PARTISANS OF FRE

PARTISANS of FREEDOM
A STUDY IN
AMERICAN ANARCHISM

By

WILLIAM O. REICHERT

Bowling Green University Popular Press
Bowling Green, Ohio 43403

CONTENTS

PREFACE

Like most Americans, I grew up in an intellectual atmosphere in which the idea of anarchism was invariably portrayed as a doctrine of willful destruction and blind violence, and thus in my youth anarchists became stereotyped in my mind as vile and unsavory creatures, enemies of all that was pure and good in life. Some years ago I chanced upon the writings of Adin Ballou, a native American Christian anarchist, and was dumbfounded to discover that not only was the idea of anarchism deeply rooted in American culture but as a political theory, anarchism does not in any way accept violence as a tactical mode of action or an essential principle. This mind-opening experience led me to delve more deeply into the writings of anarchists both at home and abroad and to think on my own in terms of what they were trying to say. As I have learned more about the subject of anarchism, I have been distressed to discover that the essential nature of anarchist thought has been seriously distorted not only by the press but by social historians as well. So great has been this distortion that with John Turner, the English anarchist writer who was turned away from our shores in 1903 because of his ideological loyalties, "I fear that trying to tell Americans what Anarchism means is like attempting to give an account of 'foreign devils' to the Chinese."

This book is the result of my concern that the record ought to be made more accurate with reference to what anarchism is all about, and thus I have attempted in the pages that follow to give as honest an account of what American anarchists have said and believed as is humanly possible. I say "humanly possible" because I fully recognize how difficult it is to construct an accurate report of what anyone believes in the realm of ideology where subjective feelings and hard objective facts stand back to back in a shadowy twilight that invites the observer to interpret what he sees after the familiar patterns of value he holds in his own mind's eye. In order to minimize the distortion that inevitably accompanies any social or political writing, I have attempted throughout this study to report what anarchists have said as closely as possible after their own viewpoints with as little interpretation of my own as possible; I may well have failed in my quest for objectivity but this has not been because of a lack of good intentions on my part.

If a candid avowal of my own ideological sympathies would be helpful to the reader in judging the authenticity of what follows, I am quite willing to confess that I am something of an anarchist myself, for I invariably find myself reacting positively to the arguments that anarchists raise concerning important social issues and I am firmly convinced that the kind of stateless world anarchists envision is the kind of world in which I would like to reside myself. But it is one thing to call oneself an anarchist and quite another to define with any precision exactly what anarchism is, for there are a great many different categories of anarchist thought. I have not sought to establish my own preference as to what particular brand of anarchist thought is most sound, for this would be special pleading, indeed, but have been content to let the reader judge for himself which is most worthy. This attempt at objectivity has led me to write a much longer book than I had originally planned, but since in the past, anarchism has not received the attention it deserves, brevity was simply not possible. In determining the points at which I should begin and end this study, the nature of my subject matter again proved to be so broad that I was forced to exercise arbitrary judgment in this regard also. And since the political developments of the post World War II era seem to have precipitated an entirely new way of viewing anarchism, I have chosen 1945 as my cut-off point, leaving the contemporary period of anarchist thought to be treated elsewhere.

When I first started this study some ten years ago, the only published histories of American anarchism were Eunice Schuster's *Native American Anarchism* and James J. Martin's *Men Against the State.* While both of these works are still valuable as a source of information concerning the ideological viewpoints of those who have embraced the idea of anarchism, they both primarily focus upon the individualist phase of the idea and thus leave out of consideration the many other facets of anarchist thought. George Woodcock's *Anarchism: A History of Libertarian Ideas and Movements* published in 1962 is a superb general history of anarchism but does not deal at any length with the development of the idea in America. In recent years several histories of anarchist thought in America have appeared but none of these has managed to avoid interpreting the idea from a predominantly liberal bias. Gerald Runkle's *Anarchism: Old and New* is written more as an epitaph than a serious analysis of what anarchists believe, while Corinne Jacker's *The Black Flag of Anarchy* discounts what the anarchist has to say because: "Fine though his dissection of the evils of the State and government may be, unanswerable though his ethical stand may be, he does not recognize the practical necessities of day-to-day living. . . ." As with all liberal accounts of anarchism, the notion that formal social control through government is the bedrock of reality misleads these authors into concluding that the idea of anarchism is wholly impractical and already dead as a viable plan for human action, and thus it is necessary that yet another book on the subject be written.

Among the more recent books that have attempted to portray anarchism nearer to the way that anarchists view the idea themselves, several deserve special mention. Yehoshua Arieli's *Individualism and Nationalism in American Ideology* is invaluable for the insight it gives into the social and economic characteristics of anarchist thought during the crucial period of the eighteenth century; while Robert Nisbet's monumental work, *The Social Philosophers: Community and Conflict in Western Thought,* is one of the most scholarly and objective treatments of anarchism that I know of. If we would really understand anarchism, of course, it is to anarchists themselves that we must turn, and hence it is necessary to mention two recently published works, Daniel Guerin's *Anarchism: From Theory to Practice,* and Giovanni Baldelli's *Social Anarchism;* if one were imited to only two books about anarchist theory, either of these would be well chosen, although neither of them deals with American anarchism in particular.

I wish to acknowledge the generosity of the University of

Chicago Press for allowing me to use material that originally appeared in *Ethics;* the Institute of Government at the University of Utah for material that appeared in *The Western Political Quarterly;* and the Extension Divison of the University of Wisconsin for permitting me to include excerpts from "Art, Nature, and Revolution," which appeared in Volume 9, Number 3, of *Arts in Society*. I also owe gratitude to The Houghton Library of Harvard University for permission to publish quotations from the letters of Josiah Warren to Stephen P. Andrews and from three unpublished manuscripts of Joseph Ishill. Finally, I am indebted to Morgan Gibson of Goddard College for permission to use his poem, "Before Undressing the Liberals," as well as his comradeship back in the days when it was difficult to find anyone in academia who would not snicker at the mere mention of the word "anarchism."

As to the other individuals who gave me assistance in completing this study, I owe particular gratitude to my students over the years who have forced me to probe ever deeper into the meaning of anarchism and to put what I have learned into writing. To Professor Mulford Q. Sibley of the University of Minnesota, I owe thanks not only for the inspiration he gave me when I was a graduate student but for my initial introduction to the idea of anarchism and its libertarian implications. I am most appreciative of the kindness of Edward Weber of the University of Michigan Library for helping me find mateials in the Labadee Collection; and the editorial board of the *Freie Arbeiter Stimme,* along with Professors Paul Avrich and David Thoreau Weick, for invaluable assistance in understanding what anarchists have been trying to say. I also gratefully acknowledge the research associateships I have received from the Faculty Research Committee of Bowling Green State University, as well as the support I have been given by Pat and Ray Browne of the Bowling Green Popular Press. Finally, I wish to express deep gratitude to my wife, Doris, for her unstinting help in editing this manuscript when she had much more interesting things of her own to do, and to my son, William Robert, for his illustration of the text.

INTRODUCTION

When the average citizen is asked to describe the image he carries in his head as to what anarchism stands for, he generally responds with the cartoon stereotype which pictures the anarchist as a wild, bomb-throwing malcontent who possesses no love whatever for the human race or any of the cherished values upon which civilization has been built. Historians and political scientists have been less given to accepting that stereotype without question but even a few of them have added to the confusion that surrounds the anarchist idea by typing at least one wing of anarchist thought as dedicated to violence as a fundamental principle. For example, shortly after the assassination of President William McKinley, it became accepted practice for American political scientists to draw a rigid distinction between philosophical anarchism and anarchist communism on the grounds that the former did not embrace the use of violence whereas the latter did. Thus in 1926 Charles E. Merriam maintained that anarchist groups in the United States may be divided into the "philosophical and the fighting anarchists, one believing in the attainment of anarchy by the peaceful processes of evolution and the other by the employment of force and by revolution."[1] A few years later Westel W. Willoughby gave support to Merriam's definition when he maintained that the philosophical anarchist is to be distinguished from the anarchist of deed or of action on the grounds that the former believes that anarchism must be established by the peaceful processes of persuasion and enlightenment, whereas the latter does not believe

1

that society will naturally evolve toward its perfection without the assistance of the revolutionary act.[2] This neat but misleading dichotomy has dogged the idea of anarchism ever since, causing that viewpoint to appear uninviting in the eyes of succeeding generations of Americans. But as a careful look at the basic political thought of American anarchists demonstrates, the conviction that violence must be deliberately employed in order to carry off a successful social revolution was not a necessary principle in the mind of any reputable American anarchist, whether he be classified as an individualist or an anarchist communist. There are, of course, real distinctions to be drawn between the many different varieties of anarchism which were found in this country but the question of the deliberate employment of violence and revolutionary force is not a meaningful categorical determinent and will not be used to choose between the various anarchist groups in this study.

When the Congress of the United States sought to ban anarchists like John Turner from our shores by law, the members of that legislative body were evidently of the impression that anarchism is a foreign ideology that could never taint the pure thoughts of the American citizenry unless it were imported from abroad like fruit flies, Japanese beetles, or some other variety of infectious pest. Where Congress went astray in formulating its immigration policy was in failing to recognize that thousands of native-born Americans had already been introduced to anarchism not by reading radical tracts imported from abroad but by a process of spontaneous intellectual combustion that was sparked at the precise moment that they first thought out for themselves the full social and philosophical implications of the concept of freedom upon which this political culture was originally formed. It cannot be stressed too strongly that both as an idea and as an ideology, anarchism focuses directly on the heritage of freedom that is fundamental to this country and is thus as "American" in character as the Fourth of July. The conviction that anarchism begins and ends with liberty is the central theme of this study and the essential foundation of the definition of anarchism to follow.

To argue that anarchism completely embraces the idea of freedom as it developed historically in America is to invite the criticism of those historians and political scientists who hold that the genius of American politics is exhausted in the liberal tradition of political thought. Building on the theoretical underfootings laid by Hobbes and Locke, the liberal view of freedom postulates the theory that liberty and government are two sides of the same coin and that one is not possible without the other.[3] The liberal, to be sure, believes in limited government, for as both Hobbes and Locke freely acknowledged, where political power is permitted to concentrate in the hands of an unapproachable sovereign, there tyranny and oppression inevitably follow. The liberal solution to the problem of maximizing freedom was to design a political system that guaranteed the individual his personal freedom on the condition that he would obey the demands of the state insofar as this was essential to the maintenance of public order. There were, of course, to be careful safeguards erected around the awesome power of government to prevent it from reenacting the lawless behavior of the monarchical tyrants of old. And thus it was that liberals drew upon the wisdom of philosophers like Montesquieu as well as Hobbes and Locke to fashion a carefully balanced political machine that would be strong enough to curb the excesses of individual egocentrism but flexible enough to permit its subjects to exercise their own tastes and desires in the realm of individual freedom.

As liberal theory worked itself out in practice, however, there has been more emphasis upon the demands of collective security than there has been on individual freedom, for implicit in the basic idea of government is the correlative principle that its own survival must come before the free exercise of rights by the individual whenever a conflict develops between them. Liberals are quick enough to sing the praises of liberty as an abstract ideal, of course, and hence they claim a deep concern for the defense of individualism. Saul K. Padover gives us a classic example of liberal theory with reference to individual freedom when he writes: "Unlike other cultures, where emphasis has been on the state or the society, in the United States the stress has been on the individual. . . . Americans have placed the individual at the center of their political life. They have taken the position that government exists for freedom, and that freedom means individual freedom vis-a-vis government."[4] However much Liberals may insist that the power of government over the individual is limited and that his rights come first, it is quite clear that there is a point at which liberalism faces a serious contradiction, and this is with reference to the basic problem of political sovereignty. If the state, which is to say, government, has the ultimate power to reverse or

veto any decision made by an individual even when acting in accordance with his own rational judgement, the Liberal is forced to admit
that individual rights and power are not in fact inalienable but very
definitely subject to limitation by a superior sovereign force. And
once he has made this admission, he can no longer fully embrace
the notion that the individual comes before any other consideration
when public policy is being forged on the political anvil; obviously
the Liberal really believes that public order and necessity come first
or he would not admit that there is any reason whatever for curtailing
the powers of the individual.

Whatever other faults it may possibly possess, anarchism, unlike
liberalism, cannot be criticized on the grounds that it accommodates
its dedication to the principle of individual freedom to the demands
of power and public order. Anarchism is distinguished from other
political ideologies, in fact, precisely because of its rejection of power
and formal organization. Anarchists recognize that power is a definite
and necessary characteristic of all social situations but they draw
a careful distinction between social and political power. So long as
there are human beings there will naturally exist subtle forces of social
control which make collective social action and cooperation possible.
Anarchists deny, however, that this control must be exercised by
government over the individuals of whom society is composed.
Viewing the world from a position of libertarian concern, anarchists
maintain that political power wielded by government can never be
acceptable in their eyes as a legitimate mode of social control because
it crushes out individual freedom. And where individual freedom is
absent, social life becomes impossible, for society is nothing more
than the sum total of the free acts of the individuals of which it is
composed.

In order to appreciate the essential nature of the anarchist idea
as it has developed in America, we must clearly understand that
anarchism is basically a species of libertarian thought. Although it is
only in the last few years that the term itself has come into prominence, anarchists have long recognized that their basic philosophic
orientation was derived from the libertarian model of freedom.[5] Peter
Kropotkin, the chief theorist of nineteenth century anarchist communism in Europe, addressed himself directly to the close relationship
that exists between anarchism and libertarianism when, in discussing
the nature of the state, he pointed out that men from the beginning

of time have fallen into one or another of two categories.[6] On the one hand are those who hold to the Roman or imperial tradition. Often called "statists," these are people who place their trust in hierarchy and formal political authority. The adherents of this view maintain that public order is impossible without the state and that men are incapable of living in peace with one another without the assistance of formal institutions of organized power and leadership. Where organized government is absent, the imperialists maintain, order and liberty are also non-existent. The centralization of government within the modern democratic state has been forced by the imperialists, for they have been highly successful in convincing the mass of men that social life without the guiding hand of the state is an impossibility. Americans need only look as far as their own Alexander Hamilton and the Federalist Party for a model of imperialist thought.

The other tradition Kropotkin makes mention of is the popular or federalist tradition. If we seek a name that will convey its precise meaning, Kropotkin wrote, we might well call it "the libertarian tradition." The libertarian, unlike the imperialist, totally distrusts hierarchy, formal political authority, and organized government. Convinced that men are created by nature for a genuine social life, although they have not yet attained any significant degree of this potential, the libertarian, according to Kropotkin, denies that external compulsion and force are essential to order and peace. To the contrary, human freedom is only possible where men abandon the state and seek instead to create social life through the principles of federalism, mutual aid, and self-discipline. Kropotkin's emphasis upon the necessity of renouncing formal orgainzed control by government and turning instead to the individual as the central focus of social life is the distinguishing characteristic of all anarchist thought and the rationale for proclaiming the philosophy of libertarianism the essential foundation of all anarchist theory.

What anarchism and libertarianism hold in common is a thoroughgoing commitment to the proposition that the one and only *modus operandi* of government is force and coercion, either actual or implied. When the actual dynamics of governmental activity are examined in depth, according to both the libertarian and the anarchist, it is clearly evident that the single device in its entire bag of tricks is the physical retribution it is capable of exercising against its subjects in a most ruthless and inhumane fashion when all other methods of control have failed. Force and coercion, however much they may be sugar-coated with deceptive language by legalists intent upon defending the reputation and sovereignty of the state, are in final analysis totally foreign elements in any formula for liberty or freedom. For "In its most fundamental sense, the sense from which the other senses stem, and the sense which is historically the earliest, liberty (or freedom) is the *absence of coercion by other human beings.* To the extent that a person is forced against his will to do something, he is not free."[7] When the libertarian announces himself the adamant enemy of government, it is because he considers government and the coercion it relies upon the moral enemy of human freedom. Hereafter, whenever an individual is identified as an anarchist in this study, it is to be taken for granted that his basic social and philosophical outlook is essentially libertarian.

However necessary it may be for the sake of accuracy to establish the connection between anarchism and libertarianism, a switch in labels is not in any way a final solution to the problem of understanding anarchism. As Pierre-Joseph Proudhon, the man who coined the anarchist label in the first place, well knew, names, like words, are always meaningless until we have plumbed the symbolic depths that lie behind them and have clearly analyzed the character of the means by which any particular philosophy would achieve its ends. If we would understand anarchism more exactly, therefore, we must address ourselves to the anarchist's claim that freedom is not only his primary value or goal but that it is the means by which he would bring about the kind of world in which he would like to live.

When anarchists speak of liberty as being fundamental to their basic philosophy, they are not engaging in mere rhetoric. "Liberty," as one American anarchist wrote, "is not a declaration, or even an inspiration, it is a science."[8] That is to say, liberty, in the anarchist frame of reference, is not so much a goal to be striven for as it is the essential means by which the goal of human freedom itself must be realized. This, of course, is why the anarchist is the sworn opponent of all attempts to achieve freedom through the use of organized government, for government, as we have already insisted, is impossible without resort to force and compulsion at some point. As strange as the idea may at first appear, this rejection of force is fundamental to the thinking of all anarchists, and is the essential foundation of anarchism's entire philosophical structure.

Undoubtedly the main reason why the noncoercive character of anarchist philosophy has never been apparent to the American people is that the basic nature of the political world we live in renders the anarchist a revolutionary. Since power *does* exist at any given time in the hands of an elite of governing leadership, the anarchist is perforce placed in the position of calling for the elimination of established power through revolution. And the word "revolution" tends to send shivers straight to the hearts of those who fear the consequences of political upheaval.

What Americans fail to realize when they condemn the anarchist for his revolutionary ardor is that revolution is by no means an alien phenomenon in America but the very basis of the freedom they profess to cherish so much. As one astute observer has pointed out, the greatest obstacle that stands in the way of a real understanding of what freedom really means in this country is the failure of Americans "to remember that a revolution gave birth to the United States and that the republic was brought into existence by no 'historical necessity' and no organic development, but by a deliberate act: the foundation of freedom."[9] That is to say, the idea of individual freedom and the concept of the American republic are for all practical purposes synonymous and we cannot understand the genius of America until we have thought out the full social and political implications of the heritage of liberty bequeathed us by the Declaration of Independence. As more and more historians are coming to see of late, the conception of human right spelled out in the Declaration is not merely a rhetorical device but a solid statement of what Americans really believed during the eighteenth century as to the nature and function of government as it pertains to the individual. Since the "right of revolution was justified by presidents as well as prophets, by politicians in power as well as by radicals out of it" during the first one hundred years of this country's existence,[10] it can hardly be charged that the anarchist is outside the pale of civilization when he, too, claims a right to it. If the right to rebellion in pursuit of freedom was an original right of the American people, it remains the most basic of civil liberties, and those who urge its exercise, as Thomas Jefferson and countless other patriots persisted in doing, are acting fully within the scope of the American conception of freedom.

Perhaps the main reason why anarchism has been so poorly interpreted in the past is that the concentration has been on its alleged dedication to violence rather than on its philosophic foundations, and so it is to its essential historical beginnings that we must return. Like most other modern political ideas, anarchism was initially inspired by the sight of the downtrodden lower orders in eighteenth century France rising in spontaneous rebellion against the heartless rule of a corrupt, effete aristocracy. One of anarchism's most pronounced characteristics is its insistence that the slave is not only entitled to rise up against his master and overthrow him if he can but that he actually has a duty to do so. But unlike many other ideological groups that applaud the struggle for freedom that was central to the French Revolution but which ignore the brutal carnage and political machinations that accompanied it, anarchists clearly recognize the negative aspects of *coup d'etat,* even when it is conducted in the name of liberty and the popular will. Slavery is always the implacable enemy of human freedom and is to be stamped out by all means. The anarchist insists, however, that the fight against tyranny be waged by autonomous groups acting in response to their own internal feelings and not by organized governments or mobs led by professional militants. For all their sympathy for the French people against the abuses of aristocracy,[11] anarchists "did not like the centralization of power they saw in the Revolution, the unitary collectivism the Revolution represented, and the stringent laws prohibiting free association of the people in cooperatives, communes, and labor unions. . . ."[12] They were moreover, greatly disturbed by the bourgeois thinking demonstrated by many followers of the Revolution in the face of the rapidly expanding industrialization and concentration of property that came in its aftermath.

As the sociologist, Robert Nisbet, perceptively notes, anarchists totally rejected the view of political modernity first advanced by the Jacobins and later given a more elaborate theoretical structure by Marx and Engels.

> The anarchists did not accept, as did Marx and the main line of radicalism in the West, the necessity of violence and terror; they did not see history as a unilinear, inexorable and irreversible process, as did the Marxists; they opposed utterly the centralized collectivism that the Revolution ushered in and that Marxism, from the Manifesto right through to Lenin and Stalin took virtually for granted. Without exception, the major anarchist philosophers, beginning with William Godwin in England . . . through Bakunin, Proudhon, and Kropotkin, down to Alexander Berkman and Emma Goldman, rejected this legacy of the French Revolution: the legacy of centralization and unitary collectivism. And with

their rejection of this went also a rejection of nationalism in any of its forms, socialist as well as capitalist.[13]

Nisbet puts his finger on the vital center of anarchist social theory when he insists that the crucial distinction in modern radical thought takes place with reference to the problem of modernity, Marxian socialists accepting "all the structural characteristics of capitalist production, including the factory system, technology, and the dominance of city over rural areas," and anarchists calling for the rejection "of the factory system, the complete decentralization of technology, and a general restoration of rural patterns of life."[14] As we shall see in the following pages, the anarchist's dedication to the idea of agrarianism as it was developed during the eighteenth century was basically determined by his fear that centralized industrialization would inevitably lead to centralized political control and thus the eventual destruction of the American notion of individual freedom. This is why the anarchist consistently places himself in opposition to the spirit of nationalism in all of its forms, including the pursuit of capitalist gain through imperialism and the creation of national wealth through state socialism.

To argue that the anarchist has historically placed himself against state socialism is not the same thing as saying that the anarchist rejects socialism. In point of fact, as Daniel Guerin points out, "Anarchism is really a synonym for socialism. The anarchist is primarily a socialist whose aim is to abolish the exploitation of man by man."[15] The anarchist quest for socialism during the first half of the nineteenth century in America largely followed the idea of mutualism worked out simultaneously but independently by Josiah Warren in this country and Pierre-Joseph Proudhon in France. Primarily individualists, both Warren and Proudhon sought to eliminate inequality and economic servitude by building a strong social collectivity based upon a population of free individuals federated together in mutual support of one another without interference or control from government. In this phase of its development, anarchism was a clear reflection of Jeffersonian agrarianism. During the last part of the nineteenth century and the first part of the twentieth, however, many anarchists, reacting to the changes that had taken place in industrial technology and the concentration of captial in the hands of powerful corporations, toyed for a time with the Marxian notion that the exploited workers needed to associate together in the trade union movement as a first but necessary step in the direction of socialism; the Chicago Anarchists and the Free Society Group were both structured in their actions by this development. But this flirtation with Marxism was never a fundamental part of the anarchist idea in this country or any other, for that matter, and by the late 1930's the mood had passed and anarchists spoke as one in rejecting the conception of collective action under the aegis of the state as it was worked out by the Bolsheviks. Anarchists continued to divide on the question of which came first, the individual or the collectivity, to be sure, but there was never any question among anarchists that the state had no legitimate role in bringing socialism about.

By now it should be perfectly clear that the central idea of anarchism is the libertarian view that the state is a totally negative force when it comes to the establishment of human freedom. By way of definition, then, the term "anarchist," as it will be used in this study, applies to all those Americans who dedicated themselves to the realization of the idea of freedom by adopting a negative attitude toward formal social control in the hands of the state. The distinctive characteristic of anarchist thought as its proponents define it, in other words, is a thoroughgoing repudiation of the concept of the modern state with its omnipresent evils of power and coercive authority in the hands of a professional bureaucracy.

Not only did American anarchists derive their political theory from the eighteenth century but their basic social and philosophical assumptions were also structured according to the major ideas of that age. If anarchists in America can make any claim to originality or greatness, it has been said, it is for their achievement of a "true synthesis of the philosophy of the Enlightenment."[16] Almost as misunderstood as anarchism itself, the eighteenth century Enlightenment has been portrayed by some historians as an age totally given to the simplistic notion that nature as it is found in the universe is to be explained according to mechanical laws set in motion by a "clockmaker" God at the beginning of time. It is on the basis of this charge that the Enlightment, with its great reliance on reason, has often been discredited. But enlightened philosophy did not in fact proceed along the lines of such a sweeping, jejune generalization as this. In the mind of the typical philosopher of the Enlightenment, the cosmos was synonymous with nature itself rather than the product of a deliberate act of an all-powerful deity who had the capability of willing the world and all that is in it. Nature on the enlightened view, that is to say, is a process to be understood through human observation and understanding and not an inscrutable pattern of necessary laws and rules forced upon us by an omnipotent power that rules from outside the human spectrum.

The distinction drawn here between nature as a reflection of the will of God and nature as process is fundamental to an intelligent analysis of anarchism as well as enlightened thought. If nature is the result of God's deliberate will, then God possesses a monopoly of power, and man, consequently, can never be anything more than a powerless creature whose very existence depends upon strict obedience to the rules laid down by his divine benefactor. Under this circumstance, it would be sheer folly for man to attempt to steer his own course through life, for he could never hope to live intelligently through the exercise of his own imperfect faculties. Where God is thought of as the creator and ruler of the universe, the only possible definition of reason left to man can be that of perfect faith and dependence upon the will of God, the supreme ruler.

Where nature is defined as process, however, man need not be relegated to a position of impotence regarding the course and quality of life. Under this view, the laws of nature are not hard and fast propositions laid down by a superior power that must be obeyed under all circumstances by the subjects for whom they have been made. The laws of nature, rather, are to be discovered by man in the process of life. "Life alone spontaneously creates real things and beings," Michael Bakunin once proclaimed.[17] This statement embraces and makes clear at one and the same time the central theme which anarchism shares with enlightened thought.

In anarchist writings of the late nineteenth century, the idea of nature as process takes the form of evolutionary theory. In the early period of its development in America, however, nature was viewed more in terms of its aesthetic qualities than its biological properties. But in both instances anarchist thought centered around the enlightened idea that there is a design of freedom imprinted in nature that must be released before human beings can realize their true being. Man, in the enlightened view, possesses a natural capacity for social life and expression, just as all living things in nature do. But in the process of becoming human, man, leaving his basic animal characteristics behind, has built a complex superstructure of institutionalized patterns of behavior that now define his character and function in a wholly artificial way. Man's basic nature is a reflection of the joy and beauty of nature itself, but the demands of advanced civilization have robbed him of his natural social heritage and have crippled his creative power. Enlightened thought proposes that this embroglio might be solved to the extent that men can learn to rely again upon their own powers of critical reason instead of the rules and laws formulated for them by others.

Enlightened thought does not conceive of reason as a facet of the intellect so much as it does the natural capacity for life that man shares with all things in nature. To possess reason, on this view, is to instinctively know the inherent form of a thing. Enlightened philosophy, however, does not subscribe to the theory that all the knower can do is to passively describe the pattern of nature he perceives through his faculties of sense. While nature is thought of as consisting of a series of essential and necessary forces that exist prior to the act of perception, the individual who does the observing is not considered to be unimportant to the process. Enlightened philosophy projects the idea "of an original spontaneity of thought; it attributes to thought not merely an imitative function but the power and task of shaping life itself."[18] Things are what they are by virtue of the inherent forces they possess and without which they could not function or exist. Yet at the very same time it is clear that the act of perception in and by itself is important to the character of the thing observed, for without that act the thing could not exist. Man does not in any literal sense create the forces he discovers in nature, since they are there prior to his act of discovery, but the rules and laws of nature remain hidden from him until he exercises his critical faculties to reveal what lies beneath the surface of illusion.

In final analysis, then, nature "is not the sum total of created things but the creative power from which the form and order of the universe are derived."[19] And the faculty of reason is primarily subsumed in the act of criticism by which man tears down the walls and veils of unexamined appearance which custom and habit have surrounded things with. Convention, tradition and authority are impediments which man must get behind before he can discover the true forms of nature, for in the realm of human affairs, as in the realm of the natural sciences, it is necessary to clear away the false theories and beliefs of the past before real understanding and perception can begin to take place. This is why Voltaire and all the other great thinkers of the Enlightenment praised the act of tearing down the structure of existing systems of thought, whether they had to do with theological truths or scientific propositions. For until the illusions and misconceptions that blind mankind to the true order of things are removed, the business of reconstructing knowledge and social life on more solid foundations cannot begin.

Nowhere is the influence of the Enlightenment more pronounced than in the conception of freedom advanced by anarchism. For most men, freedom appears to be little more than a rhetorical device by which the emotions of others may be aroused, or perhaps an empty phrase which they speak as mindlessly as they greet one another on the street. Even for the Liberal Democrat who takes freedom much more seriously than most other men, freedom is defined negatively in that the formal rights reserved to the individual are a residual product of the political process; public order maintained through the power of the state is the Liberal Democrat's first concern after which he concerns himself with freedom. For the anarchist, however, it is not enough to define freedom as a body of rights that one possesses on the sufferance of the state or society. For the anarchist as for the philosopher of the Enlightenment, freedom or liberty is intimately connected with the basic condition of human rationality and is essential to the business of being a social being. Freedom on the anarchist view is not a body of formal rights arbitrarily granted to the individual but an inherent quality the individual possesses in his very capacity as a social being, although all men must undergo an internal struggle before they can liberate themselves from the forces which prevent them from enjoying their natural condition of freedom.

Fundamental to an intelligent understanding of anarchism is the "positive doctrine of liberation by reason" which lies at the basis of all enlightened thought. Compulsion and force, in this view of freedom, play no part whatever, for the individual is envisioned as a wholly autonomous agent who has the power to direct his own actions at every point. Rather than being an artificial construct of society, freedom is conceived of as a reflection of man's rational nature. On this theory, that man is free who, knowing a thing to be necessarily true, voluntarily bends his will to conform to the rational necessity he intuitively feels within himself. There is no suggestion whatever here of force or external control, for the rational individual envisioned by enlightened thought could not if he wanted to, depart from the direction which reason relays to his will. As Isaiah Berlin puts it: "What you know, that of which you understand the necessity—the rational necessity—you cannot, while remaining rational, want to be otherwise."[20] Actual men do not always immediately recognize what is true and what is not, of course, for their passions and prejudices have a tendency to trick them into following unreasonable patterns of behavior from time to time. In point of fact, the vast majority of men at any given point in time will be found to be laboring behind a veil of illusion forced upon them by their own individual neuroses and fears as well as by the collective neuroses and fears of the society of which they are a part. To see through this veil to the rational light that lies beyond is to liberate oneself from myth, the basis of all human ignorance and social malaise.

All anarchists, however they may be classified as to their economic or philosophical beliefs, agree on the fundamental proposition that human slavery starts and ends with myth. Man as a political animal is the product of countless generations of development wherein he has progressively enslaved himself by fettering his reason with the chains of superstition and fear. The anarchist holds that the precise point at which man lost his freedom cannot be determined but we can be relatively certain that the cause of his enslavement stemmed from his forebears' readiness to grovel in the dust at the feet of the gods they erected to protect them from the things they could not understand or control. Man's greatest enemy in this regard has been himself. Unable to attain that solidarity that is essential for real community, mankind has from the earliest of times taken refuge in myth in a futile effort to find the security that is necessary to collective life. Mankind, to be sure, was never conscious of the fact that it was in the process of enslaving itself to the stultifying grip of a collective unconscious from which it might never escape again. For as Ernst Cassirer so perceptively notes, men who live under the sway of myth are never conscious of the fact that their lives are dominated by images and symbols which took form and shape in the dim recesses of the past.[21] The impulses which surge through man as he performs his rites of magic and religious atonement are deep-seated, unconscious relics of the past over which he has absolutely no control. If he were conscious of their existence, he would no longer be under their power.

There is a sense, of course, in which the idea of myth is essential to the evolution of human freedom. Karl Jaspers gives demonstration of this when he argues that mankind needs to recover the original meaning of its myths rather than destroy them altogether, for at the basis of every myth is a solid substratum of moral content which points the way toward the discovery of real religious value.[22] Laying aside for the moment the positive side of myth, it is necessary to focus upon the fact that anarchism in America has been primarily concerned with coming to grips with the negative qualities of mythical thought as it is embodied in the state idea. In the eyes of the anarchist, "the ultimate superstition of mankind is the state,"[23] and hence for him the highest form of moral act is to condemn both church and state as enemies of humanity. Firm in their conviction that reason and justice are essential properties of the human condition, anarchists have sought to make the Enlightenment's faith in freedom come true. The evolution of the anarchist idea in America is the story of a babble of voices as one freethinking son of the Enlightenment after another added his home remedy to the anarchist brew. But throughout the confusion of all this cacophony one theme is constant and this is the enlightenment idea that the beginning and end of philosophy is the concept of nature from which all human knowledge must be drawn. If man would be free, he must turn to himself in an effort to understand his enslavement to the power of the state. Anarchism, then, is essentially a theory of liberation aimed at the recovery of man's basic social nature through the destruction of the myth systems he has imposed upon himself and his progeny almost from the beginning of time.

When the anarchist speaks of freedom as being a quality implicit in nature, he reveals a deep commitment to the aesthetic as the true revolutionary force in society. In proclaiming art rather than politics the true revolutionary force in life, the anarchist does not in any way accept the argument of elitists who insist that only the noble few have the power to direct life intelligently. As Benedetto Croce points out, "the aesthetic fact is not something exceptional, produced by exceptionally gifted men, but a ceaseless activity of man as such; for man possesses the world, so far as he does possess it, only in the form of representation-expressions, and only in so far as he creates."[24] We are artists all, the anarchist insists, and the consequences of our art is inevitably a better and more just world. But we do not consciously

work toward this revolutionary end, nor do we submit to any ideological design in terms of organizing ourselves and our activity. Life
itself is our only blueprint and the methodology we discipline
ourselves by is the spontaneity that is fundamental to human nature.
At best, as Croce points out, there is a mere quantitative difference
separating the ordinary man from the great artist, for the source of
energy for both is their common human nature. Were the average
man totally lacking in imagination and aesthetic sense, no artist could
talk beyond himself. "The cult of the genius with all its attendant
superstitions has arisen from this quantitative difference having been
taken as a difference in quality," Croce points out. "It has been forgotten that genius is not something that has fallen from heaven, but
humanity itself."[25] To look toward political leadership for the initiative for social change, therefore, is to be turned in the exact opposite
direction toward which we should be pointed.

Since Pierre-Joseph Proudhon was the first to call himself an
anarchist, it is not improper that we start with his attitude toward art
and the artist. Central to all of Proudhon's social thought is the idea
that social progress stems from the activity of man's creative spirit.
If we would build a sound society in the future, Proudhon maintained, we must somehow free man from the fetters which presently
restrict his imagination and keep him in servitude to the political state
and other instruments of repression. Human progress depends, according to Proudhon, not upon the reform of political institutions but
upon the education of mankind in the ways of its own social nature,
for man is basically a creative being who has been robbed of his
natural social propensities by the crushing weight of the political
restrictions he has imposed upon himself over the centuries. To the
extent that man derives insight into the content and meaning of his
own basic nature, he becomes capable of perfecting himself and living
in freedom and social unity with his fellowman.

Displaying a genuine commitment to science in the very best
sense of the term, Proudhon refused to confine his thinking within
the rigid boundaries of any intellectual discipline, and hence he acknowledged poetry and art as being at least as important as sociology,
economics, or political economy. In Proudhon's view of things, social
progress takes place as the human race becomes reeducated in the
ways of its own social nature. According to Proudhon, this is essentially a collective rather than an individual process. Yet Proudhon saw

clearly in his own mind that it is the individual rather than the mass upon whom progress ultimately depends. Mass society has no form apart from the individual, and it follows from this that social progress can only take place to the extent that the individual differentiates himself from the mass. But, Proudhon insisted, the individual's redemptive progress cannot proceed faster than the general pace of social advance made by society as a whole, and hence it is impossible to draw a sharp line between the individual and the collective.

Central to Proudhon's contention that social progress stems from the activity of man's creative spirit is the correlative assumption that art is essential to the health of society, for the dialectical surge toward human perfection wends its way from one plateau of beauty to another. Truth, to Proudhon, was nothing less than the continuous progress of mind from poetry to prose.[26] What is really fundamental in Proudhon's social thought is his libertarian idealism which led him to hope that man might in the future realize the social strengths he is capable of by nature by giving his imagination full play. "Man is by nature a sinner,—that is, not essentially ill-doing, but rather ill-done,—and it is his destiny to perpetually re-create his ideal in himself," Proudhon wrote.[27] This is what Raphael, the "greatest of all painters," meant when he maintained that the function of the artist is not to portray man and things as nature made them but rather as they should be made, Proudhon continued. In final analysis it is the artist—painter, writer, poet, philosopher, social critic—who must give society crucial insight into its own character. Where they fail to provide such guidance, society must flounder in its efforts to establish a real social order.

Peter Kropotkin, adapting anarchist theory to the nineteenth century notion of social evolution, followed Proudhon in maintaining that mankind is inevitably progressing toward social perfection. It is still not widely understood, however, that Kropotkin's fascination with the idea of nature was not so much scientific as it was aesthetic.[28] And again, like Proudhon, Kropotkin is nowhere guilty of the superficial thinking which characterizes the outlook of the elitist, nor was he foolish enough to suppose that the purpose of art is purely didactic. The general effect of art is to inspire mankind as to what is true and beautiful, and in this task the artist is essential. But Kropotkin had no more use for the aristocratic principle in art than he did in politics. It is the people who produce great art, he maintained,

and not the chosen few. This is the reason for anarchism's total rejection of political power as a possible means of effecting social order.
For it is only when the people are uninhibited by law and formal
political authority that the creative energies of human nature may rise
to the surface of human society and display themselves.

Given the American anarchist's penchant for free thought, it is
not difficult to understand why Michael Bakunin's writings have been
widely acclaimed in the pages of the many anarchist journals published over the years in this country, for he has left us with a great deal of
helpful insight concerning the problem of overcoming mythical
thought. To this day Bakunin at first strikes those who dare to read
his writings as someone to be feared because of the apparent irrever-
ance with which he denounces the idea of God. When Bakunin argued
that it is necessary to abolish the idea of God from our minds if we
would be free, however, his iconoclasm was not without noble purpose; he was opposed to the idea of God not because he favored the
bad over the good but because it is before the God idea considered as
supreme power that mankind has prostrated itself throughout history
until today men are almost totally lacking in the strength to live in
social order with one another. If we would again become free, we
must abolish the very thought of God, i.e., myth, from our minds, for
it is only thus that we have any hope of reclaiming the pristine social
qualities of our human nature, Bakunin held.

Although Bakunin, like most everyone else who lived in the nineteenth century, was greatly affected by the philosophy of Hegel, he
departed radically from the Hegelian conception of world order when
he postulated the novel idea that history "is the revolutionary negation
of the past."[29] Man, essentially an animal, according to Bakunin, has
behind him his primitive beginnings during which he erected a social
structure built upon a foundation of language and thought. Rejecting
this heritage as grossly inadequate, Bakunin called upon men to look
forward to the development of their humanity in the future. In urging
humanity to look forward to the future rather than back to the past,
Bakunin put himself squarely within the Enlightenment view of human progress. According to Bakunin, "The only thing that can warm
and enlighten us, the only thing that can emancipate us, give us
dignity, freedom, and happiness, and realize fraternity among us, is
never at the beginning, . . . but always at the end of history."[30] What
we must do if we would become socially whole again, which is to say

free, is to reject the mythical patterns of thought the human mind became steeped in during the primitive era of history and replace them with rational patterns of behavior drawn from life.

In Bakunin's view of things, life and nature are not two separate and distinct entities but one and the same thing, and the primary quality that identifies them both is the power of human creativity which is synonymous with human rationality. Outspokenly critical of those of his contemporaries who interpreted the eye-catching achievements of nineteenth century science as an indication that the scientist is the true savior of humanity, Bakunin issued a severe warning against this kind of elitist thinking. "Life alone spontaneously creates real things and beings," he postulated. "Science creates nothing; it establishes and recognizes only the creations of life.[31] And again he urged: "The sole mission of science is to light the road. Only life, delivered from all its governmental and doctrinaire barriers, and given full liberty of action, can create."[32] When anarchists argue for spontaneity of thought and action over against a rigid adherence to formal rules and form imposed by authority, the basis of their preference is to be found in the aesthetic inclinations expressed by Michael Bakunin and others who describe life as being synonymous with nature.

Where revolution proceeds along the lines of the aesthetic paradigm, as the anarchist argues it must, human freedom becomes a distinct possibility rather than the mere rhetorical phrase it is on the lips of the politician and professional revolutionary. Far from ruling over the world through formal methods of social and political control, the artist considered as revolutionary persuades only via the means of rational influence. Where the political revolutionary—i.e., the Jacobin, the Bolshevik, or the democratic politician—utilizes power and law, the artist employs symbol and aesthetic form derived from nature to induce people voluntarily to accept the outline of a new and better kind of world. To the extent that art and nature are synonymous, anarchism thus presents itself as a highly useful guide to human freedom, and we would do well to pay heed to what those who have put themselves within this tradition have said. As the life stories of American anarchists clearly demonstrates, the idea of anarchism, although it may have become a minor phase of American political thought after a time, had much deeper roots in the culture of this country than most people realize.

NOTES

INTRODUCTION

1. *American Political Ideas* (New York, 1926), p. 349. For a more recent discussion of violence as a central issue in anarchist thought, see Billie Jeanne Hackley Stevenson, *The Ideology of American Anarchism,* 1880-1910 (unpublished Ph.D. dissertation, The University of Iowa, 1971). And for an exhaustive bibliography annotating the recent literature about anarchism, see Nicholas Walter, "Anarchism in Print: Yesterday and Today," in *Anarchism Today,* ed. by David E. Apter and James Joll (London, 1971), pp. 127-144.

2. *The Ethical Basis of Political Authority* (New York, 1930), p. 43.

3. See especially Oscar and Mary Handlin, *The Dimensions of Liberty* (Cambridge, Mass., 1961).

4. *The Genius of America: Men Whose Ideas Shaped Our Civilization* (New York, 1960), p. 14.

5. The interchangeability of the libertarian and anarchist labels is dealt with by Jerome Tuccille in his study, *Radical Libertarianism: A Right Wing Alternative* (Indianapolis, 1970), pp. 20-58. Unfortunately, Tuccille creates new confusion by suggesting that anarchism is properly described on the right of the political spectrum instead of the left where it belongs. Murray N. Rothbard's *For A New Liberty* (New York, 1973) is less extreme on this point, but he, too, considers libertarianism as essentially a facet of capitalist economics.

6. *The State: Its Historic Role* (London, 1946), p. 44.

7. John Hospers, *Libertarianism: A Political Philosophy for Tomorrow* (Los Angeles, 1971), p. 10.

8. William A. Wittick, *Bombs: The Poetry and Philosophy of Anarchy* (Philadelphia, 1894), p. 186.

9. Hanna Arendt, *On Revolution* (New York, 1963), p. 273.

10. Staughton Lynd, *Intellectual Origins of American Radicalism* (New York, 1968), p. 4.

11. See especially Peter Kropotkin, *The Great French Revolution* (London, 1909).

12. Robert Nisbet, *The Social Philosophers: Community and Conflict in Western Thought* (New York, 1973), p. 355.

13. *Ibid.,* p. 356.

14. *Ibid.*, p. 357.

15. *Anarchism: From Theory to Practice,* trans. by Mary Klopper (New York, 1970), p. 12.

16. Yehoshua Arieli, *Individualism and Nationalism in American Ideology* (Cambridge, Mass., 1964), p. 124.

17. *God and the State* (Bombay, n.d.), p. 65.

18. Ernst Cassirer, *The Philosophy of the Enlightenment*, trans. by Fritz G. A. Koelln and James P. Pettegrove (Princeton, 1951), vii.

19. *Ibid.*, p. 326.

20. *Four Essays on Liberty* (London, 1969), p. 142.

21. *The Myth of the State* (New Haven, 1961), p. 47.

22. *Myth and Christianity* (New York, 1958), p. 17.

23. Edward Dahlberg, *Do These Bones Live* (New York, 1941), p. 142.

24. *Aesthetic*, trans. by Douglass Ainslie (New York, 1953), p. 416.

25. *Ibid.*, p. 15.

26. *System of Economical Contradictions,* trans. by Benjamin R. Tucker (Boston, 1888), p. 448.

27. *Ibid.*, p. 115.

28. One who has clearly recognized this aspect of anarchist thought is Donald Drew Egbert, *Social Radicalism and the Arts: Western Europe* (New York, 1970). See especially the sections on Proudhon, Kropotkin and Bakunin.

29. *The Political Writings of Michael Bakunin,* ed. by G. P. Maximoff (Glencoe, 1953), p. 173.

30. *Ibid.*, p. 174.

31. *Ibid.*, p. 70.

32. *Ibid.*, p. 76.

Part I

Anarchism in America to 1900

TRUE FREEDOM

Wait not till the slaves pronounce the word
    To set the captives free,—
Be free yourselves, be not deferred,
    And farewell slavery.

Ye all are slaves, ye have your price,
    And gang but cries to gang;
Then rise! the highest of ye rise!—
    I hear your fetters clang.

The warmest heart the North doth breed
    Is still too cold and far;
The colored man's release must come
    From outcast Africa.

What is your whole Republic worth?
    Ye hold out vulgar lures;
Why will you be disparting Earth
    When all Heaven is yours?

He's governed well who rules himself,—
    No despot vetoes him:
There's no defaulter steals his pelf,
    Nor Revolution grim.

'Tis easier to treat with kings
    And please our country's foes,
Than treat with Conscience of the things
    That only Conscience knows.

Henry David Thoreau

The Place of Free Thought in the Anarchist Idea

CHAPTER 1

Free Thought as Ideology:
Thomas Paine and Elihu Palmer

The specific form that anarchism first assumed in America was Deism, a species of free thought which sought to attain the very same standards of philosophic integrity that had attracted Socrates and his followers in the earlier Greek Enlightenment. In many respects, Deism and free thought were identical, for they both found in Christianity the source of that philosophical confusion and obfuscation that prevented men from achieving the full social development that should be theirs in nature.[1] In rebellion against established religion and its teachings, Deism sought to find God and truth in nature rather than in ecclesiastical authority or the pronouncements of venerable seers or lawgivers. Like Epicurus and the Stoics before them, the Deists charged that the real basis of conventional religious belief was not a genuine love of goodness and truth but an irrational fear that the gods would bring retribution upon the people if they did not submit themselves to their power. Thus the effort to free men's minds from superstition and unexamined myth became the central concern of Deism as it was for free thought. Fundamentally, the Deist and the

24

freethinker were essentially libertarian in their basic philosophical outlook. The freethinker, as J. B. Bury points out, is the individual who refuses to allow his thought to be controlled or determined by any authority other than that of his own mind.[2] It was this philosophical bias, rather than any formal doctrine or ideological propositions, that demanded the allegiance of all those who have called themselves anarchists in America.

Although Deism in its early phase was confined to the well-educated, the publication of Thomas Paine's *The Age of Reason* changed it from a religion of the better classes to a popular philosophy that found expression in the rude blacksmith shops of the rural villages as well as the taverns and coffeehouses in the larger cities.[3] Accordingly, the first anarchist in America, if we exclude Anne Hutchinson and other figures of the colonial period, was Tom Paine, who more than any other individual of the age grasped the conception of natural social order that is implicit in enlightened thought. As Professor Yehoshua Arieli has pointed out, it was Paine who first perceived the "central importance of this idea of the natural society for the liberation of man from the oppressive and coercive authority of the state."[4] Like all anarchists since his time, Paine argued that the destruction of the existing framework of government would not result in chaos and confusion as conservatives implied, for there is a natural sociability in men which will prevent them from running wild when the restraints of government have been removed. "By postulating the autonomy of social life, its inherent rational structure of mutuality in exchange for service and aid, he aimed to rid the Americans of their fear and of their voluntary subjection to an exploiting and parasitic class rule." But before the people in America could reassert the natural social instincts that were theirs by nature, Paine believed that they first have to escape from the superstitions and vacuous social beliefs that obscured their sight.

Popular history sometimes has it that Paine was first and foremost an iconoclast and that his importance does not go beyond the destructive criticism that he so vehemently hurled against the major institutions of his day. Paine was indeed an iconoclast, as all vigorous thinkers are, and there can be no doubt that the major portion of his energy was directed to the task of exposing the ideas and conceptions of his fellowmen to critical examination. But it is in this very critical function that Paine's deeply religious nature is most clearly illumined.

Although he was often charged with being an atheist, Paine was in fact a profoundly religious man who saw in nature the certain signs that an intelligent pattern of order exists in the universe which is essential to the proper conduct of life. "THE WORD OF GOD IS THE CREATION WE BEHOLD"; he wrote, "and it is in *this word*, which no human invention can counterfeit or alter, that God speaketh universally to man."[5]

Paine's quarrel with Christianity was *not* that it was a religion but that it did not maintain a proper level of spirituality. The system of faith advanced by Christians, according to him, is really "a species of athiesm; a sort of religious denial of God." Instead of directly embracing the spirit of the world, Christians instead turn to a mortal man, Jesus, and direct their love to him rather than to their maker. This, in Paine's opinion, was a great mistake, for it tended to place between man and his maker an opaque screen which could have no other effect than to disorient the individual to the real nature of the moral world. Once Jesus was imposed between the individual and God, morality could never be anything more than a secondhand body of knowledge passed on and distorted by the priesthood that would of necessity be in charge of it. Christian theology, as Paine viewed it, consisted not in moral knowledge but of fragments "of human opinions and of human fancies concerning God. It is not the study of God himself in the works that he has made. . . ."[6] In time what started out as an effort to realize the beauty and reason of nature became distorted into a formal but empty ritual of pseudoworship with which men vainly preened themselves as to their supposed purity and goodness. Paine and other thinkers of the Enlightenment opposed Christianity for its failure to keep men tuned to the real nature of goodness and not simply because it was a religion; they recognized that the word of God had become so formal and structured that it was otiose. Under these circumstances there was nothing to do but escape from its spell.

In calling upon the individual to see things for himself and thus escape from the confusion and deception that clouds the mind of the ordinary man who accepts the institutions and beliefs of society as they are handed to him, Paine laid the foundations for the individualism that was to characterize the thinking of American anarchists for decades to come. Like all children of the Enlightenment, Paine was convinced that the vast bulk of the social malaise that troubles society is directly attributable to the fact that the average man accepts the opinions he holds upon the authority of others rather than his own better judgment, derived from experience. It was this thought he sought to express when he wrote: "It is impossible to calculate the moral mischief . . . that mental lying has produced in society. When a man has so far corrupted and prostituted the chastity of his own mind as to subscribe his professional belief to things he does not believe, he has prepared himself for the commission of every other crime." Under the aegis of the philosophy of the Enlightenment, Paine proclaimed the average man a reasonable creature who was capable of finding the voluntary means of living in peace and harmony with his fellowman without the benefit of the state's authority and power of coercion. In the years that followed, American anarchists returned again and again to Paine as the basic source of their philosophical inspiration.

Among the first Americans to clearly reflect a mature grasp of the anarchist idea in his social and philosophical thought was the notorious Deist, Elihu Palmer (1764-1806). Born and brought up on his father's farm at Canterbury, Connecticut, Palmer was a descendent of Walter Palmer who had settled in Charlestown, Massachusetts, in 1634.[7] After graduating from Dartmouth College in 1787, where he was elected to Phi Beta Kappa and generally recognized as a student of considerable literary ability, Elihu Palmer obtained a pulpit at Pittsfield, Massachusetts. His studies in divinity, however, led him further and further away from the ordered world of religious orthodoxy. In 1788 he received a call from the Presbyterians of Newtown, Long Island, but his parishioners soon became frightened by his radical theological views and withdrew their support after a mere six months had gone by. Moving on to Philadelphia where he preached from a Universalist pulpit, Palmer again became *persona non grata* after announcing his intention to demonstrate that Jesus was not divine but merely an inspired individual of ordinary human qualities. Convinced that the ministry now held no future for him, Palmer quit preaching and engaged himself in studying law, earning admittance to the bar in Philadelphia in 1793. But he had hardly completed his legal training when a plague of yellow fever gripped the city and Palmer suffered the double misfortune of losing both his beloved wife and his own power of sight. Unable to care for his children, he left them in the care of his father to become an itinerant deistic preacher, groping his way from place to place in an effort to lead his contemporaries away from the numbing religious darkness he feared they lived in. Settling in New York in 1794, Palmer found support for his views from the Democratic Society of that city whose members were largely recruited from among those Americans who gave their enthusiastic approval to the revolution in France and its condemnation of established religion. After several years' residence in the city, however, Palmer moved upstate to Newburgh where he became associated with the notorious Druid Society. Originally organized as a Masonic order, a number of the Druids had broken away from Masonry under the fervor of the revolutionary enthusiasm emanating from France in 1789 and had transformed themselves into a radical deistic propaganda association. The Druids were relentless in their criticism of organized Christianity and spared no one's feelings in their propaganda campaign against it, engaging in such blasphemous acts as publicly burning the Bible and an early form of guerrilla theater in which the sacraments were administered to dogs and cats.[8] Palmer's sojourn in Newburgh was apparently cut short by the public indignation which the Druids elicited and he was soon back in New York City where he turned his hand to organizing the Deistical Society which in November of 1800 began to publish a weekly paper devoted to the spreading of its point of view. *The Temple of Reason,* under the editorship of Dennis Driscol, an Irish immigrant who had been a priest in the old country, became the voice of Deism in America and served as a sounding board for the English-speaking supporters of the Enlightenment. Having married again in 1803, Palmer began publishing a paper of his own, *The Prospect: or, View of the Moral World,* which he edited until March of 1805, with the aid of his bride, Mary Powell.

The intimate connection between free thought and the anarchist idea as it evolved in America is clearly evident in Elihu Palmer's rejection of Christian doctrine and his unrestrained acceptance of the enlightened point of view. When we examine the basic writings of Christianity, Palmer complained, we find that the Church subscribes to the principle that all who exist outside its jurisdiction should be kept in a state of moral darkness and deplorable ignorance. Philosophically, he continued, this is a monstrous error. "The establishment of theological systems, claiming divine origin, has been among the most destructive causes by which the life of man has been inflicted."[9]

Where men are led to believe in prescribed truths laid down for them by others, they soon become the slaves of those who do their thinking for them. After a time, names assume a "weight and authority which in reality does not belong to them," and men become habituated to confusing the shadow of the truth with its real essence.

Acknowledging his indebtedness to the philosophic outlook established by Paine, Volney, Condorcet, Barlow, and William Godwin, Palmer enthusiastically cast his lot with that of the freethinkers. "All the opprobrious epithets in the English language have been bestowed upon that mild and peaceful philosophy, whose object is the discovery of truth, and whose first wish is to emancipate the world from the double despotism of church and state," he complained.[10] The first step toward human freedom, he held, is to overcome the debilitating effects foisted upon mankind by the builders of theological systems. "The great instrument, constantly employed by ecclesiastical despotism for the subjugation of the world has been fear," he wrote. "This despotism has made man afraid of his fellow creatures; it has made him afraid of the devil, and afraid of God."[11] If mankind is to achieve the perfection it is potentially capable of achieving, it must "rise above all the degrading impressions of theological superstition" and learn to trust its own powers of reason. "It is by the slow progress of human understanding that the evils of human life can be diminished or destroyed," Palmer held. Freeing itself from superstition and authority, mankind must clear from its mind the ancient servitudes it labors under and reclaim its heritage of freedom.

Palmer's basic quarrel with Christianity stemmed from his conviction that its teachings led mankind away from nature, the source of all social unity and harmony. "The highest delight of theology is the destruction of the beauty, order, and harmony of the universe," he charged. "To nourish the superstitious pride and folly of man, it is necessary to derange, overturn and destroy the splendid beauties and majestic grandeur of the vast empire of nature."[12] Far from being an athiest, Palmer spoke with conviction of a God that is "just, immutable, and eternal." But he was unwilling to attribute all the evils that befall man to this deity. In this regard he wrote:

> If God is good, will he be the author of your punishment? No, no; the caprice of which man complains, is not the caprice of destiny; the darkness that misleads his reason, is not the darkness of God; the source of his calamities is not the distant heavens, but near to him on earth; it is not concealed in the bosom of the divinity; it resides in himself, man bears it in his heart.[13]

Nature, in which God has his real existence, according to Palmer, consists of certain laws pertaining to man which are permanent and immutable. "The age of happiness must be that in which all theological connections shall be concentrated in the Theism of Nature, or the belief of one God," Palmer proclaimed.[14] Unlike human laws and institutions, nature, having been created by God, contains all the ingredients necessary for the reign of social harmony upon earth. In order to receive some insight into the laws of nature, however, man must learn to see things through his own reason rather than through the cannons of propriety laid down for him by his society. "It is because man has forgotten the dignity of his nature; it is because he does not realize the force of his faculties, that he consents to yield to the impositions of superstition," Palmer urged.[15] Anticipating many of the arguments which Proudhon would make some years later, Palmer secured a niche for himself among anarchist thinkers when he proclaimed that "the influence of authority ought never to triumph over evidence. . . ."[16] Taking a stand upon the side of those who have faith that human beings possess all the faculties necessary for intelligent social existence, he urged men to rise to that "exalted state of human improvement" in which reason has at last conquered superstition and idolatry.

It is likely that Elihu Palmer made many converts to free thought as a consequence of the public discourses upon moral and philosophical subjects which he delivered every Sunday evening at six o'clock at Snow's Long Room, 89 Broadway, New York. Although his interest in politics was only peripheral to his interest in religion and philosophy, it is also likely that his teachings had great impact in that realm too, for Palmer recognized full well that any discussion of the role and function of the church is bound to lead to a further discussion of the scope of the state's powers. "It is essential to the dignity of man that he be free and independent, both morally and politically," he argued. Both moral and political despotism destroy man's capacity for life to the extent that they tend to discourage him from exercising his desire for individual virtue. "It is essential to the true and elevated character of an intellectual agent," Palmer insisted, *"that he be confident of his energies*; that he hold in suitable contempt every species of moral and political despotism."[17] With the same bold self-confidence that cost Socrates his life, Palmer spoke out in emphatic condemnation of despotism in any form, urging his contemporaries to wage social revolution against tyranny. "The period is at hand, in which kings and thrones, and priests and hierarchies, and the long catalogue of mischiefs which they have produced, shall be swept away from the face of the earth, and buried in the grave of everlasting destruction."[18] But first men must emancipate themselves from "the barbarous despotism of antiquity" and rely upon "the unlimited power of human reason" to develop a true social system. Obviously influenced by Godwin, Palmer decreed that "Justice is the first great and important principle of social existence."[19] To speak of human nature is to start from the premise that man exists for the purpose of achieving a just and harmonious collective life. Man was born to be free. Left to himself, he is capable of attaining a real social existence within society. The alpha and omega of all philosophy therefore is freedom.

Like all anarchists, Palmer had no fear of freedom and held that it was a grave error to suppose that the differences of opinion to which free thought inevitably gives rise were a real threat to the basic peace of society. It is only when differences of opinion are "enabled to arm themselves with the authority of government, to form parties in the state, and to struggle for that political ascendency, which is too frequently exerted in support of or in opposition of some particular creed, that they become dangerous," he held.[20] No system of thought, whether it be in the realm of religion, politics or education, ought to be allowed to go unexamined, Palmer argued, for human progress relies upon the progression of intelligence and the moral sentiments. Where thought remains free and unobstructed, mankind can hope for the eventual elimination of the social evils it presently suffers under. To the charge that social evil can best be eliminated from society by the firm rule of authority, Palmer countered with the argument that "despotism gives no encouragement to any kind of improvement, and the hope of human amelioration from this quarter will ever prove to be fallacious." Man's intellect and moral sentiments have atrophied as he has cringed in fear before religious and political authority, Palmer urged, and thus he has come to submit to the most crude forms of servitude and degradation.[21] Human freedom upon earth will be restored when mankind has again learned to live without authority in both the religious and political realms. "Ages must elapse" before a social revolution of this magnitude can be accomplished, Palmer admitted. Yet he was confident that "the power of reason, the knowledge of printing, the overthrow of political and ecclesiastical despotism, the universal diffusion of the light of science, and the universal enjoyment of republican liberty; these will become the harbingers and procuring causes of real virtue in every individual, and universal happiness will become the lot of man."[22] The great faith in man's ability to live according to the rules and precepts of nature which Palmer reflects here is not dissimilar to the anarchist contention that freedom is the main ingredient in any formula for social evolution. Rejecting the idea that political power can work for man's good, Palmer embraced the main tenets of anarchist theory even before Proudhon was born. And since it was Proudhon who first deliberately chose to call himself an anarchist, Palmer has never been labeled under that title. His commitment to the anarchist idea is unmistakable, however, and it is to him that we must turn our thoughts when seeking for the origins of the anarchist idea in America.

Palmer did not, it is true, bring any substantial contribution to philosophy or political science. Nor was he, for that matter, among the founders of the deistic movement in America. Almost all the leading figures in this country during the revolution were confirmed Deists, including Washington, Franklin, and Jefferson.[23] And not only were the outstanding thinkers of the period proponents of Deism but the idea had passed from them to the common man, becoming the basis of that "republican religion" which characterized American society during its early years.[24] Elihu Palmer's real value was not as a philosopher but as teacher and guiding spirit of the libertarian movement in early America, for it was through Palmer that the ideas of Tom Paine were kept alive and transmitted from the freethinkers of the eighteenth century to the freethinkers of the nineteenth. When Paine landed in Baltimore in October 1802 after an absence of fifteen years from the American scene, it was Palmer who heralded his return. Unfortunately, the wide acceptance deistic philosophy had enjoyed in earlier times was now spent and the waves of reaction caused by the eruption of American patriotic fervor and religious revivalism swept away the libertarian foundations which Palmer and other Deists had built. But the essential roots of anarchism in America remained in the free thought societies which Deism had spawned in great profusion throughout the more heavily populated areas of the country. Not only did the city of Cleveland support a chapter of the United States Moral and Philosophical Society, a free thought organization, but even in rural Ohio, conventions of free-thinkers convened during the 1830's in small towns, such as Shalersville in Portage County.[25] On the East coast, where free thought was even more strongly ensconced, The Sunrise Club of New York and other groups continued to recruit members for the free thought movement right up past the first decade of the next century.[26] It was the Sunrise Club to which Ernest Howard Crosby, Benjamin Tucker, Edwin C. Walker, Emma Goldman, and other anarchists belonged. Although the major thrust of these groups was aimed at the establishment of free religious thought, the inevitable by-product of their activity was a corresponding love of freedom in the area of social and political theory as well. Elihu Palmer himself gave apt demonstration of this connection when during a Fourth of July oration in 1793 he said:

> King-craft and priest-craft, those mighty enemies of reason and liberty, were struck with death by the genius of 1776. For seventeen years they have been decaying under the influence of a mortal wound and are now in the last stages of their existence.[27]

Although American anarchists were later to find more sophisticated arguments for their beliefs, it was from this anti-clerical axiom derived from the Enlightenment's conception of progress that the movement drew its early inspiration.

NOTES

INTRODUCTION

1. Ernst Troeltsch, "Free-Thought," *Encyclopaedia of Religion and Ethics,* Vol. VI ed. by James Hastings (New York, 1924), p. 122.

2. *A History of Freedom of Thought* (New York, 1913), p. 18.

3. Herbert M. Morais, *Deism in Eighteenth Century America* (New York, 1934), p. 120.

4. Individualism and Nationalism in American Ideology (Cambridge, Mass., 1964), p. 89.

5. "The Age of Reason," *Thomas Paine: Representative Selections* (New York, 1961), p. 257.

6. *Ibid.,* p. 262.

7. "Elihu Palmer," *Dictionary of American Biography,* Vol. 14 (New York, 1934), p. 178.

8. Albert Post, *Popular Freethought in America* (New York, 1943), p. 25.

9. *Principles of Nature; or, A Development of the Moral Causes of the Happiness and Misery Among the Human Species* (New York, 1801), p. 16.

10. *Ibid.,* p. 113.

11. "Religious Fear," *Prospect; or View of the Moral World,* Vol. I (August 4, 1804), 275.

12. "Universal Deluge," *Prospect; or, View of the Moral World,* Vol. I (February 25, 1804), 89.

13. *Principles of Nature,* p. 125.

14. "Superstition," *Prospect; or, View of the Moral World,* Vol. II (March 30, 1805), 100.

15. *Principles of Nature,* p. 20.

16. "Intellectual Independence," *Prospect; or, View of the Moral World,* Vol. II (March 30, 1805), 100.

17. *Principles of Nature,* p. 191.

18. *Ibid.,* p. 200.

19. "Comments Upon the Sacred Writings of the Jews and Christians," *Prospect; or, View of the Moral World,* Vol. II (February 9, 1805), 42.

20. "Christian Heresies," *Prospect; or, View of the Moral World,* Vol. I (January 28, 1804), 71.

21. *Principles of Nature,* p. 170.

22. *Ibid.,* p. 109.

23. John M. Robertson, *A Short History of Free Thought.* (London, 1899), p. 376.

24. G. Adolf Koch, *Republican Religion: The American Revolution and the Cult of Reason* (New York, 1933), p. 16.

25. Post, *op. cit.,* p. 116.

26. Sidney Warren, *American Freethought, 1860-1914,* (New York, 1943), p. 31.

27. "Extract from an Oration Delivered at Federal Point, Near Philadelphia, on the 4th of July, 1793."

The Rebel as Anarchist: Come-Outers
and Non-Resistants

It is impossible to tell at precisely what point the anarchist idea in America first developed into recognizable form. The probability is that there were great numbers of Americans during the early years of the Republic who basically believed in anarchist principles without recognizing themselves as anarchists, since the idea had not yet been formally conceptualized. A crude form of the anarchist idea is evident in J. A. Etzler's *The Paradise Within the Reach of All Men, Without Labor, by Powers of Nature and Machinery,* which was published from Pittsburg in 1833.[1] Etzler proposed that men form themselves into voluntary associations and take advantage of nature's forces in order to release the hoard of wealth that is stored up in America. Reflecting the influence of radical individualism, Etzler warned his contemporaries that they could not realistically expect government to contribute anything positive to the progress of domestic concerns. "Men must concur freely in any measure or enterprise for their own benefit," he argued, and were they to do this they could expect a veritable utopia to be established in America within ten years.[2] But first they must organize themselves into committees or associations of some kind and learn to govern themselves. Etzler, apparently, had enjoyed very little formal education, for his exposition was noticeably defective in form and style, but what he lacked in polish and sophistication he made up in enthusiasm and integrity. One can only guess as to how much influence his book exercised over his contemporaries, since there is very little historical material available concerning his life, but most certainly here was the anarchist idea in embryonic form.

Even more pronounced in his adherence to anarchist principles was Nathaniel Peabody Rogers (1794-1846) of Plymouth, New

Hampshire. The son of Doctor John Rogers, a highly respected physician who had established a brilliant record while a student at Harvard University, Nathaniel brought much happiness to his family when he graduated with honors from Dartmouth College in 1816, thereafter taking up the study and practice of law in his home town for the next twenty years. Far back in his ancestry, however, there were deep-seated precedents for dissent: one of his forebears, the Reverend John Rogers, was the first of Bloody Queen Mary's victims to be consigned to the flames in 1555; while his grandfather, also known as the Reverend John Rogers, had been notorious around Leominster, Massachusetts, for his strong free thought sentiments and his undisguised rebellion against ecclesiastical authority. For his part, Nathaniel Rogers was completely orthodox in his religious and social views for the first forty years of his life; it was not until the stench from the festering sore of slavery reached his nostrils that he felt moved to speak out against injustice and social error.[3] But once his hackles had been raised, Nathaniel Peabody Rogers came on strong as an anarchist. Actually the more precise label one ought to attach to Roger's political views is "Come-outerism," an early form of anarchist thinking in America.[4] The Come-outers were particularly active throughout New England in antebellum America, deriving the basic pattern of their beliefs from the philosophy of free thought established by Paine and others.

Generally the Come-outers were puristic with regard to money and property, rejecting both as a hindrance to moral growth. But Rogers intuited, as did other Come-outers, that economic slavery is generally an aspect of political slavery and that one cannot stand without the other. Preoccupied as he was with moral issues, Rogers could hardly have been said to offer highly sophisticated solutions to the economic problems of his age. Yet he clearly perceived the essential connection between economic and political power. When the workingman is forced to grub and sweat from sunup to sundown in order to sustain himself and his loved ones at a mere subsistence level, he argued, that man is most likely to be kept in slavery. "It is easy for a priesthood to ride such a people," Rogers editorialized. "They have not the leisure nor the elasticity of the soul, to appreciate or assert their own freedom. Their backs are bowed, like a kneeling camel's, and the priest mounts them and rides them all their miserable lives long."[5] Totally oblivious of the fact that there was anyone in the world named Karl Marx or Friedrich Engels, Nathaniel Rogers pronounced religion the opium of the people and called upon the laboring masses of the world to throw off the parasites who clung to their backs. Formulating a crude theory of communist justice, Rogers would abolish the evil of class domination by doing away altogether with class distinctions based upon economic functions. "To till the ground and raise the bread out of it, 'the staff of life,' this is occupation," he proclaimed. "I don't mean raise it by slave labor, or even by paid labor—or the people's labor in any shape," he cautioned, "but by your own labor."[6] But before we can bring into existence such a highly moral form of social justice as this, he implied, it is first necessary to free ourselves from political domination.

It was in their attitude toward political organization that the Come-outers most closely approached the spirit of the anarchist idea. Often commonly referred to as "no-organizationists," the Come-outers were adamant in their opposition to any formal political structure and called upon all men to rely upon their own internal inclinations toward social order. "No-organizationists pursued the logic of nonresistance to its farthest reaches; all coercion is sinful."[7] It was in this spirit that Nathaniel Rogers sought to find a remedy to the problem of intemperance which so sorely troubled the socially sensitive individual of his day. Although he was personally convinced that the use of tobacco and whiskey are harmful to one's character and health, he staunchly opposed all attempts to regulate the problem through resort to formal legislation. "If we can't stop drunkenness without the paltry aid of our state house," he urged "let it go on."[8]

So affected by the slavery issue was Rogers that in 1838 he gave up the practice of law and moved to Concord, New Hampshire, where he assumed the editorial duties of the *Herald of Freedom* which had been established three years previously as the official organ of the New Hampshire Anti-slavery Society. Receiving a copy of Lysander Spooner's *The Unconstitutionality of Slavery* for review, Rogers pronounced it a thoughtful, relevant work, recommending that his readers peruse it at their earliest opportunity. Like Spooner, Nathaniel Rogers held slavery to be a fundamental violation of the basic spirit of the American republic. Accordingly, every right thinking man ought to put himself staunchly in opposition to the tyranny the nation was being forced to endure.

Implicit in the controversy over slavery, according to Rogers, is a fundamental philosophical issue that has far-reaching consequences for American society. It seems to me, he wrote in *The Herald of Freedom,* that the crucial issue that arises out of slavery is "the question between Authority, on the one hand, and the conviction of the Understanding, on the other. Can mankind ascertain what is right, or must they be authoritatively told it. . . ."[9] Certain in his own mind that freedom and self-governance were inseparable, Rogers urged his contemporaries to act upon their convictions rather than their legal responsibilities. In final analysis, he held, the slavery question must be settled according to what is ultimately right and true rather than what is legally permissible. "We in the antislavery movement," he proclaimed, "demand liberty for the slave on the ground that humanity is entitled to be free—that freedom naturally and absolutely belongs to it. [We] refuse to rest the slave's claim to freedom on any external authority whatever."

In the proposals he urged for the solution of the slavery issue, Rogers displayed a pattern of social thought almost identical to the pattern of thinking that anarchists of a later day would demonstrate. With reference to the tactics which Abolitionists should adopt to bring about the emancipation of the black man, Rogers was adamantly opposed to any resort to political methods. "Institutions make slavery," he argued, "and therefore [institutions] cannot overthrow it."[10] Turning his critical gaze upon the structure of political parties which liberals then and now place so much trust in, Rogers pronounced the entire political machinery of the country inadequate to the task of building a real social order. "The only object of party is power," he wrote. "To get it or to preserve it, is [the party's] *only possible* motive. Anything that would bring power, or perpetuate it, is always unhesitatingly and unscrupulously resorted to, and anything that would hazard it, is shunned with instinctive dread."[11] Politics, in Roger's opinion, was, like smoking or drinking or any other human vice—something to be given up by an act of individual will. That men do not do so, he urged, stands as testimony of the fact that their fundamental motives are defective. At basis, Rogers held, the politician "is but a man driver, a human teamster. His business is to control men by the whip and the goad." How, then, can we place any trust in his leadership when moral issues are at stake as they are in the problem of abolition? Not until we give up all reliance upon political machinery can we realistically look forward to an era of social harmony and peace.

Much as Voltaire or Tom Paine focused upon the priesthood as one of the main causes of mankind's enslavement, so Rogers pronounced the clergy of his day mainly responsible for the moral torpor which gripped the hearts and minds of Americans in the face of the hated institution of chattel slavery. Concerned that dissent and open discussion will tear the church apart even more than it already is, clergymen beg the people to refrain from any further talk about slavery, he complained. "They shut up the people in their Sunday prison, the meeting house, and have so holified the day, the house, and themselves, in the people's eyes, that they dare neither hear the slave's advocate, nor think a thought on any moral subject whatever."[12] Until the heavy foot of the clergy is removed from the neck of the people, Rogers roared, Americans can hope for no relief from the devastating moral evils they presently suffer. Unhappily, Rogers lamented, Christianity has been so thoroughly co-opted by the state that there is little hope that the church can ever regain any of its moral vitality. "It was the curse and ruin of the Church, when she consented to the friendship and protection of the armed State," Rogers argued. "Christianity left her at that moment, and has never since darkened her doors, except to bear testimony against her. Our modern Church is a mere creature of the State."[13] Under these circumstances, Rogers, like other Come-outers, was forced to adopt an extreme position, leaving the church and the state altogether and adopting a social stance that can only be described as anarchistic.

Although Come-outerism was confined to a very small percentage of the American population, its roots ran deep as witnessed by the fact that its major tenets again found expression in the pages of *The World's Reformer* edited by Seward Mitchell of Newport, Maine, some forty years after Rogers' death. Like Rogers before him, Mitchell argued that "the State is the great criminal, but it can never be destroyed by force but must be outgrown by higher conditions."[14] Pronouncing the ballot-box as pernicious as the cartridge-box, Mitchell joined Rogers in calling for reform through completely non-coercive means. Commenting upon the life of William Lloyd Garrison, Leo Tolstoy pointed out some years later that the important contribution made by abolitionists was not so much that the Negro has the right to be free but the more general principle that "no man, under any pretext, has the right to dominate his fellows, that is, to coerce them."[15] It is this general principle rather than any specific ideological dogma or rule that binds together all those who share the spirit of anarchism.

No American more fully embraced the essential attitudes of the anarchist idea than did Henry Clarke Wright (1789-1870). Devoutly Christian in outlook, although his views were glaringly unorthodox in character, Wright preceded Tolstoy as an advocate of the doctrines of nonviolent resistance and Christian socialism. Born in Sharon, Connecticut, Wright was descended on both sides from families which had fled to America in the 1630's to escape religious persecution in England. Perhaps it was reaction to this Puritan heritage which made him the ardent social reformer he was, for the pages of his autobiography reveal that there was a bitter war that raged within him which arrayed the theology he was taught as a young child against the social and philosophical sentiments he developed for himself in his maturity.[16] Writing in later years to his friend, William Lloyd Garrison, he expressed the conviction that no parent ought ever structure the young child's mind regarding the nature of the divine, for to do so is to impress upon the psyche an indelible theological imprint which can never be completely washed away again during maturity. Teach children "that Anthropology is the only true Theology," Wright wrote, and that they should never think about God without reference to the human relationships they find themselves enmeshed in.[17] To do otherwise, he held, is to make men the unwilling slaves of a deity which must ever remain removed from their personal control. "The gorgeous and costly phantom that men call God," Wright wrote in words that are strikingly reminiscent of the words of Max Stirner and Michael Bakunin, "that phantom has been the scourge of my life; it has haunted me, sleeping and waking, as an omnipresent, omnipotent, malignant demon."[18] It was to escape the clutches of this demon that Wright devoted his energies to the cause of free thought, thereby developing the sentiments of an anarchist without consciously recognizing that that label fitted him perfectly. For Henry C. Wright, as for many anarchists to follow, freedom was more than a slogan—it was the essential requisite for the development of a meaningful self-identity.

Growing up around Cooperstown, New York, where his father had moved the family when Henry was four, Wright suffered the torments of hell from yet another struggle which raged within him; the struggle between the natural filial devotion he felt toward his father and the equally natural revulsion he felt in the face of the things for which his father stood. Seth Wright, his father, was a hulking giant of a man who elicited strong emotional reactions from those who surrounded him. Although his neighbors found him to be a genial sort with a good word and smile for everyone, his son Henry remembered him most for his stern disciplinary attitudes and his unyielding demands that life be lived according to the strict teachings of the Calvinist faith.[19] Finding nothing incongruous between his devotion to the military and his adherence to Christian principles, the elder Wright ruled over his family with the severity of a drill sergeant, impelling Henry further and further away from the paternal course that was set for him. Many of the emotional upheavals Henry Wright experienced during his lifetime were obviously caused by the conflict between filial devotion to his father and his unconscious attempt to escape the tyranny of his father's teachings. When he was 28, Wright, who was employed in Norwich, Connecticut, as a hatter, followed his father's example and joined the Presbyterian Church under the grip of the religious fervor which swept the town during a revival meeting. Wright then entered Andover Theological Seminary, obtaining a license to preach the gospel in 1823. For the moment, it would seem, the son had bowed in submission to the father's wishes. But even as a student at Andover, Henry Wright was directed by his natural sentiments away from the Puritan heritage that had been forced upon him as a child. The God of the father was a stern god, quick to condemn human frailty and reluctant to forgive those who had broken the letter of Christian law. But the more theology the son read at Andover, the more he was convinced that the Puritan image of a stern, demanding deity who rules over the lambs of his flock with unyielding firmness was inadequate. Once he had established the futility of authority as a means of attaining perfection in his own religious experience, Wright had no trouble in applying the same precept to the realm of social and political theory. The unorthodox religious ideas which Henry Wright came to accept had far-reaching consequences in regard to his personal development in the direction of libertarianism. Whereas the elder Wright accepted the idea of God on faith, holding that the declaration of God's divinity by the fathers of Christianity was enough to demonstrate the authenticity of the idea, the younger Wright insisted that no demonstration for the existence of God can ever be made on the basis of revealed truth in any form. "I do not believe in God because of anything which I read in the Bible or in other books," he professed, "nor because of anything I see in the physical universe. . . ."[20] To accept the idea of God on faith is to follow blind authority. And authority for the freethinker, as for the anarchist, is the basis for all the evil in the world.

The only basis for an intelligent acceptance of the idea of God, according to Wright, was an intuitive awareness that God exists within nature as it is experienced by any particular individual. In this aspect of his intellectual development, Wright, like Elihu Palmer before him, was a product of the Enlightenment and the free thought movement which sprang up from the seeds it had embedded in American culture. To a man, the Deists held to the view that nature is the font of all that is good in the universe and that mankind should never be downgraded in the interest of the supernatural. "HUMAN NATURE!—It stands out in the very front of the great picture of creation, as its most beautiful and commanding object," Wright wrote. "There is nothing above the Human but the Divine; nothing above Man but God."[21] There have been social historians who have interpreted this line of argument to mean that the Deists were brazenly presumptuous in holding that man ought never to be eclipsed by the shadow of the divine, and that their ulterior motive was to foolishly cut mankind off from the source of the good and beautiful. But this is a vulgar interpretation of what Henry Wright meant by the statement. For him, the problem was epistemological rather than ideological; the problem was not to maliciously destroy the good but to discover its real essence. This is made clear in his assertion that: "As we can know nothing of God except through his manifestations, we naturally regard the Human as the most perfect manifestation of the Divine." Philosophically, Wright was not far from the position of contemporary Christian existentialism which holds that God has no existence until man gives demonstration of his being through creative acts in the face of the absurd. In terms of the philosophical structure of his day, however, the question at issue was the Calvinist concept of salvation. Whereas the followers of Calvin all agreed that eternal life can never be obtained other than as a free gift from the divine, and that good works performed here on earth have nothing to do with the matter, Wright held that the external acts of conduct performed by any individual are a precise index to the quality of his piety and his moral standing. Away with all this nonsense about visible and invisible saints which our fathers so much worried themselves with, he asserted. "When any man exhibits the spirit of Christ in his daily life, we are bound to believe that he is a Christian, no matter what name he is called, where he lives or whether he ever heard of Christ. He has the spirit, the substance."[22] Christianity, on Wright's view, was essentially a matter of ethics rather than dogma or creed. Theology, on the other hand, conceived as the demonstration of a divine power based upon abstract principles of right, was for him a "fathomless abyss" which could provide man with no intelligent guide to human development.

In Wright's hands the idea of Christian perfection led directly to the idea of anarchism, as it did in the case of all the Tolstoyans who were to follow him. Actually the Tolstoyan label was inappropriate to Wright, for both he and his friend, Adin Ballou of the Hopedale Community, had preceded Tolstoy in developing a philosophy of Christian socialism and an accompanying theory of nonviolent resistance to force and violence. Rejecting Saint Paul's suggestion that the Christian ought to obey the powers of God and the state with equal humility, Wright self-confidently proclaimed the institution of government a "costly farce." The American people sit spellbound at the feet of the state, he charged, bowing down in submission to its powers on the belief that the institution of government is the only possible means of maintaining law and order within society. It is on the authority of this idea that the jailor locks up the social deviate, the hangman kills his victim, and the general orders his soldiers to slaughter the enemy. The supporters of the state idea argue that since the institution of government was originally established by God as an act of generosity toward men, it is a sacred institution which men must never overthrow. But "the Being whom I worship as God never committed such a folly," Wright contended. "God never established an institution, and then enpowered men to destroy one another to preserve the instition."[23] It is this very myth which men must somehow eliminate from their minds if they are ever to live a truly social existence.

The extent to which Wright embraced the anarchist idea is clearly evident in the humanistic character of the social philosophy he espoused. Finding himself as a youth in a Christian culture which had proceeded dangerously far down the hazardous path of formalism, Wright warned his contemporaries against the religious institutionalism they were so wont to indulge themselves in. Christianity, as

Wright saw it, was not an end in itself but a mere means to an end. Where an institution such as state or church becomes omnipotent, the people who are molded by its forms and powers soon become enslaved to its authority. This was why Wright fought so vigorously against the notion of church and state as sacred instruments of God's will. "Man, not the church," he wrote, "is the image of God. Through man, not through the church, does God reveal himself and give his law. Man, not the church, is the Ark of the Covenant. . . ."[24] The institutions of church and state are mere human expedients which man may choose to use for his social purposes. A monstrous social evil is created where men and women reverse this arrangement and sacrifice themselves to the institutions they have made by their own hands. Laying the foundations for the movement of American anarchism that was to follow, Wright urged his fellowmen to refuse to sacrifice themselves to the institutions of church and state. "Let us give all that is ours to give for liberty," he wrote. "Attach no sacredness to any institution; but all sanctity to man." For no church or state has ever advanced any ideal other than the tired remedy of authoritarian prescription designed to perpetuate its own power. The chief aim of all institutionalized government, whether it be temporal or spiritual, is to "sustain and perpetuate the ideas, maxims and customs of the Dead Past." Let us break with the eternal yesterday, he proposed, and turn to man, the hope of all that is creative and libertarian.

And it is indeed as a libertarian that Wright, so much ignored by American historians, breaks through the crust of accepted opinion concerning our past. For all his dedication to the ideal of Christ and his tendency to write in the language of religious commitment, Henry C. Wright was primarily a champion of mankind's liberation from all forms of human slavery. Writing years before the development of modern concepts of social and psychological theory, his books tend to present him as a religious fanatic rather than as a strong-minded radical with much to offer in the way of social criticism. On closer examination, however, his published writings indicate that his focus was always upon the methods of liberating mankind from its self-imposed servitude to the madness of authoritarianism, however spiritual the language he used may have been. Wright, in fact, like many of the leading social critics of his age, was a convinced Spiritualist for a time, believing in a transcendental force of beauty and truth which permeated the universe. In the vein of Emerson and Thoreau he held that mankind possesses something of the divine and that there is no other god before it. Human government, he held, is a weak reed upon which to lean if man would stand upright in the full glory of his natural endowment. Man, on the other hand, is a product of nature, the matrix from which all social value takes form. Born with a capacity for social development that is limited only by his own capacity to recognize the laws of his own being, man is duty bound to search out the design of justice and beauty from which he was fashioned. "By virtue of his existence man owes allegiance to the laws of life and health under which he exists," Wright opined. "These are God's laws, and from his obligations to obey them, no power in the universe can release him."[25] God, as Wright defined the concept, was not so much a power or authority as a standard of beauty which has no form aside from the moral acts to which it gives rise. God, that is to say, is conterminous with nature, albeit we are given to describing the idea in anthropomorphic terms. Wright, no less than any other serious-minded person of his day, was restricted to referring to God as a person or thing even though it was perfectly clear in his mind that what he made reference to was essentially an aesthetic quality or standard. It remained for later day anarchists, such as Horace Traubel and other aesthetically tuned individuals, to more sharply define the essential connection between beauty and liberty; that Henry C. Wright was aware of the connection at all is enough to earn him a niche in libertarianism's hall of fame.

With reference to the question of war, Henry C. Wright, like Adin Ballou and William Lloyd Garrison, was an ardent peace man. Encouraged in his pacifism by his connection with William Ladd's American Peace Society, Wright was a founding member of the New England Non-Resistance Society which was organized in Boston in September of 1838.[26] It was at this meeting, dominated by such fire-eating radicals as Wendell Phillips, Amasa Walker, Abby Kelly, and Garrison and Ballou, that the famous Declaration of Principles was adopted, one of the most pronounced statements of anarchism ever made in America. Not only did the Non-Resistants declare themselves totally opposed to the institution of war but they took a firm stand against any use of force or coercion as a means of regulating people within society. Non-Resistants pledged themselves unwilling to take life as a penalty for crime or even to resort to the courts as a means of controlling wrongdoing. Responding to the primitive Christian bias of Restorationists like Adin Ballou who still hoped that some kind of reconciliation might be brought off within the larger Christian community,[27] The Statement of Principles did advise its members to refrain from any organized attempts to overthrow established government and to generally obey political authority when matters of conscience were not at issue. But on the other hand, the Statement pledged its members to prior commitment not to take an oath in support of any government or even give it tacit allegiance. Non-Resistants would under no circumstances hold office, fight in war, or give any kind of support to any man who employed force for the defense of life, liberty, property, or religion. In short, the New England Non-Resistance Society, of which there were less than 200 members, was committed to a totally nonviolent rejection of formal government on the grounds that political power and war so intertwined that it is not possible to have one without the other. In this they anticipated the finding of modern political scientists who recognize that "Power is linked with war, and a society wishing to limit war's ravages can find no other way than by limiting the scope of Power."[28]

Historians who have depicted anarchists as a breed of essentially violent nihilists have missed the import of such figures as Adin Ballou and Henry C. Wright. Among those historians who have not stumbled into this trap is Staughton Lynd who acknowledged anarchism as a vital connection between nineteenth and early twentieth century nonviolence in this country. "The ultimate goal of all anarchists," Lynd notes, "was a society that would function nonviolently without need of the aggressive state."[29] Nonresistants like Wright who hurled their invective against the trend of events America was caught up in were not so much politically angry as they were morally indignant that politicians and jurists should presume to take power into their own hands on the pretext of serving the good of humanity. It was this which moved Wright to proclaim that "America, once a wilderness, now sits in high places of the earth and sings like a harlot." Recognizing that integrity and honor within American society would be swallowed up by the demands of legality as the country turned more and more to the courts in search of justice and social order, Wright had dark forebodings of things to come.

The first step toward declaring one's independence from the twin evils of power and war, according to Wright, is to refuse to profess loyalty to the state, for like the early Christians, he was aware that any formal oath of loyalty is to abandon one's commitment to independent moral judgment. "To swear allegiance to any human government," he argued, "is to call God to witness that you will obey a power that assumes the right to reverse his decisions at pleasure."[30] It was to preserve the right to moral independence that Wright took a stand upon the side of the philosophy of individualism. Popular opinion has it today that the philosophy of individualism is essentially an outgrowth of economic groups which merely desire independence of movement for the purpose of their financial self-aggrandizement. But Wright, characteristic of the whole anarchist movement in this country, was an individualist not because he wanted economic freedom but because he recognized that moral perfection was obtainable in no other way. This was why he insisted that the individual must have final say as to what is ethically correct in any given situation. As he put it:

> The power to decide what is law, is placed by God in the man, as a man, not in the state. The combination is or should be subject to the individual, not the individual to the combination; the state to the man, not the man to the state. When the government dictates law to individuals, it arrays itself against Nature; creates and fosters antagonism between individuals, and between itself and individuals; and substitutes the enactments and decisions of a soulless, irresponsible organization as rules of domestic, social and commercial life, instead of individual institutions, sympathy, reason and conscience. It dethrones God, and inaugurates the reign of a soulless, godless combination, for whose decisions and acts no individual man or woman is held responsible.[31]

It was in pursuit of a philosophy of individualism that Wright developed a keen interest in the problem of raising children to be free men and women, becoming an agent of the American Sunday School Union and the author of a host of books dealing with marriage and early education of the child. Aware of the crippling effect of religious authority upon the developing mind of the child, Wright was totally opposed to giving formal religious instruction to the young. The development of a libertarian society can only proceed, he held, where the individual is left free to determine right and wrong according to his own experiences and insights. If children are taught anything, it should be "to know the laws of their physical, social, and spiritual nature, and to find their heaven in obeying them."[32] Recalling his own childhood experience, Wright warned that any attempt to harness the mind of the child within formal rules of moral or social instruction is tantamount to crippling his ability to perceive the eternal verities of the universe he inhabits. Let the child free to search out his own truths according to the energies he finds within himself, Wright urged, and he cannot help but come in contact with the sublime truths of human nature which underly all the particular experiences men feel in their lifetimes. "There is but one rightful government, but one divine statute book," he wrote, and that "is engraven on the physical, intellectual, social and moral universe" we find ourselves in. In order to know this universe, it is first necessary to scourge one's basic personality of the vision of the sacred, implanted there by well-meaning but misguided parents who fear that without formal religious and moral instruction, the child is lost forever. In short, Henry C. Wright held to the view that a truly libertarian society must start with a libertarian theory of education at the lowest levels of the educational system. It was this which led him to take the adamant stand against authority that he did. For as he knew so well from his own experience, the negative attitudes that are implanted in the heart and mind of the individual during infancy are graven images which stand in the way of his knowing real beauty later on. And where men fail to perceive the form of the good with their own eyes, they become the easy victims of power-crazed priests and politicians who lead them to indulge in all kinds of collective madness. Many an American anarchist was to discover the validity of Henry C. Wright's outlook in the years to follow, although few of them were aware that this noble soul had any significance aside from his participation in the abolitionist movement.

NOTES

SECTION I - CHAPTER 2

1. Rudolph Rocker, *Pioneers of American Freedom* (Los Angeles, 1949), pp. 51-52. For a more recent treatment of Etzler, see William H. G. Armytage, "J. A. Etzler, An American Utopist," *American Journal of Economics and Sociology*, XVI (October, 1956), 83-88.

2. *The Paradise Within the Reach of All Men, Without Labor, by Powers of Nature and Machinery* (Pittsburg, 1833), p. 105.

3. "Nathaniel Peabody Rogers," *The National Cyclopedia of American Biography*, Vol. II (New York, 1921), p. 320.

4. Lewis Curtis Perry, *Antislavery and Anarchy: A Study of the Ideas of Abolitionism before the Civil War* (Ithaca, 1967), p. 6.

5. "Labor," *Miscellaneous Writings of N. P. Rogers* (n. p., 1849), p. 311.

6. "Tilling the Ground," *Ibid.*, p. 373.

7. Perry, *op. cit.*, p. 96.

8. Rogers, "The Fifteen Gallon Law," *op. cit.*, p. 88.

9. "The Great Question of the Age," *Ibid.*, p. 311.

10. "The Anti-Slavery Movement," *Ibid.*, p. 308.

11. "Politics," *Ibid.*, p. 264.

12. "Newburyport Jail," *Ibid.*, p. 242.

13. "Church and State," *Ibid.*, p. 221.

14. "The Nature of the State," *The World's Reformer*, #286 (Newport, Maine, n.d.), 1.

15. "Introduction to a Short Biography of William Lloyd Garrison," in *The Works of Leo N. Tolstoy* (Oxford, 1928), p. 577.

16. *Human Life: Illustrated in My Individual Experience as a Child, a Youth, and a Man* (Boston, 1849), p. 21. Hereafter referred to as *Autobiography*.

17. *Ibid.*, p. 116.

18. *Ibid.*, p. 353.

19. Louis C. Jones, *Growing Up in Cooper County* (Syracuse, 1965), p. 15.

20. *Autobiography*, p. 201.

21. *The Self-Abrogationist, or the True King and Queen* (Boston, 1863), p. 21.

22. *Autobiography*, p. 219.

23. *Ibid.,* p. 348.

24. *The Self-Abrogationist,* p. 138.

25. *Ibid.,* p. 115.

26. Merle Curti, "Non-Resistance in New England," *The New England Quarterly,* II (January, 1929), p. 42-45.

27. For an analysis of Adin Ballou's social and political thought, see William O. Reichert, "The Philosophical Anarchism of Adin Ballou," *The Huntington Library Quarterly,* XXVII (August, 1964).

28. Bertrand de Jouvenel, *On Power* (Boston, 1962), p. 143.

29. Stoughton Lynd, *Non-violence in America: A Documentary History* (Indianapolis, 1966), p. XXXI.

30. *The Self-Abrogationist,* p. 115.

31. *Ibid.,* p. 116.

32. *Autobiography,* p. 37.

CHAPTER 3

Sidney H. Morse and the Free Religious Association

Although Sidney H. Morse (1832-1903) is largely remembered as an American sculptor, he stands out among anarchists as one who arrived at the anarchist idea via the avenue of religion. Born at Rochester, New York, Morse studied at Antioch and later prepared for the ministry at Harvard. Labelling himself a Unitarian, he held a numer of pulpits in the West before he abandoned his ministerial robes for the smock of the artist. Along with Benjamin R. Tucker, Morse as a young man was a member of a "parlor meeting" in Boston which met to discuss the mutualist theories of Josiah Warren. Becoming an ardent disciple of the "first American anarchist," he accepted Warren's principle of labor exchange as the essential first step in social reform. In his declining years, Josiah Warren, reciprocating the devotion of his young protege, made Morse literary executor of his estate. Among his intimate friends Morse counted Emerson, Samuel Johnson, A. B. Alcott, Samuel Longfellow, and a host of other outstanding literary and social figures. Later, when he turned to sculptor as the main vehicle for the expression of his views, the subjects he chose as models included many of the most prominent Americans—Walt Whitman, Thomas Paine, Abraham Lincoln, Oliver Wendell Holmes, William Ellery Channing, Theodore Parker, James Martineau, and President Cleveland. His bust of Emerson was deposited in the Second Chuch of Boston, a reminder that radical libertarianism has received a great deal of its support from individuals who were principally interested in the arts and only secondarily interested in politics.

In his early years it was as a writer and lecturer that Sidney H. Morse attempted to advance the libertarian idea. In 1865 Morse helped establish *The Radical,* a journal of religious reform that re-

flected the views of the Free Religious Association, of which O. B.
Forthingham was president. Serving as editor until 1872, Morse
steered the *Radical,* which was the successor to the *Dial,* further and
further to the religious left. Convinced in his own mind that Christianity as it was then practiced was a "wornout theological system" that
must be discarded before any real religious progress was possible,
Morse called for a revolution in the spiritual processes of his generation. The typical Christian, he complained, is one who accepts the
notion of spiritual monarchy, submitting himself to the authority of
a superior being. But authority of this sort is not so much spiritual as
it is political, he argued, for the one commanded is little else than the
slave of a master.[1] If we are ever to claim our birthright of freedom,
Morse reasoned, we must first reject all attempts to fetter the Spirit. It
is time that we cease thinking of ourselves as sheep to be led by Jesus
into the paths of righteousness. The notion of Jesus as savior has cut
the lines of communication between the individual and the religious
forces of nature, forcing Christianity into a *cul de sac* from which
there seems to be no escape. Let us be done with Jesus, then, Morse
urged, for he has become a "stumbling block to the generation" that
must be removed before any further progress can be made. "Let the
people today speak of themselves, in their own name, in their own
Spirit."[2] The similarity of Morse's religious views and those of
Nicholas Berdyaev are striking, despite the wide cultural differences
that separate them.

Confident that human beings function best within an environment of freedom, Morse maintained that religion must depart
radically from the structure and organization it was then contained
by. Religion, as he conceived it, was not a formal body of theological
rules to be imposed upon people but a spontaneous outpouring of
social concern directed toward the general improvement of the social
condition. True religion, he argued, is not consciously introduced into
the world but the product of the evolutionary process we find everywhere in nature. "The movement was in the time, in the needs and
aspirations of the people."[3] Reflecting a supreme confidence in the
ability of people to govern themselves, Morse advocated the theory
that the first and only rule of moral and social reform is freedom. Give
the individual the reins and he will guide himself to the goals he now
appears incapable of attaining. If we desire the realization of justice
and truth on earth, we ought to turn men loose, allowing human

nature to seek its own level. Give thought to the winds, without concern for the outcome, and humanity can be expected to reflect the same amazing order that physical nature manifests all about us. "Waiting minds are at every point of the compass. They know their own truth. They can manage it. They need no pastor, no divine Doctor."[4] The people can succeed where kings and politicians have failed, Morse proclaimed.

Reflecting the soul of the artist that he was, even when he was still primarily concerned with questions of religious reform, Sidney Morse set himself in opposition to formalism as the chief obstacle in the path of the free society. The first of the false idols to be knocked down is that personal authority by which men in former times were bound to a supreme being. Declaring himself a radical, Morse defined the radical position as belief in the controlling influence of sentiment rather than control by authority, whether in the realm of morals or politics. Radicalism thus defined, he argued, is "a leaven in the nature of man," a force to lead him out of slavery into the freedom of a libertarian society. The conservative, according to Morse, clings to the myth of Jesus as the supernatural lord of men, with the consequence that the latter are relegated to the role of mere subjects, powerless to do anything other than follow their leader wherever he might beckon. The mere reformation of Christianity is not enough, therefore, for the idea "represents a dying and disappearing civilization" which we ought not to save even if we could. It is a revolution that we need, then, Morse urged, and not just the reform of our existing religious structure.[5] As revolutionists, our work is not to be done within the old body of the church but outside of it. We must declare our independence and replace the old spiritual notions with new ones more adequate to the times.

Having cut himself off completely from the religious institutions of his generation, Morse faced the task of finding some new conceptualization of spiritual value which would not display the same rigidity that he had so recently criticized in Christianity. Displaying a pronounced libertarian bias, he advised his contemporaries to avoid all formal religious organization and structure and turn instead to a *laissez faire* arrangement wherein the individual's efforts would be centered in his own undirected attempt to perfect a personal "religious sentiment" without reference to creeds or clergy. Finding no basis for morality other than in the free conscience of the individual,

Morse maintained that any new society must develop out of the spontaneity of the people. "Culture," he argued in his column "Chips From My Studio" which regularly appeared in Tucker's *Radical Review,* "is the liberation of self from rules and laws."[6] We must be extremely careful, therefore, not to organize the religious sentiment or to make any effort to propagate it by means of structured pedagogic devices. Just as poetry becomes hard and brittle when we attempt to use it for didactic purposes, so the religious sentiment withers and dies when we consciously employ it for the reformation of society by turning it over to trained ministers. "It becomes dogma, as poetry prose, on the lips of professionalists."[7] Let us put our trust, then, in the spontaneous native impulses of the individual in our quest for spiritual advancement. For "human nature is a flower that is unfolding" and we must do nothing to disturb its natural growth toward perfection, Morse insisted. To date the perfect blossom has appeared in individuals but never yet in the race. Tomorrow, perhaps, the race itself will blossom into the perfection we have long dreamed about but have not been wise enough to cultivate. Likening human nature to a "plant that has a self-conscious and self-directing growth," Morse maintained that the answer to the moral problem was to put our trust in freedom and the individual's ability to steer himself according to the unwritten laws within his breast. For in final analysis there is no other road to social peace than the way of individual responsibility and self-direction. As Morse put it:

> If the law is within, there is liberty. If it is without there is bondage. What was the heroism of Jesus but his endeavor to abolish for himself the exterior law? What was his superiority but the degree of his triumph? What is his proper influence but the excitement of others for their own victory? Willingness to obey, from pure delight in the recognition of the law, is man's religion.[9]

In his political theory Morse was as staunch a friend of liberty as he was in his religious thought. Although he was reluctant to attach any particular label to himself, and was critical of his dear friend Benjamin Tucker for calling the libertarian idea anarchism,[10] Morse was as much an anarchist in his basic sentiments as any man who ever carried the black flag. As a result of his studies in theology, Morse had learned that power from the point of view of the individual is a hindrance to the development of spiritual being. "Mere power is gross and an illusion," he wrote. "The worship of it, is not only the sign of a servile spirit, but the most futile method of guarding one's self."[11] In the realm of politics, Morse lamented, most people display the very same sycophancy in the face of power that they do before the pulpit on Sunday. Lacking a genuine faith in liberty, yet aware that liberty is generally the most highly praised of all human values, they indulge themselves in sham genuflections to its glory. In their hearts, unfortunately, they are as devoted to the despotic principle as is the Czar of Russia. For the Czar, according to Morse, "has the same 'divine' distrust of liberty that they have, and they have the same misgivings that he has."[12] But just as God must remain unreal to humanity so long as people lack a genuine faith in the religious sentiment, so liberty must remain an empty cry upon our lips so long as we lack a real belief in its power to effect social order. When will we learn, Morse queried with heavy heart, that liberty does not stem from the refinement of the methods of despotism but from the methods of freedom.

The great mistake of those who seek refuge in despotism, according to Morse, is that they fail to realize that behind the "Babel of confusion and strife" which characterizes existing human institutions is an order and harmony stemming from nature that is far superior to any system of law and order that men can create through power. Many political theorists worship formal political institutions, considering them the manifestation of an advanced science. But just as the turtle or armadillo that seeks protection in the hard shell it wears on its back has not progressed beyond the first crude stages of self-defense, so a humanity that seeks safety in institutions is not yet sufficiently advanced to deserve the name "society." The state, on this view, may well have been a useful device in its day, furnishing people with protection from one another in the time before they had learned to control themselves from within. Yet it becomes increasingly evident, Morse argued, that the law and order maintained by the state is a far cry from the genuine social order of a real society. Since society is a thing of the future rather than an existing fact, men despair, accepting the discord and strife which they see all about them as the essential character of the human will. And thus they redouble their efforts to build safeguards and restraints around the spontaneity of the human spirit. But the libertarian cannot be satisfied with the superficial peace of the state. "We are not to be cheated with a false alarm," Morse wrote, "as though whatever did not conform to the 'law and order' enforced by the State was a menace to Society. Society is of the future. All things must flow on towards it,—the State no less than all else,—and be *lost* in it. Society is to be created."[13] The fact that brutality and violence are common in existing society should not dissuade us from our faith in liberty, for social disorder is merely the stuff out of which social order is created; our task is to learn the technique of effecting its transformation.

According to Morse, the "genius of Rationalism invites solely to the perfecting of peace. Not to be victorious in battle, but, by the diffusion of light, to make the battle impossible, is the nobler aim."[14] For more than one hundred years, Morse complained, we in this country have tried to forge a strong union on the anvil of authority, force, and compulsion. "Not through liberty, but without it, we sought our peace." But peace has been denied us, as it is denied to every people who seek order through the wrong means. "Union, harmony, peace, are not to be taken by violence. Every gift of such sort laid on Union's altar has been spurned. 'Thou Fool! First go and be reconciled to thy brother.' "[15] For liberty alone is peace. Force and compulsion may well succeed in organizing men behind the plans imposed upon them by their leaders. They cannot, however, lead to the creation of a genuine social order. Only freedom and individual responsibility are capable of doing that. "We must each see for ourselves. And just to the extent that we and others do see for ourselves, the very possibility of dispute ceases; there is no longer strife or contention."[16]

Just as anarchists of a later era were to be stirred to the development of a political theory by the "legal" murder of such anarchist martyrs as the Haymarket victims and Sacco and Venzetti, so Sidney H. Morse lamented the hanging of Captain John Brown nine years before by the State of Virginia, finding the outline of his own political philosophy in the compassion he felt for the courageous adventurer who had attempted to end slavery by an act of "propaganda by deed." Instructed by such noble souls as Captain John Brown, Morse ejaculated, we are beginning to recognize that government is not the standard of absolute right just because it has enjoyed a long and unquestioned existence. The State of Virginia has condemned John Brown on a charge of treason. But while Brown may have been guilty of violating political law, he was clearly in the right in regard to the moral issue of slavery, Morse reflected. In failing to observe the moral law, it was the state, and not John Brown, who was guilty of treason. "If John Brown's act was treasonable, his treason and that of the State of Virginia were as dissimilar in character as light and darkness. His was the presence of the moral light which ignored or sought to banish political darkness."[17] We may regret that Captain John Brown felt compelled to take up arms to settle his grievance against the immoral state, Morse held. Yet when we analyze his motives we find that he acted upon the very best of sentiments. It was for the purpose of making America what she ought to be that he became a revolutionary. "He accepted the Declaration of Independence fully. To his mind it meant what it said. . . . He wrote his own constitution, making the golden rule the cornerstone."[18] Can we ask any more of a citizen than this? John Brown should have been rewarded for his deed, not hung for it; like Socrates, he was entitled to demand free room and board for life from the State of Virginia, so well had he served her. When he was put to death instead, Morse proclaimed, the basic rottenness of government became plain for all honest men to see. Only a knave or a fool can continue to serve the state once her basic nature has been found out.

For all his commitment to the pacifist ideal, Sidney Morse was unwilling to define peace as the total submission of the enslaved and oppressed to the will of the powerful few who control the existing social machinery. As social violence flared up into a general conflagration in the seventies, Morse came to labor's aid, defending it against the accusations of its detractors. It is true, he admitted, that labor has been driven to violence on occasion and that it has employed the heavy-handed tactics of organized force to compel capital to meet its demands. Yet there is a basic difference, he insisted, between the actions of labor and the conduct of the state. Playing an active role in the New England Labor Reform League, Morse, along with other libertarians such as Ezra Heywood and William B. Greene, formulated the theory that social violence is created by the state and not the working men and women who compose society. Before we condemn labor for disturbing the peace, Morse argued, we first should ask who is responsible for initiating social discord. "If it is seen that government itself is the real invader—the lawless party that robs and murders without restraint—then the 'Revolution' may assume the aspect of the party that is striving—not always wisely, perhaps, but striving after what sort it can—to protect society and insure domestic welfare and peace."[19] Abject submission to the demands of the state is no solution to the social problem. Nor does a citizen serve justice merely by remaining obedient to those who control society through the prior control of government. Before we submit to power, we must ascertain if the authority behind it is legitimate. It is time that we learned, Morse wrote, "that loyalty is not fealty to reigning usurpation, though it be clothed in sacred robes of State." With these words Sidney H. Morse assured himself a place in the history of the evolving idea of anarchism in America.

On the subject of the ballot, Morse was consistently faithful to the anarchist conception. Although he was unwilling to deny the equal right of suffrage to women,[20] and spoke in favor of a Civil Rights Bill to assure the newly freed Negro that he would be protected as a voter,[21] Morse placed very little trust in the ballot box as a method of attaining social justice. If we seek a practical reform for the evils of society, he maintained, we are more likely to find it in the abandonment of politics itself than in the processes of government. "Political affairs are at best but a remedy for an evil; a remedy to check the ravages of evil; but utterly impotent to effect a cure."[22] As he said in his address before the 1873 convention of the New England Labor Reform League, true social order can only grow when men appreciate the capacity of human nature to function without the assistance of political leadership and imposed social control by government.[23] If we would become free, he reasoned, we must first place our trust in freedom, convinced that men will act justly and prudently if given the chance. For "When the attempt is made to establish institutions by a system of *coercive co-operation,* the evil begins, and there is no end to it. Voluntary co-operation," Morse held, "is not only the one method consistent with liberty, it is by far the most practical and effective."[24] It is this strain in his thought that leads us to think of Sidney Morse as an anarchist.

It is to be noted, however, that the philosophical foundations of Morse's anarchism were derived from his association with the Free Religious Association, an offshoot of New England Unitarianism. The official publication of the Free Religious Association was the *Index* which was issued from Toledo, Ohio, where its editor, Francis Ellingwood Abbot, made his living as minister of the Unitarian Society in that city. Serving under Abbot as associate editors were some of the most stalwart of American freethinkers—Octavius Brooks

Frothingham, Thomas Wentworth Higginson, Richard P. Hallowell, and William J. Potter. The *Index*, published from Toledo from 1870 to 1880, was read by many anarchists, including Henry Appleton, C. L. James, Dyer D. Lum, and Benjamin R. Tucker, and on occasion published pieces written by Josiah Warren. Although its stated purpose was totally nonpolitical, the freethinkers who wrote it were all anarchists at heart.

Nowhere is the connection between free thought and anarchism more clear than in the lectures which the Reverend William J. Potter delivered in Horticultural Hall, Boston, sponsored by the Free Religious Association during the seventies. Reprinted in the *Index*, these lectures must have had a deep impact upon the developing social thought of subscribers like Tucker. It was Potter, in fact, who gave Tucker his first instruction in religion during his youth, teaching him that the idea of God as power is one of the most pernicious thoughts ever to enter the mind of man. And it was Potter who now argued that conventional religious thought, based as it is upon fear of the unknown, can be nothing better than superstition and unreflective submission to forces outside of the individual so long as it remains uninformed. "The progress of mankind in religion has always been from a spirit of fear to a spirit of confidence and love," Potter urged.[25] As knowledge takes the place of ignorance, man, instead of fearing nature, will learn to discover the outline of his true being in its forces. "The more perfectly he unfolds his own being, and brings to exercise his various gifts and faculties according to their normal design—that is, the higher he rises in the scale of intelligence and power as a true human being—the more completely does he come into sympathy with Nature's Laws to find her ends his own." In this tendency of thought, Potter was as much a child of the Enlightenment as Thomas Paine or William Godwin.

Although Potter as a freethinker directed himself almost exclusively to philosophical questions and was only peripherally interested in politics, there were political conclusions that could easily be drawn from his propositions. When we come to consider the origins of both religion and government, Potter argued, we discover that "both had a natural origin in the mind itself, far back in the primitive ages, when it first began to meet and struggle with the experiences of conscious existence."[26] That is to say, the idea of the state, like the idea of God, is mythical in character and has its beginning in man's fear of that which he does not understand. In both religion and politics, therefore, the path to human progress leads along the way of enlightenment and self-instruction. Just as in the natural sciences there was no science worthy of the name until men had learned to overcome the foibles and deceptions of the mind in perceiving reality, so there can be no science in religion or politics until men emancipate themselves from bondage to dogmatism and superstition.[27] If freedom is ever to become meaningful in America, we must probe into the collective psyche to discover the roots of human bondage which nurture men in their self-enslavement. When mankind has come face to face with the fears of its childhood, it will be capable of negating the symbols which have heretofore compelled it to adopt patterns of irrational behavior in the realm of religion and politics. As Tom Paine had discovered many years previously, we must break the hold which the "hag of superstition" presently exerts over our minds before we can discover the beauty and charm of the goddess of truth.

NOTES

SECTION I - CHAPTER 3

1. "Notes," *The Radical,* III (April, 1868), 572.

2. "Notes," *The Radical,* II (August, 1867), 760.

3. "Notes," *The Radical,* X (June, 1872), 467.

4. "Notes," *The Radical,* III (September 1867), 55.

5. "Radicals and Unitarians," *The Radical,* II (November, 1866), 185.

6. "Chips from My Studio," *The Radical Review,* I (May, 1877), 189.

7. "Notes," *The Radical,* X (June, 1872), 467.

8. "Liberty and Wealth," *Liberty,* II (June 14, 1884), 5.

9. "Concerning The Nation's Soul," *The Radical,* I (April, 1866), 284.

10. Benjamin R. Tucker, "A Lie Disposed Of," *Liberty,* VI (October 13, 1888), 7. For a further clarification of his ideological position, see: "Conservator, Radical, Liberal," *The Conservator,* I (May, 1890), 19.

11. "Waifs," *The Radical,* V (January, 1869), 61.

12. "Placing Responsibility," *Liberty,* III (June 20, 1885), 4. Morse signed this piece "H," which was his usual practice when he wrote for *Liberty.* His articles in the *Irish World,* to which he was a frequent contributor, were usually signed "Phillip," but he used his own name when writing for *The Word, The Radical,* and *The Radical Review.*

13. "Chips from My Studio," *The Radical Review,* I (November, 1877), 604.

14. "Notes," *The Radical,* VIII (February, 1871), 76.

15. "Chips from My Studio," *The Radical Review,* I (May, 1877), 186.

16. "The Individual," *Liberty,* III (December 26, 1885), 5.

17. "The Second Day of December, 1859," *The Radical,* IV (December, 1868), 453.

18. *Ibid.,* 460.

19. "Chips from My Studio," *The Radical Review,* I (August, 1877), 384.

20. "Editorial," *The Radical,* IV (August, 1868), 145.

21. "Public Affairs," *The Radical,* II (September, 1866), 57.

22. "Notes," *The Radical,* II (August, 1867), 339.

23. *The Word,* II (July, 1873), 2.

24. "A Conscience for Liberty," *The Index,* VI (February 25, 1875), 89.

25. "Fear, Knowledge, and Love in the Development of Religion," *The Index,* II (February 18, 1871), 49.

26. "Religion in Politics and the State," *The Index,* VII (September 28, 1876), 458.

27. "The Positive Content of Rationalism in Religion," *The Index,* III (March 30, 1872), 97.

Individualist Influences in Anarchist Thought

CHAPTER 1

Josiah Warren: Chief Architect of Libertarianism

Josiah Warren (c. 1798-1874), known as "the first American anarchist" ever since that label was pinned on him by his biographer in 1901,[1] was as much a child of the Enlightenment as was Elihu Palmer. Descended from one of the old New England families, although his precise pedigree is not exactly known, he was active as a member of the Boston Free Discussion Society, holding forth on the topic of social reform at the Sunday Lyceums sponsored by these freethinkers from 1846 onward.[2] However, Warren was less concerned with the formal categories of philosophical thought and theological issues than was Elihu Palmer and the earlier freethinkers, turning his attention instead to the more practical economic and social questions that the Enlightenment had given rise to in America. Like so many of his contemporaries, Warren was exhilarated by the notion of individual freedom which had been the justification for the political revolution so recently concluded. Philosophically, Warren was closely related to Emerson, whose pronouncement that there is a spark of the divine in every individual, colored the social thought of most Americans around the middle of the nineteenth century. God for Emerson and the Transcendentalists was not some untouchable power at the zenith of a hierarchical universe but a living force inherent in the soul of every man that could be developed to the extent that the individual had the personal courage and fortitude to find it within himself. To possess truth and justice, one must first love them, which for Emerson, as for Plato, meant that the individual must demonstrate exceptional courage in asserting his spiritual self-reliance and dedication in the face of his philosophical enemies. Freedom, on this view, was something to be fought for, not a gift to be laid at one's feet with no demands in return. Emerson, however, was more concerned with the philosophical aspects of the idea of individualism than he was with its political implications. And thus it remained for Josiah Warren, assisted by Stephen Pearl Andrews, Benjamin R. Tucker, and a whole line of lesser prophets, to popularize the political and economic undertones of the idea.[3]

Little is known about the circumstances of Warren's early years other than the fact that he received a fairly good education from one source or another.[4] Apparently he possessed considerable native musical talent, for he supported himself while very young by performing with local bands. Shortly after his twentieth birthday Warren took a wife and moved west to Cincinnati in search of their fortunes where he made a living by teaching music and leading an orchestra. Warren, however, had no patience with the "vulgar" old proverb which holds that "the jack of all trades is good at none," for he advocated that the best citizen is the one who has perfected himself in a number of different ways of making a living.[5] Demonstrating his own commitment to the notion of individual self-reliance and hard thought, Warren obtained a patent on February 28, 1821 for a lamp which was fueled by common lard, and later opened a factory from which he successfully sold his invention to the public. Some years later he brought out yet another invention, a cylinder press which automatically inked itself and printed upon a continuous roll of paper instead of individual sheets used by the old hand presses. Put into actual use in February of 1840 by the *South-Western Sentinel* of Evansville, Indiana, the press aptly demonstrated Warren's "yankee ingenuity." Unfortunately, the printers employed on the paper did not view his invention as a blessing but rather as a grave threat to their continued employment and a number of acts of sabotage at their hands finally forced Warren to put the sledgehammer to his creation. Ironically, it was as a liberator and champion of the workingman and his rights that Josiah Warren directed the major part of his life's work, seemingly unaffected by the personal anguish he suffered as a result of this incident.

Warren's destiny as a social reformer was initially shaped by a lecture he heard delivered by Robert Owen in Cincinnati. Persuaded by Owen to the view that the most efficacious way of eliminating social evil from society is to withdraw from the established social and economic system into voluntary communities, Warren moved his wife and baby daughter to New Harmony in 1825 where he imbibed a number of new ideas, not the least important of which were the educational theories of Pestalozzi which were enthusiastically championed by Owen, Joseph Neef, and other residents of the community. Warren found the theory of environmental determinism advanced by Owen highly plausible but his own proclivity to think in terms of individual autonomy made him distrustful of Owen's role as leader of New Harmony. As his own social philosophy took more definite shape, it became increasingly evident to Warren that the individual differences which distinguish one man from another in regard to their productivity and ingenuity were not sufficiently given weight within Owen's system. The failure of the New Harmony experiment found Warren struggling with the difficult problem of reconciling liberty and equality in such a way that neither would be compromised. Although he never repudiated Owen but remained personally faithful to him to the end, it would appear that Owen's influence upon Warren was much less important than was the latter's philosophical indebtedness to such notable social thinkers as William B. Greene and other American exponents of radical individualism.[6]

Undismayed by his experiences at New Harmony, Warren plunged into a new experimental village in Tuscarawas County, Ohio, in 1835, along with five other families comprising 24 persons in all. Unhappily, the ground upon which the village was constructed was not properly drained and the effect of this upon the health of the community soon appeared disastrous, causing the experiment to break up after one year. Eleven years later Warren tried again with a small colony called Utopia which was located on the Ohio River twenty-five miles south of Cincinnati. Sometimes referred to as 'Trialville,' the community was composed of a number of families that had previously been involved in the unsuccessful Clermont Phalanx, which had been structured according to Fourierite principles of joint ownership and responsibility. In 1844 Warren had met with the principals of this group then in the planning stage of organization in Cincinnati and had warned them that since the financing of any experimental settlement by joint stock necessitated joint management, it would be wise to avoid such an arrangement. However good our intentions may be, he cautioned his audience of future communitarians, "we cannot construct any *verbal organization* that will not wear itself out by its own friction. . . ."[7] Failing to heed his warning, the Clermont Phalanx soon came to grief and the more hardy of its survivors came together to build Utopia, this time according to Warren's specifications.

The essential principle upon which Utopia was founded was the "labor cost principle," which was in turn the main foundation of Warren's economic theory. Rejecting the accepted argument that the cost of any commodity should be determined by the value assigned to it by the laws of supply and demand, Warren held that the only sane index to price ought to be the actual cost to the producer of making the item. To charge what a commodity would bring on the open market rather than what it actually cost to produce, according to Warren, was a form of that "civilized cannibalism" which lies at the base of all the social strife mankind suffers from. Where speculators buy in a cheap market in order to sell when the price has risen, those who are forced to buy at inflated prices must in turn seek to take advantage of others in order to recoup their losses to the first speculator. The effect of this is morally disastrous to society, for people who are conditioned within such a system cannot help but value cunning and competitive spirit, since to be without them is to stand naked in the face of a determined enemy. The only basis upon which a truly just and orderly society can be built, Warren insisted, is an economic system in which all price is determined by the actual cost of the trouble or sacrifice one puts into the commodity he has to sell. "When we begin to think from this starting point," he wrote, "we see that the all-pervading viciousness of trade, and dire confusion and distress that everywhere prevails, have originated, not in our primary nature, as has been so extensively thought and taught, but in this subtle and undetected error in one of the starting-points of our intercourse with each other."[8] The "Time Store" that Warren operated in Cincinnati from 1827-1829, and later at New Harmony from 1842-1844, was based on the principle that the equitable marketing of the goods produced by individual workmen would automatically lead toward a social system in which freedom would be maintained at a maximum. Warren offered those who supplied goods and services to his store paper script entitling them to a like amount of labor time from anyone who would accept it. The intention of the system was the elimination of unearned increment in the form of profit and interest. The exchange of "labor for labor" left no room for the exploitation and profit gouging which characterized the ordinary market system Warren sought to revamp. A time store was established at Utopia and all participants in the experiment, carefully chosen by the original members, were permitted to buy a piece of land at a fixed price of fifteen dollars. Exchanging goods and services according to the principles of cooperation rather than the laws of supply and demand, the members of the community seemed to prosper for the first few years. Unhindered by any kind of formal governmental machinery or judicial structure, life flowed smoothly and little strife seemed to have arisen, causing Warren to pronounce the experiment an unqualified success. But like all utopian communities of this period, the corrupting influences of the outside world gradually drew away the participants and by 1875 only a few of the most hardy utopians were left in residence. Warren himself had moved East to establish himself at Modern Times, the third and best known of the experimental communities he sponsored.

In 1833 Warren established *The Peaceful Revolutionist,* the first of a long line of anarchist publications to be circulated in America. As the title of the journal suggested, Warren sought to frame his political ideas within the context of nonviolence, for he was inclined by nature toward social solutions which eschewed power and force. If there is anything that warrants calling Warren an anarchist, it is his attitude toward power. "The man of virtuous soul commands not nor obeys," he wrote with poetic rapture in his notebook. For "Power, like a desolating pestilence, withers all it touches; and obedience, bare of all genius, virtue, freedom, truth, makes slaves of men, and of the human frame a mechanized automation."[9] Like William Godwin, Warren held that the only possible road to human freedom lies down the path of individual sovereignty. As he viewed the problem, "the great mistake of all society is the compromise or surrender of the sovereignty of the individual." Unless society can be reconstituted without this surrender of individual sovereignty, freedom must forever remain unknown to mankind. Warren firmly held the conviction that individual men are perfectly capable of determining their own social actions without assistance from the state or even private associations. The laws of natural liberty teach us, he wrote, "that our own happiness depends upon a proper respect for that of others, and therefore not to make any social arrangements which require compulsion, or the violation of the natural liberty of the individual." Since the natural liberty of the individual is not possible where we combine into mass organizations in which the interests and responsibilities of one person become merged with those of another, "we are hereby taught *not to form them.*" In the tradition of Emerson and Thoreau, Josiah Warren insisted that free society can only survive where the individual stands as his own highest authority in matters having to do with social and moral actions. Long before the shadow of Herbert Spencer's social and political philosophy was to fall over the land, Josiah Warren was exhorting his fellow Americans to beware of giving up even a modicum of their rights as individuals. It is doubtful if any social prophet in America ever made a stronger case for self-autonomy than Warren did when he wrote:

> Our surrounding institutions, customs, and public opinion call for *conformity:* they require us to act in masses like herds of cattle: they do not recognize that we think and feel *individually* and ought to be at liberty to act individually; but this liberty cannot be enjoyed in combinations, masses, and connections in which one cannot move without affecting another.[10]

Many observers have been critical of individualist anarchists like Warren because they suppose that his reverence for individual sovereignty was very much like the attitude reflected by the initiates of the American cult of unrestrained wealth-getting, but this is emphatically not so. Warren was indeed a believer in the virtue of the private ownership of property, for he believed that only thus could mankind avoid a situation in which the producer is robbed of the fruit of his toil.[11] But he valued the private ownership of property because he believed that this was the only way men might achieve equality and not because he believed in inequality as an end in itself. Throughout all his efforts to establish decentralized economic communities, such as "Utopia" and "Modern Times," his aim was to help men discover the natural laws of cooperative living while at the same time preserving their individual sovereignty. Adopting Warren's system of labor exchange, the members helped each other to prosper as individuals. Aware that men are not presently perfect and that they may indeed violate their neighbor's rights as a consequence of their human falli- bility, Warren admitted the necessity for some kind of machinery for the resolution of conflict. But Warren, like all anarchists, denied that the state with its monopoly of force is essential to the preservation of social order. Just as men form temporary associations to advance their economic purposes, so can they form temporary associations for the purpose of protecting themselves from fire, theft, and other forms of danger. There is nothing that the state can do that voluntary organizations of individuals could not do better. And as men cooper- ate together in the business of living, they gradually come to learn the natural laws of social harmony, thereby drawing closer to the ideal standards of the human species. Benjamin Tucker was later to take over this theme from Warren, making it the cement that held his movement of philosophical anarchism together.

But it is not so much his individualism as his dedication to the ideal of freedom and the concept of libertarian education that iden- tifies Warren as an anarchist. Like many later anarchists, he was impressed with the necessity of developing a theory of education which would eliminate the authority of the teacher over the pupil. It was this interest which led him to contribute his services for most of a year to a communal school for orphans at Spring Hill, Ohio, where the principles of mutalism were introduced. Somewhat later Warren turned his attention to the question of national aid to education and concluded in an editorial in *The Peaceful Revolutionist* that it would be like "paying the fox to take care of the chickens" to take the responsibility of education out of the hands of parents and turn it over to the lawmakers,[12] for those who govern never understand the real interests of the child as the parent does. All we should ask of law- makers is to stand aside and allow us to take care of our own needs in our own way. If Congress undertook the supervision of the nation's education as was then proposed, Warren predicted, the intellectual development of the American people would be shackled with bonds which would ultimately crush out almost all spontaneity and indi- vidual initiative amongst them.

Nowhere did Warren demonstrate his dedication to the principles of libertarianism more clearly than in his attitude toward the problem of nullification. Unimpressed with the argument that the national interest required individuals and groups from time to time to subordinate their own private desires to the general good, Warren maintained that "liberty is the . . . only safe principle to which we can pledge ourselves." It may well be, he argued, that certain national goals may be unattainable where individual citizens are permitted complete personal freedom. But the goals of the nation must never be used as fetters to bind the private liberties of the citizens. To those who see a contradiction between the goal of the individual and the goals of the nation, Warren wrote:

> . . . I reply that there can be no national object greater than national happiness— that this, as I understand it, consists of the happiness of the individuals who compose the nation, and that individual happiness consists in nothing so much as the liberty of person and property. If this is unattainable in large masses, it shows us one circumstance with which we have to contend, and proves that society will have to dissolve its *imaginary masses and combinations* and RESOLVE ITSELF INTO INDIVIDUALS *before liberty can be anything but a word.* [13]

In final analysis Warren's objection to mass political organization was sociological rather than economic. However much his contemporaries might sing hosannas to the freedom they professed to enjoy under the newly formed federal union, Warren was completely critical of the whole national arrangement, insisting that the American people "are at this moment under the most unqualified despotism that exists on earth!"[14] Rather than having attained an advanced stage of civilized life, Warren charged, the American people, whether they know it or not, have not advanced beyond the crude barbarism of tribal life. Clanship, in his opinion, was the lowest form of social organization in that it coerced the individual into giving his allegiance to the leaders of the group without regard to the necessities of freedom or justice. "As soon as different tribes are formed, each member prefers, or is compelled to profess to prefer, his own clan or tribe to all others, on pain of being murdered as a 'traitor,' " Warren proclaimed. The individual's "motto must be, like that of Daniel Webster, 'My tribe, my whole tribe, and nothing but my tribe!' "[15]

In many respects Peter Kropotkin was correct when he held that Warren's individualism was peculiar to America, for only in a land in which potential wealth lay everywhere underfoot could such a social philosophy make sense. In Europe, where class lines were already tightly drawn and land and wealth were firmly in the grasp of an established oligarchy, the doctrine of the sovereign individual was not so readily believable. Yet it is wrong to suggest as some commentators have, that Warren's individualism was outside the purview of the anarchist idea on the grounds that his political theory was essentially peaceful, whereas the political theory of communist anarchism is essentially violent;[16] the very same antipathy to state control at the hands of a power elite which characterizes the philosophy of communist anarchism is evident in Josiah Warren's writings. Denying that governments and their laws secure the individual in his private property or personal security, Warren argued that governments "commit more crimes upon persons and property and contribute more to their insecurity than all criminals put together."[17] Although he was firmly committed to the idea of nonviolence, arguing that force and compulsion should never be directed by one person toward another, he concurred with Jefferson in the proposition that liberty can never be attained by any society unless some blood is spilled from time to time, for ruling elites never give up power cheerfully but fight on to the bitter end. So long as society is composed of rulers and the ruled, social conflict is inevitable, since no equilibrium is possible where the interests of such widely separated parties are constantly in opposition. We need not be surprised, therefore, that corruption and strife are everywhere evident in the social order, for violence breeds violence and ill will perpetuates itself with increased tempo from one generation to the next. "The word Rebellion is only a barbarian name for the exercise of Freedom," Warren wrote, "and crushing out rebellion is CRUSHING OUT LIBERTY!"[18] No less than Samuel Adams or any of the other fire-eaters of the revolution, Josiah Warren stood ready to break out of his shackles should government ever attempt to enslave him. Anarchism, as Josiah Warren defined the idea, aimed not so much at destroying the law as making every man "a law unto himself." Only thus, he maintained, might freedom be established on earth.

But Warren was no bloody-eyed radical spoiling for a fight, nor did he advocate change for change's sake. Wary of instigating "sudden or great changes" in the social system according to some master plan of utopian hope, Warren suggested instead that the real source of all social change is to be found in the economic structure of society rather than in the abstract schemes which reformers dream up. One cannot help but notice in this regard that there is a striking similarity between the basic philosophical viewpoints of Karl Marx and Josiah

Warren, despite the many differences that separate them from one another. On the question of collective action, they were miles apart, Warren holding that mass political action is totally illegitimate as a means of bringing about social change. Yet the respective writings of Warren and Marx were in essential agreement that the political structure of capitalist civilization must be somehow transformed before justice can be achieved by living men. Referring to the clash between North and South that was soon to erupt into civil war, Warren, like Marx, insisted that its basis was economic rather than spiritual or moral. We have no one to blame for the hated tariff which divides the nation into two warring camps but the "foreign and domestic capitalists" who doggedly pursue their private profits without regard to the national interest, he charged.[19] Under the technique of capitalist production, the worker, for both Marx and Warren, becomes a mere pawn to be used by the tycoons of industry for their own economic benefit. Several years before Marx got around to saying it, Warren had already proclaimed the principle that the social and political institutions of men are basically a reflection of the economic circumstances that shape their lives. "Surrounding circumstances alone produce the differences between the people of different nations," Warren wrote in 1833. "It is the influence of circumstances which produces different classes in society, and that influence only, which divides men into different political parties and ranges them under different banners of religion."[20] Clear thought would lead us to conclude from this, according to Warren, that mankind is "not to reverence or perpetuate bad circumstances simply because we are born under them."

Unwilling to give his assent to revolutionary mass action, Warren advocated resistance to economic tyranny on an individual basis, each working man and woman standing on his own unique right to sovereignty. The individual's "duty towards all political creeds and theories is the same," Warren wrote. "They are all entitled to forbearance till some attempt is made to enforce them on the unwilling. This attempt is an encroachment upon the great sacred right of self-sovereignty—an attack upon the Divine law of Individuality, and will always beget resistance and war."[21] And thus Warren no less than Marx admitted that the ultimate remedy for economic and political tyranny is rebellion against the existing power structure so that the life of the alienated worker-producer might be made whole again. Warren, however, looking out over the virgin forests and untilled fields of early nineteenth century America, concluded that the battle against corruption in high places might best be carried out by individuals skirmishing on their own, whereas Marx, conscious of the deep roots which organized political power had planted in the old world, called upon the workers of the world to organize themselves for the impending battle. In years to come when the industrial revolution reached its advanced stages in America, the theoretical differences which separated Warren and Marx would be swallowed up in the excruciating social agony the workers suffered under capitalism. But by that time Warren would not be around to bring his philosophical position up to date. This is not to suggest, however, that there were not deep political differences which separated Marx and Warren but merely to argue that they were more in agreement on economic questions than many anarchists of a later day were willing to admit.

What little fame Josiah Warren has managed to gain among American historians has been derived from his association with Modern Times, that brief haven for eccentrics and freethinkers which so thoroughly shocked the moral sensibilities of New Yorkers during the third quarter of the nineteenth century. Despite the poor condition of the soil upon which the village was established some forty miles out from the city, the project from the very beginning was an economic success and very quickly comfortable but unconventional little houses sprang up among the scrub oaks to liven the drab Long Island typography. So optimistic was Warren concerning the venture that he pronounced it a success almost at once. But unfortunately, one of the residents of the community wrote a letter to the *New York Tribune* describing the libertarian sentiments of its members and before long hoards of curiosity seekers descended upon it to complicate its existence. The effect of this unwanted publicity, as Warren described it, was an influx of "crochets," each dragging with him his "particular hobby" by which he projected the total and immediate salvation of the world and all in it.[22] One of the "imposters" assured the community that the liberation of mankind would follow at once if only all of its children were brought up without the burden of wearing clothing. So reasonable did this proposition appear to another of the newcomers that she immediately put the theory into practice, forcing her child to go naked despite the severity of the bitter winds that blew in from the Sound during the winter. One old man of German origin sought to cure the infliction of blindness from which he suffered by walking the streets *sans* clothing, while some of the female residents took to the habit of dressing themselves in men's clothing as a sign of their emancipation. More serious in its consequences were the dietary notions of another of the female inhabitants who would eat nothing but beans on the theory that it was good for her health. "She tottered about a living skeleton for about a year," according to Warren, "and then sank down and died (if we can say that there was enough left to die)." As if this kind of notoriety were not enough for the community, one of the male residents surrounded himself with three young women whom he treated as wives of equal standing, while the group collectively defended their free love theories in the pages of a newspaper they published for that purpose. Although Warren believed that complete social freedom must be guaranteed every individual no matter what the consequences might be, he was personally opposed to the practice of free love on the grounds that the complications it brought to the lives of its practitioners were usually more "troublesome than a crown of thorns." But true to his principle of individual sovereignty, he refused to erect any formal rule prohibiting the practice, insisting that the persons involved must always be accorded the freedom of controlling all regulation over their own lives. Undoubtedly the bad public relations all this caused Modern Times contributed to its demise. Warren, however, preferred to let the experiment fail rather than to violate the libertarian principles he had dedicated himself to. For Josiah Warren, no less than John Stuart Mill, was firmly committed to the precept that society has no right to interfere with the activities of the individual, even to protect him from harm, where no one else's interests are involved. It was from Warren, in fact, that Mill got much of the inspiration for the conception of individual sovereignty that formed the foundations of his *Essay on Liberty.*[23] Totally suspicious of all formal constitutions and codes, Warren would substitute a " 'Union,' not only on paper, but rooted in the heart" whose members would be rendered completely social as a consequence of the conditioning they would undergo while living in a libertarian society in which force and compulsion would be unknown. Any reform of society short of this fundamental shift in philosophical and political perspective was doomed to failure, he insisted. Anarchists of a later day, both individualists and communists, would come around to adopting this outlook too, even when

NOTES

SECTION II - CHAPTER 1

1. In December of 1901 William Bailie contributed an unsigned article to the *Boston Globe* in which he made this claim. Later he published his biographical study under the title *Josiah Warren, The First American Anarchist* (Boston, 1906). For a largely negative appraisal of Warren's anarchism, see Harold Barclay, "Josiah Warren: The Incomplete Anarchist," *Anarchy* 85 (March, 1968), 90-96.

2. Albert Post, *Popular Freethought in America, 1825-1850* (New York, 1943), p. 109.

3. Yehoshua Arieli, *Individualism and Nationalism in American Ideology* (Cambridge, Mass., 1964), p. 283.

4. *Dictionary of American Biography,* XIX (New York, 1936), p. 483. The most complete description of Warren's background is to be found in James J. Martin, *Men Against the State* (New York, 1957).

5. *Modern Education* (Modern Times, L.I., December, 1861), p. 1.

6. *Men Against the State,* p. 8.

7. *Practical Applications of the Elementary Principles of "True Civilization"* (Princeton, Mass., 1873), p. 8.

8. *True Civilization An Immediate Necessity and the Last Ground of Hope for Mankind.* (Boston, 1963), p. 95.

9. The unpublished *Notebook of Josiah Warren* (1840) is to be found in the library of the Workingman's Institute, New Harmony, Indiana.

10. "Individuality," *The Peaceful Revolutionist* I (April 5, 1833), 1.

11. *The Periodical Letter on the Principles and Progress of the Equity Movement,* I (August, 1854), p. 22.

12. "Editorial," *The Peaceful Revolutionist,* I (April 5, 1833), 16.

13. "Of Our State Difficulties," *The Peaceful Revolutionist,* I (February 5, 1833), 6.

14. *True Civilization,* p. 138.

15. *Ibid.,* p. 47.

16. See, for example: Charles E. Merriam, *American Political*

Ideas (New York, 1926), p. 349; and Westel W. Willoughby, *The Ethical Basis of Political Authority* (New York, 1930), p. 43.

17. "A Brush at Old Cobwebs," *The Peaceful Revolutionist*, I (April 5, 1833), 14.

18. *True Civilization*, p. 158.

19. "Of Our State Difficulties," *Ibid.*

20. "Surrounding Circumstances," *The Peaceful Revolutionist*, I (February 5, 1833), 1.

21. *True Civilization*, p. 145.

22. *Practical Applications*, p. 18.

23. Bailie, *op. cit.*, p. 99.

CHAPTER 2

Stephen Pearl Andrews:
Pedantic Libertine or Prophetic Libertarian?

Closely allied with Josiah Warren in his efforts to propagate the idea of the sovereign individual was Stephen Pearl Andrews (1812-1886), one of the most colorful of all the native American anarchists. Starting out as a follower of Fourier, Pearl Andrews, as he was affectionately called by his intimates, was introduced to Warren's social thought as a consequence of their mutual interest in the free thought movement and their association in the New England Labor Reform League. In time Andrews and Warren became closely associated with one another in the work of social reform, both giving enthusiastic support to any idea which furthered the creation of a libertarian society in America. The degree to which they identified with each other in the realm of social theory stands out in the following letter which Warren wrote to Andrews:

> It is gratifying, is it not, to see that our works will bear the test of time, and even exhibit new powers, new value, by age, instead of being outgrown by time . . .; and having once done our work we may consider it finished—not to be done over again at every new turn of the wheel of accidents. A store of simple truths remain unaltered by time; even our attempts at improvement cannot improve them, and like the elements of arithmetic, we have only to improve our modes of presenting them, multiply examples, and supply demand for them.[1]

Pearl Andrews, like Josiah Warren, was essentially a product of the Enlightenment, and the search for new methods to open the secrets of nature was the preoccupation of his lifetime. A long-time subscriber and contributor to *The Truth Seeker*, the "Journal of Free Thought and Reform," he thought of himself as "a scientist, a positivist" rather than an activist or agitator. Known as "the Socrates" of the Manhatten Liberal Club to which he belonged, he welcomed speaking

79

opportunities, whether as the featured speaker on the occasion of Tom Paine's birthday, or to debate some unreconstructed champion of orthodox religion. When the Union Reform League was organized in 1879 by such stalwart radicals as J. Flora Tilton, Ezra and Angela Heywood, and Henry Appleton, it was Pearl Andrews who was tapped for president, since he, more than anyone else they could call upon, was certain to remain faithful to the League's goal of repealing all restrictions on the individual's enjoyment of his natural rights and encouraging cooperative action in all progressive movements.[2] For a time it appeared that Pearl Andrews would single-handedly defeat the forces of reaction and ignorance in America, so omnipresent was he in the councils of enlightened social action. In the end, however, Pearl Andrews, like all other men, proved to be a mere mortal after all and his voice was stilled before his dream of a libertarian society could be attained.

Born to affluence as well as a better than average intellectual heritage, Andrews was the youngest of the nine children of the Reverend Elisha Andrews who had married wealth when he took Ann Lanthrop for his wife. Educated at Amherst College, Pearl Andrews moved in his nineteenth year to Clinton, Louisiana, where he took up the study of law under the tutelage of an elder brother, Thomas. Something of a genius in his mastery of languages, he gave lessons in Greek and Latin at a girls' school while completing his legal training and in 1832 held an instructorship at Louisiana State University. Later in life he taught himself Chinese, Hebrew, and Sanskrit, and was reputed to be proficient in a total of thirty-two languages. At the request of the Congress of Texas, he translated the republic's laws and constitution into Spanish.[3] Discovering Issac Pitman's system of shorthand just as he was to speak before an antislavery convention in England, he was responsible for introducing shorthand into the United States and later became the author of several books on the subject of phonography. One of the uses to which Andrews hoped to put shorthand was as a simplified method of teaching the illiterate slave to read and write. His most enthusiastic venture in the field of linguistics, although not his greatest success, was the invention of "Alwato," a universal "scientific" language by which he hoped to overcome the intellectual confusion and lack of communication among the different peoples of the world.

After completing his legal training, Andrews practiced law in

New Orleans from 1835 to 1839 during which time the sentiments of ardent abolitionism became more and more fixed in his social conscience. Meanwhile the brother whom he came to live with married a Southern lady of libertarian sentiments whose dowry included a plantation and more than one hundred slaves. Acting upon their abolitionist sentiments, the courageous couple sold their land and moved to southern Illinois where they engaged themselves in the work of erecting houses for the fortunate Negroes whom they had endowed with freedom. Undoubtedly this example of applied idealism had a strong impact upon the younger brother's impressionable mind, causing him to become even more fervently dedicated to the idea of abolition. Deciding to throw himself into the battle against slavery, Pearl Andrews packed up his belongings and moved on to Texas with the specific purpose of helping to make it a free state at whatever cost. But Andrews, apparently, was wise enough at first to mute his thoughts in public concerning the slave issue, for he seemed to have enjoyed a great deal of success practicing law in his new home. Not only did he stand in well with President Sam Houston but one of the papers in Galveston proclaimed him "the foremost lawyer in Texas," undoubtedly on the strength of the exceptionally fine work he did in the area of conflicting land titles where his ability to read Spanish was a great asset.[4] As the slavery issue became increasingly more bitter, Andrews' abolitionist sentiments caused him to lose favor with his neighbors in Houston where he had established himself with his newly acquired wife. After a time he refused to accept any case which involved slavery on the grounds that no one had the right to deny another man his freedom, whatever the laws of Texas or the United States might have to say about the matter. Goaded by his opposition to their cherished institution of chattel bondage, an angry mob attacked his home in 1843 and Andrews and his wife were lucky to escape with their lives, melodramatically fleeing by horse and carriage at the very last minute through the dark and stormy night. Never at a loss for an idea, Andrews left at once for New York City where he spoke to a number of influential people, including William Cullen Bryant and Theodore Sedgewick, about his plan to obtain a loan in England which would permit the republic of Texas to purchase and free her slaves. Proceeding to Boston with Lewis Tappan, he obtained the encouragement of John Quincy Adams and on June first the two reformers set sail for England on the ship *Caledonia.* Tappan was instrumental in getting Pearl Andrews presented to Lord Aberdeen and for a time it appeared that they might be successful in this grandiose abolitionist scheme. Later, however, a representative of Texas exposed the plan as a private affair rather than one officially sponsored by his government and Andrews was unmasked as a dealer in international intrigue.

Andrews' main contribution to social thought was his *Science of Society,* published in 1851, the work which established his fame and endeared him to the followers of the anarchist idea in America. *The Science of Society* was praised by anarchists of the day as the most intelligent interpretation of Warren's philosophy that had then been published, and few issues of *Liberty* appeared without a large advertisement describing its contents. While Benjamin Tucker's language may have been a bit extravagant when he wrote that it was "the most important political and economical work ever printed in the English language,"[5] there can be no doubt that the book was instrumental in spreading the libertarian teachings of individualist anarchism throughout the United States. Less successful as a source of inspiration for his contemporaries was *The Propagandist,* a journal of social opinion which fought a losing battle from its introduction by Andrews in November of 1850 till its inglorious demise two years later as a result of a lack of interest upon the part of the public.

The Science of Society develops the theme of an oration Andrews delivered on the Fourth of July while still in New Orleans during the first year of his law practice. Of all the sentiments basic to man's nature, the young lawyer ejaculated on that occasion, none is more deeply rooted than his love of independence and freedom. Written constitutions, laws, and governments cannot increase the freedom of the individual in any instance, nor is it to any avail to trust one's lot to political parties and politicians. In fact, Andrews held, one of the most insidious dangers of our times is the tendency of people to find succor and strength in the collective mass, whether it takes the form of party, sect, or church. The freedom of the people can only be maintained where "absolute independence" of thought and deed are held to be their birthright. For, he argued:

> The principles of party are a blind and passive reception of the doctrines of others, prepared and distilled at some great fountain-head of pretended patriotism; a willing and unconditional obedience to the dictates and determinations of self-constituted dictators and rulers, and an absolute surrender of the right of thinking

and judging for ourselves. It imposes a bondage unworthy of freemen, and reduces us to a set of pliant and convenient tools in the hands of demagogues and political aspirants.[6]

These were not so much the sentiments of a Democrat or Republican as they were the deeply held convictions of one who had drunk deeply of the exhilerating doctrine of individualism and had been transported into a state of euphoria by its spirits. Throughout the pages of *The Science of Society* the argument is made again and again that the individual must be perfectly free to make all choices and decisions by himself. Calling this principle "the sovereignty of the individual" after the phrase coined by Warren, Andrews held that it is fundamental not only to protestantism and democracy but to socialism as well. No social science can develop where this truth is not recognized, he maintained. Just as in religion the individual must be free to determine exactly what the laws of God are, so in politics there can be no court or legislature superior to the individual judgements of the citizen. The sovereignty of the individual, according to Andrews, is not merely a grandiloquent phrase to be used by sophists who would persuade belief in their theories without offering any genuine proof of a rational nature. To the contrary, individuality is the fundamental and indispensable principle of the universe and serves as the very apex of the human imagination. Not only is it the "best image of the Infinite" that the finite mind is capable of perceiving, but it is the foundation of all rational law and justice. Infinite diversity, according to Andrews, is the sum and substance of the universal law itself and must serve as the initial benchmark of any intelligent social system. Since no two individuals, events, or things are exactly alike, it is futile to attempt the mechanical regulation of any phase of the universe. "This diversity reigns throughout every kingdom of nature," Andrews wrote, "and mocks at all attempts to make laws, or constitutions, or regulations of any sort, which shall work justly and harmoniously amidst the unforeseen contingencies of the future."[7]

Andrews' argument for absolute individual freedom cannot be lightly dismissed as the work of a crank. Arguing that social unity can only arise where each separate nomad is free to follow its own individual course of development, he maintained that "the essential condition of freedom is disconnection-individualization-disintegration of interest."[8] Where every individual is perfectly at liberty to pursue his own individual goals and desires without external restriction, there naturally arises a social harmony which will be as complete and perfect as the individuals who contribute to it are free to develop themselves. In its initial stages, no doubt, such a libertarian social system will frighten those conservative natures among us who crave for personal security and who are intimidated by the uncertainties of social change. Yet "What is feared by the timid conservative as the dissolution of order, is, in fact, merely the preliminary stage of the true harmonic Constitution of Society—the necessary analysis prior to its genuine and legitimate synthesis." If we are to enjoy freedom, Andrews seems to suggest, we must be content to live dangerously until we have learned the social skills necessary to its maintenance.

One of the most frequently expressed sentiments of those who champion authority and the state is the argument that genuine self-government is impossible within human society, given the inevitability of human error and corruption. Where individuals are left free to govern themselves without the aid of appointed leaders, every advocate of statecraft from Machiavelli on has argued, social chaos and violence are sure to arise. But this conclusion, according to Andrews, is wholly without validity and has been one of the main roadblocks in the path of social science in America, as elsewhere. Undoubtedly individual persons will at first misuse their freedom, and even abuse it on occasion. This will cause observers of the social scene to conclude that order is not possible where force is not exercised by rulers in the name of the general welfare. But if freedom is ever to be realized on earth, Andrews argued, it is essential that the individual be allowed to exercise his right to decide the course of his own conduct for himself in every case, whatever the consequences of his action might be to himself or to others. "He must be left absolutely free to commit every conceivable breach of the principle itself. . . ." For social science is nothing more than a personal knowledge of the principles of freedom which individuals can only discover where they have been allowed to follow their own inner feelings and convictions. "Men have sought for ages to discover the science of government; and lo! here it is, that men *cease totally to attempt to govern each other at all.* . . ." Instead of writing lamentations because the "true kings and governors of mankind" have refused to fulfill their supposed obligations, Carlyle ought to write paeans to their good judgement. As Andrews chided Horace Greeley some years later, the beginning of wisdom is to give up the attempt to cure the evils of government by the foolish course of encouraging the growth of even more government.[9]

Among the important corallary principles of the science of freedom proposed by Andrews was the rule that "Objects bound together contrary to their nature, must and will seek to rectify themselves by breaking the bonds which confine them, while those which come together by their own affinities remain quiescent and content.[10] The violent social upheavals experienced from time to time by mankind, on this view, are the consequence of the violation of this rule, just as social peace and order is the fruit of its faithful observance. In order to develop a widespread condition of peace among men it is necessary that the principle of universal self-election be made applicable to the day-to-day affairs of life instead of being reserved solely for election day as it is in American democracy. If you would have freedom, Andrews urged, "make the pulpit, the school-room, the workshop, the manufactory, the shipyard, and the storehouse the universal ballot-boxes of the people. Make every day an election day, and every day and hour its full and unlimited franchise."[11]

The economic doctrine Andrews projected for the realization of his libertarian dream was, as he freely acknowledged, derived from the social teachings of Josiah Warren. Directing his attention to the fundamental economic question of value, Andrews argued that Warren was right when he maintained that an equitable system for the free exchange of labor is the very alpha and omega of social liberty. Under conventional economic theories, the value of goods are determined by what they will bring in the marketplace and do not take sufficient account of what they cost the worker in order to produce them. But no producer of economic goods can make an intelligent judgement as to the true cost of the things offered for sale—that is the function of the consumer. All the worker or businessman can legitimately concern himself with is the question of the fair cost of what he has produced. Under the existing rules of commerce, the exact opposite condition is in operation. Price is not determined by the producer, whether he be worker or manufacturer, but by the speculator whose only concern is to make the greatest possible margin of profit with the least expenditure of effort on his own part. The result of this is that social irresponsibility characterizes every facet of modern commerce. Men do not value honesty or integrity, for to do so under the existing rules must inevitably lead to their own economic ruin. Human intelligence, consequently, is employed not for constructive purposes of social progress but for the domination and ruin of those who are unable to protect themselves, either because they cannot or will not.[12]

Contrary to what is generally believed, Andrews argued, competition itself is not socially negative. This is one of the most misunderstood of all economic principles. Correctly employed, economic competition ultimately leads to the growth of a perfectly balanced system of social cooperation in which disharmony and guile would be completely absent. But this pertains only to a perfectly libertarian society within which all avenues of self-development and improvement would be completely open to the individual. Where the cost principle is in operation and not subject to any artificial restraints from outside the natural economic system, each individual automatically adjusts his actions to the exigencies of the situation he finds himself in. Free to move about as he pleases, the worker who is supernumerary in one trade or profession will automatically shift to another where the opportunities are greater. Likewise, those who manufacture goods and services will set their individual courses according to the actual opportunities which open up for them within the dynamics of a free economy. Andrews held that under such unrestrictive conditions, there would not result the unemployment and deflation which ordinarily plague society. For where complete freedom is assured the individual, economic relations automatically adjust themselves to the exclusion of overproduction and underprotection of goods. Supply will, of course, catch up with demand from time to time. But since the wants of men are infinite when they are permitted to develop their tastes without artificial restraint, new needs and markets will constantly open up, offering economic opportunity for all. At present, Andrews insisted, men are unprepared to take advantage of opportunity when it knocks, so stultified have they become as a consequence of the social and economic bondage they are habituated to. In a system in which the cost principle is in full operation, the fetters which bind the individual will disintegrate, for man has an unlimited potential for development where his actions are determined by his own internal guidance mechanism. Where men now hoard knowledge and otherwise establish barriers to freedom, in a libertarian society all will be enabled to function according to the natural laws of their individual personalities. Whatever anarchists of later generations might think of Andrews' economic theories, none would take issue with his insistence that "the artistic and cultural tastes of men, although conditioned by the institutions within which they live, are basically capable of infinite growth and variety." To bring about society's full social and artistic development, it is merely necessary to remove all impediments from the path of the individual.

Along with Warren and Greene, Andrews understood full well that no change in the superstructure of the economy can be effected until the defects in its foundation have been eliminated. In the monetary system maintained under conventional economic theory, currency is not only difficult to obtain due to its scarcity but the interest charges added to it by banks and bankers renders it expensive. What we need is a "Labor Note System" which would free money from the heavy hand laid upon it by government sponsored institutions and restrictions.[13] The suggestions Andrews proposed in this regard did not add anything significantly different from those made by Warren and Greene, although he did go further than they in portraying the probable results monetary reform would have upon culture and society. As Andrews viewed the problem, a properly functioning labor note system would "make every man his own banker," since the character and skill a particular man possesses serve as the basis for his credit in the marketplace, and hence he always has as much money as he actually needs. "He has only to take his pen from his pocket and make it at will." In part, this is what Andrews probably had in mind when he asserted that it was accidental, not essential, that money bears the imprint of government. "Money, as an instrument of trade, never grew up out of the social necessities of the people, and probably existed long before there was any government properly so-called."[14] Were many people convinced of the validity of this argument, there would be a lot more anarchists in the world than there are at present, for it is devastating in its political ramifications.

Like all the disciples of Josiah Warren, Pearl Andrews was a determined foe of economic collectivism and lost no opportunity to cast stones at the theory. The basic flaw in collectivism is that it imposes a false equality upon those who reside under its influence. In obliterating the lines of ownership and administration of private property, the collectivist makes social chaos and confusion inevitable. If the individual is to be truly sovereign over his own destiny and development, he must always be allowed to be his own master and leader. Nothing more thoroughly stifles the growth of human freedom than the bureaucracy and despotism which are inevitable in a collective society. Collectivists, in turn, reject the idea of individualism because it supposedly forces competition upon the individuals of which society is composed and thus destroys social solidarity. But individualism, as Andrews defined it, does not lead to social isolation but to true social and economic cooperation. "Competition is a motive power, like steam or electricity, and is either destructive or genial according to its application!" Where competition is used to induce individual moral and cultural excellence rather than private economic gain within an economy of scarcity, it will have the exact opposite effect to the one it has today. The real enemy of social solidarity, Andrews cautioned, is not the wage system but the imposition of arbitrary restraints upon the free flux of talent and energy within the economy. Stifle individual initiative and development and you have at once produced a dangerous force which can only cause harm to society; allow each individual within society to seek his own level and you have unloosed a genie that can work wonders where all the administrators of government can only wreck havoc.

At the risk of being misunderstood by other social reformers, Andrews maintained that the acceptance of freedom as the highest possible value means that there must be no interference with the natural balance of the social universe, even for purposes of supposed benevolence. For "true society is a growth from true principles, not an artifical formation—a growth from seeds implanted in the soil of such society as now exists—the only soil we have."[15] Although he had once sat at Fourier's feet, Andrews now rejected the concept of utopia as an impediment in the attainment of social reform, just as he rejected the conventional socialist argument that the first step in social reform is the abandonment of the wage system. Voicing the argument of anarchists of all ages, Andrews insisted that the first and final reform is to refuse to acknowledge the function of organized government within the social process. This means that individuals will be forced to accept the full consequences of their own actions, even when their total effect is negative. Since all men within any given economic or social system cannot perch on the top rung of the ladder, this will necessitate a class division very much similar to the one envisioned by Plato. Andrews, refusing to distort reality, acknowledged that it will also be necessary for some men within such a system to labor for a wage. But where freedom is observed as the highest of all possible principles, such restraints will not prove onerous, for they will not be permanent. Those in the lower strata of society may well become disgruntled with their lot as they become more intellectually and culturally mature. The remedy for this dissatisfaction is not to establish a social welfare state but to grant each individual full scope for his own energies, permitting him to rise or sink as he desires. Some men, of course, will become leaders, while the vast majority will be content to be followers. Yet where each is free to determine his own fate, the idea of social and economic differentiation is not negative. Here Andrews' words deserve to be quoted in full.

> When mankind graduates out of the period of brute force, that man will be the greatest hero and conqueror who levies the heaviest tribute of homage by excellence of achievement in any department of human performance. The avenues to distinction will not be then, as now, open only to the few. Each individual will truly govern the minds, and hearts, and conduct of others. Those who have the most power to impress themselves upon the community in which they live, will govern in smaller spheres. All will be priests and kings, serving at the innumerable altars and sitting upon the thrones of that manifold hierarchy, the foundations of which God himself has laid in the constitution of man. Genius, talent, industry, discovery, the power to please, every development of individuality, in fine, which meets the approbation of another, will be freely recognized as the divine annointing which constitutes him a sovereign over others—a sovereign having sovereigns for his subjects—subjects whose loyalty is proved and known, because they are ever free to transfer their fealty to other lords. [16]

As individuality becomes more and more widespread through society, the opportunities for the further employment of social initiative and leadership will progressively increase. In time all distinctions between persons will fade away of their own accord, for socially developed individuals will automatically adapt themselves to the natural harmony of interests a real social system suggests.

In asserting that nature demands that individuals exert leadership when they are capable of doing so, Andrews had made a great contribution to the philosophy of anarchism. One of the great problems of anarchist theory is to provide an alternative to the control now exercised by government within a centralized society. "Will we not have chaos if government should disappear?" people again and again demand. Andrews' answer to this question was that only a free organization of talent within a system of total individuality is capable of solving this problem. Where each individual is allowed to be his own master, he is forced to observe the rules of rational conduct or suffer as a consequence. Individuals, under such circumstances, will inevitably learn to cooperate in carrying on the necessary functions of everyday industry and social life. As things now stand, the favors granted to privileged groups by government forces those who are thereby deprived to combine their interests with other deprived individuals in a quest for power whereby such privilege might be ended. But this leads in turn to a new system of privilege and consequent discrimination others will be forced to fight against. Hence the vicious circle of power is created which in all ages prevents men from developing the fundamental social aspects of their nature. Not only does individualism lead to greater cooperation within society, according to Andrews, but it equips the individual with the psychological vigor and strength to live in real social solidarity with others. Anticipating many of the arguments to be made in a later day by such social philosophers as Paul Goodman and Erich Fromm, Stephen Pearl Andrews argued that "it is through the individualization of interest alone that harmonic co-operation and universal brotherhood can be attained."[17] It is only where individuals are secure and confident in their own lives that they can enter into satisfactory social relationships with others. "The more distinct the personalities, and the more they are guarded and preserved," Andrews wrote, "the more intimate the relations may be, without collision or disturbance."

It goes without saying that the libertarian social teachings espoused by Andrews demand a great deal from the mortals to be governed by them. If freedom is to be preserved inviolate, each individual must in every instance be accorded the power to determine when and how he is to act, and to be allowed to experience the full consequences of his decisions. For where individuals have no freedom to do wrong, they can never acquire the experience necessary to know right. Under conventional moral systems, according to Andrews, men are taught the duty of submitting themselves to false social relationships. They are urged to accept a code of social ethics which has almost no connection with their individual personalities. Right and wrong are arbitrarily established, and each individual is taught from earliest childhood to feel pangs of conscience when one of these imposed rules has been breached. But the science of society Andrews proposed "graduates the individual out of the sphere of Ethics into that of Personality—out of the sphere of duty of submission to the wants of others into the sphere of integral development and freedom." No longer is the individual expected to respond to moral preachments aimed at him from pulpit and throne. From henceforth "The individual must be kept absolutely above all institutions." Free to violate the law at will, the individual can only be restrained by constraint excercised over himself by his own free perception of the "true principles" of social harmony. The only exception to the rule of the Sovereignty of the individual, Andrews held, is where the individual is incapable of assuming the consequences of his actions himself. If the "cost" or burden of one's conduct must be born by others, as in the case of a young child or mental defective, this principle may be compromised; in all other instances it is absolute. Only thus, he urged, is it possible for men to escape from the power complex which currently grips their minds so that they may learn to live in a libertarian society.

That Pearl Andrews' mind traveled in advance of conventional morality is clearly evident in the series of exchanges on government and social philosophy he carried on with Henry James and Horace Greeley in the pages of the *New York Tribune* which were titled "Love, Marriage, Divorce, and the Sovereignty of the Individual," and which were reprinted by Tucker in *Liberty*. The world must come to see, Andrews argued in his best forensic style, that human beings do not need to be regulated and cared for by forces external to themselves. When all the rhetoric and bombast is distilled away from the science of politics there remain two fundamental but contradictory principles which serve as basic archetypes for all successive political theories, he wrote:

> (1) that man is *not* capable of governing himself, and hence needs *some other man* (or men) to govern him; (2), that man *is* capable of self-government, potentially, and that, if he is not so actually, he needs more experience in the practice of it including more evil consequences from failure; that he must learn it for himself, as he learns other things; that he is entitled of right to his own self-government, whether good or bad in the judgement of others, whenever he exercises it at his own cost,—that is, without encroachment upon the equal rights of others to govern themselves. [18]

The notion that man is incapable of governing himself is the primordial myth from which all the more advanced theories of authoritarian social control stem, Andrews maintained. Wherever human servitude is found in society there will also be found the theory that the individuals involved are incapable of taking care of their own needs and hence must be managed by some superior intelligence. This principle pertains as much to the enslavement of woman as it does to man. One of the leading advocates of woman's liberation in his day, Andrews condemned the institution of marriage and the corollary principle of male supremacy as a "house of bondage and the slaughter-house of the female sex." Women must be accorded the same right to self-determination as men are, and both must be given far greater freedom than they presently enjoy if we are ever to establish a free society, he urged.

To boldly champion the liberation of woman was enough in itself to brand Pearl Andrews a dangerous eccentric, as it did all the other advocates of that ideal. But the luster of Andrews' reputation was further discolored by his association with Victoria Woodhull, the sensational advocate of free love who made New York an exciting place to live during this era. As inscrutable as she was beautiful, Victoria had the effect of either charming her listener into complete submission or goading him into uncontrollable rage, and hence she was viewed as both saint and sinner at the same time, depending upon the perspective of the viewer in question. Brought together by their respective interests in social reform, Pearl Andrews, who was then close to sixty years of age, and Victoria Woodhull, who was at the height of her career and beauty, found much in common and they became closely associated in the work they both loved. As one of the chief editors of Woodhull and Claflin's Weekly, Andrews had occasion to closet himself with Victoria from time to time and this soon led to the persistant rumor that they shared more in the way of furniture than an editorial desk, especially when Andrews established the practice of moving into Victoria's house whenever his wife chanced to be away. For all we know, their relationship may have been perfectly platonic. But beautiful women who consort with eccentric social philosophers cannot expect to keep their reputations pure, especially when they publicly advocate social theories as sensational as the idea of free love. This is not to suggest that Andrews was insincere in his libertarian professions, or that his understanding of the theory of free love was superficial. To the contrary, it was in pursuit of this principle that he developed his notorious theory of the Pantarchy, a proposed voluntary community of free souls, both male and female, who would live together in complete freedom in an effort to withdraw themselves from the authoritarian practices and institutions of the outside world. An inveterate joiner of any communitarian project that aimed at the actual practice of libertarian theory, Andrews had not only participated in Modern Times but had lived with a communal group in New York City after Modern Times broke up. Andrews' wife, in addition to being a licensed physician, was a dedicated advocate of woman's emancipation, and she apparently plunged into each successive social experiment with enthusiasm equal to that of her husband. Although the records are sketchy about the incident, one of the last things Andrews did before he died was to establish an actual Pantarchy. His granddaughter, Andrela, whose first name was made from the universal language Pearl Andrews invented, was born in the Pantarchy. Barely six when the old gentleman died, Andrela remembered her grandfather as a kind and considerate person who "always greeted me with the utmost courtesy as if I were a grown person—and this—I was always told out of his respect for the Individuality whose Sovereignty he believed commanded recognition even in children."[19] Although the Pantarchy had the reputation in some people's minds of being nothing more than "a training school for wayward wives," nothing in Pearl Andrews' character or writings would lend any credence whatever to the insinuation that he was in any way lewd or immoral. Pearl Andrews, no more than Rousseau or any other social philosopher, can be accurately judged by the company he kept or the rumors that circulated about him. Whatever the state of his personal morality might have been in his advanced years, we have it on the word of his biographer that he was highly critical of the loose sexual attitudes he found among young men in the South and on one occasion at least he demonstrated that his own personal standards were incorruptible.[20] Although one act of virtue does not make a saint, neither does a pack of unsubstantiated tales make a sinner.

If Andrews is to be criticized for anything, it is for the extravagant heights to which he allowed his imagination to soar at times. Scattered throughout the unpublished manuscripts and notebooks he left to posterity are some of the most grandiose social schemes ever to come from the pen of man.[21] Influenced by the writings of Swedenborg, Comte, and other initiates of scientific sociology, Andrews confidently boasted that another thirty years of study would be sufficient to effect the "Grand Reconciliation" of all knowledge. To hasten this process, he proposed the establishment of a "Normal University of the Pantarchy," a sort of multi-university designed to "stand in the same relation to the control of man in which the polytechnic institute stands to the control of nature."[22] Such an institution was actually chartered by Andrews during the years 1875 and 1876, although its structure never progressed beyond the most rudimentary of forms. On paper, however, it was projected that the institution was soon to have one hundred and nineteen professorships in such esoteric subjects as Alwato, Integralism, Universology, and Frangkwa, the "universal popular or people's language," and ultimately Andrews hoped that it would grow to ten thousand professorships and a student body of at least a "half million souls." Centered in Washington, D.C. with the view of making that city the educational center of the world, the Normal University of the Pantarchy, once it was established, would lead to "the Friendly Rivalry and Co-operation in Advancement of Progress of all the Nations to the Grand Mutual Reconciliation of Humanity and to the Virtual Inauguration of a Midevial (sic) Order on this Planet through Science and Wise Organization." In order to circumvent the central-ization of power that characterizes existing international relations, Andrews proposed that present governments of the world be replaced by "a new government" that would exhibit the qualities of a "mon-archical mind." While still a young man in Louisiana, Andrews became elated by what he believed was the discovery of a universal science which would integrate all the various philosophical schools then known to the world. Among the numerous published works he left behind is *The Basic Outline of Universology* (1887), a large tome which he hoped would become the textbook for those who, like him, sought for a unified system of social thought. The concept of a "monarchical mind" that he now advanced stemmed from his belief that the social sciences had progressed far enough to warrant the actual implementation of his theory of Universology. As if to apolo-gize for the apparent authoritarian qualities of the "monarchical mind" he proposed, Andrews quickly added that the kind of mind he desired to see at the control of intellectual things would be paternal. Like Rousseau's legislator who serves only the general will rather than his own interests, the monarchical mind "will look upon the highest good of each and all the members of the national family" whenever it acts in its official capacity.[23] Andrews, apparently, fancied himself the logical choice for grand pantarch, if not the monarchical mind, for although intellectuals might rally around

Emerson and scholars around Bancroft, only he had acquired enough knowledge of science of universology to attract all the various peoples of the world to follow his lead without employing force or compulsion. In an address before the Union Reform League, Andrews admitted as much when he confided: "That I should assume this office myself, at least for the time being, is inevitable, if the thing is to be done, as there is nobody else who appreciates the conception, and is willing to give the necessary time, labor, and devotion to its practical working."[24] In fairness to Andrews it should be stressed that what he was after was a social science that would remove all the contradictions and cross-purposes of the many different voices that caused social reform in the nineteenth century to appear cacophonous. But the elaborate schemes and organizations which Pearl Andrews indulged himself in, as his biographer quipped, made him appear "supremely logical and absurdly mad."[25]

That Pearl Andrews was not absolutely mad but only relatively so is attested by the fact that he carried on a rational dialogue with George Fitzhugh and George Frederick Holmes, the leading sociologists of the South, seeking a common ground upon which they might resolve their sociological differences.[26] Men who appear to froth at the mouth as a consequence of the strange social doctrines they profess are often less mad than their contemporaries think them to be, and Pearl Andrews is a case in point. However, on occasion he could indulge himself in gibberish, as when he wrote:

> The whole world speaks instinctively of an upright man, associating Moral Integrity with Perpendicularity. A man whose highest *rule of right* is his own *disinclination* is neither positively base nor positively upright, but has little true moral quality. . . . If the observer think a perpendicular straight line passing through the point at which he stands and connecting the zenith above with the nadir below, the figure so constituted in his mind by these three straight lines crossing each other at right angles will be the Cosmical-Tri-equiaxe—in its normal or most governing position the figure by which all our ideas of structure and cosmical relations are unconsciously regulated. Whoever deviates by disinclination, or inclination from conformity to this figure, is abnormal, irregular or exceptional to our apprehension.[27]

Yet Pearl Andrews was no more mad than Thomas Hobbes was when he boasted that he had squared the circle or had found the key to all philosophy in the theorems of geometry he was so fond of proving. Essential to a fair assessment of Andrews' work is his awareness of the intricate relationship that exists between liberty and authority, a

relationship that is all too often hidden from the eyes of social reformers who attempt to establish freedom within a flimsy utopian
frame. Taking issue with Benjamin Tucker for too boldly asserting
that liberty and authority are mutually exclusive principles, Andrews
argued that no such easy proposition can be successfully maintained,
for these two forms of human action always stand in juxtaposition.
Without doubt, Andrews held, freedom is the fundamental pre-
requisite of a libertarian society, and it is the necessary condition for
any true moral act. Yet it is impossible to live one's life in such a way
that authority plays no part whatever in one's actions. "We all *do*
and *must* serve two masters, from the cradle to the grave; two fundamental opposite principles, always and everywhere existing in the
nature of things, and the whole art of life consists in reconciling
them approximately or relatively, as they can never be reconciled
absolutely."[28] In openly acknowledging the full complexity of social
life, Pearl Andrews followed the pattern set by Proudhon when he
declared anarchism unafraid of ordinary contradictions.

Adding to the haze that obscures the character of the real Pearl
Andrews was his attraction to Marxian socialist ideas. One of the
first Americans to discover Marx, Andrews was among the original
organizers of an American section of the First International in 1869.
Two years later, Andrews, caught up in the whirl of attention that
was set off by the Paris Commune, had the honor of being the first
journalist to publish the *Communist Manifesto* in this country.[29]
Andrews' attraction to Marxian ideas, however, was not motivated
by profound ideological considerations or a well-conceived theoretical analysis but by a rather loose identity of general intellectual
sympathy. Since they were both socialists of a sort, Pearl Andrews
was ready to stand beside his co-patriot while he had his say. Undoubtedly there were deep-seated questions of value and principle
over which they might have quarreled had their brief ideological
flirtation lasted for any length of time. But before they could get
down to serious discussion of basic issues, Pearl Andrews, along with
the Claflin sisters and the rest of the membership of Section 12 of the
International, were unceremoniously expelled for their "borgeois"
intellectual sympathies. Perhaps it was just as well, for some years
later Andrews described Marx' archenemy, Michael Bakunin, as
"a profound thinker, an original genius, a scholar and a philosopher."[30] Sooner or later Pearl Andrews, like Proudhon and other

anarchists, would have come into bitter personal conflict with Marx, however much they might have been in basic sympathy on the idea of social justice.

NOTES

SECTION II - CHAPTER 2

1. Letter from Josiah Warren to Stephen Pearl Andrews, (April 13, 1825). This letter is one of a series of 21 letters (1825-1852) contained in the Catalogs of Charles Coffin Jewett, Houghton Library, Harvard University. The 1825 date cannot possibly be correct as Warren and Andrews did not meet until 1846.

2. *The Evolutionists; Principles, Purposes and Methods of the Union Reform League, as Revealed in its Three Conventions Held in Princeton, Massachusetts 1879, 1880, 1881* (Princeton, Mass., 1882), p. 4.

3. Charles Shively, "An Option For Freedom in Texas, 1840-1844," *The Journal of Negro History*, L (April, 1965), 80.

4. *Ibid.*, 91.

5. "On Picket Duty," *Liberty*, III (May, 1885), 1.

6. *An Oration Delivered on the 4th of July, 1835, Before the East Feliciana Temperance Society, Clinton, Louisiana* (New Orleans, 1836), p. 4.

7. *The Science of Society* (New York, 1851), pp. 19-20.

8. *Ibid.*, p. 46.

9. "Love, Marriage, and Divorce, and the Sovereignty of the Individual," *Liberty*, VI (August, 1888), p. 2.

10. *The Science of Society*, p. 23.

11. *Ibid.*, p. 61.

12. *Ibid.*, p. 119.

13. *Ibid.*, p. 163.

14. "Money and Its Meaning," *The Truth Seeker*, XI (March 8, 1884), 154.

15. *The Science of Society*, p. 157.

16. *Ibid.*, pp. 53-54.

17. *Ibid.*, p. 69.

18. "Love, Marriage, and Divorce, and the Sovereignty of the Individual," *Liberty*, V (June 9, 1888), 2.

19. Letter from Andrela Lilian McReavy to Professor Richard T. Ely, Bellingham, Washington (February 24, 1925), State Historical Society of Wisconsin.

20. Madeline B. Stern, *The Pantarch* (Austin, 1968) p. 17. For a more sympathetic interpretation of Andrews' views by one who

knew him in life, see George E. MacDonald. *Fifty Years of Free Thought*, I (New York, 1929), pp. 406-7.

21. The Archives of the State Historical Society of Wisconsin contains several boxes of such materials.

22. "What Mr. Andrews Told the Union Reform League," *The Truth Seeker*, XL (August 2, 1884), 486.

23. Unpublished Manuscript titled "Address to the People of the United States of America," State Historical Society of Wisconsin.

24. "What Mr. Andrews Told the Union Reform League," *op. cit.*

25. Stern, *op. cit.*, p. 4.

26. Harvey Wish, "Stephen Pearl Andrews, American Pioneer Sociologist," *Social Forces,* XIX (May, 1941), 477.

27. Unpublished Notebook, State Historical Society of Wisconsin.

28. "Mr. Tucker Differed With," *The Truth Seeker*, X (October 27, 1883), 675. This piece was reprinted by Burnett Haskell in *Truth* as he was the subject of Tucker's original attack. Pearl Andrews was not personally acquainted with Haskell but knew him only through his journal.

29. Stern, *op. cit.*, p. 115.

30. Charles Shively, "Introduction," *The Science of Society* (Weston, Mass., 1970), p. 21.

CHAPTER 3

William B. Greene: Prince of American Proudhonians

Although Josiah Warren may be remembered as "the first
American anarchist," William Batchelder Greene (1819-1878) of
Haverhill, Massachusetts, has a better claim to the title of chief
philosopher of the anarchist idea in nineteenth century America, for
his powers as an original thinker far surpassed those of Warren. As
authentically "American" as it is possible to be for one who did not
actually come over on the Mayflower, Greene had deep family roots
in the American soil. His father, Nathaniel Greene, founder of the
Boston *Statesman*, was a descendent of one of the founders of
Warwick, Rhode Island, and was postmaster of Boston from 1829 to
1841 and again from 1844 to 1849. His mother, Susan, was the
daughter of the Reverend William Batchelder, and was in all probability at least partly responsible for her son's decision to study
theology. Appointed to West Point in 1835 when he was sixteen,
Greene apparently contemplated a career in the military. He left the
academy before graduating, however, but fought as a second
lieutenant of the Seventh Infantry Regiment during the Indian Wars
in Florida and later as a colonel in the Fourteenth Massachusetts
Infantry during the Civil War, serving as the commander of Fort
Albany for a time and later as the officer in charge of the earth works
erected between the Arlington House and the City of Alexandria.
More than six feet tall, slender and erect, he retained the military
posture he developed at West Point throughout life, although as he
grew older he progressively became more disenchanted with the social
attitudes which are typically associated with the military mind.

In 1841 Greene associated himself for a few months with the
Brook Farm movement, apparently in search of a new social ideal by
which he might order his life. Turning his interests toward theology,
he graduated from Harvard Divinity School in 1845 and took up the

career of a Unitarian clergyman in Brookfield, Massachusetts. Here he became known as a militant champion of free speech, woman's rights, and labor reform. Judged by the fact that he served as a member of the Massachusett's Constitutional Convention in 1853, Greene seems to have still retained some hope that the institution of government might be employed to improve social conditions. Sometime later, Greene went to Europe, there establishing a strong friendship with Pierre-Joseph Proudhon, the leading light of early nineteenth century anarchism. When he returned to the United States in 1861, he found himself compelled to take a starring role in the abolitionist movement, although he never attained the notoriety that William Lloyd Garrison or Wendel Phillips did.

Known as a fine mathematician and scholar of Hebrew literature as well as of Egyptian and Hebrew history, Greene very rapidly established himself as a vigorous writer of radical tracts. Along with Ezra Heywood, Greene was one of the founders of the New England Labor Reform League. When he died in May of 1878 at the age of 59 in Weston Super Mare, England, where he was then living, many remembered him as the honored president for many years of the League, as well as the inspiration for much of the talk about social revolution that took place in the country at the time. Those who had personal contact with Greene during his prime are unanimous in describing him as an imposing figure of manhood, the center of attention of any group in which he and his attractive wife found themselves. As a young man, Greene's bushy jet black hair and penetrating dark eyes transfixed those who had occasion to converse with him, adding extra authority to the convincing logic of his mind. And when the advancing years had changed his massive shock of hair to pure white, his appearance retained all the charm and charisma it had reflected in his youth. Upon his death Ezra Heywood paid great tribute to his companion in reform when he wrote that William B. Greene not only outweighed Josiah Warren as a social philosopher but that he greatly overshadowed those great libertarians, John Stuart Mill and Adam Smith, "in understanding those principles of liberty which, demolishing compulsive systems revolutionizing to redeem, will make human society possible."[1]

One of the distinctive characteristics of Greene's intellectual development was that his conversion to anarchism stemmed directly from his religious experiences. Profoundly influenced by Proudhon, whom he remembered as "an extraordinarily religious man" who "spent as much time in meditations upon God and eternity as upon the emancipation of the laboring people,"[2] Greene thought of social reform and religious activity as essentially different sides of a single coin. But for him, as for Proudhon, religion was not some musty, authoritarian teaching handed down from the past but the living, subjective experience one felt as he discovered his ego and its relationship to the surrounding world. Taking issue with the writings of Jonathan Edwards, the last of the great theologians of Puritanism in America, Greene denied that the concept of a sacred soul was in any way essential to religion. What is ordinarily called the soul, he argued, is nothing other than that state of consciousness the individual feels when he becomes aware of himself as a social and moral agent. Where Edwards thought of all of man's actions as the deliberate choice of an all-powerful God who completely controlled the winds and currents of the spiritual world, Greene visualized human activity as a process of cause and effect set in motion by man's consciousness of himself as a free being. ". . . as soon as [man] acts, wills, perceives," Greene urged, "he begins to learn the nature of efficient causes, by observing the operations of his own spiritual existence."[3] As he digests the consequences of his individual experiences, he comes to appreciate the importance of his will in the affairs of the world. Man is free to do good or evil through either action or inaction, and the choice he makes is primarily determined by him alone. "I do not conceive that freedom consists in a man's willing as he wills to will; but I hold that man *wills,* and that the very word *will* includes the idea of freedom," Greene wrote. "I choose between two outward objects, and my freedom consists of my ability to choose between these objects, and this power I possess."[4] Obviously Greene was led to the adoption of a libertarian social philosophy as a consequence of the libertarian principles he espoused in the realm of religion.

Some thirty years later Greene entered into yet another controversy concerning the nature of consciousness, this time with Herbert Spencer, the dazzling theorist of nineteenth century liberalism. As if to defend himself against the accusation that he, like Spencer, was committed to a theory of thoroughgoing materialism, Greene composed a careful brief in which he outlined the precise points wherein his epistomological beliefs differed from those of Spencer. Scolding Spencer for asserting that "there is no method of acquiring knowledge except the one used by naturalists in the prosecution of physical investigations," Greene charged him with ignoring "the whole spiritual nature of man" in the construction of a social system which was really a "thinly-disguised system of materialism."[5] Far from being a mere reflection of the material world within which he resides, man, according to Greene, is capable of intuiting knowledge that goes beyond the laws of chemistry and physics. We may speak of "the life of the soul." But the soul of which we speak, Greene insisted, is not some mysterious force implanted in man by a supreme being but the faculty of intelligence that man shares with all other men and which distinguishes him from the animal from which he descended. Man does indeed intuit truth. But the truth he intuits is generally confined to the subjective feelings he experiences as a social animal who has acquired the ability to analyze the facts of his own consciousness.

In the popular mind, social philosophers like Greene and Proudhon who deny the theist's belief in a supreme being are equally guilty of denying the whole realm of religious value. But this is a highly superficial reading of their actual positions, as a careful analysis of their respective writings will demonstrate.[6] In point of fact, Greene, like Proudhon, was a deeply religious man, if by religion we mean a sincere concern for the moral and social condition of humanity. Transposed into the terms of his own individual credo, the religious equation worked out by Greene was sufficiently broad so as to include all the great humanistic philosophers from Socrates and Plato to the social revolutionaries of his own age who totally rejected all creeds and church organization in their quest for moral perfection. All Greene asked of those who claimed religious purpose and commitment was that they actively involve themselves in the fundamental questions of human concern and that they recognize the ongoing nature of religious truth. The fundamental test of authenticity of any social or religious philosophy, according to Greene, is that it must be valid to all men in all ages and that it be arrived at spontaneously and without aid from any established canons of orthodoxy or hierarchy of priests or teachers.

It is true that Greene thought of himself as an atheist; indeed, he almost boasted about the fact. But atheism for him was not a crude, unthinking repudiation of religious value but the conscious attempt to establish oneself as an intelligent social being. Ordinarily we impute atheism to the savages of the primitive past who labored under the burdens of witchcraft and black magic. For Greene, however, atheism was a phenomenon that appears only in the advanced stages of civilization when men are finally capable of the conscious repudiation of their enslavement to their gods, superstition, and the cloying sentimentality of their fathers.[7] With Proudhon, Greene held that the idea of God as lord and master must first be cast out of the human consciousness before any real religious experience can become widely spread among men, for where men bow down in slavish obedience to mindless authority, their actions are devoid of true religious significance. The godless, according to Greene, are not those individuals who purposely reject the undigested notion of the godhead they were spoon-fed during early childhood but those who crassly worship the graven images of power or money, allowing these false gods to exert the predominant influence in their lives. The practical application of Greene's religious commitment is reflected in the vigorous crusade he waged against the evil of "usury," which he felt was the main source of corruption and evil in American society. The deeply religious quality of his social and political theory is evident in a letter Greene wrote to a clergyman in Boston who had championed wealth as a sign of intelligence and self-denial, if not election and grace.[8] Denying that the possession of wealth is very often anything more than sheer luck, "which is the blessing of the prince of the powers of the air," Greene maintained that it is the unscrupulous who have the advantage in obtaining it. Morality, especially since the beginning of the Civil War, he argued, has precious little effect upon the operations of those who thirst for gain, and business men are generally no more honest or public-spirited than the politicians who brazenly manipulate public power for their own advantage. The true Christian, according to Greene, can place no value upon material success on earth but directs all his efforts toward the attainment of the treasure he is promised in heaven. Since very few Christians have any real faith in the ideal they profess to believe in, Greene urged that the beginning of religion is the destruction of the myth which now sustains such individuals in their hypocrisy and self-deceit. Very much after the fashion of Proudhon, Greene sought for religious truth in social philosophy rather than mysticism and theology. And the first step in this process was to unroot the stultifying idea of God from one's mind.

Although Greene today is most remembered, if he is remembered at all, for his book *Mutual Banking*, American anarchists of an earlier era were endeared to him by virtue of his *Blazing Star*, a moving essay in which he attempted to make clear the basic libertarian design of individualism.[9] The blazing star, according to Greene, is "an ideal, a mental picture," of the perfection that any man is theoretically capable of achieving. Hovering above us just out of reach, "the Blazing Star is the transfigured image of man—the Ideal that removes farther and farther, making always higher and higher claims" as to what man ought to be.[10] Individualism, Greene earlier wrote, "is a holy doctrine."[11] As man becomes progressively conscious of himself as a social animal, he increasingly comes to see that his life is not accidental and meaningless but shaped by the "mysterious designs of a holy providence." This holy providence, in Greene's mind, is not a supernatural force or being but an idea—*the idea of the free individual*. Greene, like Godwin, had something like a religious commitment to the idea of human progress, going so far as to suggest that it is the individual's duty to achieve as great a measure of the pattern of harmonious social order implicit in nature as he is capable of. Walking in the footprints of Paine, Emerson, Jefferson, and Thoreau, Greene was clearly influenced in this regard by the philosophy of the Enlightenment. Convinced that the individual is capable of infinite evolutionary development once he frees himself from outmoded institutions and stultifying myth, Greene called for a social revolution in which the basic character of humanity as we have known it through history would be transformed. And like all Enlightenment thinkers, he held that the possibility of actually effecting such a far-reaching social revolution was wholly realistic. The author of a number of small volumes of poetry,[12] Greene imagined a time not too distant in the future when men would overcome the shortcomings they revealed in the past to achieve a uniformly high level of cultural attainment. But equally important in the shaping of his philosophical disposition were his studies in the symbolism of the Jewish Kabbalah, the radical strain in the Hebraic religious tradition. Like a lonely voice crying in the wilderness, Greene called his fellow Americans to account for their failure to observe the great spirit of brotherhood and human compassion which the Kabbalists had fashioned out of their ancient faith.

It is easy to understand why Greene was attracted to the Kabbalah, for the philosophical premises underlying the radical tradition in Hebraic religious teachings were compatible with his interests in mysticism and the study of nature while they at the same time fitted in with his rejection of formal authority in political and social life.[13] Orthodox Christians and Jews ordinarily turn to the idea of God and search for religious truth in His revelations, thereby firmly fixing themselves within a metaphysical outlook in which the process of creation must start with an act of God's will. But Greene, like the Kabbalists, reversed the process and sought for the outline of an adequate and meaningful theory of creation within the recognizable patterns of nature we find ourselves surrounded by, thereby constructing what was essentially an existential explanation for the human situation. Dispensing with the notion of a formal act of creation, the Kabbalah holds that "It is the spectacle of the world that elevates mankind to the idea of God; it is the unity governing the work of Creation which demonstrates at one and the same time the one source of wisdom of the Creator."[14] Man, on this view, since he has not been created from nothing by God as a demonstration of His omnipotence, cannot be thought of as the powerless creature of his maker. Following the Kabbalah, Greene thought of nature as complete, the source of energy and value for all living creatures, including man.

In the beginning, according to both Greene and the Kabbalah, the world was nothing, an Abyss without form or value. "From that Abyss all created things were drawn forth," Greene wrote. "the world [was] created out of *nothing.* "[15] The act of creation in Greene's mind was not a spiritual process, nor was it a physical one either. In the manner of the major tradition in German philosophy during the last half of the nineteenth century,[16] the Kabbalists believed that the essential property of the creative process is a flow of mind or thought and not a physical transformation concerned with matter. Greene gave demonstration of his debt to the Kabbalists when he held that the world "is in one aspect, a poem; in another, it is a logical argument. In every aspect, the universe is a work of art."[17] Unhindered by the staggering notion of an all-powerful God which most men carry about in their minds, Greene was free to develop a humanistic conception of creation. If God did not create the firmament as Genesis holds, then it is man who is the actual author of the events and happenings we observe upon the stage of life. Man, to be sure, does not possess supernatural powers, any more than does the Godhead which conventional theology posits as the sources of the world. But man can be said to possess the power to create reality, according to Greene, for there can be no other plausible explanation for the universe we inhabit. "In truth," Greene wrote, "if all outward things depend for their being and manner of existence upon ourselves, and upon our inward states, a change in these states involves a change in outward nature." If we can then discover the link which connects our inner thoughts and feelings with the phenomena of nature which surrounds us, "the whole universe is in our power; and we may, by a modification of ourselves, change the world from its present state into what we wish it might become."[18] In effect what Greene maintained here was that both matter and spirit are forces which man discovers by virtue of his relationship to them. Man, that is to say, is the "Kabbalistic Balance" wherein both matter and spirit take form and shape.[19] Well-read in the philosophy of Plato, Greene echoed the thoughts of that ancient philosopher when he maintained that things may be said to exist in potential form only until they are given philosophic substance. "When they come forth from potentiality, they do so by entering into relations." All things, that is to say, are what they are by virtue of the existential meaning that man imparts to them. The existential qualities of Greene's philosophical stance were sharply illumined when he wrote:

> There is no life in the Abyss, where all relations have vanished; there is no life in pure essence, but only in existence. Life ceases when man enters the Abyss: it commences when he emerges from the Abyss, and enters into relations. Man's life is in concurrence, in relations. The activity of the soul, whereby it enters into relations, is the life of the world. The act of passing from the state of essence into that of existence, is life. Life, therefore, depends upon the soul, and upon that with which it is in relation; for the activity, which is the life, changes its character according as it is in relation with different objects.[20]

It is necessary at this point to suggest, at the risk of appearing inconsistent, that for all his commitment to the philosophy of individualism, Greene was basically a socialist in his social and economic thinking. Given to the reconciliation of contradictions, as was Proudhon, Greene was not at all perturbed by the evidence of antithetic propositions that showed up from time to time in his writings, and one of his favorite criticisms of Herbert Spencer was that the great architect of social Darwinism, ordinarily so fearless in the face of hard facts, was as fearful as a lost child when it came to the difficult task of thinking his way through two apparently contradictory propositions. "When he is in the presence of a contradiction," Greene charged, Spencer "expunges everything on either side that conflicts with anything on the other. The residium, which he presents as something large and comprehensive, is, usually, a fact, not of knowledge, but of ignorance . . . ."[21] Rather than turn tail and run when confronted with a philosophical dilemma, Greene much preferred to stand fast, allowing apparent contradictions to work themselves out. And thus he could write with self-confidence that "Individualism is good in its place, as qualified and balanced by socialism, but the experience of the world shows clearly that individualism unbalanced by socialism, and socialism unbalanced by individualism, lead always to disastrous social and political crises."[22] The amalgam which he forged out of the normally irreconcilable philosophies of individualism and socialism was what Greene and his successors called anarchism, as did Proudhon in France.

At the outset we must be clear that when Greene spoke of anarchism, he, like Proudhon, conceived of the social and economic organization of society in terms of the mutualist paradigm wherein the individual attains autonomy and self-sufficiency to the extent that he is capable of aligning himself with one voluntary group or other for specific limited ends. Social Darwinists such as William Graham Summer and Herbert Spencer might deceive themselves that there is strength and comfort for the solitary individual plying his preditory trade but both Greene and Proudhon were dedicated to the view that all real social progress is social rather than individual. As Martin Buber wrote of Proudhon, the essential pattern of his social thought is not properly described as individualistic. "What he opposes to the State is not the individual as such but the individual in organic connection with his group, the group being a voluntary association of individuals."[23] Mankind, on this view, forges ahead toward social perfection to the extent that individual men and women join forces with one another for the solution of their common social and economic problems. All association for any purpose, however, must be informal and strictly voluntary rather than regulated or enforced by the established instruments and agencies of government. This distinction made by both Greene and Proudhon between the social and political organization of society on the basis of whether it was voluntary or enforced is central to the idea of anarchism and the essential starting point for all succeeding generations of anarchists.

On the other side of the question of socialism, Greene took the view that social progress must be borne forward on the sweaty backs and shoulders of the working people marching in legion against the bastions of organized capital supported by the state. Counselling the workers to be wary of false prophets, however, Greene warned them not to follow those who would lead them toward social reform by passing new and better laws for the alleviation of poverty and inequality. The achievement of socialism and the "emancipation of the working-class must come, the nature of the State being what it is, from politcal action, resulting, not in the making of new laws, . . . but in the repeal of all existing laws that breed and hatch out privilege."[24] Unlike the liberal and those state socialists who believe that equality can be established and maintained by law, Greene was adamant in his belief that equality can never be said to exist except within a social community in which no special or artificial privileges are given to any man or class of people. Although goverment cannot establish equality by statute or decree, it can stifle the growth of progress by giving aid and support to special groups of privileged people. Greene's *Mutual Banking,* the best known of all his many books, was written to portray the evils which result where government uses its power to interfere with natural equality by setting up monopolies in favor of the few, and to urge that the opposite course be followed. It was widely read at the time and undoubtedly influenced many men to follow the anarchist standard.

The argument that unfolds in the pages of *Mutual Banking* is a highly volatile, radical economic doctrine. Distinguishing between legal and actual value, Greene held that legal value results from fiscal manipulations of money at the hands of government and not from natural causes. The national debt of a country such as England, he held, consists chiefly of interest payments which have accumulated over the years on the money the government originally borrowed. Were the legal value of this debt wiped away, the country would be as wealthy after the event as before, for no actual value would have been destroyed. No doubt the holders of debt would suffer a loss in their pocketbooks but the people of the country who pay taxes to cover the interest on the debt would immediately become richer to the extent that the debt holders became poorer. The practical effect of this monetary system is that the people of the country are divided into classes, depending upon whether they pay off the debt through taxes or are recipients of the interest and are thus enabled to live without working.[25] Altogether independent of Marx and Engels, Greene arrived at a theory of class conflict and domination which was strikingly similar to theirs. But the social and economic facts from which he constructed his conclusions were drawn largely from the American scene and were the honest observations of a genuine yankee.

"At the present day," Greene wrote in 1849, "chartered corporations, enjoying special privileges, disarrange our social organization, and make the just distribution of the products of labor impossible."[26] The annual income which flows into the pockets of stockholders in the form of interest, he maintained, is entirely unearned by them and rests on nothing more substantial than a legal fiction. Unlike the workingman, who pays for his sustenance with the sweat of his brow, the stockholder is completely parasitic, offering nothing in return for the wealth which accumulates to him. Actually what we have right here and now in the State of Massachusetts, Greene argued, is an essentially socialistic society in which the government distributes the wealth according to artificial methods maintained by law. Socialism *"is precisely this intervention of society for the distribution of wealth in some order other than that which would follow from the prevalence of* FREE COMPETITION." Taking issue with the economic doctrines formulated by Alexander Hamilton, Greene maintained that the establishment of gold and silver as a circulating medium virtually amounts to a grant of power to a financial elite whereby they might exercise a rigid monopoly over the monetary system. Where gold and silver are used to back currency, money cannot obtain its natural level but is subject to artificial controls by those who possess the power to influence government. Thus they have a veto power over all exchanges and the natural economic laws are prevented from taking their normal course.

Foremost among those who stifle free competition in the money market, according to Greene, are the banks which receive their charters from government, whether state or national. When a group of individuals pool their capital to establish a bank, they have engaged in what might be described as a conspiracy to destroy competition among capitalists. Had they each attempted to employ their capital as independent investors, they would find themselves in competition, under ordinary circumstances, which would have the effect of driving downward the rate of interest any one of them might obtain. But where the law permits them to invest their money in concert, they are able to escape competition. And competition, as Greene saw it, is the life-blood of liberty and equality.[27] Whoever prevents competition destroys the natural liberties of the people.

With Proudhon, Greene subscribed to the view that "property is theft." This assertion was not the ranting of an irresponsible malcontent but the reasoned judgment of a lifelong student of economics. Greene, along with Proudhon, did not object to the possession of property which was based upon honest labor or initiative. His complaint was directed against an economic system which rewarded fraud and privilege rather than hard work and frugality. And this, in his opinion, is exactly what takes place under conventional banking laws. By regulating the amount of money in actual circulation, the banks actually reach into the pocket of the ordinary citizen, increasing or decreasing the value of his wealth to suit their own pleasure.

> They make great issues, and money becomes plenty; that is to say, *every other commodity becomes dear.* The capitalist sells what he has to sell while prices are high. The banks draw in their issues, and money becomes scarce; that is, *all other commodities become cheap.* The community is distressed for money. Individuals are forced to sell property to raise money to pay their debts, and to sell at a loss on account of the state of the market. Then the capitalist buys what he desires to buy while prices are low. These operations are the upper and the nether mill-stones, between which the hopes of the people are ground to powder.[28]

Far from being honorable, the money made by capitalists in the controlled economy maintained by the conventional banking system is actually stolen from the pockets of the working people, Greene charged. No term describes such profits as well as the word "usury," and no man of good conscience can rest so long as the present capitalist system continues in operation.

The remedy Greene outlined for the reform of capitalist society was one of the most thoroughly anarchistic proposals ever to have come from the pen of an American writer. Since the evils of the existing system were the result of actions initiated by government, Greene proposed that the state be eliminated as a factor in the economic process. This could be done by employing the cooperation of individuals; working together, farmers and working people must replace the existing banking structure with a system of mutual free banks unsupported by government favoritism and privilege. It would of course require a great surge of voluntarism upon the part of the people to effect such a drastic reform, but Greene, like all anarchists of his day, was confident that it was realistic to suppose that such a social transformation might be expected in the future if only the proper educational foundations were laid, and hence he threw himself into the work of making known the nature of the anarchist idea as he conceived of it.

The system of mutual banking that took form in Greene's imagination was an ingenious adaptation of the anarchist idea to the frontier conditions which still largely characterized America during the middle years of the nineteenth century. One of the most serious complaints Greene directed at the conventional banks of his day was that they were controlled by men who were unable to think in terms of human problems, so preoccupied were they with the mechanics of the fiscal world wherein they dwelt. But "If there were no banks, the (mere) capitalist would unfold his hands, would become human, would have a feeling for the common accidents and infirmities; he would no longer . . . make it his pride to cultivate a patrician haughtiness calculated to give him an immediate ascendency over all who approach him."[29] The mutual banks advocated by Greene, like the Time Store advocated by Josiah Warren, were designed to eliminate those speculators and adventurers who exploit the honest workers under conventional financial arrangements. After the fashion of Proudhon, the banks were to be owned and operated by the people themselves rather than the scions of wealth established and maintained by Hamilton's Leviathan state.

The rules of Greene's mutual bank plan were very simple and were obviously intended to realize the dream of equality which he felt was being denied to the American people. Any individual might become a member of a mutual bank merely by pledging himself to do so.[30] Thereafter he was morally obligated to receive the money issued by the bank whenever it was offered in payment of debts owed to him. If he desired to borrow money from the bank, which was only to be issued in paper form, he was required to give his note, pledging his property as collateral. No one could borrow more than one half of the property he was able to pledge but no interest was to be charged on the loan beyond a small charge based upon the exact cost of the expenses incurred by the bank in processing it. One might release himself from the debt he had pledged merely by repaying his loan at any time.

Unfortunately, Greene did not make clear exactly what he meant by property. In one instance he maintained that "Mutual money, which neither is nor can be merchandise, escapes the law of supply and demand, which is applicable to merchandise only."[31] But did property include land? If so, Greene might be charged with inconsistency, for he had previously argued that inherited wealth is usury as much as is interest collected on legal debts. Benjamin Tucker came to his rescue some years later, maintaining that Greene had not intended to include land itself within the category of property but only the improvements which had been made upon it by the individual.[32] Land itself, although currently monopolized by individuals who had somehow managed to obtain a legal title to it from the state, was primarily the property of society rather than persons. One might use the land to support himself but Greene's economic theories entitled the individual to claim possession only of those products that had been created wholly by his own labor. Since no individual can create the land itself, he can not sell it but only the value of the improvements which he may have made upon it.

For those who value social freedom above any other consideration, the advantages of mutual banking, were any people ever able to sustain such a system, are immediately obvious. Since wealth under a system of mutual banking would depend upon the initiative and efforts of the individual rather than legal title conferred by the state, equality would be within the actual reach of all who really desire it. Thus, Greene wrote: "Whoever, in the times of the Mutual Bank, has property, will have money also; and the laborer who has no property will find it very easy to get it; for every capitalist will seek to secure him as a partner."[33] Like all anarchists, Greene was convinced that the greater part of the corruption and social injustice society now experiences is ultimately traceable to the power the state possesses to force people to carry out its will. Where the state is invested with monopolistic powers over the economy, as it has been from Hamilton's day forward, myriad currents of distrust and discontent are generated which prevent individual persons from acquiring even a fraction of their potential for moral development. Hence the state is our social enemy rather than our benefactor and it becomes our duty to erase it from the face of the earth. But violence begats violence, and this fact prevents us from mounting an all-out physical war upon the machinery of government. Social reform therefore, Greene urged, must come from the people themselves and not their leaders. And it must take the form of a social revolution rather than a political one.

Having been conditioned by more than a half century of government sponsored economic discrimination, the American people, although born free, are burdened down with chains. A system of mutual banking, since it is dependent upon voluntarism for energy rather than compulsion and artificial law, is capable of allowing people the freedom necessary to their further social development.

It has been fashionable in recent years to draw a sharp division between the individualist anarchists as opposed to the communist anarchists, and Greene's writings clearly support this dichotomy to some extent. Condemning communist societies because all power within them has been concentrated in the tribal chief, Greene voiced strong opposition to any social system wherein the leader is obeyed "as something extra-natural and ruling by a mysterious inscrutable right."[34] Social progress, for this reason, is likely to be by the way of mutualism rather than communism, he held, for in communism, the individual is perforce sacrificed to the welfare and unity of the whole. Within a mutualist society, on the other hand, unlimited individualism "is the essential and necessary prior condition of its own existence, and coordinates individuals without any sacrifice of individuality, into one collective whole, by spontaneous confederation or solidarity." The flavor of Greene's language is strikingly similar to that of Kropotkin, although he had proabaly never even heard of "the anarchist Prince" at this time. When Greene wrote that "the principle of mutuality in social economy is identical with the principle of federation in politics," he unknowingly summed up the essential principle of Kropotkin's teaching. A year after he wrote these words Greene joined with other French speaking members of the Boston Section, Number One, of the Working People's International Association in proclaiming that "The identical spirit . . . now works in the entire proletariat of the world, that worked formerly in the insurgent Hebrews, when . . . marching by fives, they broke forth from the bondage of the Pharaonic civilization."[35] However much he might profess his intellectual allegiance to Proudhon, the basic outline of Kropotkin's version of the anarchist idea was not something alien to Greene. As in the case of many later American anarchists, the standards of the various anarchist schools were cut from the same piece of cloth more than those who bore them realized at the time.

NOTES

SECTION II - CHAPTER 3

1. "Colonel William B. Greene," *The Word*, VII (July, 1878), 2.
2. "Is Property Robbery," *The Word,* II (January, 1874), 4.
3. *Remarks In Refutation of Jonathan Edwards on the Freedom of the Will* (West Brookfield, Mass., 1848), p. 9.
4. *Ibid.*, p. 21.
5. *The Facts of Consciousness and the Philosophy of Mr. Herbert Spencer* (Boston, 1871), p. 18.
6. For an analysis of Proudhon's religious position, see William O. Reichert, "Proudhon and Kropotkin on Church and State," *A Journal of Church and State*, IX (Winter, 1967), 87-100.
7. *Socialistic, Communistic, Mutualistic, and Financial Fragments* (Boston, 1875), p. 194.
8. A letter to the Rev. Henry W. Foote, *In Vindication of the Poorer Class of the Boston Working-Women* (Princeton, Mass., 1873), p. 8.
9. "Anarchism and the Anglo-Saxons," *Road to Freedom*, II (August 1926), 2.
10. *The Blazing Star; With An Appendix Treating of the Jewish Kabbala* (Boston, 1872), p. 4.
11. *Equality* (West Brookfield, Mass., 1849), p. 73.
12. Two volumes of Greene's poetry, *Three Vows and Other Poems* (1881), and *Thought Sketches* (1887), were put into print after his death by a son, also named William Batchelder Greene. The younger Greene was also a poet and published a number of volumes of poetry himself, the most notable of which was *Cloudrifts At Twilight* (1888).
13. For a sympathetic account of the Kabbalah, see: Gershom G. Scholem, *On the Kabbalah and its Symbolism,* trans. by Ralph Manheim (New York, 1965).
14. Adolph Franck, *The Kabbalah; The Religious Philosophy of the Hebrews,* trans. by John C. Wilson. (n.p., 1967), p. 67. Franck originally published his work from Paris in 1843 and it is possible that Greene was familiar with it, for ten years later he spent some time in France acquainting himself with Proudhon and other intellectuals who shared his interests in radical religion and politics.
15. "The Jewish Kabbalah," in *The Blazing Star, op. cit.,* p. 80.

16. Franck, *op. cit.*, pp. 77-78.

17. "The Jewish Kabbalah," *op. cit.*, p. 80.

18. *Transcendentalism* (West Brookfield, Mass., 1849), p. 6.

19. "The Jewish Kabbalah," *op. cit.*, p. 51.

20. *Transcendentalism*, p. 42.

21. "The Jewish Kabbalah," p. 131.

22. *The Sovereignty of the People* (Boston, 1868), p. 31.

23. *Paths in Utopia* (Boston, 1960), p. 28.

24. *Socialistic, Communistic, Mutualistic, and Financial Fragments*, p. 254.

25. *Mutual Banking* (Worcester, Mass., 1870), p. 10.

26. *Equality*, p. 67.

27. *Ibid.*, p. 2.

28. *Mutual Banking*, p. 46.

29. *Equality*, p. 7.

30. *Mutual Banking*, p. 29.

31. *Ibid.*, p. 35.

32. "On Picket Duty," *Liberty*, II (October, 1883), 1.

33. *Mutual Banking*, p. 50.

34. "Communism Versus Mutualism," *The Word*, III (November, 1874), 1.

35. *Socialistic, Communistic, Mutualistic, and Financial Fragments*, p. 233.

CHAPTER 4

Lysander Spooner:
Stentorian of Enlightened Rebellion

One of the most penetrating criticisms of the state idea was made by Lysander Spooner (1808-1887), who needed no teacher to discover the beauty of the anarchist idea. Tracing his ancestry to William Spooner who settled in Plymouth around 1637, Lysander Spooner might have been expected to lie back and bask in the warmth of the heritage his forbears had left to him. And so far as is known he gave no indication while working on his father's farm near Anthol, Massachusetts, where he remained until he was twenty-five years of age, that any radical blood coursed through his veins. Although uneducated beyond the learning he had acquired in the country schools near his home, he succeeded in obtaining a clerkship in the Registry of Deeds in Worcester. The next year at the age of twenty-six he began to read law, working at first in the law office of John Davis and later in the office of Charles Allen, both of whom were among the most famous lawyers in Massachusetts at the time. Sometime later, Spooner opened his own law office in Worcester but did not practice for very long, although he continued to cogitate upon the nature of law for the rest of his long life. His thinking progressively structured by the libertarian philosophy which he seems to have discovered entirely on his own, Lysander Spooner could not force himself to practice a trade which he felt to be a fraud and a cheat.

Like all the other native American anarchists who came of age during the early years of the Republic, Spooner's social and political philosophy was primarily shaped by his commitment to free thought. Unwilling and unable to submit his judgment to any principle or dictum that did not bear the test of rational examination, Spooner, in the tradition of Tom Paine, proclaimed reason the only legitimate authority in human relations. To accept a thing as true on the basis of revelation, Spooner charged, is to humiliate oneself in the most

117

destructive manner, for it crushes out that self-respect which is essential to individual growth and development.[1] In what must surely be one of the most vitriolic attacks ever directed at organized religion by an American, Spooner ridiculed those "who pretend to be Christians" for the superficiality of the arguments which they put up in defense of their beliefs. Many believe in the Bible because they find that belief useful, he charged, but few so-called Christians stand ready to present rational reasons for believing as they do. "If men were but to read the New Testament with the same tone and emphasis with which they do other books, and were to keep out of mind the idea of its being sacred," he wrote, "they would be disgusted with the credulity, and the want of intellect, reason and judgment, that is apparent in it."[2] Turning his wrath on the Apostles, Spooner was forced to admit that Paul stood out from the others in that he had "some talents," although his intellect was "muddy" and his judgement bad. But he charged, Paul was "violent, precipitate, and unreflecting," not to mention "bigoted, superstitious and dogmatic." So "crafty and deceitful" was Paul, according to Spooner, that he conspired with the other Apostles in concocting imaginative stories about Jesus' powers to perform miracles which "constituted the bait" by which the people were drawn into the net of Christianity like so many herring or sardines. Turning away from Christianity as though it were some sort of offensive odor, Spooner applied his critical faculties to an equally rigorous examination of American social and political theory.

Perhaps the most important influence to cause Spooner to don the coat of radicalism was his bitter experience with the various governments with which he came in contact. After leaving his ancestral home in Massachusetts, Spooner moved westward to Ohio, settling briefly in Perrysburg, Toledo, and finally in Columbus. While in Perrysburg, he waged a legal feud with the State of Ohio, suing it in 1838 after its drainage of the Maumee River had caused alleged damage to land which he had purchased on its shores.[3] Losing the suit, Spooner returned to the East in 1844, no doubt with bitter memories of the institution of government. Establishing the American Letter Mail Company, a private postal service to operate between the cities of Boston and New York, Spooner again had his hackles raised by government when the United States squashed his venture in private enterprise by ruling that his operations violated the government's "exclusive right" to maintain a mail service for the nation, holding that every letter his company carried was a separate violation of the law punishable by a fine.[4] Stung to the quick by the heavy-handed ways of his own government, Spooner dashed off *The Unconstitutionality of the Laws of Congress Prohibiting Private Mails* (1844) in denunciation of it. The constitutional stipulation allowing Congress to establish post offices and post roads, according to him, did not give the national government any exclusive power to the function of carrying mail. Congress may establish agencies of its own for the delivery of mail but it has not been given the power to prevent others from doing the same thing, he argued, for nowhere in the Constitution are there any words denying this privilege to private citizens. If the founding fathers had intended to give Congress an exclusive right to operate the postal service, it would have been "required" to establish a post office, not merely permitted to do so. Nor can it be argued, Spooner continued, that just because a thing done by a private person is similar to a thing done by the government, it is unconstitutional. If this logic were to be followed, it would be unconstitutional for private persons to borrow money, since the government is also permitted to do this. There is absolutely no reason why the carrying of mail should be made a monopoly either in the hands of government or private persons, Spooner declared. The fact that his company had forced the government to reduce its own rates indicated that the public was served at least as well by private competition as it was by a public enterprise.[5]

The only other conceivable justification for the government's postal monopoly, according to Spooner, would be that the freedom of public communication and intelligence might be better protected in this way. But the fact is, Spooner argued, that those who desire a postal monopoly in the hands of government intend that this power should be used as "an engine of the police" during periods of civil disturbance and not as a means of increasing the free flow of ideas.[6] In government as in commerce, the primary function of monopoly is to stifle freedom, not secure it. And hence a government monopoly over the mails "has no adaptation to facilitate anything but the operations of tyranny"; it has no aspect whatever, that is favorable either to the liberty or the interests of the people. As the scales fell away from his eyes, Lysander Spooner's lost innocence was converted into a deep and lasting hostility toward a government which would hypocritically abuse its powers in the name of liberty.

Championing the poor and propertyless worker, Spooner declared that the employment of public power to secure the banking system was the cardinal sin from which a host of lesser evils flowed.[7] Where legislation is used to establish the terms under which money may be loaned, the worker who does not originally possess property is put at a severe disadvantage when he tries to obtain capital with which to begin his economic climb. In order to borrow money, one must establish credit by demonstrating title to tangible property that can be used as collateral. This the rich have no difficulty in doing; but for the poor, according to Spooner, it is an entirely different story. When the rich borrow money, they borrow on property, such as houses and lands, which they continue to use and enjoy. Hence the return realized on this borrowed money is pure gain, since it cost nothing but the risk involved in borrowing it. Possessing no property to begin with, the poor cannot obtain a loan on credit. When they borrow money, it is real cash which they are borrowing, to be repaid out of the actual sweat from their brows. "The effect of usury laws, then," Spooner asserted, "is to give a monopoly of the right of borrowing money to those few who can offer the most approved security." For them, money is readily available at the standard rate of interest and is never in short supply. Those without credit, however, find it extremely difficult to borrow money at all, even when they are willing to pay a substantially higher rate of interest, for who will chance lending money to one without credit when others can be found who possess adequate security for the money they wish to borrow? Like many of the other native American anarchists, Spooner insisted that the answer to this problem lay in the complete withdrawal of government from the business of regulating banks.

Although Spooner's sympathies were predominantly with the working classes as against the rich, he did not allow himself to be led into a doctrinaire defense of labor in support of a general program of leveling property rights. No economic communist, Spooner did not condemn the private ownership of property itself; what he opposed was the injustice meted out by government when it interfered with the natural laws of economics. Foremost among the tyrannic acts perpetrated by government within the economy, according to Spooner, are the patent and copyright laws which interfere with the individual's right to enjoy the full fruit of his own labor. Obviously influenced by the economic theories of John Locke, Spooner asserted that it is the act of adding one's labor to the natural products of the earth that renders them valuable. And once this has been done, no one may interfere with the enjoyment of wealth so created. But it is not only by hammer and hand that property is produced; "A man's ideas are his property," too, and no other man may thus lay claim to the value which results from their application. When government limits a man's claim to the fruits of his inventions to a specific period of years, it interferes with his natural right of property ownership. Spooner favored giving the inventor perpetual claim to the value produced by his invention. Although this in effect gives him a monopoly over the thing in question, we must recognize, he argued, "that all property is a monopoly."[8] And monopolies are undesirable only when they are unjustly maintained by law for the benefit of those who have no moral claim to them. It is one thing for the law to protect a certain few industrialists in a monopoly of an industry but an entirely different matter when it comes to allowing inventors and designers to claim the product of their own ingenuity. For one thing, their inventions are as much the product of their own labor as are the potatoes a farmer digs from the ground after having planted and cultivated them. Moreover, where inventors are granted a perpetual claim to the value created by their idea, society itself must benefit, for other men will consequently be spurred into perfecting an even better idea. Not only would more inventions thus be made, thereby vastly increasing the general wealth of society, but those already made would not be as long-lived as at present, since competition among inventors would be very keen. Unusually fine ideas would undoubtedly lead to the enrichment of those who create them, Spooner reasoned, but since other men would also be free to improve upon the existing science and technology, "it would consequently require vastly more actual wealth to make a man relatively rich." In Spooner's view of things, the copyright and patent laws are a prime example of "that pretended wisdom" by which governments rationalize their interference with the rights and liberties of their peoples. "When will mankind learn—and compel their governments to conform to the knowledge—that justice is better policy than any scheme of robbery, that was ever devised?"[9] Spooner's proposal that the living descendants of the great inventors of the past are entitled to the full proceeds of the thing invented by their forebears may well have been an extravagant statement, as Benjamin Tucker asserted some years later.[10] But Spooner made no claim to moderation of thought or opinion; for him it was enough to tell things like they are, even at the cost of offending one's contemporaries beyond redemption.

On the question of slavery, Lysander Spooner was a veritable lion, loudly raging against all who would defend the dread system which he hated with passion and unrestraint. It is reported that upon receipt of the news of John Brown's daring exploit at Harper's Ferry, he sought to enlist the aid of other sympathetic souls in a scheme aimed at kidnapping the governor of Virginia and trading him off for Brown.[11] We can never know whether Spooner was serious about this project but it was most certainly characteristic of his boldness and moral determination. In his mind there was only one significant consideration—is slavery constitutional or is it not? Referring back to the original colonial charters, Spooner pointed out that none of them allowed the institution. As a matter of fact, he argued, a decision by the Court of King's Bench in 1772 established the rule that any slave brought into England even temporarily, should have his freedom under law. And since the colonies were considered to be an integral part of England at that time, it clearly followed that the institution of slavery was from almost the very beginning illegal in America. It might well have been that England "tolerated" the African slave-trade and did not take any overt steps to stamp it out. But, Spooner retorted, "toleration of a wrong is not law."[12]

The fact is that liberty was declared a "self-evident" truth in America with the break from the mother country, Spooner maintained. The nation might well have chosen to deny this principle had it decided to do so. But this has not been done, for the claim that "*all* men have liberty, and the pursuit of happiness" has been daily woven into the very fabric of American life ever since. No court in the land would deny immediate freedom to any man brought before it in chains who was not black, Spooner held. Then why do the courts not set the African free likewise? Mincing no words, Spooner declared that: "It is because the courts are parties to an understanding, prevailing among the white race, but expressed in no authentic constitutional form, that the negro may be deprived of his rights at the pleasure of avarice and power." And this is done in open and premeditated defiance of the fundamental law of the nation. The partisans of slavery, to be sure, make an attempt to find legal foundations for their vicious prejudices when they argue that a sanction for slavery may be found in the debates which accompanied the writing of the constitution. Yet after the convention tumult had died out, the framers agreed upon a legal instrument which gave no official standing whatever to chattel bondage.[13] How then can it be maintained that the framers wished to give standing under the law to slavery? To be perfectly accurate, Spooner continued, when the Constitution of the United States was adopted, all the people who were not then slaves under their state constitution were declared to be citizens. And since the state constitution of that day did not permit slavery, the national Constitution made everyone a citizen, without regard to color or place of origin.[14] Obviously it was too late for the state governments to undo something that had already been accomplished in law. Spooner would have none of the hypocrisy that characterized the state rights position. The real issue before the nation, he opined, is not whether slavery shall be extended from the existing states into the territory of states yet to be created, but whether there shall be slavery at all. Those politicians of the Republican party who attempt to make the state rights argument into a moral proposition, Spooner asserted, "are either smitten with stupidity, as with a disease, or what is more probable, are nothing else than selfish, cowardly, hypocritical, and unprincipled men, who, for the sake of gaining or retaining power, are simply making a useless noise about nothing, with the purpose of diverting men's minds from the true issue . . . ."[15] Some years later Spooner again insisted that the notion that the Civil War was fought primarily to end the injustice of slavery was sheer fraud. Those who abolished slavery did so for purposes of expediency and not to sustain their moral principles. Anxious to get on with the business of wealth-getting, the leaders of the industrial part of the nation considered it necessary to abolish chattel slavery.[16] But they were not opposed to another kind of slavey, as the industrial empires they were busily engaged in erecting soon demonstrated.

Reacting strongly to the Hobbesian principles that are implicit in the structure of American political development, Lysander Spooner was one of the first "angry young men" to declare the bankruptcy of the idea of parliamentary democracy as it had come to be practiced in this country. We often hear it said that the government of the United States is a "sovereign government," Spooner charged. But aside from the sonorous tones of its rhetoric, what does this phrase actually contain, Spooner indignantly asked. With anarchists of all ages, Spooner maintained that for practical purposes a "sovereign government" is one that denies the natural rights of its subjects, demanding from them absolute obedience and submission to its will. To pretend that the people of this country, or any other country, ever openly chose to live under such insane conditions is ridiculous, for it supposes that the people "intended, not only to authorize every injustice, and arouse universal violence, among themselves, but that they intended also to avow themselves the open enemies of the rights of all the rest of mankind."[17] If we would put political philosophy on a sound foundation, Spooner countered, it must be clearly understood that "the only real 'sovereignty,' or right of 'sovereignty,' in this or any other country, is that right of sovereignty which each and every human being has over his or her own person and property, so long as he or she obeys the one law of justice towards the person or property of every other human being."

Utterly unable to content himself with political ideas that did not ring true to his ear, Spooner was goaded to fury when faced with the argument that the Constitution of the United States is not only the supreme law of the land but also in some sense sacred. Far from being holy, he held, it "has been an utter fraud from the beginning." Whatever the intentions of those who wrote the Constitution may have been, the words they chose by which to express their thoughts suggest that it was their hope that that instrument "might prove useful and acceptable to their posterity." But nowhere does the language of the Constitution imply the right of the framers to compel future generations of Americans to bind themselves to its terms. Had they intended to force future generations to obey the Constitution's edicts, they would not have proclaimed that their purpose was " 'to secure to them the blessings of liberty,' but to make slaves of them; for if their 'posterity' are bound to live under it, they are nothing less than the slaves of their foolish, tyrannical, and dead grandfathers."[18] Then how does it come about that this document, about which very few Americans have any real knowledge, has been able to stand for over ninety years and has been "used for such audacious and criminal purposes?" Challenging the right of all "so-called Senators and Representatives in Congress to exercise any legislative power whatever over the people of the United States," Spooner advanced the thesis that the Constitution "has been sustained by the same kind of conspiracy as that by which it was established; that is, by the wealth and power of those few who were to profit by the arbitrary dominion it was assumed to give them over others."[19] And all this time the innocent as well as the ignorant among the people "who were to be cheated, plundered, and enslaved by it, have been told, and some of them doubtless made to believe, that it is a sacred instrument, designed for the preservation of their rights."

In one of the many vitriolic epistles he addressed to the officials of government, Spooner insisted that it is not the Constitution that is the supreme law of the land but justice. "And if you do not know it," he wrote one of his unfortunate victims, "your ignorance is so dense as to be pitiable."[20] There are those who argue that liberty is lost to the American people because the Constitution has been neglected, he rasped, but freedom can never be sustained in the land where people are taught to slavishly follow the exact letter of the Constitution as though it were a book of commandments bequeathed to them by a supreme lawgiver. Only justice possesses enough majesty to be accorded a place of honor in our consciences.

Turning his wrath on John Marshall, Spooner castigated him for his part in the great American conspiracy. Marshall, the chief "oracle of all the rapacious classes in America," had no conception whatever of the value of the natural rights philosophy. In Marshall's mind, Spooner charged, the people do not possess any right other than their obligation to obey the laws laid down for them by the government.[21] Concerned above all else with securing the property rights of the upper orders of society rather than the rights and liberties of all the people, Marshall engineered one of the most brazen *coups* of power known in all history when he led the supreme court to assume absolute power concerning the limits of freedom in America.

But Marshall was not alone in the game of fleecing the people of their heritage of freedom; aiding and abetting him was that motley crew of statists who deem the legislative power the savior of the people. "Substantially all the tyranny and robbery and crime that governments have ever committed," Spooner wrote, "have been committed under the pretense of making laws."[22] When individual persons act, he argued, they invariably recognize that there are some limits to their actions, whether these derive from their own consciences or the mores of society which are imposed upon them by their social group. But when legislators act, there are no restraints to the power they claim to possess. The self-appointed saviors of the people, lawmakers are no more concerned with the liberties of the people than the shepherd is concerned with the feelings of his sheep. " 'Our liberty' is in danger *only* from the lawmakers," Spooner asserted, "because it is only through the agency of lawmaking, that anyone pretends to be able to take away 'our liberty.' "[23]

Concerning the natural rights of the individual, Spooner maintained that every man has perfect freedom to do anything whatever with himself and his property that is consistent with the demands of justice toward others. Fundamental to the individual's basic natural rights is the right to be free from all compulsion exercised over him by others.[24] Unless a man is absolutely free to determine his social actions by his own internal feelings concerning justice, Spooner claimed, it is utter nonsense to prattle about natural rights. Singling out the President of the United States for special treatment, Spooner chided him unmercifully for his lack of faith in the people. "Your 'country-men' would be perfectly competent to take care of their own 'interests' and provide for their own 'welfare,' " he castigated Grover Cleveland, "if their hands were not tied, and their powers crippled, by such fetters as men like you and your lawmakers have fastened upon them."[25] The people have no need for any leadership other than that which they are capable of providing themselves. "Are you so stupid as to imagine that putting chains on men's hands, and fetters on their feet, and insurmountable obstacles in their paths, is the way to supply their 'needs' and promote their 'welfare'?" Like the dog who has treed a cat and is unable to pull himself away from his quarry, Spooner had difficulty in restraining himself once he got started on the subject of the usurpations of political powers. "Are you an idiot," he pressed the chief executive, "that you talk as you do, about what you and your lawmakers are doing to provide for the real wants, and promote the real 'welfare' of fifty millions of people?" Since he, like Thoreau, was confident in his own mind that all the verbosity of politicians, statesmen, and divines amounts to little more than the rantings of a feeble minded old woman, Spooner did not wait for an answer but went on with his indictment against the state. As he pointed out to the president, government, if it is to provide substantially equal justice to everyone, must not attempt to use its powers at all in support of the general welfare. Where it attempts to do this, it inevitably finds itself in the position of favoring some one person or group of persons with favors of one kind or another. But government, since it possesses absolutely nothing in the way of property of its own, can only give to one person what it takes away from another. When certain individuals are granted exemptions, privileges, or monopolies by the state, they have been given something that the state has had to wrest from another, employing its power of coercion to do so.

True to the concern with moral questions that has characterized the thinking of anarchists of all ages, Spooner was primarily opposed to the coercive power of government because it interfered with the natural development of the individual's social power. Acknowledging that individuals have duties and obligations to one another, he yet maintained that it can be no business of government as to how these are fulfilled. The beginning of all political science, he urged, is "the science of justice. . . ."[26] If we would give it a name sufficiently broad to include all of its many facets, we might call it "the science of peace." Endowed by nature with certain basic judicial powers or rights, every man must develop his own internal mechanism of social control whereby he fulfills his obligations to others. But in each instance he must act only in accord with his own conception of right, being fully aware of his personal responsibility for his failures. And this is why, Spooner argued, government is antithetical to the development of an adequate social system. For government allows no such freedom to individuals. It is true, of course, that even the most brutal despotism will give individual citizens enough liberty to support themselves, pay their taxes, and otherwise serve the interests of the state. *"But it will do this for its own good, and not for theirs.* In allowing them this liberty, it does not at all recognize their right to it, but only consults its own interest."[27] A flagrant example of the state's callous attitude toward the moral development of the individual, according to Spooner, is its demands regarding the military function. "The government not only denies a man's right, as a moral human being, to have any will, any judgment, any conscience of his own, as to whether he himself will be killed in battle, but it equally denies his right to have any will, any judgment, any conscience of his own, as a moral human being, as to whether he shall be used as a mere weapon for killing other men."[28] And thus before the individual has fully reached manhood he has been taught that his ultimate duty is not to God, or truth, or mercy, but to success of the state. Could there be a more thoroughgoing corruption of the youth than this?

It is not widely recognized, even among anarchists themselves, that Lysander Spooner was the author of some of the soundest libertarian political philosophy ever to have been written by an American. This claim is substantiated by his writings concerning the nature of law and its function within society. Unhappily, Spooner wrote, the concept of law has become synonymous with the arbitrary commands of a government which compels submission to its demands by virtue of its immense physical powers of coercion. But this is a complete perversion of the true nature of law. And what is even more to be deplored, Spooner continued,

> such has been the superstition of the people, and such their blind veneration for physical power that this injustice has not opened their eyes to the distinction between law and force, between the sacred requirements of natural justice, and the criminal exactions of unrestrained selfishness and power. They have thus not only suffered the name of law to be stolen . . . but they have rendered homage and obedience to crime, under the name of law, until the very name of law, instead of signifying in their minds, an immutable principle of right, has come to signify little more than an arbitrary command of power, without reference to its justice or its injustice, its innocence or its criminality.[29]

Unless we hold justice to be a natural principle of society superior to all others, according to Spooner, the entire history of man's struggle for right takes on the proportions of a fantasy within which all is false and unreal. "If there be no such science as justice, there can be no science of government. . . ." The implications of such an admission are far-reaching and deadly serious. If justice is unknown in nature, Spooner argued, there can be no moral standard introduced into social conflicts which divide man from man. Thus unable to appeal to any objective standard of right, "the inevitable doom of the human race must consequently be to be forever at war; forever striving to plunder, enslave, and murder each other; with no instrumentalities but fraud and force to end the conflict."[30] If justice is a mere word upon our lips with no substance apart from the expediency we gain by uttering it, "the world is a mere abyss of moral darkness; with no sun, no light, no rule of duty, to guide men in their conduct towards each other." In short, Spooner asserted, men must either acknowledge the validity of the principle of justice or completely abandon all pretense regarding the reign of law within society.

Within the province of nature, Spooner urged, every particular object is governed by some unalterable, universal principle. Thus matter responds to gravity, animals are governed by their essential natures, and the stars follow irregular pattern in the heavens. In the case of man, the universal rule which determines his correct form of conduct is the principle of natural justice. Ultimately the principle of justice is seen to be deeply rooted within human nature itself. But men do not automatically attain perfection in its outline in the process of social evolution; through their contacts with one another necessitated by the currents of social intercourse, men are constantly engaged in a process of education in the essential nature of natural justice. No man can escape the demands forced upon his conscience regarding the right and wrong of his actions toward others and their corresponding responses toward him. Daily there is pressed upon his mind a consciousness of the existence of a natural law of human behavior which is basically alike wherever men are found.[31] Man, left to himself, can no more escape the necessity of this conclusion than fish can walk upon dry land.

But men are not presently allowed to freely develop their social consciences, according to Spooner, for government intrudes into their private worlds to the extent that individuals have been denied the right to make their own contracts with one another. The power to make our own contracts is a basic right of natural law and is fundamental to the maintenance of a free society. "Natural law recognizes the validity of all contracts which men have a *natural* right to make, and which justice requires to be fulfilled. . . ."[32] It follows from this, of course, that men may enter into a contract of government if they wish, thereby obligating themselves to observe certain duties to their fellowmen prescribed by the law so established. But no contract of government may be deemed legitimate which denies men the full benefit of the natural rights they began with. Such a contract "cannot lawfully authorize government to destroy or take from men their natural rights: for natural rights are inalienable, and can no more be surrendered to government — which is but an association of individuals — than to a single individual." Moreover, the prohibition or qualification of any single right of the individual to freely enter into contracts of his own choosing is tantamount to the virtual denial of all of his natural rights.

Nowhere does Spooner more forcefully express his anarchist sentiments than in his refusal to acknowledge the right of government to legislate for the individual. To begin with, he urged, most men spontaneously develop a knowledge of natural law even before they can talk and hence need no official legal code to restrain them from wrongdoing. Jurists often defend positive law on the grounds that most do not have the ability to recognize right from wrong without the assistance of their governments. But, Spooner argued, "legislation does not even profess to remove the obscurity of natural law," nor does it even make a feeble attempt to do so. The fact is that the primary object of most legislation is not to assist men in discovering the principles of natural justice but to "overturn natural law and substitute for it the arbitrary will of power."[33] And all the while the defenders of positive law are engaged in perpetrating the fraud that no law is possible whatever where the legislature does not make it. Obviously, the purpose of such deception is to "secure to the government the authority of making laws that never ought to be known."

Spooner's *Trial By Jury* (1852) is a valiant attempt to provide those who love liberty with a legal means of saving her from the ravages of that firebreathing monster, government. For all practical purposes, Spooner held, "there can be no legal right to resist the oppression of government unless there be some legal tribunal, other than the government, and wholly independent of, and above, the government, to judge between the government and those who resist its oppressions. . . ."[34] For unless we can find such an independent agency, the will of the government over its citizens is absolute, rendering them nothing more than slaves. The only agency known to Anglo-American law that might serve as an effective arbiter between the government and the people is the jury. To deny an individual the right of being defended by jury when resisting an oppressive decree of government is to deny him all protection against despotism. It is ridiculous to argue here that the oppressed citizen may resort to revolution for redress of his grievances, for revolution has no practical legal utility. As Spooner put it in his own words:

> The right of revolution, which tyrants in mockery accord to mankind, is no legal right under a government; it is only a natural right to overturn a government. The government itself never acknowledges this right. And the right is practically established only when and because the government exists no longer to call it in question. The right, therefore, can be exercised with impunity, only when it is exercised victoriously. All unsuccessful attempts at revolution, however justifiable in themselves, are punished as treason, if the government be permitted to judge of the treason. The government itself never admits the injustice of its laws, as legal defense for those who have attempted a revolution and failed. The right of revolution, therefore, is a right of no practical value, except for those who are stronger than the government. So long, therefore, as the oppressions of the government are kept within such limits as simply not to exasperate against it a power greater than

its own, the right of revolution cannot be appealed to, and is therefore inapplicable
to the case. This affords a wide field for tyranny; and if a jury cannot here intervene, the oppressed are utterly defenseless.[35]

Spooner's unrestrained enthusiasm for the principle of trial by
jury serves to illustrate the libertarian nature of his anarchist sentiments. Unlike the liberal democrat who desires to see the individual
free but who yet possesses no faith that he is capable of living in
freedom, Spooner was prepared here and now to establish direct
democracy upon earth. Under the existing judicial system, he argued,
the jurors who sit in judgment of one of their peers are not permitted
the free exercise of their own sympathies and opinions. Dominating
the court by virtue of his superior training in the law, the typical
judge sits with the arrogance of a Greek god, forcing the jury to
accept his rulings as authoritative and final. But if we would see
justice enthroned amongst us in any realistic sense, such judicial
tyranny cannot be permitted. Reaching back to the foundations
of the Anglo-American legal tradition, Spooner insisted that one of
the outstanding features of the common law was the principle of the
free administration of justice; and this principle "must necessarily
be a part of every system of government which is not designed to be
an engine in the hands of the rich for the oppression of the poor."[36]
In the early years of English history when the modern jury system
was taking form, there was no attempt made by any court to interfere
with the free judgement of the jurors. The members of the jury
determined all questions of law for themselves and were not subjected
to any prompting from sheriffs, bailiffs, or stewards. And not only
were they free of dictation from the court but they actually made
their judgements independent of the laws of the King. Since the
King's laws were not anywhere written, and since the jurors—largely
illiterate—could not have read them had they been written, it is
evident that the government had no say over the decisions rendered
by juries.[37] Had the officers of the courts been empowered to force
the jurors to accept their rulings as authoritative, we would not now
be entitled to refer to the early Anglo-American jury system as the
seedbed of modern liberty, for the illiterate jurors would have perforce
been compelled to submit completely to such domination. Where
government is permitted to dictate the letter of the law to juries,
according to Spooner, "it is no longer a 'trial by the country,' but a
trial by the government; because the jury then try the accused . . . by

the standards dictated to them by government."[38] And even a child can see, Spooner maintained, that the standard of liberty enjoyed by the people will of necessity be the standards permitted by the government and not those liberties which the people feel are their basic rights under nature. How can we realistically speak of freedom where government is allowed to have the last say regarding the limits of what is permitted and what is not? Demonstrating a strong feeling for history as well as a dedication to the basic values of the libertarian concept of freedom, Spooner wrote:

> For more than six hundred years—that is, since Magna Carta, in 1215—there has been no clearer principle of English or American constitutional law, then that, in criminal cases, it is not only the right and duty of juries to judge what are the facts, what is the law, and what was the moral intent of the accused; *but that it is also their right, and their primary and paramount duty, to judge of the justice of the law, and to hold all laws invalid, that are, in their opinion, unjust or oppressive, and all persons guiltless in violating or resisting the execution of, such laws.*
>
> Unless such be the right and duty of jurors, it is plain that, instead of juries being a 'palladium of liberty'—a barrier against the tyranny and oppression of government—they are really mere tools in their hands, for carrying into execution any injustice and oppression it might desire to have executed.[39]

Surely these are the words of one who clearly understood the role of the people in a libertarian society.

Anticipating the argument that the people are not fully competent to serve as judge of what is true law and what is not, Spooner insisted that a jury chosen by lot without regard to the professional background of its individual members is infinitely more capable of seeing justice done than any legal system dominated by professional lawmakers and judges, however learned they might be. "Legislators and judges," Spooner declared, "are necessarily exposed to all the temptation of money, fame, and power, to induce them to disregard justice between parties, and sell the rights and violate the liberties of the people." A freely chosen jury, on the other hand, cannot be accused of this failing, since its members would have nothing to gain from giving false decisions. Selected from among the people, they must return to the people after their service to the law has been completed. Professional judges are subject to no such intimate accounting to society. As for the consistency of juries in arriving at a reasonable and uniform perception of what is naturally just, it is "hardly credible that twelve men, taken at random from the people at large, should unanimously decide a question of natural justice one way, and that twelve other men, selected in the same manner, should unanimously decide the same question the other way, unless they were misled by the justices."

One might argue, of course, that freely selected jurors, lacking formal training in the law, will in many instances be unable to make an intelligent judgement where highly complicated issues of jurisprudence are involved. But Spooner countered, "Legitimate government can be formed only by the voluntary association of all who contribute to its support. As a voluntary association, it can have for its objects only those things in which the members of the association are all agreed."[40] Where parliamentary democrats make their mistake is in their willingness to use the power of government to force unity upon society, even where a vast multitude of the people are unable to understand the social and moral principles involved. But this is tyranny, albeit that the wielders of power have good ends as their motive. Liberty is only possible, Spooner argued, where government confines its administrative function to those things upon which all the people are agreed. Positive law, in other words, must never precede natural law but must in every instance be based upon what the people "can comprehend and see the justice of." This it can only do where jurors are permitted total freedom in exercising their right to judge the law. To be sure, Spooner admitted, there will inevitably be instances in which the written law cannot be reconciled with natural law. Where this occurs, the positive law ought not to be enacted at all, for no degree of legal efficiency can compensate for injustice. Speaking for Americans of all ages who might cherish freedom above any other good, Spooner declaimed that "it is the purpose of our system of government to maintain in force only those principles of justice which the people generally can understand, and in which they are agreed; and not to invest one portion of the people, either minority or majority, with unlimited power over the other."[41] Wherever this principle is not observed, tyranny reigns, whatever the label applied to that form of government might be.

Like all anarchists, Lysander Spooner was basically revolutionary in his political philosophy, although his exhortations to man the barricades bore the "made in America" label. "The right and the physical power of the people to resist injustice," he held, "are really the only securities any people ever can have for their liberties,"[42] for seldom do governments consider anything but their own political interests except when they are compelled to do otherwise by the forcefully expressed discontent of their people. This is not simply because those in places of power are more vicious or unprincipled than other men but because the pressures and temptations of political office are much too powerful for ordinary men to withstand. In Spooner's opinion, the constitution of the United States does not require those who live under it to abjectly submit to the usurpation of power committed by the government or the "lawless violence" of those who hold office. Endowed with the natural right to keep and bear arms, the people may also be credited with the right to use them in the protection of their liberties. "The constitution takes it for granted," Spooner wrote, "that as the people have the right, they will have the sense, to use arms, whenever the necessity of the case justifies it."[43] It makes no sense whatever to argue as some people do, he continued, that the remedy of the people in the face of injustice is to change the nature of the government through discussion and the ballot. In the final analysis, discussion by itself is impotent to deter a despotic government unless it clearly understood that actual resistance is to follow if the people's grievances are not alleviated.[44]

Spooner was impatient with those who cry "treason" upon the assertion that actual resistance to the laws of government are sometimes necessary for the preservation of liberty. Correctly defined, he held, the word treason implies deceitfulness, treachery, and a conscious breach of faith upon the part of the actor involved. When we revolt against government, we break no contract with anyone. A free government by definition is one that is maintained not by force and coercion but by voluntary support freely given. With a clarity of vision that is extremely rare among modern day political scientists, Spooner went right to the heart of the matter when he declared that: "There is no other criterion whatever, by which to determine whether a government is a free one, or not, than the single one of its depending, or not depending, solely on voluntary support."[45] Any government, however inefficient or despotic it might be, is a free government in the eyes of those who voluntarily chose to support it. Conversely, however benevolent or efficient it may be, a government which rules over its subjects without their free consent is a tyranny. It can thus hardly be called treason when unwilling subjects choose to sever their relationship with a government they never bound themselves to serve, as in the case of the rebellious colonists who demanded their freedom from George III.

Taking note of the fact that those who find strength in the cult of the Constitution have given undue emphasis to the principle of majority rule, Spooner denied that there is anything sacred about the opinion of the majority. In the first place, he pointed out, if the opinion of the majority had been given priority in 1776, we would never have obtained independence, for our fathers were much less numerous than the Englishmen from whom they revolted. When there is a principle of justice involved, all talk of either the majority or minority view is absurd. "Men are dunces," he declared, for giving their support to any laws or government other than those they can give their complete support to. And any government that does not have the complete consent of all its citizens can only sustain itself by using force and fraud. It jars the American ear to be told, Spooner insisted, that our government rests upon force like any other. But we have only to consider the Civil War to realize that *"our power is our right."*[46] Oblivious to everything but its own survival, the government of the United States demonstrated that it is not one wit more worthy of the people's confidence than the worst of tyrannies of the past. As he indignantly declared to the President:

> To preserve 'the constitution' . . . could it ever have been necessitated to send into the field millions of ignorant young men, to cut the throats of other young men as ignorant as themselves—few of whom, on either side, had ever read the constitution, or had any real knowledge of its legal meaning; and not one of whom had ever signed it, or promised to support it, or was under the least obligation to support it?
>   The truth was that the government was in peril, *solely because it was not fit to exist.* It, and the state governments—all but parts of one and the same system—were rotten with tyranny and crime. And being bound together by no honest tie, and existing for no honest purpose, destruction was the only honest doom to which any of them were entitled. And if we had spent the same money and blood to destroy them, that we did to preserve them, it would have been ten thousand times more creditable to our intelligence and character as a people.[47]

Like the true anarchist he was, Spooner recognized only one principle as being binding upon himself as an individual and that was the principle of justice. In his view of things, "natural justice either is law, or it is not," and anything that contradicts it or is inconsistent with it cannot be given the color of legality.[48] Where justice is pushed aside so that the interests of the state may advance unhindered, any laws made under this influence are illegal and can make no claim upon the allegiance of the individual. One cannot have it both ways, Spooner argued; if justice has no bearing upon the actions of the state, the authority of law rests on nothing more sub-stantial than the state's power to compel its citizens to submit to its demands—in which case the individual is under no moral obligation to obey it. The only obligation the individual has to an unjust law is "disobedience, resistance, destruction."[49] Lacking justice, law and the state have no more moral authority over our lives than the rude oaths of pirates and brigands. As Spooner pointed out to the Irish people, the propertied classes who dominate the social structure of any given society derive their power from the lands which their descendants originally obtained without any great expenditure of effort or intelligence. Over the years those who possess wealth join the conspiracy of organized government which has as its chief aim the preservation of the property right of the possessing classes. Since such wealth is actually "stolen property" which has been obtained "through centuries of robbery and extortion," the possessing classes are never so secure as they think they are, for injustice breeds social violence. "If those, and the descendants of those, from whom all this wealth has been taken, shall combine to take it from you," Spooner warned the rich, "it will be only an act of just and lawful reprisal and retribution."[50] Speaking with devastating candor, Spooner permitted himself none of the polite generalities by which most men hide their innermost feelings when he wrote:

> All the great governments of the world—those now existing, as well as those that have passed away—have been of this character. They have been mere bands of robbers, who have associated for purposes of plunder, conquest, and the enslavement of their fellow men. And their laws, as they have called them, have been only such agreements as they have found it necessary to enter into, in order to maintain their organizations, and act together in plundering and enslaving others, and in securing to each his agreed share of the spoils.[51]

In short, legislation, reduced to its essential properties, is nothing more than the means by which one set of men subject the rest of their fellowmen into giving up their natural rights to spend the rest of their lives in slavery.

Spooner's dedication to the concept of social revolution puts an entirely new light upon his economic theories, placing him in a different category from the economic individualist who demands personal liberty for conservative purposes. Unlike the economic conservative and the state socialist, who, despite their widely divergent ideologies, both look toward government for the power to implement their social theories, Spooner, like all libertarians, viewed government control and support of the economy as the first step toward despotism. If the American people would protect their natural right to freedom, Spooner argued, they must jealously guard their pocketbooks from the greedy hands of government, for "every man who puts money into the hands of a 'government' (so called), puts into its hands a sword which will be used against himself, to extort more money from him, and also to keep him in subjection to its arbitrary will."[52] If men want real protection and security from each other, they will be well advised to provide it for themselves and not to turn this function over to the state. Unhappily, Spooner noted, taxation had already been made compulsory, enmeshing men in the suffocating webb of government and thereby permitting unscrupulous politicians to argue that the fact that men vote to protect themselves from further taxation is a sign of their consent that they wish to be governed. Nor is this the full extent of the guile and cunning demonstrated by the statists. Aware that most working people have little familiarity with economic theory, Spooner claimed that the ruling classes justify a whole host of abuses of power on the grounds that the maintenance of a monopoly of money by government is essential to the preservation of its value. But this is a specious argument designed to obscure the fact that government monetary policies are intended to enrich one class of people at the expense of another.[53] The erection of a monopoly over the monetary system, Spooner argued, "is equivalent to the establishment of monopolies in all the businesses that are carried on by means of money—to wit, all businesses that are carried on at all in civilized society; and to establish such monopolies as these is equivalent to condemning all persons, except those holding the monopolies, to the condition of tributaries, dependents, servants, paupers, beggars, or slaves."[54] Those who demand proof of the validity of this argument need merely reflect upon the fact that the industrial progress of American industry depends upon a certain degree of poverty among the working classes in Europe and elsewhere and that the specific purpose of much legislation passed by Congress has been to effect this design.[55] Knowing all this, Spooner was not content to cry "the least government the better" but went further, demanding that government ought not to exist at all.

A bachelor and a recluse, Spooner spent long hours reading political philosophy and economy in the Boston Athenaeum. At his death in May of 1887 his tiny room on Myrtle Street was crammed

NOTES

SECTION II - CHAPTER 4

1. *The Deist's Immortality, and an Essay on Man's Account-ability* (Boston, 1834), p. 11.

2. *The Deist's Reply to the Alleged Supernatural Evidences of Christianity* (Boston, 1834), p. 3.

3. John Alexander, "The Ideas of Lysander Spooner," *The New England Quarterly*, XXIII (June, 1950), 201.

4. "Our Nestor Taken From Us," *Liberty*, IV (May, 1887), 4.

5. *Dictionary of American Biography*, XVII, p. 466.

6. *The Unconstitutionality of the Laws of Congress Prohibiting Private Mails.* (New York, 1844), p. 8.

7. *Poverty: Its Illegal Causes and Legal Cure.* (Boston, 1846), p. 14.

8. *The Law of Intellectual Property.* (Boston, 1855), p. 156.

9. *Ibid.*, p. 14.

10. "On Picket Duty," *Liberty*, II (July, 1884), 1.

11. Lewis Perry, "Versions of Anarchism in the Antislavery Movement," *The American Quarterly*, XX (Winter, 1968), 215.

12. *The Unconstitutionality of Slavery* (Boston, 1853), p. 24.

13. *Ibid.*, p. 117.

14. *Ibid.*, p. 56.

15. *Address of the Free Constitutionalists to the People of the United States* (Boston, 1860), pp. 3-4.

16. *No Treason.* VI (Boston, 1870), p. 56.

17. "A Letter to Grover Cleveland," *Liberty*, III (March, 1886), 7.

18. *No Treason*, VI, p. 5.

19. "A Letter to Thomas F. Bayard," *Liberty*, II (May, 1884), 6.

20. "A Second Letter to Thomas F. Bayard," *Liberty*, II (May, 1884), 6.

21. "A Letter to Grover Cleveland," *Liberty*, IV (April, 1886), 3.

22. "Against Woman Suffrage," *Liberty*, I (June, 1882), 4.

23. "A Letter to Grover Cleveland," *Liberty*, III (October, 1885), 2.

24. "A Letter to Grover Cleveland," *Liberty*, IV (May, 1886), 6.

25. "A Letter to Grover Cleveland," *Liberty*, III (September, 1885), 6.

26. *Natural Law; or The Science of Justice* (Boston, 1882), p. 56.

27. "A Letter to Grover Cleveland," *Liberty*, III (October,

1885), 2.

28. *Ibid.*

29. *The Unconstitutionality of Slavery,* p. 10.

30. *Natural Law*, p. 15.

31. *Ibid.*, p. 9.

32. *The Unconstitutionality of Slavery*, p. 7.

33. *Trial by Jury* (Boston, 1852), p. 139.

34. *Ibid.*, p. 16.

35. *Ibid.*, pp. 15-16.

36. *Ibid.*, p. 140.

37. *Ibid.*, p. 83.

38. *Ibid.*, p. 9.

39. *Ibid.*, p. 1.

40. *Ibid.*, p. 130.

41. *Address of the Free Constitutionalists,* p. 28.

42. *A Defense for Fugitive Slaves* (Boston, 1850), p. 30.

43. *Ibid.*, p. 28.

44. *Trial by Jury*, p. 13.

45. *No Treason,* II (Boston, 1867), p. 13.

46. *No Treason,* I (Boston, 1867), p. 5.

47. "A Letter to Grover Cleveland," *Liberty,* III (February, 1886), 6.

48. *The Unconstitutionality of Slavery,* p. 145.

49. *Ibid.*, p. 9.

50. *Revolution: The Only Remedy for the Oppressed Classes of Ireland, England, and Other Parts of the British Empire* (Boston, 1880), p. 7.

51. *Natural Law,* p. 21.

52. *No Treason*, VI, p. 17.

53. "Gold and Silver as Standards of Value: The Flagrant Cheat in Regard to Them," *The Radical Review*, I (February, 1887), 751.

54. "Our Financiers: Their Ignorance, Usurpations, and Frauds," *The Radical Review*, I (May, 1877), 150.

55. "A Letter to Grover Cleveland," *Liberty,* III (December, 1885), 3.

56. Alexander, *op. cit.*, 216.

CHAPTER 5

The Reign of Benjamin R. Tucker, The Terrible

As English utilitarianism had its John Stuart Mill, so American anarchism had its Benjamin Ricketson Tucker (1854-1939). Born of Quaker and old colonial stock, his great-grandfather on his maternal side being a follower of Thomas Paine, Tucker seems to have been destined for a life of nonconformity and dissent from the very start. His father, a whaling outfitter and later a prosperous wholesale and retail grocer, was himself something of a rebel, having been "turned away from the Quaker society for marrying outside the faith,"[1] although only a Jeffersonian democrat in his politics, Tucker's mother was a radical in her own right, not only in her adherence to the extreme Unitarian viewpoint but in her dedication to the tradition of political dissent within which she had been raised. Born at South Dartmouth, Massachusetts, a mecca of nonconformity and religious unorthodoxy, Tucker attended the Friends' Academy at nearby New Bedford where the family moved when he was seven. Reading English fluently at the age of two, he was exceptionally well versed in the Bible by the time he was four and gained early family fame by pointing out to an Episcopalian aunt that there was a discrepancy between the prayer book she had asked him to read to her and the exact text of the Bible.[2] Despite the fact that the religious training to which he was exposed was derived at the hands of the radical W. J. Potter, President of the Free Religious Association, he soon gagged on what loose theology he had been fed and at the age of twelve adamantly refused to swallow another Sunday school lesson, much to the consternation of his mother. Tucker was exceptionally bright in school and his proud parents undoubtedly hoped that he would receive a good higher education so that he might assume the same prominence within enlightened New England society that they enjoyed. But another family crisis occured when he refused at the age of sixteen to enter Harvard University, finally compromising by attending Massachusetts Institute of Technology for several years but without graduating. True to his heritage of nonconformity, he broke away from every aspect of structured education and jealously guarded his independence of mind from all intrusion by adults. Tucker wanted no teachers but insisted upon seeking out knowledge for himself, for he was convinced that only in this way could he retain his integrity. From the age of twelve he vociferously consumed daily all that was worthy of his attention in the *New York Tribune* and was reading the works of Spencer, Darwin, Tyndall, Huxley, Mill, and Buckle by the time he was fourteen, as well as attending lectures by Ralph Waldo Emerson, William Lloyd Garrison, and Wendell Phillips whenever they lectured at the Lyceum at New Bedford.

As radical as he might be in his religion and philosophy, there was nothing in Tucker's appearance to distinguish him from any other well-bred New Englander of good family background. Always neat and fashionably dressed, he was exceptionally handsome as a young man, his swarthy complexion and flashing black eyes set off by his dark hair and neatly trimmed mustache. Later in life he was to gain distinction by adding a neatly trimmed beard, perhaps as compensation for his rather light body build and the nervous laugh which characterized his appearance as a youth. Completely absorbed in the development of his intellect, Tucker expended an enormous flow of his youthful energy in reading, almost to the exclusion of any other diversion. Speaking of his youth, Tucker wrote of himself:

> Athletic sports did not attract me. Marbles during my early 'teens, billiards (occasionally bowling) during the latter, and now and then a game of cards—these were my only amusements. Luckily I had an iron constitution and perfect digestion, and these preserved my health. But my manner was rather that of a weakling. I was bashful, shy, timid, ill at ease, in a degree exceptional. I had to be driven to dances, parties, and every sort of social diversion. Anything that excercised my mind attracted me; almost any other form of exercise I found repellent. Toward girls I felt a special indifference. I would walk around the block to avoid meeting one. And, so far as I know, no girl had the slightest use for me. I had read much on sexual problems and sexual physiology. On these subjects I was more than usually well-informed. But my sexual instincts had not been awakened. And so it was that at the age of nineteen I was still virgin.[3]

Tucker's life reads like something from Greek mythology from this point on, for it was that goddess of love, Victoria Woodhull, who introduced him to the mysteries of sex. Tucker's first glimpse of the beautiful Mrs. Woodhull took place in 1872 when he was in his second year of M.I.T. Attending her lecture on "The Principles of

Social Freedom" delivered in the Old Boston Music Hall, Tucker enthusiastically joined the claque which sought to drown out the boos and hisses that burst forth when she declared her right to change lovers every day if she wanted to, and he became convinced then and there by her determination and courage that she was destined to play a leading role in the war to attain social freedom then being fought. Little did he know at the time that in the next year he was to have the honor of being seduced by that lovely and sexually aggressive lady. Laying aside the ways of his boyhood, he was never again quite the same after tasting the sweetness of Victoria's largess. Challenged by the harassment and the obstructionism that Mrs. Woodhull experienced in attempting to place her views before the public, Tucker, in defense of free speech, served as her tour manager for a time and later joined the melange of lovers and social reformers who hung out at the Woodhull establishment in New York, accompanying that colorful troop to Europe in the summer of 1874, paying for his own passage from funds given him by his parents for the furtherance of his education. Fending off the advances of Victoria's sister, Tennie Claflin, his education was advanced more than his parents dared suspect. Yet intellect always played a greater part in his life than emotion and Tucker never really stood in danger of being corrupted by his seducers.

Tucker's fertile mind, never able to compromise truth, gradually came to the conclusion that Victoria Woodhull was a fraud. Undoubtedly she was sincere enough when it come to her espousal of the doctrine of free love, for she never demanded anything from her many lovers other than the right to please them. But Victoria, despite her eloquence and charm on the lecture platform, could barely manage to write more than her own name, according to Tucker, and had little grasp of the essential nature of the many social theories expressed in *Woodhull and Claflin's Weekly*, which was edited by her second husband, Colonel Blood, as well as Stephen Pearl Andrews and others. Here as in the brokerage firm they maintained in New York with the backing of Commodore Vanderbilt, the notorious Claflin sisters, according to some of their detractors, were mouthing the social sentiments of the many males who flocked about them and were incapable of adhering to any developed principles of their own. Even before Victoria married into English polite society, having divorced Colonel Blood and renounced her free love activities, Tucker came to scorn her as an unprincipled woman, a disgrace to the sex she so flamboyantly championed. And when Tucker cooled toward someone, he became as forbidding as the New England winter. Parting from the sisters in Europe, he was embarrassed that he had been deceived into once aiding and abetting their propaganda, especially after *Woodhull and Claflin's Weekly* began to print Biblical aphorisms "as nauseating as they were silly. . . ." But chivalrous to the end, he expressed no regrets for the warmth and tenderness he found while clasped in Victoria's embrace, however much he might repudiate her intellectual position.

Benjamin Tucker's addiction to the idea of anarchism dates from the year 1872 when he attended a convention of the New England Labor Reform League and was introduced to those brilliant stars of native American anarchism, Josiah Warren, Colonel William B. Greene, Ezra Heywood, and Lysander Spooner. Reading Warren's *True Civilization*, he experienced a revelation and quickly came to understand that the social system of force and compulsion which he had previously accepted was an impossibility. From henceforth the guiding stars in Tucker's firmament were to be these fathers of individualist anarchism. To Ezra Heywood he not only owed his first formal introduction to Victoria Woodhull but also his association with the New England Free Love League and the American Woman's Emancipation Society. Becoming associate editor of Heywood's *Word* in April 1875, his growing anarchist sympathies caused him to refuse to pay Massachusetts' poll tax, just as Thoreau had done before him. But in December of the next year, Tucker, dissatisfied with Heywood's preoccupation with the free love issue, decided to resign, stating in a final editorial that his course of action was not based upon any diminuation of his regard for the doctrine of sexual freedom but his desire to pay increased attention to the more important question of labor reform.[4] When in 1877 Heywood was imprisoned in Dedham jail for printing *Cupid's Yoke*, however, Tucker came to his rescue by filling in as editor of *The Word* in his absence. Differ as they might about the relative importance of free love versus free labor, they both emphatically agreed that all laws against obscene literature ought to be repealed in the name of freedom.

It was William B. Greene who first advised Tucker to take up and read the writings of Pierre-Joseph Proudhon, which quickly became an influential current in his social thought. Fascinated by the French language and culture, Tucker, upon establishing *The Radical Review* in 1877 on the strength of a small bequest he had received upon coming of age, began the translation and publication of Proudhon's entire literary production, serializing the first volume of the *System of Eonomical Contradictions* in his new journal; the entire repertoire of Proudhon's social and political writings was to be made available to the public in this way for less than five dollars. This caused Tucker to write some years later, "Can the people of America—the country in which Proudhon is said to have expected his ideas to be first realized—afford to remain in ignorance of them?"[5] Unfortunately, the bequest gave out at the end of one year and *The Radical Review* came to an abrupt end with the publication of its fourth quarterly issue. Finding full-time employment with the *Boston Globe,* where he remained for the next eleven years in a variety of jobs from printer to copy reader, Tucker founded his famous *Liberty* in 1881, publishing it at first on the side. Although he was to serve on the editorial staff of the *Engineering Magazine* in 1892 and the *Home Journal* in 1894, both of which were published in New York, he continued to publish *Liberty* almost continuously for the next twenty-seven years, later supporting the venture from the sizable inheritance he received upon the final settlement of his family's estate.

It is impossible to overemphasize the influence *Liberty* had over the development of libertarian thought in America. ". . . kind, gentle, and always smiling," Tucker was an affable soul, never known to speak a harsh word to anyone's face, according to his friend, the poet, J. William Lloyd.[6] But in the role of *Liberty's* editor, this lamb, ordinarily so considerate of everyone's feelings, became a veritable lion, roaring out at anyone he thought to be in error. As Lloyd said, Tucker, "was dogmatic to the extreme, arrogantly positive, browbeating and dominating, true to his 'plumbline' no matter who was slain, and brooked no difference, contradiction, or denial." And yet there was no more devoted literary audience in the America of his day than the anarchists and fellow travelers who subscribed to *Liberty.* Although Tucker was the master of a trenchant prose style, it was not his literary ability alone that endeared him to his followers but his phenomenal philosophical breadth, his piercing logic and criticism, and above all his contagious enthusiasm for the anarchist idea. As Emile Armand put it from France, "to establish contact with Tucker meant inquiring into everything which his predecessors, or those to whom he alluded, had written. . . ."[7] And thus it was that the pages of *Liberty* carried translations and articles from many of the most seminal thinkers of both Europe and America. It was Tucker who introduced Americans to the writings of Josiah Warren, Michael Bakunin, Max Stirner, Stephen Pearl Andrews, Edward Carpenter, John Henry Mackay, and a score of other hitherto unknown writers. Much of his fame outside the anarchist circle was derived from his translation of Tolstoy's *Kreutzer Sonata,* one of the many reprints issued by the Tucker Publishing Company. At a time when most Americans were incapable of thinking of sex and marriage in anything other than the vapid sentimental terms of Victorian morality, Tucker dared to place Tolstoy's frank and open discussion of conventional marital relations squarely at everyone's eye level without adorning the naked truth with fig leaves or other camouflage. Utterly devoted to the libertarian idea, and convinced without a doubt that truth will win out above error where free thought is maintained, Tucker was relentless in his pursuit of intellectural honesty. Disturbed by a book by the German writer, Max Nordeau, in which the thesis was advanced that all art is pathological, he contacted George Bernard Shaw, offering him a generous sum for an article that would challenge the anti-libertarian viewpoint expressed in *Entartung.* When Shaw compiled, Tucker absorbed the tremendous expense of distributing a reprint of the article to every editor in America and as many as he could reach in Europe, much to Shaw's eternal gratitude. When it came to the truth, Tucker was indefatigable. For again like John Stuart Mill, he was convinced that falsehood could not exist in the bright light of public examination—a proposition to which he, like his English counterpart, devoted his life.

One of the most persistent myths about Tucker is the assertion that he was a "philosophical anarchist," as opposed to the communist-anarchist, and that he earned this title because he was primarily an intellectural who chose to employ only argument and discussion to bring about the anarchist society he proposed.[8] It is true, of course, that Tucker was very much an intellectual and that he shared the same optimism concerning human rationality that Mill did. It is also true that Tucker was an extremely sensitive individual for whom violence was ordinarily an unthinkable means. But as Tucker himself pointed out, the adjective "philosophic" originally was pinned on the American anarchists not by themselves but by outsiders who did not accept their teachings. As for himself, Tucker wrote: "I have never accepted it, and rarely, if ever, have I used it. Every fool thinks himself a philosopher."[9] Nor did Tucker think of himself as the originator of a unique social philosophy which had been created by "immaculate cognition" after the fashion of Thomas Hobbes. The roots of the anarchist idea were planted thousands of years ago, he wrote, "when the first glimmer of the idea of liberty dawned upon the human mind, and has been advancing ever since,—not steadily advancing, to be sure, but fitfully, with an occasional reversal of the current."[10]

In the very first issue of *Liberty*, Tucker locked arms with anarchists everywhere when he declared that the chief foe of libertarianism is authority, whatever shape or form it might take. Among the major forces of authoritarianism, according to Tucker, are the Roman Catholic establishment, manchester individualism, and the socialism of Karl Marx. In this, his thinking was in essential harmony with most anarchists. It soon becomes evident, however, that the evolutionary theories of Darwin and Spencer, so enthusiastically championed in the United States, exerted considerable influence over Tucker's social thought. "The law of liberty," he proclaimed, "is spontaneous association by natural selection."[11] In order for a free society to develop, the individual, who is "the basic factor of social existence," must be allowed complete freedom in determining his own course of action in regard to the feelings and interests of the other equally free individuals with whom he coexists. Undoubtedly, Tucker admitted, the self-restraint exercised by such individuals constitutes a form of social regulation. "But regulation, under the law of liberty, comes of selection and voluntary assent" and must not contain an element of external coercion. Although Herbert Spencer's influence is undeniably present in Tucker's social philosophy, especially in his early years, it is not true that his viewpoint was exclusively, or even predominantly, Spencerian. "Anarchists recognize in Herbert Spencer a kindred spirit, and offer to his memory their tribute of admiration and gratitude," Tucker wrote some years later, "but they cannot accept him as a trustworthy exponent of their political philosophy."[12] For although Spencer recognized the individual's right to free decision in economic matters, he wound up justifying the interference of the state in the area of national defense and the maintenance of social order. And this, Tucker perceptively noted, destroyed any claim Herbert Spencer might otherwise have made to being a libertarian.

Philosophically, Benjamin Tucker owed a great deal to those outspoken iconoclasts, Pierre-Joseph Proudhon and Michael Bakunin. Although he needed no help in finding his way to atheism, Tucker was greatly comforted by their writings about God and the state and made it his business to direct as many customers as he could to their stalls in the marketplace of ideas. Like Proudhon, Tucker was convinced that "humanitarian atheism" is an advanced phase of scientific development and is an attitude of mind essential to the reconstruction of philosophy. Where many people interpreted Proudhon's argument against the existence of God as an irreverent stupidity, Tucker interpreted it as the sincere conviction of a thoroughly honest man who would search for truth above every other human consideration.

The first step in the reconstruction of a scientific social philosophy, Tucker held, following Proudhon, is to free ourselves of the notion of an all-powerful, unapproachable deity, whether it be in the area of religion or of government. "Liberty denies the authority of anybody's god to bind those who do not accept it through persuasion and natural selection," Tucker wrote. "Liberty denies the authority of anybody's state to bind those who do not lend voluntary allegiance to it."[13] The inherent difficulty with all systems of organized religion, Tucker argued, is that they utilize the very same degenerate social machinery that the state employs to carry out its designs. Playing upon the susceptibility and superstition of the people, organized religions sustain themselves through a process of calculated indoctrination whereby the individual is taught to accept all manner of belief on nothing more substantial than authority. The Christian, for example, is commanded to love his neighbor as he loves himself. Aside from the authoritarian nature of such an injunction, Tucker asserted, the very attempt to order an individual to love his neighbor is a gross perversion of the human phenomenon of love. To demand love indiscriminately from all men, he wrote, "is a stifling of all natural attraction to that which is lovable and of all natural repugnance to that which is hateful—a rigid, formal, heartless, soulless, and sort of unconsciously hypocritical joining of hand."[14] At basis the Christian's slavish obedience to the authority of Christ is little different than the blind obedience of a Roman legioneer to his commander.

Although the ideals of Christianity are clearly of a higher character than those of Caesar, the adoption of wrong means negates the distinction, reducing the Christian soldier to the same level as his secular counterpart. Anarchists would do well to read Bakunin's *God and the State*, Tucker asserted, for Bakunin clearly understands that at the root of all the human misery and evil which is committed under the name of authority is that "illusion called God."[15] Until man frees his mind of the notion of a supreme being, social morality can never rise above the level of mere cant and hypocrisy. For church and state are inseparable from one another and together form the matrix from which all subsequent social evil stems. From the very beginning of organized society, Tucker insisted, church and state, presumptuously claiming the blessings of God, have "had all the money, all the land, all the saints, all the bayonets, and all the fools (whose name is legion) to work with. . . ."[16] Surely goodness and mercy shall evade us all the days of our lives so long as we set upon our quest for social justice in such a ridiculous fashion.

     No anarchist worthy of the name, Tucker asserted, can attempt to live his life through an appeal to authority, and hence the Christian is perforce excluded from the anarchist fold. "A society negating all authority," he wrote, "would differ from a society affirming the authority of Christ very much as white differs from black."[17] In order to call a libertarian society into existence, individual men and women must learn to be autonomous social agents, capable of determining their own moral conduct. What the Christian fails to see, Tucker opined, is that "God to be God must be a governing power." But as soon as the individual relies upon external authority for his social choices, his primary powers of moral judgment begin to atrophy and soon become utterly useless. Anarchism correctly defined, therefore, is a genuine love of justice, demonstrated by the ability of the individual to remain true to his natural inclinations, whatever the pains and penalties that might be inflicted upon him.

     Taking the famous quotation from Proudhon—"Liberty, not the daughter, but the mother of order"—for the motto of his journal, Tucker sought to light the way to the kind of society envisioned by his French predecessor. When Proudhon made reference to social order, Tucker pointed out, he did not mean merely the condition which exists when violence is absent but a highly advanced form of society in terms of its organization and development.[18] The princes and statesmen of the existing social world think of order as the product of force and coercion, deluding themselves into believing that the only kind of science they need know is, as Machiavelli counselled, the science of war. But Tucker would not accept the argument that political science is coeval with the science of political force. We anarchists believe in force, he declared, for nature itself consists of a complex of various kinds of force. "But we want native, healthy, spontaneous forces in social life," he continued, and "not arbitrary, extraneous, usurping forces."[19] The anarchist is willing to go further, in fact, admitting that he also believes in authority. But the kind of authority anarchism subscribes to is not the moral slavery of the orthodox religionists but the authority of rationally derived ideas and feelings, each individual man being his own judge of truth and falsehood. Christian moralists attempt to determine the principles of right and wrong upon the revealed truths of Christian culture. Sincere as they may be in their beliefs, Tucker urged, they overlook the fact that truth, as Proudhon pointed out, can never be absolute. Truth differs from individual to individual and only freedom can bring order out of the heterogeneity that forms the basis of every social group. "Right and wrong are principles that must ever be defined, qualified, and circumscribed by the individual in his associative capacity," Tucker asserted, subject only to the further qualification "that all action, individual and associative, shall be at the sole cost of the party or parties" involved.[20] According to this law, every individual is entitled to complete freedom in all his actions, subject only to the condition that he accept full responsibility for their consequences.

Tucker's insatiable thirst for individual freedom led him into one of the many inbroglios which shook the ranks of individualist anarchism during his lifetime. In support of the principle of individual autonomy, Tucker argued that "the mother who uses force upon her child invades nobody."[21] Apparently Tucker's approval of force and authority in this instance wounded the sensibilities of other anarchists, for his statement gave rise to a howl of criticism from his readers. In denying the possibility of invading the rights of the undeveloped child, Tucker did not mean to imply that children are not entitled to freedom. But he saw, as John Stuart Mill did, that liberty can only be secure if the individual is guaranteed full control over his own affairs. If a mother is to be free to conduct her life according to reason, Tucker insisted, she must be allowed full responsibility over her children until they reach maturity and are capable of determining their own actions. Undeniably, Tucker had been forced to compromise here when he sacrificed the child's welfare to that of the mother. But in the end he was true to his libertarian convictions. For as contemporary anarchists have concluded, where responsibility for the child's development is relinquished by the parents, the state will force itself into the vacuum thus created, with even more dire consequences for the condition of human freedom.

In basic disagreement with Locke, and other exponents of the social contract theory, Tucker maintained that the idea of natural right as an inalienable and prior fact of nature is sheer nonsense. Rights do not descend upon man in the pre-social state but are the result of well-defined conventions which develop within the context of society. "They are not the liberties that exist through natural power, but the liberties that are created by mutual guarantee."[22] Anticipating many of the arguments that Kropotkin was later to make in his *Ethics,* Tucker asserted that the whole concept of morality as a system of well-defined rights and duties inherent in nature must be totally discarded. Instead, the anarchist conceives of rights and duties as the product of social intercourse. Unknown in nature itself, although they are undeniably based upon the human characteristic of social solidarity, social obligations arise from contracts freely entered into by unrestrained social man. There is no room for the state, with its instruments of force and compulsion, within the scope of anarchist ethics. Anarchist morality is essentially voluntaristic and does not permit either church or state to intervene into the affairs of men. Completely free to determine his own actions, the individual must thus necessarily develop a social consciousness of his own or risk total failure as a social creature. In every instance, he is his own court of social judgment. "Instead of making oath to God and his prince," Tucker wrote, "the citizen swears upon his conscience, before his brothers, and before humanity. Between these two oaths there is the same difference as between slavery and liberty, faith and science, courts and justice, usury and labor, government and economy, non-existence and being, God and man."[23] In short, Tucker argued, "scientific politics" completely rejects the rule that the individual citizen is in any way bound by moral obligations to the state. At the foundation of Tucker's political philosophy was Josiah Warren's teaching that it is the individual alone who is the final sovereign force in society. Anarchism, as Tucker conceived it, arose out of the contradiction that exists between the sovereign individual and the sovereign state. One or the other must emerge supreme, and in Tucker's opinion, this must be the individual.[24]

The notion that "philosophical anarchists" completely eschew violence, whereas the "revolutionary" wing of anarchist thought permits violent means, is predicated upon the popular myth that Tucker was an absolute pacifist and an unyielding foe of all compulsion and force. While it is true that Tucker, like most anarchists, was personally and philosophically repelled by the idea of violence and compulsion, it is not in fact true that he was doctrinaire in his rejection of it. Toward the end of his life Tucker wrote that it was emphatically *"not true* that I was a pacifist and advocated an absence of all compulsion," nor was it true that "I held all coercion immoral."[25] The essential key to his attitude toward violence and compulsion is contained in his assertion that anarchism is most precisely defined as "the belief in the greatest amount of liberty compatible with equality of liberty; or, in other words, the belief in every liberty except the liberty to invade."[26] The only freedom Tucker would deny the individual was the freedom to trespass upon the liberty or interests of another human being. Obviously this would preclude the use of force or violence against the person of another under ordinary circumstances. The one exception to the rule was in the case of genuine instances of self-defense when no other means would assure self-survival short of physical force. "I insist that there is nothing sacred in the life of an invader," Tucker wrote.[27] When attacked, one has a perfect right to defend himself by any means adequate to the situation. "I am no Christian, no non-resistant," he proclaimed, for "I believe in combatting evil; I never turn the other cheek, but often repay my adversaries in kind and with interest. . . ."[28]

Yet for all his disclaimer of pacifism and non-resistance, Benjamin Tucker had much in common with the Tolstoyan point of view. As his one-time disciple, Victor S. Yarrow, pointed out, the Quaker influence in Tucker's background again and again asserted itself. An athiest according to his own confession, Tucker nevertheless embossed a high moral tone on all he wrote. "He spoke earnestly of right and wrong. Human rights, he declared, were 'an august thing.' It was a sin to support government. It was the duty of the right-thinking person to work for the gradual overthrow of the state."[29] The tendency to disown religious influences that was so pronounced in Tucker's utterances was due not to indecision but to his prior commitment to liberty and justice as the first and foremost principles of social order. "Anarchism favors peace," he professed, "but knows no peace without liberty."[30] The technique of nonviolence is not a sacred thing to be preserved by and for itself but a mere means to an end. "It is because peaceful agitation and passive resistance are, in *Liberty's* hands, weapons more deadly to tyranny than any others that I uphold them," Tucker professed, "and it is because brute force strengthens tyranny that I condemn it."[31] Consistent within his own apparent inconsistency, Tucker opposed war not for moral reasons but because it destroys liberty. Consequently, he could not even condone wars that might be fought in the name of liberty, for wars always "breed the spirit of authority, with aftereffects unforeseen and incalculable." For the same reason, he was opposed to the employment of force and compulsion in domestic relations. Just as "the surest way to make a man a desperate criminal is to treat him as an outlaw," so, Tucker held, the most certain road to social amelioration is to accord all potential offenders of the social order complete freedom to regulate their own conduct. Although there will be exceptions to this rule, we must nevertheless hold true to it. For, as he wisely concluded, "it is the rule, and not the exceptions, that must govern our course,"[32] if we are to develop a true science of freedom.

And yet Benjamin Tucker, for all the peaceful sentiments that found shelter in his thoughts, stood back to back with anarchists everywhere in defense of the view that the state is a thoroughly corrupting influence within society which must be plucked out root and branch if men are ever to develop a higher form of civilization. The chief indictment against the state is that it is the primary source of human brutality and bloodshed. "Just as truly as Liberty is the mother of order," Tucker wrote, so "is the State the mother of violence."[33] Tucker did not hold to the oversimplified premise that the evil states perpetrate is done consciously and willfully, for he recognized full well that the state has an inertia of its own which is to a great degree independent of the wills of its citizens. And yet, he argued, it is not incorrect to view "government as a machine invented by a few designing schemers to excite discord and war, and profit by the spoils."[34] The state, according to Tucker is essentially a "mammoth organization, held together by usurpation and force."[35] Compelling the individual citizen to bow to its will rather than allowing him to follow his own internal mechanisms of control, the state forces all minor forms of organization within a society to become fashioned after its image. When the state takes life on gallows or battlefield, it gives sanction to private persons to follow its lead in other situations. How can one maintain that it is the individual who commits violence when all he knows and is permitted to think is hammered into him by the iron hand of the state? The institution of government, moreover, despite its own inability to make any intelligent moral choices when it formulates social policy, rides like a jaugernaught over the feelings and interest of individuals. As a case in point, Tucker cited the imprisonment of Oscar Wilde as an outrageous example of the state's violation of the doctrine of individual freedom. "A man who has done nothing in the least degree invasive of any one; a man whose entire life, so far as known or charged, has been one of strict conformity with the idea of equal liberty; a man whose sole offence is that he has done something which most of the rest of us (at least such is the presumption) prefer not to do—is condemned to spend two years in cruel imprisonment at hard labor."[36] By what authority, other than his own filthy mind, does the presiding judge condemn this as the "most heinous crime" ever to be heard in his court room? Is it not fair to conclude that those who dare punish other men who have injured no one are themselves criminals, Tucker demanded? How can we respect a government which is itself the most monstrous antisocial force known to man? Tucker, it would seem, wrote the scenario for the Watergate Affair 75 years before it took place.

Anarchist that he was, Benjamin Tucker, like Thoreau, Garrison, and John Brown, was convinced that the government of the United States is as much a lawless despotism as any other despotism in the world. "The rag upon which is emblazoned the stars and stripes," this disillusioned yankee wrote, "is a painted fraud. The robber bird is alone truthful among our national symbols."[37] It did not change matters to argue that since American democracy determines its policies on the basis of popular will, democratic government possess virtues that other forms of government lack. As Proudhon maintained, the liberal principle of majority rule is basically a reactionary instrument by which justice and freedom are denied existence. It is true, of course, that the American people are allowed to elect their own representatives and that their rulers are consequently subject to some popular direction and control. But it is equally true, according to Tucker, that the politicians and so-called statesmen of the world know full well in this day of mass culture how to appeal to superstition and authority for the purposes of controlling the people. Unfortunately, Tucker held, where despotism takes the form of mass rule as it does in this country, it is impossible to strike down tyranny by assassinating the ruling monarch. And consequently, he wrote, it is extremely difficult to devise an effective means of rooting out the species of despotism we suffer from in America.

> If it were a single head, it could not stay on long. If it were any moderate number of heads upon which the whole responsibility could be distinctly fixed, those heads would probably be taken off. The fact is that the root of majority despotism in this country is a superstition found in almost everybody's head, and which could not be exterminated even if millions of heads were taken off. On grounds of utility as well as humanity, then, the American anarchist must trouble no man's head any further than to get the superstition out and to get something better in.[38]

And yet, Tucker confessed, were it not for the futility of using violence to overturn the demonic state, violence would be an altogether legitimate means. ". . . I would use dynamite if I thought that thereby I could best help the cause of freedom," he proclaimed, and would justify the action "squarely on the excellent doctrine that the end justifies the means."[39] For as he argued with his friend and compatriot, John Beverley Robinson, "violence, like every other policy, is advisable when it will accomplish the desired end and inadvisable when it will not."[40] Anarchism does not reject the use of force and violence so much, then, because these means are bad in themselves as it does because these means are inefficacious in achieving the goals anarchists desire to accomplish.[41]

In view of these words, it is incorrect to place Tucker in complete opposition to the anarchist-communists on the grounds that he rejected violence as a strategy, whereas they did not. In fact, as we shall see later, Tucker's attitude toward violence is hardly distinguishable from the view held by most anarchist-communists. We anarchists, he maintained, prefer the methods of peace and we refuse to engage ourselves in any organized conspiracy to overthrow the state by assassination and revolution. And yet, he continued, we find "words of approval for the Hartmans and tyrant-slayers who in secrecy plot the revenges of fate."[42] By what twist of logic do we justify this apparent contradiction, Tucker sternly asked?; on no other grounds than that we are forced to choose between the working classes who are oppressed and the owning classes who do the oppressing. Those who employ violence to strike off the chains of their masters are justified in doing so, whereas those who employ violence to keep others in slavery are hardly to be forgiven for their actions. Is there a real distinction to be drawn between these two categories of force, Tucker questioned? "You know there is, you editors who mouth about assassination," Tucker charged, "and if you say there isn't, we take the liberty to say that the truth is not in you." In Tucker's eyes, since freedom is the sum and substance of life, nothing must be allowed to stand in the way of its implementation. If this necessitates violence, then violence there must be, however much we regret to see it employed by man against man.

It is to be noted, however, that Tucker's revolutionary ardor was of the same kind as that displayed by William Godwin, Pierre-Joseph Proudhon and the liberal, John Stuart Mill. Convinced that social change can come about only to the degree that men voluntarily change their basic attitudes through social and political education, this triumvirate of liberty maintained that every man must make himself a revolutionary of ideas. The only possible justification for violence, therefore, is to break down the barriers that tyrants erect in order to keep men from the truth. When all avenues to education and discussion within society have been deliberately blocked by despots who desire to keep the people in subjection, the sons of liberty will be in the right when they employ force to strike down these barriers. But short of this condition, violence is always to be abjured. Tucker seems to have had exactly this principle in mind when he wrote:

> Bloodshed in itself is pure loss. When we must have freedom of affiliation, and when nothing but bloodshed will secure it, then bloodshed is wise. But it must be remembered that it can never accomplish the Social Revolution proper; that that can never be accomplished except by means of agitation, investigation, experiment, and passive resistance; and that after all the bloodshed, we shall be exactly where we were before, except in our possession of the power to use these means.[43]

One of the most misunderstood aspects of Tucker's social philosophy has to do with the distinction he drew between anarchism and socialism.[44] Although he definitely thought of himself as a socialist, he often spoke of socialism and anarchism as being in basic opposition. The explanation for this apparent confusion lies in Tucker's deep-seated enmity to Marxian social theory which he for the most part derived secondhand from his reading of the works of Proudhon and Bakunin. Like Proudhon, Tucker was an "un-marxian socialist" who saw in marxism the frightful spector of totalitarianism.[45] In his opinion, economic communism inevitably leads to an increase of social regimentation and coercion. He could not, therefore, ally himself with the socialist camp without establishing the precise points at which he was in disagreement with other socialists.

Rather than being generally opposed to socialism, Tucker was actually opposed only to what he and other anarchists termed "state socialism." As he put it: "It is compulsory communism of the Bismarckian stamp that we combat. It is the needle-gun socialism of Ferdinand Lasalle that we oppose. Statecraft is our enemy."[46] And Marx, in Tucker's opinion, was the high priest of state socialism. Revealing his own fundamental dedication to the position staked out by Proudhon, Tucker maintained that there is a basic choice every man must make when contemplating a commitment to the values of socialism and this has to do with the matter of liberty versus authority. Where communism and state socialism "propose to set up by force a rival and antagonistic machine" in opposition to the existing political structure, anarchism places itself in complete opposition to all political systems. Placing Josiah Warren and Pierre-Joseph Proudhon in fundamental opposition to Marx, Tucker insisted that the split between anarchism and socialism occurs at the point at which any particular social reformer chooses to follow either the path of authority or the path of liberty. It is impossible to escape this choice. And here we must note that the crucial difference between the anarchist and state socialist is that anarchism completely eschews the idea that social reform can be achieved by employing the power of the state as a vehicle for establishing Utopia, Tucker maintained.

As Tucker defined it, state socialism is *"the doctrine that all the affairs of men should be managed by the government, regardless of individual choice."*[47] That Marx was responsible for the formulation of this viewpoint, according to Tucker, is seen in the Marxian precept that the social revolution can never be accomplished except where social reformers acquire political power and use it for the purpose of expropriating capital and administering the economic system thus acquired for the general welfare. Such a use of power, he charged, is no less authoritarian because democratic instead of patriarchal."[48] Socialists everywhere, Tucker proclaimed, owe a tremendous debt to Karl Marx, and thus *Liberty* mourned his death in 1883, since he was "one of the most faithful friends labor ever had." But we must nevertheless understand, Tucker continued, that the differences in the social viewpoints of Marx and Proudhon are of tremendous importance to those who cherish the idea of a libertarian society. Focusing upon the respective social remedies proposed by Marx and Proudhon, Tucker pointed out that:

> Marx would nationalize the productive and distributive forces; Proudhon would individualize and associate them. Marx would make the laborers political master; Proudhon would abolish political mastership entirely. Marx would abolish usury by having the State lay violent hands on all industry and business and conduct it on the cost principle; Proudhon would abolish usury by disconnecting the State entirely from industry and business and forming a system of free banks which would furnish credit at cost to every industrious and deserving person and thus place the means of production within the reach of all; Proudhon believed in the voluntary principle; Marx believed in compulsory majority rule. In short, Marx was an *authoritaire,* Proudhon was a champion of liberty.[49]

We make a tremendous mistake, Tucker argued, when we accept the viewpoint that the only way the monopoly of economic power now enjoyed by capital can be broken is to transfer that monopoly to the state. Rather than place their trust in the state, socialists should turn instead to the natural forces found in nature for an intelligent outline of the principles of a libertarian society. Among the most misunderstood forces of nature, according to Tucker, is the phenomenon of human competition. "The contention of Individualist Socialism," according to Tucker, "is that competition, when left free, is possible throughout nearly the whole of industry and commerce, and that, whenever thus possible, it abolishes usury and secures labor in the ownership of its entire product."[50] Rather than work for the further centralization of economic and political power in an effort to beat capital at its own game, therefore, socialists ought to pay heed to the anarchist contention that social reform can never be brought about by the centralization of economic power in the hands of the state.

Contrary to what is generally believed, Tucker argued, individualism and socialism are not antithetical terms but are basically compatible with one another. In fact, he maintained, "the most perfect socialism is possible only on condition of the most individualism" and we must consequently rid our minds of the myth that individualism is fundamentally a conservative doctrine. We individualist-socialists fully recognize the antisocial attributes of unrestrained capital, Tucker asserted, for we are aware of the callous disregard for human life manifested by the captains of industry where their profits are apt to be diminished by the introduction of safety measures. We individualist-socialists also believe in human solidarity and call upon the working people of the world to unite in the overthrow of the existing capitalist system. But we must nevertheless remain clear on the fact that social cooperation is not fundamentally anti-individualistic; that to the contrary, "voluntary co-operation is clearly individualistic."[51]

The degree to which Tucker veered away from the centralization of economic power is revealed in a comparison of his views with those of Henry George. Where George would retain the super-landlord invested with the power to collect rents from individuals who occupy lands, Tucker would abolish the state along with the present system of taxation and economic regulation. In Book III of *Progresss and Poverty*, Tucker complained, Henry George "entered upon a defense of usury more damaging in its influence than the studied reasoning of Bastiat and the other political economists."[52] George cries out loud enough against usury when it is committed by private individuals, Tucker urged, but he finds nothing to condemn when usury is committed by the state. But wrong is wrong whoever commits it, and the superior strength of the state does not modify the nature of its actions in the least. To a very great degree, George's "regime of universal rent spoilation" is a step toward the state socialism advocated by Marx. For once the state has been invested with the power to collect rents, by what twist of logic can George deny it the power to regulate profits, wages, or any other aspect of the economy it feels is within the national interest?

Calling for the freeing of all lands not occupied and employed by the owner for his own support, Tucker would deny a legal right to anyone to obtain income from land he did not actually reside upon, thereby destroying the possibility of large scale speculative and monopolistic rent, although he was forced to admit that economic rent—income derived from renting part of the land one lives upon—would still be possible.[53] In Tucker's opinion, economic rent "is one of nature's inequalities" that man must tolerate, just as he must live with the fact that some individuals are born beautiful and some are not. Aside from this one small breech of equality, an economic order regulated by the forces of nature rather than the power of the state would soon lead men to the realization of the libertarian idea, for where men are left completely free to regulate their own affairs, inequality and injustice can no longer flourish but must wither as does the vine that is cut off from its roots in the soil. According to Tucker, "monopoly is impossible in nature and under liberty."[54] Where men are left to regulate themselves according to their own individual self-interests and their "native sense of equity," social order inevitably asserts itself without any artificial assistance. With impeccable logic, Tucker argued that monopoly is never present in nature but only in organized society in which power has been concentrated in the hands of government. "The root and great feeder of monopoly is the State, and all monopolies are simply appendages of it." Consequently, radical reformers who would destroy inequality must first slay its parent, authority.

In final analysis, then, Tucker argued, there are only two ways open to us when it comes to the distribution of wealth. We may, on the one hand, choose to allow it to freely distribute itself according to the natural mechanisms of economic law. Or if we prefer, we may choose to legislate statute laws which provide for its arbitrary distribution to those who stand first in the line of political power. Between these two extremes, according to Tucker, there is no possibility of compromise. In answer to the charge that a free economic order would soon be dominated by the great trusts, Tucker, speaking before the Chicago Civic Federation in September of 1899, pointed out that anarchism advocates no measures of governmental regulation to meet this problem.[55] Trusts, no doubt, are harmful to the interests of the consumer as society is now organized. But in a free society in which the state had no right to regulate the economy, countervailing forces would soon appear to curb the antisocial actions now practiced by the great trusts. We anarchists, Tucker boasted, have faith in nature and its ways. We would, therefore, trust men to follow their natural sentiments of social equality and solidarity, rather than impose "justice" upon them through the power of the state.

We would be wise in this regard, Tucker urged, to investigate the social theories of the Mutualists, for they fully understood the problem of liberty versus authority. "When Warren and Proudhon, in prosecuting their search for justice to labor, came face to face with the obstacle of class monopolies, they saw that these monopolies rested upon Authority, and concluded that the thing to be done was,

not to strengthen this Authority and thus make the monopoly universal, but to utterly uproot Authority and give full sway to the opposite
principle, Liberty, by making competition, the antithesis of monopoly,
universal."[56] Anarchists would be well advised, Tucker argued, to
note that man's first step toward totalitarianism was at the point at
which he decided that the only way labor might be guaranteed equality
was to divest all private individuals of their capital goods, thereby
"making the government everything and the individual nothing."
Warren and Proudhon, on the other hand, by taking all power and
authority away from the state, start down the path of "making the
individual everything and the government nothing." Tucker's quarrel
with anarchists communists was not so much that they were angry
young men who sometimes used intemperate language as that they
did not clearly recognize the importance of the individual in the
march toward the libertarian goal. In itself, the expropriation of
capital is not socially negative, Tucker argued. But once this step
has been taken there invariably arises a move toward the reestablish-
ment of privilege in favor of the class in power. It does not change
things to argue that the proletariat, now starving, will be the beneficiary after the revolution. For a ruling class, by whatever name it is
known, is antithetical to the freedom of the individual. "Any communistic attempt to interfere with the *freedom of individual production and exchange* will result in still another revolution," Tucker
warned.[57] Let us not, then, ever compromise with the foundation of
all social life, which is freedom. For this is the very core of the
anarchist idea, the alpha and omega of its libertarian doctrine.

In reconciling individualism and socialism, and calling the
amalgam thus created "anarchism," Benjamin Tucker stands out as
one of the most original thinkers in the entire history of American
libertarianism. It is only now, in this late day of Leviathan's march
to near total dominance over free society, that the wisdom of Tucker's
viewpoint is becoming fully apparent. Drawing upon Proudhon's
distrust of the masses, Tucker warned his anarchist compatriots
that there is serious danger in any attempt to lead the masses to
Armageddon through organization and military methods of control.
With anarchists everywhere, Tucker took a firm stand on the principle
that "the philosophy of liberty is emphatically opposed to organization
as generally understood."[58] This did not mean, he argued, that social
groups, possessing a common purpose, could not find rational

methods of acting in concert. Referring to the plight of the laboring classes during the textile strike in Lawrence, Massachusetts, he deplored the fact that no natural leaders stepped forward from the ranks to lead the assault against the citadel of capitalist injustice. Where social organization springs from spontaneous forces within the group itself, Tucker had nothing but good to say of it. What he stood opposed to was the principle of military organization and hierarchy, whether in the ranks of labor or the state. Taking issue with Auberon Herbert, the famous English anarchist, Tucker denied that the trades union is at basis a "force institution."[59] So long as labor depends upon the spontaneity and enthusiasm of its own natural leaders for its motivation, it cannot be charged that unions belong in the same category as organized government. It is only when the labor union, in imitation of the state, adopts the paraphernalia of a legislative body and acts upon its members as well as the public through threats, force, and compulsion, that its essentially libertarian character is perverted. Anarchism, as Tucker defined it, is indistinguishable from the natural sociability of human beings which leads them to cooperate with one another in the realization of mutual social ends when left free to do so. "It is State Socialism," Tucker charged, "which dreads the growth of voluntary cooperation, since men familiar with the advantages of the latter will never take kindly to the compulsory features inseparable from the former." Speaking past each other, Tucker and Kropotkin would have been chagrined to discover that they stood on essentially the same philosophical ground, for all the polemical differences which seemed to separate them.

The true depth of Tucker's commitment to the libertarian idea is seen in the strategy he worked out as his plan to realize the social revolution. Wary of all attempts to organize the unenlightened masses, since this can only be done through compulsion or deception, Tucker echoed Plato's belief that the assent from the cave of human ignorance must of necessity be an individual effort. Radicals who attempt to lead the people in a frontal assault upon the barricades of injustice inevitably discover that the rule in which they find themselves differs little from that of the generals and statesmen of the existing world. To bring about a true social revolution that will be in keeping with the values of the libertarian idea, social reform must spring from individuals who act upon genuine humanitarian convictions of their own. "Whoever . . . waits for the masses will wait till his deluded class is itself swept into the great struggling heap, and naught remains but unchallenged despots and hopeless slaves. The true law of social dynamics knows nothing about the masses."[60] It was this gem of Proudhonian wisdom that led Tucker to the conclusion that the only means of bringing social change about that would not bear the traces of authoritarian side effects was passive resistance. And hence Tucker, even before Gandhi, called upon individual citizens to resist injustice whenever it was indulged in by their government. "The time will come," he prophesied, "when passive resistance to taxation will be recognized as the most effective method of abolishing the State."[61] To be utterly realistic, Tucker argued, it is futile to take on Leviathan using conventional tactics of revolutionary warfare. For the state can easily put down any effort of violence by launching a superior show of violence itself. But when any considerable number of individuals, deciding to withhold their taxes from the public treasury, quietly refuse to honor the demands of the tax collector, a serious rupture has been inflicted in a main artery of the state system. "If one fifth of the people were to resist taxation, it would cost more to collect their taxes, or try to collect them, than the other four fifths would consent to pay into the treasury."

Anarchists of a later era who attacked Tucker for his alleged indifference to the plight of the working classes missed the point that his passive resistance was as much based upon distrust of organized government as was that of the bomb throwers.[62] When he urged the "student of Liberty" to "disassociate his imagination from sanguinary dramas of assassination and revolt," he did so not because he had less revolutionary ardor than others but because he recognized that force and violence are not an efficacious means of realizing social freedom. As Emma Goldman and Alexander Berkman themselves were later to argue, violent outbursts of revolutionary discontent are not integral parts of libertarian philosophy but are ultimately caused by the inability of those who control the state to allow peaceful social change to freely take place.[63] Tucker, for all his preference for the ways of passive resistance, was a veritable fire-brand when it came to the question of the nature of the state.

Liberals who believe that power can be used for good ends delude themselves, Tucker argued, for public regulation invariably necessitates the invasion of the rights of others. The only way power can be trusted is to confine its use to individuals in their private affairs, which means that no large concentrations of force can exist within society. Left to himself, an individual may well injure another person, invading his property and trampling his rights under foot. But political science reveals that violence never breaks out in the social order without cause. Where violence occurs between individual and individual, or group and group, the means of settlement for the dispute is inherent within the persons involved and will be invoked when the interests of all concerned dictate that they should be. It might occasionally be necessary to combine one's resources with that of others to create a more efficient instrument of self-defense. But so long as the function of social order is left up to individuals, Tucker held, power can never become highly concentrated, for the natural laws of social balance militate against this. It is only where a monopoly of power is held by the state that power becomes an evil.

No starry-eyed dreamer, Tucker readily recognized that it is inevitable that large numbers of people at any given point in time will lack the personal resources to perfectly control themselves and will thus be forced to rely upon others for guidance and support. This was why Tucker argued that individuals might voluntarily join together in forming private protective associations for one limited purpose or another. They might, for example, organize fire companies or police forces. But in each instance these functions should remain limited and private in structure rather than being given the form of permanent public organizations. Tucker was aware, of course, that there is a certain amount of efficiency derived from turning over essential functions to professionals, as in the case of the police or fire fighting. But he also wisely recognized that any efficiency thus gained would soon be lost in the bureaucratic tendencies which professional organizations inevitably develop. As society becomes increasingly complex in its administrative structure, the gains which were originally made when basic social functions were taken over by professionals are lost as inflexibility and obsolescence become increasingly evident. Even more serious is the fact that a professional administrative class is tantamount to a ruling elite, provoking the violence which inevitably accompanies class rule. For where formal methods of social control are imposed upon people, as they must be by professional administrators, the point at which force need not increasingly be employed is perpetually just beyond our reach. As a consequence, simple problems become complex and two evils appear where there had formerly been one. Force begats violence, thereby calling forth even more stringent methods of social control. In the end, administration by professionals is the certain road to slavery.

It is much better, according to Tucker, to allow people to bumble along in their own inefficient way than to remove the control of their own destiny from their hands. Undoubtedly a thoroughgoing system of private enterprise would be one in which large concentrations of wealth and power would be impossible. But if no few people would be extremely rich, no large class of people would be extremely poor either. It is ridiculous to advance the Hamiltonian argument that government protection is necessary for the growth of a strong, prosperous economy. In Tucker's opinion, just the opposite is true, for it is clear that governments inevitably spend the greater part of their efforts in perpetuating themselves and not in serving the real needs of the people. How else are we to explain the insanity of organized warfare from the beginning of the state's history? And how are we to explain the gigantic police organizations which currently exist within every advanced country and which threaten to wipe out every last vestige of the individual liberties men once enjoyed? Turn men loose to manage their own affairs without the aid of government, Tucker insisted, and the natural laws of social and economic progress will assert themselves. No longer will the state then frustrate men in their quest for social solidarity. But while they persist in relying upon the state for support in the conduct of life, the full satisfaction of human sociability is bound to elude them.

Tucker's fear of centralized political power led him to reject the system of organized political parties which American liberals cling to so tenaciously. Within every party system, Tucker urged, the party in power is inevitably in favor of a further centralization of power. Although the party out of power always favors decentralization, as soon as it gets into power it suddenly reverses itself and calls for the exact opposite of what it previously championed. This proves, according to Tucker, that "only those who despise power altogether can be steadfast friends of liberty." In America, to be sure, political scientists tend to overlook the negative aspects of political power on the argument that power is here made responsive to the majority. But, Tucker retorted, the true friends of liberty understand that power is always socially negative, whoever may wield it. Here we must be especially careful, he warned, to avoid the subtle deception we find in the authoritarian "democracy" of Rousseau, whose theism "is only a modification of Roman Catholicism, and has its political results in the despotism of Robespierre and its social results in the monstrous schemes of Karl Marx and Lasalle to wipe out individual liberty," Tucker held.[64] For all his professed animosity toward the authoritarian aspects of organized religion, Rousseau was as guilty of enslaving man to the superstition of God as any of the clerics he attacked. By the same token, Tucker continued, we must be wary of revolutionaries who promise us that the nature of political power will somehow be changed once it rests in the hands of the working class. With an uncanny degree of accuracy, Tucker predicted that there will "be one article in the constitution of a State Socialistic country: 'The right of the majority is absolute.' "[65] Young anarchists such as Emma Goldman may not have realized it at the time but they would one day acknowledge the wisdom of Tucker's warning.

In his own life, Benjamin Tucker was highly successful in putting his anarchist theories into operation. In demonstration of his free love doctrine in which he insisted that monogamy, with or without the benefit of formal vows, ought to be avoided for the sake of the complete freedom of both parties, he entered into the love tryst with Pearl Johnson in which either individual was free to escape at any time. But just as Tucker suspected, love soon bound the two of them together and their "friendship" resembled a conventional marriage in every way except the legal trappings of that institution. A daughter was born to them in New York and was named Oriole after the daughter of Tucker's friend, J. William Lloyd. When Tucker retired to Europe after his establishment went up in flames in 1908, Pearl and Oriole went with him, just as all happily integrated families do. To the end, Tucker needed no external coercion to tell him how to live his life. For like all anarchists, he was convinced that it is the individual who knows the secret of harmonious social relationships and not those who place themselves in positions of political power.

Unhappily, Tucker, in his last years, lost some of the determination and fortitude he displayed as a younger man, if we can believe one of his colleagues, the Stirnerite, Stephen T. Byington.[66] An undisguised Francophile, Tucker early in life adopted a love of things French from which he never deviated. Not only did he consider French the most advanced of languages but he considered French culture as superior to all others. As World War I came on, Tucker, to the dismay of his anarchist friends, professed his allegiance to the Allies on the grounds that French culture ought not to be allowed to perish from the earth. Retiring to Monaco in 1908, where he frittered away his time collecting materials for a book which never got written, Tucker was overcome with a deep melancholy concerning the future of mankind.[67] As Tucker analyzed the modern scene, the greatest threat to human survival was technology, the source of man's material blessings as it was the scourge of his spiritual being. Recognizing the potential for destruction which technology held out for the human race should it ever get out of hand, Tucker lost faith that anarchism would be successful in turning back the forces of authoritarianism in time to prevent a social and political cataclysm. Writing to his friends and compatriot, Clarence Lee Swartz in July of 1930, Tucker revealed that his mind was indeed gripped by a black mood when he said:

> the insurmountable obstacle to the realization of Anarchy is no longer the power of the trusts, but the indisputable fact that our civilization is in its death throes. We may last a couple of centuries yet; on the other hand, a decade may precipitate our finish. As Clemenceau said, 'Perhaps there may still remain a few negroes wandering in the Congo.' The dark ages, sure enough. The monster, Mechanism, is devouring mankind.[68]

To be sure, these are the words of a tired old man who had struggled mightily against the main currents of social development only to see all of his theories come to naught. Tucker's pessimism, on the other hand, was completely justified by the deterioration in social conditions since his youth. After all, Tucker did not invent the state. And he did speak out against it, urging his fellowmen to overthrow government by employing whatever means were necessary to the task. That they did not do so can hardly be blamed on him, for Tucker stood ready to perform any "propaganda of deed" that the situation demanded, whether that was the education of his fellowmen or the refusal to support government through taxes. In his last years, Tucker realized that political power had been so highly concentrated that nothing short of widespread violence could effect the social revolution. But this was exactly what he had predicted throughout the years. If percipience is the mark of a great man, Benjamin Ricketson Tucker was certainly one of the most towering figures in the annals of anarchism.

NOTES

SECTION II - CHAPTER 5

1. Joseph Ishill, "Benjamin R. Tucker," in *Free Vistas,* II, ed. by Joseph Ishill (Berkeley Heights, N.J., 1937), p. 267.

2. George Schumm, "Benjamin R. Tucker—A Brief Sketch of his Life and Work," *The Freethinker's Magazine,* XI (July, 1893), 436.

3. Quoted in Emanie Sachs, *The Terrible Siren; Victoria Woodhull* (New York, 1938), pp. 250-251.

4. *The Word,* V (December, 1876), 2.

5. "Announcement Extraordinary," *Liberty,* IV (January, 1887), 4.

6. "Memories of Benjamin R. Tucker," *Free Vistas,* II, p. 281.

7. "The Influence of Tucker's Ideas in France," *Free Vistas,* II, p. 284.

8. For a typical example of this viewpoint, see James W. Garner, *Political Science and Government* (New York, 1928).

9. *Liberty,* XII (July, 1896), 4.

10. "On Picket Duty," *Liberty,* XIV (December, 1900), 1.

11. "The Root of Despotism," *Liberty,* I (August, 1881), 2.

12. "On Picket Duty," *Liberty,* XIV (January, 1904), 1.

13. "The Root of Despotism."

14. "Moralism the Denial of Love," *Liberty,* X (April, 1895), 2.

15. "On Picket Duty," *Liberty,* I (July, 1882), 1.

16. "The Twin Children of Tyranny," *Liberty,* II (March, 1883), 3.

17. "Anarchy Necessarily Atheistic," *Liberty,* III (January, 1886), 3.

18. "The Meaning of Liberty's Motto," *Liberty,* IX (June, 1893), 3.

19. "The Root of Despotism."

20. "The Philosophy of Right and Wrong," *Liberty,* I, (October, 1882), 2.

21. "What Is Prosperity," *Liberty,* XI (September, 1895), 5.

22. "Rights and Contract," *Liberty,* XI (December, 1895), 4.

23. "The Relation of the State to the Individual," *Liberty,* VII (November, 1890), 7.

24. Florence Finch Kelly, *Flowing Stream* (New York, 1939), p. 192.

25. This letter dated April 11, 1936, originally published in *The*

American Journal of Sociology, was reprinted in *Free Vistas*, II, *op. cit.*, p. 307.

26. "Armies that Overlap," *Liberty*, VI (March, 1890), 4.

27. "A Word about Capital Punishment," *Liberty*, VII (August 30, 1890), 4.

28. "Political or Other Tyranny," *Liberty*, XI (November, 1895), 5.

29. "Philosophical Anarchism (1880-1920)," *The Journal of Social Philosophy*, VI (April, 1941), 260.

30. "Reform it Altogether," *Liberty*, II (November, 1882), 3.

31. "The 'Philosophical Anarchists,' " *Liberty*, IV (July, 1886), 1.

32. "Political or Other Tyranny," 4.

33. "Liberty and Violence," *Liberty*, IV (May, 1866), 4.

34. "The Doctrine of Assent," *Liberty*, I (September, 1881), 2.

35. "Do Liberals Know Themselves," *Liberty*, I (February, 1882), 2.

36. "The Criminal Jailers of Oscar Wilde," *Liberty*, X (June, 1895), 2.

37. "American Czardom Unmasked," *Liberty*, II (November, 1882), 2.

38. *Ibid.*

39. "Principle, Policy, and Politics," *Liberty*, XII (November, 1896), 5.

40. "The Advisability of Violence," *Liberty*, VIII (January, 1892), 3.

41. "A Plea for Non-Resistance," *Liberty*, V (February, 1888), 5.

42. "Liberty's Weapons," *Liberty*, I (September, 1881), 2.

43. "Liberty and Violence," 4.

44. For a recent analysis of Tucker's thought, see David Henry Leon, *The American as Anarchist: A Socio-Historical Interpretation* (unpublished Ph. D. thesis, The University of Iowa, 1972).

45. See Henri de Lubac, *The Un-Marxian Socialist* (New York, 1948).

46. "Two Kinds of Communism," *Liberty*, I (September, 1881), 3.

47. "State Socialism and Anarchism: How Far They Agree, and Wherein They Differ," *Liberty*, V (March, 1888), 2.

48. "After 'Freiheit,' 'Der Sozialist,' " *Liberty*, V (April, 1888), 4.

49. "Karl Marx as Friend and Foe," *Liberty*, II (April, 1883), 2.

50. "The Mistakes of Merlino," *Liberty*, VIII (July 16, 1892), 2.

51. "On Picket Duty," *Liberty*, VII (February, 1892), 1.

52. "Michale Davitt and His Seducer," *Liberty*, I (June, 1882), 2.

53. "Economic Rent," *Liberty*, IX (November, 1892), 3.

54. "The Telegrapher's Strike," *Liberty*, II (August, 1883), 2.

55. "The Attitude of Anarchism Toward Industrial Combinations," *Liberty*, XIV (December, 1902), 4.

56. "State Socialism and Anarchism: How Far They Agree, and Wherein They Differ," 3.

57. "Blind as Well as Brutal," *Liberty*, II (February, 1883), 2.

58. "Organization, False and True," *Liberty*, I (April, 1882), 2.

59. "On Picket Duty," *Liberty*, X (June, 1894), 1.

60. "Lessons of the Hour," *Liberty*, III (October, 1884), 4.

61. "On Picket Duty," *Liberty*, I (May, 1882), 1.

62. "The Power of Passive Resistance," *Liberty*, II (October, 1883), 4.

63. "Liberty's Aims and Methods," *Liberty*, II (January, 1883), 2.

64. "Has Truth Become a Liar," *Liberty*, II (October, 1883), 2.

65. "State Socialism and Anarchism:How Far They Agree, and Wherein They Differ."

66. "Bengamin Ricketson Tucker," *Man!* (August, 1939), 5.

67. Charles Madison, *Critics and Crusaders*, (New York, 1947), p. 212.

68. "My Contact with Benjamin R. Tucker," *Free Vistas*, II, p. 301.

CHAPTER 6

The "Boston Anarchists" and Philosophical Egoists

It is difficult to arrive at an exact classification of Tucker's follow-ers, for the wide range of opinion expressed by the individuals who contributed to *Liberty* made the doctrine of individualist anarchism sound hopelessly cacophonous at times. Yet if one listened carefully enough, a definite pattern was discernible within the great variety of diverse viewpoints prompted by Tucker's editorial permissiveness. In general the harmonious note which sounds through all the pages of *Liberty* in the early years of its publication was the radical complaint that capitalist society abuses the worker, denying him the full fruits of his labor.

While Alan P. Kelly, one of Tucker's early editorial assistants, may by no means be designated as typical of his followers, he did express anarchist leanings when he argued that the American social structure is as definitely divided into "the masters and the slaves, the idlers and the workers, the robbers and the robbed" as any social system that ever existed.[1] Those who attempt to deny the reality of class distinctions in America, Kelly charged, do so to cover up their servile obeisance to those in power. A Boston journalist by trade, Kelly was an outspoken critic of the railroad monopolies which he felt had denied many of the American people their rightful in-heritance to the land. When this forerunner of the muckrakers spoke of class rule, he was not mouthing the empty platitudes of an abstract ideology but the sincere convictions of an American indignant in the face of capitalist injustice.

Yet individualist anarchism was racked by the same ideological disputes that have sapped the energy of all left-wing movements in the American past. Ironically, it was the labor movement, the main source of radical strength, that gave rise to the issues which first divided American anarchism. Already in the eighties there were rumblings of concern in *Liberty* which centered in the question of

171

the propriety of anarchists participating in the movement of organized
labor. When in 1883 John Swinton undertook the publication of a
radical labor paper in New York, Tucker wished him well but expressed some concern, based upon Swinton's testimony before the
Senate Labor Committee, that the paper might "fly the flag of authority."[2] A fiery radical in his demeanor, Swinton the year previously
had spoken at a mammoth labor rally in Cooper Union against New
York's infamous penal code, denouncing lawyers as shysters who
were a menace to liberty in this Republic.[3] On the surface, therefore,
Swinton could make as good a claim to being libertarian as anyone.
But Tucker was a keen judge of people and had detected a weak
spot in Swinton's anarchist commitment and refused to place the
official imprimatur upon his views. Throughout the entire life of
Liberty, Tucker rode herd upon his followers, often chiding them
in strong words for their failures in remaining true to the libertarian
idea. Always completely candid in his remarks, he sometimes alienated those he castigated for their ideological shortcomings, although
more often than not his honesty won him increased devotion.

Henry Appleton, another of Tucker's editorial assistants who
sometimes wrote under the pseudonym "X," was one of those unfortunates who became the object of Tucker's wrath for joining the
Knights of Labor. Tucker had no objection to Appleton attending
meetings of organized labor and there speaking out in support of
anarchist doctrines but he was seriously disturbed by his associate's
acceptance of ideas which were basically alien to the anarchist idea
of liberty. "It is because he goes to such meetings and does not
emphasize Anarchist doctrines, but on the contrary emphasizes
Knights of Labor doctrines as superior to Anarchist doctrines, that I
condemn him," Tucker wrote.[4]

It would be wholly incorrect to assume, however, that Tucker's
outspoken criticism of those who disagreed with him was a reflection
of an authoritarian strain in his own intellect. Tucker may well have
demanded rigorous adherence to libertarian principles from his
followers, but they were always free to disagree with him as much as
they liked so long as they possessed rational grounds for the views
they held. Tucker would not equivocate, to be sure, on the fundamental principle of force versus liberty. The central concern of all
anarchist doctrine and activity, as he saw it, must focus upon the
libertarian idea of human freedom. Tucker used the pages of liberty

as a "plumb-line," subjecting all social argumentation to rigorous scrutiny in terms of its compatibility with libertarian principles. The greatest of all doctrinal errors, as Tucker saw it, was to become confused as to the basic character of political power. As Proudhon had warned, the attempt to use organized political power for good ends must inevitably result in failure, for the means one chooses to attain any given goal always conditions the outcome of the overall situation. Organized power, since it is fundamentally authoritarian in character, can only result in a further growth of authoritarianism. This was why Tucker insisted that labor tread on dangerous ground when it began to think in terms of organized force and political power. The tendency of labor to mobilize its force for a showdown in the political arena, he warned, is a most disastrous decision that can only lead away from a true social revolution.

Still another of Tucker's trusted editorial associates was Gertrude Kelly, whom he spoke of as "one of the foremost radical writers of this country or any other country." Basically determined in her anarchism by Josiah Warren's philosophy of individual responsibility, Gertrude Kelly maintained, as Tucker did, that true peace can only arise from a social situation in which each and every person is guaranteed complete autonomy. A real social order is *not* secured, she argued, by binding ourselves together into organized groups or by establishing a hierarchy of force within which the individual is compelled to function according to an imposed pattern. True social cooperation can only grow from a situation in which our aims and interests are identical. Where these conditions exist, cooperation will spring forth spontaneously without any conscious effort or formal planning.[5] Libertarian to the core, Gertrude Kelly held firm to the anarchist theory that freedom is the antidote for all social ills, whereas repression and force can only lead to a further deterioration of social solidarity.

Completely sympathetic with the plight of the workingman and convinced that capitalism was nothing more than a system of legalized embezzlement, Gertrude Kelly called for a social revolution which would thoroughly transform the nature of existing society. But while she was unrestrained in her loyalty to the welfare of labor, she was equally unrestrained in her condemnation of the theories of class rule that were then being advocated by social reformers who saw the state's power as the perfect model to copy. When labor places itself in opposition to capital and threatens to use force to realize its aims, it gives vent to the same "spirit of robbery" that capital displays when it exploits the worker without regard for his welfare, Kelly argued. But a libertarian society cannot operate upon this low level of moral concern. Might makes right is adequate as a law of the jungle, she urged; among human beings who have once tasted the delights of freedom, however, it is completely unacceptable. We cannot, of course, blame the workingman who concludes that his only recourse is to fight back against the system with the very same weapons that are employed against him. But it is an entirely different thing when men who have adopted the libertarian philosophy endorse the use of violence and class rule.

It is important to notice here that like Tucker, Gertrude Kelly drew a careful distinction between legitimate and illegitimate force. On the one hand she maintained that the strike was a potent weapon which might be used to bring capital to agree to a more equitable distribution of wealth. Addressing herself to labor she argued that "it is in your power, when you wish it and thoroughly understand your position, to cause capital to come on its knees to you, begging you to employ it, instead of as heretofore, you begging capital to employ you."[6] The kind of strike she envisioned, however, was one in which the individual, acting upon genuine social convictions of his own, joined with others in spontaneous but concerted action against injustice. Such a course of social action, to be sure, demanded a great deal from ordinary men and women. But American anarchists like Tucker and Gertrude Kelly were in substantial agreement with anarchist communists like Kropotkin and Emma Goldman regarding the nature of human potential for social solidarity. Libertarians all, they concurred that there is an inherent urge for social justice within every man which inevitably asserts itself wherever he lives in freedom. To bring it out, however, those who call for the reform of the social order must first demonstrate their own willingness to lay aside the weapons of force and work through libertarian means. In condemning the tendencies of organized labor to adopt the techniques of force and class rule, the individualists voiced sound anarchist principles.

Not all of Tucker's followers, to be sure, remained loyal to him to the end. Like the butterfly that starts out as one thing but soon becomes another, Victor S. Yarros' career as an anarchist was subject to a series of metamorphic changes which moved him from one end of the political spectrum almost to the other. While only a lad in his native Ukraine, Yarros threw in his lot with the Social Revolutionaries and as a consequence was forced to flee for his life to America where he continued at first to dwell on the idea of imminent revolutionary upheaval. Writing from New Haven, Connecticut, where he had settled during the 1880's, Yarros first came to the attention of American anarchists with a daring criticism of its leading light, Benjamin R. Tucker. Referring to Tucker's acrimonious tirades against John Most and the Chicago anarchists, Yarros castigated *Liberty's* editor for being too hard on those who fight back against oppression. Although he himself professed a personal unwillingness to engage in violence when it was unnecessary, Yarros insisted that there was nothing more repugnant than "Christian meekness and all-forgiving love in a radical."[7] Many people, Yarros complained, have come to think of anarchism as "a harmless thing, a sort of spiritual amusement for kid-gloved reformers," which has no real relevance to the hard facts of political life, and thus they "begin to smile on 'philosophical anarchism,' pronouncing it a very sweet and charming thing—to be realized a thousand years hence. . . ." Brushing away all such overtures toward reconciliation and compromise, Yarros vehemently denied that the followers of *Liberty*, among whom he now counted himself, were harmless pacifists who could be depended on to remain nonviolent under all circumstances. With a ferocious mien almost as frightening as that which was affected by the notorious John Most, Yarros heated up the pages of *Liberty* when he thundered:

> Anarchism means war—war upon all government, all authority, and all forms of slavery. We have a right to use force and resist by all means the invasion of the self-constituted rulers, and we shall not hesitate to bring into play the "resources of civilization" when necessity calls for it and when maddened authority leaves us no alternative. We are all "rebels to the law," and the monopolists and the prostituted editorial Mammon worshippers need not favor us more than they do the Chicago "fiends." The followers of *Liberty* are even more dangerous to "law and order" than the bomb-throwers, and, judging from certain indications, we may be compelled to do a little bomb-throwing of our own before long. Let tyranny beware, and let respectability undeceive itself.[8]

For all his bellicosity, however, Yarros posed no more of a clear and present danger to the existing institutions of government than Tucker, under whom he came to labor as second in command of *Liberty*. In response to the English anarchist, Auberon Herbert, Yarros could argue that "where force is the only weapon, where the choice is between force and entire inactivity, force may and should be used for the purposes of acquiring the liberty of using the other and better weapons."[9] But all propaganda by deed can do, according to Yarros, is prepare society for that propaganda by word through which men must ultimately be won over to anarchism. In the advanced state of society of the future, he argued in an exchange with Dyer D. Lum, "bloodless revolutions will be a historical fact. Radical changes and reforms will be inaugurated without any violence or civil war. Where we can speak openly and freely, educate and agitate, the propaganda by deed is needless and will do more harm than good."[10]

Actually, Yarros' position regarding the employment of violence was very similar to Tucker's. Like Tucker, he felt that where passive resistance was possible in the fight against the state, this was preferable to physical conflict. But the question as to whether armed combat is necessary or not was not the primary responsibility of the anarchist. We must be clear in our minds, Yarros argued, that it is at the hands of the state that violence initiates and not at the hands of the people. The violent conflict which emerges from all revolutionary situations is the direct consequence of the invasive actions of government as it forces its unwelcome attention upon the individual persons who make up society. Where our rights are denied by the actions of the state, he urged, we not only have the right but the duty of resisting such encroachment.[11] Yarros did not make the common mistake of confusing nonviolence with civil disobedience. Writing in reference to Ernest Howard Crosby, whose personal sincerity and dedication he greatly admired, Yarros found the theory of nonresistance to which Crosby subscribed "wholly unscientific," and the doctrine of Christian ethics he advanced "impracticable and undesirable."[12] In Yarros' mind, government and "Machiavellianism" were synonymous and hence it was inevitable that men would find themselves at war with the state until its power over their lives was brought to an end by revolutionary upheaval. One could not, therefore, dedicate himself to peace under all circumstances, as Crosby did, for where the basic nature of government is aggressive, private individuals must of necessity group together in self-defense when circumstances demand it. Those who band together in mutual defense against the invasive powers of the state, Yarros insisted, cannot be said to have erected a government themselves, for "defense against aggression is not government" but merely the means of perpetuating one's own survival against illigitimate power.[13] With Thoreau, Yarros viewed civil disobedience as an essential factor in the political process. Government, on this view, is a constant threat to the civil liberty of the individual and only a determined effort to maintain freedom against the inevitable incursions of the hostile state can preserve the heritage of democratic polity which Americans so greatly cherish.

As the years went by Yarros became less and less convinced that revolution is an inevitable fact of social progress. In order for revolution to occur, he held, it is essential that there be widespread discontent in society and that there be an equally predominant class of "ardent and skilled conspirators" to give leadership to the disaffected. Reassessing the situation from his new perspective within American society, Yarros concluded that "not only Anarchists, but even State Socialists, are discarding the 'catastrophic' policy."[14] Perhaps the most mellowing influence upon Yarros' ideological development was the Boston Anarchist Club, of which he was a founding member. Stealing a page from the English Fabian Club's book of tactics, the Boston Anarchists advocated a gradual progression to anarchism carried forward by public meetings, lectures and debates, and the distribution of anarchist literature. As solidly as they were themselves convinced that the state is the source of all social evil, the Boston Anarchists recognized the wide span of understanding and misunderstanding which existed among the American public in general. And since it would be a denial of man's fundamental right to individual freedom if anarchists forced those who did not accept that political view to go along with revolution unwillingly, the actual day of revolutionary upheaval must wait until men convince themselves of its rightness.[15]

Having abandoned his passion for revolution, Yarros flirted for a time with the idea of egoism which Tucker and other members of the *Liberty* group found appealing, but in his later years a noticeable lack of conviction began to creep into Yarros' discussion of anarchism. During the height of his commitment to the idea, he could hardly contain himself when faced with the argument that the ballot is a possible form of political action for those who love liberty. In reply to kindly old Moses Harman, who, despite his staunch opposition to government tyranny throughout a lifetime, never really saw the impossibility of changing society through the vote, Yarros stormed that he would rather choose dynamite than the ballot. "To propagate anarchism while regularly visiting the polls is impossible," he insisted.

Yet a mere five years later Yarros sorely perplexed the readers of *Liberty* when he soberly editorialized that there was "no trace of absurdity or inconsistency in the proposal of some Anarchists to give their votes or other form of aid to the Democrats with the purpose of helping them to defeat the Republicans."[16] Before long Yarros backed off some distance from the movement, now writing from a position of impersonal detachment. In a series of scholarly articles, he bloodlessly delineated the shape of the anarchist idea as though he were a surgeon who had never before seen the patient he was working on.[17] Where once he proudly referred to himself as a dedicated anarchist, Yarros now thought of himself as an "independent radical," which he defined as a person who was halfway between the positions of the philosophical anarchist and the state socialist. The degree to which Yarros had shifted his course is clearly evident in his description of the independent radical as one who:

> though individualistic in his philosophy, perceives that it is foolish, idle and re-actionary to oppose, for example, child labor laws, shorter workday laws, social insurance, old-age pensions, insurance against unemployment, and the like. He sees that to oppose such ameliorative measures is to give aid and comfort to toryism, to alienate labor and its middleclass sympathizers, and to retard the reform process. He realizes that so long as the State exists, and is being used by social groups with power enough to shape and influence legislation, it is utterly irrational to expect that labor and the humanities will be induced . . . to ignore the State or refrain from utilizing its machinery and authority. In short, he knows that life obeys no dogmatic formulas, and that progress is a resultant of many forces and factors.[18]

From his retirement home in France where he lived like a deposed monarch with aspirations of winning back his former subjects, Benjamin Tucker let loose a mighty blast against his erstwhile protege. In the good old days Tucker had been proud to acknowledge that "The name of Mr. Yarros has been more steadily and conspicuously identified with *Liberty* than that of any other person, save myself,"[19] but there was little goodwill in Tucker's vitriolic reply to Yarros' article in the *American Journal of Sociology* in April of 1936. After somewhat pedantically correcting a series of misinterpretations which Yarros had made regarding his social and philosophical views, Tucker ended all hope for reconciliation between them when he wrote in an open letter: "It remains only to add that Victor Yarros, who now parades in the role of a mere observer, was for years my most active participant in Anarchistic propagandism,—a fact which he is now careful to conceal. I once admired him; I now despise him."[20] Like a jealous lover, Tucker would rather destroy his former admirer than see him live to love another.

To James L. Walker (1845-1904) belongs the distinction of being among the first, if not the first, American anarchist to point out the importance of Max Stirner's *The Ego and His Own,* which he first discovered as early as the spring of 1872. Born in Manchester, England, and educated there as well as in Germany, Walker was a quiet, scholarly individual who had been schooled in ten languages and was proficient in Latin, Greek, and Sanskrit.[21] Making his living as a journalist, first with *The London Times* and later with a series of papers in cities stretching from Chicago to Galveston, Texas, where he eventually settled, one of his first journalistic ventures after coming to America was the editorship of an anti-theological paper published in Chicago. Forced to leave Chicago because of deteriorating health, he became the chief editorial writer for *The Galveston Daily News.* It was about this time that Walker discovered the doctrine of anarchism through Moses Harman and before long he was a frequent contributor to *Lucifer the Light-Bearer, Liberty,* and Henry Replogle's *Egoism,* often writing under the pseudonym "Tak Kak." Walker was living in Mexico in 1904 when he suffered from successive attacks of yellow fever and small pox which brought on his death in Houston where he had gone to recuperate. Other than his articles and letters which he scattered about through *Liberty* and other anarchist journals, his major philosophical effort is his *Philosophy of Egoism* which was published posthumously by his wife, Katherine Walker, in 1905. It was Walker who wrote the introduction to Stephen T. Byington's translation of *The Ego And His Own* which Tucker issued in 1907 three years after Walker's death.

Always enthusiastic in his reaction to ideas when he thought them worthy of his love, Tucker had in his turn heralded Stirner's *The Ego and His Own* as "the greatest work of political philosophy and ethics ever written," and advertised it for sale to his readers for years, thus establishing a school of Stirnerites in America who were dedicated to the root idea of utilitarian psychology. Although some of the original subscribers to *Liberty* were alienated by Tucker's new found enthusiam, there was a striking similarity between the idea of philosophical egoism urged by Stirner and the doctrine of libertarianism advocated by American anarchists. Among Tucker's followers who happily embraced Stirner's teachings were George Schumm, who could read *Der Einzige* in the original German, and Joseph Labadee, who could not; Labadee, however, paid tribute to Stirner when he named his widely-printed column "Crankey Notions" after a phrase which Stirner used in his book.

What American anarchists found so appealing in Stirner's pyschology was his thoroughgoing commitment to the idea of the free individual. Breaking totally with the authoritarian idea that the individual person must always submit himself to the control of his appointed leaders, Stirner took the position that the human being in his physical aspects is nothing more than the vehicle by which the ego establishes itself as a power in human relations. Apart from the ego, Stirner maintained, nothing has any value or meaning. It is only when the courageous individual asserts his unique creative power that "truth" comes into being. Thoroughly existential in his outlook, Stirner insisted that there is no truth apart from the actions of the individual as he struggles to stamp his mark upon the face of history. But Stirner would not have the individual embrace the product of his own action too firmly, for tyranny comes into being at the point at which men raise their values into sacred precepts and force them upon their fellow beings. Like Proudhon, whom he often cited as a reliable source of libertarian thought, Stirner subscribed to the theory that freedom is possible only on an individual basis and on a relative plane. Once men attempt to formalize their truths into systems of morality and right, the foundations are laid for that totalitarian spectre that haunts the modern age. The state, in Stirner's opinion, is the product of man's proclivity to run society through law, the courts, and the police. Where right becomes codified and established as the motive force for all social relations, social power becomes a fixed idea, a sacred font of authority, before which each and all must bow down in total submission. To circumvent these impossible conditions, Stirner advocated with Proudhon that no principle of right or truth ever be considered final or beyond question, for the beginning of all human tyranny is precisely the point at which ideas become revered by those who submit to them.

Demonstrating the direct line that extends from the free thought movement to American anarchism, Walker held with Stirner that the basis of all human systems of slavery and servitude is man's proclivity to make his tyrants as he makes his gods. Both God and the state, according to Walker, exist in the minds of men because they have been taught to look upon institutions with awe and unquestioning obedience. Egoism, to the extent that it can help men to understand their own existential worth, frees men from the "awe, reverence, and obedience upon which all despotism thrives."[22] In order for freedom to exist for the individual, he argued, it is necessary "to make Ego—the I, master, rather than the slave of his environment."[23] Under the theory of democracy, the individual is burdened by his relationship to the will of the majority which acts as a major force of repression when the person concerned is not in agreement with the direction the majority has chosen to take. But, argued Walker, "the basic principle of consistent Social Polity is not a relation of the Majority with the Individual or of the Individual with the Majority, but of Individual with Individual, as of nation with nation in international relations." Where each individual is left on his own to maneuver as he pleases in regard to the actions of those with whom he is in social proximity, a real community becomes a possibility, for the lines of ethical and social responsibility become untangled, permitting everyone to understand the dynamics of social life. Under the influence of such ponderous social concepts as Christianity, democracy, and civil marriage, Walker warned, the individual becomes involved in a skein of moral and legal obligations which are presented to him as sacred and unalterable. And thus he is soon lost in a philosophical maze from which there can be no escape so long as he continues to accept the metaphysical laws laid down for him by church and state.

The history of human freedom begins at the point that the individual ceases to look to the state and God for his rights and turns instead to a contemplation of his own personal resources of social and political power, Walker proclaimed. "There can be no liberty of action," he wrote, "till it is understood that each of us finds his law in his will and pleasure and that wherein our wills and pleasures agree we make our law, which we enforce on others who come into our domain, because we must or it is our convenience to do so."[24] The pragmatic candor with which he wrote might make it appear that Walker was out of sympathy with the Platonic notion of a universal idea of justice and right which is applicable to all men; Gertrude Kelly accused him of as much in a letter to *Liberty*.[25] But Walker envisioned egoism not so much as a denial of the idea of justice as the proposition that justice and right must remain nonexistent until they are brought into being by individuals acting with regard to their own pleasures and pains in parrticular situations. Law, on this view, takes on a flexibility and adaptability which is completely lacking in the formal legal systems maintained by states and churches of the conventional world. Once established, ordinary legal precepts bend so slowly that they more often than not become fetters which bind the individual rather than aids to his liberation. But where law is tailored to the needs of particular individuals acting in particular situations according to their personal needs and capabilities, Walker urged, a genuine social order is developed wherein the maximum amount of good is apt to result. Where state and church impose law upon unreflective subjects, the real social will of those concerned is swallowed up by the blind demands of authority which can never know the real needs of those it commands. Under the logic of egoism, by contrast, the individual's rights and liberties consist of those things he can do for himself with the aid and assistance of those whose own private interests permit them to lend support to his project. No particular man, on this view of things can ride rough-shod over others, since he is limited in what he can do by the voluntary cooperation and support of others. Unlike governments, which possess an unalterable monopoly over power and force, individuals can never become tyrants so long as they are devoid of the means to force blind obedience from awed subjects who have been charmed by the irresistable powers of authority. In final analysis, Walker saw both egoism and anarchism as logical extentions of the idea of *laissez faire* whereby men are permitted to form social and political associations according to their free impulses and desires. Proclaiming Proudhon the inspiration of this school of thought, Walker argued that "Anarchy in its strict and proper philosophical sense means 'no tyranny,'—the regulation of business altogether by voluntary and mutual contract."[26] Philosophically there is much to be said for Walker's definition of anarchism, as many of his contemporaries came to see in their turn.

When John Beverley Robinson (1853-1923) went to Ann Arbor in the fall of 1916 to spend the last years of his retirement in the home of his son, he found a kindred soul in Agnes Inglis, the founder of the Labadee Collection of anarchist literature at the University of Michigan. Working on the foundations laid by Professor R. M. Wenley and other libertarian members of the University's faculty, Robinson charmed the students who gathered in Agnes Inglis' home periodically for the free discussion of social and political issues, inspiring them to a new understanding of what anarchism is all about.[27] An architect by trade, Robinson started out as a single taxer, channeling his zeal for reform into the movement to return the land to the American people. Joining forces with Louis Post and R. Heber Newton, he was one of the publishers of *The Free Soiler* issued from New York in 1884 as the official organ of the American Free Soil Society.[28] Sometime after this he shifted over to the camp of Tolstoyan anarchism but by the late 1880's he was a frequent contributor to Tucker's *Liberty,* eventually abandoning his former trust in the idea of Christianity for a thorough-going devotion to the Stirnerite philosophy of egoism. In many respects, Robinson was the most gifted interpreter of the egoist idea ever to write for *Liberty*.

The foundation of Robinson's anarchism was a deep concern for the libertarian conception of personal freedom and a well-founded fear of the corrosive effects of organized power upon American democracy. A long-time resident of New York City, Robinson discharged a volley of criticism against the board of health in Brooklyn when it attempted to make vaccination compulsory in June of 1894. If the American people wish to preserve their cherished freedoms as social beings, he warned, they must jealously guard their right to choose their own doctor and their own form of treatment. "The contrary opinion ends in the establishment of a compulsory State medical practice to the detriment of scientific advance in medicine, and of a compulsory State church to the detriment of scientific advance in ethics."[29] Nowadays, it is the economic conservative who fulminates against the creeping influence of government and the swarm of rapidly multiplying bureaucrats which it inevitably spawns. But the original formulation of the anti-state idea was at the hands of anarchists like Robinson who feared that every gain in power by those who run government is a further defeat for the people upon whom bureaucrats feed. This fear was obviously behind his argument that if you "give a man, or set of men, the power to tax you, you give them power over your life. Keep the money in your control, so that you may contribute or not, as you choose, and you are above society."[30] Robinson opined that the principle of compulsory taxation in which people are forced to pay for services they do not want or ask for "is at bottom a principle of warfare, of robbery; and everything that stands upon it is inevitably permeated with dishonesty."[31] Defining the state as "an organization of the propertied classes to maintain property," Robinson maintained that throughout history men have submitted to the power of government on the supposition that such submission would bring them increased personal benefits, when in fact the advance of civilization has been retarded to the extent that government has had power over the lives of the people. Since the institution of property is inextricably entwined in the institution of government, Robinson argued, they must be abandoned simultaneously. But government cannot be eliminated through physical force directed against the structure of power, he warned, for those who control property inevitably come out ahead when force is pitted against force. When men are clear in their minds that property and government "are brothers in arms," and that one cannot be abandoned without the other, they will of necessity attack them both at once. But the attack must be philosophical rather than physical. Steadfastly refusing to take part in either of these institutions or to countenance them in any way, libertarians will have vanquished them at one blow, he urged.

The basic principles of Robinson's philosophy of egoism are contained in an article titled "Ethics" which originally appeared in *Liberty* in 1897. Acknowledging that "the times call for a practical code of action" rather than any more homiletical excursions into the Christian past, Robinson founded his system of social thought upon the conviction that the proper basis of all action is the natural desires of the individual. Past generations, operating according to the Christian doctrine of original sin, have held the natural desires felt by persons suspect, Robinson urged. But the idea of human depravity does not hold up under careful examination, he charged, and thus we cannot attribute any particular person's actions to innate drives over which he has no control. It is the actual circumstances and pressures a man feels rather than any natural tendency to do evil or good which determine the character of that individual's actions. Obviously impressed with Stirner's philosophy of egoism, Robinson argued that "we have learned to regard desire as an indication of the needs of the organism, which must be to some extent gratified, under penalty of partial death."[32] Human social action, on this view, is prompted by the individual as he seeks to adapt himself to his environment. Seeking to maximize his pleasures and minimize his pains, the individual naturally does those things which bring him into the most satisfactory relationship that is possible with those with whom he is in daily contact. But it is because he wants comfort and pleasure for himself that the individual treats others with respect and decency and not because he directly hopes to further their pleasures in some altruistic fashion. In final analysis, Robinson argued, the individual serves as the real guide post for mankind, for "each one of us stands alone in the midst of the universe."[33] We experience sensations through our organs of sense, and we interpret what these experiences mean in terms of our own individual reactions to them, but we have no source of knowledge concerning ultimate truth outside of ourselves and our efforts to think out the meaning of what we have experienced. Each of us is a unique being, experiencing life in his own individual way. There can be no general code of morality for all men everywhere, therefore, since men, far from having standardized experiences, each respond as particular entities according to their respective backgrounds and character. Hence we must search beyond Christianity for the basis of our ethics.

With Stirner and Nietzsche, John Beverley Robinson turned to the individual and sought to make him the center of the moral world, insofar as we may speak of a moral world at all. The philosophy of egoism starts with the proposition that the individual "is above all institutions and all formulas" and that law consists only of those precepts which the individual freely chooses to acknowledge as binding upon himself. As the ultimate source of power in society, the individual can be said to wish into being only those things which he wants to see realized. Like Stirner, Robinson proclaimed the individual the sovereign power in all human relationships and insisted that he had the capability of determining the ultimate shape of social reality. Things are like they are not because a power outside of man has willed them so but because man, the ultimate force in the world, has permitted them to develop as they have. The reformation of society, therefore, must begin with the individual's desire to see things transformed into a new and better configuration of social relations. But to effect this goal, it is first necessary to abandon the idea of the state as the umpire of human affairs. Unhappily, Robinson complained, " 'The State' or 'The Government' is idealized by the many as a thing above them, to be reverenced and feared."[34] Patterning his language after Stirner's, Robinson declared the concept of the state to be similar to the "fixed idea" of the lunatic who lives a fool's existence among vague shadows and nonexistent terrors which drive him hither and yon without intelligent plan or reason. Overcome with the passion of patriotism, the citizen of the modern nation state is ever ready to sacrifice his life and the lives of his loved one's to the mythical good which politicians foist upon him, never once realizing that the ideals which motivate him are pneumatic and without ethical substance. Fortunately, Robinson held, the authority by which government sustains itself is a "figment of the imagination" and can thus be modified to the extent that men gain new visions of how life should be lived. The wise man, according to Robinson, "has no reverence for 'The State.' He knows that 'The Government' is but a set of men—mostly as big fools as he is himself, many of them bigger. If the State does things that benefit him, he will support it; if it attacks him and encroaches on his liberty, he will evade it by any means in his power." The idea of anarchism stems from the proposition that freedom is impossible where an established order is imposed upon people from above. Either each of us takes personal responsibility for our own actions or we must surrender our rights to the state. In this connection "we have yet to learn that, with the most benevolent intentions in the world, no one can rule over another without oppressing him," Robinson urged. "If we grant power to anybody to order us about, we soon find that their notion of what is good for us is very different from our notion."[35] Tyranny thus starts at the precise point at which we abandon our own powers of self-rule.

Like most anarchists, Robinson applied his convictions to the relations between the sexes, arguing that marriage as it was then practiced among men and women was not the "happy and voluntary living together of men and women" but an unhappy situation in which the institution dominated the lives of those it was supposed to serve. "Marriage is a club," Robinson laconically proclaimed: "Now I have got you; if you try to get away, I will club you."[36] To make compulsion under law the cement which binds couples together is to render marriage a form of human slavery. How much more satisfactory it would be if people were left to their own devices. Were force eliminated from the marriage scene, only people who truly loved each other would remain joined together, thereby making the institution a joyful one rather than the miserable hell it now so often is. In answer to those who pessimistically prophesied the end of all normal sexual relations, Robinson, with the faith in man's social nature which is characteristic of all anarchists, asked: "Is it possible, if people ever loved each other, that they would leave each other lightly!" Happily joined to a woman in his own personal life, John Beverley Robinson was ready to leave all structured social institutions behind and fly for safety into nature's arms, confident that the love he experienced was not unique but the common possession of all humanity.

The life of Stephen Tracy Byington (1868-1957) once again illustrates the proposition that any attempt to define anarchism in hard and fast ideological terms is bound to be deceptive. Born in Benson, Vermont, where his father, a graduate of Andover Theological Seminary, celebrated the initiation of his first parish, Stephen Byington received a better than average secondary education, studying in Burlington High School and Castelton Normal School before matriculating at the University of Vermont from which he graduated Phi Beta Kappa and *cum laude* in 1891. Familiar with ten languages, he could read and write classical Greek with ease and was proficient in Hebrew and Arabic which he taught himself as an undergraduate. Byington then spent the next two years studying theology at Union and Oberlin but never chose to follow the call to the ministry, taking up school teaching instead, first at Eddytown, New York, and later in Flushing Institute on Long Island. When he was thirteen Byington resolved to translate the Bible when he was able, and this became a major goal of his life. Completing his mission at the age of 87, he was disappointed to find that no publisher was willing to risk the huge outlay of cash which the publication of his translation would necessitate.

Known as "the Bard of Ballardvale," in Massachusetts, where he had settled down in the family's ancestral home, Byington commuted daily to Boston for several decades where he worked as a proofreader for Ginn and Company until his death in 1957 at the age of eighty-eight. Writing to Agnes Inglis, the archivist of American anarchism, Pearl Tucker Johnson aptly characterized Byington when she observed that "he was a good churchman but not a bigot."[37] From time to time Byington preached a sermon from the pulpit of Union Congregational Church in Ballardvale, of which he was a member, and it was said that he never climbed into his bed without first saying his prayers on bended knees. Ostensibly, it would appear Byington had not totally broken with the "god idea" which Proudhon and Bakunin so vehemently warned anarchists against. But Byington's training in theology and his commitment to Christianity apparently had no adverse effect upon his social thinking, for it was from the Bible with which he was so familiar that he derived at least one of his favorite arguments in support of anarchism. Referring to the books of Judges and Samuel,

Byington took as his text the argument that "where once 'there was no king in Israel, every man did that which was right in his own eyes,' and when the people wanted to establish a regular government God said they were 'rejecting him,' giving the king the allegiance that belonged to God."[38] Like many other American anarchists, Byington found nothing contradictory between his commitment to Christianity and his eternal allegiance to anarchism.

Hardly had Byington graduated from college when he became an ardent Tuckerite, contributing frequent pieces to *Liberty* until that organ closed up shop. In the initial stages of his intellectual development, Byington, much like Tucker, emphasized the deep roots which anarchism had in the American political tradition. Related to ancestors who had come over on the Mayflower, Byington further traced his lineage to Roger Sherman, a signer of the Declaration of Independence and a coauthor of the Constitution of the United States. Nurtured by such deep roots in Yankee culture, Byington could speak with self-confidence as to the nature of the American dream. Just as the Founding Fathers of the republic were forced to resort to passive resistance in order to protect themselves from tyranny, he argued, so later day Americans must resort to active opposition when government attempts to trespass on their rights and privileges. Much too well-bred to savor the idea of violence, however, Byington rejected the tactics of propaganda by deed in favor of propaganda by idea. Although not every anarchist is necessarily a nonresistant, he held, all genuine nonresistants are necessarily anarchists. Where free speech is maintained as in America, the followers of the anarchist idea properly rely upon education as a means of carrying off the social revolution. It was in pursuit of this idea that he orgainzed a letter writing corp among the readership of *Liberty* and other anarchist journals for the purpose of swaying popular opinion in the direction of libertarian goals. A new "target" was chosen from time to time—a particular newspaper, public official, or group of people—and the members of the corp were pledged to shoot their arrows at the designated mark. Another of the projects that Byington sponsored was the sale of stickers which bore anarchist messages designed to be affixed to letters sent through the mails.

But Byington did not subscribe to the notion that anarchists must be totally passive and ineffectual in the face of tyranny at the hands of government. Following Tucker's view, Byington argued that the employment of force is wrong wherever it invades the privacy of another individual, and to this extent all anarchists are pacifists. But where force is used by another individual or organization against the rights or privacy of an innocent party, the proper remedy is a like amount of force for the purposes of discouraging the invader. Since all anarchists see government as a fundamental threat to the individual, Byington was of the opinion that the proper outlook for the anarchist is a "practical disregard of law whenever possible, and passive resistance when there is a hope of accomplishing anything."[39] In the tradition of Thoreau, Byington went so far as to urge that no self-respecting anarchist should pay any tax or tariff imposed upon him by government when there is the least possibility that the penalty for not doing so will be less than the cost of evading the law. "We are lost among so large a throng that the danger of persecution is slight; yet that throng is materially strengthened, and this branch of contempt for law materially forwarded, by the presence of even a few who practice tax-dodging as an intelligent and public-spirited policy."[40] Obviously Byington felt that a healthy contempt for the existing law is an essential principle of anarchist theory.

But Byington, like all the plumb-liners of the Tuckerite school, was far from being a nihilist, for he visualized a society in which order was very much a part of the everyday world of social and business life. An individualist to the core, Byington argued that the best source of social regulation in society is the ego of the individual concerned, and hence he insisted that all social order be generated spontaneously by those who feel the need for it. Practically, of course, no social order could ever hope to be totally free of conflict and violence, and the anarchist must thus be prepared to meet the demand for a working solution to this problem. Byington met this question by arguing that in an anarchist society all law and order would be the product of voluntary groups of individuals who would unite for specific purposes and goals. In a large city, for example, groups of property owners might band together to provide themselves with fire protection, sanitation and welfare services, and even a police force to keep the peace in some specific instance when disorder made self-defense absolutely imperative. So long as these kinds of services are voluntary on the part of those who wish to support them and no one is forced to participate against his will, Byington argued, this would not be government. For "government is not government unless it monopolizes its business within its boundaries," he insisted.[41]

However farfetched it may appear to us in the advanced stages of centralization and hierarchy we now suffer, Byington's solution to the problem of social conflict and disorder was eminently sensible. Rather than treat the social offender to prison as punishment for his misdeeds, Byington proposed that the community use "the one weapon whose use is strictly non-invasive, yet whose disciplinary power cannot be surpassed," the boycott.[42] As uncomfortable as it may be for the individual who suffers social ostracism, surely it is less cruel for the community to cut him off from all social intercourse than it is to lock him up or hang him, as is presently done. Rejecting the state, as all libertarians must, Byington would leave all discipline to voluntary groups within society so that the formal lines of oppression and injustice would have no chance to take form. Reflecting the influence of pragmatism, he reminded some of his friends that "Anarchists ought to be the last of men to imagine that people can be made either free or prosperous by any device but teaching them to care for themselves; and human nature must have taken a new twist if most men can learn anything practical except by experience."[43] Like all the native American individualists, Byington saw liberation as primarily a private affair in which each of us counts as one, steering himself by some individual scheme of utilitarian pains and pleasures.

It was to be expected that Byington, like Tucker, would have a confrontation at some point with the newly emerging forces of anarchist communism, and this was decidedly the case. Reconciled to the view that the differences between individualists and collectivists were "largely congenital, and cannot be gotten rid of by education," Byington nevertheless maintained contact with all branches of the movement, writing frequently, albeit critically, for the *Firebrand* (later *Free Society*) and other papers of a collectivist outlook. There were a number of occasions when heated differences of opinion separated him and some of the communists, as when he was referred to as rich and well-born by one of his critics in the *Firebrand* group. In self-defense, Byington retorted that in the five years since he had graduated from college in 1891 and ceased to any longer depend upon his father's support, he had been unemployed two and a half years and had had just a little over four hundred dollars a year to live on which he had earned or borrowed.[44] Another minor flurry in which he became caught up was on the question of voting, Byington insisting that it was permissible for anarchists to take to the polls as a show of their strength, thereby lessening the possibility that the established order would attempt to repress the social revolution that anarchism supports.[45] But in every instance, Byington agreed to disagree on minor points of policy or ideology but he never abandoned his belief in anarchism, insisting to the end that in a libertarian society there will be plenty of room for individualists as well as communists. "The truth in this matter is that Anarchism allows both Communism and Commercialism," he wrote. "Those who wish to unite in the communistic enjoyment of the products of their labor will be free to do so; those who wish to hold the products of their labor as private property will be equally free to do so."[46] Anyone who would interfere with another person's wishes in this regard, he argued, is no anarchist. In answer to the communist's argument that man's basic nature requires him to unite with others in society, Byington conceded the point but went on to maintain that social order does not necessitate that the individual give up his freedom which is the essential mark of a real libertarian society. Where men are free to unite voluntarily, or stay apart if that is what they desire, the possibility of a real social unity opens up.[47]

To the end of his days Byington remained both an individualist and an anarchist, consistently denying that there was any conflict between these two positions. Shuffling about Ballardvale in an old tattered greatcoat and sneakers, his head bared to the heat of summer and the chill of winter, he became something of a local celebrity in his particular corner of Massachusetts, climbing mountains until he was 82. Byington never married, and for most of his years he lived with his mother who was blind. Although he stuttered in personal conversation, his voice never faltered when speaking from pulpit or lectern and he was widely sought after as a public speaker. Very responsive to young people, he endeared himself to his fellow townspeople by his hearty individualism, his eccentricity, and his genuine love of life. Serenaded with carols at Christmas time, he would stand in the doorway of his mother's home, his long white beard flowing in the wind, singing back carols in many different languages.[48] Anarchists like Stephen Byington, it would seem, were overlooked when Congress sought to curb their entry into this country, for they were already widely distributed throughout the population and could not be recognized from the ordinary citizens until they held forth on their views toward government.

It was not at all incongruous that Edward H. Fulton, of Columbus Junction, Iowa, chose July Fourth as the date to launch his *Age of
Thought* in 1896, for Fulton, like all the followers of Benjamin
Tucker, was solidly American in his outlook and opinions. Nestled
close to the soil among the rows of mid-west corn which surrounded
him, Fulton drew inspiration from many of the original Warrenites,
such as William B. Greene and Stephen Pearl Andrews. Dedicating
his journal to a libertarian program of freedom, including the free
use of land, free banking, and an unalterable opposition to all special
privilege and arbitrary authority, Fulton serves as an example of the
radical implications which individualism can have in the hands of an
American patriot. Although he was not in the least unsympathetic to
the ideas of Bakunin and Kropotkin, as witnessed by the fact that he
habitually advertised their writings for sale in the five different
journals that he edited at one time or another during his libertarian
career, Fulton derived the outline of his political philosophy directly
from the American experience in good pragmatic fashion. The great
American Revolution might well have been over at his coming of age
but Fulton was not willing to let go of the political principles for
which his ancestors had fought and died. Speaking out with boldness
and moral indignation seldom seen since the days of the Boston Tea
Party, Fulton proclaimed the ultra-radical view that "All compulsory
taxation is robbery, and should be resisted with the most prudent and
effective forces at command at any given time."⁴⁹ When Fulton spoke
of resistance to invasion by government, he was not speaking ir-
responsibly but merely drew from the heritage of rebellion laid down
by another staunch American, Wendell Phillips, who had argued that
'Nihilism is the righteous and honorable resistance of a people crushed
under an iron rule."⁵⁰ Heir to the kind of moral courage expressed by
Phillips, Fulton subscribed to the view that it is the right of every
American to enjoy complete freedom from the tyranny of unwanted
governmental control.

Had Fulton stopped here, he would have been indistinguishable
from the Liberal who substantiates his cherished individual freedoms
upon the theory of natural rights outlined by Locke. But Fulton, a
long-time subscriber to Tucker's *Liberty,* had been won over to the
libertarian position and would have none of the watered-down political philosophy brewed by Liberals. In the second of the journals he
was to edit, *The New Order,* which was first issued in July of 1919,

Fulton acknowledged his allegiance to the ideas of Tucker when he proclaimed that "the most satisfactory solution of all the political, industrial, and social problems of the world" lies in the theory of non-invasive liberty originally formulated by Josiah Warren and made a household remedy among American radicals by Tucker. Unfortunately Tucker had expatriated himself to France after the disastrous fire in his New York store had destroyed the last reserve of will which had kept him going as the uncrowned leader of the native-born American anarchists. It was undoubtedly to fill the conspicuous gap left by Tucker's departure ten years before that Fulton struggled to launch a worthy successor to *Liberty*. Although Tucker lived until 1939 in his self-imposed exile, and always promised to reissue *Liberty* when his mood should move him in that direction, "he lacked the drive to rouse himself out of his strange lethargy,"[51] and so Fulton felt the need to step into the empty shoes of his mentor. Supported by Stephen T. Byington, who was listed on the mast-head of *The New Order* as an "Editorial Contributor," Fulton condemned all government, including the newly emerged "Soviet Bolshevism," because of the state's tendency always to exert absolute authority over the individual. Government, as Fulton defined it, is "All authoritative regulation of manners and customs . . . exercised by any majority or minority whatever. . . ." Thoroughly consistent in his individualism, he was insistent that the basic outline of all anarchist thought must be the conviction that "the Individual should have complete liberty to pursue his own ends at his own responsibility; inviting the resistance of others by becoming invasive, just as others becoming invasive would meet resistance by him.[52] Fulton, like Byington, would trust to voluntary protective associations formed spontaneously by groups of individuals for the protection of their private interests on a temporary basis rather than in the institution of permanent government which must of necessity be built on a monopoly of force and power. Advocating equal freedom for all people upon a basis of voluntary cooperation, the brand of individualism that he supported contained none of the hypocrisy so evident in the individualism of the Spencerian variety. "Competition, when not truly and completely free, is deplorable," Fulton wrote.[53] Aiming his barbs at the Hamiltonian system of protected industries, he argued that where special classes are benefited by legislation which restricts the operation of other individuals and groups, those who are so benefited become "monopolists or industrial 'despots.' " Fulton voiced the sentiments of all anarchists when he maintained that "Privilege cannot exist without government, nor can government exist without creating special privileges in diverse and sundry forms." The beginning of human freedom, therefore, can only be established when the state is put asunder.

Unhappily *The New Order* was short lived, but its indefatigable editor replaced it with *The 1776 American* starting in January of 1920. Before a year was out, however, this floundered, too, but Fulton stubbornly launched yet another journal in January of 1921, calling it *The Ego* in obvious reference to the inspiration which he, like so many other Tuckerites, had derived from the writings of Max Stirner. Most certainly it was under the influence of Stirner's philosophy that Fulton expressed the thought in *The Ego* that "the one great curse of the human race is the use of force in the imposing of one's will, religion, habit, custom, or moral code upon another."[54] Another prominent Stirnerite was John Basil Barnhill who edited *The Eagle and the Serpent* from London during the late 1890's but who was a native of Xenia, Illinois.[55] Forging an amalgam of the philosophies of such profound thinkers as Nietzsche, Ibsen, Thoreau, Goethe, as well as Stirner, *The Eagle and the Serpent* faithfully reflected the anti-Christian basis of American anarchism when it rejected the idea of altruistic social effort as a condition for personal salvation. Salvation comes not as a gift but as the fruit of individual self-fulfillment. Let us have no more of that foggy notion that a beneficent god sits ready to distribute impartial goodness and mercy to all his creatures, egoists like Stirner and Barnhill urged. "The only remedy for social injustice is this: the exploited must save themselves by enlightened self-interest."[56] Urging his readers to become "as proud as the eagle and as wise as the serpent," Barnhill advocated the thoroughly American precept that resistance to tyranny is the only possible path to freedom. "The great are great only because we are on our knees," Barnhill proclaimed in good libertarian fashion. If we would be free, he cryptically remarked, "Let us rise!" Seldom has there been a more accurate expression of the basic revolutionary nature of philosophic egoism than this.

Taking off from where Barnhill left off, Fulton saw individualism as the common ground upon which all libertarians stand. Although he was a convinced individualist himself, Fulton saw no basic contradiction between the respective viewpoints held by individualists and communists, at least so far as economic questions were concerned. "Economic forms or ways of life are matters of individual choice," he held, "and anarchism covers any form that does not deny or infringe on non-invasive individual liberty."[57] An interesting new twist was brought to the pattern of anarchist theory when Fulton sought to revive the name "mutualism" which William B. Greene had brought to American anarchism from the writings of Proudhon. In an effort to circumvent the thicket of misunderstanding which the many different lines of American anarchism had worked themselves into by the Twenties, Fulton launched a new journal called *The Mutualist* in October of 1925. As he explained the change in names, "the word Mutualism has been chosen in the place of anarchism by the disciples of Tucker" because it more adequately expressed their demand that "all the affairs of men should be managed by individuals or voluntary associations" rather than by the state.[58] Where the state is acknowledged as the central source of authority and action in society, the individual perforce is implicated in a concentric spiral of power and command over which he has no control. Rejecting the Burkean theory of social contract in which each individual shares power not only with his contemporaries but with the full range of his ancestors, and the Hobbesian notion of contract in which power is monopolized by a government whose very legitimacy is determined by its ability to keep a Roman peace, the "social contract of Mutualism" would be "based on the free contract of those living, not a 'contract' made for them by men long dead, and forced upon them." Unlike existing governments, which jealously demand total allegiance from their subjects from the cradle to the grave, and which are always ready to excommunicate those who would question the basic structure of authority, Mutualism would not prevent any member of society from withdrawing from any social or political relationship he might have entered. The chief source of evil under existing systems of government, according to Fulton, is that states, which possess a monopoly of power and are therefore unchecked in all that they might do, are "bound to be arrogant, invasive, tyrannical and despotic." But, he argued, "the preposterous idea that the State or the majority can rightfully do that which is wrong for the individual to do, is a lingering stain of the ancient view that 'the King can do no wrong.' The doctrine of authority, or force, is man's most disastrous error."[59] The virtue of Mutualism, according to Clarence Lee Swartz, an ardent Tuckerite, an associate of Moses

Harman at one time, and a frequent contributor to *The Mutualist,* is that it is "a social system based on reciprocal and non-invasive relations among free individuals."[60] Undoubtedly influenced by the writings of Max Stirner, as all the Tuckerites were during this period, Swartz went on to hold that it was nothing but the sheerest of nonsense to talk about natural or inalienable rights, as so many Lockeans do, for "fundamentally and elementally, there is only one right—the right of might."[61] Let everyone do what he has the strength and the will to do, Swartz argued, and human conduct will again reflect the underlying patterns of social harmony and voluntary cooperation that are to be found in nature. Certain individuals may on occasion seek to tyrannize their neighbors but the pains visited upon them in return would soon teach them to find better ways of getting what they want. Such a system of genuine *laissez-faire,* as distinguished from the ersatz version fashioned by Spencer and the later-day liberals, would not make the elementary mistake of retaining the state as the source of all social and economic regulation, according to Fulton. In theory the state or government is supposed to protect the weak as well as the strong in their rights and privileges, he argued, but in practice it more often "aids the rich against the poor" and gives indescribable advantages to those who have the ability to influence its policies. "A supreme, monopolistic, sovereign state is a dangerous thing, not a necessity," Fulton urged, and the path to liberty lies in the opposite direction from the one we are now taking with regard to governmental control of social and economic relationships. The depth of Fulton's commitment to libertarian philosophy is evident in his assertion that the "present public schools are State communistic institutions— owned by the State."[62] Arguing that ownership implies control, Fulton warned his contemporaries that their unrestrained enthusiasm for public education was an extremely dangerous preoccupation. Fifty years later we can begin to appreciate the validity of Fulton's concern.

However much he might have desired to see himself called by another name, Fulton was thoroughly and consistently anarchistic in his social philosophy. "I do not advocate the mere reforming of laws to render them less objectionable," he wrote, "for that would be a virtual admission of the fundamental right of the law, which I deny. I am out-and-out for the absolute repeal of every and any law that assaults non-invasive individual liberty."[63] It is this fundamental distinction that separates the anarchist from the liberal and makes him the thoroughgoing libertarian he is. Although Edward H. Fulton was not the best known of American anarchists, he was certainly one of the most persistent. Unhappily the momentum which anarchism had enjoyed in Tucker's heydey was now spent and Edward H. Fulton's efforts to revive the movement were futile; times had changed and the arguments of individualism fell upon deaf ears, at least for the moment.[64]

NOTES

SECTION II - CHAPTER 6

1. A. P. Kelly, "Masters and Slaves," *Liberty*, II (September, 1884), 4.

2. "On Picket Duty," *Liberty*, II (October, 1883), 1.

3. "John Swinton on Lawyers," *Liberty*, I (June 1882), 2.

4. "Plumb-Line or Cork-Screw, Which?" *Liberty*, IV (April, 1886), 5.

5. Gertrude Kelly, "Association as a Means of Reform," *Liberty*, IV (November 26, 1886), 5.

6. Gertrude Kelly, "Stemming the Tide with a Pitchfork," *Liberty*, III (March 6, 1886), 4.

7. *Liberty*, IV (July 31, 1886), 1.

8. *Ibid.*

9. "Auberon Herbert on Dynamite," *Liberty*, X (July 14, 1894), 4.

10. "Man of Principle Vs. Time Server," *Lucifer the Light Bearer* (April 16, 1887), 2.

11. "Passive Resistance," *Liberty*, VI (October 13, 1888), 4.

12. "A Consistent Christian Reformer," *Liberty*, X (December 14, 1895).

13. "Individualism in Ethics," *Liberty*, IX (September 12, 1893), 3.

14. "Evolution of Revolutionary Thought," *Liberty*, VI (May 18, 1889), 5.

15. *Anarchism: Its Aims and Methods* (Boston, 1887), p. 17.

16. "Political Salvationists," *Liberty*, IX (October 29, 1892), 3.

17. See: "Individualist on Philosophical Anarchism," *The New Encyclopedia of Social Reform*, ed. by William D. P. Bliss and Rudolph M. Binder (New York, 1908); "Philosophical Anarchism (1880-1910), *"The Journal of Social Philosophy*, VI (April, 1941); "Philsophical Anarchism: Its Rise, Decline, and Eclipse," *The American Journal of Sociology*, LXI (January, 1936).

18. *Our Revolution; Essays in Interpretation* (Boston, 1920), p. 7.

19. *Liberty*, X (June 1, 1895), 4.

20. In: *Free Vistas*, II, ed. by Joseph Ishill (Berkley Heights, New Jersey: 1937), p. 307.

21. Biographical Sketch by Henry Replogle, in James Walker's, *The Philosophy of Egoism* (Denver, 1905).

22. Introduction, "Egoism," *Liberty*, IV (April 9, 1887), 7.

23. "Egoism's Purpose and Whyfore," *Egoism*, IV (May, 1890), 1.

24. *The Philosophy of Egoism, op. cit.*, p. 52.

25. "A Letter of Protest," *Liberty*, V (August 13, 1887), 7.

26. *The Philosophy of Egoism, op. cit.*, p. 2.

27. Unpublished notes of Agnes Inglis, Labadie Collection, The University of Michigan.

28. James J. Martin, *Men Against the State*, (New York, 1957), p. 267.

29. "Compulsory Vaccination," *Liberty*, X (June 2, 1894), 2.

30. *Rebuilding the World*. (n.p., 1917), p. 16.

31. "A Business Government," *Liberty*, X (November 17, 1894), 2.

32. "Ethics," *Liberty*, XIII (December 2, 1897), 6.

33. "Egoism," *Reedy's Mirror* (September, 1915), 1.

34. *Ibid.*, 5.

35. *Rebuilding the World, op. cit.*, p. 15.

36. "The Abolition of Marriage," *Liberty*, VI (July 20, 1889), 6. [Originally read as a lecture before the Manhatten Liberal Club.]

37. Letter from Pearl Johnson to Agnes Inglis, May 27, 1942, Labadie Collection, The University of Michigan.

38. "Items of Anarchist History," *The Firebrand*, II (July 5, 1896), 4.

39. "What Anarchism Means," *Liberty*, XIII (October, 1897), 5.

40. "Passive Resistance Today," *Liberty*, XIV (July, 1903), 2.

41. "What is Anarchism?" *Liberty*, XIII (May, 1899), 2.

42. "Quasi-Invasion and the Boycott," *Liberty*, X (May 19, 1894), 2.

43. "A Difference in Opinion," *The Firebrand*, II (March 29, 1896), 2.

44. "Commercialism and Anarchism," *The Firebrand*, II (April 26, 1896), 2.

45. "More of How to Get It," *The Firebrand*, II (August 2, 1896), 4.

46. "Propaganda Methods," *The Firebrand*, II (August 2, 1896), 2.

47. "Apologies for Governmentalism," *Liberty,* X (September 8, 1894), 3.

48. Letter from Ruth A. Sharpe to William O. Reichert, August 25, 1969.

49. "Statement of Principles," *Age of Thought,* I (July 4, 1896), 4.

50. "The Scholar in a Republic," *Speeches, Lectures, and Letters,* II (Boston, 1900), p. 357.

51. Charles A. Madison, "Benjamin R. Tucker: Individualist and Anarchist," *The New England Quarterly,* XVI (September, 1943), 467.

52. "Statement of Principles," *Age of Thought, op. cit.*

53. "Editorial," *Age of Thought,* II (December 11, 1897), 5.

54. *The Ego,* III (January 1, 1921), 1.

55. James J. Martin, *op. cit.,* p. 267 f.n.

56. *The Eagle and the Serpent* (February 15, 1898), 3.

57. "The Tolerant Attitude," *The Mutualist,* VI (March-April, 1927), 14.

58. "Editorial," *The Mutualist,* V (October 11, 1926), 5.

59. "Editorial," *The Mutualist,* V (December 1, 1926), 14.

60. "The Practicability of Mutualism—I," *The Mutualist,* V (December 1, 1926), 2.

61. "The Practicability of Mutualism—II," *The Mutualist,* VI (January 1, 1927), 6.

62. "Public and Private School Control," *The Mutualist,* I (October, 1925), 17.

63. "The Question of Method," *The Mutualist,* V (August 1, 1926), 5.

64. In recent years a number of journals have appeared which reflect the extreme individualist point of view once again. See for example: *Fragments, A Quarterly Journal of Individual Opinion; Outlook, The Libertarian Monthly;* and *The Modern Utopian.* Among the books that express the individualist point of view are Murray N. Rothbard, *For A New Liberty* (New York: Macmillan Co., 1973); Jerome Tuccille, *Radical Libertarianism* (Indianapolis: Bobbs-Merrill Co., 1970); and John Hospers, *Libertarianism* (Los Angeles: Nash Publishing Co., 1971).

Conflicting Pressures: The Red and the Black

CHAPTER 1

Burnette G. Haskell: Grand Sachem of Anarchism's Epigoni

Like the roaring surf that pounds against the California shore with majestic fury but which soon spends itself to become a gentle ebbing flow of sea spray and foam, Burnette Gregg Haskell (1857-1907) brought considerable tumult to the idea of anarchism in America but ultimately left no lasting philosophical imprint of his own upon its form and substance. Born of pioneer parents who had prospered in their new home in California's Sierra County, Haskell was destined to become a professional man and was accordingly sent off to a number of different educational institutions to be polished and refined. Always erratic and undisciplined in his personal conduct, however, Haskell was an unsteady student and had difficulty in staying long with any established course of study, despite a certain native brilliance of mind. Flitting from one college to another, he entered Oberlin without completing any courses, became a first year student in mining engineering at the University of Illinois at age eighteen, without completing the requirements, and sojourned briefly at the University of California. Somewhere along the way he picked up enough

201

legal training to pass the California bar exams in 1879 but his career at law, like everything else he attempted, was spasmodic and unpredictable. An uncle, acting no doubt in answer to the plea of Haskell's worried parents, offered the young dilettante the editorship of the weekly newspaper he had established in San Francisco called *Truth*, and Haskell, who had studied the printing trade at one time, eagerly accepted the offer sometime after his twenty-fifth birthday. As far as can be determined, Haskell, up to this point of his life, was conventional in his politics, even if he were erratic in his personal actions. But as editor of *Truth* the new Burnette Haskell came into being and the anarchist movement felt the reverberations of his ideological rebirth for years to come.

No sooner had Haskell tacked up an editor-in-chief sign over his door when the one-man operation he was involved in necessitated that he cover a meeting of the Trades and Labor Assembly, one of the earliest labor organizations to be formed in California. Listening to the impassioned diatribes against management delivered by the union leadership, Haskell was immediately persuaded to the side of the workingman and he impetuously offered to devote the full services of *Truth* to the Trades and Labor Assembly.[1] No doubt Haskell's uncle was furious at not being consulted by his nephew before this momentous decision was made but the problem was resolved when the union leadership became frightened by the rapid progress the young man was making in his flight into the arms of labor and before many months had passed the deal was called off. Refusing to be deterred in his newly-discovered interest, Haskell read vociferously on the subject of labor unrest until "he was known as the best read man in the California labor movement." As energetic as he was enthusiastic, he embraced the labor movement with an overpowering bear-hug, totally oblivious to the fact that his affections were not altogether welcome. "A tall, slender, blond man, rather good-looking, with his bright eyes and fair mustache, he was soon a familiar figure at every gathering of workers." Before long Haskell referred to himself as a socialist, and soon thereafter he pinned the colors of anarchism to his masthead, without ever reconciling the possible contradictions which these two commitments might in some circumstances cause. When Burnette G. Haskell decided upon a course of political action or a shift in ideological commitment, it was full speed ahead and damn the consequences.

Spurned by the labor union people he had sought to befriend,

Haskell, who displayed very definite characteristics of the Romantic mood in his thinking, gave vent to his imagination and invented a radical organization of his own complete with secret membership lists and elaborate machinery for concealing the identities of its members. Known at first as "The Invisible Republic," Haskell thought better of the title, renaming it "The Illuminati," and then, finally, "The International Workingmen's Association." Fashioned after the First International in which Marx and Engels had been active, Haskell's organization was stronger in organizational structure than it was in ideology or political theory, its most distinctive feature being a system of interlocking memberships which permitted each member to know no more than sixteen other members. Attached to a basic cell comprised of a total of nine individuals, each member of the cell was responsible for the formation of a new cell, so that a membership explosion could take place without any possibility of a mass crackdown by the authorities. Once again Haskell offered *Truth* to the new organization. And since he was largely in charge of the International's helm, this time the offer was graciously accepted, plunging *Truth* into the maelstrom of labor dissent and subsequently into the shifting pattern of anarchist ideas.

In the initial stages of his editorship, Haskell seemed to have difficulty finding his bearings and his reading public must have in turn found it difficult to comprehend just where it was being taken. On the one hand, *Truth* appeared to steer the straight course of American patriotism, paying unabashed tribute to God and country. ". . . we claim the right to do our little toward preserving and purifying the splendid State whose mighty hand extends its gracious protection over our earthly destinies," the audacious young editor wrote at one point.[2] Not content to do the work of the California Chamber of Commerce free of charge, Haskell sung the praises of his nation state as well. "Every child in our public schools, should be taught to reverence and love this Republic, bound as it is by the seas, walled by the wild air, domed by heaven's blue and lit with the eternal stars," Haskell wrote in a burst of patriotic inspiration. "They should be taught hourly to love this, our country, and to keep it pure; because to love it is to love liberty; because liberty is religion, and because those states fall where the national banner are (sic) degraded by the men who should bear them aloft."[3] In later years after he had drunk his fill from the cask of anarchism and found that its spirits did not

mix well with his intellectual juices, Haskell joined the forces of
Bellamy's nationalist movement, giving full vent to the patriotic feelings he obviously harbored in the deeper regions of his psyche. But in
his youth he rarely stood still long enough to really understand the
full implications of his own professed beliefs. Most surely this must
have been the case when *Truth* reported in all seriousness the in-
corporation of the California Improvement Corporation which
claimed that it had perfected a method of helping men to grow to the
height of twelve feet, although the company had not as yet fixed the
schedule of prices it would charge for this service.[4] In another issue
it was announced that a demonstration had been conducted in which
the human soul was made plainly evident to the naked eye, while a
little later *Truth* revealed that some Chicago scientists had "caught
and caged" human mental power in a little black bottle[5] and that the
planet Mars had "flashed a telegram in living light to the scientific
expert of *Truth.*"[6] If Haskell had his tongue in cheek through all
this, the bulge in his jaw was not evident to those who stood closest to
him, for those who knew him best never for a moment doubted his
seriousness of purpose. The truth was that Haskell was not a lighthearted or jocular individual and we are led to conclude that everything that appeared in *Truth* was written in dead earnest, however
wild it might appear to its readers.

One of the earliest windmills against which Haskell tilted was on
the Chinese question, an issue which was red-hot among west coast
laboring men. All through 1882 and in subsequent years *Truth*
editorialized again and again on the dangers of cheap Chinese labor to
the labor movement of this country. Stealing a page from Karl Marx
whom he badly interpreted, Haskell called upon laboring men and
women to organize against the yellow peril in the same way that
captialists combine and consolidate themselves in order to gain an
advantage in strength. "God helps those who help themselves," he
wrote. "The soldiers of honest industry who wield the sword of labor
in the battle ranks of life are the hope and reliance of the good people
of our golden State. Any relief from the mongolian curse must come
from them as the source of power."[7] Not only should workers write
their congressmen and senators to legislate against cheap Chinese
labor, Haskell emoted in very dubious anarchist fashion, but they
should support in every way the League of Deliverance which had been
formed for the specific purpose of combatting the Chinese workman

as he sucked the life-blood from the veins of the American working-man. Trying his hand at more subtle methods of propaganda, Haskell ran a story titled "Smoke," which described the plight of a beautiful young American girl, Nellie Brown, convicted of prostitution she was forced to turn to when she could not find a job as a consequence of cheap immigrant labor. "Nellie Brown is crouching now on the damp and filthy floor of a prison cell. She is friendless, loveless, and home-less," Haskell maudlinly observed.[8] "Do you have a Chinaman to do your washing and housework?" he candidly queried his readers. "Do you buy Chinese cigars and shoes? Are you one of those SCOUN-DRELS who act as procurers to drive the pure girls of free America to SHAME and a PRISON CELL." Although Haskell's tears for Nellie Brown might have been strained, his concern for the plight of the American cigar makers was undoubtedly genuine, for the situa-tion in that industry on the west coast was very perilous with over three-fourths of the workers being of Chinese origin. In October of 1885 a strike took place among the Chinese workers of the firm of Koenigsberger, Falk and Mayer when forty of them refused to work alongside white workers, indicating that both sides in the conflict had adopted the same rules and methods of combat.[9] But no anarchist would ever assume the stance on this issue that Haskell did, unless of course, he was not really an anarchist at all.

A rough content analysis of *Truth* reveals that Haskell had ex-cellent intentions so far as his commitment to anarchism was con-cerned, for he consistently made room for material that had an authentic anarchist flavor, running serialized versions of the works of Bakunin, Kropotkin, Johann Most, Proudhon, Albert Parsons, and Henry Appleton. But Haskell's editorial tastes were as broad as the Pacific horizon his native San Francisco looked out on and there seemed to be little rhyme or reason to the selections he made. Ap-parently Haskell considered the ideas of Patrick Henry and Henry George to be of equal weight to those of John Swinton, H. M. Hynd-man, and Karl Marx. There is, to be sure, much that is compatible in the ideological viewpoints of Marxism and anarchism. But Haskell, like the indiscriminate lovers of wine or philosophy Plato warned us against, embraced all radical ideas with equal enthusiasm just so long as they were sufficiently radical to wet his taste for social action. Few anarchists would find anything to quarrel with in *Truth's* asser-tion that the bayoneting of an innocent bystander by militia called out to keep order in the labor dispute with the Burlington and Missouri Railroad in Omaha, Nebraska in 1882 was a species of state crime which clearly demonstrated the moral degradation of government.[10] But when Haskell rambled on to the further proposal that the existing political order, once it had been overthrown by the oppressed, should be replaced by "a cooperative form of government instituted for the benefit of the workers and not the loafers of the world," one could not blame anarchists like Benjamin Tucker for raising their eyebrows, or for even blurting out as Tucker did in an editorial that he had come to regard Haskell as "mentally lost, intellectually untrustworthy and an unsafe guide for the multitude of persons just awakening to an interest in the labor cause."[11] Tucker was correct when he accused Haskell of flying into the arms of authority in his efforts to secure the laboring man the full share of his labor power, for as an avowed state socialist Haskell had no objection whatever to force and compulsion as techniques of government rule so long as they were firmly gripped in the hands of labor. Like all state socialists, the weakness of Haskell's position is clearly visible in the formula by which he would establish social justice. On the one hand he insisted that workingmen should be guaranteed equal opportunities to labor and an equitable share of the rewards which industry brings to society. Yet he saw nothing amiss in the proposition that "Society should compel all people to labor,"[12] or that "The State must be the only employer and distributor of the products of labor."[13] In opposition to Tucker, who on this issue had almost every anarchist who ever lived behind him, Haskell advanced the ridiculous proposition that "the capitalistic state founded on force and fraud is entirely distinct from the Socialistic state founded on free association and justice."[14] How Haskell could have made such a monumental mistake in judgment as to argue for any form of state after reading the works of Proudhon, Kropotkin, and Bakunin must remain one of the unsolved mysteries of nineteenth-century anarchism, unless one concludes that he did not bother to read the copy he inserted in his journal to fill the interstices of his scattered and confused thoughts.

An even more glaring example of Haskell's ideological confusion is evident in his treatment of the problem of violence. Many anarchists have argued that violence is something inherent in the structure of an organized society and that its outbreak is inevitable as those on the bottom of the social pile seek to shake those above them off their

backs. But to glorify violence in the way that Haskell did, as though
it were a positive principle of anarchist doctrine, is to go much too far.
In fairness to Haskell it should be pointed out that the game of violence is one in which there can be unlimited players, and Haskell was
not the first person on the west coast to enter the fray. During the
sailor's strike of 1891-1893, the Ship Owners Association made an
all-out effort to crush the Coast Seamans Union which Haskell had
helped establish. There were acts of malicious destruction perpetrated
by both sides of the controversy. Dynamite charges were discovered in
the holds of ships, rioting swept up and down the wharves, and the
police were used again and again in support of the ship owners. In
December of 1893 Haskell went to court to defend a sailor charged
with placing a suitcase full of dynamite in front of a non-union board-
ing house in San Francisco which had killed eight men. Haskell won
the case, arguing that the dynamite had been planted by the ship
owners as an effort to discredit the union in the eyes of the public. Yet
Haskell was given at times to extremely loose talk concerning the
employment of violence, running an article titled "Dynamite; The
Plain Directions For Making It" in *Truth* in April of 1883, and following this up with an editorial which held that the leaders of the New
York Central Labor Union fully approved of its use.[15] On another
occasion Haskell revealed to an academician who was interviewing
him that "he had manufactured bombs and hidden them in valises,
with a view to blowing up the Hall of Records in San Francisco and
so causing an inextricable confusion in land titles."[16] Haskell's
willingness to give public approval to the deliberate use of violence
would indicate that an inability to understand the ultimate consequences of the ideas he expressed was his fatal weakness, for as all
anarchists admit, violence is only legitimate when it is spontaneous
and free from calculated design but never excusable when it is aimed
at the domination of other people or groups. One cannot help but
conclude that it was a mere reflection of Haskell's romanticism that
led *Truth* to carry the announcement that "*Truth* is five cents a copy
and dynamite is forty cents a pound," or to proclaim as its motto:
"War to the palace, peace to the cottage, death to luxurious idleness."
Obviously Haskell never outgrew the political naivity of his youth.

However wild and undisciplined Haskel might have been in his
political philosophy, it is nevertheless true that his efforts in organizing the International Workingmen's Association gave him considerable

influence over the direction of radical politics. Divided into two branches, one on the west coast which Haskell headed, and one for the Rocky Mountain region under the direction of Joseph R. Buchanan, editor of the *Denver Labor Inquirer* and a leading light of the Knights of Labor, the IWA made great progress in organizing American labor, drawing somewhere around six thousand workers into its membership. The IWA drew a great deal of its strength from The Knights of Labor which was then struggling to find a course to follow. But the IWA was not alone in the field of labor organization and it soon received a call to attend a conference of socialists to be held in Pittsburg in October of 1883, the purpose of which was to devise a more centralized organizational structure and a more effective plan of agitation and propaganda. In addition to Haskell's IWA, the other groups involved were the loosely federated autonomous groups of socialists and anarchists on the east coast who generally recognized Johann Most as their chief spokesman, and the revolutionary socialists of the midwest led by Albert Parsons, August Spies, and other members of the Alarm group, who had formed the International Working Peoples Association several years before. Also invited to the Pittsburg Congress was Benjamin Tucker, who more than anyone else spoke for the native American anarchists and individualists who descended from the influence of Josiah Warren. Tucker, however, declined the invitation, although he did send his regrets at not being able to attend and wished the delegates success in their efforts to reconcile the various currents of socialist thought in America.[17] As it turned out, Haskell was himself unable to attend the Pittsburg meeting. But since his head as always was crammed full of schemes and plans, he dashed off an elaborate design of revolutionary action which he sent to August Spies and Joseph Labadie to be presented in his absence. A potpourri which attempted to blend the liberal notion of natural rights with the Marxian theory of labor value, the single tax theory of Henry George, and a smattering of theory from the writings of Proudhon, Bakunin, and other anarchists, Haskell's plan for uniting American labor was doomed from the start. Attempting to placate Tucker and the native Americans by formally rejecting the use of violence, Haskell apparently alienated Most, who made himself the chief antagonist of Haskell's proposal and led the fight on the floor of the congress in opposition to it.[18] Having suffered his Waterloo, Haskell apparently withdrew from revolutionary politics and the labor movement altogether to turn instead to the idea of communal living.

Joining the Kaweah Co-operative Commonwealth in Tulare County, which was located within what is presently California's Sequoia National Park, Burnette Haskell once again allied himself, it would appear, with a facet of the radical movement in America which sought for the liberation of mankind according to its own theory of utopia. Founded in 1886, the colony was composed largely of the followers of Edward Bellamy who were committed to the idea of national socialism. Ostensibly, therefore, Haskell and his associates were engaged in a venture that would deliver yet another blow to the weakening structure of American capitalism. But if Frank Roney, one of the outstanding figures in the labor movement on the West Coast can be believed, the Kaweah Cooperative Colony was far from being a genuine socialistic experiment aimed at the extinction of capitalism. Actually, according to Roney, the colony was "a scheme on the part of Haskell and some of his associates to take up what was supposed to be a large tract of government timber land as individual preemptors, pool it all when title had been acquired, and go into the saw mill and lumber business on an extensive scale."[19] Some of the members of the Coast Seaman's Union were principals in the operation, their palms having been greased by the ever-scheming Haskell. Unfortunately for Haskel and his co-conspirators, powerful lumber and real estate firms in the area were better at playing the game of fraud than they, and Haskell soon found himself in dire economic straights. At his death in November of 1907 Haskell was so impecunious that his corpse would have been unceremoniously cast into Potter's Field in his native San Francisco had not the Sailor's Union he had helped to organize stepped in to give him a decent burial in its own cemetery.[20] During the last fifteen years of his life Haskell had been active in the Nationalist Club of San Francisco, a group whose platform and program were so broad that almost anyone could find shelter under them. From cradle to grave Burnette G. Haskell, it would appear, was consistent in his inconsistency, flitting from pillar to post and never quite certain where he really stood or what he believed in. In the end one cannot help but agree with George Woodcock who argued that Haskell's "links with real anarchism were too slight to be taken seriously."[21]

And yet in one sense Burnette G. Haskell had a profound impact upon the direction that radical politics in America took, for his efforts in bringing the International to this country introduced the very same division between the "Reds" and the "Blacks" that had come out of the organizational meeting of The International Workmen's Association held in London in August of 1862. Socialists all, the more "radical" members of the International lined up behind Bakunin and the black flag of anarchism, while the more "conservative" members, who were the majority in the convention, stuck it out behind the red flag of communism after the design of Marx.[22] Under the guidance of Haskell, the International became organized up and down the West Coast, introducing many American workingmen to their first lessons in Marxian economic and political theory. Joseph R. Buchanan, one of the leading organizers of the movement, acknowledges Haskell as the key figure in the development of Marxian thinking in America. There were, to be sure, natural-born revolutionaries such as Orestes Brownson who developed an untutored form of revolutionary socialism without specific reference to Marx, as well as acknowledged followers of Marx who came to America to escape persecution for their convictions, such as Weydemeyer and Herman Kriege.[23] But Brownson's efforts to organize a revolutionary party came too early to be effective, whereas the German refugees were compelled to confine their operations within the German speaking working class population and were likewise ineffective from the point of view of the mass of Americans. Haskell, for all his intellectual frivolity, was on the spot with the right idea at the right time, and hence his influence on radical political thought in America was immense. From his time forward anarchism in America had to concern itself with tension between the reds and the blacks, those who were predominantly concerned with the introduction of communism as opposed to those who were primarily concerned with stamping out the idea of the state. In the years to come the revolutionary forces in America found it increasingly difficult to focus on a concerted program of action, leading detached observers to conclude that they would all have been better off if they had remained color-blind from the start.

NOTES

CHAPTER XV

1. Miriam Allen deFord, *These Were San Franciscans* (Caldwell, Idaho: 1947), pp. 211-217.

2. "Our Future Course," *Truth* (January 28, 1882), 2.

3. *Truth* (February 4, 1882), 2.

4. *Truth* (February 18, 1882), 1.

5. *Truth* (March 4, 1882), 1.

6. *Truth* (March 11, 1882), 1.

7. *Truth* (February 11, 1882), 2.

8. *Truth* (April 8, 1882), 1.

9. *University of California Publications in Economics,* Vol. XIV (1935), p. 169.

10. "Cold Steel; The Answer that Cruel Capitalists Give the Poor," *Truth* (March 18, 1882), 3.

11. "Has 'Truth' Become a Liar," *Liberty,* (October 6, 1883), 2.

12. "Governments," *Truth* (October 13, 1883), 3.

13. "Salut," *Truth* (February 7, 1883), 1.

14. "The Anarchists," *Truth* (October 27, 1883), 3.

15. "Dynamite," *Truth* (May 19, 1883), 1.

16. deFord, *op. cit.,* p. 216.

17. "On Picket Duty," *Liberty* II (October 6, 1883), 1.

18. Chester McArthur Destler, "Shall Red and Black Unite? An American Revolutionary Document of 1883," *The Pacific Historical Review,* XIV (December, 1945), 437.

19. *Frank Roney; An Autobiography,* ed. by Ira B. Cross (Berkeley, 1931), p. 475.

20. *Ibid.,* p. 391.

21. *Anarchism* (Cleveland, 1962), p. 461.

22. Joseph R. Buchanan, *A Labor Agitator* (New York, 1903), pp. 265-268.

23. David Herreshoff, *American Disciples of Marx* (Detroit, 1967), passim.

CHAPTER 2

Albert R. Parsons and the "Chicago Anarchists"

Had Albert Parsons (1848-1887) been born at a different time or a different place, he would in all probability have lived to a much riper age, and his name, most certainly, would be less well-known than it is. But it was his sad fate to have come upon the American scene precisely at that moment that the nation desperately needed a victim to sacrifice to Moloch, and hence he left this world with a noose burning into the flesh of his neck and the sound of his deathrattle haunting the ears of sensitive Americans for generations to come. This was indeed a strange end for Parsons to come to, for on the record his heritage was as favorable as any American youth might want. His ancestors, passengers on the second voyage of the Mayflower, had been among the pious Puritans who had risked all in the clamor for religious freedom in seventeenth century England.[1] Here in the new world, having found the religious peace they sought, they were active in the political turmoil which had been engendered by the growth of the democratic idea and were all courageous fighters for freedom. One of his paternal grandfathers had carried a musket in the revolution against the mother country, while his great grandfather on his mother's side of the family (the Tompkins-Broadwells of New Jersey) had fought under Washington in some of the most important battles of the war — Trenton, Brandywine, Valley Forge. Samuel Parsons, Albert's father, was a native of Maine and a dedicated Universalist and temperance reformer who moved his family in 1830 to Montgomery, Alabama, where he established a shoe and leather factory to support his ten children. When Samuel Parsons died, Albert, who was then four, was raised by an older brother who was in later years to become inspector of customs at Newport News, Virginia. At the time, however, Parson's brother was engaged in operating a cattle ranch in Johnston County, Texas, and so Albert became an expert horseman as well as a crack shot with a rifle. Coming to manhood in the early

212

years of the Civil War, Albert Parsons could not wait to enlist in the army and impetuously ran away from home at age fifteen to join an artillery unit that was stationed at Sabine Pass, Texas, where another of his brothers, Captain Richard Parsons, commanded an infantry company. When that hitch was up, Albert joined a cavalry brigade, The Lone Star Grays, under the command of his older brother and guardian, Major General William H. "Wild Bill" Parsons, and soon found himself facing the dangers of reconnaissance duty as one of the renowned McInoly Scouts.[2] After four years of war service, Parsons, a hardened veteran of nineteen, mustered out to become a university student in Waco, Texas, concentrating his studies in what was then called "moral philosophy and political economy," or what we would today call political science. Undoubtedly the theoretical foundations of the social beliefs for which he later was to die on the scaffold were laid during this period of his life.

Although we do not know what kind of student Parsons was in terms of academic performance, it is clear that he had a mind of his own, for at the age of twenty he had already started to outgrow the Southern attitudes he had been indoctrinated in as a child.[3] So far had he progressed away from his Southern upbringing that when he was ready to take a wife he chose to marry a girl of Mexican-Indian blood, the beautiful Lucy Eldine Gonzalez, who was not only devoted to him through the years as a spouse but completely faithful to the social values he held. Marrying across racial lines as Parsons had done was then defined as the crime of miscegenation in Austin, Texas, where the event took place, and thus constituted the first of his several encounters with the law. His courage and daring in undertaking such a radical break with social convention is remindful not only of his ancestors' devotion to conscience but his own later martyrdom to an idea. Yet Parsons was not yet ready to break completely with organized political society, for he was elected secretary of the Texas Senate in 1870 and in the following year received an appointment as a deputy of the United States Internal Revenue Service. So far as one could tell from his actions, Albert Parsons fancied himself entitled to enjoy all the benefits and privileges of his native land and was well on his way in the climb to success within the establishment.

In 1875 the Parsons moved east to Chicago where they became increasingly involved in political activity of a different and more dangerous kind. In many ways Albert Parsons' education was just beginning, as he was learning many things as a member of a great mid-western city's labor force that his teachers of political philosophy had failed to mention. He learned, for instance, that major dislocations of the national economy have more serious personal implications for the workingman than they do for the owners and manager of capital. He learned that the worker, who ordinarily owns little beyond his weekly wage and his few meager household possessions, suffers the torments of hell when unemployed during hard times. A devoted family man himself, Parsons knew what it was to come home empty-handed to a wife and hungry children day after day. As his heart swelled with sympathy for the industrial poor, his brain throbbed with resentment of the overfed rich whom he held responsible as the prime cause of all this social discontent. Joining the Knights of Labor and later the Social-Democratic Party, he became an outspoken critic of capitalism, availing himself of every opportunity to inform his fellow proletarians of the injustice of the system. As economic conditions worsened throughout the country, spontaneous outbursts of social unrest took place here and there, making it evident for all to see that the nation was in for even more serious difficulties as a consequence of the clash between the forces of labor and capital. In the summer of 1877 the discontent of railroad employees burgeoned into the first nationwide strike against management and gave labor agitators a perfect opportunity to further the organization of American workingmen. When the railroad strikers in Pittsburg were put down by force in July, Albert Parsons was the principal speaker at a meeting called to protest the incident. For this, according to Alan Calmer, his biographer, Parsons was discharged as a typesetter for the Chicago Times and kept from finding employment for many months by a conspiracy of management which was determined to snuff out the labor trouble once and for all before it spread too far. On one occasion Parsons was physically manhandled and forced to submit to two hours of abuse at the hands of some thirty prominent members of the city's power structure, including the Chief of Police himself; on another, he was warned not to visit the printing shop where he was once employed if he wanted to live out the year. The threat of personal danger only served to cause Parsons to become more determined in his radicalism, however, and he now devoted full time to the revolution he saw just beyond the horizon.

Urging labor to make itself felt at the polls, Albert Parsons threw his support behind the eight hour day movement, then the focal point of labor's program, and pressed for any political action that might strengthen the workingman in his struggle with management. For a time Parsons was perfectly content to work within the established political process, convinced, apparently, that the workingmen and women of the country would ultimately receive justice at its hands. As he learned more and more about the subterranean currents that swirl beneath the mainstream of American politics, however, he gradually developed a class consciousness that brought him into contact with the forces of Marxian thought that were then taking shape in America. By 1878 Parsons had formally begun to think of himself as a socialist, for it was in that year that he took on the editorship of *The Socialist,* an organ of Daniel DeLeon's Socialist Labor Party. One of the organizers of the Social Revolutionary Club, Parsons figured large in the formulation of the "Chicago Idea," which projected the militant trade union as being the vanguard in the proletariat's march to victory.[4] More closely resembling syndicalism than it did anarchism, the Chicago Idea was a reflection of the Marxian precept that the working people of the world were destined to taste the sweetness of victory over capital if only their leaders were sufficiently energetic in their labors. Accordingly, Albert Parsons worked feverishly in the movement then underway to make the working people of America aware of the power that was theirs for the asking. Adopting the view that class warfare is not an abstract doctrine of the future but the chief fact of the existing social structure, Parsons called upon the American working classes to arise and throw off their chains, for the social revolution was under way and nothing further could be gained by waiting.

This is not to suggest, however, that Albert Parsons was chiefly responsible for the fact that the workers of Chicago began to arm themselves for the violence that soon burst into the open. Three years before Parsons became editor of *The Socialist,* a group of German-speaking laboring men formed and began to call themselves the *Lehr und Wehr Vereine.* The counterpart of today's Black Panther organization, the *Lehr und Wehr Vereine* acquainted its members not only with social and political theory but with the techniques of armed resistance to be used in self-defense when attacked by the police. Undoubtedly it was from the *Lehr und Wehr Vereine,* at least in part, that Albert Parsons and other Chicago radicals got the idea of defending themselves with armed force if necessary. However this may have been, Parsons very quickly adopted the view that only armed resistance could be successful in the worker's fight for survival against capital.

Sometime around 1880 Parsons began to refer to himself as an "Anarchist." Actually the practice was not altogether original with him; increasingly referred to as an anarchist by the hostile press, Parsons and other radicals adopted the title more as a matter of convenience than ideological commitment. "We began to allude to ourselves as anarchist," Parsons wrote, "and that name which was at first imputed to us as a dishonor, we came to cherish and to defend with pride."[5]

Becoming editor of *The Alarm* in 1884, Parsons, already a socialist, sought for a means to give expression to the anarchist ideas which increasingly appealed to his common sense as well as the sharply etched patterns of justice that always predominated in his social thought. The rapid pace of his intellectual development during this phase of his life very often left him confused as to who or what he really was or where he stood on crucial social and political questions. But one thing was perfectly clear in his mind and that was that the working classes would have to fight for their freedom from capital.

In a meeting of the English-speaking group of the Canton, Ohio, chapter of the International Working People's Association held just three months before the Haymarket incident, Parsons and his associates distributed red cards amongst the assembled workers which bore the inflammatory inscription: "Private Capital is public theft. Get lead and you'll get bread."[6] And in his address to the disgruntled workingmen who were there assembled, Parsons informed them that in his opinion it was perfectly legitimate for the working classes to fight back against military force if things should come to that. Sounding very much like his ancestors who took down their guns in self-defense in 1776, Parsons argued that liberty is something that one must be prepared to shed his blood for if necessary. "We hold that a people up in arms are a free people," he declaimed. Less American were the economic theories that flavored his words. Taking the same view of historical necessity that characterized the thinking of Marx and Engels, Parsons lectured his audience on the dialectics of the "materialist view" of social development and stressed the need of the working people of America to clear away the tottering ruins of capitalistic civilization so that a new order might be born. "We are destroyers," he admitted, "but only of the bad." Picturing the revolutionary as being in the same desperate position as the trapped animal who must fight his way out of his hazardous predicament if he is to survive, Parsons argued that: "Our struggle is against the present economic institutions, not against men. But insofar as men represent these institutions, they must suffer." Undoubtedly these were the words of a desperate man who had been so totally alienated from the values and institutions of society that he saw no hope save through the instrument of bloody revolution and relentless class conflict; they were also the words of a man who was somewhat unclear as to the precise pattern of his own ideological commitment.

Whatever one may think of the moral implications of Parson's argument, it would be extremely unfair to suggest that he alone was responsible for the violence that so sorely troubled Chicago in his day. As a number of reputable historians have pointed out, the class conflict that gripped Chicago in the last quarter of the nineteenth century was intensified by the hard-nosed opposition of the city's business community in the face of the urgent necessity for social change. "In no city in America," Louis Adamic has written, "was the capitalist's contempt for the public interest stronger than in Chicago. . . ."[7] Openly hostile to the working classes, the rich defiantly paraded their opulence as their brazen answer to the growing social discontent, while their hearts were at the same time gripped by the fear that social warfare would sweep away all the wealth that they had accumulated. Deciding on a policy of crushing the social agitation before it got completely out of hand, a "Citizen's Committee" made up of prominent businessmen urged public officials to take measures adequate to the threat that was presented by labor. Accordingly, units of the state militia were called out, the Chicago Police Department was strengthened by Pinkerton agents and special deputies, and the city girded itself for civil war. With ominous prophecy the Chicago *Mail* appeared on May Day, denouncing Albert Parsons and August Spies as the chief troublemakers in the city and calling for their severe punishment as an object lesson to others should trouble break out. It was not long before the forces of reaction found their opportunity to strike down those who dared to question established authority in Chicago.[8]

The tragic events of the Haymarket bombing is one of the black-

blackest pages of all American history. Brazenly flaunting every principle of civilized behavior, the Chicago Police Department, long known for its brutality and lawlessness, was deliberately used to crush the leaders of the growing social unrest. Rushing into every public meeting of labor with upraised nightsticks, the police seemed to delight in inflicting pain upon the workers without regard as to whether they were disturbing anyone or not. Under these circumstances it became generally agreed that labor could not expect to get a fair hearing in Chicago through conventional political means and the necessity of protecting themselves from police atrocities became real in the minds of such labor agitators as Albert Parsons. As the Haymarket bombing made painfully evident, the police, maintained by public tax funds, were being used to protect the interest of the privileged few.[9]

The events of the Haymarket incident have been too well-documented to require detailed reiteration here. Excited by the trend of events, a huge crowd had assembled in Haymarket Square on the night of May 4, 1886, upon the call of several labor unions, to demonstrate against the police brutality suffered the previous day by strikes at the McCormick Harvester Works. Although only one person had been killed in the McCormick clash, the police had been bestial in their attack, unnecessarily wounding a number of strikers. August Spies had witnessed the bloody melee and had been revolted by the sight of police officers viciously clubbing and firing upon helpless workers who had been knocked to the ground. It was in a belligerent mood, therefore, that the Haymarket meeting had been called by the leaders of the labor movement. Addressed by Spies, Parsons, and Samuel Fielden, the crowd was orderly, although definitely sympathetic to the radical views of those who addressed it. Carter Harrison, the mayor of Chicago, had mingled with those on the edge of the crowd, concluding that since the meeting was peaceful, he could afford to leave it and go home. Driven off by the sudden threat of rain, a crowd was rapidly dwindling when it was approached by a large contingent of police led by Captain John Bonfield, one of the most notorious of those who delighted in breaking the heads of strikers. Confronting the startled speakers who were seated on a wagon before the crowd, the police had just issued the command that the meeting must break up at once when a bomb was thrown from nowhere into the ranks of the police, killing one and wounding almost seventy more, six of whom were ultimately to die of their injuries. As soon as the shock of the bomb's blast had worn off, the police, regrouping themselves under their officers, set upon the crowd of assembled workmen and sent it flying, firing wildly into the terrified mass of humanity as though it was composed of vermin that must be wiped off the face of the earth. Hospitals and drug stores throughout the city were kept busy all night long treating the wounds of the victims who were estimated to be over 200 in number.

Almost immediately a wave of hysteria swept the city, prompted by the sensational headlines of the Chicago newspapers, many of which were outright fabrications. Although the person who threw the bomb was never apprehended or definitely identified, the press spread the word that the deed was the work of an "anarchist" conspiracy designed to completely destroy law and order in the city. Businesses closed their doors and the citizens of Chicago, the victims of an irresponsible press, howled for vengeance for this act of "propaganda by deed." The police, recognizing a good opportunity when it presented itself, hurled themselves into a frenzied search for the perpetrators of this "foul crime," and bombs of all shapes and sizes were soon found all over town in the most unlikely places. Unable to find the specific individual who hurled the bomb, the object of the manhunt became reds and radicals in general rather than any particular person. Led by Captain Michael J. Schacck, an unprincipled incompetent who seized upon this opportunity to satiate his craving for fame and glory, droves of "anarchists" and "communists" were herded into police stations with a melodramatic flourish seldom seen off the stage. When the curtain was finally lowered on the first act of Chicago's greatest extravaganza, thirty-one persons were indicted for murder and a total of sixty-nine lesser crimes, although only eight were finally brought to trial.

As Henry David aptly demonstrates in his *History of the Haymarket Affair,* the trial of the Chicago anarchists—August Spies, Michael Schwab, Adolph Fischer, George Engel, Louis Lingg, Oscar Neebe, and Albert Parsons—was one of the most glaring travesties of justice ever witnessed in this country. The proceedings in the courtroom were more like a comic opera than a serious judicial proceeding. Some years after the trial a prominent Chicago jurist, commenting upon the conduct of Judge Gary, who presided, expressed dismay at the irregularity of what had taken place, writing:

I never was in the courtroom during the trial when Judge Gary did not have on the bench, sitting with him, 3 to 5 women. He seemed to treat the affair as a Roman holiday and so did the women, and the thumbs were all down from the start. One day my wife sat on the bench and Gary showed her a puzzle. [10]

Not only had the police ignored all established rules of procedure in conducting their investigation before the trial but the hysteria that gripped the public made a fair trial impossible, even had the judge been big enough to have permitted one. Although it is difficult to establish the exact truth at this late date, there is strong probability that the Haymarket bomb was not thrown by an "anarchist" at all but by an *agent provocateur* named Rudolph Schnaubelt who was in the employ of the police. Schnaubelt was spirited out of the country before the trial got underway and lived out his life abroad, very likely haunted by the specter of what he had left behind. But the court was not as much concerned with finding the real bomber as it was in trying the defendants it had in hand for their alleged anarchist beliefs. Had the general public been allowed to act upon its impulses, the accused would not have been heard at all but hung at once from the nearest lamp post. Albert Parsons, correctly concluding that he could not expect fair play from the police, had left the city immediately after the bomb had burst and his hideout in Waukasha, Wisconsin was never discovered by the officials. As soon as the trial got under way, however, he dramatically returned and voluntarily presented himself before the court. Parsons believed no doubt that his voluntary return would have the result of demonstrating the strength of his personal character and integrity, thereby aiding the other accused in their defense. But his actions were even more determined by his basic honesty and his sense of social responsibility; not only did he refuse to abandon his co-defendants in their hour of need but he was determined to speak out in praise of the social ideas he loved, whatever the cost might be to himself. The thought that he might hang for his convictions must have entered his mind as he hugged his loving children to his breast as they ran to him each morning before the court proceedings began. Idealist that he was, however, Albert Parsons undoubtedly felt in his heart that the goddess of justice would miraculously appear at the last moment to prevent innocent men from being sacrificed once again to human ignorance and ill will. That he was mistaken in his idealism was not so much to his discredit as it was to that of the social system before which he was on trial.

Although the prosecution announced at the beginning of the trial that it would produce the individual responsible for throwing the bomb, it never made good its claim, and most of its witnesses turned out to be professional informers of highly dubious character and judgment. The defense attorneys were repeatedly informed that since the defendants were being tried for murder, testimony that related to the social convictions of the accused was irrelevant and out of order. Yet when the prosecution summed up its case for the jury in the final hours of the trial, it insisted that anarchism itself was the issue and that society could not rest easy until its nefarious doctrines had been destroyed. Since Parsons and the other prisoners personified anarchism in the minds of the jurors, it was evident that they would never leave prison alive. Parsons and the others, however, were less interested in saving their necks than they were in establishing the exact nature of the social beliefs that they were being tried for.

In regard to the question of whether Parsons was deliberately willing to employ violence as a means of affecting social change, it is extremely difficult to arrive at a clear conclusion. As chief editor of *The Alarm,* Parsons no doubt permitted statements to appear in print which were indeed inflammatory, as when in 1884 *Alarm* editorialized that "Gunpowder brought the world some liberty and dynamite will bring the world as much more as it is stronger than gunpowder."[11] A few weeks later *Alarm* made the terrifying prophecy that "there will be deprived and starving people enough in the United States this winter to strike the first deadly blow at this ancient property system" and announced its determination to incite the people to revolutionary action. "We know of no way to strike," *Alarm* intoned, "but to make a raid on all stores, warehouses, vacant tenements, etc., and open them to the free access of the general public."[12] These were undoubtedly the words of a revolutionary-minded individual who was not afraid of leading his followers to the barricades, at least in theory.

It is to be noted, however, that Albert Parsons, whatever else he may have believed, did not expect that blood would actually flow in the streets. In fact, pressed to act in a real situation, Parsons, like Proudhon, might well have abandoned the barricades to take refuge again in his books and theories, for he was a very sensitive individual and personally had no stomach for violence. Somewhat naively, perhaps, Parsons seemed to have placed his faith in the hope that a revolutionary confrontation of the sort he advocated could be carried off without widespread bloodshed or human suffering. Whether or not blood will be spilled during a revolutionary situation, he argued, will depend upon how ancient the social injustice to be overthrown is and how determined its defenders are in preserving it. Where the revolutionary forces are extremely strong, or at least believed to be strong, he urged, a determined show of power may well bring a bloodless victory. "This is why," he wrote in *Alarm*, "The Communist and Anarchist urges the people to study their schoolbooks on chemistry and read the dictionaries on the composition and construction of all kinds of explosives, and make themselves too strong to be opposed with deadly weapons. This alone can assure against bloodshed."[13] Like the inhabitants of the Kremlin or Pentagon, Parson's mind was clouded by the romantic notion that force can actually bring peace to men on earth. In his opinion the fact that labor had been subjected to violence made it legitimate for the harassed worker to fight back with the same weapons that had been used against him. Yet for all the fire of his language, he thought of himself as basically a pacifist and a devotee of the anarchist idea that force and compulsion should never be exerted against any human being.

Perhaps the most vague area of Parson's thinking was his uncritical acceptance of collectivism as the "only solution" to the conflict between capital and labor. As many anarchists have discovered, Plato knew of what he spoke when he insisted that the quest for social justice must proceed largely along individualistic lines rather than those of mass political action. Where social reformers have chosen the technique of collective force after the fashion of a Lenin or a Stalin, there is acute danger that what starts out as a positive movement for social reform will soon change into an authoritarian organization that is antithetical not only to the original enemy but to its own members as well. Mass organization, as Proudhon so perceptively noted, inevitably necessitates the development of leaders and administrative machinery. And once social reform is thus burdened with a formal structure, there is bound to be a progressive development toward increased authoritarian control, for public administration, whoever controls it, is in essence authoritarian to the extent it leads ever toward more centralization of power. Enthusiastically embracing the attitude of collectivism, the Chicago anarchists opened themselves to the charge that they had broken with the *force majeure* of libertarian philosophy which is a basic commitment to the idea of individual freedom and autonomy. The schism between the individualists and collectivists was present even before Haymarket, of course, but it was not brought out into the open until Parsons, Spies, and the other Chicago anarchists were placed on trial for their beliefs. When *Alarm* made its first appearance in 1884, Benjamin Tucker, speaking for the individualists, welcomed Parsons to the anarchist ranks but reserved final judgment as to whether the paper was authentically libertarian until he had learned more about the views of its editor. It was not long before Tucker observed that *Alarm* "spoils all its support of liberty by opposing the private ownership of capital."[14] Apparently Parsons did not understand, Tucker complained, that all the liberties in the world are useless where the individual does not possess the freedom to own his own tools.

But the economic question was not Tucker's most important criticism of Parsons' anarchism. More fundamental in his opinion was the tendency of the Chicago anarchists to advise the use of force in carrying off their plans for social revolution. Referring to Parsons' claim during the trial that he had not publicly advised the employment of violence in his Haymarket address, Tucker pointed out that whatever he may or may not have said on that particular evening, *Alarm* had for several years advocated a policy of expropriating the instruments of production by any means, employing force and violence if necessary.[15] Observing that August Spies had argued that the bomb would never have been thrown if the police had not attacked the meeting, Tucker found it difficult to accept this line of reasoning. "How do they know?" he demanded. "Have they not been preaching for years that the laborers need no other provocation than their steady oppression by capital to warrant them in wholesale destruction of life and property? Was not this very meeting held for the purpose of advising the laborers to pursue such a policy? Why, then, should they not expect some ardent follower to act upon their advice?"[16] In Tucker's opinion, the Haymarket affair had one beneficial effect and that was to focus attention upon the basic question of how far an anarchist might go in advising armed revolution. Conceding that the right to resist oppression and violence is inviolable, Tucker, engaging in some fancy footwork, danced all around the issue when he maintained that the only remaining question was how far the individual is justified in exercising that right. Holding to his "plumb line" with even more tenacity than usual, Tucker doggedly argued that the only legitimate excuse for the exercise of armed revolution is the necessity of overthrowing a regime that seeks to suppress all freedom of thought, speech, and the press. In Tucker's mind, apparently, violence as a means of self-defense was permissible only when all other alternatives had been tried and found wanting. It never seemed to occur to him that Albert Parsons and the other supporters of the International Workingmen's Association had already concluded that capitalist America was a regime that sought to suppress all freedom of thought, speech, and the press, and that they thought they had good evidence to prove it.

Looking back upon the doctrinal disputes that separated the native born individualist anarchists from the anarchist communists represented by Albert Parsons, it is clear that the credibility gap that divided them was more a matter of changing life styles than it was a question of social or political principles. Tuned to the more simple needs of the pre-industrial era of American development, and steeped in the philosophy of individualism that Emerson and others had preached, Tucker found it difficult to recognize the enormity of the immediate threat that capitalism presented to the workingman. For Parsons and the other wage earners without capital, however, violence at the hands of the capitalist state was not an abstract concept but a real category of everyday experience. Exacerbating the situation was the foreign origin of many of Parsons' associates. August Spies, for example, a native of Central Germany, was a youth of seventeen when he first came to America. Settling in Chicago where he had a number of well-to-do relatives, he worked principally as a furniture maker and after a time found himself the proprietor of a small shop of his own. Upon his arrival in this country he was politically untutored, although he had enjoyed a better than average education in Germany before his father's premature death forced him to go to work. Shocked by the squallor and brutality he witnessed in industrial America, Spies very rapidly became radicalized and determined that he would educate himself in social and political theory. In 1875 he attended his first lecture on the principles of socialism; two years later he joined the Socialist Labor Party, having made up his mind by that time that Marx had more than a little to offer the individual who sought for a real answer to industrial strife. Judged by the fact that he next associated himself with the *Lehr und Wehr Verein,* Spies had come a long way in accepting the concept of class conflict. In the spring of

1880 Spies took over the management of the *Arbeiter Zeitung,* a German language worker's daily, and soon thereafter was made the editor of this largest German paper in the city of Chicago.[17] From that point on, Spies, like Parsons, assumed a major role in educating the proletariat in America to the realities of capitalist society. Not the least of August Spies' transgressions against the American establishment was a statement he issued along with Joseph Labadie at the International's Workingmen's Association Congress held in Pittsburg in October of 1883. "We ought to adopt a method of creating revolutionists," Spies and Labadie exhorted the workers. "Why not begin to proselyte among the young men of America?"[18] Like many another reformer, August Spies soon came to understand how dangerous it is to advocate the corruption of the youth in a land dominated by a powerful ruling class. Allowed to speak in defense of his anarchist convictions after the guilty verdict had been delivered in court, Spies declared that Buckle, Paine, Jefferson, Emerson and Spencer had been the inspiration for his ideological development. From them, as well as from his own bitter experience, he had discovered that the worst of all social orders is a state in which one class dominates and exploits another for its own convenience and supremacy.[19]

Dyer D. Lum who frequently visited the Haymarket anarchists in their death row cells found Spies, a lighthearted "ladies man" in his social relations, to be a clear-sighted realist when it came to recognizing the political implications of radical agitation. Totally composed when the police arrived at the *Arbeiter Zeitung* office after the Haymarket blast to lead him away to jail, Spies, even before the trial began, was convinced that they would all hang.[20] Admitting that he and his confreres had "preached dynamite" as an antidote to the viciousness of industrial capitalism, Spies gave poignant demonstration of his penetrating realism when he said at the trial: "Yes, we have predicted from the lessons history teaches, that the ruling classes of today would no more listen to the voice of reason than their predecessors; that they would attempt by brute force to stay the wheel of progress. Is it a lie, or was it the truth we told?"[21] Few people who have taken the trouble to read the details of the Haymarket proceedings can deny that August Spies' greatest crime against society was to speak too openly and bluntly about its deficiencies, and hence, like Socrates before him, he was forced to pay with his life. Before he died, however, August Spies unburdened himself totally when he blurted out at the trial:

The ground upon which you stand is on fire. You can't understand it. You don't believe in magical arts, as your grandfathers did who burned witches at the stake, but you do believe in conspiracies; you believe that all these occurances of late are the work of conspirators! You resemble the child that is looking for his picture behind the mirror. What you see is . . . nothing but the deceptive reflex of the stings of your bad conscience.[22]

No wonder those who controlled political power in the City of Chicago decided to silence this firebrand of proletarian discontent.

Louis Lingg, the gay young Bohemian who in life divided his previous vitality between the making of bombs and his consuming passion to make love to beautiful women, was very much like August Spies in respect to his devotion to the idea of revolution and his unyielding realism. Arriving in Chicago from his native Mannheim, Germany in July of 1885, Lingg, who was then just twenty-one years of age, hardly had time to get oriented to life in his new home before the Haymarket incident caused him to be hauled off to jail. Despite his youthful idealism, Lingg was already a confirmed political cynic and was convinced that no social reform will ever come about until the world is jarred out of its complacency by a blast of dynamite. Resigned to his fate as an unsuccessful revolutionary, he won Benjamin Tucker's praise for his unflinching realism in acknowledging that all he and his friends could expect from the state was the death penalty. Although Lingg, in Tucker's opinion, was no more representative of anarchy than the others with whom he was implicated, he at least understood that those who challenge authority to a duel to the death can expect to be killed for their pains. "We must cry out against the viciousness of this gross miscarriage of justice at the hands of government and do what we can to snatch these mistreated men from the jaws of death," Tucker announced. But "if we cannot save these men except by resorting to their own erroneous methods and thus indefinitely postponing the objects we have in view," Tucker rasped in his inimitable style of brutal frankness, "then the wild beast must have its prey. Nothing requires us to save misguided men from consequences which we did nothing to bring upon them. Those who think this cruelty may make the most of it."[23] Unfortunately for the anarchist movement in America, Tucker's dogged pursuit of truth, although obviously well-intentioned, appeared to be perversity in the eyes of many other anarchists. Holding dogmatically to his "plumb line," Tucker navigated anarchism directly into the eyes of the storm. Had he been more willing to talk, the movement might never have broken up on the reefs of doctrine, for in final analysis the disputes which shook it were superficial rather than basic, however deep the emotions and misunderstandings that accompanied them might have been.

From among the Proudhonians, Gertrude B. Kelly took issue with Tucker's ideological obduracy, arguing that the violence created in the Haymarket was directly caused by capitalism as a system and not by any irrational statements that might have been made by Spies, Parsons, or any of the other Chicago anarchists. Comparing social conditions in this country with those just preceding the French Revolution, she pointed out that there was great danger in the extreme and contradictory views which American public opinion had divided itself into; "On the one side we see the almost blind despair, the sense that things are becoming more and more hopeless . . . , and on the other a blind confidence that this is a mere temporary insurrection, fraught with no far-reaching dangers, which need not at all interrupt us in our pursuit of pleasure, as it can be met by the 'bravery and prowess of the police.' . . ."[24] True to the art of critical thinking which she had learned as an associate of Tucker's, Gertrude Kelly understood full well that the labor question could never be resolved by force or dynamite and that reason alone held a true solution to the problem. But she denied that an anarchist need necessarily reject all theories of class conflict, as Tucker now seemed to suggest. "As Proudhon has demonstrated in a masterly manner, society being divided into two classes, one of which controls all the means of production and the other only the labor of its hands or brains, which labor it is obliged to sell at the lowest figure compatible with the maintenance of its life as a class, all the deeds of violence which are commited are necessarily the encroachments of the latter class upon the privilege of the former. . . ."[25] The fact that she stated her opinion in *Alarm* rather than in *Liberty* would seem to indicate that Gertrude Kelly found nothing in the communist version of anarchism that was basically alien to her own libertarian values.

In keeping with his lust for freedom and justice, Louis Lingg, aware of the futility of all his idealism, ended his life as dramatically as he had lived it when he blew his head off with a dynamite cartridge clamped between his teeth the day before he was to be executed. Lingg's basic ideological viewpoint was expressed in an article written by him, translated from the German and published in *Alarm* after his death, in which he pointed out that the major development in American anarchism was a sharp decline in the number of individualists and a definite swing to the modern school which accepted the viewpoint of the communist teachings. "The adherents of this advanced or modern school of anarchists, to which I belong," Lingg wrote, "call themselves communistic anarchists, being opposed to a centralized organization of society—the state—but at the same time preferring co-operative production and consumption."[26] Reflecting Kropotkin's faith in the ability of people to voluntarily organize themselves into efficient economic and social groups without resorting to the formal political process or the machinery of a centralized state, Lingg insisted that "our advocacy of decentralization distinguishes us from the social democrats or state socialists, who are *not* opposed to the state. . . ." Not only was Lingg correct in his description of the fundamental viewpoint of anarchist communism but he was right when he argued that the forces of individualist anarchism were rapidly dwindling to insignificance. During the early and middle years of the nineteenth century it made sense to talk about freedom in terms of individualist philosophy, for the American economy, still largely agrarian, left ample room for newcomers who were the least bit lucky and who were willing to sacrifice enough. By the 1800's, individualism as an economic solution had just about run its course, for industry and finance had become so tightly centralized with the aid of government that it was unrealistic to maintain that the average American youth could make it primarily on his own any longer. For the individual of middle-class background who had access to capital, the economy was still ripe for plucking. But for the sons and daughters of the working classes there was very little room left at the top of the social structure into which they might squeeze, however hard they might work and save. As the waves of immigrants succeeded each other upon American shores and the nation's cities became ever more crowded with unskilled workers, Tucker's brand of individualist anarchism inevitably declined in appeal, for it made little sense to those of an industrial proletariat in that age of giant corporations. Faced with a well-entrenched system of privilege and inequality, the oppressed workers found Kropotkin's theory of social solidarity and collective action much more realistic than Proudhon's economic mutualism, although the latter's social philosophy was as relevant for those who could see it as it ever was. Unfortunately, the execution of the Chicago anarchists caused such chaos in American social thought that it became virtually impossible to talk sense about anarchism for years to come.

When the State of Illinois murdered Albert Parsons, August Spies, George Engel, and Adolph Fischer on November 11, 1887, a sore took growth upon the American social body which has not been healed to this day. It is impossible to overstate the enormity of the injustice done to the Chicago anarchists. Not only was there no legal case presented against them but much of the evidence presented by the prosecution was either sheer fabrication or the perjured testimony of paid witnesses hired by the police.[27] Even more clearly than in the recent trial of Jerry Rubin and the other so-called Chicago conspirators, the prosecution found itself compelled to deal with a small band of determined idealists whose love of truth and injustice was greater than their personal desire for freedom. The game of charades enacted out in the courtroom in 1886 was a deadly serious affair for Albert Parsons and his compatriots, for they genuinely believed in the validity of their social ideals. If they were guilty of anything, in fact, it was the crime of taking themselves and their social beliefs too seriously. As Harry Kelly, a communist anarchist of a later day pointed out:

> One of the most beautiful and most touching features of the trial was the faith of most of the men in the sense of justice in mankind in general and in their accusers in particular. Parsons, with his great love of humanity welling up in his heart, could not believe in the possibility of their conviction. All his traditions were against it. Was he not a descendant of men who had fought and bled in the revolution against George III! How could he believe that a nation that exalted freedom could possibly turn her back on it?[28]

The pathos of what was taking place in the courtroom was not missed by the public and huge rallies and processions were staged in support of the men on trial for their lives. Parsons, a born actor, made the most of his brief moment in the limelight; when brought before the bench to hear the verdict, he pulled a bright red hankerchief from his pocket and waved it to the crowd waiting down below in the street. As the words "guilty and condemned to death by hanging" were droned out by the clerk, Parsons, turning toward the window behind him, whistled in mock compassion for himself and making a loop in the cord that dangled down from the shade, held it out in symbolic gesture of the fate that was in store for him.[29] On the eve of his execution Parsons was in a loquacious mood and engaged his guards in a long conversation concerning the loves of his life—his sweet wife and loving children, the principles of socialism and anarchism, and his visions of what a just world would be like. After the lights had been turned out and the prisoners settled down for the night, the deadly silence of death-row was broken by Parsons' voice reciting Whitier's poem, *The Reformer*. "With clear intonation verse after verse flowed from his lips, ringing through the gloomy corridors and awakening prisoners to listen as if to the death-song of a dying hero."[30] Later in the night he broke the silence once again, this time to make the walls of the prison reverberate with the meloncholy strains of "Annie Laurie." On the scaffold, just before the trap door was sprung from under his feet, Parsons valiantly attempted to deliver a last message to the people for whom he was making the supreme sacrifice but the masks and ropes which his executioners hastily bound him with prevented him from uttering more than a few words. August Spies, however, left his murderers something to think about when he managed to warn them that "There will come a time when our silence will be more powerful than the voices you strangle today." Almost as cruel and barbaric as the execution itself was the inhumane treatment that Parsons' wife, Lucy, was subjected to at the hands of the ever vicious Chicago police force. When she, along with her children and her friend Lizzie Holmes, attempted to visit Parsons just before the execution, she was brutally turned away and finally thrown in a jail cell when she could not accept the fact that she would be denied one last embrace from the man she loved. For years after the execution Lucy Parsons wandered the four corners of the land explaining to all who would listen what the real beliefs of the silenced Albert Parsons were. Founding a journal of her own, *The Liberator*, in 1905, the widow of one of American anarchism's most faithful sons continued the work that her slain lover had begun.

It is not easy to establish the precise depth of Albert Parsons' attachment to anarchist philosophy. Judged by the face value of his declarations before the court and in his writings published by his wife after his death, Parsons was in fact deeply committed to the anarchist idea and had a profound understanding of its essential meaning. "Anarchy," he correctly concluded, "is a free society where there is no concentrated or centralized power, no state. . . ."[31] Objecting to the principle of compulsion exercised by one person over the actions of

another, he insisted that it is wrong to interfere with the natural inclinations of the individual, for only nature has enough wisdom to
establish the pattern of right conduct. "In a natural state, intelligence
of necessity controls ignorance, the strong, the weak, the good, the
bad." In final analysis, then, anarchy is a social situation in which
natural laws are given free play and in which all man-made law is
excluded. Like all anarchists, Parsons displayed a basic rejection of
all formalized social control and legal machinery. "Whoever pre-
scribes a rule of action for another to obey," he insisted, "is a tyrant,
usurper, and an enemy of liberty." Writing in the style and manner of
Gerard Winstanley, Parsons pronounced an anathema upon all man-
made statutes, charging them with being the "last and greatest curse
of man" and the one remaining obstacle in the path of a free society.
"The statute book is a book of laws by which one class of people can
safely trespass upon the rights of another," he charged. Here in
America, the lawmaking process is dominated by the capitalists who
will fight and kill "before they permit laws to be made, or repealed,
which deprive them of their power to rule and rob. This is demonstrated by every strike which threatens their power; by every lock-out,
by every discharge, by every black list. Their exercise of these powers
is based upon force, and every law, every government, is in the last
analysis resolved into force." We anarchists are often accused of
advising the use of force as a means to our social ends, Parsons complained, but this charge is utterly false. To the contrary, he argued,
existing capitalistic society is held together by force and could not last
another day if it were not for the guns and clubs of the police, backed
up by the bayonets of the militia. There was more than a little bitterness in Parsons' heart when he wrote:

> The political economy that prevails was written to justify the taking of something
> for nothing; it was written to hide the blushes of the rich when they look into the
> faces of the poor. These are they who brand anarchy as a compound of 'incendiar-
> ism, robbery, and murder'; these are they who despoil the people; they love power
> and hate equality; they who dominate, degrade and exploit their fellow men; they
> who employ brute force, violence and wholesale murder, to perpetuate and main-
> tain their privileges.[32]

In the light of the deliberate attempt made by the industrial barons
of Chicago to crush out the forces of social reform by any means,
fair or foul, and the willingness of public officials to serve as the
tools of wealth, one can hardly make good the claim that Albert
Parsons did not comprehend the true nature of the political monster

he sought to slay.

Embracing the liberatarian ideal of a free society held together by voluntaristic forces arising spontaneously from the people, Parsons, in theory, would have abandoned all political control of the individual's actions, for politically inspired laws were, in his opinion, "violations of the laws of nature and the rights of man." We anarchists have complete faith in the average man's ability to control himself when given the opportunity to do so, he declared. The anarchist believes that "if each man held all laws within himself, he would be held to a just execution of them by every other man."[33] Contrary to what religionists may tell us, Parsons maintained, evil does not arise in the human will but in the thwarting of the laws of nature by those who control the machinery of government. The anarchist believes that "evil in man only appears when some natural law or some natural right of that man has been violated, and therefore, as all statutes only operate when they oppose the natural will, they can only operate to produce evil." Only in a libertarian society where all formal political controls have been jettisoned can we hope for the perfection of man as a social being.

No final assessment of Parsons' anarchism can be made without reference to the opinion of William Holmes, his longtime friend and confidant, and one of the moving spirits of the anarchist movement in America in the decade following Parsons' execution. It was at the home of William and Lizzie Holmes in Denver, where they moved after the tragic event of November, 1887, that Emma Goldman would stop off for succor on her way West when making one of her many speaking tours. The Holmes' household, in fact, was something akin to a shrine for Emma, for it was the execution of the Haymarket martyrs that had won her over to anarchism; William and Lizzie Holmes, therefore, were a vital spiritual link between her and her fallen hero. As William Holmes recalled the events of his friend's political transformation, at the time of the Haymarket affair all of the followers of anarchist-communism in America, of which he considered himself to be one, had not yet come to a mature and final understanding of the philosophy they sought to establish. Genuinely dedicated to the libertarian idea of free will, they nevertheless clung to the liberal notion that the state could somehow help mankind to realize social equality and justice. Again and again the Parsons and the Holmes would come together with Fielden, Spies, and Fischer to try to untie the Gordian Knot that would free mankind from servitude to ignorance and superstition. Although all of them had originally been members of the Socialist Labor Party, and had therefore drunk deeply of the spirits of Marxism, all had by the time of Haymarket severed their connections with DeLeon and had become affiliated with the International from which they imbibed Bakunin's distaste for the idea of the state. From this moment on they never wavered in calling themselves anarchists. Seeking for a rational basis on which to ground their newfound social vision, Parsons and his companions, according to William Holmes, read voraciously. "We read Proudhon, Warren, Spooner, Tucker and other anarchist writers; we also read Kropotkin's and Malatesta's works, and gradually the truth dawned on us."[34] Incarcerated for over a year and a half in the Cook County Jail before their execution, Parsons and the others were visited daily by William Holmes and Dyer D. Lum, both of whom were confirmed in their acceptance of the anarchist idea. With nothing but time on their hands, Parsons, Fielden, and Fischer, according to Holmes, had thought deeply and had broken completely with the idea of state socialism that they had formerly held, although Spies and Schwab had read so much Marx that it was more difficult for them to give up the idea of state power altogether.

Even more important in assessing the ideological position of the Chicago anarchists was their basic commitment to the philosophy of the Enlightenment. Each of the Haymarket martyrs had in one way or another discovered the beauty of free thought sometime in his ideological development and had accordingly been led to anarchism by virtue of it. Louis Lingg aptly captured the catholic nature of the tradition when he described himself as "naturally a freethinker, a domain in which greater men than I have trod, and still greater will continue to walk."[35] Once the cobwebs of superstition have been brushed away from the mind in the realm of religion, new vistas suddenly become possible in the political realm as well. The Chicago anarchists, freethinkers all, were in this respect completely within the libertarian tradition of American anarchism and rightfully take their place alongside of Greene, Spooner, Warren, Tucker, and other noble souls who have tasted the delight of freedom.

NOTES

SECTION III - CHAPTER 2

1. Lucy Parsons, *The Life of Albert R. Parsons* (Chicago, 1903).

2. *The Autobiographies of the Haymarket Martyrs,* ed. by Philip S. Foner (New York, 1969), p. 20.

3. Alan Calmer, *Labor Agitator: The Story of Albert R. Parsons* (New York, 1937), p. 34.

4. Samuel Yeller, *American Labor Struggles* (New York, 1936), p. 46.

5. *Autobiography of the Haymarket Martyrs,* p. 43.

6. *The Canton Daily Repository* (February 6, 1886), 1.

7. *Dynamite: The Story of Class Violence in America* (New York, 1931), p. 60.

8. Henry David, *The History of the Haymarket Affair* (New York, 1936).

9. Philip S. Foner, *History of the Labor Movement in the United States* (New York, 1955), p. 111.

10. Samuel P. McConnell, "The Chicago Bomb Case," *Harper's Magazine,* (May, 1934), 733.

11. *The Alarm,* I (November 15, 1884), 2.

12. *The Alarm,* I (December 6, 1884), 2.

13. *The Alarm,* I (October 25, 1884), 2.

14. "On Picket Duty," *Liberty,* III (October 25, 1884), 1.

15. "On Picket Duty," *Liberty,* IV (September 18, 1886), 1.

16. "Liberty and Violence," *Liberty,* IV (September 18, 1886), 1.

17. *The Autobiographies of the Haymarket Martyrs,* p. 69.

18. *International Workingman's Association Congress,* (Pittsburg, October 14-16, 1883), p. 18.

19. Lucy Parsons, *Famous Speeches of the Eight Chicago Anarchists* (New York, 1969), p. 14. This is a reprint of the 1910 edition.

20. Dyer D. Lum, "Pen Pictures of the Prisoners," *Liberty,* IV (February 12, 1887), 1.

21. Albert R. Parsons, *Anarchism: Its Philosophy and Scientific Basis* (Chicago, 1887), p. 56.

22. *Ibid.,* p. 57.

23. "Why Expect Justice From the Senate," *Liberty,* IV (September 18, 1886), 4.

24. Gertrude B. Kelly, "The Wages of Sin," *Liberty*, IV (May 22, 1886), 5.

25. Gertrude B. Kelly, "Anarchy No Disease," *The Alarm*, I (December 17, 1887), 1.

26. *The Alarm*, 1 (December 17, 1887), 2.

27. John P. Altgeld, *Reasons For Pardoning Fielden, Neebe, and Schwab* (n.d., n.p.), p. 50.

28. "The Eleventh of November," *Road to Freedom*, II (November, 1925), 2.

29. *The Chicago Tribune*, XLVI (August 21, 1886), 1.

30. *The Alarm*, I (November 19, 1887), 1.

31. *Anarchism; Its Philosophy and Scientific Basis*, p. 95.

32. *Ibid.*, p. 98.

33. *The Alarm*, I (November 15, 1884), 2.

34. "Were The Chicago Martyrs Anarchists?" *Free Society*, XV (September 18, 1904), 2-3.

35. *Autobiographies of the Haymarket Martyrs*, p. 178.

CHAPTER 3

Dyer D. Lum and C. L. James:
Anarchist Scholars of the Midwest

The life of Dyer D. Lum (1839-1893) completely destroys the notion that anarchist-communism as a theory of revolution was largely a foreign import. Like Albert Parsons, Lum was a native-born American of Puritan, revolutionary and abolitionist descent, tracing his family's sojourn in this country to Samuel L. Lum who immigrated to New England from Scotland in the year 1732. Lum's great-grandfather was one of the minutemen who hailed from Northampton, Massachusetts, where Lum himself was born and buried. In his youth, Lum, again like Albert Parsons, seemed to be perfectly well-adjusted to the conventions and institutions of society. During the Civil War, he served in the 14th New York Cavalry, and in 1876 stood unsuccessfully for the Lieutenant Governorship of Massachusetts on the Greenback ticket. But Lum, an extremely modest and sensitive young man, soon became disenchanted with the ordinary political process and turned increasingly to radical ideas. A bookbinder by trade, his real introduction to radical politics was the Pittsburg riots which accompanied the railroad strike of 1877. Witnessing the brutality and false patriotism of those who serve the state in the maintenance of law and order, Lum, like Parsons, was so revolted by the hypocrisy and deception he saw that he could hardly remain civil in the presence of authority, going so far as to refuse to accept the government pension to which he was entitled for his services during the war. By the end of his life the gentleness and warmth which were basic to his character had been replaced by a "certain uncouthness, wholly assumed out of a detestation of the conventionalities and shams of society. . . ."[1] But if Lum's mannerisms alienated him from conventional society, he was deeply loved in the anarchist circles in which he moved. What endeared him to his libertarian friends was his sincere faith in humanity and his devotion to the cause

236

with which he identified himself. When his friend, Albert Parsons, was plucked from the helm of *Alarm* as a consequence of the Haymarket incident, Lum gave up a prosperous business to fill in as editor without any thought for his personal fortune. And when Alexander Berkman stood almost alone facing the wrath of society for his reckless act against Frick, Lum, despite his tendency toward shyness and modesty, stepped forward to stand alongside the anarchist martyr. Essentially nonviolent by temperament, Lum nevertheless felt that since he shared the basic values and convictions that Berkman did, it was his duty to assume a portion of the punishment which was being meted out to his comrade, even though he might not know him personally.[2] Like all anarchists, Lum was guided in his actions by the light he found within himself and not by any external forces. His deep felt compassion at the thought of social injustice is aptly illustrated by the opening lines of his poem, "The Modern Nirvana," in which he queried with a heavy heart:

> Why is the path by which mankind has risen
> Traced in the life-blood of its martyrs slain?
> Must life to souls refined e'er prove a prison
> Till death can loose the captive from his chain?[3]

But if Lum resembled the Quaker in his spiritual methods, he publicly disclaimed the notion of total nonviolence advocated by the Society of Friends and other convinced pacifists. His attitude in this regard is extremely difficult to comprehend, for Dyer D. Lum was essentially nonviolent by temperament and conviction. Like his former friend and teacher, Benjamin Tucker, Lum identified himself with the idea that intellectual persuasion alone is capable of bringing about real social change within society. Upon assuming the editorship of *Alarm* after Parsons' incarceration, he editorialized that since "anarchist-socialism" is best realized within an atmosphere of progress and industrial peace, *Alarm* "shall calmly and dispassionately advocate its principles . . . less in an aggressive and belligerent mood than in a sober and rational one. . . . "[4] Although Lum was thoroughly distraught by the fact that Parsons and his companions had been "strangled to death by the state" without so much as the courtesy of an impartial trial, he continued to see the problem as an infringement of free speech which was best resolved at the level of rational discourse. With the haunting scene of his dear comrades struggling for life on the gallows still fresh in his mind, Lum wrote:

The duty of the hour is now to wage the battle for a free press. *Revolt must be that of the mind. To the state leave coercion, force, tyranny. Let our revenge be the nobler one of raising a higher ideal than that symbolized in a brutal policeman or a heartless judge.* For our dead comrades no excuses need be made. Their battle for free speech has ended in temporary defeat. Let our's be for a free press wherein their views can be intelligently discussed. (Italics mine.)[5]

In the light of the moderation and caution demonstrated here, it is difficult to accept Henry David's conclusion that Lum was the author of "a carefully planned defense of the theory of violence" who had "appealed to the 'wage slaves of America' to arm themselves because it provided the only way out of their misery."[6] Lum's dogged defense of the industrial proletariat might well have sounded violent to the ears of the upper orders of his day, but nowhere did he recommend deliberate or premeditated violence as a means of social revolution.

That Lum was greatly influenced by the same forces that influenced Marx—either directly or indirectly—is clearly evident in the sociological foundations he built for his political theory. Sharing the Marxist's conviction that history determines the basic social relationships of men, Lum maintained that people are largely incapable of changing or retarding the revolutionary fevers that wrack the social body from time to time during the modern industrial age. "Our wishes, our plans, our rights are unavailing to arrest coming events," he counselled his fellow radicals, for the essential characteristic of all public questions of the nineteenth century has been that they have been basically economic in nature.[7] It is ridiculous, on this view, to condemn the laboring classes for violent acts in which they may engage in their struggles to free themselves from the hold of capital. Like Marx, Lum seemed to conclude that man's existence is imposed upon him by the economic forces he meets in the course of living. Without becoming a thoroughgoing Marxist, Lum, along with many other anarchists of this period, accepted the theory of inevitable class conflict outlined in *The Communist Manifesto*. In the one hand he waved the traditional black flag of anarchy, calling for the end of the state and its oppressive rule. In the other, Lum clutched the red flag as a token of his support for laboring men and women everywhere who seek to escape the tyranny of capital.[8] Lum's willingness to stand under both red and black banners clearly indicates that his philosophic values rested somewhere between the anarchism of Bakunin and the communism of Marx.

Yet for all his tendency to express himself in the sociological precepts of Marxism, Lum remained an anarchist through and through. On the subject of power, for example, he was adamant in his conviction that social control exercised from above the people cannot lead to anything other than increased centralization and the further enslavement of human beings. "Power from the people," on the other hand, "is human, relative, dispensive, subject to the changes of social growth; ever tending to widen out from the theoretic centre to individuals in spite of forced restraints privilege seeks to erect."[9] Reflecting a sincere dedication to the principles of libertarian philosophy, Lum maintained that as a social being, man's own personal interests inevitably lead him to a harmonious relationship with his fellowmen when left to his own devices. "Remove restrictions," he argued, "and the incentive to greed and selfishness disappears. Proclaim liberty and the better nature of man will assume control. . . ."[10] In the mature phase of his intellectual development, Lum drew his essential inspiration from the social theories of communist anarchism outlined by Kropotkin. "True individualism," Lum wrote in words which were greatly reminiscent of those of the "anarchist prince," is "based on mutualism, on the voluntary co-operation of each to the common end."[11] Where freedom is established as the highest of all possible social values, men naturally broaden their sympathies, finding friendship in their hearts for men they formerly suspicioned. "As compulsory co-operation has relaxed, as individual initiative has been given greater scope of action, our emotional natures are affected and mutual accord follows as naturally as water gravitates to a level." Confident that the human race was caught up in a torrential stream of progress, Lum substantiated his optimism with the defense that this moral growth is clearly evident all around us. In his opinion the liberatarian philosophy of freedom, once put into practice, would work wonders in the social realm.[12]

That Lum was sincerely devoted to the libertarian ideal is evident in his vigorous support of the Mormons who were then despised for their practice of polygomy. In the face of the self-righteous indignation of the vast majority of his countrymen, Lum had the courage to take his stand by the side of the Mormon who insisted that his freedom was infringed at the point at which the state sought to regulate his marital relations. Not that Lum sang the praises of marriage in any of its forms, for if he had his choice he would have chosen the more rigorous anarchist ideal of free love above any other arrangement.

Denying the right of law and society to force any opinion whatever on the individual, Lum maintained that monogamy, like virtue itself, needs no assistance from the coercive forces of the state to maintain itself if it is natural to man. Siding with Macaulay, Lum insisted that " 'The true remedy for the abuses of freedom is more freedom.' "[13] Wherever we find an institution which requires the heavy hand of the state to sustain it, he urged, that institution has already been judged in advance. In this connection he wrote:

> If polygamy be barbarian, our superior civilization will crush it out. But right or wrong, be careful how you deny to even a "deluded" people the right of self-government, brand their children bastards, and turn them over for relief to the sense of equity possessed by a board of politicians.[14]

As his words make perfectly clear, Lum was sincerely dedicated to the proposition that human freedom is the necessary condition for the growth of a healthy society. This was not the superficial conclusion of a half-informed casual observer but the result of a sociological study Lum had conducted when visiting Utah in an "official capacity" in 1879. Having gathered the facts for himself, he was compelled to take his stand upon the side of reason, as any basically honest man would.

In taking the stance he did on the Mormon question, Lum once again gave witness to the fact that the philosophy of anarchism equips its adherents to peer into shadowy depths which are often impenetrable to those with ordinary vision. On the issue of the extension of slavery into the territories, as an example, Lum clearly perceived that many of those who opposed it did so for economic reasons and not because they adhered to any sharply defined moral or social principle. Acting upon the rule that the end justifies the means, many who fought to keep the slave from working the virgin lands of Kansas and Nebraska were guided in their exertions by the demands of economic survival rather than by a genuine love of freedom and the desire to bestow the blessings of liberty on all men regardless of color. When Congress took action to secure the practical economic advantage of white labor in the territories, falsely masking the real purpose of its action behind a flimsy facade of sentimentality and patriotism, it seriously weakened the foundations of the social community in America. "Our fathers ate sour grapes," Lum admonished his countrymen, "and we wonder that our teeth are set on edge." In twisting the construction of the Constitution into the grotesque shape Congress did when it furthered the power demands of white labor under a false standard of freedom, the integrity and sincerity of government itself was brought under suspicion. It is now evident, Lum thundered, that "the anti-slavery sentiment gave the government power to secure ideal freedom and actual centralization."[15] Northern capital, untouched by the moral issues at stake in the fight against the extension of slave labor, in turn displayed the true color of its patriotism when it replaced chattel slavery with an equally abominable system of "cheap labor." In the light of this historical precedent, Lum proclaimed, the Morman's quarrel with the government has real significance for working people in America. "The Eastern demand is that of Caesar," Lum wrote. "The despised Mormon is, an unconscious ally of what is not as yet a lost cause. Before giving assent to new coercive Acts now before Congress, let us endeavor to understand Mormondom."[16] From Lum's vantage point the Mormon was not a symbol of social maladjustment or perversity but an example of the heroic type who has the courage to stand up and fight back against the state when it employs its power to destroy the basic freedoms of the individual. This was why he advised laboring men and women to think carefully before they joined the forces of opposition to the Mormon.

A careful reading of Lum's words reveals that although he recognized labor's necessity to organize itself, he adamantly proclaimed that the basic structure of that organization must be libertarian rather than a copy of the authoritarian state.[17] The basic framework of Lum's attitude toward labor was the revolutionary philosophy of the International Working People's Association which he had helped revive along with Albert Parsons and August Spies at Pittsburg in October of 1883. Abandoning the principles of the old Socialist Labor Party, the I.W.P.A. totally rejected the existing political establishment as a legitimate instrument of social progress and put in its place a philosophy of revolutionary direct action. Rather than attempt the reform of existing society through such limited feats of social engineering as the proposed eight-hour law, the I.W.P.A. called upon labor to totally reject politics and involve itself instead in a direct and final confrontation with capital. The owners of wealth and industry, of course, correctly interpreted this policy as a serious threat to the established social order and hence set out to crush it with every ounce of force that was available to it. For as Albert Parsons had stressed, the social disorder of the age was the outcome of a basic struggle for survival between the proletariat and the bourgeoise. In recognizing this in outspoken and unequivocal terms, the I.W.P.A. made it inevitable that violence would follow. Yet as Lum argued, the blame for this could not be laid upon labor alone, for it had not chosen to voluntarily put itself under the power of capital but had been forced into that position by social and economic pressures over which it had absolutely no control. Labor, therefore, could no more be held responsible for violence than the slave can when he fights to free himself from his chains.

Consistent with the framework of communist anarchist philosophy he had adopted, the idea of Christianity played little part in Lum's social thought. In fact, socialism and Christianity, in his opinion were totally incompatible ideas which could never be brought into harmony. Following the path which Proudhon and Bakunin had blazed, Lum insisted that the notion of God is a totalitarian concept and can never play any part in libertarian thought. "We can imagine Christian Caesarism," he argued, "but not Caesarian Socialism."[18] Turning to the ancient world in order to gain insight into the origins of political development, Lum argued that the modern state is the eventual outgrowth of the enforced "peace" established by Rome. "The civilization of Rome had authority for its corner-stone, and freedom languished in chains."[19] The Christian Church in turn, profiting by the example which the secular power set, likewise embraced the dogma of authority as the basic technique it was to employ in governing the spiritual development of its members. Throughout the length and breath of European history, Lum stated, a heated battle has raged between those who take their stand on the side of authority and force and those who place their entire trust in liberty as the most powerful of all social mechanisms. In thus rejecting Christianity, Lum sought to clear the way for the development of a more efficient and realistic approach to moral problems. Like Kropotkin, Lum was not so much opposed to religion as he was to hypocrisy and deceit. It might well be that his reaction to Christianity was stronger than it need have been, but it cannot be denied that Dyer D. Lum, for all his professions against established religion, had a large measure of that "ultimate concern" Professor Paul Tillich sees as the essential stuff of religion. It was indeed a concern for the ultimate fate of man which led Lum to throw in his hat with the

I.W.P.A. in its struggle against industrial capital. With Albert Parsons and a few other stalwart libertarians, Lum early recognized that social justice can never be realized within a social system where inequality is maintained by a wealthy minority that holds a monopoly of political power.

It is interesting to note that Lum was catholic in his anarchist views, contributing frequently to all the various anarchist journals without regard for doctrinal fine points. When Benjamin Tucker showed restraint in defending Albert Parsons and his fellow martyrs, Lum criticized him severely, arguing that it was not manly for the anarchist to show undue concern for his philosophical reputation at so crucial a point in mankind's struggle for freedom and justice. "If, as you say, there is a real menace to liberty in the *madness* of constitutional authorities," he admonished Tucker, "it seems to me that it is a practical duty for us to show our faith by our works, and to take steps to see that the men under arrest in Chicago are defended and acquitted."[20] Certainly it is not my duty as an anarchist, Lum continued, "merely to carefully distinguish my cause from the cause of less cultured and more unfortunate men?" The generosity of mind Lum displayed here was characteristic of him and one must conclude that he was genuinely devoted to the cause of mankind's liberation from tyranny and intolerance. His falling-out with Tucker should not be assumed as a sign that he had joined the communist anarchists in opposition to the "philosophical" school headed by *Liberty's* editor. More likely his devotion to Parsons and his fellow martyrs was prompted by his conviction that the proof of any philosophy's correctness lies in the practical results it brings in the arena of human relations. If the anarchist loves freedom and is convinced that it is the only means by which justice might be attained, then it is imperative that he demonstrate his inner devotion in his social and political activities. "Thought, which necessarily clothes itself in action," Lum wrote, is needed to make the truly self-reliant man."[21] And the anarchist, in his opinion, was nothing if he was not a courageous, independent soul capable of remaining true to his commitment to freedom and justice whatever the pressures upon him might be.

Unfortunately, Lum in his personal habits was incapable of affecting the same high ideals that he displayed in his philosophical development. Addicted to alcohol, he had to sruggle constantly to keep himself from drowning his better nature in drink. Were it not for his niece, Voltairine de Cleyre, whose "solemn, imploring eyes" haunted him in his moments of weakness, Lum would have been totally helpless before the demon that plagued him.[22] Perhaps the deep love of truth that made Lum the magnificent social philosopher he was drove him to peer in dark recesses within himself that were better left unexplored. At any rate, the anarchist movement in America lost one of its most outstanding members when death took Dyer D. Lum at the age of fifty-four.

No American anarchist departed more radically from the stereotype of the bomb thrower than Charles Leigh James (1846-1911). Born in Baden-Baden, Germany, James was the youngest son of George Payne Rainsford James, the distinguished English historian and novelist. During the early 1850's the elder James served as British counsul at Norfolk and Richmond, Virginia, and later as British counsul-general for the ports of the Adriatic. C. L. James, therefore, had not only traveled extensively as a youngster but had made the acquaintance of many of the notable literary figures who visitied in his father's home. When his father died at Venice in 1860, C. L. James returned to England with his family, studying at Cheltenham and Brighton Colleges under the guardianship of the Duke of Wellington. Here he broadened his knowledge of languages and developed a deep love of Shakespeare and the Bible, both of which subjects he became something of an authority on in later years. In 1865, the James family immigrated to Wisconsin, settling in the town of Eau Claire, where the elder James had earlier invested in land.

During his first years in America, C. L. James, like many immigrants, found the business of making a living a somewhat precarious affair. In November of 1866 James opened a grocery store but that venture apparently did not bring him the prosperity for which he had hoped, for the wife he had recently taken was forced to supplement the family income by the sale of doughnuts she baked in her kitchen. With three bright daughters to raise, James' classical education was better suited to feeding their minds than it was their stomachs and the family was to know many lean years before the two eldest girls were able to go to work to help out. C. L. James, meanwhile, lectured on temperance and religious subjects, supporting the family as best he could as a journalist for some of the local papers. One of the guiding spirits of the Free Religious society in Eau Claire,

James quickly gained a reputation for eccentricity in the community. A colorful description of James' character is furnished us by one of his townsmen who affectionately wrote:

> As a boy in highschool I remember him as a kind of Rumpelstiltskin figure, someone a bit sinister as well as exotic and strange. My recollection of him is of a small, spare figure, in a long, worn overcoat, a broad-brimmed faded felt hat, a preoccupied person always thinking and sometimes mumbling as he sped along, a bundle of newspapers or a large book under his arm. For some reason I remember him only in winter or cold weather, his overcoat tails flying in the wind, his long white hair streaming, his ample moustache stiff with the cold. He was a small, intense, preoccupied figure in the wind. [23]

Needless to say, James did not gain in popularity when he assumed a role of leadership in the water works strike which shook Eau Claire in 1885. And when it became locally known that he was contributing to various anarchist publications throughout the country, C. L. James must have indeed become a notorious figure among his townsmen on the banks of the Chippewa River as it flowed toward the Mississippi.

Although James, like most prophets, may not have been highly honored by his neighbors, he enjoyed a sound reputation among anarchists in America. Voltairine de Cleyre bestowed upon him the distinction of being "the most learned of American Anarchists,"[24] while Hippolyte Havel thought of him as "one of the most striking figures" of the entire movement in this country.[25] And he had gained this reputation while leading the quiet life of the scholar in Eau Calire, rarely venturing more than a few miles from his home. When he did venture out it was to address some gathering of anarchists or to attend one of their conventions. It was at just such a meeting in Chicago in the fall of 1893 that Voltairine de Cleyre first laid eyes on James. So little is known about C. L. James as an individual that her description of him deserves to be quoted in its entirety.

> . . . though he said almost nothing, his personality was not easily forgotten. There was nothing imposing in his figure, which was quite ordinary; but his clear, restless dark eyes, set in a skin tinted with morning, glittered intensely upon everything, had compelled notice; one might have thought them coals of life. Although he was then about 47, and looked even younger, his hair was snowy, and fell like a mane; its color had already grown old and died, while yet the luxuriance of youth thickened it. [26]

The natural reticence that was so pronounced in James' personality seems to have been akin to the reticence of Plato's philosopher-king, for James had no taste for the bitter sensations of active struggle although his intelligence and daring spirit would not allow him to let any issue go unchallenged. However dauntless he may have been in courage, he was essentially a quiet, reflective scholar whose chief weapon was his penetrating logic and his great store of knowledge. A careful reading of James' voluminous writings, which appeared in *Free Society, Lucifer the Lightbearer, Mother Earth,* and other anarchist periodicals reveals that he was indeed a highly erudite political philosopher and a serious historian of political ideas.

It is virtually impossible to place James within any sharply defined category of anarchist thought, for James skillfully avoided the dangerous ideological quagmire in which many of his anarchist compatriots so often became enslaved. One of the most heated controversies which separated anarchists in James' day was the argument that raged between the Spiritualists and the Materialists. The Spiritualists, of whom Ezra Heywood was one of the outstanding examples, reflected a deep prejudice against scientific method because they believed that modern science was essentially based upon the materialist dogma. But James emphatically denied that science and materialism are synonymous, for the scientist makes no absolute pronouncement upon the nature of matter but merely suggests a hypothesis concerning its properties. On the other hand, James, unlike many others who called themselves anarchists, stoutly maintained that the particular religious beliefs an individual ascribed to had nothing whatever to do with his being an anarchist. Brought up in the Evangelical wing of the Church of England, James, at the age of twenty-four, had rejected Christianity when he discovered that Brahmins, Freethinkers, and Buddhists could lay as good a claim to "the perfect sacrifice of actual self to that ideal self which conscience sets before us" as Christians could.[27] To call oneself a Christian, therefore, was in James' opinion, to make religion a partisan affair, thereby setting oneself in opposition to those of other religious persuasions. And yet, James confessed, when we set aside the "dogmatisms, the intolerance, the priestcraft, and the pseudo-science" of systematic Christianity we are forced to acknowledge that the fundamental ideals of Christianity derive from the sound conclusion that humanity can progress only to the extent that men receive the "atonement-conviction" and mend their ways. Thus, according to James, the Tolstoyan anarchist who accepts the teachings of Jesus as they are portrayed in scripture has not violated any basic canon of anarchist philosophy so long as he does so through conviction based upon experience and not blind authority. In his own case, James held that his acceptance of the anarchist idea had brought him closer to Christianity as a moral ideal rather than away from it. Like Proudhon and Kropotkin, James fully accepted the basic values and spirit of Jesus although he totally rejected the authoritarian method to which the Church had tied itself.[28]

Unlike many other American anarchists who sought for the genius of the anarchist idea in Trancendentalism, Spiritualism, Christianity, Egoism, or Materialism, C. L. James held, with Kropotkin and Bakunin, that "Anarchism should be regarded as a product of the modern scientific method, or the inductive Baconian philosophy."[29] This was not to say that Christians, Spiritualists, and others could not be anarchists but merely to state that whoever is "hostile to science is hostile to Anarchism." James' reasoning, in this regard, was wholly sound. The true value of the inductive method, he held, is that induction is the only method of thought available to man which does not ultimately depend upon dogma or authority for proof of its propositions. Consequently, induction "furnishes a true basis of reconciliation, a common ground of friendship, to the champions, hitherto so hostile, of every extra-scientific opinion, not only by giving them an abundant field in which their equal right to labor admits of no dispute, but also by allowing proper space and weight to the proofs of all their theories, while simply ignoring such theories so far as they fail to offer any proof."[30] And thus James established the right of all wings of the anarchist movement to labor toward their common goal of defining the generic idea of libertarianism while he at the same time laid down the rules whereby the fruit of their labors must be judged.

In denying that anarchism as a philosophy is not fundamentally based upon materialism, James supported his argument by the observation that materialists are no more prone to adopt the idea than those who are not materialists. Among the advocates and supporters of the anarchist idea, James wrote:

> Burke was a sound churchman; Godwin a deist; Proudhon a Catholic; Emerson, Thoreau, and Whitman, transcendentalists; Garrison, as he always took pains to state, a Christian; Tolstoy a Christian indeed—in whom there is no guile; Heywood a Spiritualist. Shelley, Byron, Paine, Jefferson, Condorcet, Marx, Bakunin, Voltaire, and Rousseau, were indeed known as decided opponents of religious dogma. But excepting perhaps Condorcet and Marx, there were no materialsts among them.[31]

It was not ignorance or fuzzy thinking which caused James to include Burke and Marx in his roll-call of anarchist luminaries. Like many American anarchists of his day, James was convinced that Burke's *Vindication of Natural Society* was not originally intended to be satirical, as the father of modern conservative thought maintained in his later years, but was rather the reflection of genuine misgivings in his mind concerning the nature of government.[32] Actually, James maintained, "Two thoughts operated as centripetal and centrifugal forces in all Burke's philosophy—that human nature is indefinately improvable, and that precedent is the logic of authority."[33] Taken together, these two propositions led Burke to thunder his celebrated phrase: "In vain you tell me that artificial government is good, and that I fall out only with the abuse. The thing!, the thing itself is the abuse." But unfortunately, James held, Burke eventually allowed the idea of human progress to dim in his mind, leading him to place all his trust and hope in authority itself as the savior of mankind. From that point on, Burke, originally a libertarian, was "carried away from the sun into the chaos and darkness." Repelled by the abuses and tyrannies of the French Revolution, Burke reversed himself and now came to argue with Saint Augustine that government is a divine remedy for human sin and folly. What Burke did not realize, according to James, is that revolutions do not come about as the result of radical agitation or even conservative tyranny; to the contrary, revolutions "always spring from encroachments upon previously existing freedom. . . ."[34] But there was no longer room for subtle nuances of this kind in Burke's mind, James charged. Henceforth Burke branded all those who sympathized with the Revolution as dissenters, leading members of the English religious establishment to go over to the side of the Roman hierarchy, one of the most disastrous events in the entire history of intellectual thought.[35] And thus Burke, originally one of the most clearheaded of political philosophers, muddied the stream so badly that the cause of freedom has been set back tragically.

As for Marx, James insisted, of all the philosophical ideas that have dawned upon the mind of man in the modern era, his scientific socialism alone deserves to be compared with the anarchist idea. At basis, Marx, along with Proudhon and Bakunin, belongs to the Hegelian Left which rejects the notion that law can ever arise from outside the individual. Too often, according to James, American anarchists are prone to accept the Quaker idea of the Inner Light as the ultimate in man's struggle for freedom of conscience. Yet the Quaker must eventually seek for a theory to explain the origin and nature of the Light he finds within himself. And so soon as he does, he "smothers it under a metaphysical bushel, for he is again caught in the act of manufacturing a deity through the process of deduction. The virtue of those who stand on the Hegelian Left is that the inductive method they embrace never leads them to deduce the presence of a supreme power in the universe which acts upon men or serves as the source of their consciences.[36] Marx, to be sure, made use of deduction at the point at which he arrived at his synthesis of the historical forces he had under observation. In a very real sense, therefore, his social convictions were based upon emotion and imagination as well as particular events in the evolution of human society. But the deductive function, in Marx's hands, was not both the beginning and end of knowledge, as it is for the strict religionist, but merely an aid to the inductive method he followed. Marx's social convictions, that is to say, were general hypotheses he deduced as the result of his reasoning from particular to particular. As such they were not absolute principles of social good but merely tentative statements of principle which were open to further analysis, refinement, and revision. When Marx announced that the central fact of capitalist civilization is that it is ultimately heading toward economic communism, he did not claim to have established "THE economic Law, but [merely] *an* economic Tendency. All capital must be sooner or later concentrated in a single cooperation—unless something hinders."[37] In this respect, James held, Marx made a very great advance upon the social science practiced by his contemporaries and we must honor him as one of the great minds of the radical tradition in the West.

Yet James saw glaring inadequacies in the social philosophy Marx had so ingeniously produced. Foremost among the errors of which he was guilty was his conclusion that the military strife of earlier European civilization had been superceded altogether by commercial strife. "The school of Marx and Engels claims to have discovered a law of social progress, which they accuse the Anarchists of ignoring, misunderstanding, or evading." But, James wrote, the inductive method advocated by anarchism is much superior to that of Marx and Engels in that it does not rest on economic tendencies alone but takes note of the problems of war, religion, morals, and aesthetics.[38] Having stood the Hegelian philosophy upon its head,

Marx was unable to see the full range of the forces which lay at his feet, forces which had plagued mankind from the very beginning and which have become exacerbated as the world has progressed through the scientific era. It is not the institution of capitalism alone that explains the phenomenon of war, James argued. Equally important to its explanation is the institution of government, with its reliance upon force and compulsion as the regulator of men's social relationships. Originally an anarchist in his social thought, Marx at the outset of his creative labors understood clearly enough that the idea of state socialism must end at the point at which the military spirit dies out among men, James argued. But the military spirit will never die so long as men retain any vestige of the governmental method. Marx, being unable to bring himself to break completely with the government idea, was persuaded to accept the view that political action is legitimate where its end is based upon the interests of the proletariat. In compromising himself in this manner, James maintained, Marx largely placed himself outside of the libertarian tradition, for as all anarchists well know, human freedom and social justice can never be realized where any resort whatever is made to the force idea. Nevertheless, James continued, anarchists and Marxists need not sever all relations with one another. Referring specifically to the work of William H. Van Ornum, the American anarchist who fashioned his anarchist principles within a basically Marxist frame of reference, James argued that where "a party on the Marx and Van Ornum principle seems likely to increase the number of Anarchists by drawing attention to their principles, to break down some portion of the existing law, to bring Anarchy a little nearer realization by any means, then it is good for so much, and [the Anarchist] gives it all the encouragement it seems worth."[39] In thus effecting a partial reconciliation between anarchism and Marxism, James did not conceive of himself as accepting the principle that the end justified the means but merely of following the inductive method which judges all ideas on their intrinsic value rather than by any nebulous aura derived from ideological considerations.

In extolling the virtues of the inductive method, James was not guilty of placing his hopes in a vain and ineffectual scientism. Implicit in all of James' writings is an awareness that a scientific method which depends exclusively on the physical aspects of nature for its proofs is inadequate for the purposes of giving man realistic knowledge of his true social condition. Man, to be sure, is an integral part of the physical universe, but he is not, like other animals, limited by absolute and unchangeable rules of behavior. No doubt man manifests definite patterns of conduct at any one point in time, thereby enabling us to predict his actions with a certain degree of reliability, James argued. Yet with the advent of the Baconian spirit we are no longer forced to conclude, as men once did, that progress is impossible. In point of fact, James maintained, the idea of progress now presents itself as the acme of all scientific thought. This, according to James, was Herbert Spencer's real contribution to social science. Recognizing experimentation and adaptation as the central requisites for human progress, Spencer decreed that freedom is the essential condition mankind must honor if the tyranny of the past is ever to be conquered. To this extent, Spencer was almost persuaded to be an anarchist. Unfortunately, James continued, Spencer was "a little afraid of his logic" and he wound up by making the unfortunate compromise of retaining the state as the ultimate guarantor of social order.[40] While anarchists reject Spencer in this aspect of his philosophy, they wholeheartedly agree with him that social change is from the homogeneous to the heterogeneous, and that the concept of an improvable human nature is not a vain fancy but a reliable scientific phenomenon.

Attempting to place his finger on the essential wisdom of anarchist thought, James stated what he considered to be the highly important thesis that "every advance in knowledge must be the fruit of departure from rule. Only by presuming to think for himself can a man add anything to the general stock of reason. . . ."[41] He did not mean by this that human thought takes place in a vacuum, for he was well aware that "new truth cannot be spun out of the human brain, which long ago evolved its whole stock of original creations, but comes from increased familiarity with nature, that is from experiment, which means from independent action." In thus turning to nature as the source of all social wisdom, C. L. James brought the anarchist movement in America into close proximity with the theories of anarchist communism worked out by Kropotkin in Europe. Like Kropotkin, James viewed nature as the mother of all human social order as well as the generator of all correct social action. Man's task is not to use nature, but to discover in it the outlines of a wholesome social science of behavior. Social disorder, as James viewed it, was not something man consciously engages in but a product of his ignorance. To the extent that men know what is right, they invariably do what they should. But men have lived within the confines of corrupt institutions for so long that they are no longer capable of embracing the truths of nature spontaneously. They must, therefore, be reconditioned to an awareness of the moral content of the natural world they live in but do not readily recognize.

Since anarchism totally rejects the notion of any conception of authority that depends upon force and compusion, James, like all anarchists, ruled out any resort to formal power in the building of a free society. To be sure, he held, all patterns of human relationships depend upon power of one kind or another for the unity which is essential to the creation and maintenance of social order. But formal political power, in James' view of things, was not social but antisocial. As he put it, "The desire of power, the dominion of man over man, is the ignorant barbarian's way" of establishing social order. "The greatness of men is their power over nature. That is founded in their knowledge. To the progress of knowledge, and therefore of collective power, there is no drawback, like the waste of time and energy involved in men's strife to rule each other."[42] When James spoke of men's knowledge, it was not scientific nor technological skills that he had in mind. Like all anarchists, he thought of knowledge as being essentially social in character. "The strength of the Anarchist doctrine that to conform is to be wicked, to be wicked is to be weak, and to be weak is to be miserable," James wrote, "lies mainly in their scientific character."[43] Man's goal, as social scientist, is to pursue truth within a framework of social freedom which permits all men to be their own masters rather than the servants of another. To accomplish this task, the anarchist turns to nature, the source of all freedom, in an attempt to discover the true laws of social progress. But here, James noted, we must be careful not to define science too narrowly, for as recent studies in psychiatry have revealed, human knowledge proceeds on principally two levels—the scientific and the poetic. To pursue one to the exclusion of the other is the main source of philosophic confusion in the world today.[44]

Although C. L. James had little knowledge of modern psychiatry, his intuition led him to arrive at substantially the same conclusions that modern psychiatry arrived at some sixty odd years later. In discussing the merits of the various wings of the native American school of anarchism, for example, James praised the Spiritualists for "their very important distinction of being the first to adequately recognize the subjection of women as the basis of all tyranny, and their emancipation as the necessary condition of freedom."[45] For as James clearly understood, the poetic function, whereby man comes to understand himself as a social being, is essentially feminine in character, as opposed to the masculine qualities of knowledge derived from the physical sciences. This was why the subject of art loomed so large in James' social thought. Where the artistic function is excluded from the realm of science, power comes to dominate all human organization and man's progress toward justice and freedom must come to an abrupt halt.

In the realm of human conduct, James proclaimed, art and religion in turn cannot be rigidly separated, as all too many moderns have attempted to do. For "Art which is not essentially religious, is not Art but dilettantism. Religion which is not essentially artistic, is not religion but metaphysics or casuistry."[46] Obviously influenced by Tolstoy, James held that although the artist can never consciously use his art for propagandistic purposes, all genuine art nevertheless contains a moral content which serves to advance the human race along the road of progress. At basis, both art and religion are rooted in the emotions, the matrix of the human imagination. Through art man gains wisdom into the nature of his essential being and devises forms of social organization which are compatible with his basic love of freedom. But in both art and religion, it is tradition—the dead hand of the past—which fetters man's imagination and prevents him from realizing his potential for harmonious social unity. "The example of good artists are to art what the practices handed down from the ancestral Totem are to piety," James wrote. "Such a servitude to precedent is obviously incompatible with improvement."[47] All meaningful art, therefore, must break with the past and proceed in new directions of its own. In this regard James fully understood, again as Tolstoy did, that the artistic function is not reserved to the gifted few alone. For, as he said: ". . . while those who possess the faculty of casting beautiful conceptions into melodies, form, or color, are few; anyone may aspire to the highest art, which is that of making action beautiful and experience sublime." In a vein of thought which seemingly anticipated the highly perceptive anarchistic insights of that latter-day anarchist, Herbert Read, James pronounced art to be everyone's business and called upon the people to take the lead in discovering new conceptions of beauty. In holding art and beauty as the essential stuff of which social revolution is made, James led American anarchists to accept Peter Kropotkin's work in aesthetics as a valuable source of libertarian philosophy.

In many respects, C.L. James' contribution to anarchist theory stands as the dividing line which separates the native American school from the collectivist version of the idea which rapidly gained ascendency during the first two decades of the twentieth century. As has been previously noted, most of the native Americans were individualists who drew their inspiration from the writing of Pierre-Joseph Proudhon. But James, although he had considerable respect for Proudhon as an "agitator" for the anarchist idea, was not as convinced of his greatness as were William B. Greene and Benjamin Tucker. For although Proudhon was a master at epigram and had won many great victories with his pithy, scintillating prose style, still he was, in James' opinion, primarily a journalist rather than a profound political philosopher, "the bulk of whose fifty volumes consists in tracts and articles often written without much previous reading, often, therefore, about what he did not understand."[48] Taking issue with the *Liberty* group, James chided Tucker, who had been his former teacher, for his failure to see the validity of the anarchist-communist viewpoint.[49] In the beginning, James wrote, "Proudhon, Josiah Warren, Marx, Bakunin, Tucker, and I, all set out with the radical idea that possession is natural; that property, as distinguished from possession, is robbery; and that this robbery is artificial, being made possible only by government."[50] But James felt forced to a parting of the ways with the *Liberty* group at the point at which Tucker "concluded that 'peace' under the sword of the state, and 'property' are of more value than humanity." In making this accusation, James was perhaps too hard on his former friend, for Tucker, for all his faults, never made any such ignominious peace with the Establishment. If Tucker had sinned at all, it was in his hardheaded refusal to see anything good whatever in Marxism and his tendency to always think of his own viewpoint as holier than anyone else's. Without wishing to make excuses for either party to the dispute, it is fair to conclude that the seemingly unreconcilable antagonism which separated the individualists from the collectivists was of the same nature as the antagonism which always separates one generation from another. The members of the *Liberty* group, largely agrarian in their outlook, had little feeling for the problems which faced labor in the full-grown industrial society of twentieth-century America, whereas Marx and his ideas could have little relevance to American anarchists during the early nineteenth century. But by the end of the century his writings had taken on new significance, causing many who called themselves anarchists to shift their perspectives. Tucker's inability to find a place for Marx in his libertarian philosophy and his tenacious loyalty to Proudhon tells us more about his age than it does about his basic values.

It would be a mistake, however, to conclude that C. L. James had become a full-fledged Marxist simply because he argued against Tucker and other exponents of individualist anarchism that there was a large measure of validity in Marx's social criticism. By no stretch of the imagination can it be said that James had gone over to the Marxian camp, nor had he totally broken with the philosophical tendencies of Proudhon. Essentially eclectic in outlook, James always insisted that anarchism does not rest "on any dogma older than itself, but on Induction, whose evidences are alike for all men whatever dogmas they were taught to believe."[51] For all his criticism of Proudhon, James remained faithful to the end to the Proudhonian precept that all social ideas are to be held tentatively rather than absolutely, and that superstition is the basic evil with which anarchists must contend. He was aware, to be sure, that "because men can always be found in every stage of intellectual evolution, all superstitions are immortal, and government will doubtless always have its advocates."[52] The remedy for this illness, in James' opinion, was to maintain a steady barrage of criticism against the bastions of superstition, all of which center in the state idea, for he was firmly convinced that "superstitions, once called in question, soon lose the respect of the intelligent class; and after that are pretty harmless." James, no doubt, was much too optimistic when he proclaimed that the government superstition had already lost the sympathy of most intelligent people and would "in another thirty years . . . be like the belief in witchcraft, an object of general ridicule." But he was certainly on the right track when he maintained that although government "pretends to fear the bullets of the Anarchists, it is infinitely more afraid of their pens and their tongues. The petroleum of knowledge, the nitroglycerine of ideas, are what it dreads. . . ."

In an effort to sum up the main tenets of anarchist philosophy, James correctly noted that there is general agreement among anarchists that the institution of government is a direct result of the human institution of war.[53] Were it not for the fears of "the enemy" instilled in the citizen when he is very young and susceptible to conditioning, politicians and the ruling classes would never succeed in enslaving the mass of humanity as they have. All anarchists, accordingly, are basically opposed to war, for they clearly recognize that it is the germ from which all human regimentation and oppression grow. If we would escape from servitude to government, we must start by uncovering the many layers of primordial myth that clutter up the human unconscious and prevent social man from realizing the justice and unity that could be his. Political institutions, James maintained, "never represent modern civilization, but always antiquated barbarism; we are used to accepting them not because we have considered their merits but because we have not."[54] The chief task of the anarchist, therefore, is to take up the work of the Enlightenment; human reason must be brought to bear upon institutions so that mankind will begin to become conscious of the web of complicity in which it is caught. In this regard, James wrote, "The use of anarchistic literature is obvious. It is to teach the deluded multitude by what arts they are imposed on."[55] In carrying on the work of iconoclasm, the anarchist will perforce cause shock and fear in the hearts of those who presently control society, for people who understand the controlling qualities of power instinctively fear those who would undermine it. Here it is helpful to keep Garrison's teachings on the subject of militancy in mind. The literature of reform is to be gauged by the reaction it elicits from those against whom it is directed. If our words fail to cause fear in the hearts of those who oppress us, they are worthless and do not deserve to be expressed. "All Proudhon's other services to humanity pale before this single one that he dared to call anarchy anarchy," James proclaimed. In eulogy of the Haymarket martyrs, James sought to understand why extremists as unlike as Socrates and Saint Paul are remembered by posterity, whereas those who are responsible for prosecuting them for their militancy are ignominiously ignored by succeeding generations. We come close to understanding the quintessence of anarchism when we see that "Every sincere conviction for which a man will die is original, and every originality is an incipient revolution," James intoned. "This is the voice of the creative spirit in man. Its antagonist, 'Law and Order,' is the voice of the mowing, imitating ape."[56]

NOTES

SECTION III - CHAPTER 3

1. Lizzie M. Holmes, "Dyer D. Lum," *Lucifer, The Light Bearer* (April 21, 1893), 3.

2. Voltairine de Cleyre, *Selected Works* (New York, 1914), p. 289.

3. *The Radical Review,* I (August, 1877), 261.

4. *Alarm,* I (November 5, 1887), 2.

5. *Alarm,* I (November 19, 1887), 2.

6. *History of the Haymarket Affair* (New York, 1936), p. 123.

7. Dyer D. Lum, *A Concise History of the Great Trial of the Chicago Anarchists in 1886* (Chicago, n.d.), p. 7.

8. Dyer D. Lum, *The Red Flag; An Address Before the Sun-Set Club* (Chicago, 1890), p. 8.

9. Dyer D. Lum, "Eighteen Christian Centuries," *Liberty,* IV (June 19, 1886), 2.

10. Dyer D. Lum, "Anarchy and Its Aims," *The Liberator,* I (September 24, 1905), 2.

11. Dyer D. Lum, *The Philosophy of Trade Unions* (Chicago, 1892), p. 9.

12. Dyer D. Lum, "The Fiction of Natural Rights," *Road to Freedom,* IV (June, July, 1928), 7.

13. Dyer D. Lum, *The Mormon Question* (Port Jervis, New York 1886), p. 80.

14. Dyer D. Lum, *Utah and Its People* (New York, 1882), p. 46.

15. *Ibid.,* p. 6.

16. *Ibid.,* p. 7.

17. For a statement of Lum's attitude in this regard, see "The Knights of Labor," *Liberty,* IV (June 19, 1886), 7.

18. "Christian Socialism," *Liberty,* III (November 28, 1885), 5.

19. "Eighteen Christian Centuries," 3.

20. Dyer D. Lum, "Mr. Lum Finds Liberty Wanting," *Liberty,* IV (June 19, 1886), 5.

21. Dyer D. Lum, *The Spiritual Delusion* (Philadelphia, 1873), p. 82.

22. *73 Letters from Dyer D. Lum to Voltairine de Cleyre,* 1889-1893, Houghton Library, Harvard University.

23. Personal letter from Ralph W. Owen to William O. Reichert,

May 10, 1967. See also: James F. Morton, "C. L. James," *Mother Earth*, VI (August, 1911;, 172-174; and, Abe Isaak, Jr., "C. L. James," *Mother Earth*, VI (October, 1911), 245-249.

24. *Selected Works*, p. 97.

25. "An Anarchist Scholar," *Road to Freedom*, IV (May, 1928), 5.

26. "C. L. James," *Mother Earth*, VI (July, 1911), 142.

27. C. L. James, "The Confession of a 'Christian Anarchist,' " *Free Society*, XV (November 6, 1904), 4.

28. For a discussion of Proudhon and Kropotkin's attitude toward Christianity, see William O. Reichert, "Proudhon and Kropotkin on Church and State," *A Journal of Church and State*, IX (Winter, 1967).

29. "A Vindication of Anarchism—I" *Free Society*, X (January 4, 1903), 6.

30. "A Vindication of Anarchism—X," *Free Society*, X (August 16, 1903), 6.

31. "A Vindication of Anarchism—X," *Free Society*, X (August 9, 1903), 6.

32. Burke's "Vindication of Natural Society" was included in Charles T. Sprading's anthology of anarchist writings titled *Liberty and the Great Liberatarians* (Los Angeles, 1913).

33. "A Vindication of Anarchism—IX," *Free Society*, X (July 19, 1903), 6.

34. C. L. James, *A History of the French Revolution* (Chicago, 1902), p. 26. Originally serialized in *Free Society* during the year 1901.

35. *Ibid.*, p. 123.

36. "A Vindication of Anarchism—VIII," *Free Society*, X (June 28, 1903), 7.

37. "A Vindication of Anarchism—IX," *Free Society*, X (July 12, 1903), 6.

38. "A Vindication of Anarchism—VIII," *Free Society*, X (July 5, 1903), 7.

39. "A Vindication of Anarchism—IX," *Free Society*, X (August 2, 1903), 6.

40. "A Vindication of Anarchism—IX," *Free Society*, X (June 18, 1903), 7.

41. "A Vindication of Anarchism—II," *Free Society*, X (January 18, 1903), 6.

42. "A Teacher is Learning," *Free Society,* XV (July 24, 1904), 2.

43. "Ethics for the Times," *Free Soceity,* XV (October 9, 1904), 2.

44. Karl Stern, *The Flight from Woman* (New York, 1965), p. 49.

45. "A Vindication of Anarchism—IX," *Free Society,* X (July 19, 1903), 7.

46. "A Vindication of Anarchism—VIII," *Free Society,* X (June 21, 1903), 6.

47. "A Vindication of Anarchism—VIII," *Free Society,* X (July 5, 1903), 6.

48. "A Vindication of Anarchism—IX," *Free Society,* X (July 26, 1903), 7.

49. See especially "A Reply to Some Critics," *Free Society,* X (July 5, 1903), 5.

50. "Comments," *Free Society,* XV (October 16, 1904), 3.

51. "Replies to Critics," *Free Society,* X (August 30, 1903), 2.

52. "An Open Letter," *Free Society,* VI (September 16, 1900), 1.

53. *Ibid.*

54. "A Vindication of Anarchism—I," *Free Society,* X (January 11, 1903), 7.

55. "Comments," *Lucifer the Lightbearer* (January 21, 1899), 22.

56. "Labor Martyrs Remembered," *Lucifer the Lightbearer* (November 19, 1893), 370.

CHAPTER 4

The Firebrand-Free Society Group

From 1895 to 1904 one of the most authentic voices of anarchism in America was *The Firebrand* (called *Free Society* after 1900). Published at first from Portland, Oregon, then San Francisco, and later Chicago, *The Firebrand* was the mouthpiece of native born Americans who came upon the philosophy of anarchism without the aid of any formal instruction or ideological indoctrination. Advertising itself as a torch "For the Burning Away of the Cobwebs of Superstition and Fear," most of those who wrote for it were free-thinkers who sought to break down the stultifying myths that prevented the American people from realizing the peace and brotherhood they were promised every July 4th. Above and beyond this they were "common old working men" who had picked up their social and political ideas not from reading books but as a by-product of the sweat and tears they had shed working in the mills and factories of capitalist America. In keeping with its anarchist inclinations, *The Firebrand* had no formal editor or editorial board, that function being performed on an *ad libitum* basis by any who were willing and able. Good Americans all, they possessed solid Yankee names and were dedicated to the reform of American society before the defects in its social structure became so deep and bitter that they would destroy the land of hope and freedom.

Giving the lie to the often heard assertion that communism is an import from abroad, the supporters of *The Firebrand* demonstrated in their writings that their acceptance of communist doctrine was spontaneous and wholly unpremeditated. Denying that there were any creeds or doctrines involved, J. H. Morris, reflecting a definite tendency to think in individualistic terms, argued that "communism is voluntary association, and proceeds upon mutuality of interests, not upon obligations."[1] But it would be incorrect to conclude that Morris and his comrades were opposed in any way to collectivism, for as

Lizzie M. Holmes argued, there is really very little difference of opinion between "a Communist-Anarchist who advocates voluntary association on a communistic basis, but who would not force any one to live that sort of life, and an Individualist Anarchist who believes in liberty and would not prevent the organization of any number of voluntary communistic societies."[2] To a man, the anarchists, whether calling themselves individualists or communists, agreed that the common objective was freedom. Where they basically differed was on the question of the means to be employed to bring them to their cherished libertarian goal. The individualists, for the most part, were content to remain within an economic system which permitted all the same freedom to acquire the good things of life through the exertion of individual efforts. But the collectivists, viewing the world from the prospective of the proletariat, manifested no confidence that the American economic system permitted the individual any fair share of the rewards. Displaying an unconscious predilection to accept the notion of class consciousness outlined by Marx, the anarchist communists understood full well that those who do not own the instruments of production cannot realistically hope to share equally in the economic value produced under capitalism. And yet they were not "Marxians," for they completely rejected the political solution that Marx and Engels offered the proletariat.

Turning their backs on both the trade unionism of Gompers and the scientific socialism of Marx, the *Firebrand* anarchists manifested contempt for those who proposed that peace and social progress might be realized by working within the established system of state sponsored social legislation. Clear in their minds that the end of all human effort is a libertarian society in which law and force are nonexistent, they argued that it is making a fatal mistake to entertain the idea of state socialism as a conditioning period for the communism to come. No doubt it is difficult to make the transition from capitalist society to anarchism in one stage, they suggested, but it is either that or submit to the authoritarianism of the state while the conditioning takes place. Where the state is appealed to for assistance, "the producers must be forced into their places and held there by the strong arm of law," thereby continuing the very tyranny we are seeking to escape.[3] With remorseless logic Henry Addis added that "The more the powers of the State are curtailed the more nearly we approach a condition of Anarchy: the more the powers of the State are increased the further we drift from it. How then can State Socialism, the governmentalization of everything, lead to Anarchy?"[4]

Taking Henry Addis as typical of the *Firebrand* group, a stark contrast presents itself when we compare his social ideas with those of Gompers. Gompers, as John R. Commons once pointed out, had no patience with the impractical ideas of social revolutionaires.[5] Pragmatic to the core, Gompers rejected the grand schemes of social revolution in favor of the practical tactics of the labor movement as it emulated the actions of its capitalist enemies. Marx could call upon labor to arise *en masse* all he pleased; Gompers, for his part, placed his faith in the individual workman organized in the ranks of the labor movement. Alone the workingman was weak and helpless; united in a labor union with other workingmen he was the mightiest of powers. It was for his genius in discovering this, according to Commons, that Gompers was entitled to be called the "most scientific" of all American social theorists, as well as the "greatest" of all American intellectuals.

Henry Addis, on the other hand, typical of all nineteenth century American anarchists, was basically an idealist, a voluntarist, and an individualist. "The Anarchist ideal in matters of propaganda and revolutionary methods, as well as all things else, is personal choice," he wrote. "Everybody to determine, for himself or herself, what to do and how to do it."[6] So adamantly did Addis cling to the individualist ideal that he found himself, like Emerson and Thoreau, defending the notion that law and order is primarily a matter between the individual and the forces of nature he discovers in the universe. Human freedom is only possible, according to Addis, where the individual frees himself from formal political authority and joins with other free individuals in voluntary cooperation designed to achieve the liberty of every member of the group. Flying in the face of the major tradition of modern democracy, he argued that the firmament of law which most people accept as the basic foundation of social order is not worthy of the respect it has been accorded. "Law is not synonymous with order," he urged, for the simple reason that it lacks all authority in human relations where it is not supported by penalties and brute force.[7] Contrary to what most people believe, law and disorder are logical correlates of each other, for "where brute force is used to compel obedience, or prevent action, disorder begins."

Convinced that morality owes nothing to law, Addis reasoned

that the truly good man is the individual who breaks the law rather than the subject who compulsively obeys commands which have no fundamental meaning to him.[8] Addis viewed government as a gigantic "conspiracy of the rich to rob the poor." Impatient with the rationalization and circumlocution which characterizes the political thinking of most men, he went right to the heart of the matter and spoke his mind without fear of the consequences. "Government is the control of one or more persons by one or more other persons, and is fundamentally vicious, being founded on assumption and upheld by force."[9] The fact that the mass of people seem to accept the political authority which ties them to government does not make it legitimate. Popular government signifies nothing more than that most people are easily manipulated into believing what the politically astute few wish them to believe. If we really desire freedom, Addis argued, we must seek it in a social configuration from which formal political control and direction have been eliminated.

If we are to create a better world, it is "absolutely" necessary to begin by "overturning" existing economic and political arrangements. Addis did not conceive of revolution as something one manufactures, however, but as something "forced" upon humanity by those who control the social order and who prevent change from taking place when they keep things as they are so as not to lose their private advantage. Taking issue with the "philosophical anarchists" who rallied behind Benjamin Tucker, Addis rejected the doctrine of "passive resistance" which the *Liberty* group generally extolled. "Resistance and slavery are the two horns of the dilemma which faces us today. Which horn will you choose?" Addis asked. "For my part," he answered, "I prefer to resist, and my resistance will always be just what the surrounding conditions indicate as most expedient, all things considered."[10] Fully cognizant that violence begets violence, he would avoid bloody conflict wherever possible. The decision to avoid violence, however, is not for the citizen to make but for those who control political power. As he saw things, "Should the 'powers that be' refrain from violence henceforward, no necessity of it would every occur."[11] To expect that any ruling elite would be content to remain nonviolent when confronted by a powerful competing group within the sphere of political conflict, however, was totally unrealistic. As much as he professed an abhorrence of violence, Addis had to admit that he preferred the actual outbreak of hostilities between rulers and ruled to the stultifying atmosphere which prevails where all social change is suppressed by a moribund political regime which does not know when to call it quits. "The storm destroys some but purifies the atmosphere leaving it good for all to breathe, but the unpurified atmosphere noiselessly but effectually destroys all."[12]

During the early years of its publication *The Firebrand* was jointly owned by Abner J. Pope, an "utterly irrational" advocate of Tolstoyan nonresistance; Henry Addis, an outspoken critic of religious fundamentalism and a dedicated freethinker; and Ezekial Slabs. In real life Ezekial Slabs was none other than Abraham Isaak (1856-1907), who had been born in a Menonite Colony in Russia and had become a member of the revolutionary underground movement in Odessa while a very young man.[13] Joining the Socialist Labor Party in Portland, Oregon where he had immigrated, Isaak went over to anarchism as a consequence of the stormy proceedings of the Second International in 1889, refusing after that date to ever associate himself with any political party again, whether it was socialist or not. Unfortunately the firebrands stoked their fire so energetically that they soon drew the attention of the United States Government and Isaak, Addis, and Pope were arrested and charged with sending obscene literature through the mails when they printed Walt Whitman's "The Woman Who Waits for Me," and *The Firebrand's* torch was temporarily snuffed out. Revived as *Free Society* from San Francisco, where Isaak now lived, the paper became a family affair, with Abraham being assisted by his wife, Mary, and his children, who not only performed all the editorial and printing chores but took in boarders to support the operation when subscriptions dropped off.[14] Committed to the Jeffersonian principle that real freedom is only possible when one lives close to the soil, the Isaak family founded the Aurora Colony at Lincoln, California, where they sought to give expression to the idea of anarchism by living in close cooperation with other homesteaders. After Abraham's death in 1907, Mary Isaak stayed on at Aurora where she died in 1934 at the age of 83.

In many respects *Free Society* was merely a continuation of *The Alarm,* for not only were its subscribers old customers of Albert Parsons but the ideas and attitudes expressed by its contributors were fashioned out of the same white-hot social issues that Parsons had hammered on his anvil. Among those who helped *Free Society* continue to beat the tocsin of revolt in memory of the fallen warrior,

Albert Parsons, was his former assistant, Lizzie Holmes and her husband William, who now lived in La Veta, Colorado. William Holmes, a devoted disciple of Benjamin Tucker, found nothing in communist anarchism to frighten him and he contributed to *The Firebrand* and *Free Society* as generously as he had formerly contributed to *Liberty*. Totally unsubdued by what had happened to his dear friend, Albert Parsons, Holmes refused to equivocate or soften the tone of his language. "The state is a monster, and we, the people, are its victims," he wrote. "It is none the less an evil because sanctioned by the majority."[15] The fact that he called himself a communist anarchist and that he freely admitted to a feeling of social outrage against the ruling class might make it appear that William Holmes had drunk ideological spirits from abroad but this was definitely not the case. It was precisely because he felt himself entitled to all the privileges and duties of an American, in fact, that Holmes fought so bravely against the specter of tyranny he saw settling over the land. Sounding like a northern version of John Calhoun, Holmes argued that "the right of the individual is supreme," and that "secession and rebellion are inalienable rights." Drawing inspiration from the writings of Emerson, William Ellery Channing, and Washington Irving, Holmes envisioned anarchism as a mere extenstion of the revolt against tyranny precipitated by the American Revolution when he wrote:

> The first slave who freed himself from the chains of a despotic master, the first enthusiast who denied the creed of his spiritual advisor, unconsciously planted the germs of that lofty principle which is destined to emancipate mankind. For the history of anarchy is the history of human revolt. The history of anarchy began with the first struggle against coercive authority; it will end only when invasion shall have ceased. Whatever degree of freedom we now enjoy has been gained only by resistance, first to the authority of the church; second, to the authority of the state and of individuals.[16]

It is doubtful if any more perceptive analysis of the anarchist idea has ever been written.

When *Free Society* shifted its base of operations from San Francisco to Chicago, many of the former contributors of the *Liberty* group, such as Stephen T. Byington, C. L. James, and W. C. Owen continued to write for it. The move from the west coast to the geographical center of America, however, seemed to open the way for a more sophisticated style of anarchist journalism. *Free Society* now started to carry pieces by some of the outstanding anarchists of

Europe—Leo Tolstoy, Maurice Maeterlinck, John Turner, Elisee Reclus, and Errico Maletesta. It is also to be noted that American Tolstoyans, including Ernest Howard Crosby and Voltairine de Cleyre, found themselves as much at home in its pages as they formerly did in *Liberty*. Although *The Firebrand* and *Free Society* were always published on Sunday in tribute to the working classes, the flavor of its journalism continued to emphasize the individualist philosophy which was still the dominant mood in America. Despite the running dispute which continued from issue to issue starting in the spring of 1900 as to whether American anarchists were communists or individualists, the *Firebrand-Free Society* group was marvelously consistent with this aspect of American culture.

Any doubt that the communist anarchists were unequivocally devoted to the ideal of individualism is dispelled by the pronouncements on the subject by Peter Kropotkin, who was recognized on both sides of the Atlantic Ocean as the chief philosopher of anarchist communisim. In a series of articles on Herbert Spencer which appeared in *Free Society* during October of 1904, Kropotkin set out to explain the contradictions which mar the work of England's greatest social scientist. In his *Social Statics,* which was his best work, Spencer displayed "a breath of idealism" which indicates that he was not at all hostile to the basic values of communism, Kropotkin maintained. Opposed to all economic, religious, political, and intellectual oppression, Spencer was something of a radical and set himself on the side of the victims of social injustice rather than with those who waged it. So long as Spencer is concerned with the facts of biology, chemistry, or any of the other physical sciences, there is a sharp precision which characterizes all of his work. When it comes to the social sciences, however, Kropotkin complained, Spencer was not content to report nature exactly as he found it but turned instead to the practice of allowing the values he derived from his middle class origins to color his perception. Brought up in a society which accepted the ethics of Calvinism as its world view, Spencer believed in the religious conception of *just retribution* whereby each individual in society is rewarded according to his actions as they conformed, or failed to conform, to God's will. For Spencer, that is to say, the "laws of nature" were framed against the Calvinist ethic and his work in the social sciences can hardly be classified as that of a naturalist. "It is not an observer of nature that speaks to us, but a lawyer and an economist that moralizes."[17]

In his attitude toward the state, likewise, the same ambiguity that mars his view of nature characterizes Spencer's work. On the one hand Spencer knows full well the limitations of government and warns us that human freedom can only flourish where the state is absent. Breaking with all those philosophers before him who sacrificed the individual to the state, he develops a social system which has the virtue of enthroning the individual as the sovereign power in all human activity. No longer is the individual to be the subject of the state; from henceforth he is to be the source of value, free to determine how far he will give himself to society and how far he will preserve his privacy. "Spencer teaches us that in man we have to fight, not his independence of character, but his too great submission to the common herd; while all religious and all social systems have, on the contrary, fought the independent spirit in their fear of making revolutionists."[18] Unhappily, Kropotkin lamented, Spencer is again inconsistent, for no sooner has he curtailed the powers of the state in the interest of the individual when he compromises his position by admitting that the state may in fact exercise certain powers legitimately. In the economic realm the state's hands are tied. But the state may, Spencer concedes, preserve the rights of private property and carry on the activities necessary for the preservation and defense of society. "And once on this road [Spencer] is obliged to proceed from one concession to another so that at the last he compromises the whole of his work." In the end, Spencer, while freeing the individual from state interference in economic matters, gives government a great deal of power over him wherever the question of social control and security are involved. "After having given the insolent title 'Man Versus the State' to one part of his 'sociology,' " Kropotkin complained, "he goes on to admit a negative and conservative part for the State."[19] Spencer, adamant in his conviction that government has no right to spend public money for the educational uplift of the individual, is guilty of gross inconsistency when he grandly proclaims that the State must take upon itself the mission of protecting the lives and fortunes of its citizens as they engage in social and economic intercourse with one another in daily life. In making the State the major power in man's quest for social order and justice, Spencer created a theory of society which could only lead to the individual's impotence as a social animal. Were Spencer truly concerned for the status of human freedom, Kropotkin suggested, he would have been consistent in denying the State control over *every* aspect of human intercourse, for then the individual would have had no option other than acting out the role of the social creature he basically is and must be. Thus Spencer's stature as a philosopher is to be measured by the failure of nerve which leads him to admit the state into his social philosophy through the back door after he had grandly tossed it out the front door. In defining the anarchist position as one which rejects the state in the interest of individual autonomy, Kropotkin clearly demonstrated that all the furor which arose from the clash between philosophical and anarchist Communists was basically a tempest in a teapot. Unfortunately for anarchism, no one thought to take the pot off the fire and thus the controversy between individuals and collectivists went on for years. Much of the pointless debate which separated American anarchists into two warring camps might have been avoided if more people had clearly seen that the anarchist communists were not advocating the adoption of communism as an end but merely as a means to an end. To assume that the erection and maintenance of a communistic society is the ultimate end of anarchist philosophy, as one communist anarchist pointed out, is to distort the essential principles of the idea. "We cannot imagine free men sacrificing their freedom merely for the sake of maintaining a communistic form of society, any more than we can imagine free men maintaining an individual property form after the primary conditions of existence had rendered it positively useless and harmful."[20] Had both sides of the controversy listened more and talked less, the anarchist idea in America might never have suffered the reverses it did.

Although the anarchist idea did not flourish in the South as bountifully as it did in the North, it found one of its most ardent champions in the person of Ross Winn (1871-1912) of Dallas, Texas. Born to poor dirt farmers, Ross Winn, possessed by a dauntless spirit and a rare spark of human ingenuity, dared to dream of a better world—a world in which humanity would liberate itself from the ignorance and stupidity that everywhere characterized its present stage of development. Setting out by himself at the age of sixteen without a penny to his name, he worked as a hired man on one cotton farm after another, always just a jump ahead of the grim pangs of poverty. Like so many other anarchists of the period, Winn was won over to the anarchist cause by the shocking spectacle of lawlessness presented by the State of Illinois when it coldly and methodically murdered the Haymarket martyrs.[21] It was Ross Winn who first took over the publication of *The Alarm* after Parson's execution until he was relieved of his editorial duties by the more experienced Dyer D. Lum.[22] A faithful contributor to such anarchist communist journals as *The Rebel* and *The Firebrand* (later *Free Society*), Winn did what he could to spread the anarchist idea among the Populists and Single Taxers of his native state. "We are arranging a series of street meetings for this winter," he informed the readers of *The Firebrand,* and "we propose to make Anarchism a burning issue here in Texas before long. Populists are very strong here and some of their prominent leaders are avowed anarchists."[23] Borrowing money to purchase type and a press, he established a series of radical journals of his own, starting with the *Co-operative Commonwealth* in 1894, the *Coming Era* in 1898, and *Winn's Freelance* in 1899.

Acknowledging Josiah Warren, Lysander Spooner, and Stephen Pearl Andrews as the major influences of his intellectual development, Winn, reflecting their commitment to the philosophy of free thought, proclaimed the idea of organized religion a block in the path of mankind's progress toward freedom. In Winn's conception of things, anarchism and free thought were synonymous, for the institutions of church and state were not two distinct and unrelated instruments of human repression but "twin vultures that had been hatched from the same egg of iniquity."[24] If we are to break the monopoly of government enjoyed by the state, we must simultaneously attack mankind's dependence upon the gods for his security and peace of mind. "Man, the creator of the gods," Winn complained, "has ever been the worshipper of his handiwork."[25] And thus mankind has labored over the centuries perpetuating the false relationship of ruler and ruled that stems from the mythical idea of God as ultimate power. And yet, like his libertarian forebears, Winn recognized the fact that religious concern is an intricate part of man's basic makeup. "Every man, they say, has a religion"; Winn wrote, "my religion is Anarchism."[26] In his secret dreams Winn envisioned the dawn of a new era for humanity in which the principles of anarchism would be openly accepted throughout the four corners of the earth; in a state of philosophical euphoria, he mused:

> The hideous nightmare of government—the subjection of man to man—is gone and I hear the happy sound of many voices of men and women singing of liberty, and mingled with it the laughter of children. I see a grand civilization dawning

upon the world—a new heaven on a new earth, in which every man and woman shall be a sovereign with his or her own individuality; an empire in which authority shall have no place, and in which national boundaries shall be blotted from the map and the flags of all nations shall be merged into the red emblem of universal brotherhood. I see the grim specter of war fade forever from the scene and over all spread the white pinions of peace. I see the jails turned into workshops, courthouses into institutions of learning, and where once fell the awful shadow of the gallow, I see the flowers bloom.

Five years later, however, Winn had begun to lose some of his youthful effervescence, for he complained: "I am tired of having the grand name of Anarchy covered with the slime and slander of ignorant abuse; tired of having people regard me with fear and suspicion, on account of the avowal of my convictions.[27] Apparently Texans did not readily cotton-up to the anarchist viewpoint, even when it was presented by one of their own kind.

It was somewhat naive, of course, for Ross Winn to expect his neighbors to accept his social views without fear and trembling, for his analysis of the political scene was too incisive and revealing to suit the tastes of the ordinary citizen. After the fashion of a modern-day Machiavelli, Winn described conditions exactly as they were rather than as he would have preferred to see them. Although he himself would have preferred, had he a choice, to live in a world where justice and mercy were the rule rather than the exception in everyday human affairs, in all honesty he had to admit that "the unwritten creed" that motivates people in high places is the ancient precept, "might makes right." Americans indulge themselves in the fanciful notion that this country operates according to the noble ideals of democracy, Winn growled, when in fact the "rulers" of society know only one law, the use of force to crush those who are weak and defenseless. "The dominant power in a nation does not wish to argue, it fears to discuss, and dares not hear the other side. It has a short simple and effective method of settling controversies—the sword," Winn wrote.[28] When the working classes learn to think as sharply as their rulers do, he urged, oppression and tyranny will at long last cease. The political state, according to Winn, "is essentially a military establishment; it never manifests itself except through force and violence . . ."[29] It is sheer folly to suppose that anything less than violent conflict could characterize the main stages of social evolution, Winn argued. In view of the fact that "all human advance has been from tyranny to freedom," it is clearly impossible that peace and harmony should accompany social change.[30] In Winn's opinion no social theory is more "damnable" than the doctrine of nonresistance, for nowhere in nature can we find a life style that completely eschews all resistance to force and coercion. In the physical world, Winn insisted, "every atom asserts the instinct of resistance to extraneous force."[31] And hence human society must also evolve toward freedom by virtue of the struggle carried on by its members against the rule of its oppressors. "I have not one ounce of sympathy for the oppressed, the downtrodden," Winn wrote. "They who weld the chains about their own slavish necks merit the misery of their self-debasement." In the tradition of Thoreau and John Brown, Ross Winn held to the conviction that freedom is not something one automatically receives at birth but a cherished dream one must fight for against the deliberate opposition of established authority. The prevalent condition of the mass of humanity, according to Winn, is slavery. It is as individuals that we arise one by one and make our way to the light above, always with the knowledge that only as we save ourselves from ignorance can we aid the rest of mankind. The rules of the game dictate that blood will be spilled somewhere along the way, for those who hold the instruments of social and political control never hesitate to use all the force and coercion that is necessary for their ends. To fight back against oppression and tyranny, however, was a very different thing than using force to effect one's control over others, and so Winn was willing to defend the use of violence as a defensive measure when all else had failed.

Shortly after the turn of the century, Ross Winn left the plains of his native Texas to settle down in the greener pastures surrounding Mount Juliet, Tennessee, where he eked out a precarious existence for his wife, Gussie, and their young son by operating a small farm while he continued to practice the art of social criticism on the side. Here he established yet another radical journal which closely resembled the anarchist publications that he had contributed to over the years. So closely, in fact, did *Winn's Firebrand* copy the style of the earlier *Firebrand* published from Portland and Chicago, that it, too, advertised itself as "an exponent of Anarchist Communism" and stated that its mission was to "Burn Away the Cobwebs of Ignorance and Superstition." Publishing his journals intermittently whenever money could be found for paper and ink, Winn changed its title to *The Advance* and later the *Red Phalanx*. But by whatever title it was known, Winn's journalism carried on in the tradition of dissent he had adopted when he discovered the anarchist idea in the agony suffered by Albert Parsons and his companions. One of the high points in his life was his meeting with Emma Goldman in 1901, and he frequently contributed articles to *Mother Earth* thereafter, while the readers of *Mother Earth* on at least one occasion contributed funds to save the impoverished Winn family from starvation. Succumbing to the ravages of tuberculosis at the age of forty-one with just nine dollars left in his pocket, anarchism lost one of its most valuable exponents when it lost Ross Winn.

It is a commonplace fact that anyone who has anything worth saying is bound to be misunderstood, and Ross Winn is no exception to the rule. Acknowledging Winn as the "outstanding anti-statist writer and publisher in the South," the historian, James J. Martin has charged him with failing to remain true to the libertarian ideal to the extent that "the tone of his philosophy gradually slid over to socialism."[32] Winn, to be sure, was a socialist, if by socialism we mean the equitable distribution of the wealth of the world to those who earn and create it. But it is emphatically *not* true that he failed to remain faithful to the basic philosophy of libertarianism as it was outlined by Josiah Warren and other adherents of the anarchist idea in America. Winn may not have added anything original to anarchist theory but his thinking was crystal clear as regards the correct balance to be maintained between individualism and collectivism in a free society. Shortly before his death Winn editorialized that anarchism is "the doctrine of individual sovereignty" whereby it is possible to reconcile the needs of the individual with the demands of the social collectivity.[33] This could be done not by seizing political power and using the state for radical ends, as the socialist wants to do, but by trusting to man's instinct for social cooperation and unity. "Anarchism reconciles cooperation with free competition—social unity with individualism," Winn wrote. "As political authority and the government monopoly of everything is the Socialist panacea, cooperation is the economic program of Anarchy." To the very end of his days on earth Ross Winn remained firm in his commitment to individualism as the chief means to preserve freedom at the same time that he was possessed by an unyielding hostility to the idea of collective social action under the auspices of the state. "Co-operation has often been confounded with collectivism," Winn complained, but the difference between them is fundamental, for collectivism would dispense with the inalienable rights of the individual as a social creature to make the state sovereign over all without regard to private desire or inclination. "Under collectivism," Winn warned, "society would be swallowed up by the all-embracing State, which would represent simply the will of the majority." Sounding ominously like Alexis de Tocqueville or José Ortega y Gasset, Ross Winn cautioned his countrymen to be wary of the masses as they began to stake out their claim to inherit the earth, for their's was a desire of the lower appetities and not a necessary social need tempered with justice. "The desire to rule and the stupid veneration of authority has been the bane of humanity," Winn charged, and the placing of power into the hands of the masses does not alter the nature of the situation one bit.[34] With anarchists of all ages Winn maintained that only as individuals erect an island of freedom in the seething seas of human confusion can mankind save itself from ultimate destruction.

NOTES

SECTION III - CHAPTER 4

1. "The Discussion on Duty," *The Firebrand,* I (April 21, 1895), 1.

2. "The Firebrand Symposium," *The Firebrand,* I (October 6, 1895), 2.

3. W. P. Boreland, "Communism Vs. State Socialism," *The Firebrand,* II (May 10, 1896), 1.

4. "Through State Socialism into Anarchism," *The Firebrand,* II (June 21, 1896), 3.

5. "Karl Marx and Samuel Gompers," *Political Science Quarterly,* XLI (June, 1926), p. 286.

6. "Revolutionary Methods," *The Firebrand,* I (November 17, 1895), 1.

7. "Reply," *The Firebrand,* I (December 29, 1895), 3.

8. "Law and Lawbreakers," *The Firebrand,* I (April 14, 1895), 3.

9. "Popular Government," *The Firebrand,* I (April 28, 1895), 2.

10. "Passive Resistance," *The Firebrand,* I (February 24, 1895), 2.

11. "Violence-Resistance," *The Firebrand,* I (February 28, 1895), 2.

12. "Revolution Inevitable," *The Firebrand,* I (November 10, 1895), 2.

13. Harry Kelly, "Abraham Isaak," *Man!,* VI (December, 1938), 450.

14. Marcus Graham, "Mary Isaak," *Man!,* II (June-July, 1934), 126.

15. *The Historical, Philosophical, and Economical Basis of Anarchy.* (Columbus Junction, Iowa, 1895), p. 8.

16. *Ibid.,* p. 3.

17. "Herbert Spencer-III," *Free Society,* XV (October 23, 1904), 4.

18. "Herbert Spencer-IV, *Free Society,* XV (October 30, 1904), 3.

19. *Ibid.*

20. W. P. Boreland, "The Status of Communism," *The Firebrand,* II (May 17, 1896), 2.

21. "A Voice from Texas," *The Rebel,* I (October 20, 1895), 15.

22. Emma Goldman, "Ross Winn," *Mother Earth,* VII (September, 1912), 209.

23. "Anarchism in the South," *The Firebrand,* I (December 15, 1895), 3.

24. "Editorial," *The Advance,* I (December, 1911), 1.

25. "Editorial Comment," [Winn's] *Firebrand,* III (October 16, 1909), 1.

26. "A Vision of Anarchy," *The Firebrand,* I (October 13, 1895), 2.

27. "Anarchism Organization," *Free Society,* VI (December 16, 1900), 3.

28. "The Man in the Tower," *Free Society,* VI (July 29, 1900), 1.

29. "War," *Free Society,* VI (December 10, 1899), 1.

30. "Editorial," [Winn's] *Firebrand,* III (October 30, 1909), 2.

31. "Violence and Resistance," [Winn's] *Firebrand,* II (May, 1903), 3.

32. *Men Against the State,* (New York, 1957), p. 250.

33. "Editorial," *The Advance,* I (March 2, 1912), 1.

34. "Editorial Comment," [Winn's] *Firebrand,* III (November 27, 1909), 3.

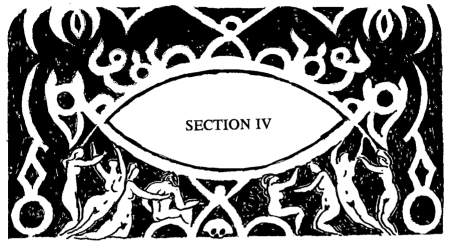

SECTION IV

The Place of Eros and the Aesthetic in Anarchist Thought

CHAPTER 1

Free Lovers and Free Thinkers:
Joseph Déjacque, James A. Clay, and Ezra H. Heywood

One of the first anarchist periodicals to be printed in a foreign tongue in America was established by a Frenchman, Joseph Déjacque, a political refugee who settled in New York City after a brief sojourn (1852-1853) on the Island of Jersey off the coast of France which was at that time a collecting point for persons fleeing persecution. A painter and paperhanger by trade, Déjacque had undoubtedly incurred the wrath of the French authorities for his outspoken call for the "abolishment of the government in all its forms, monarchy or republic," as well as for his vehement condemnation of organized religion and the priesthood which supports it.[1] In 1855, Déjacque had already settled in New York, for he was one of the French-speaking comrades of that city who undersigned the program of the International Association which was founded in London in that year.[2] We learn from correspondence which he exchanged with Proudhon that Déjacque was living in New Orleans during the years between 1856 and 1858, but in June of the latter year he was back in New York City

277

where he began publishing *Libertaire,* the second anarchist journal to be introduced on American soil. All told, he was to singlehandedly produce twenty-seven numbers of his journal before he closed down shop on February 7, 1861 to return via London to Paris where he died in poverty and deteriorating mental health at the home of his brother somewhere between 1864 and 1867.

A perceptive critic of the American scene, Déjacque must have acted as a major force for radical change among the French-speaking population of New York City who were exposed to his journalism. Moved by John Brown's death on the gallows of Charlestown, Déjacque pointed out to his readers the striking similarity between Brown's martyrdom and that of Jesus. The slave owners of the South might well have felt themselves triumphant as they "rushed like an insane hoard" at Brown, "as if in destroying this man they would also destroy his vibrant blow," Déjacque observed.[3] But it is futile to try to place a crown of thorns upon the head of idealism, he editorialized, for the ideal may appeal at first to very few of the people but in time it "becomes the universal stand, the rise of the new social order and the toll of the dying old social order." Like all anarchists, Déjacque had an abiding faith in the social judgement of the "people" and was confident that they would at some point rise up to put things right within the new republic they had established. "It is not a man, even Washington, who can save the Republic," he wrote, "nor a hundred, nor a thousand, nor a hundred thousand; it is the whole people." He continued that unfortunately, after freeing themselves from the English tyranny they labored under for so long, the American people delivered themselves over to still another tyrant, a written constitution. "Down with the written constitution of the majestic and antique American Union!" Déjacque flamboyantly ejaculated, for "it contradicts the moral constitution of the people." Rather than putting their faith in constitutions and politicians, the American people ought rather to put their trust in their own ability to live together without guidance from outside themselves. Déjacque undoubtedly meant to establish the second declaration of independence of the American people when he advised them that "direct and universal legislation is the only remedy for the ailment that is rotting you." If the American people really desire to be free, they must jealously guard their independence from all who would establish themselves as leaders. For Déjacque warned:

As long as you will vote in your booth for men that praised you yesterday and will
eat you up tomorrow instead of voting directly and universally for the law, as
long as you will give up the power within your hands to your always unfaithful
representatives instead of doing your own governing by your own laws, as long
as you will not realize your first right, your right of direct sovereignty, you will
be the dupes of the corrupt, the victims of their deeds, who will treat you as
subjects, as if you were defeated; from the one who holds the highest seat in the
White House to the . . . thugs who steal and will kill you without remorse in the
name of political and authoritarian order under the latent protection of the
courts and the police, their allies in corruption.[4]

Much as Wendell Phillips and other Americans went on from
their rejection of chattel slavery to a rejection of economic servitude,
so Déjacque clearly perceived that "once black slavery will be a-
bolished, the issue of white slavery will be raised too, and it also will
have to be abolished." In fact, he concluded, "the white proletarian is
the natural brother of the slave" and together they must fight for their
freedom. The only thing that prevents them from uniting forces are
the governments in both the North and South which painstakingly keep the mass of the people so confused with propaganda
and prejudice that they are not able to follow their natural social
inclinations.

Déjacque, like Proudhon and Godwin, was essentially individualistic in his social attitudes. He had a deep and unyielding fear of man
in the mass; his faith in the individual, on the other hand, knew no
bounds, for he was confident that human nature is capable of infinite
social progress and perfection. Reflecting much of the libertarian
outlook that moved both Proudhon and Godwin to adopt the anarchist
idea, he saw the courageous individual as the hope of mankind's
liberation. "Act, put your creative spirit in your work, produce and
discover," he urged his contemporaries. "Accomplishments and
discoveries bespeak liberty. Idle men do not enjoy life. Life is motion.
Work is life. Inertia is death."[5] The supreme form of individual
action, for Déjacque, as for Proudhon and Godwin, was to act as an
agent of social revolution. Although the individual must extract
himself from the mass before he can become a free man, it is for the
sake of humanity that he must establish his identity as an individual.
Déjacque, who proudly spoke of himself as an anarchist, also referred
to himself as a socialist, for in his mind, there was no contradiction
whatever between these two ideas. The intimate connection between
individualism and socialism is clearly expressed in the following
paragraph he wrote for Le Libertaire:

Just as man is made up of organs, and his organs of molecules, so man is, in turn, a molecule of the social body; the commune then is the organism. It is then with the individual or molecule and with the organic or communal system, with which you must first start if you hope to revolutionize society. The organization of work is not different than the communal organization, a group of compatible individuals and personalities, whose center of gravity is the expansion of the productive and consuming forces.[6]

In the years to come, many Americans who had been attracted to the anarchist idea would rediscover this truth so precociously intuited by this emigré from France.

If a claim to greatness can be made for Déjacque, it must be made upon his philosophical ruminations concerning woman as an agent within the social realm. In most respects, Déjacque's glory was obscured by the blinding brilliance of his compatriot in ideas, Pierre-Joseph Proudhon, one of the greatest, if not the greatest, of all the philosophers of anarchism. But on the question of woman, Déjacque stole the show from this master of dialectics. In a letter to Proudhon written from "the depths of Louisiana" where he had "been driven by the vicissitudes of [his] exile," Déjacque chided his correspondent for his reactionary attitude toward the female sex. "Is it possible great publicist," he impudently asked, "that under your lion's skin so much of the ass may be found. You have in your veins such powerful revolutionary pulsations for all that pertain to labor . . . but are stupid and reactionary, when you come to consider emotions of the heart and sentiments."[7] "You cry out against the robber-barons of capitalism," he chided his countryman, and yet "you would rebuild a proud barony of man on vassel-woman." Do you not know, Déjacque asked, that man depends upon woman for the energy that is vital to his social development, just as woman in turn depends upon man for the strength she needs to create! "There is not an idea in your deformed brain, no, nor in the brain of any other man, that was not given life by woman," he added. "All man's heroism, all his physical and moral valor, come from love." And love on earth can only arise out of a social environment in which man and woman exist in equipoise, neither one dominating the other but both freely giving of the precious human resources which have been entrusted to them by nature. Social progress, on Déjacque's view, proceeds most freely where the masculine attributes of physical strength and power are tempered with the feminine concern for compassion and beauty. Undoubtedly it takes shock troops and sappers to carry off a revolutionary action, Déjacque acknowledged, for the existing institutions of society will yield before nothing less than superior force directed against them. Yet if revolution is to lead to anything more than the horrors of social violence, it is essential that mankind use woman, with her concern for life and social unity, as its model. Where man depends exclusively on his masculine penchant for order and organization, the full force of his activities are confined to the realm of the political. This is why the history of western Christian civilization, which has been essentially a male dominated culture, has given so much power to the state, the most masculine of all institutions. It was this which prompted Déjacque to admonish Proudhon to:

> Raise your voice . . . against the exploitation of woman by man. Proclaim to the world . . . that man without the aid of woman, is unable to drag the revolution out of the mire, to pluck it out of the filthy and bloodstained rut into which it has fallen; that alone he is powerless; that he must have the support of woman's heart and brain; that in the path of progress they should march forward together, side by side, hand in hand. . . .[8]

A few years later, Ezra Heywood and Moses Harman would also pick up this theme and make it the *leitmotif* of their lives' work. But the seeds of woman's liberation were first cast by Joseph Déjacque, a product of the Enlightment and the free thought movement which was a part of it.

All anarchists believe in the idea of free love, but some anarchists have demonstrated this principle more faithfully in their own personal lives than others. James A. Clay and Ezra H. Heywood were two who lived the idea so fervently that they were early marked as enemies of the state and shut up in prison for their beliefs. When the final chapter in the history of woman's liberation is written, these two champions of freedom will at long last receive the acknowledgement they are due as two of the world's most faithful devotees of the idea that woman was created equal to man.

James Arrington Clay, a "down easter" whose basic philosophical position was essentially Tolstoyan, was a native of Gardiner, Maine. Coming from a poor country background, Clay received a common-school education until his fourteenth year when he went to work as a handyman in a local groggery, measuring out whiskey and, no doubt, learning much about human nature on the side. Typical of the serious person of his day, he was extremely well versed in the idea of Christianity and seemed to practice his religion with faithfulness and enthusiasm. But much like Adin Ballou, with whom he maintained intellectual liason, Clay soon discovered that the Christian concept of individual moral responsibility was difficult to practice in conventional society and he very quickly came to lean toward the communitarian notion of withdrawal so that he could live his life as his conscience dictated. A strict Baptist, he practiced total immersion daily and refrained from eating meat in demonstration of his love for all of God's creation. As the years went by, however, he gradually outgrew his early theological attitudes and became something of a perfectionist Come-outer, refusing to acknowledge any religious precept whatever as dogma.

In his political theory there is a certain restlessness and dissatisfaction with the notion of authority which permits us to label Clay an anarchist, although he himself seems to have been unfamiliar with the term. " 'Liberty' to me means something more than to think, speak, and act, as others shall dictate, and 'happiness' more than to drink, eat, and sleep," Clay proclaimed.[9] The good life, in Clay's opinion, was one in which the individual aimed toward the realization of the universal principle of love bequeathed to mankind by God, unhindered by the Augustinian notion of the state. "I wish to have a life —to live a life in love and wisdom in God," he wrote. "I feel myself an individual sovereign, wishing not to encroach on the rights of anyone, and wishing my rights not to be encroached on by anyone." Rather than obey the laws of the state, Clay preferred to obey the higher laws of nature which he felt God in his wisdom had decreed. But like the young Luther, Clay would have the individual do the judging as to what is right and what is not.

That Clay was essentially libertarian in his political theory is well documented in the pages of David's Sling, a monthly journal of independent social opinion which he co-edited with Isaac Rowell until their funds ran out. "I believe, were it possible, at a breath, to annihilate every human law, that men would be much sooner, and with less violence, restored to harmony with all that was created," he intoned in the first issue of David's Sling.[10] In subsequent editorials, Clay argued that were men content with the simple life, and were they content to live out their lives without resort to the dubious services of lawyers, politicians, and state officials, there would be little necessity for them to toil the back-breaking hours they then imposed upon themselves. Chiding the workingmen of his time for their inability to see that their cherished values of liberty, equality, and freedom were "little else than idle tales," Clay exhorted them to take a realistic view of social reality rather than the superficial outlook which dominated their political thinking. Mincing no words, Clay charged the working classes with a large measure of the responsibility for the web of social malfeasance they were themselves caught in. "You are slaves to capital which you are fast accumulating in the hands of your masters by your imaginary wants, you are in slavery to vitiated appetites and unnatural lusts—it is time to strike the axe at the root of all bondage, white as well as black, mental as well as physical," he intoned in Tolstoyan fashion.[11] Only an anarchist could adopt the thoroughgoing libertarian stance that these words implied.

Clay, like all good anarchists, had very little good to say about the role that government plays in the lives of people. The notion that law and order depend primarily upon government was, in his opinion, a "mere farce." All states "protect themselves as states," he argued, "while the people yield their life, their liberty, their happiness, for an idle frame."[12] Nothing, therefore, could be expected from the political process and Clay refused to vote or otherwise give respectability to an institution which he deemed to be worse than useless. When Elihu Burritt was nominated by the Abolitionists for the post of Lieutenant Governor of the State of Massachusetts, Clay expressed astonishment that so worthy a radical could even think of accepting an office in a government which was committed to upholding a "war-making, slave-holding" union, even if it was in the cause of abolition, which Clay supported. "Can Burritt in good faith and with a clear conscience, lift up his hand and swear that he would with the sword repel the blacks, were they to rise to throw off their yoke of bondage?" he asked. "Can he as editor of a Christian paper, become in any way one of a government whose whole structure is the sword and bayonet, dungeon and gallows?"[13] Going much further in his social views than most American radicals, Clay assumed something akin to the uncompromising Christian radicalism voiced by Jerard Winstanley, the English Digger, two centuries earlier. There is, in fact, a striking resemblance in the viewpoints of Clay and Winstanley which is clearly evident in the following paragraphs Clay wrote for *David's Sling:*

> Why is the soil withheld from a large portion of the race of mankind? It as rightfully belongs to the great family as the air they breathe. . . . Life and liberty

are no more justly the right of men than the land on which they labor to earn their daily bread. In fact, one cannot enjoy life or liberty without the soil; for when he is deprived of this he is subject to another's will, and may be obligated to become a slave in order to acquire a subsistence. . . .

When one is dispossessed of the right to the soil, he is also dispossessed of the right to live, save at the will of another. Every person has a right to as much soil as he needs to cultivate for his subsistence, and no person has a righteous claim to more. [14]

Had Clay been born a half century sooner, this outlook would have made him a Jeffersonian democrat. But writing in the 1840's, his attitude toward land made him one of the earliest of the mutualist anarchists who saw the problem of land ownership as basic to the further development of a libertarian society. In this respect, James Arrington Clay was related to William C. Owen, William B. Greene, and a host of other libertarians who preceded the School for Living organized by Ralph Borsodi.

At the basis of all of Clay's social and political thought was his insistence that life should be lived according to the natural law set forth by God rather than the positive law formulated by men. Here, as in all other aspects of his life, his thoughts were guided by the conception of radical Christianity that he had formed for himself. Honest to the core himself, Clay attributed the same quality to others, insisting that all men have the means to live a good Christian life if only they are left to their own resources and not forced into a mold by the state. Reflecting the influence of Josiah Warren, with whom he was later to have communion as a member of Modern Times, Clay subscribed to the libertarian formula which holds that "Freedom is the sovereign remedy for all bondage or slavery, and love for all enmity or discord."[15] The proper foundation for a good social order is a social system in which each individual trusts the integrity of his neighbors, thereby eliminating the need for regulation by government and its positive law. "The ruling power must be love, or God, the only power which does not destroy," Clay maintained. Earthly governments profess that they have the mission of saving man from harm and injury but in fact they are "soulless organizations" which have no other function than perpetuating themselves, even at the expense of destroying humanity if necessary. Adamant in his religious outlook, Clay argued that "There cannot be any harmonious combination of individuals, except through our living head, which is God. Mankind must come to him and there be united." Again like Adin Ballou, Clay

saw the problem of politics as a mere extension of the moral or
religious dimension of life.

Clay's importance in the history of the anarchist idea lies in his
views concerning sexual freedom, for he precedes Ezra Heywood and
Moses Harman as a champion of the idea of free love. Possessed by a
highly sensitive personal conscience and a painstaking devotion to
Christian duty, Clay was disgruntled with his lot in conventional
society and dreamed of joining one of the many Christian communities of his day where he might find relief from the evils of
capitalism and the slovenly moral practices of self-seeking men.
Unhappily, Clay's wife, Emily, who had provided him with a son and
daughter, did not fully share his social dreams and was unwilling to
drop out of conventional society, however imperfect it might be. By
1854, when Clay had his first brush with the law, relations within the
Clay family had apparently progressed to a stalemate on the issue of
copping out, and it appears that his wife finally separated herself from
him upon the urging of some of her friends. According to the marital
laws of the time, Clay could have chosen to move his family to the site
of some utopian community without his wife's consent, for she was
legally obligated to "love, honor, and obey" her husband under all
circumstances. But being inclined toward libertarianism and unwilling to force his will upon his spouse, Clay would not act until he had
the family's voluntary consent, which was never forthcoming. Left
without wife or children, Clay consoled himself after some time by
inviting a young woman to share his domicile with him, causing
tongues to wag in Gardiner with the fury of the winter winds that
lashed the nearby Maine coast. But the relationship between Maria
Cole, the Jezebel at issue, and Clay was founded upon a substantial
philosophical affinity rather than a casual erotic impulse of the
moment. In an open letter he wrote to Maria in *The Eastern Light,* a
journal which he published on an occasional basis after his release
from prison, Clay revealed that his attraction to her was primarily
motivated by the libertarian sentiments which were so pronounced in
her make-up. ". . . when I heard you reject time honored authority
and express a disbelief in all religious dogmas," he wrote her, "I felt
a great interest in you; I knew you had outgrown all those old shackles
that bind the human soul and I felt that you were free for flight."[16]
But the local authorities cared little for such libertarian sentimentality
and Clay and his love were charged with adultery. When the testimony

of two medical doctors proved without a doubt that his partner in crime was a virgin, the adultery charge had to be dropped. But the police authorities, unwilling to let their quarry escape, now charged him and his untouched mistress with "lewd and lascivious cohabitation," sentencing him to six months in prison or a two hundred dollar fine, and her to four months or fifty dollars. The girl, understandably, fled Gardiner, after Clay paid her fine, but Clay, refusing to submit to what he considered armed robbery at the hands of the state, was locked up in jail to serve out his term. It was in the gloom of his prison cell that Clay composed the text of the book he left to posterity in explanation of his actions. *A Voice From Prison* (1856) is not only a revealing account of the social implications of radical Christianity but is one of the most genuine expressions of the anarchist idea ever to be published in America.

In arguing that "the marriage law, as it now is, is the deepest and biggest root of the tree of evil," Clay went right to the heart of the social problem as anarchists see it. Approaching the question with disarming sincerity and innocence, Clay revealed a fundamental discrepancy in the logic of American social and political theory that has again and again plagued those who would defend the system. "The marriage institution," Clay pointed out, "is a religious ordinance, and the constitution of the State [of Maine] and the United States pretends to guarantee free religious toleration." Cutting through the rhetoric which ordinarily clouds the vision of legalists, Clay insisted that "If the marriage institution be not a religious rite, then marriages are not divine—are not of God, but a mere civil contract. . . ." If this is the way the courts would have it, Clay continued, "shall the Constitution of free America not allow her subjects to make and unmake civil contracts, if they choose? Will it not be more wise to leave matters of love with God, who is love?"[17] Clay's neighbors, puffed-up with moral indignation and self-righteousness, turned a deaf ear to his pleas and could find no better solution to the social problems they faced than putting the gadfly who had stung them into prison. But a less impassioned examination of his case indicates that there was considerable philosophical substance to his arguments.

Those who approve of legal restraint and penalties regarding marriage, Clay maintained, assume that it is possible to lead people to truth and righteousness by force of arms. But any personal relationship as intimate as marriage can never be properly regulated by so artificial a means. "Freedom and love are two distinct principles, harmonious in themselves and with each other, and neither can be trespassed on without evil consequences following."[18] If we desire to establish harmonious relations between men and women in society, "let us all be perfectly free, and hold only by the affinity that exists, and the congeniality will be enhanced."[19] Familiar with the writing of Stephen Pearl Andrews, Clay no doubt derived some of his opinions from the notorious "Pantarch." But basically his free love views were the natural consequence of his radical Christianity which led him to critically examine every aspect of life with regard to its moral implications. If God is love, as Clay and other perfectionists held, then every facet of life must reflect this fact. And in fact this is just what Clay preached. "Freedom is a universal desire of our natures, whether we be good or evil, and love is hardly less so. Each is as firmly rooted in our lives; our very existence is dependent upon the two principles combined."[20] Clay would leave every individual free to do what he pleased in regard to sexual relations, making him fully responsible for the consequences of his actions. There would, of course, be those who would abuse such a privilege. But this, in Clay's mind, was no reason for curtailing the individual's freedom, for the overall social relations of society can be no better than those of the individual men and women who make it up. A society in which men and women are restricted in their sexual relations will be one in which freedom is restricted on the higher plane of social relations. Convinced that men possess tremendous resources for good, Clay would turn everyone loose and trust to the spiritual forces that bind men together in social communion for the regulation which is necessary to social order.

It would be a great mistake to brush Clay aside as a half-literate eccentric as his contemporaries did, for there is profound wisdom and majestic beauty in his thoughts concerning woman and her function within the social order. Seldom has any man paid woman a higher compliment than did James Arrington Clay when he acknowledged her as the source of all that is noble and good in society. When Clay argued for free love, it was because he recognized that there is a direct connection between social order and the quality of the sexual relations which men and women have with one another. The sexes were made for each other, Clay maintained, and society suffers when unnatural barriers are placed between them. "Physical love is no less a demand of our natures than spiritual," he wrote, "and its freedom should no more be restrained."[21] Whatever others might believe regarding sexual morality, Clay would impose no restrictions whatever on the individual, for "God was a wicked being if he made us to love each other and then made it a sin to gratify the passion."[22] Clay harbored no fear that such a loose system of sexual morality would lead to widespread licentiousness. To the contrary, he held, "so far as my observation extends, where there has been the most freedom in social connection of the opposite sexes, there has also been the most virtuous beings and the least outbreaks of the lower passions." Unencumbered with the social blinders which prevent most ordinary men from seeing beyond the obvious, James Clay intuited much of what has since become accepted as fact by scientific psychology, as when he held that "the very reservedness with which we are held by society stultifies the nobler passions of the soul and causes an outbreak of other and lower passions." For his own part, Clay candidly acknowledged that the practice of free love had been most beneficial in the development of his spiritual capacities.

> For much that I am,—good it seems to me comparatively; others may call it evil if they must,—I am indebted to love in freedom—to good women who could take me to their bosoms in love when I wished to go there, and let me go in freedom when I chose to do so; neither of us giving or receiving any earthly bond whatever. I never had a more healthful, ennobling, refining influence exerted over me than was done by women, free, independent, truthful women, who loved in accordance with nature's laws, rather than according with the prostitution of statute law.[23]

Lest it be thought that Clay considered the erotic aspect of love the whole of the question, it should be noted that he was well aware that woman is important not as a sexual object but as the bearer of those traits which mankind depends upon for social harmony and unity. "Love is life," Clay mused, and it is the feminine quality of human nature which insures us its perpetuation, for woman is designed by nature to operate in harmony with the natural forces in the universe. The masculine quality, which Clay typed as "wisdom," was undoubtedly essential to prevent love from becoming weak and overly sentimental, and was equally necessary to the establishment of a correct balance within society. "Love and wisdom united savour of God," Clay wrote. "Woman as properly developed is the embodiment of love; man, wisdom."[24] Where one dominates the other, as was the case in America at the time, there is bound to be felt serious reverberations throughout the social structure. And hence Clay called for the practice of total freedom in sexual relations. After all, Clay argued, nature has made us in such a fashion that one love is insufficient in the life of any particular individual. "Are we not one great brotherhood, and God the Father of us all, and our interests a unit?" Clay queried. "And how shall we realize such a fact, except by a freedom to love all?"[25] Making his judgment by the same measure that Plato did when he distinguished between the natural and unnatural appetites, Clay challenged any man or woman to deny that he had never loved but a single individual, however much he had been indoctrinated to believe that any other course of action but monogamy was sinful and wrong. At least a century before his time in his social views, Clay was destined to suffer ostracism for such bold thoughts. But libertarians of a later era would look back at him as one of the most precocious social theorists ever to make himself heard in America.

The last record we have of Clay's activities is a letter to his daughter which reveals that he had taken up residence in *Modern Times,* the community established on Long Island by Josiah Warren and Stephen Pearl Andrews. Again like Jerard Winstanley whose life so closely parallels his own, the beginning and end of Clay's life are obscure but the impact of his active years has left a definite impress upon the evolution of the anarchist idea.

One of the most colorful figures to emerge from among the native American anarchists was Ezra H. Heywood of Princeton, Massachusetts. Heywood was one of several children born to Ezra Hoar, an energetic Quaker farmer who traced his family connections to Senator George H. Hoar and ultimately to John Locke.[26] The name Heywood was conferred upon the Hoar children by legislative enactment after their father's death. Born at Westminister, Massachusetts, in 1829, Ezra Heywood graduated from Brown University in 1856 but stayed on for two additional year's study as preparation for the Congregational ministry, which he never entered. Heywood appears to have been one of those precocious souls who develop a love for liberty almost before they reach maturity, for he was already a convinced defender of women's rights during his undergraduate days. Hearing William Lloyd Garrison address an abolitionist meeting, he was at once won over to Garrison's cause, becoming a vigorous agent of the Massachusetts Anti-Slavery Society. When the war came, however, he was just as vigorous in condemning it as a convinced pacifist. Throughout his life he remained faithful to the principles of non-violence, although many observers have mistaken his outspoken condemnation of social injustice for violence.

Among the decisive influences in Heywood's early intellectual development were the writings of Josiah Warren, which seem to have led him to a formal commitment to the principles of anarchism, although it is evident that he was naturally impelled toward anarchism by every fiber of his moral disposition and thus needed no teacher. First meeting Warren in 1863, Heywood understood at once that liberty and justice could only be attained within a society in which men resist the enticements of political power. Like Josiah Warren, he committed himself unreservedly to the proposition that the state can never be used as an instrument for social reform. Although they were later to develop differences in viewpoint on specific issues, Heywood never lost basic respect for his philosophical mentor.

It was as an agitator for labor reform that Heywood first came into prominence, and it was also in this role that he first clashed with Warren. In 1867 he was instrumental in the creation of the Labor Reform League of Worcestor, Massachusetts. Where Warren was basically suspicious of any move in the direction of collective action upon the part of workingmen, Heywood preached that only thus could they hope to survive in a hostile world. Addressing the League, he warned that "workingmen, unless allied by religious convictions to the organized movement, may be obedient and serviceable to their principles for awhile, but are liable to break and scatter when the old party bugle sounds on election day."[27] Hence, in his opinion, it was essential that labor organize so that it might remain clear as to its objectives and that its collective weight might be felt. In a society where the legislative power counts for a great deal, Heywood had to admit that labor must of necessity employ its strength to keep the balance of power from being used as a club against itself. But he at the same time felt that it must be careful never to align itself too completely with any political party. The New England Reform League, which was organized in January of 1869 largely because of Heywood's efforts, was extremely radical in orientation, drawing heavily upon anarchists for its members. With the formation of the American Labor Reform League in May of 1871, the reform movement became predominantly anarchist in flavor, as witnessed by the fact that

William B. Greene was elected president and Heywood corresponding secretary.[28]

It was for the purpose of providing a means to give expression to the viewpoint of the labor reform leagues that Heywood launched *The Word* in 1872, although he was later to devote more and more space to interests which were more peculiarly his own. In the first number of *The Word* Heywood made it clear that his paper would not be content with halfway measures of social reform but would insist upon a thoroughgoing revision of society. Not only did *The Word* favor the abolition of all income derived from speculation but it regarded "all claims to property not founded on a labor title as void. . . ." The basis for this radical doctrine was the clause in the constitution of the New England Labor-Reform League which stated that since "Labor creates all wealth," all forms of unearned income derived from the exploitation of working people is inherently wrong. "Except as they represent work done, or risk incurred, interest is extortion; rent robbery; and profit, only another name for plunder."[29] Thus Heywood took a stand alongside Karl Marx as a vigorous critic of capitalist civilization. In arguing that "labor is the sole possible ground on which ownership of property can be defended,"[30] Heywood, like Marx, adopted a theory of value that could only lead to a radical restructuring of the basic institutions of society. Calling upon the barons of American wealth to give up their ill-gained holdings, Heywood proclaimed that the only basis upon which property might be given legitimacy was the sweat of the worker's brow. "These empires of mining and prairie lands 'given' by Congress and the states to corporations, must be returned to their rightful owners, those, and those only, who can till them," Heywood proclaimed. "One failing to show a deed from the creator, that is, a labor-title, has no more right to hold land, than to hold slaves."[31]

It is important to note here, however, that Heywood's attitude toward capital was not derived from reading revolutionary writings imported from abroad but from his own sincere reactions to events as they developed in his own native country. When trouble broke out between labor and management of the Baltimore and Ohio Railroad at Martinsburg, West Virginia, on July 16, 1877, Heywood quickly observed that the willingness of government to take the side of capital against labor revealed the class bias of the state, making "plain to all eyes the kind of 'law and order' which good citizens are called upon to support."[32] There was much talk that the burning of railroad property by the strikers justified the actions of the government. But Heywood responded that this argument did not stand up, since the burning of property was provoked by the act of the "over-zealous and misinformed" troops when they fired upon innocent citizens. Incited to action by the injustice dealt them by the soldiers, the crowd in Heywood's opinion was no more guilty of criminal violence than were the citizens who dumped the British tea into Boston Harbor some years earlier. "The different sections of the labor reform movement with which I have the honor to serve," Heywood wrote, "do not think the destruction of life or property a judicious method of advancing any reform." Personally a nonresistant, he continued, he could never condone the taking of life for any cause, even to save his own. Nor was he convinced that the strike was a legitimate method for labor to employ in advancing its interests. But when honest men and women are denied the fruit of their own labor and shot down in the streets for protesting their lot, one has no other alternative than to become a vociferous critic of the existing economic system. Much as the communist-anarchists were to argue twenty years later, Heywood maintained that the individual of good conscience and integrity must of necessity sympathize with the slave against his master, the exploited against exploiter, the striker against those who would deny him a living wage. If those who are enslaved are compelled to use force against their captors in breaking free of their chains, they can hardly be held accountable for the blood that is thus shed. The authors of our dictionaries "in defining strikes as essentially mutinous and revolutionary . . . conspire with capitalists against liberty and the natural rights of working people to property in the fruits of their labor." Yet it is not the harassed workingman who acts immorally, Heywood countered, but those who profit from the economy without making any contribution to it in the form of work. The existing property system deserves to be destroyed, Heywood proclaimed, and thus all "intelligent friends of *natural law* and order will conspire to overthrow it."

The strident tones of Heywood's condemnation of property ownership were painful to Josiah Warren's ears and it was not long before he publicly chided his former student for his intemperance. Heywood, obviously no man's vassal, was not in the least intimidated by his former teacher's criticism. "If Mr. Warren supposes that one can intelligently befriend labor without attacking vigorously, land ownership, interest, rent, and all other forms of speculative profit," Heywood countered, "he is seriously mistaken."[33] There can be no doubt that Heywood walked a precarious line where he insisted that the violence which is unwittingly created by labor in defending its rights is wholly justifiable. But it is clear that Warren trod an equally precarious line when he insisted that one can unreservedly value the private ownership of the means of production at the same time that one sincerely values social justice. The difference of opinion that developed between teacher and student was not so much due to conflict in their basic value or ideological systems as it was to the changing nature of the social system they were attempting to reform. In the more simple economy which prevailed when Warren was a young man, it was entirely plausible to argue, as he did, that social justice can best be served by allowing every man to keep the full proceeds of his own efforts. But by the 1870's the industrial system had advanced to the point that Warren's individualist teachings were outmoded. So much social injustice had been experienced by that time that Heywood was right in arguing that any attempt to reform the economy was bound to lead to suffering upon the part of the entrenched property owners. Throughout American history this dilemma has been experienced over and over again.

An additional point of disagreement between Warren and Heywood was the latter's view on free love. When Heywood married Angela Fiducia Tilton in 1865, one of the attributes he most cherished in his bride was her radical opinion regarding the controversial topic of free love. As they grew older together they became more and more convinced that the institution of marriage was not only superfluous but an outright obstacle in the path of true love. Accordingly, they established a printing press under the name of The Co-operative Publishing Company and used it to bombard the country with salvos of propaganda intended to reduce the institution of matrimony to rubble. In 1873 Heywood and his wife established yet another organization for the reformation of society, the New England Free Love League. So important did Heywood consider this event that he henceforth dated his correspondence with the chronological designation "Y.L." to distinguish the "Year of Love" from the Christian era which preceded it.

In their crusade to make women free, Heywood's chief enemy

became Anthony Comstock, the prime mover behind the federal
statute of 1873 banning obscene matter from the mails. Heywood's
conviction under this statute in 1878 was primarily based upon
evidence supplied by Comstock, who had entrapped his victim by
ordering some pamphlets on free love under an assumed name.
During the trial the writing which most offended the court was Heywood's *Cupid's Yokes,* in which he maintained that marriage does not
add anything to the development of true love between any two individuals but actually impedes its growth. Reading this pamphlet today,
it is difficult to understand how it could have been labled obscenity.
But as one observer of the trial pointed out, *Cupid's Yokes* was not
condemned by the standards applied to other literature but solely
upon the individual tastes of the judge, who was in no mood to see
the props of traditional morality tampered with.[34] Making little effort
to hide its prejudices, the court at one point in the proceedings advised
the jury that Heywood's teachings on marriage were apt to "turn the
State of Massachusetts into one great house of prostitution." The jury
was further frightened with the warning that *Cupid's Yokes* was
bound to corrupt the morals of the young, although no evidence was
presented that Heywood had ever permitted his writings to be sent to
youthful individuals. That Heywood and his wife were devoted to each
other and their four children, Hermes, Angelo, Vesta and Psyche
Ceres, was of absolutely no interest to the court. Sentenced to a
hundred dollar fine and confinement for two years at hard labor, Heywood was strengthened in his conviction that the state is a thoroughly
immoral and unjust institution, although he was pardoned by President Hayes after serving six months of his sentence. The fact that six
thousand people publicly demonstrated in Boston against Heywood's
imprisonment would indicate that other Americans shared something
of his sentiments. In actual life, few men have been as high-minded
as Ezra Heywood and purient ideas never seemed to have entered his
head. In fact, Heywood was one of the most outspoken critics of the
promiscuous life as led by Henry Ward Beecher and other libertines.

The libertarian flavor of Heywood's social thought is nowhere
more pronounced than in his attitude toward the question of free love
and women's rights, which he linked closely together. Nowhere in
Cupid's Yokes is there any suggestion of sensuality or insincerity. In
advocating the right of women to sexual activity outside the bonds of
marriage, Heywood did not intend to grant them license for frivolity

but rather the right to govern themselves in this most sacred area of human relationships. In Heywood's opinion, woman is equal to man in every respect, and consequently, she has the same right to self-government in sexual matters as the male. We need not fear, Heywood urged, that woman, having been granted freedom, will abuse her newfound rights and become socially degenerate. With all libertarians, Heywood concurred in the notion that in a free society woman would naturally be true to her nature. How could freedom possibly make the female any less feminine, he queried.[35]

Published in 1876, *Cupid's Yokes* aimed directly at the heart of the Comstock Laws, which were ultimately based upon the proposition that people are unable to regulate themselves intelligently where sex is concerned. In calling for the immediate and unconditional repeal of all obscenity laws, *Cupid's Yokes* asked for much more than the mere right of the individual to indulge in sexual activity according to his own free tastes; it demanded the right of the individual to judge for himself what is morally proper and what is not. In taking such an uncompromising stand with reference to sexual freedom, Heywood no doubt caused himself to appear a radical extremist in the eyes of his more timid contemporaries but in retrospect it is clear that he was in actuality a most dedicated libertarian whose only crime was that his social thought was far in advance of his age.

If there is any question as to whether Heywood's political thought falls within the scope of anarchist theory, it is dispelled by his words regarding the nature and function of government. In Heywood's opinion, no human institution may claim immunity from change. Just as it is our right as human beings to withdraw support from any prevailing opinion, he argued, so may we choose to abolish any existing institution, such as marriage or the church. In fact, he continued, it is our "legal right to abolish the government itself, it is our constitutional right . . . to destroy the Constitution and improvise new and better guarantees of freedom and order if we can do it."[36] Unconsciously reflecting the idea of human progress that plays so large a role in the thinking of other nineteenth century anarchists like Proudhon, Heywood pointed out that the tendency to progress from one stage of development to the next is basic to human society. We can no more retard social change than we can stop the cycle of the seasons we discover in nature, and hence Heywood stood ready to dispense with government itself should it prove to be a block in the path of human progress.

That Ezra Heywood was not a babe in the woods when it came to political philosophy is demonstrated by the fact that he reprinted Michael Bakunin's "Gospel of Nihilism" in *The Word* in April of 1880, in which Bakunin argued the frightening doctrine that the first step in social reform must be the total "destruction and annihilation of everything as it now exists."[37] Like all anarchists, Heywood's ultimate desire was not to reform government but to abolish it entirely. Needless to say, Heywood was impatient with liberals who sought to preserve the institution itself after making superficial alterations in its superstructure. One occasion on which he expressed this impatience was in reply to a letter from Susan B. Anthony, in which she requested his support of Grant and the Republican Party on the grounds that that party had constructed a platform promising a serious consideration of woman's grievances in the political campaign that was to follow. Heywood acknowledged the National Woman's Suffrage Association as one of the leading forces of civil liberties of the past but expressed great concern for its fortunes should it adopt the political position advocated by Susan Anthony. Having enjoyed political rule for twelve years, the Republicans, in Heywood's opinion, were guilty of supporting a "male usurpation" of power which denied one half of the citizens of the nation any control whatever over their own destiny. Rather than use her ballot to support such tyranny, he pontificated, Susan Anthony would be well advised to use it to abolish government entirely.[38]

Heywood's condemnation of government did not arise from a mere personal distaste toward it but from a sincere and reasoned commitment to the proposition that government is basically antithetical to human freedom. Where people live under authority for any appreciable length of time, he argued, their ability to govern themselves is bound to atrophy. This was why he was constrained to take a strong stand against the political methods chosen by the temperance movement to achieve what would have otherwise been a good end. "The habit of taking authority, the denial of the inalienable prerogative of persons to judge for themselves what is right," he wrote, has led many otherwise intelligent persons to attempt to abolish the evil of drink by erecting prohibition laws against it. It is bad enough to allow one's senses to be dulled by rum, Heywood chided the Temperants, but it is even worse to become intoxicated on "invasive frenzy." A good society is one which is held together by a webb of voluntary social reciprocity, based upon an "intelligent sense of what is right and best, in the Nature of Things, irrespective of what superstitious ignorance, intolerant greed, or irrational frenzy may enact as 'law.' " In such a society each individual must be left free to determine his own fate, regardless of the consequences to himself. No doubt many will at first abuse the freedom that is given to them, much to their own personal grief. "It is one's right to go to hell at one's own risk and cost," Heywood wrote. But no individual has the right to concern himself with the moral and personal obligations of others. Nor may people appeal to their government to act in their name in this regard. "Freedom, not invasive authority, redeeming love, not punitive force, brings temperance."[39] Where resort is made to law for the purpose of forcing individuals to perform social duties which their consciences do not voluntarily recognize, social violence must inevitably result. Men are made brutal not from any cause inherent in human nature but as the result of their exercise of arbitrary power over other human beings.

Supporting themselves by keeping the "Mountain Home," a retreat for summer boarders in Princeton, Massachusetts, Ezra and Angela Heywood were hosts to some of America's famous anarchists, including Josiah Warren and Stephen Pearl Andrews. Andrews, in fact, spent his last years enjoying their hospitality. Pearl Andrews and Ezra Heywood had much in common; for years they had both maintained subscriptions to the *Truth Seeker* and had often contributed articles and letters to its pages. Both, moreover, were fascinated with the spirit world, as were many other prominent reformers of the era. A participant at the Eighth Annual Convention of the New England Anti-Death League, Heywood publicly proclaimed his conviction that the spirit survives after death. Not all anarchists of this era were spiritualists, of course, but there is, nevertheless, much in the idea of spiritualism that is compatible with the anarchist viewpoint. For one thing, spiritualists, like anarchists, were totally suspicious of any form of organization or ritual.[40] And both the spiritualist and the anarchist were thoroughgoing individualists, refusing to receive any truth or teaching that did not originate within their own human experience. Heywood, perhaps, summed up the common ground of anarchism and spiritualism when he wrote that the "impulse, duty, and necessity to judge for ourselves what is right, to prove all things . . . is inseparable

NOTES

SECTION IV - CHAPTER 1

1. Max Nettlau, *Der Vonfriihliug der Anarchie* (Berlin, 1925), p. 214.

2. Letter to Agnes Inglis from A. Muller Lehning, Institute for Social History, Amsterdam (December 15, 1936).

3. "The American Question," *Le Libertaire* (February 4, 1861), 1.

4. *Ibid.*

5. "Authority and Laziness," in *Free Vistas,* II, ed. by Joseph Ishill (Berkley Heights, 1937), p. 216.

6. "The Organization of Work," *Le Libertaire* (November 2, 1860), 2.

7. "Letter to P. J. Proudhon from Joseph Déjacque, 1857." Trans. from *Les Temps Nouveaux* by Jonathan Mayo Crane, in *Lucifer the Light Bearer* (March 18, 1899), 81-2.

8. *Ibid.,* 90.

9. "Adultery," *The Eastern Light,* I (August 27, 1853), 1.

10. "Law," *David's Sling,* I (May 13, 1845), 1.

11. "Editorial," *David's Sling,* I (September 23, 1845), 3.

12. *A Voice From Prison* (Boston, 1856), p. 20.

13. "The Abolitionists," *David's Sling,* I (October 24, 1845), 3.

14. "The Land," *David's Sling,* I (November 25, 1845), 3.

15. *A Voice From Prison,* p. 71.

16. "Letter from James Arrington Clay to Maria Cole," *The Eastern Light,* I (August 27, 1853), 4.

17. *A Voice From Prison,* p. 27.

18. *Ibid.,* p. 42.

19. "The Marriage Question and Kindred Subjects," *The Eastern Light,* I (September 1, 1853), 1.

20. *A Voice From Prison,* p. 43.

21. *Ibid.,* p. 59.

22. "Letter from James Arrington Clay to Maria Cole."

23. *A Voice From Prison,* p. 46.

24. "Love and Wisdom," *The Eastern Light,* I (August 27, 1853), 1.

25. *A Voice From Prison,* p. 67.

26. *Dictionary of American Biography,* VIII, pp. 609-10.

27. *The Labor Party* (New York, 1868), p. 7.

28. James J. Martin, *Men Against the State* (New York, 1957), p. 117.

29. *Declaration of Sentiments and Constitution of the New England Labor-Reform League* (Boston, 1869), p. 4.

30. *Hard Cash* (Princeton, Massachusetts, 1874), p. 4.

31. *Yours or Mine* (Boston, 1869), p. 19.

32. *The Great Strike: Its Relation to Labor, Property, and Government* (Princeton, Massachusetts, 1878), p. 11. First published in *The Radical Review,* I (November, 1877).

33. *The Word,* II (July 1873), 2.

34. Sidney H. Morse, "Chips from my Studio," *The Radical Review,* I (February, 1878), 823.

35. Ezra H. Heywood, *Uncivil Liberty; An Essay to Show the Injustice and Impolicy of Ruling Woman without her Consent* (Princeton, Massachusetts, 1877), p. 14.

36. *Free Speech; Report of Ezra H. Heywood's Defense* (Boston, 1882), p. 13.

37. *The Word,* III (April, 1880), 1.

38. *The Word,* I (September, 1872), 2.

39. Ezra H. Heywood, *Social Ethics* (Princeton, Massachusetts, 1881), p. 3.

40. Geoffrey K. Nelson, *Spiritualism and Society* (New York, 1969), p. 84.

41. *Lucifer the Light Bearer* (March 19, E.M. 286), 2.

Moses Harman:
Militant Dean of Enlightened Feminity and Woman's Liberation

When Moses Harman (1830-1910) breathed his last at the age of
79, George Bernard Shaw, one of his many admirers, summed up the
story of Harman's life by commenting that it was something of a
miracle that a man of such enlightened opinions and staunch courage
had survived for so long in as dangerous a country as America.[1]
Editing *Lucifer The Light Bearer* from Valley Falls, Kansas, and
later Chicago for over thirty years, Harman seems to have been
identified with Satan himself, so thoroughly was he hated and reviled
by the authorities in charge of keeping America's morality pure. Imprisoned four times for violating the crude laws against obscenity that
were in force at the time, and hounded unbelievably for ten years by
administrative fiat and whim, Harman was persecuted as though he
were the most dangerous of criminals. The last time he was imprisoned at the age of 74, he was forced, despite his obvious frail health,
to break rock at Joliet Prison as if the very survival of society depended
upon the dissipation of his rapidly dwindling energy upon so futile a
task. What manner of man, then, was this Moses Harman? And why
was he considered so dangerous?

Born on a mountain ridge in Pendleton County, Virginia (now
West Virginia) that was so steep that it could be reached only on the
back of a horse or mule, Harman was of Germanic stock which had
originally come from Wurtemburg, Germany. Hardly had Moses
learned to walk when his family packed bag and baggage in a covered
wagon and moved on to a new frontier home in Mercer County, Ohio,
close to the banks of the St. Mary's River in what was then a raw
wilderness. In the Fall of 1838 another move was made, this time to
the hills of Southern Missouri. The Harman brood being large, Moses
was compelled to learn to support himself very early and he thus
learned the skills of an expert woodsman while still a boy. But his

301

mind ran to book learning and he soon acquired enough education to make his living by teaching school, working his way through college at the same time. Since his parents were of the Methodist faith, Moses himself joined that church in his sixteenth year, and by the age of twenty was licensed to preach the gospel. But shortly after this event, Moses Harman, displaying the independence of thought and character which were to characterize all of his actions throughout his long life, concluded that a god who would commit the very creatures he had created to eternal damnation for their sins was no god of his, and he forthwith turned his back upon Christianity, never to hesitate one moment in his resolve. The finality of Harman's break with Christianity is evident in the fact that *Lucifer* was dated not after the conventional Christian chronology which starts with Christ's coming but with the execution of Giordano Bruno in Rome in February of 1601, who, along with Galileo and Copernicus, demonstrated the incredibility of the orthodox idea of a heaven and life after death. Martyred for his service to science by a church which preferred to educate the people after superstition and ignorance rather than reason and truth, Bruno, in Harman's opinion, was more worthy a moral guide than all the saints in Christendom. Accordingly, the first issue of *Lucifer The Light-Bearer,* which was issued in 1872 bore the inscription "Era of Man 271" so that no one would confuse the journal with the missals of propaganda supported by Christians and other religious groups.

When Moses Harman thus entered the ranks of the freethinkers, he had in effect become an anarchist, at least so far as religious questions are concerned. Free thought, as Harman saw it, was more a matter of basic personal temperament than it was of intellectual commitment. Having contemplated the state of the universe and his place in it, he wrote: "I cannot be other than a rebel, a heretic, an iconoclast, a breaker of idols—of idols that have been set up by men whose main effort seems to have been to rule their fellow human beings, and by ruling exploit or rob others of their equitable share of the earth and its opportunities."[2] The essential link between anarchy and free thought is plainly evident in an editorial Harman wrote for *Lucifer the Light-Bearer,* in which he said:

> We of the Lucifer office follow the logic of free thought further still. We deny the right of any archy to dictate to us in the domestic or sex-relations; we repudiate the right of any government to exercise sovereign power over the individual in

trade or commerce, in the issue of legal currency or legal tender, in the control of public lands, etc. In short, we maintain that the denial of the sovereignty of God through kings and priests implies and necessitates the affirmation of the sovereignty of the individual be conceded, that there can be no rightful sovereignty of a state or nation over that individual. He who is a subject cannot, at the same time be a sovereign.[3]

Although Harman on several occasions disclaimed the formal anarchist label, preferring to think of *Lucifer* as the organ of no particular sect or party, he was spiritually and ideologically allied to Benjamin Tucker, Emma Goldman, and Peter Kropotkin to the extent that they were freethinkers too. Proposing the formation of a radical league to bring all freethinkers together, Harman envisioned his mission as being twofold; not only must *Lucifer* "help destroy the vested wrongs of the centuries" but it must "help in the reorganization of society upon the basis of liberty, industry and equity."[4] Taking a stance which was essentially the same as that taken by today's new left, Harman proclaimed that the primary goal of *Lucifer* would be to "preach the gospel of discontent," for "until people become discontented with their environment it is utterly hopeless to expect them to make an effort to better themselves, or their condition."[5] The first step toward liberation is to *"get people to think for themselves;* to convince the people that the present system is wrong. . . ."[6]

True to the philosophy of the Enlightenment and its central idea of progress, Harman, like all libertarians, looked forward to the day when the human race will have overcome its present condition of ignorance and superstition. But Harman's conception of progress was not a vapid, romantic notion. His opposition to organized religion, for example, was based on the fact that its foundations are all too often man's "ignorance and fear—ignorance of nature's methods and forces; fear of the unseen powers that are supposed to be waving over human destinies—fear of man, whom theology represents as totally depraved."[7] Men who fear one another, Harman concluded, soon learn to hate one another. And hate invariably leads to oppression, war and the spilling of blood. To bring about the liberation of society, he maintained, it is essential that educational forces predominate, thereby remaking human beings into the independent individuals they must be if government is ever to become superfluous. "Every man and woman," he held, "must learn no longer to depend upon a priest, a Jesus, or a god for salvation. Each must learn that he must be his own priest, his own God and Savior,—his own King, Priest, and Governor."[8] Then and only then will it be realistic to talk of doing away with the oppressive instruments of the state. As Harman viewed the evolution of American politics, "the Declaration of Independence was a grand strike in the direction of individualism—of Anarchism—but nearly all that had been gained while fighting under that banner was lost in the constitutional convention."[9] Adhering to a literal interpretation of the American idea of freedom, Harman maintained that the Declaration of Independence guaranteed sovereignty to every individual born in the land, whereas the United States Constitution wrests that sovereignty from the citizen's hands and places it in the firm grip of a ruling elite. The framers of the Constitution, far from being revered figures, were, for Harman, *"traitors"* to the noble cause for which the revolution had been fought. And Alexander Hamilton was the "evil genius" who carried off the grand deception which accompanied the writing of the new Constitution. "With clearer prevision than that possessed by Franklin, Washington, and many older heads who signed the compromise document," Harman wrote, "Hamilton foresaw that this Constitution could and would be made the shelter and shield behind which the forces of aristocracy, of monarchy, of militarism and imperialism could establish and entrench themselves, and thus would be gained by strategy the advantages that could not be achieved by frank and open avowal."[10] This "New Federalism," Harman insisted, far from being the extention of democracy and self-government it was purported to be, was actually the introduction of a system of "corporate capitalism" which would in the years to come enslave the American people and make them the servants and slaves of the ruling class thus enthroned.[11]

Harman, for all his inclination toward individualism, proclaimed himself a friend of socialism. Walking boldly where others stepped with fear and trembling, he self-confidently asserted that there is in fact no real contradiction between the individualist and communist positions. "As I understand the purpose or end of socialism, that is, of 'economic collectivism,' he wrote, "its aim is the production of more nearly perfect individuals, which would mean not the destruction but triumph of individualism."[12] The workingmen and women of America, he held, will never achieve their emancipation until they have the strength and courage to take themselves outside the currents of the conventional political process. Following Proudhon, Harman insisted that the people must come to understand that the majority will in politics is as fraught with danger to liberty and justice as the will of a corrupt minority. No Rousseaun collectivist, Harman was completely suspicious of the concept of a general will which is higher than the will of the individual citizen.

> . . . God in politics, as expressed in the formula, 'The voice of the people is the voice of God,' is the most dangerous superstitution extant, because it takes away the sense of personal responsibility from the individual and puts it upon an irresponsible abstraction called the state or society, whose edict must be obeyed because they have an element of the divine in them. It makes human machines of men, mere automatons, ready to invade and take away the rights—the liberties, the property and even the lives of their fellow citizens at the command of their divine, their almighty master.[13]

Rather than trust his fortunes and happiness to the state and the political process as it has developed in such democratic societies as America, Harman advocated the complete withdrawal of the individual from the established system. "The only rational cure for the curse of politics," he argued, "is to cease voting for and working for the present party machines; cease voting for president and congressmen."[14] In the place of the present party machinery, workingmen should organize all kinds of voluntary labor exchanges and societies so that they might again begin to exert some real influence upon the policy-making process. According to Harman, the salvation of labor lies in the formation of local and national cooperative industries which will serve as a means for returning the fruit of the workingman's efforts to him. Beyond this, workingmen and women must be prepared to follow Robert Ingersoll's advice when he counselled them to "agitate for the repeal of laws." Drawing upon the political style of the abolitionists, among whom he had counted himself some years previously, Harman urged that "it will be necessary to *ignore* all invasive laws, or even violate and defy them, for it may safely be assumed that no law ever was repealed or ever will be repealed until someone was or is courageous enough to ignore or violate it."[15] Citing the opinion of Ralph Waldo Emerson, whom he considered "one of the purest and best of Americans," Harman echoed Emerson's dictum that "The best citizens are not the 'law-abiding' ones, but rather they who by breaking laws, make way for progress." If there is any doubt that Emerson was an anarchist, or that anarchism embraces the philosophy of individualism propounded by him, surely it is dispelled by

Harman's response to his influence.

But it is not for his political theory especially that we remember Moses Harman but for his contributions to the emancipation of women in America and his outspoken defense of the doctrine of free love. When Harman came upon the scene, the indomitable Ezra Heywood had done much to call the country's attention to the primitive notions which determined woman's status and was a veritable human dynamo in the business of marshalling opposition to the time-worn tyrannies which relegated her to the position of a second class citizen. But Heywood and his wife Angela stood almost alone and badly needed reinforcements in their uphill battle. Convinced that there was very little chance that the male will of his own volition make the female his equal, Harman turned to woman herself and called upon her to make herself a polititcal activist in the struggle to come.[16] Addressing himself "especially and almost exclusively to women," Harman saw the American female as the most important factor in bringing off social revolution, much as Marx saw the proletarian as the primary agent of social change. In this regard Harman wrote:

> While *Lucifer* clasps hands with all reformers who work for human liberty, and who demand equal justice for all, it recognizes that there is a reform more important than all other reforms, viz., the reform that would strike the shackles from the bodies and minds of the *mothers* of man. Lucifer recognizes that while men are enslaved, governmentally, etc., women are enslaved not only in all these regards but also in their sex-natures; that while man is a slave, woman is the slave of a slave.[17]

Harman's championing of woman was based upon what he considered to be formidable philosophical foundations and not mere sentimentality or the frothy notion of chivalry which was passed around so glibly by our Victorian ancestors. "I regard man-made laws and ecclesiastical assumption of control over the person of woman as the most prolific, most fruitful, of all the sources of vice, crime and misery to the human race," he wrote.[18] Even today many people are oblivious to the important truth urged by Harman that power relationships, such as the one that exists when the male is considered to be superior legally and socially to the female as in the nineteenth century, are destructive to both parties. Not only is the female's creative potential dulled by her position of subservience but the male in turn is injured to the extent that he has adopted a role which is detrimental to the development of his character. Libertarian that he was, Harman argued that power and force are out of place in all healthy human relations. How can man possibly evolve toward social perfection when he insists upon treating his mate as something less than his social equal? Just as freedom is an empty phrase in politics without equality, so in the social realm man can never know love until he unequivocally accepts his mate as his equal. Harman understood that the basic role structure which man assumes determines the ultimate shape of his character and personality. Accordingly, it was of the utmost importance that the social structure of society reflect the libertarian value of freedom to the maximum extent.

At the base of Harman's attitude toward women was his philosophical conception of the sexes and their nature. Years before his time in his sociological theories, Harman's views were rejected by his contemporaries as the work of a charlatan or a soft-headed old crank. But in recent years it is instructive to note that modern research bears out many of the basic premises advanced by Harman.[19] In terms of her relative effect upon society, Harman urged, woman is normally a constructive force, whereas the male is generally negative in his influence. As Harman put it in his own words:

> Woman—feminine man—is the centripetal force; the constructive, the organizing, the peace-loving, the civilizing, the humanizing, the conservative, the saving force in the human equation.
> Man—masculine man—is the centrifugal force; the distributing, the disintegrating, the aggressive, the war-loving, the brutalizing, the iconoclastic, the destructive force in the human equation.[20]

This was not to suggest that there is an absolute difference between the sexes, or that they stood in totally separate camps, for Harman was aware that any individual merely approximates masculinity or feminity and is never absolutely one or the other. Each of us, he argued, embraces psychological characteristics and biological traits which make us members of one or another of the sexes. To the extent any individual is predominantly masculine in his human orientation, he will tend to emphasize the male characteristic in his social relations, which is the resort to force and compulsion as a basic problem-solving technique. That is why politicians and generals are usually recruited from among the male sex. Faced with a social problem, the male characteristically chooses to employ force as a means of attaining his end. And since the male has almost monopolized the political scene from the beginning of recorded time, it is natural that the history of the human race should reflect war and physical strife as normal aspects of life. Since the structure of society everywhere is determined after the masculine prerogative of power, the political process is basically one which considers compulsion and force as real agents of progress and rejects the feminine quality of love and accommodation as unworkable. The basic myth by which man shapes his existence, Harman seems to suggest, is what ultimately determines the nature of human reality. Mankind will never know an end to the vicious circle of power politics until philosophers learn to utilize the feminine qualities in drawing the design of future society. As Harman put it: "woman must be the savior of the race, if it is ever saved, from the social hells in which the rule of physical force—man's rule—has placed it."

A world in which woman holds an equal position with man, and in which the feminine qualities assume a perfect balance with the masculine, may well be utopian in character. But Moses Harman was no starry-eyed idealist, shooting for an impossible dream. To the contrary, he was one of the most effective propagandists ever to have operated on the American scene, which accounts for the viciousness by which he was persecuted by the United States Government. As Gilbert E. Roe, the famous civil libertarian and law partner to Robert LaFollette eulogized on his death, Harman was persecuted by his government because he dared to confront it with a scheme of social reform which threatened the United States Government with the one thing all governments abhor—change. "And so it was that Moses Harman grievously offended, and it was for that that he was punished."[21]

Persecute him as it might, the Government of the United States lacked the power to deprive the prophet of followers, and so he became the center of a free love movement which persists down to the present day. According to one of his supporters, Harman did for free love what Marx did for socialism. Even today his writings serve as a manifesto for all those who would break with the conventional attitudes toward love and marriage. In his lifetime Harman's most enthusiastic disciple, without doubt, was his daughter, Lillian, his faithful assistant to the last days of his life. Possessing an enormous capacity to love, Moses Harman was twice married and twice widowed. When his first wife died he was left with two small children to raise.

Some measure of Harman's character is gathered from his daughter's testimony that she could never remember a single instance when harsh words were exchanged between her father and her mother. But Moses Harman, for all his exemplary qualities, did not stand in good grace in Valley Falls, Kansas, where he edited *Lucifer the Light-Bearer* (originally called the *Valley Falls Liberal*). It was obviously under Harman's influence that his daughter Lillian ran afoul of the laws of Kansas in regard to cohabitation without benefit of license and marriage. In her sixteenth year, Lillian Harman, deeply in love with Edwin C. Walker, who was then employed as an editorial assistant to her father, entered into a "common-sense arrangement" whereby she became his wife without benefit of a formal ceremony or governmental decree. "I love you," she whispered to Walker in keeping with her father's libertarian teachings, "but I will not be tied to you." Unimpressed by the depth of her devotion and her painstaking adherence to the idea of liberty, the State of Kansas sentenced her to 45 days in jail, while her lover, who had not yet received a divorce from his first wife by whom he had two children, was sentenced to 75 days for the more serious charge of adultery. Considering herself the compatriot of Emma Goldman and Voltairine de Cleyre, Lillian Harman was one of America's most outspoken advocates of total freedom in the area of personal human relationships. Lillian Harman was actually one of the purest of women in her personal affairs, however shocking her theories might have seemed in print. Although she argued that a woman might choose to have a child by a lover while still married to her husband if the husband suffered from a hereditary disease such as consumption, so long as all parties in the triangle freely consented to that arrangement,[22] she definitely did not advocate promiscuity but to the contrary opposed it.[23] Like her father, Lillian Harman maintained that the love relationship of any two or more persons was no one's business but their own. The state, above all, was incompetent to regulate affairs of the heart, even where offspring are involved. So tenaciously did she cling to her beliefs that she never complained a moment when Walker's appointment to the editorship of *The Truth Seeker* in 1893 led him to reside in New York City while she and their daughter continued to live on with Moses in Chicago. When Lillian Harman offered a man freedom, she meant what she said.

Perhaps because he was himself incapable of deception or

310 PARTISANS OF FREEDOM

PARTISANS OF FREEDOM

infidelity, Moses Harman insisted that the institution of marriage was detrimental to real love between a man and a woman and that it should be jettisoned at once if mankind is sincere in its quest for social progress. The essential ingredients of a wholesome society, according to Harman, are ". . . Freedom (the negation of all slaveries) . . . Love (the negation of all hate) . . . and Wisdom or Knowledge utilized (the negation of all ignorance)."[24] Freedom, Harman carefully pointed out in yet another demonstration of his proclivity to think in libertarian terms, is basic and prior to all other considerations, for "until Freedom prepares the way, neither Love nor Wisdom can have room to live and grow." The ultimate weapon in man's fight to free himself from social strife and disorganization, however, is love. "I believe in Love; because love is the uniting, the combining, the organizing, the creative force of the universe," Harman wrote. "Whoever or whatever debases or kills love, debases or kills life; for life is evolved and preserved through love. Without love, life is a desert—not worth having." Harman's objection to marriage as an institution was primarily that it destroyed love by attempting to contain it within the legal restraints imposed upon it by the government. Love, to be genuine, must be spontaneous and wholly without external restriction. The true lover, like Plato's philosopher, must be one who possesses an unwavering thirst for the object of his desire. There is no more need to chain a real lover to his love than there is to compel the lover of wine to drink, for the basic qualities of his appetite and tastes have already been determined by the circumstances of his birth and his breeding. Concerned above all with the problem of building toward a world in which man could be more social, Harman opposed marriage because it destroyed the freedom so necessary to the development of the individual's capacity to love freely and spontaneously. "Marriage kills love and incarnates hate," Harman proclaimed. "The attempt to bind love kills it, or changes it to jealousy and hate." Is it any wonder, he continued, that deception and hypocrisy abound when everywhere around us men and women live a lie every day of their lives and see nothing incongruous in doing so?

Perhaps the outstanding accomplishment of Harman's entire career as a radical journalist was the good grace with which he suffered persecution at the hand of his government. Gentle to the core, and completely without guile or evil intentions, Harman ironically was harassed by the postal authorities for violating the Comstock Laws which prohibited the sending of "obscene" literature through the mails. It did not seem to matter to the powers that were that *Lucifer* contained nothing that could be considered purient by any stretch of the imagination. Actually the persecution which Harman suffered was not due to anything he had said, for he never indulged himself in profanity or erotica, but for publishing the uncensored writings of others. On one occasion, for example, *Lucifer* was condemned by the postal authorities because Harman had printed an excerpt from *The Home Cyclopedia of Popular Medical, Social and Sexual Science,* written by his friend, Doctor E. B. Foote, a New York City physician, despite the fact that the book itself was regularly permitted to be sent through the mails. The purient sentence of the excerpt singled out as objectionable by the postal authorities was the thought that "it is natural and reasonable that a prospective mother should be exempt from the sexual relation during gestation."[25] On another occasion an entire issue of *Lucifer* was seized because it contained a letter from a reader that too openly discussed woman's right to control her own body in the sexual relationship. On still another occasion Harman was harassed because he had published an editorial from a popular woman's magazine which was critical of the postal authorities. That the authorities were deserving of criticism is plainly evident in the circumstance that the magazine the article had originally been published in was not excluded from the mails as *Lucifer* was. Yet however much Harman was plagued by the bumbling postal authorities, he never retaliated with invective or hate against them, preferring to bear his crown of thorns with good cheer and human generosity.

Shortly before he died Harman finally heeded the arguments of his friends and changed *Lucifer's* title to the *American Journal of Eugenics.* Although the subject matter of his new publication was not significantly different from that of the old one, the change in the title seemed to have had almost an immediate impact upon its success, and the new subscriptions began to come in as Harman's reputation soared. Avoiding all tobacco and hard drink, Harman led a Spartan existence, permitting himself only fruit as a luxury. But unfortunately his years in prison and the killing pace he set for himself sapped his energy in spite of the rigorous diet and health rules he forced himself to observe. Given to taking long vacations in different parts of the country for the sake of his health, Harman, who lived in Chicago during his last years, was sojourning in California when he died. His

NOTES

SECTION IV - CHAPTER 2

1. See the Memorial to Moses Harman published in *The American Journal of Eugenics* (January, 1910).

2. "Where We are At," *Lucifer the Light-Bearer* (June 8, 1901), 164.

3. "Anarchism Again," *Lucifer the Light-Bearer* (March 19, 1886), 2.

4. "Editorial," *Lucifer the Light-Bearer* (January 1, 1872), 3.

5. "The Gospel of Discontent," *Lucifer the Light-Bearer* (April 7, 1897), 109.

6. "Practical Anarchism," *Lucifer the Light-Bearer* (January 8, 1886), 2.

7. "The Power of Hating," *Lucifer the Light-Bearer* (January 8, 1872), 3.

8. "Our Object," *Lucifer the Light-Bearer* (April 9, 1886), 3.

9. "Another Centennial," *Lucifer the Light-Bearer* (August 26, 1887), 1.

10. "Militarism, Nationalism, Imperialism," *Lucifer the Light-Bearer* (May 8, 1902), 131.

11. "The New Feudalism," *Lucifer the Light-Bearer* (July 15, 1899), 212.

12. "Individualism or Collectivism—Which or Both," *Lucifer the Light-Bearer* (August 18, 1905), 148.

13. "God in Politics," *Lucifer the Light-Bearer* (November 18, 1887), 3.

14. "Politics," *Lucifer the Light-Bearer* (December 22, 1900), 388.

15. "The Statute," *Lucifer the Light-Bearer* (July 1, 1887), 3.

16. R. B. Kerr, "Moses Harman: On Appreciation," *Lucifer the Light-Bearer* (October 11, 1906), 600.

17. "The Gospel of Discontent," *Lucifer the Light-Bearer* (April 7, 1897), 109.

18. "Continence or Abstinence," *Lucifer the Light-Bearer* (June 2, 1900), 285.

19. See, for example, Karl Stern, *The Flight from Woman* (New York, 1965).

20. "Hear All Sides," *Lucifer the Light-Bearer* (March 16, 1898), 85.

21. "Moses Harman and the Imported and Americanized Administrative Process," *American Journal of Eugenics* (January, 1910), 22.

22. "Freedom of Choice, The Foundation Principle," *Lucifer the Light-Bearer* (February 24, 1897), 58.

23. "From My Point of View," *Lucifer the Light-Bearer* (September 24, 1898), 309.

24. "A Free Man's Creed," *Lucifer the Light-Bearer* (April 7, 1897), 106.

25. Alice Stone Blackwell, "Moses Harman," *The Woman's Journal* (February 12, 1910), 28.

CHAPTER 3

Bards and Troubadours: Incendiaries of the Anarchist Idea

There is a little of the poet in every man, it has often been observed, and so it comes as no surprise that many American anarchists chose the medium of poetry as their way of advancing the anarchist idea. Although most of these anarchist poets have had little lasting popularity, they undoubtedly had considerable influence in their day in making the anarchist idea known to more and more people. Patron of the arts for many of these poets was the omnipresent Benjamin R. Tucker, who kept the pages of *Liberty* opened wide to anyone who wished to sing of freedom's glories. Two of the little-known poets whom Tucker encouraged were Harry Lyman Koopman and William Walstein Gordak. Koopman's collected verse was published under the titles, *Morrow Songs* and *At The Gates of the Century* around 1900. Gordak, who was much better known than Koopman, "slowly died in obscurity" at his home in North Scituate, Massachusetts, in March of 1903, a victim of Bright's disease. After his death Tucker revealed that Gordak, who had been greatly influenced by the aesthetic theories advanced by William Morris, was possessed by a "growing yearning and tendency toward free communism."[1] But Gordak, Tucker was quick to point out, was not taken in by the false promises of state socialism as Morris had been, remaining to the end of his days an outspoken critic of the political art. One of Tucker's favorite poems was Gordak's "The Politician" whose closing stanza read:

> Statesman, knave, tyrant, meddler, fool,
> I would not *dare* the risk to take;
> For I am of an older school,
> Nor ever can I be the tool
> Of those who slaves and weaklings make.
> The victim I—but time moves on.
> The stern Avenger looks at you.
> You—horrible to gaze upon,
> While murder, rape, and theft you do.

Like Tucker, Gordak saw freedom as something one had to fight for.

315

And he clearly recognized that it is the simpleminded person, who looks to law and politics for his wisdom, that must be guarded against. This, no doubt, was why Gordak urged his readers to:

> Think for thyself; and let no clown
> In trappings wield thee for his gain.[2]

In these few lines Gordak compressed the substance of the anarchist spirit and established himself for all time as a true libertarian.

Another of the poets who was initially sustained by Tucker was J. William Lloyd of Westfield, New Jersey. Secluded on his little farm on which he grew vegetables and chickens and occasionally turned out a verse or two, Lloyd was considered "queer" by his neighbors. Lloyd's frequent controversy with Tucker in the pages of *Liberty,* sometimes prompted others to seriously question his sanity, too, as when he publicly renounced his affiliation with anarchism after a heated argument with Tucker. Tucker castigated Lloyd unmercifully for this, pointing out that since he did not own anarchism, he was in no position to accept Lloyd's escutcheon now that he no longer wanted it.[3] After giving up the anarchist label, Lloyd referred to himself thereafter as a socialist and even went so far as to join "the Socialist Party." From 1900 to 1910 Lloyd edited a journal called *The Free Comrade,* although he was frequently forced to temporarily suspend publication due to a lack of funds and reader enthusiasm. *The Free Comrade* advocated a broad humanism and favored any idea that liberated human growth. But Lloyd had indeed moved far from the anarchist fold, for toward the end of his life he could argue in all seriousness that "the only possible chance the workingman has today to save himself is to use the ballot and by organization and voting put himself into position to defend himself and liberate the race."[4] It is difficult to understand how Lloyd thought he could substitute legislative force and coercion for freedom as the integer in his equation and still make the sum come out to be liberty. It was for just such fuzzy thinking as this that Tucker questioned Lloyd's anarchism in the first place and in retrospect his doubts about Lloyd's ideological stability appear well-founded.

Although Horace Logo Traubel (1858-1919) never formally referred to himself as an anarchist, he was one of the most vigorous propagandists of the idea that America ever produced. Born in Camden, New Jersey, of an American mother and a German-Jewish

father, Traubel's childhood was serene and pleasant as a consequence
of the strong libertarian instincts possessed by his parents and in his
later years he looked back upon his youthful experiences as the source
of his own libertarianism. Whereas Traubels' neighbors saw their
infamous townsman, Walt Whitman, as a dirty old man to be
shunned and avoided, Horace Traubel saw him as a great inspiration
and a noble soul, and he spent the rest of his life trying to explain
Whitman to America. Leaving school when he had reached his twelfth
birthday, Traubel supported himself as an errand boy, newsboy,
printers devil, and compositer, later becoming a free-lance journalist.
"All his life he endured poverty heroically that he might be able to say
his say about men, books, and ideas."[5] And Horace Traubel had a
great deal to say, although like the poet he was, everything he said
was said with regard to beauty and form above all else and only
secondarily with regard to social and political "truths."

From 1890 to 1919 when death stilled his hand, Horace Traubel
edited and published *The Conservator* whose primary mission was to
"keep itself free to welcome all the broader tendencies and ethical
growths, in orthodox life as in radical."[6] Although Traubel has
sometimes been presented as "probably the leading writer in this
country, if not in the world, whose work is completely saturated with
Socialism and, indeed, grows excusively out of Socialism," his writing
is marvelously free of dogma or ideological bias. It is true that Traubel
was one of the staunchest friends the laboring man has ever had and
that he was always ready to come to labor's defense. In an age when
other men made a fetish of personal industry and thrift after the
Calvinistic teachings their fathers had instilled into them, Traubel
lightly soared above the prejudices of his age as though he were a bird
and they were huge oaks firmly rooted in the soil. While Andrew
Carnegie and Henry Ford trumpeted the virtues of hard work and
made a religion of obedience to the time clock, Traubel proclaimed
that "the right to loaf is the right to life" and that there shall be no
other right before it.[7] And with what must have appeared to be outrageous impertinence to these haughty lords and barons of the Gilded
Age, he went so far as to reverse the order of their cosmos, putting
their angels in hell and their devils in heaven. "Labor is not going to
let you loaf any longer," he warned the high and the mighty of
American capitalism. "For labor has decreed that the loafer shall
not loaf. Only the worker shall loaf. Labor says that when you have

earned your loaf you shall have it."[8] Traubel taunted his capitalist
foes to: "Come now, you with your yachts and your perfumes, you
with your margins and priorities, you with your lorded lands and
palaces, come bringing along your dollars. Explain them." Not even
Eugene Debs, for whom Traubel had great personal regard, could
boast of greater socialist militancy than this.

And yet Horace Traubel, true to his vocation of poet, completely
avoided the ideological snare into which so many other socialists
have wandered. For this he had his great friend and inspiration,
Walt Whitman, to thank, for it was from Whitman that he had
gleaned the essential germ of his own libertarianism. Like the true
anarchist he was, Walt Whitman was a profoundly rebellious individual, refusing to submit himself to the formal rules and regulations
of organized society. "No man more delights in revelations of revolt
against rigid rules, in spontaneity and individuality" than Whitman,
Traubel argued. ". . . no label will stick to him."[9] Cutting himself
loose from all the philosophical moorings of his age, Whitman,
according to Traubel, "vindicates the declaration that in all the
essentials of culture, nature provides the profoundest resources,"
thereby placing himself within the influence of the Enlightenment.[10]
Far from being the drillmaster of America's massed hoards, Whitman
was, "by virtue of this inherent genius which went straight through
all cries of sect and model, past all danger-signs, across deepest
streams and impenetrable fastnesses . . . to primal spirit and law,"
the archetype of the enlightened thinker who will be bound by no
rules but his own inner urgings. Like that other great poet, Shelley,
whose anarchism was derived from the enlightened idea that "to
impose our wills upon others is to endanger our souls,"[11] Walt
Whitman trusted no authority other than that which has been implanted in man by nature itself.

Nothing is more pronounced in Traubel's own writing than this
Whitmanesque celebration of nature and the natural man. Political
scientists could prostrate themselves in the dust at the feet of the
goddess of science all they wished but Horace Traubel would have
none of this scientism, with its emphasis upon the behavioral aspects
of collective humanity. For him the greatest of errors was to look
toward the state and its bureaucratic entourage for guidance through
life, for all that government can do for man is to burden him down
under a veritable mountain of rules, regulations, prohibitions and

restraints which no mortal, however agile or determined he might be, could ever hope to climb. The air is full of injunction," Traubel complained. "The hat you put on your head is enjoined. The love you put in your heart is enjoined. The thought you put in your head is enjoined. Democracy has given way to injunction."[12] Exuding a confidence in the social qualities of human nature that made him appear eccentric in his time, Traubel sincerely believed that there was still hope that the control of life could be wrested from the hands of those who placed all their faith in the negative agency of law and the penal system. "He enjoins best who enjoins last," he proclaimed, and we have still to hear from the people. "Nothing is logical but the people." The courts have done their best to convince us that wisdom and justice reside in them and that the people must therefore place all their hope and trust in their decrees, but "when the people awake the injunction sinks to chaos." Under the powdered wig of the learned jurist is a bald pate that thumps like a hollow gourd when compared with the natural wisdom and integrity of the people. "The worst of the people are potentially better than the best of your courts," Traubel taunted the worshippers of statecraft. We may yet see the day, he urged, when the people kick off the traces that bind them to the monstrous evil of government, which they drag behind them like their own hearse, to once again run free.

A prolific contributor to all of the radical journals of his day, Traubel never missed an opportunity to urge the individual to action. "Do not come to me confessing moral bankruptcy," he admonished the man in the street. "I do not ask you to commit yourself before your time. But as soon as you have freely seen you must commence to freely do. Your time for doing is now. Your way of doing is to do."[13] The worst of all sins, according to Traubel, is "to trick your soul by postponements." To those who pleaded intellectual poverty, arguing that their spirit was willing enough but their brains were unable to lead the way, Traubel had a ready reply. "The laws of the state may be written by intellect," he argued. But the laws of man are written by the heart."[14] It is the heart, rather than the head, in which we must put our trust. And it is the individual, rather than the state and its rulers upon whom we must rely. No American has ever made a more impassioned plea in defense of anarchism than Traubel did when he wrote:

> The individual must be left to himself. Unencroached upon, free to live out his career according to the instincts which possess him, he will offer the social body

its richest contribution of health and job. Legislation is mainly contradiction—it
flies in the face of nature—it is the survival of the instinct of distrust—it would
make character a useless mendicant.[15]

To the would-be author in search of inspiration, Traubel's advice was
the same as it was for the citizen. "You writers who are trying to
write," he intoned, "Stop trying to write. Then you can write. Live.
Let the writing take care of itself. Trust yourselves to moods."[16] No
one but an anarchist could urge "oblivion to rules and traditions" as
self-confidently as Traubel did, for to trust oneself so completely to
nature is to live dangerously indeed. But in Horace Traubel's opinion,
there was no element of recklessness whatever in "letting the soul
retreat to nebula every time it wishes to advance to creation"; this for
him was tantamount to letting "the law take its course," and there
was not a shadow of doubt in his mind that nature has equipped man
with all the essentials for leading a social life. No amount of intimida-
tion or threat could quiet this kind of agitation and so Horace Traubel
and other incendiaries kindled the fires of rebellion against tryanny
with their verses and prose with telling effect upon the foundations of
established political institutions.

Perhaps the most trenchant criticism ever made of anarchism is
that its adherents all too often are given to an extreme seriousness of
expression that stems from a rigid adherence to ideological commitment. But this charge could not be made to stick on Charles Joseph
Antoine Labadie (1850-1933), jovial poet-philosopher from Michigan.
Descended from French-Indian racial stock, Jo Labadie as he was
called, expounded the philosophy of anarchism with the same lighthearted abandon that a child displays when blowing soap bubbles
from his pipe. "Sweet-souled, hard working, loved and respected,"
Labadie followed Rudyard Kipling's advice to the letter, standing up
boldly to rulers and politicians while retaining a common touch which
endeared him to all who knew him.[17] With a frowzy coat on his back
and a crumpled hat on his head, he looked more like a wandering
troubadour than he did a philosopher. If Jo Labadie was not a great
poet, he was certainly one of the most poetical souls ever to call himself an anarchist and it is high time that his countrymen should get
to know him.

Born in Paw-Paw, Michigan where his descendents on the
paternal side looked back 250 years to the time when Pierre Descompts
dit Labadie left Rochelle, France, to come to the new world, Jo

Labadie was firmly convinced that he had royal blood in his veins, for one of his ancestors had married the daughter of an Indian chief somewhere along the line and thus it could be said that there was a princess in the family.[18] Wandering through the woods of Northern Michigan where his father earned the family's living by serving as an interpreter for the Jesuits as they made treaties with the Indian tribes of that region, Jo Labadie received very little formal education, although his love of life and his appreciation of beauty must have been heightened by the wild and beautiful scenery he saw daily. At age sixteen Jo Labadie became a printer's devil in South Bend, Indiana. After his training in the trade was completed, he set out as an itinerant printer and spent the next eleven years wandering in search of work and adventure until he finally settled down in Detroit where he came into contact with the explosive social questions that accompanied the growth of advanced capitalism and industrialism.[19] From the very beginning Jo Labadie identified himself with the proletariat and before long he was a regular contributor to every major radical publication of the age.

Starting out as a member of the Socialist Labor Party, Labadie first began to veer toward anarchism when he was in his early thirties. Subscribing to Burnette Haskell's *Truth*, Jo Labadie was shaken by the superficiality of its editor's social views and he soon became an irate contributor to its pages. Chiding Haskell for his tendency to make himself the savior of the human race and his habit of concocting elaborate plans for the implementation of the perfect society, Labadie insisted that the first step in social reform is to free the land so that all who would use it would have access to it. "Your duty," he admonished Haskell, "is not to enter into the discussion of details as to how this is to be brought about but simply to declare the truth, and out of the discussion which it will create among people will evolve some plan by which it will be done."[20] By 1887 Labadie was editor of a paper of his own, *The Labor Leaf*, and one of his most vigorous crusades was as a defender of his compatriots in the struggle against capital, the condemned Chicago anarchists. Some time before this, he had become a regular subscriber to *Liberty;* undoubtedly it was Tucker's influence that led him to totally repudiate the faith he had previously had in the state as an agent of social reform. "If rent is wrong when paid to an individual," Jo Labadie asked himself after reading Henry George, "does it become right when paid to the State? Is it right for the State to do that which is wrong for the individual to do?"[21] Unable to answer the question he had put to himself in the affirmative, he abandoned his former faith in politics to become one of the most enthusiastic of all the Tuckerites.

In January of 1888 Labadie began to contribute a regular column to *Liberty*, which he titled "Crankey Notions," and from thenceforth he was anarchist all the way. Yet even after his conversion, Jo Labadie was no purist when it came to the labor question, for he was not at first able to see any basic conflict between the aims of trade unionism and those of anarchism. Instrumental in organizing the Knights of Labor in Detroit, Labadie went on to become the first president of the Michigan Federation of labor which was established in 1888. In the early years of his novitiate in the labor movement, he still held on to the hope that the transition to socialism could be furthered within the confines of the established political superstructure. "We anarchists recognize the inherent defects of the ballot," he wrote. "And yet, as defective as it is, can it not be utilized by us to advance the principles of liberty?"[22] As the years went by, however, it became progressively more evident to him that it was futile to place any hope in the machinery of representative democracy. Everybody in this country knows, he proclaimed, that "honest men rarely ever get into Congress." Moreover, he continued, "Government, or more strictly speaking, the State, is not a voluntary body organized by men and women for their protection against invasion. The few really organize the State and the others are compelled to live according to its decrees."[23] Having thus discovered the real nature of the political world, he never again wavered in his rejection of it.

Apparently a late bloomer, Labadie claimed that he had never so much as written a single line of poetry prior to his fiftieth birthday. But once he got started he found it difficult to restrain himself. Operating a print shop in Detroit with the aid of his wife who had helped him to educate himself, he issued anarchist tract after anarchist tract, using old wallpaper samples and scraps of leather and ribbon for materials. If the doggerel he produced was lacking in literary perfection, it was strong in sincerity and candor. Addressing himself to the working men and women of America, he pleaded with them to discover the truths he had just discovered for himself:

As you value freedom,
As you appreciate liberty,

> . . .
> As you love home and family and friends and country,
> I warn you, watch the courts!
>
> . . .
> The politician is the braggert and brawler of the hustings.
> The common disturber of the peace,
> The bungling purloiner of our goods,
> And more times than not you know him as liar and knave. [24]

But while Labadie was dedicated to the interests of the laboring man, he was unable to wink at his shortcomings or to excuse him for his transgressions against liberty and justice, as he made clear in a poem which appeared in a collection called *The Red Flag and Other Verses* in 1910.

> I like you, ye working men and women,
> Ye who earn your bread and clothes and shelter
> by the skill of your hands and the sweat of your hide.
> . . .
> But I hate your supineness, your ignorance,
>   your crawling on your hungry bellies like swine to your swill;
> I hate your scabbin, your moral fear,
>   your distrust of liberty and justice;
> I hate your race prejudices, your low-browed
>   submission to flinthearted authority;
> I hate your mockery of high ideals of brave
>   fighters on the field of freedom;
> I hate your poverty, your lack of education,
>   your want of culture;
> I hate your rags, your bare tables,
>   your cheerless hearths,
> And I would cram your hearts with the spirit
>   of revolt
> Against conditions that make you mean and slavish! [25]

Coming to full social bloom well past middle age when his hair had begun to whiten and his temperament to mellow, Jo Labadie, like the rambling rose, gave the appearance of gentleness and serenity but always stood ready to jab his prick-thorns into those who wandered off the path of liberty and justice. The mission of anarchism, as he saw it, was to put an end to the "saturnalia of crime" that had descended upon man like the plague, with the advent of the state. For in imposing its rule upon the non-invasive individual, he argued, the state violates the basic rules of human freedom and consequently ushers in a whole host of accompanying social evils. "All who believe in authority and government, deny freedom, [and] can consistently resort to violence and crime, because to hold authority, physical force, control over others, is itself a crime. Aggression, denial of freedom, is the fundamental concept of their scheme of politics."[26] Without fear or doubt, Labadie called upon the captives of the state machine to smash the infamous thing which held them prisoner and robbed them of their humanity. If this ultimately led to violence, Labadie proclaimed, we must be prepared to accept that consequence:

> The sunshine of peace can gladden our
> hearts only when the blackening clouds
> of injustice roll away.
>   Pleasing progress ordains that the fashioners
> of the world's wealth shall not bow
> in meek assent to the power of privilege;
>   And nature says the underdog in the fight
> may bark, bite, bruise, damage, hurt,
> tear, injure, lacerate, aye, even kill if necessary!
>   The end justifies the means, and
> the cause of the workers is defensible indeed,
>   Therefore, for those who toil and tire,
> who work and sweat and produce,
> who are denied the fullness of their efforts,
>   I have no protesting frown when they
> strike, vote, fight, appeal, struggle, contest, agitate,
> for the right to life, liberty, property, happiness,
>   Be it by individuals, mobs, or unions,
> by brigades, by armies,
>   Or strive with bluster or passivity or embattled warfare,
>   With winning words or moral suasion or
> abuse or satire or argument or lies or truth,
>   With fists or clubs or ballots, or bullets or
> cannon or dynamite,
>   To throw off the deadly load of industrial
> spoilation.
>   Think not we dare not when we do not.
>   It is war, and war is hell, and hell is
> disorder.[27]

Like Emma Goldman, Jo Labadie was goaded into taking the outspoken stand he did as a consequence of the violent surge of moral indignation he felt in the face of the undisguised social injustice of his age. Acting like lawless brigands, the industrial giants of capitalism had forced worker and public alike to bow to their power without regard for right or mercy. To hold one's tongue under such circumstances was, in Labadie's opinion, the greatest of sins, a virtual abdication of one's duty under the higher laws of the social universe. As to the nature of law, Labadie held that "The best laws, the safest laws, and . . . the only laws necessary for the guidance of human action are natural laws."[28] Natural laws, according to him, are self-enforcing and require no political machinery to give them effect. Although he admitted that he had not made an exhaustive study of the subject, he was of the general opinion that "any human action that does not produce pain is not a violation of natural laws, and that conversely, all human actions that produce pleasure and happiness are in harmony with natural laws." In short, Jo Labadie stood ready to hand life back to the people, so confident was he that human beings are social animals fully capable of governing themselves when given the opportunity.

Although anarchists differ widely as to theoretical principles, Labadie held, they all concur in the basic conviction that freedom is the alpha and omega of all human aspirations. To know freedom is to love it, as the connoisseur of fine wine loves the perfect vintage and will be satisfied with no less. Anarchists very well know, he continued, "that you must become an Anarchist before Anarchism can be; that *you* must have an intelligent desire to be free before timid freedom ventures within your reach—that freedom is only for those who want it."[29] With the abandon of an opium-crazed militant, Labadie proclaimed the virtue of a ceaseless and remorseless frontal attack upon the bastions of the state idea. In imitation of the communards of Paris, he would throw himself totally into the battle against authoritarian power, cutting off all avenues of retreat. For him the social revolution was not a glittering generality but the hard glint in the eye of the worker-rebel. As to the methods of revolt and revolution, Jo Labadie leaned strongly toward the syndicalist conception of the general strike. For him the general strike was the sure road to universal peace and harmony. "It is destined to take the munitions of war and human butchery out of the hands of trained murderers and put axes and hoes and other industrial tools in their stead."[30] One of the great virtues of the general strike is that it does not require a trained philosopher to understand its potential in the struggle for liberty. The worker "has within himself the power to win himself from bondage. All he has to do is not to load his enemy's gun." Jo Labadie would have the worker demand his fair share from the capitalist, since what he demands is no more than what belongs to him by right. In the face of a negative response, Labadie counselled the workers to:

> Fold your brawny arms across your brawny breast, my clear eyed comrade; wreath your sweat-stained face with confident smiles; out of your straight-cut mouth say "Thus far and no further, greedy brother"; stand like a mountain against the boisterous blasts of balked frenzy—and the world is yours.[31]

To the charge that anarchism is synonymous with destruction and disorder, Labadie penned a ready reply:

Grim-visioned chaos Anarchy is not.
But with tranquil grace and confident feet,
It walks the paths of the garden of reason,
Restful and radiant as a leisure season,
And the people, simple, unthoughtful,
          welcome and love it;
Tho alas, by that name they know it not.[32]

To the argument that anarchists engage in criminal acts, Labadie retorted that "no one who commits crime can be an Anarchist, because crime is the doing of injury to another by aggression—the very opposite of Anarchism."[33] Although he steadfastly denied that he himself was a pacifist, he readily conceded that no anarchist could ever take another person's life, liberty, or property. It was true, of course, that a person calling himself an anarchist might do injury to another individual on occasion. But this did not logically warrant the total condemnation of the philosophical views he professed to believe in. For, Labadie intoned:

Do not some Christians set at naught the principles of Jesus Christ? some vegetarians eat meat occasionally? some mothers destroy their children? But does the Anarchist invade *because* he is an Anarchist? does the Christian fly in the face of Christ *because* he is Christian? does the hungry vegetarian eat meat *because* he is vegetarian? [Or] are these victims of conditions which drive them to do things contrary to their general principles?[34]

In reference to the hapless Czolgosz, Labadie pronounced him the victim of a power-oriented social system which corrupts both ruler and ruled alike. If the crazed lad did injury to McKinley, McKinley in turn did injury to his assassin. But in any event, he held, the doctrine of anarchism could hardly be held responsible for the crime, since Czolgosz was a registered Republican at the time of the deed. As for the anarchist, no true believer in the idea could consciously choose the method of violence so long as he remained in his right mind. For all his denial that he harbored Tolstoyan sympathies, Labadie proclaimed that "The price of peace is peace. We cannot adopt warlike tactics and methods and have peace. Whoever aids and abets war is a disturber of the peace and responsible for the disasters that follow."[35] But to commit oneself to peace is not to submit oneself to the state and allow it to do what it wished without hindrance, for Jo Labadie knew that it is the state itself that is the real sponsor of violence among men. Were he living today we would undoubtedly find him lying in the halls of the Pentagon, his arms folded firmly across his chest, but with a bright twinkle in his eye and the sly grin of a mischievous angel from one end of his cherub-like face to the other as he spread himself like so much grit in the cogs and wheels of the military machine.

NOTES

SECTION IV - CHAPTER 3

1. "William Walstein Gordak," *Liberty,* XIV (April, 1903), 5.

2. "Think for Thyself," *The Firebrand,* II (April 26, 1896), 1.

3. "Mr. Lloyd's Departure," *Liberty,* XI (November 30, 1895), 4.

4. "Editorial," *The Free Comrade,* I (July, 1910), 6.

5. "Horace Traubel," *The Dictionary of American Biography,* XVIII, ed. by Dumas Malone, (New York, 1936), p. 627.

6. William E. Walling, *Whitman and Traubel* (New York, 1916), p. 40.

7. "Collect," *The Conservator,* XIII (October, 1902), 113.

8. Horace Traubel, *Chants Communal* (Boston,1904), p. 68.

9. "Walt Whitman At Date," *In re Walt Whitman,* ed. by Horace L. Traubel, Richard M. Bucke, and Thomas B. Hanned (Philadelphia, 1893), p. 135.

10. "Walt Whitman: Poet and Philosopher and Man," *Ibid.,* p. 208.

11. Carl Grabo, *The Magic Plant* (Chapel Hill, 1936), p. 304.

12. *Chants Communal,* p. 40.

13. "From *The Worker,*" *Free Society,* X (June 5, 1904), 6.

14. "Collect," *The Conservator,* IX (October, 1898), 114.

15. "Collect," *The Conservator,* VI (March, 1895), 3.

16. *Collects* (New York, 1914), p. 44.

17. Lawrence H. Conrad, "Jo Labadie—Poet," *Michigan History Magazine,* XVI (Spring, 1932), 221.

18. Letter from Laurence Labadie to William O. Reichert, September, 1968.

19. Charles Lutzky, *Reform Editors and Their Press* (Unpublished Ph.D. Dissertation; The University of Iowa, 1951).

20. "Sensible," *Truth,* IV (December 6, 1882), 1.

21. "Letters to the Editor," *Liberty,* II (June 9, 1883), 3.

22. "Cranky Notions," *Liberty,* VI (November 10, 1888), 1.

23. "All Government Rotten," *Essays* (n. d. or p.), p. 52.

24. "Watch the Courts," (Detroit, 1911).

25. "I Like You, But Hate Some Things You Do." *The Red Flag and Other Verses* (Detroit, 1910), pp. 41-42.

26. *Anarchism* (Detroit, 1932), p. 10.

27. *A Welcome Disorder* (Detroit, 1910). First published in *The Valley Magazine*, I (January, 1903).

28. "Cranky Notions," *Liberty*, VI (December 5, 1888), 1.

29. *Anarchism*, p. 21.

30. "The General Strike," *Essays*, p. 43.

31. *Ibid.*

32. "Anarchy," in *Anarchism: Genuine and Asinine* (Bubbling Waters, Wixon, Michigan, 1925), p. 61.

33. *Anarchism: What It Is, and What It Is Not* (A paper read before the Board of Psychic Research at Detroit, Michigan, p. 4.

34. "Anarchism and Crime," in *Anarchism: Genuine and Asinine*, p. 10.

35. "The Great Taboo," *Road to Freedom*, II (April, 1926), 7.

CHAPTER 4

The Tolstoyans:
Ernest Howard Crosby, Voltairine de Cleyre, and Others

One of the great paradoxes of American anarchism is that for all its rejection of organized religion and theology, many of those who embraced the anarchist idea were profoundly religious individuals even while they professed themselves to be dedicated to enlightened free thought. But a careful reading of what anarchists really hold reveals that the apparent contradiction is without basis in fact, for there is much that the Christian holds in common with the anarchist. Both, for example, renounce power and force as legitimate means of attaining community. The more conservative Christian, to be sure, is wary of dispensing altogether with the state as an agency of social control on earth. But the radical Christian, like the anarchist, is convinced that secular government is an insurmountable obstacle in the path of true social community and hence he joins the anarchist in calling for its rejection. Anarchists and Christians even find agreement on so provocative a conception as "love," for the idea of "mutual aid" outlined by Kropotkin was essentially what Tolstoy and other Christian perfectionists had in mind when they spoke of "love."[1] To speak of Christian anarchism, therefore, is wholly proper, as the case histories of some of its most outstanding figures bear out.

Ernest Howard Crosby (1856-1907) was one of the best known of the early Tolstoyan anarchists in America. The son of Doctor Howard Crosby, a distinguished member of the Presbyterian clergy, he traced his ancestry to Rip Van Dam, president of the council and acting governor of the province of New Netherland, and to General William Floyd, a member of the Continental Congress and one of the signers of the Declaration of Independence. After completing his education at the fashionable Mohegan Lake School in Westchester County, New York, Crosby graduated with first honors from N.Y.U. in 1876 and then repeated the performance at Columbia Law School, graduating in 1878.[2] After passing his bar exams and taking up the practice of law, he became active in the Republican Party and was elected to the state legislature in 1887 as successor to Theodore Roosevelt. Two years later Crosby was appointed to a judgeship of the international court at Alexandria, Egypt, and it appeared that he was well on his way toward success in his chosen profession. In 1894, however, after having served five years on the bench, he left Egypt to return to New York where he renounced many of his former political views and immersed himself in the work of social reform. Taking a strong stand against America's imperialistic policies in the Philippines, he moved progressively to the left. It was Tolstoy who most influenced his philosophical development, although many others, such as Walt Whitman, Emerson, Henry George, Peter Kropotkin, and St. Francis of Assisi contributed fuel to the fires that raged within him.[3]

Well-groomed, well-bred, and well read, Crosby projected the image of impeccable integrity to all who knew him and was fully accepted by society. Living in quiet splendor on the banks of the Hudson in Rinebeck with his wife, who was a Schiefflin and the heir of the estate upon which they resided, Crosby resembled Tolstoy in more ways than one. Upon Crosby's death in 1907 Benjamin Tucker commented upon his "inspiring and truly noble presence and personality," likening him to another of his friends, Wendell Phillips, who also imparted the same "sense of modest majesty" to all who conversed with him. But having acknowledged the finer qualities displayed by his competitor, the quarrelsome Tucker could not refrain from commenting that he doubted if Crosby's many books would live on after his death, a prophecy which appears now to have been all too accurate.[4]

In retrospect it is clear that Crosby's immense stature as a representative of the anarchist idea during the last years of the nineteenth century rested more upon the strength and warmth of his personality than the specific ideas he advanced. Sincerely devoted to Christian perfectionism as an ethical concept, Crosby reflected its values in every aspect of his life. In his eating habits, as an example, he tended toward vegetarianism because "the idea of butchery for food is cruel, and you cannot be cruel humanely." With unerring logic Crosby argued that since those who eat meat are responsible for the slaughterhouses which produce it, he, as an individual, could not avoid culpability for the crime if he continued to allow meat on his table.[5] On the question of war, his devotion to Christian perfection drove him reluctantly to the conclusion that organized Christianity had failed miserably in the matter of attaining the peace. The proper remedy for war, according to Crosby, is not to enact a new commandment against it but to make use of the "legacy of love" left to us by Christ. Since "we cannot love men with bombshells," Christianity must inspire its followers to so firm a love for other men, even including Filipinos and Boers, that it becomes unthinkable for one man to contemplate shoving a bayonet into another. "All that we need do," Crosby maintained, "is to become as little children and look at war afresh, free from all the prejudices that a perverted education has rooted in us."[6]

What attracted Crosby to Tolstoy was the libertarian character of the educational theories he advocated. Tolstoy condemns the prevailing educational systems of the day, Crosby wrote, because they are based upon a moral despotism which seeks to mold everyone in the same pattern, and this is a gross violation of the ethical rights of the individual. Rejecting authority as a legitimate aspect of education, Tolstoy would replace it with freedom. People have a right to organize their own schools in any fashion they please and to "make up their own minds as to what they will learn and how they will learn it."[7] Undoubtedly there is some risk in allowing the individual to follow his thought patterns wherever they might lead him, Crosby conceded, and a certain amount of surface disorder is bound to appear where education is established on the principle of complete freedom. But this disorder, or "free order," as Tolstoy called it, only appears chaotic because we do not understand it and thus have no confidence that things will work out as they should. Young people can be trusted with much more freedom than they ordinarily are given simply because they are naturally in "harmony with the true, the beautiful, and the good which we carry in us. . . ."[8] The secret of successful teaching, according to Crosby, is not to guide the student to his goal but to turn him loose upon his own resources, for human creativity can only take place as the result of spontaneity and individual enthusiasm.

Crosby's first attempt at anarchist propaganda resulted in the publication of his *Plain Talk in Psalm and Parable* (1899), which Tolstoy liked "very, very much."[9] Benjamin Tucker, however, was unable to share Tolstoy's unqualified enthusiasm, for there was too much superstition and altruistic preaching in the book to satisfy the tastes of an egoist such as himself. The pity of it is, according to Tucker, that Crosby reflects so much "grand egoism" in his writing that he would make a wonderful philosophical egoist were he once to realize the futility of the Christian faith he professes.[10] "Possessed of the false idea that the salvation of the world depends on charity and self-sacrifice instead of on self-assertion and self-vindication," Crosby barely stands on the first rung of the ladder of philosophy, Tucker proclaimed. And yet, Tucker was forced to admit that for all his religious devotion Crosby was as solid an anarchist as one could hope to find.

Taking over the editorship of *The Whim* in February of 1902 on the eve of its first birthday, Crosby sought to give expression to both his religious and aesthetic feelings at one and the same time. "The real reason why art does not flourish more at the present time is that society has an uneasy conscience," he wrote. "The first and most pressing duty of mankind is to right the wrong, and the art of the epoch must of necessity grow out of a sense of this obligation."[11] Denouncing America's foreign policy in the Philippines, and defending anarchism and socialism at home, he set forth to demonstrate that art and politics, correctly defined, are as compatible a marriage as ever took place. Convinced that the state is "drunk with the sense of its divine right," Crosby adamantly refused to allow government to determine the attitudes he held toward his fellowmen. "Who are you at Washington," he queried, "to declare me the enemy of anybody or to declare any nation my enemy." For all the state's control of physical force, Crosby denied its authority to plant the seeds of hatred and brutality in the souls of its subjects. "Away with all your superstition of a statecraft worse than priestcraft!"[12] he intoned, let us entertain no longer the notion that the state is the friend and benefactor of mankind.

The most important of the heroes that led Crosby to adopt the viewpoint of anarchism was William Lloyd Garrison. Although Garrison is known largely for his abolitionist sentiments, Crosby maintained, his primary importance stems from his libertarian teachings. As much as he hated slavery and demanded its abolition, Garrison was first and foremost a devotee of the idea of nonresistance. In Garrison's mind, the institution of chattel slavery, as odious and hateful as it may appear to us, is not the root of the sickness but merely one of its symptoms. The coercion of man by man is the real cause of slavery; and this evil, practiced by men almost from the beginning of human history, will not suddenly disappear simply because the government of the United States dispatches its troops against the South. "Slavery was a crying evil," Crosby wrote. "In a thousand ways it was a disgrace to this country and to mankind, and it should have been abolished; but it was abolished the wrong way."[13] Garrison clearly understood this and had no desire to support the power claims of the politicians who sought to end the war by force and bloodshed. "Garrison had just one thing to accomplish and that was to make slavery intolerable, and this he succeeded in doing. When it had once become intolerable, it was doomed; but the method of its abolition was a matter of choice in which he was overruled." Long before he had become notable for his stand against slavery Garrison was already a confirmed advocate of nonviolent resistance to power. Like Tolstoy, he was conscious of a basic moral obligation to refrain from any kind of violence in all situations.

Garrison was correct in his attitude, according to Crosby, for the war did not settle the basic issue involved in the race question that divided the nation, but merely aggravated it. There can be no doubt that the Negro is much better off as a free economic agent since the end of slavery than he was before when he was completely subject to his owner's will. When we assess the overall social results of the war, however, we cannot escape the conclusion that there has been an intensification of the evils which so troubled the nation before the conflict. In the first place, the differences of circumstance and opinion which divided the North from the South have not been eased but have actually been exacerbated. Within the South, moreover, both Negro and White have been corrupted in their basic moral dispositions by the "rude and ruthless manner of bringing the change about." People cannot indulge themselves in four years of licensed slaughter, rapine, arson, and rape without becoming brutalized by the means they have adopted. Crosby argued that it would have been much wiser to have allowed the South to secede from the union rather than attempt to keep it in by force. As it stands, he urged, the forty years which had elapsed since the end of the war had not brought the Negro one step closer to emancipation than he was before. Had the South been permitted to determine its own course of action free from coercion from without, slavery as an institution would of necessity have come to a natural death when the economic and social circumstances were ripe for that to happen. ". . . the Southerners would have felt that they had consented to its demise, and they would have accepted the new order with that attitude of acquiescence which is necessary to the success of any social experiment."[14] The Southerner, Crosby intimated, is not so much an evil man as one who is boxed in, like the rest of us, by the institutions and misunderstandings we have erected around ourselves. Any attempt to force such a creature to give himself to imposed moral rules which he has not freely chosen can only end in failure. The real evil, Crosby suggested, comes from the statist who resorts to force and power under the influence of the fear of his fellowman which he feels rumbling through his bowels.

With the very same expression of disgust for constituted authority which was to characterize the social thought of anarchists such as Emma Goldman and Alexander Berkman, Crosby followed Garrison in declaring himself an avowed enemy of political power and the conventional political process which engenders it. The only legitimate form of social power, according to Crosby, is non-violent resistance to evil. Order is necessary and proper to social life, of course, and this must be our ultimate goal as a community, he conceded. But those who urge us to establish government as a means of attaining such order give us poor counsel indeed. Dedicated to the anarchist ideal of social revolution, Crosby was careful to point out that those reformers who reach out for power in an attempt to further their revolutionary aims stand in peril of vitiating any positive gains they might otherwise realize. "The lesson of all history," according to Crosby, "is that men are not to be trusted with the power of life and death over their fellows; and any revolution which claims for itself any such power carries in its bosom the seeds of a countermovement which will bring in again the supremacy of the party of reaction."[15] True revolution is only possible within a social process which relies completely upon "the higher powers of influence, persuasion, and truth" rather than the power of the courts, the police, and the institutions of formalized political control.

Crosby's anarchism was primarily determined by the uneasiness he felt concerning the elaborate system of legal rules and regulations which the American people had imposed upon themselves and to which they had become enslaved. What are those who uphold every law regardless of its merits but fetish-worshipers, Crosby asked.

"We talk of the majesty of the law as we used to talk of the majesty of our rulers; but the two absurdities must vanish together, for laws are not a whit more majestic than those who make and enforce them."[16] There may well be majesty in the actions of a good man, Crosby intoned, but rarely if ever is there majesty in the law, for as Emerson argued, our laws are handed to us by the dead hand of the past and thus have little relevance to contemporary life. "I saw laws and customs and creeds and Bibles rising like emanations from men and women," Crosby philosophized in the fashion of Walt Whitman whom he and his fellow anarchists so greatly admired. "I saw men and women bowing down and worshiping these cloudy shapes, and I saw the shapes turn upon them and rend them."[17]

Crosby, for his part, recognized only one authority and that was the divine presence as it is felt by every man. Like Emerson, who believed that "a man should learn to detect and watch that gleam of light which flashes across his mind from within," Crosby saw men and women as "the supreme facts." Let the individual reverse the "truly respectable" while holding himself aloof from the ancient tyrannies which have enslaved him.

> Respect for tyrants and despots, for lying priests and blind teachers, how it has darkened the pages of history!
> There is only one true respect, the respect for the conscious life that fulfills its true function.
> Revere humanity wherever you find it, in the judge or in the farm hand, but do not revere any institution or office or writing.
> As soon as anything outside of divine humanity is revered and respected, it becomes dangerous,—
> And every step forward in the annals of man has been over the prostrate corpse of some ancient unmasked reverence.[18]

Crosby, like Whitman, heard America singing and he hastened to open wide the doors of life to the people. And yet, Crosby, by his own admission, was not an Abolitionist. "I would abolish nothing except by disuse," he held, for "anything is good enough for the man who believes in it, and the first step forward is not abolition but disbelief." Rather than spend his time tinkering with the machinery of reform, Crosby preferred to give the people their head on the assumption that they knew best where they were going.

> And who will lead the way?
> The good and wise must lead.
> He that loves most is the best and wisest and
> he it is that leads already.
> Where the best lover sits is always the

head of the table.
>Tell the great secret to the people.
>*Let the people love and they will lead.*
>No cunning device of ballot-machinery can give them
>the power.
>>No system of common-schools, spending its energies on
>mind alone, can give them the power.
>>No campaign against monopoly and oppression, however
>it may promise, to succeed, can give them the power.
>>Nay, but let the people love, and theirs is the power![19]

As much as he admired Garrison's commitment to the spirit of nonviolence, however, Crosby was forced to be critical of his mentor for failing to be sensitive to labor's anguish and suffering.[20] Contributing to *The Comrade*, an "illustrated socialist monthly" which was then edited by John Spargo, Crosby's poem, "The Cotton Mill," read in part:

>And you, makers of laws!
>Who are true to the gold-bag's cause—
>Who will not interfere—
>To whom commerce alone is dear,
>And who pay any price—
>Child's life, or woman's, or man's—
>For its plans—
>Makers of devil's laws, breakers of God's,
>Open your eyes!
>See what it means to succeed!
>Confess once for all that you worship the Ogre of Greed.[21]

Recognizing the disadvantage of labor's position in relationship to captial, Crosby had deep understanding and sympathy when the deprived workingman struck back at those who oppressed him, even when bloodshed was involved. "Let us condemn violence by all means," Crosby insisted, "but let us not forget that the very savagery of the men who commit the violence may be the result of the economic position in which they are kept."[22] There was, in Crosby's opinion, no finer principle than that of the golden rule by which the Christian commits himself to means which are consistent with Christ's devotion and love for humanity. We make a serious mistake, however, when we attempt to "behave in accordance with a rigid formula expressing a principle which is still too far beyond us."[23] Jesus was capable of perfect love for his fellowmen, and this is the ideal which we must strive for, too. But until we have perfected the qualities of the soul which He demonstrated, it is best that we refrain from attempting too much. Nonviolent resistance to evil is something to be learned and not a simple technique that can be practiced without effort, Crosby argued. Crosby urged reformers everywhere to recognize that "it is the ethical foundation of society itself that must be over-hauled. The trouble is dishonesty, and this dishonesty pervades the whole social fabric."[24] Unable to view social reform apart from the structure of Christian ethics within which he oriented himself, Crosby held that "the chief work of the church in relation to the labor question must be the awakening of that spirit of co-operation, of brotherhood, of love, which is to be the motive power of the new society, and which sums up the law and the prophets." And thus, though he felt real compassion for the workingman, he took little stock in labor's efforts to organize itself as a political force within American society. Anarchism and Christianity, for Crosby, were so intricately related to one another that one could not be a Christian without being an anarchist and socialist at the same time. The labor question will be solved, he intimated, when all men become Christian. Like Tolstoy, Ernest Howard Crosby saw a blueprint for the perfect society of the future in the doctrine of perfect love advocated by Christ. And like Tolstoy, he viewed the Bible, especially the Old Testament, as that "perfect art" by which we may teach our children to love themselves and their fellowmen.

In assaying Crosby's importance within the tradition of American anarchism, one might well question Emma Goldman's pronounce-ment that he was a "gifted poet and writer." Of all his writings, the only one that appears to have had lasting influence was his *Captain Jenks,* a lively satire on the folly of war and the military mind.[25] Yet, as Leonard D. Abbott says, Ernest Howard Crosby must be ac-knowledged as a "great intellectual figure" among Americans at the turn of the century. Crosby was great, Abbott holds, not because of any original contributions to social thought but precisely because he so faithfully represented the vital struggle that was then taking place within the breasts of so many Americans in all walks of life. Confined within the rigid framework of their Puritan heritage, many Americans of Crosby's day shared his inability to enjoy life openly and without anxiety. Calvin's jealous and demeaning God had perhaps taught them how to be morally responsible and worthy but had told them little about freedom and love. Devotion to God and duty was no problem for Crosby, for his conscience rarely failed to set him on approximately the right path. On the question of personal freedom, however, Crosby, for all his attraction to the anarchist idea, found himself unable to reconcile the antagonistic forces he found raging within. "In certain matters his soul remained, to the end, an arena of warring forces."²⁶ Foremost among the torments that robbed him of his peace of mind was the problem of sex. Crosby understood as a consequence of his reading of Edward Carpenter's writings on aesthetics and art that mankind's inability to find beauty and peace in the world is to a large extent attributable to the rigid notions society holds about sex. But Crosby could never quite overcome his Puritan background. "I confess that I feel no call to undertake the settlement of these troublesome questions of sex," he wrote. "In some future incarnation I may have them forced upon me, but for the present I see no solution and do not know in which direction to search for one."²⁷ Conscious of his limitations in this regard, Crosby could only lament his shortcomings, leaving the troublesome problem of human aliena- tion and liberation to others who had more familiarity with psychology.

What was of lasting importance in Crosby's philosophy was his ability to retain his faith and trust even in those men whom society condemns as criminals. Thus, when Emma Goldman came to Crosby for his support in obtaining the release of Alexander Berkman from prison, he did not turn her away as Benjamin Tucker did, but graciously offered to go to Andrew Carnegie and ask that Berkman be given his precious freedom once again. Cringe as he might before the tempting beauty of Eve, Ernest Howard Crosby could on occasion rise to noble heights of courage. Yet, as Leonard Abbott again noted, Crosby's anarchism was marred by a certain measure of philosophical superficiality. For a number of years Crosby refrained on principle from voting, as all good anarchists do. But in his last years he demonstrated considerable interest in the political process and even went so far as to participate in elections as though he believed in the legitimacy of parliamentary democracy.²⁸ In his effort to reconcile himself to all points of view, Ernest Howard Crosby lost touch with the central thrust of libertarian thought. Although he remained a pacifist to the end, his interpretation of anarchism left something to be de- sired and it is easy to see why anarchists of today view him as something of an interesting historical figure but not one to be consulted in terms of philosophical foundations.

One of the most beautiful souls ever to adopt the libertarian teachings of anarchism was Voltairine de Cleyre (1866-1912). Born in the town of Leslie, Michigan, she was descended from American Puritan stock on her mother's side. Her father, Auguste de Cleyre,

a French native of Western Flanders, seems to have been responsible
for giving her her unusual name, for he was a freethinker who held
Voltaire in great respect for his services to truth. Unfortunately, the
father, plagued by poverty, did not remain loyal to his earlier convictions, and when his daughter reached the proper age, he entered
her in the Convent of Our Lady of Lake Huron at Sarnia, Canada,
where she was to become a nun. But though her father might recant
his libertarian attitudes, Voltairine from her earliest years seems
to have had a natural devotion to truth and freedom as well as
inexhaustible resources of courage. Displaying the same fierce independence and determination which characterized her thought and
action throughout life, she fled the convent and refused to return
to it again, however hard her father tried to make her.

    In her twenty-first year, Voltairine became an avowed anarchist
as a result of the murder of Albert Parsons and his companions by
the State of Illinois. Still at the time thinking of herself as merely a
believer in free thought and without any well-defined ideological
commitment, she found herself at first swept along with the crowd
which clamored for the execution of the Haymarket anarchists. But
as the enormity of the injustice done these men became evident to
her intellect, she became completely ashamed of her earlier behavior
and vowed that she would atone for her social blindness by pursuing
the ideal for which Parsons and the others had died. Spending most of
her life in the ghettos of Philadelphia, New York, and Chicago, she
supported her mother and herself from the meager earnings she
derived from giving piano and English lessons to the great masses of
immigrants who huddled in these cities. Voltairine devoted her life to
the service of the poor unfortunates she lived amongst, much as if
she belonged to a formal religious order. Denying herself even the
ordinary comforts, she fully accepted the squalor and deprivation
which was the lot of the slum dwellers she sought to teach so that
she might sympathize more honestly with them. Frail and sickly from
childhood, her self-denial was not good for her health. But veritable
saint that she was, she persisted in remaining true to her vow of
poverty to the end without regard for her own welfare.

    The ascetic was only one side of Voltairine de Cleyre's person-
ality, however. Equally strong in her nature was a love of beauty which
expressed itself in her great talent for poetry and music. As Emma
Goldman, her good friend and comrade in the social struggle, pointed

out, Voltairine's worship of the goddess of beauty and her devotion to the idea of anarchism often caused a fierce conflict to take place inside her. "Her life was a ceaseless struggle between the two; the ascetic determinedly stifling her longing for beauty, but the poet in her determinedly yearning for it, worshipping it to utter abandonment, only to be dragged back by the ascetic to the other deity, her social ideal, her devotion to humanity."[29] Intensifying the conflict between the ascetic and aesthetic aspects of her personality was her physical appearance. For all her love of the beautiful, according to Emma Goldman, Voltairine was completely without feminine charm or attraction and was destined to undergo a series of frustrations in her love affairs. At one point, while she lay critically ill of a bullet wound, a former lover whom she had supported through medical school and who was then a successful practicing physician, refused to contribute a penny to her care. Another of the great tragedies which wrecked her personal life was the complete lack of motherly instinct she felt for the son that had been born to her. Like Rousseau, she could develop a carefully wrought theory by which to educate the children of the world but had no ability to love children of her own. Intensely aware of her inadequacies in this regard, she suffered a great deal because of it, throwing herself completely into her writing as compensation. No higher tribute could have been given to Voltairine de Cleyre than the one Emma Goldman gave her when she called her "the most gifted and brilliant anarchist woman America ever produced." Rather than being an exaggeration, her friend's assertion did not go far enough, for there were few men who were her equal in the development of a libertarian social philosophy.

In her early years with the individualists, Voltairine reflected Benjamin Tucker's bias for atheism, holding that a belief in anarchism and a belief in God are incompatible with one another. As she evolved a distinctive view of her own, however, she came more and more to hold that the metaphysical position one accepts really has very little to do with one's being an anarchist. Anarchists sometimes fail to realize the tremendous power ideas have in changing the nature of the real world, she argued. Looking back toward the medieval age, Voltairine insisted that anarchism might benefit by emulating the religious enthusiasm that was so prevalent in that period. Demonstrating a breadth of vision and an ability to think outside of predetermined philosophical lines which is all too rare in human beings, she could call herself an anarchist and yet appreciate the importance of the religious impulse which dominated medieval man.[30]

Yet for all the attraction the religious life held out for her, Voltairine de Cleyre called herself an anarchist and not a Christian. The distinction she drew here is of tremendous importance to an understanding of libertarian philosophy. Basically a moralist, Voltairine reflected the same profound grasp of the power of ethical thought as did Peter Kropotkin. The anarchist, no less than the Christian or any other religious individual, is primarily concerned with questions of good and evil, right and wrong, love and hate. But where moralists of traditional religious persuasion tend to establish creeds and laws to judge the acts of others, the anarchist insists that morality is wholly a private matter that permits no interference with the complete liberty of the individual to determine his own course of social conduct. Basing its ethical concept not upon any revelation from a superior power or the prescribed word of traditional authority, anarchism insists that good and evil can only have intelligent application to human society where compulsion and force are eliminated as legitimate means of dealing with the problem of social value.

What most people fail to realize, according to Voltairine, is that authority is fundamentally a negative force wherever it is employed as a means of effecting order within the sphere of church, state, or any other aspect of human activity. For as soon as a supreme authority is established among human beings, the individuals who make up the group are necessarily denied rights. For all practical purposes, the supreme authority possesses all the rights and individuals are only permitted such liberties as the ruling power decides to offer them. Within the secular sphere, therefore, "your government becomes your God, from whom you accept privileges, and in whose hands all rights are invested."[31] And within the sphere of the church, the right of moral judgment belongs likewise to the supreme authority, whether this be conceived as a book, an individual, or a tradition. Whatever form it might take, therefore, authority destroys all possibility for the growth of individual freedom and development within the social order.

In calling upon the individual to break with traditional religious forms, then, the anarchist is not engaged in any subversive plot to destroy good. To the contrary, anarchism, as Voltairine de Cleyre defined it, was a philosophy which bore good news for the individual. For this ideal is "the only one that has power to stir the moral pulses of the world, the only Word that can quicken 'Dead Souls' who wait this moral resurrection, the Word which can animate the dreamer, poet, sculptor, painter, musician, artist of chisel or pen, with power to fashion forth his dream. . . ."[32] Much more than a mere ideological doctrine, anarchism, in final analysis, is synonymous with the "feelness of being" which the ancient Greeks so vigorously sought. Anarchism seeks the radiance of life, the love of truth and beauty, that the Greeks sought without assuming that indifference toward the rights of the common man which they practiced. Yet anarchism also embraces the Christian exaltation of love and communism without accepting the fanaticism, gloom, and tyranny which have so often characterize Christian society. In short, "anarchism means freedom to the soul as to the body,—in every aspiration, every growth."

When we look back over the centuries, Voltairine declared, we find that human history has been dominated by two principal ideas. On the one hand there is the idea of authority under which men place their faith in force and compulsion as the chief means of bringing about order within society. The concept of God posited by the Church is a reflection of the authoritarian mentality. God is a supreme power, a jealous being, who insists upon a rigorous observance of his will and the certain punishment of those who dare to disobey. Under the idea of God as authority, Christians have burned fellow Christians at the stake and have otherwise brutalized the society which they sought to improve. Over against the authoritarian concept is the libertarian idea in which individual liberty is considered the very highest social value by which all thought and action are to be judged. The libertarian view of necessity must abandon the control of thought and deed which Christian society exercised through the institutions of Church and State. For authority, "clad in the purple and scarlet of pomp and of power," can only work where the individual is bound and fettered by controls and sanctions which are not his own and is thus antithetical to human liberty. The libertarian idea, on the other hand, "stands a glorious shining center in the white radiance of freedom," trusting wholly in the autonomous individual as the motive force of orderly society. The libertarian totally distrusts all methods of formal control which interfere with the natural feelings of the individual considered as a social being. For the individual is a product of nature and possesses all the attributes of a moral agent. While he may not at present have developed his social potential to its greatest height, he nevertheless possesses the means to do so. Institutions such as the Church and State, on the other hand, are artificial creations of men and not of nature, and thus lack the capabilities necessary for moral action. They can legislate, threaten, punish and destroy, but they cannot escape the character which was imposed upon them when men sought to effect their will by creating them. Only natural man has a certain feeling for freedom; where man has bent his own will for the sake of the institutions he has created, authority has invariably crushed out liberty within human society. "Anarchism, to me," Voltairine de Cleyre wrote, "means not only the denial of authority, not only a new economy, but a revision of the principles of morality. It means self-responsibility and not leader worship."[33]

Anarchism, to be sure, is a doctrine of revolution and its adherents must be prepared to effect far-reaching changes in the structure of society. But the word revolution, Voltairine insisted, must be properly defined before we can understand what libertarianism, has to offer. For Americans, the meaning of the word "revolution" is particularly impervious, in that our penchant for "name-worship" has generated a thick fog through which the keenest eyes can hardly hope to penetrate. Holding the "American Revolution" as something sacred, although the substance from which it was made was nothing but pure force, Americans generally have come to fear any further revolution within the social order.[34] Thus, though they actually sing the praises of force and violence, they insist that the advocacy of force and violence is a cardinal sin. What hope is there that a people so confused in their basic social outlook can see their way to a higher form of social development?

Finding support for her views in the writings of Emerson, Channing, and Thoreau, Voltairine de Cleyre announced that the "triumphant word" of anarchism is that the moral feelings of the individual is a much more valid source of moral authority than man-made law can ever be. Whatever the mass of the American people may now seem to hold, she argued, the genius of American life is not centralized legal force but the ideal of a perfectly free man. Anarchism is often calumniated as the wildest of schemes because it purports to establish social order without the assistance of organized government with its laws, courts, and police systems, she held. But "the wildest dream that ever entered the heart of man is the dream that mankind can ever help itself through an appeal to law. . . ."[35]

Turning to the problem of crime, Voltairine took issue with those of her generation who saw crime as a disease of character or the willful act of a depraved individual. "Crime is not a thing-in-itself, not a plant without roots, not a something proceeding from nothing," she wrote.[36] What we loosely call crime invariably has a cause or causes, if only we are successful in recognizing it. To be meaningful, criminology must isolate and describe the causes of crime with regard to the power of those who are primarily responsible for it. Like Proudon, she insisted that it is the institution of property that constitutes the "giant social mistake today," for where law supports a particular class of people in demanding tribute from the rest, it is inevitable that those who are deprived will emulate the actions of their oppressors. Like Plato's drone that stings, the victim of class privilege merely gives expression to the dominant circumstances of the social system, seen from the perspective of one who has personally experienced injustice. Unfortunately, she argued, the seeds of our present economic plight were sown long ago by Alexander Hamilton who, as Secretary of the Treasury, sought to perpetuate the advantage enjoyed by property owners by creating a financial system which had two main objects. On the one hand, finance was expressly made to appear complex so that the average man and woman upon whom the system really rests was unable to comprehend how it actually functioned. Secondly, Hamilton clearly foresaw that if those who controlled the legislative power stood personally to gain by perpetuating that economic system, it would be almost impossible to destroy it once it was set into motion and maintained for a few years. The property owning class, "bound together by mutual corruption and mutual desire for plunder," thus came to have a standard of interest and welfare which was entirely distinct from that of the wage earning class.[37] Those who cry out against the idea of class struggle and economic conflict ought to reflect upon the fact that it was in Alexander Hamilton's logical mind that the design of our present economic turmoil was first conceived.

But the crime of economic slavery is not the only form of violence that plagues America, according to Voltairine de Cleyre. Like so many other nineteenth century American anarchists, she recognized the antiquated sexual codes of the Victorian era as a source of social

violence which was as horrible in its own way as the abuses perpetu-
ated under the institution of negro slavery had been. In total rebellion
against the tradition of puritanism which her generation had inherited,
Voltairine refused to observe the narrow standards of propriety that
were then in vogue, insisting upon the right to speak her mind fully
and without reservation on any subject. The married woman who
submits to the sexual demands of her husband without any real desire
on her part for the sole purpose of "keeping him at home" is as much
guilty of adultery as Jezebel ever was, she argued. For the male's
part, he who forces himself upon his wife against her will is guilty of
rape, whatever the existing marriage laws might say. Reflecting her
commitment to libertarian values, Voltairine flew in the face of her age
when she argued that only the principle of total liberty can work in
the area of sexual morality. "If everyone would learn that the limit
of his right to demand a certain course of conduct in sex relations
is himself; that the relation of his beloved ones to others is not a
matter for him to regulate, any more than the relations of those whom
he does not love; if the freedom of each is unquestioned, and whatever
moral rigors are exacted are exacted of oneself only; if this principle
is followed, crimes of jealousy will cease."[38] As in any other aspect
of life, liberty is the only possible remedy for a society that sees sex
as dirty and obscene. "Centuries upon centuries of liberty is the only
thing that will cause the disintegration and decay of these pestiferous
ideas." The sooner we turn complete control of this most sacred of
human functions over to the individual, the sooner shall mankind
see an end to the crimes of violence which now mar man's relation
with woman. Along with anarchists such as Bakunin, Voltairine
de Cleyre called for an end to the power of both church and state
over the affairs of the individual. The church in particular was a
harmful influence in this regard, for in perpetuating the myth of Eve's
temptation of Adam, woman had become symbolic of evil itself and
thus an object to be controlled by others. Following Proudhon's
example, Voltairine declared that social reform must commence
with the destruction of the god-idea itself. Short of this, she argued,
there is no hope that humanity will ever overcome the insanity that
now grips it.

Like Peter Kropotkin, whom she greatly admired, Voltairine de
Cleyre had no illusions that anarchism might be actually implemented
in her lifetime—or ever, for that matter. Anarchism, as a possible

form of social organization, is a dream of the future and not a concrete proposal for the immediate reorganization of society. It is thus impossible for any mortal to lay down precise plans for its realization or to predict the manner in which it will be brought about, she argued. "Liberty and experiment alone can determine the best forms of society." And since the existing social order permits very little room for either freedom or experimentation, the only thing we can do is visualize in our mind's eye what life would be like in a free society. Make no mistake, she cautioned, the anarchist is no idle dreamer, no soft-headed believer in utopian schemes for the immediate rejuvenation of society. He is above all else an activist, willing to immerse himself in the social struggle for freedom and human dignity. We must be clear here, however, she urged, that political action and direct action are not one and the same thing. From the point of view of the workingman, political action, though it at first appears to hold out great hopes to labor, is not likely to bring about a real social revolution. Wherever labor has sought to improve its circumstances by the enactment of laws, those very laws have ultimately been used against it or have proven to be empty shells. Labor must come to realize that its power is not at the polls but in its ability to stop production in factory and shop. Sharing the mood of the I.W.W., Voltairine de Cleyre wrote that "what the working-class can do, when once they grow into a solidified organization, is to show the possessing classes, through a sudden cessation of all work, that the whole structure rests on them; that the possessions of the others are absolutely worthless to them without the worker's activity; that such protests, such strikes, are inherent in the system of property, and will continually recur until the whole thing is abolished. . . ."[39] Thus placing herself in advance of the majority of social reformers of her age, she proclaimed the necessity of a militant attitude toward the idea of social revolution and a willingness to accept responsibility for any violence which might be generated as a by-product.

Taking issue with those anarchists whose imaginations had been captured by Marx's conception of the state as the reflection of economic forces, Voltairine de Cleyre maintained that it was a mistake to think of government as having such a simple origin. ". . . the State is not merely the tool of the governing classes; it has its roots far down in the religious development of human nature, and will not fall apart merely through the abolition of classes and property. There is other work to be done."[40] Foremost among the pressing tasks before the anarchist was the necessity of educating the people to a new social understanding. Aware of the tremendous influence which industrialism had come to exert over society, she sided with those libertarians who called for a return to the countryside. Mankind, in her opinion, had been rendered completely insufficient as the result of its conditioning within the sprawling urban areas that the industrial revolution had spawned. Drawing upon her own experiences in the ghetto, she saw no hope for mankind while it remained confined in its prison of brick and mortar, forced to breath "poisoned" air and to live without sunshine or hope. Writing on the subject of "modern educational reform," Voltairine de Cleyre insisted that children can never be properly educated while they reside in urban environments, far from nature and the great outdoors. "It is the city that is wrong, and its creations can never be right. . . ."[41] One can improve conditions within a city by virtue of certain key reforms but urban life can never be made adequate to the needs of the young with regard to their education. "Until the whole atrocious system of herding working people in close-built cities, by way of making them serviceable cogwheels in the capitalistic machine of grinding out rent and profit, comes to an end," she wrote, "the physical education of children will remain at best a pathetic compromise." Thus in the end Voltairine de Cleyre once again reconciled the divergent viewpoints of individualist anarchism with anarchist communism, demonstrating once more that there is no real conflict between them.

For all her commitment to the radical way of life and the role of the social activist, Voltairine de Cleyre never quite managed to overcome her love of beauty and her devotion to prose and poetry as the best road to the social revolution. When we reflect upon the matter, she urged, we find that our deeds as social reformers, although generous in motive, are apt to be extremely "chary in practice." Like "mites gesticulating at the stars and imagining they are afraid because they twinkle," we must beware that we do not become like so many Don Quixotes, forever waging battles that lead us nowhere. How much wiser it is to seek the elevation of man by causing a genuine revolution to take place in his brain, his heart, his soul, as we do when we touch his understanding and his sense of truth and beauty. Literature, "the mirror of man," becomes a potent weapon in the waging of this war, allowing us to develop a composite image not only of man as he is but as he would be if only his dreams and hopes were to be realized. And in each instance, our task is not to preach at man, to quote scripture or homilies, but to lead him to an understanding of himself and his nature were the heavy hand of the state removed from his shoulder. Voltairine de Cleyre, her heart bursting with ecstasy and love for her fellowman, poured out her libertarian sentiments when she wrote:

> Ah, once to stand unflinchingly on the brink of that dark gulf of passions and desires, once at last to send a bold, straight-driven gaze down into the volcanic Me, *once*, and in that once, and in the once *forever*, to throw off the command to cover and flee from the knowledge of that abyss,—nay, to dare it to hiss and seethe if it will, and make us writhe and shiver with its force! Once and forever to realize that one is not a bundle of well-regulated little reasons bound up in the front room of the brain to be sermonized and held with copy-book maxims or moved and stopped by a syllogism, but a bottomless, bottomless depth of all strange sensations, a rocking sea of feeling wherever sweep strong storms of unaccountable hate and rage, invisible contortions of disappointment, low ebbs of meanness, quakings and shudderings of love that drives to madness and will not be controlled, hungerings and moanings and sobbing that smite upon the inner ear, now first bent to listen, as if all the sadness of the sea and the wailing of the great pine forests of the North had met to weep together there in that silence audible to you alone. To look down into that, to know the blackness, the midnight, the dead ages in oneself, to feel the jungle and the beast within,—and the swamp and the slime, and the desolate desert of the heart's despair—to see, to know, to feel to the uttermost,—and then to look at one's fellow, sitting across from one in the street-car, so decorous, so well got up, so nicely combed and brushed and oiled and to wonder what lies beneath that commonplace exterior,— to picture the caravan in him which somewhere far below has a narrow gallery running into your own—to imagine the pain that racks him to the finger-tips perhaps while he wears that placid ironed-shirt-front countenance—to conceive how he too shudders at himself and writhes and feels from the lava of his heart and aches in his prison-house not daring to see himself—to draw back respectfully from the Self-gate of the plainest, most unpromising creature, even from the most debased criminal, because one knows the nonentity and the criminal in oneself—to spare all condemnation (how much more trial and sentence) because one knows the stuff of which man is made and recoils at nothings since all is in himself,—this is what Anarchism may mean to you. It means that to me.
>
>   And then, to turn cloudward, starward, skyward, and let the dreams rush over one—no longer awed by outside powers of any order—recognizing nothing superior to oneself—painting, painting endless pictures, creating unheard symphonies that sing dream sounds to you alone, extending sympathies to the dumb brutes as equal brothers, kissing the flowers as one did when a child, letting oneself go free, go free beyond what the bounds of what *fear* and *custom* call the "possible," this too Anarchism may mean to you, if you dare to apply it so.[42]

It is impossible to miss the existentialist undertones that run through these words, indicating the depth of Voltairine de Cleyre's religious feelings. With her, religion was no hollow mockery but a living, consuming belief in her fellowman. When she called for the realization of the anarchist idea, she did so not for political reasons but for the sake of her fundamental religious values. Avoiding the dualism of religion and culture which characterizes the modern age, Voltairine de Cleyre insisted with Peter Kropotkin that society must reflect man's spiritual concern for his fellowman or acknowledge that religious values have no real existence. Anarchism, therefore, was more a matter of ethics, broadly conceived, than it was of politics. And the great "sin our fathers sinned was that they did not trust liberty wholly." Turning our backs upon the "Authority idea," we must once again learn to be free men, trusting our innermost feelings and inclinations rather than the formal controls of government. Failing in our efforts to effect a real social revolution, we can expect one day to hear a "terrible leaden groan," whereupon we will know that here in America "beneath the floating banner of the stars and stripes, more than fifty million human hearts have burst. A dynamite bomb that will shock the continent to its foundations and knock the sea back from its shores."

Brand Whitlock (1869-1934) was another well-known Tolstoyan of nineteenth century American anarchism, although he is ultimately located on the fringes of libertarian thought rather than at its core. Born the son of a Methodist minister in the quiet rural community of Urbana, Ohio, where his maternal grandfather had maintained one of the stations in the underground railroad for escaping slaves, Whitlock's political career was initially shaped by the idealism that surrounded him in his youth.[43] After serving time as a reporter on the *Toledo Blade*, Whitlock went to Chicago where he found work on the *Herald* and later became Secretary of State under Governor John P. Altgeld. Not only did Whitlock derive the essentials of his progressive political views from Altgeld but it was also by him that he was introduced to Clarence Darrow, who in turn introduced him to the social views of Tolstoy.[44]

After studying law and passing his bar exams, Whitlock returned to Ohio, settling in Toledo where he set up a legal practice and did freelance writing on the side. Here he came under the influence of the mayor, "Golden Rule" Jones, a Welsh immigrant who had succeeded in building a prosperous manufacturing concern which he ran according to the principles of the Christian doctrine as interpreted by Tolstoy. Teaming up together, the old Mayor and the young, idealistic lawyer made a practice of visiting the city's jails where they sought out worthy individuals who needed help in escaping from the sticky tentacles of the impersonal legal system, Jones paying the court fees and Whitlock representing them in court without charge.[45] Never before nor since has the City of Toledo enjoyed so much justice as it did under these two Tolstoyans. After Jones' retirement, Brand Whitlock was elected mayor in 1905. His administration was a faithful reflection of the charitable acts he had seen performed by his grandfather, Governor Altgeld, Golden Rule Jones, and other heroes he chanced to know and admire. In an era when municipal government was uniformly corrupt, Toledo under Mayor Whitlock enjoyed the reputation of being one of the cleanest and safest urban communities in the nation and Brand Whitlock soon enjoyed the reputation of being one of the country's finest and most progressive mayors. When he was not too busy with his official duties in running the city, Whitlock moonlighted as a writer, producing a number of novels which cast a great deal of light on the workings of the Progressive mind even if they did not possess lasting literary significance.

There were, to be sure, those who were critical of Whitlock and his administration. Clergymen were particularly bitter with respect to Whitlock, for not only did he allow wine and beer to be drunk in the city on Sundays but he openly professed himself to be sympathetic to religious free thought. But the most harsh criticism to burn Whitlock's ears came from Emma Goldman after a meeting which she was to address in Toledo was broken up by the police. Of this incident she wrote years later, "The action of the authorities in Toledo was especially reprehensible because the Mayor, Brand Whitlock, was supposed to be a man of advanced ideas, known as a Tolstoyan and a 'philosophical' anarchist." Like all those who feel compelled to soften their position by hedging it with the adjective "philosophical," Emma harped, Whitlock proved himself to be neither an anarchist nor a philosopher when he failed to insist that free speech be protected in Toledo whatever the cost.[46]

In retrospect it appears clear that Emma Goldman was correct in her assessment of Whitlock's libertarian qualities, for he was more an anarchist in name than he was in deed. Had it not been for the fact that his Tolstoyan leanings brought him under the anarchist standard, he would never have been recognized as more than a Progressive in politics. Despite all the doubts he harbored about the political process and the low esteem in which he held politicians, Brand Whitlock was not at all certain that people are capable of leading their own lives without the help of law and authority. When in Woodrow Wilson's administration he was appointed ambassador to Belgium, Whitlock again became revered by the people whom he served, for he was truly a man of noble sentiments and high ideals who conscientiously sought to give the best that was in him. But he never appears to have been thoroughly convinced that life is possible without government to regulate and control the people when they come into conflict with one another. Writing to his dear friend, Clarence Darrow, Whitlock, after noting that the nations of the world were about to engage in a disastrous restriction of trade by imposing tariffs upon one another's goods, wrote, "How incredibly stupid the human race is to persist in clutching at these economic heresies for salvation, and above all for not listening to us! Haven't we told them plainly and often enough what they ought to do?"[47] Whitlock, no doubt, meant this remark to be interpreted as frivolous jest but the imperious tone these words convey is probably a reflection of his true political sentiments.

As he became older, Whitlock became more conservative in bearing and deed with each passing year until he had pretty much repudiated most of the libertarian ideals he professed as a younger man. Not even the distrust of organized religion and moral indoctrination he had espoused as a Tolstoyan were free from doubt and in his last years he took active membership in the Episcopal Church. The actual ideological distance he stood from anarchism is most accurately measured by the melancholy thoughts that filled his head as be came to recognize that he could never complete the book on Walt Whitman he had been planning for years. Writing to his publisher, he was forced to confess that much of what Whitman wrote now left him unmoved, and that in his opinion, the true beauty of America was to be found "in the old-fashioned mid-western life" he had experienced as a boy. "I wish that I could think that it was there still as it was when I was a boy, and that nothing, not even democracy or democratic poets, could change it or make it other than it was," he wrote.[48] Brand Whitlock, to be sure, remained the same high-minded individual he had always been but his pretentions toward being an anarchist were obviously more fanciful than real.

One of the most genuinely libertarian Tolstoyans was Clarence Darrow (1857-1938), whose upbringing and career greatly resembled that of Brand Whitlock, albeit there were essential differences in their basic ideological positions. Born and raised in the rural village of Kinsman, Ohio, Darrow's character was greatly shaped by the free thought convictions his unusual parents held despite the deep-rooted provincialism that surrounded them on all sides. When Darrow had reached the impressionable age of five, the charismatic John Brown had come to call upon his father in connection with the Underground Railroad and had sent shivers up the boy's spine when he exhorted the bright-eyed youngster never to deny his friendship to the oppressed Negro as he went through life.[49] When in later years Darrow found himself coming again and again to the aid of black people who had been victimized by the law, usually at great financial loss to himself, it was undoubtedly the spirit of John Brown's example that haunted him. After studying law, Darrow, too, made his way to Chicago where he became one of the inner circle who had the confidence of Governor Altgeld. It was Altgeld's book, *Our Penal Code and Its Victims*, that helped Darrow decide to devote his life to the defense of the poor unfortunates who get caught up in the impersonal but vicious machinery of the American system of law. Observing the courts and the police from behind the scenes as they went about the impossible task of trying to make men good by imposing archaic modes of punishment upon them, Darrow became a convinced anarchist.[50]

In 1902 Darrow published *Resist Not Evil* in which he revealed not only his commitment to the Tolystoyan philosophy of nonresistance but a deep and abiding faith in the libertarian theory advanced by anarchism. As society is presently structured, Darrow complained, "violence and wrong" are the foundations upon which all social relationships rest. Behind the laws and court system of modern society is a system of property rights that determines who shall enjoy freedom and who shall not. Almost all the offenses punishable under our criminal code, he argued, relate in one way or another to the preservation of private property in the hands of those in which it presently rests. Although almost ninety per cent of the people who find themselves in prison got there for crimes against property, everywhere one turns the wealthy few remain securely in control of the vast preponderance of wealth. Surely this indicates, Darrow told the inmates of Cook County Jail, that the real purpose of the law is not the pursuit of justice but the support of the property right of those who control it.[51] Were it not for the soldier with his bayonet and the policeman with his club, he mused, the entire social system would collapse under the dead weight of the hatred and ill will that such injustice engenders.

Unlike his friend, Brand Whitlock, Clarence Darrow did not merely pay lip service to the anarchist idea but sincerely believed that it held the key by which men might open the doors of freedom. Darrow, to be sure, shared with Whitlock the conviction that popular democracy as it was practiced in the modern age was not necessarily the best of all possible systems. Popular democracy, Darrow proclaimed, "is the mediocre, the thimble riggers, the cheap players to the crowd, the men who take the customs and thoughts of the common people, who weave them into song and oratory, and feed them back to the crowd to get their votes."[52] His disillusionment with democracy, however, was not because he did not think that men can rule themselves but because he did not think that democracy gave them a fair chance to do so. The architects of modern democracy, Darrow argued, made the serious mistake of assuming that without rule from above, people cannot govern themselves, and hence even in democracies the few govern the many, whatever rhetorical arguments the few may make to disguise that fact. "The history of the past and the present alike proves beyond a doubt that if there is, or ever was any large class, from which society needed to be saved, it is those same rulers who have been placed in absolute charge of the lives and destinies of their fellowmen."[53] Rather than making an abrupt and final break with the tradition of tyranny maintained by the autocratic regimes of the past, Darrow pointed out, modern democracy merely continues in the pattern set by the absolute monarchs of old. Authority is authority by whatever name it may be known, and its effect upon people is the same, whether it is called democracy or something else.

Like Tolstoy, Darrow called for a thorough revamping of the existing social structure and the adoption of new and more rational techniques whereby men might govern themselves. "The non-resistant pleads for a better order," he wrote, "one in which the law of love and mercy will be the foundation of every relationship of man with man."[54] A keen student of social psychology, Darrow harbored no illusion that the transition to a free society would be an easy thing to accomplish. Even if by some miracle the jails and prisons of existing society were to be immediately torn down, he warned, force and violence exercised by one man over another would persist for some time, for once men have learned authoritarian patterns of behavior, great effort is required to help them unlearn them. The first step in the direction of a genuine social revolution in which force and violence would be eliminated from society, according to Darrow, would be the adoption of a policy in which force and violence would be declared inappropriate as a device for controlling men. Once society took this crucial step, the social atmosphere would begin to clear and the possibility of real social order would begin to grow. At the basis of all Darrow's thinking about social and political questions was the libertarian belief that "To change the individual you must change the heart, and then the conduct must be free." Hatred cannot cure hatred, he argued, for men always respond to others as they have themselves been treated. "You may force men against their will to do certain things," he cautioned, "but their heart is a seething mass waiting for a time when they may accomplish other things by violence."[55]

Although Darrow, like all libertarians, was adamantly opposed to employing force against other men to determine their behavior, he did not advocate a supine surrender upon the part of the individual when confronted with tyranny from the hands of his rulers. "Nothing is so loved by tyrants as obedient subjects," he wrote in this connection. "Nothing so soon destroys freedom as cowardly and servile acquiescence. Men will never have any more liberty than they are ready to fight to take and preserve."[56] But his call to resist oppression was not designed to stir men to take up arms and shed blood, although he did recognize that there might possibly be instances when such bloodshed was justifiable. The German advance on Belgium during the First World War was one such instance when freedom could only be preserved by means of violence, in Darrow's opinion, and hence he joined Kropotkin and Tucker in supporting the allied cause. Under ordinary circumstances, however, to fight back against tyranny meant in Darrow's mind to stand firm against those authoritarians who have no trust in freedom and who therefore take every opportunity to fasten mankind ever more securely in the web of legalism spun by the state. Every man must choose his own weapons in this never-ending battle, and the weapon of Darrow's choice was the phenomenal skill he developed as a defender of the underdog in America's courts of law. To the very end of his long life he fought case after case in order to wrest from the bloody talons of the state those victims it sought to devour. Unlike some lawyers who adopt a slavish and unthinking devotion to the legal system they make their living from whether or not it warrants or deserves respect, Darrow considered positive law as being far from sacred. "To violate law is often the highest, most sacred duty that can devolve upon the citizen," he wrote. The fact is, Darrow argued, "The world worships and venerates many of its dead because they violated law. Every new religion, every social advancement has been carried on in violation of human law."[57] To the end of his brilliant career as a trial lawyer, Darrow continued to maintain that law is actually a hindrance in the path of justice rather than the means to attain it, and that the true order that society might effect in the absence of a rigid, unyielding legal system must wait until people learn to live without law and constituted government.

In final analysis it is Clarence Darrow's penetrating criticism of law and not merely the Tolstoyan label he attached to himself that permits us to claim him for anarchism. In the early days of his career, as the historian, Ray Ginger, points out, Clarence Darrow, like all men, did the things he did in response to mixed motives, and hence he dabbled in politics at the same time that he sought to serve the high ideals that made claim to his heart. "He spent his evenings alternately: some giving stump speeches in front of flophouses and brothels for the outrageously corrupt Democratic machine in the first Ward; others giving stump speeches in front of saloons and factories asking clemency for the Haymarket prisoners," Ginger wrote.[58] Darrow's experience with law led him increasingly to the conviction that the American legal system is a veritable jungle in which all kinds of man-eating beasts lurk in the shadows waiting for the innocent and defenseless to stumble into their trap. This is particularly true in the area of criminal law, according to Darrow, for the poor and uneducated individuals who fall victim to the legal technicalities it works by are no match for the tremendous power of the state. "Every criminal trial is a man-hunt where the object of the pack is to get the prey," Darrow wrote. "The purpose of the defense is to effect his escape. It is a game where the dice are loaded, and the victim is almost sure to lose."[59]

Even more destructive to the freedom of the individual, according to Darrow, are those laws designated under the vague and amorphous label of conspiracy. "If there are still any citizens interested in

protecting human liberty," Darrow wrote in his declining years,
"let them study the conspiracy laws of the United States. They have
grown apace in the last forty years until today no one's liberty is
safe."[60] Under the conspiracy laws, according to Darrow, zealous
public prosecutors can turn relatively innocuous breeches of civic
conduct into the most monstrous of crimes simply by connecting
the actions of two or more individuals together and claiming that they
were designed to overthrow the existing political order. In the hands
of such unbalanced power mongers as Attorney General A. Mitchel
Palmer, Darrow charged, the conspiracy laws become a veritable
"drag-net for compassing the imprisonment and death of men whom
the ruling class does not like."[61] When courts convene for the purpose
of hearing conspiracy charges, Darrow argued, the most ridiculous
of evidence is permitted to be entered in the record on the grounds
that a direct linkage in the actions of the defendants may later be
demonstrated. But we all know, he hastened to point out, that no
human being is capable of holding opinions with mental reservations
and hence even after the evidence has been conclusively demonstrated
to be false, the testimony against the accused remains active in the
minds of the jurrors. With the spectacle of the Chicago Conspiracy
Trial of Jerry Rubin and others fresh in mind, one must credit
Clarence Darrow with remarkable foresight.

Molded as he was in the pattern of enlightened free thought he
had learned from his father and the other important influences who
had shaped his character, Clarence Darrow continued throughout
his long life to grow and change with the times, searching always
for new insights that would liberate his mind from the dead hand
of the past. "Once we have learnt from science that nothing held
evil today has not in historic times been held good, that nothing held
good today has not similarly been held evil," he opined, "what else
can we do but seek new truth as we examine the unexploded truths
of mankind."[62] A dramatic demonstration of his ability to readjust
his mind to new circumstances and evidence was given during the
closing months of World War I when the British Government invited
him to Europe for a briefing on the atrocities that German troops
were alledgedly committing against women and children. Although
in 1917 Darrow had renounced his former pacifism to support the
war, he had become notorious during the early war years for his
defense of conscientious objectors who were hauled before the courts

NOTES

SECTION IV - CHAPTER 4

1. Woodcock, *Anarchism,* (New York, 1962), p. 224.

2. "Ernest Howard Crosby," *The National Cyclopedia of American Biography,* X (New York, 1909), p. 61. See also: *Addresses in Memory of Ernest Howard Crosby* (New York, 1907); and, Perry E. Gianakos, "Ernest Howard Crosby: A Forgotten Tolstoyan Anti-Militarist and Anti-Imperialist," *American Studies*, XIII (Spring, 1972), 11-29.

3. Leonard D. Abbot, *Ernest Howard Crosby: A Valuation and a Tribute* (Westwood, Massachusetts, 1907), p. 11.

4. "On Picket Duty," *Liberty,* XV (April, 1907), 3.

5. Ernest Howard Crosby and Elisee Reclus, *The Meat Fetish: Two Essays on Vegetarianism* (London, 1905), p. 7.

6. *War from the Christian Point of View* (Boston, 1900), p. 11.

7. *Tolstoy as a School Teacher* (London, 1904), p. 45. See also, "Count Tolstoy's Philosophy of Life," *The Arena*, XV (December, 1895), 281.

8. *Ibid*, 30.

9. *Free Society*, VI (January 14, 1900), 4.

10. *Liberty*, XIV (September, 1899), 5.

11. *The Whim*, IV (September, 1902), 40.

12. *Swords and Plowshares* (New York, 1902), p. 15.

13. *Garrison the Non-Resident* (Chicago, 1905), p. 123.

14. *Ibid.*, p. 95.

15. *Ibid.*, p. 140.

16. *Ibid.*, p. 128.

17. *Broad-Cast* (New York, 1905).

18. *Ibid.*

19. *Ibid.*

20. *Garrison the Non-Resistant*, p. 52.

21. *The Comrade*, I (March, 1902), 61.

22. *Garrison the Non-Resistant*, p. 52.

23. *Labor and Neighbor* (Chicago, 1908), p. 94.

24. *Garrison the Non-Resistant*, p. 78.

25. Recently reissued by the Gregg Press, Crosby's middle initial was incorrectly given as S. instead of H.

26. Abbott, *op. cit.*, p. 12.

27. *Edward Carpenter*, p. 47.

28. Leonard D. Abbott, "Ernest Howard Crosby," *Mother Earth*, I (February, 1907), 22.

29. Emma Goldman, *Voltairine de Cleyre* (Berkley Heights, 1932), p. 30. See also: Harry Kelly et al, "Voltairine de Cleyre; A Tribute," *Mother Earth*, VII (July, 1911), 146-155.

30. Voltairine de Cleyre, *Selected Works*, ed. by Alexander Berkman (New York, 1914), pp. 85-86.

31. Voltairine de Cleyre, "The Economic Tendency of Free Thought," *Liberty*, VI (February 15, 1890), 3.

32. *Selected Works*, p. 138.

33. *Ibid.*, p. 216.

34. *Ibid.*, p. 131.

35. *Ibid.*, p. 170.

36. "Crime and Punishment," a lecture delivered before the Social Science Club of Philadelphia, March 15, 1903. Reprinted in *Selected Works.*

37. "Anarchism and American Traditions," *Mother Earth*, III (December, 1908), 386.

38. *Selected Works*, p. 197.

39. *Direct Action* (New York, 1912), pp. 18-19. Reprinted in *Selected Works.*

40. *Selected Works*, p. 105.

41. *Ibid.*, p. 336.

42. *Ibid.*, pp. 113-114.

43. *Forty Years of It* (New York, 1914), p. 6.

44. Robert M. Crunden, *A Hero in Spite of Himself: Brand Whitlock in Art, Politics, and War* (New York, 1969), p. 77.

45. *Ibid.*, p. 97. See also, "Biographical Introduction," *The Letters of Brand Whitlock*, ed. by Allan Nevins (New York, 1936).

46. *Living My Life*, p. 396.

47. *Letters of Brand Whitlock*, p. 514.

48. *Ibid.*, p. 292.

49. Irving Stone, *Clarence Darrow; For the Defense* (Garden City, 1941), p. 470.

50. *Liberation*, II (April, 1957), 3. For a statement of the exact opposite point of view, see Victor S. Yarros, *My Eleven Years with Clarence Darrow* (Girard, Kansas; 1950), p. 9.

51. *Crime and Criminals* (Chicago, 1919), p. 28.

52. "Will Democracy Cure the Social Evils of the World," *The Modern School*, III (March, 1917), 215.

53. *Resist Not Evil* (Chicago, 1902), p. 18.

54. *Ibid.*, p. 159.

55. *Darrow-Lewis Debate on the Theory of Non-Resistance* (Chicago, 1910), p. 35.

56. *The Story of My Life* (New York, 1932), p. 297.

57. *Resist Not Evil*, p. 127.

58. *Altgeld's America* (Chicago, 1965), p. 56.

59. *The Story of My Life,* p. 332.

60. *Ibid.*, p. 64.

61. *Ibid.*, p. 144.

62. *Infidels and Heretics: An Agnostic's Anthology*, ed. by Clarence Darrow and Wallace Rice (Boston, 1929), p. viii.

63. Stone, *op. cit.*, p. 359.

Part II

Anarchism in the Twentieth Century

BEFORE UNDRESSING THE LIBERALS

Before undressing the Liberals
the left-headed Liberals
the split-level Liberals
with picture window souls
before undressing
and dressing them down

I noted the assortment
of political afflictions
impediments of vision
behind dark glasses
a hand of aluminum
waving a pink petition
for Soviet-American Friendship:

"We're what's left
of the Progressive Party."

So I had no recourse
but to goose their graven image
and rip off their clothes
and run into the snow
towards the constellations
left of any party
as they shrieked and scrambled
for their best china
smashed upon the carpet
in a heap with their glasses
and elegant clothes.

                    Morgan Gibson

SECTION V

Anarchist Communism and the Rejection of Authoritarian Socialism

CHAPTER 1

Yiddish and German Libertarians from Abroad

No history of the anarchist idea in America would be complete without mention of the great contributions made to it by foreign language groups.

It is not without significance that the idea of anarchism in nineteenth century America received tremendous support from Jewish freethinkers concentrated in New York City and its environs, most of whom were faithful subscribers to DeRobigne M. Bennett's *Truthseeker,* one of the main organs for the expression of free thought ideas between 1873 and 1879. Most of the Jewish anarchists in America were political refugees from Russia whose radical libertarian sentiments had led them to adopt the viewpoint of anarcho-syndicalism three decades and more before revolution was finally to engulf their homeland.[1] Other than Victor Yarros, the only Yiddish-speaking anarchist formally to join Benjamin Tucker's *Liberty* group was Joseph Bovshover, and his affiliation with the native American individualist anarchists was more a literary farce than a forthright act of ideological transcendence. A frequent contributor to the *Arbeiter*

362

Freind of London and the *Freie Arbeiter Stimme* of New York, Bovshover's poetry had always appeared in Yiddish until he brought his poem, "To the Toilers," to Benjamin Tucker's editorial office in 1896 under the assumed name of Basil Dahl. Unaware that the young man who stood before him was an old hand at writing revolutionary poetry, Tucker printed "To the Toilers" in *Liberty* along with paens of praise for the author's ability.[2] Tucker did not realize the *faux pas* he had committed until his good friend, Joseph Ishill, revealed it to him some years later. Unhappily, the story ultimately has a sad ending, for Joseph Bovshover went insane a few years after the publication of his poem, spending the rest of his youth in a mental asylum.[3]

Most large industrial cities in late nineteenth century America supported large concentrations of Yiddish-speaking anarchists. In Chicago, a number of freethinking Jews gathered together to form the "Anarchist Red Cross," a mutual aid society intended by Russian émigrees of that city to lend support to anarchists who fled from persecution back home.[4] From the late 1880's right up to World War II, the Jewish libertarian community in Chicago ran benefits to raise funds intended to assuage the suffering of broken Russian revolutionaries, the victims at first of the anti-revolutionary Czar as they were later the victims of the anti-czarist revolutionaries. Organizing themselves into the *Free Society* group, the Chicago Jews received a good bit of their impetus from the efforts of Boris Yelensky, active in the anarchist movement for sixty years, and Abe Isaac, editor of *The Firebrand*. Although there was no central nerve system to coordinate the activities of the various Jewish anarchist groups that were sprinkled about the country, there was a distinct feeling of comaraderie that bound them together, as illustrated by the fact that the Chicago group held a public dinner in honor of Alexander Berkman in 1930 and on numerous occasions sponsored public lectures by Emma Goldman, many of which drew over 2000 paid admissions. The Chicago group acknowledged financial and moral support of its activities from other anarchist circles, such as the Russian group of New York, the Kropotkin branch of Los Angeles, and groups in Detroit and Washington, D.C., further illustrating the solidarity that bound them together into a loosely federated movement.[5]

Despite the cultural identity that drew them together in search of shelter from the perilous political storms that buffeted them in America, these foreign-born anarchist groups were, like all libertarians, disdainful of any national symbols or attachments. Samuel Polinow, for example, a member of the Jewish anarchist group in Philadelphia, berated other Jews for their ethnic loyalties and advised them to give up the anarchist label if they could not rise to its demands of universalism.[6] And from Chicago G. P. Maximoff proclaimed that his "fatherland is Liberty," adding that he felt just as much animosity toward those Bolshevik Russians who tyrannized the Russian people after the Revolution as he had sympathy for these same individuals when they were themselves victims of the Czar. "Communism and Capitalism both teach the masses not to respect, but disdain freedom," he complained. "The struggle between these two mad actors, both of whom belong in a lunatic asylum, drags mankind ever more deeply into a state of stupor."[7] Calling upon mankind to liberate itself from ignorance and superstition, Maximoff, consistent with the teaching of native American anarchists, was basically committed to the libertarian philosophy of the Enlightenment as mankind struggled with the forces of darkness.

Born in the tiny village of Mitushino in the province of Smolensk, Russia, Gregori Petrovich Maximoff (1893-1950) was entered by his father into the theological seminary in Vladimir in preparation for the life of a priest.[8] Unable to accept the logic of organized religion, however, he refused after graduation to go on with a clerical career, becoming an agronomist instead. Stumbling upon the writings of Stepniak and Kropotkin, Maximoff quickly recognized himself as an anarchist and before long was an avid reader of everything that Bakunin, who was to become his favorite author, wrote. Entering with fervor into the revolutionary activities of the student underground in St. Petersburg, as well as the agitation among workers in the shops and factories, Maximoff looked with great anticipation toward the day when the hated system of injustice and oppression maintained by the Czar would at long last fall. When the Revolution did finally come, Maximoff was dismayed when the Bolsheviks forced themselves upon the people and put a damper on the spontaneity upon which the Revolution had initially been fueled. Although he joined the Red Army to throw back the forces of reaction directed against the Revolution, he was condemned to death by the Bolsheviks when he spoke out against the repression and secret police activities in which the troops became increasingly engaged. After fate stepped in to save him from execution, he was arrested during the Kronstadt Rebellion of 1921 on no other charge than that he held anarchist beliefs. Exiled from Russia, he made his way to Chicago via Berlin and Paris where he became editor of *Golos Truzhenika,* a Russian language paper directed toward labor, and supported himself by hanging wallpaper. When the *Free Society* group celebrated its 25th anniversary in 1948, it singled out Maximoff for special honor as a consequence of his untiring efforts in behalf of anarchism over the years. Not the least of his accomplishments in this regard was his translation of Bakunin's writings, published under the title of *The Political Philosophy of Bakunin;* and *The Guillotine at Work,* an exposé of the terror perpetrated by the Bolsheviks after their acquisition of power.

William Shulman (1881-1935), one of the mainstays of the Yiddish-speaking anarchist group in Philadelphia, was also a devotee of enlightened thought. Emigrating from Russia in 1903, Shulman was a genuine scholar, thoroughly devoted to a life of reason. "Relentlessly and fearlessly he preached his adopted theory of a free society, based on freedom and equality for all. Like a true soldier, he stood his post in the movement, lecturing, propagating, and expounding the doctrines of Bakuninism and Kropotkinism, as the only medium by which humanity could liberate itself."[9] Although Shulman, like thousands of other Yiddish-speaking anarchists, never won widespread acclaim for his contributions to the movement, he was representative of the kind of enthusiast that anarchism attracted in the large city ghetto.

In New York the crusade against authoritarianism and social chaos was carried on by the *Freie Arbeiter Stimme,* a Yiddish language paper established on July 4, 1890, and published continuously since then right up to the present. Devoted to the cause of free thought as much as it was to free labor, the *Freie Arbeiter Stimme* has never been a strict party organ devoted to any sharply defined ideological viewpoint; rather, it has devoted itself as much to the arts as to politics and has permitted the expression of any viewpoint that is genuinely aimed at the kind of freedom endorsed by the philosophers of the Enlightenment. Although its editorial policy has always reflected the anarcho-syndicalist outlook of the Jewish Anarchist Federation, the *Freie Arbeiter Stimme,* thanks to the freethinking editors who have given it guidance, has served reason and truth first and only secondarily concerned itself with ideological consistency. Thus in the dim years of the Depression the *Freie Arbeiter Stimme,* for all its dedication to the principle of social solidarity amongst working people, influenced the Jewish labor unions away from any alliance with the Communist Party.

Space does not permit a detailed description of the long list of editors who have labored in behalf of the *Freie Arbeiter Stimme*; it suffices to say that from Saul Yanofsky (1864-1939), the first editor, to the editorial board that presently gives it direction, its pages have born witness to the high level of intellectual attainment characteristic of the Jewish immigrant in America. But it would be deceptive to conclude from its Yiddish format that the *Freie Arbeiter Stimme* has been to any degree Zionistic. Despite the fact that the paper has never been published in anything but Yiddish, it has constantly stood firm in the face of the tendency of individual Jews to cling to the Hebraic religion and to make a fetish of their native tongue. Nowhere is this more aptly illustrated than in the life experience of Joseph J. Cohen (1878-1953), one of the editors of the *Freie Arbeiter Stimme* during the thirties. Born in White Russia and destined by his family to become a rabbi, Cohen became an anarchist after he rejected the Jewish faith. Upon immigrating to America in 1902, he became active among the Yiddish-speaking anarchists of Philadelphia and was instrumental in establishing the Radical Library, one of the chief educational instruments of the Jewish libertarian movement in this country. From 1933 to 1938 Cohen was engaged in The Sunrise Co-operative Farm Community, an experiment in communist life located in Michigan's Saginaw Valley. Among the hardships which the members of this commune had to fight was an internal division centered around those who favored the promotion of Yiddish culture and language as opposed to those libertarians who were unwilling to allow any national loyalty to interfere with their dedication to all mankind. Cohen's memoirs, *In Quest of Heaven,* is essential reading for anyone who plans to engage in communal life and work. In the very first formal discussion to be held in the community, Cohen took the floor to oppose the ethnocentrism of the "Yiddishers" who insisted upon having all intellectual intercourse carried on in the Yiddish tongue. "I opened that discussion by explaining the Anarchist view," Cohen wrote. "I maintained that all languages, like all people, are equal, and that each individual has the right to live and to speak in the way he wishes. At the same time, I pointed out that language has no particular sanctity which justifies one in making it a fetish or a cause of dispute."[10] For Cohen, as for all anarchists, the one luxury the community could not permit itself was the ancient practice of discrimination based upon religious prejudices formed in the deep, dark recesses of the past.

During the nineteen fifties the *Freie Arbiter Stimme* was guided by Dr. Herman Frank, an intellectual compatriot of Eric Fromme, who attacked the problem of human ignorance and superstition at the level it had then attained, the recurring problem of anti-Semitism as a phase of human brutality. Acknowledging the deep, psychological foundations of modern anti-Semitism, Frank brought the libertarian tradition in America into sharp contemporary focus when he argued that those who persecute ethnic minorities are engaging in a form of sadism that has long been known to mankind and warned that there was not much time left in which to gain insight into the problem.[11] Victims of persecution and oppression for centuries, Jewish anarchists in America were not only familiar with theories of social violence but were experts on the subject of what violence does psychologically to those who suffer it.

Among German-speaking anarchists in America, Robert Reitzel (1849-1898), deserves special mention. Born in Baden in the Black Forest region of Germany, Reitzel spent a miserable childhood due to the tyrannical nature of his father, a weak-willed schoolmaster utterly lacking in generosity and human compassion. His mother, a tanner's daughter, was a warm and compassionate soul, however, and it was from her that Reitzel acquired his fine social consciousness and his love of life. From the days of his early youth Reitzel displayed a fondness for poetry and good literature and it was because of his love for these that he neglected his assigned lessons in the gymnasium and was finally expelled. Entering Heidelberg University, Reitzel majored in history and philosophy but found beer drinking and other pleasures of the flesh more compelling ways of expressing his individuality. Unfortunately, his personal finances were inadequate to support his tastes and he was forced to leave the university. Advised by his father to seek his fortune in America, Robert Reitzel was among those immigrants who trooped to these shores in 1870.

But Reitzel, like most immigrants, found America less hospitable than he thought she would be, for the city of Baltimore had nothing to offer the likes of him. Overcoming the strong impulse of personal pride that always characterized his personality, Reitzel, in desperate poverty, took to the streets to beg for bread. Knocking on the door of a clergyman, he was advised to enter the ministry as a profession and in 1871 he was appointed pastor of the German Reformed Church in Washington, D. C. A year later Reitzel married and it appeared that the young emigré had at last made his mark in the world. But Reitzel, idealist that he was, expected more from his parishioners than they could give. Approaching the ministry with the same abundant enthusiasm with which he had drunk wine at Heidelberg, Reitzel "Had vague dreams of bringing together religion and science, of initiating a reformation of the Church on a large scale, of becoming a Luther or Calvin of the nineteenth century."[12] Unable to accept their pastor's religious liberalism, not to mention his radical social views, Reitzel's congregation soon rebelled against his leadership and he was finally invited to leave his post after many incidents of anguish and disharmony. Reitzel then became a free-lance lecturer on social and literary topics and soon had the reputation of being one of the most accomplished of German-American speakers. Settling in Detroit, a number of his friends and admirers raised funds to start him a newspaper and thus the *Arme Teufel* was launched on December 6, 1884, the pride and joy of German-speaking citizens of that city for the next fifteen years.

The *Arme Teufel,* although it expressed Reitzel's political philosophy, was not the organ of any party or movement. The first issue did carry the news that the black flag of anarchy had been unfurled by August Spies and other German-Americans in Chicago in symbolic support of the hard-pressed proletariat, but Reitzel loved life too much to make himself an ideological drudge, however deeply committed he was to the idea of libertarianism. His dedication, moreover, was to mankind rather than to any party or movement and thus he remained on cordial terms with John Most at the same time that he considered Benjamin Tucker his philosophical compatriot.[13] Despite the fact that the *Arme Teufel* was published in German while *Liberty* was written in English, there was a great deal that their respective editors held in common, including a profound respect for the ideas of Max Stirner. It was from Reitzel, no doubt, that Tucker discovered John Henry Mackay and other Stirnerites. Most of the copy that filled the pages of the *Arme Teufel* was written by Reitzel himself in a jovial style that revealed his warm heart and his unquenchable love of freedom. A favorite speaker at Turn-Vereins and free thought societies, Reitzel took every opportunity to speak out against the idea of organized religion and structured theological thought. It was in this mood that he poked fun at the Anglican Bishop of the diocese of Hong Kong who was alleged to have replaced the wine used in the sacrament with tea, Reitzel observing that under this logic the blood of Christ would turn into beer in Germany, whiskey in Ireland, and water in Kansas.[14] Undoubtedly this kind of sacrilegious banter won him many enemies among confirmed religionists but it also won him friends as witnessed by the fact that there were *Arme Teufel* clubs in cities with large German-speaking populations such as Toledo, Cincinnati, and St. Louis.

As with many other libertarians, the trial and execution of Albert Parsons, August Spies, and the other Haymarket Martyrs killed something in Reitzel himself and from that bleak moment on there was a note of melancholy evident in the pages of the *Arme Teufel*. A personal friend of both Parsons and Spies, Reitzel viewed their persecution and legal murder as one of the most infamous crimes ever committed by man against man and he carried on a determined campaign in the *Arme Teufel* in an effort to rally his readers to their support. A week before the execution was scheduled to take place, Reitzel journeyed to Chicago determined to save his comrades at any cost, even if this meant giving his own life in a violent confrontation with those who were determined to murder them.[15] Reitzel's valiant efforts to obtain justice, of course, could be no more successful than the efforts of the thousands of other humanitarians who had tried to save them and so all he could do was to return to Detroit in deep anguish after delivering the funeral speech over the graves of the slain martyrs.

To the end of his days Reitzel remained loyal to the libertarian idea and was frequently visited by Emma Goldman and other workers in the movement. Individualist to the core, Reitzel was said to carry his independence of thought to the point of rudeness on occasion but for the most part he was a much sought-after drinking companion and parlor debater. Always game for drink or song, Reitzel carried his love for alcohol to extremes, frequently going off on long drinking adventures that left the *Arme Teufel* without a hand on the rudder for weeks on end.[16] Eventually, however, Reitzel would come back on the job, convinced that only through a revolution of the mind could mankind throw off the penchant for authoritarianism it had picked up during its infancy.

Another outstanding representative of German-American anarchism was Carl Nold (1869-1934). Born in the south of Germany in the town of Wensberg, Nold came to America in 1883 at the age of fourteen. By eighteen he was already widely read in the literature of anarchism, buying every pamphlet he could get his hands on. A skilled machinist by trade, Nold was a conscientious hard worker, very frugal and conventional in his living habits. In regard to politics, however, his sympathies were always with the oppressed and exploited. During the Homestead steel strike, Nold and his roommate, Henry Bauer, who were then living in Pittsburg, were approached by a gaunt, pensive young man who asked if they could give him shelter for the night. Attracted by the radical ideas expressed by the man, they consented, only to discover the next day that their guest of the night before was none other than Alexander Berkman who had come to the city to administer the *coup de grace* to capitalism when he attempted to murder Frick. The police, seeing a conspiracy where none existed, arrested Nold and his roommate as accomplices and these two innocents spent five years in prison for a crime with which they had only an accidental connection.

After his release from prison. Nold made his way to Arkansas where he helped organize a cooperative farm near the town of Little Rock. The experiment, unfortunately, was short-lived and Nold, who had found cooperative farming a delightful way of life, was forced to move on to St. Louis where he organized an anarchist discussion group. Here he discovered Kate Austin, one of the more enthusiastic workers of midwestern anarchism, and Nold thereafter spent many delightful summers on the Austin farm near Caplinger Mills, Missouri.[17] An outgoing, good-natured individual, Carl Nold made friends without difficulty and counted some of the most outstanding anarchists among his correspondents, including Lucy Parsons, Abe Isaak, Robert Reitzel, and Marcus Graham. Like Reitzel, he loved to sing and his jovial sense of humor and love for life endeared him to all who knew him. Under other circumstances, he might have become an accomplished scholar, for he had a phenomenal memory and could recite any poem, however long it was, without missing a single word. But in the kind of world in which he was born, the only idea that made sense to Nold was the philosophy of anarchism and so he poured his limitless energy into his collaboration with Marcus Graham, the editor of *Man!* Before he died in 1934 he rendered American anarchism a priceless favor when he cooperated with Anges Inglis in laying the foundations for the Labadee Collection at the University of Michigan. Much of the rare material in that collection was personally contributed by Nold.

The most notorious, if not the most important, of all foreign-born American anarchists of this period was Johann Most (1846-1906). It is extremely difficult to place Most precisely within the spectrum of anarchist thought for the real Johann Most fades at many points into the mythical Johann Most created by the sensational press and his other detractors. The facts of his upbringing are certain enough; born by chance as the consequence of a lighthearted adventure in eroticism, he had no moral or legal existence until his parents solemnized his birth by getting married after the event. His father, a poor office clerk, and his mother, a governess to one of the wealthy families of Augsburg where Most was born, seem to have been kind enough to their unplanned child. In fact, as Most related the events of his early life to the ever sympathetic Emma Goldman one evening shortly after they first met, the first seven years of his life were calm and serene. Not only did his mother give him her maternal love without stint or hesitation but she imparted to him a love of learning and ideas without burdening his young mind with the weight of religious dogma or superstition which most parents feel compelled to heap onto the shoulders of their offspring.[18] Undoubtedly it was to a great extent the influence of this wise and loving mother that made Johann Most so sensitive in later years to beauty as well as to the wrongness of social injustice and human suffering. But unhappily, a series of personal tragedies embittered him so thoroughly that it was often difficult for those who knew him to see through the gnarled exterior shell behind which he took refuge, to the better self that was hidden within.

Undoubtedly the most crucial event of Most's life was a childhood illness, an abscess of the face that was allowed to go untended due to the carelessness of the family doctor. By the time a competent physician was finally called in, the abscess had gotten out of control and an operation had to be performed that left the youngster with a hideously twisted jaw which he carried throughout life, much to the detriment of his personality and self-confidence. The bristling beard that Most cultivated as a young man was not so much a declaration that he had "dropped out and turned off" as an attempt to hide the facial disfigurement that plagued his existence, making him shy and defensive in the presence of others. Growing up in the Bavarian city of Augsburg where Catholicism was preached and practiced with dogmatism and intolerance seldom equalled elsewhere, Most, according to one of his contemporaries, became more and more rebellious.[19] At the age of nine Most's beloved mother died and the agony which raged within him was exacerbated by the remarriage of his father to a woman who found it impossible to give her deformed stepson the love that he so desperately needed.

Already typed as one who was not likely to succeed, Johann fulfilled the harsh prophecy of his unsympathetic superiors when at the age of twelve he led his schoolmates in an organized strike against the tyranny of a brutal teacher, and for this he was punished with expulsion. Threatened with a beating at one point if he did not attend confession, the young Most retaliated by giving his parish priest a thrashing, thereby incurring the first of the many prison sentences he suffered. Taking a vow to himself never to enter any church again, he remained a cynic and a determined unbeliever to the end of his days.

While in his youth, Most was apprenticed to a bookbinder, becoming a journeyman of that trade at the age of seventeen, when he set out on his own in search of his fortune. Wandering from place to place, he was educated in politics and sociology with a thoroughness far beyond anything he had experienced in the Augsburg schools and he was well on his way to becoming a militant radical.

If Most had been allowed to choose his own calling, he would have become an actor, for he had a deep and abiding love for the theater. The tragedy of his life was his disfigurement which prevented him from ever appearing on the stage. Seeking an outlet for the dammed-up aesthetic currents that pulsed within him, Most gave vent to his innate acting ability and his fine Rebellaisian wit by developing a powerful style of political and social oratory which he practiced at every opportunity, and before long he was widely sought after as a speaker in Zurich and other centers of worker unrest. Leaving Switzerland just as the leaves started falling from the trees in 1868, Most made his way to Austria where he offered his services to the leaders of the socialist movement in Vienna. In the Spring of 1869 Most became involved in a confrontation with the Austrian government that was to lead to his imprisonment, this time for the crime of "high treason." Actually all that Most had done was to serve as one of the featured speakers before an assembly of workingmen who had gone on general strike in protest of a decree by the Minister of the Interior suspending all civil liberties. All the members of the delegation that had been sent to present the worker's grievances to the government were indicted for the act of defiance but Most and two other defendants were sentenced to five years imprisonment rather than the lighter terms given the rest on the grounds that they were the most dangerous. While languishing in prison, Most founded the *Nusskracker*, an underground newspaper that circulated among the prison's inmates written in cipher to keep it hidden from the eyes of the authorities. After his release, Most's reputation among the socialist forces in Germany was solidly established by the free publicity the Austrian government had unwittingly given him when it singled him out for special treatment and his influence over the workers soared.

Proceeding to the industrial city of Chemnitz in Saxony, Most took over the editorship of a local socialist paper and here quickly became a figure to be reckoned with among radical agaitators. In the Fall of 1871 Most was again asked to speak at a worker gathering, this time a counter-demonstration against Prussian patriots who loudly celebrated Prussia's recent victory over Napoleon III, and again he was imprisoned, although only for eight months. Upon his release from prison, worker delegations vied with one another to strew flowers in his path and he was soon elected to a seat in the Reichstag. But Bismarck, employing a number of skillful political ploys, introduced a policy intended to outlaw the Social Democratic Party in Germany and thus bring the fortunes of the rising young socialist movement tumbling down. Using an isolated act of terror that had no logical connection with the Social Democratic Party as a pretext, he generated a fear of socialism in the minds of the people so that he had no difficulty in getting the Reichstag to dissolve itself over the objections of Most and the other socialists who held seats. Then, calling for a new election, the Iron Chancellor succeeded in getting majority support in the Reichstag to back him in his efforts to root socialism out of the German soil. Failing to get elected back to the Reichstag, Most was fair game for his enemies who quickly succeeded in getting him thrown in prison again for a five month term on the most insubstantial of charges. Reading the handwriting on the wall, Johann Most decided to expatriate himself to London. Founding a

German language newspaper there, the *Freiheit*, Most became the acknowledged leader of those German socialists who had already taken refuge from political repression at the hands of Bismarck; and when *Freiheit* was smuggled back into Germany and passed eagerly from hand to hand by the socialists who had been deprived of all their own publications by the orders of the government, Most became a veritable lion among German revolutionaries everywhere.

It was while he was at the height of his popularity among German workers both in London and at home that Most was unceremoniously dumped from his membership in the Social-Democratic Party. None of the prison sentences Most endured was more bitterly felt by him than this act of injustice and it no doubt chafted his political soul for years after. As Max Nomad describes the incident, at least a part of the responsibility for his expulsion from the Social-Democratic Party can be attributed to Marx, for Karl Marx and Johann Most had been at ideological odds for some time prior to this event.[20] The basis for the animosity that existed between these two was Most's support for the ideas of Professor Eugen Dühring, one of Marx's hated adver-saries. Dühring, in opposition to Marx, took the libertarian view that it is the centralized state with its monopoly of violence that is the true source of the exploitation of the proletariat rather than the economic forces of capitalist society. Thus, like Bakunin, Dühring took a stance against the Marxian conception of state socialism, arguing that the means of production must be controlled by dispersed social groups rather than any centralized proletarian party apparatus. Most, moreover, believed that a cataclysmic overthrow of the capitalist political state was an unrealistic goal and hence he tended to think more and more in terms of the educational methods of anarchism. Whatever the ideological differences between the two may have been, Marx and Engels initiated a whispering campaign against Johann Most which succeeded in eroding the basis of his popular support and the party threw him out on a charge of having "committed actions which were opposed to all laws of honesty." Not only was Most under attack from his friends but now his enemies came into the act when he published an editorial in *Freiheit* expressing favor at the assassination of Alexander II, felled by the shot of a terrorist.

After spending a year and a half in Clerkenwell Prison for the crime of writing an editorial, Most, like many another disenchanted European libertarian, eagerly snatched at the chance of changing his luck when he was invited by the Social Revolutionary Club of New York to tour the United States as a spokesman for its point of view. Arriving in New York just before Christmas of 1882, he was enthusiastically welcomed by thousands of German-speaking workers, the backbone of the urban radical movement at that time. Before many months had past, Johann Most was generally recognized as the leader of the German-speaking social revolutionary movement in this country.

While it is not altogether correct to say, as many political historians do, that there was no organized radical movement in the United States before Most's arrival, it is true that he pulled the scattered fragments of the social revolutionary movement together, giving it new energy and a more sharply defined sense of purpose. Before Most's arrival, native American anarchists like Josiah Warren, Stephen Pearl Andrews, and Ezra Heywood carried on a determined educational campaign against the idea of the state with its tendency to centralize and monopolize all power. But aside from Heywood, who was more concerned with the labor situation than his individualistic compatriots, the native Americans did not speak directly or relevantly to the vast majority of skilled and semiskilled laboring men who kept the mills and factories going in the urban areas. Establishing another German language periodical in New York, again called *Freiheit,* Most aimed his editorials at those workers who were essential to the humming machines of capitalism, the experienced machinists, pattern-makers, and sundry craftsmen who had learned their trades before leaving the old country. In quest of complete accuracy it is to be noted, however, that Most aimed *Freiheit* more at the workers back home in Germany than he did at those surrounding him in America, at least in the first years after his arrival. "It was in Germany where Most's heart and mind lay. At best, he only became reconciled to his life of exile in the United States."[21] It would not be fair to charge Most with any major responsibility for revolutionary agitation in this country during the first decade of his stay here, for the only influence he exerted was over those German expatriates who could read *Freiheit.* As the years went by, however, and the number of German speaking workers who labored in the mills and factories of America swelled, there can be no doubt that his activities as an editor and a speaker at worker gatherings had increasing relevance to radical political events as these Germans became assimilated to the political culture of their new environment.

A dramatic, fiery speaker, Johann Most preached a theory of social revolution that struck fear into the hearts of those who supported the political establishment of the day. Calling upon the proletariat to rise up in rebellion against their capitalist masters, he urged that "the war of the poor against the rich" was the only way that the exploited worker could deliver himself from oppression. For the institution of property, in Most's opinion, transformed the capitalist from a man into a beast who had no feeling whatever for those whom he exploited. "The life of the poor is valued as nothing by the rich," Most held, and therefore women and children are treated as objects within the dreaded factory system that modern capitalism has built. Calling upon the oppressed workers to organize themselves for the warfare ahead, Most sent shivers of terror down the spines of the capitalist class when he wrote: "If the people do not crush [the capitalists and their supporters], they will crush the people, drown the revolution in the blood of the best, and rivet the chains of slavery more firmly than ever. Kill or be killed is the alternative. Therefore massacres of the people's enemies must be instituted."[22]

If Most's words are taken at face value, it would appear that his personal hatred of capitalism compelled him to accept violence as a legitimate form of political action and that he actually planned the physical overthrow of existing society. And indeed there is evidence to support the view that Johann Most's head was filled with dangerous thoughts that might well lead to overt acts of terror and destruction. On more than one occasion Most filled the pages of *Freiheit* with technical details concerning dynamite and its use. That this might well have been more than an idle exercise in revolutionary fantasy is evidenced by the fact that Most actually obtained employment in an explosives factory in Jersey City, after which he published his notorious pamphlet, *Revolutionäre Kriegswissenschaft*, which contained exact instructions for those who wished to perpetrate violence and destruction against the existing order.[23] Although he himself, so far as is known, never employed violence in any of his actions, some of his followers, going further, perhaps, than Most would have liked, participated in acts of arson, using the directions for making exploding kerosene lamps that he had provided them with. It was widely rumored at the time that the insurance payments that were fraudulently collected by some social revolutionaries in this manner were turned over to the movement, when they were not stuffed into private pockets. When called to account for this by the ever vitriolic Benjamin Tucker, Most refused to publicly repudiate any social revolutionary, no matter now dark his deed, on the grounds that his first loyalty was to those who stood against the existing structure of corrupt society. The genial Justus Schwab, whose East Side New York saloon was the meeting place for radicals of all persuasions, broke with Johann Most soon after this, as did Robert Reitzel in Detroit, burdening the social revolutionary movement with yet another internal division.

In all fairness to Most it must be emphasized that his defense of violence was not based upon nihilistic foundations but was rather the logical outcome of his revolutionary morality—a morality incomprehensible to his capitalist adversaries, of course, but a sincerely held set of moral convictions nevertheless. In Most's mind, as one of his anonymous disciples pointed out, there was a fine but definite line to be drawn between violence as an act of social indifference and violence as a reflection of concern for the well-being of society. In the pages of *Freiheit*, Most condemned all those who undertake acts of violence that are not motivated by the sincere goal of liberating the working men and women of the world from industrial slavery.[24] Murder or brutality are not justifiable for their own sakes but only when they arise spontaneously as natural patterns of human behavior in answer to events that take place within the social order, he argued. Most was ready enough to admit that he, like most anarchists, believed that the reform of corrupt society could never be brought off without some resort to violence and revolutionary warfare. But, he insisted, "that is a question of tactics which has nothing to do with principles."[25] In terms of principle, the anarchist's fundamental aim is to "prevent all command over man by his fellowmen, to make state, government, laws, or whatsoever form of existing compulsion, a thing of the past, to establish freedom for all." In point of fact, Most vehemently argued, anarchism not only does not teach violence but it is the very negation of violence. In existing society, according to Most, we are faced with violence every moment of our day-to-day existence and hence we must sometimes resort to violence as a practical means of survival. But that violence, he insisted, is generated by the authorities of the state whose only mission is to keep the lower orders of society subservient to the power of the middle and upper classes. When that formal power complex is eliminated, human beings, drawing upon nature, will find ways to live that do not institutionalize violence.

Although there was naturally little sympathy for Johann Most's theories about violence among the supporters of the established political system, his views were widely shared by other Americans with libertarian tendencies. Wendell Phillips, for example, one of the most straight thinking of all Americans, defended nihilism as an inevitable aspect of a society which enslaves a part of its population, as was the case under chattel slavery in the United States. When the slave breaks his chains and strikes back at his master, Phillips urged, he has done nothing more than exercise that longing for freedom that nature has planted in us all. Violence, on this explanation, stems from the actions of the slaveholders and not those who struggle to free themsleves from captivity and subjugation. One can no more hold the slave morally responsible for his act of violence than we can condemn the man who fights for his life when he is subjected to surprise attack on the street at night. Since no one except the absolute pacifist renounces his right to self-defense, most men can be said to embrace violence to the same extent that Most did.

It is also to be taken into account that Most was persecuted by the police authorities in so vicious and illegal a fashion that only a fool could have retained respect for "law and order" after experiencing such injustice. Whatever Most might have proclaimed in print concerning the employment of violence, he, as a naturalized American, had as much right as anyone else to his opinions until his action presented a real and immediate threat to public safety. Most, however, was persecuted not for what he did, nor even for what he said, but for who he was. As Hippolyte Havel, an on-the-scene observer, put it:

> the police made it a sort of specialty of arresting Most on every possible occasion and hauling him to court. Newspaper reporters and journalists, whose ability as translators was more than doubtful, were in the habit of placing in his mouth the most ridiculous of expressions, for which he was in all seriousness held responsible by the stupidity of the public and the courts. He was villified, persecuted, and thrown into prison on general principles, so to speak, because he was the Anarchist Most.[26]

After the Haymarket bombing in 1886, for example, Most, although he was in New York and could have had no connection with the incident, was arrested for making dangerous statements in a talk which he delivered several days later. The evidence used to convict Most in court turned out to be his pamphlet, *Revolutionäre Kriegswissenschaft*, which he had written a number of years previously and which had not even been mentioned in his speech.[27] That Most did not receive a fair trial is demonstrated by the viewpoint of Henry Appleton, one of Tucker's editorial assistants and a most reliable reporter. "Only the other day the prosecuting officer in a court of so-called justice ranted to the jury that, if they failed to convict, he would shoot Most with as little compunction as he would a rattlesnake," Appleton complained.[28] With piercing logic Appleton charged the prosecuting attorney with the exact same crime that Most had been convicted of and chided the court for smiling while this immoral harangue was delivered and the courtroom audience for applauding it.

The double standard of political morality that was observed in the United States was again brought painfully to Most's attention when he was sentenced to a year in prison in 1901 as a consequence of the McKinley assassination. Plagued by misfortune throughout his tragic existence, Most's undoing this time resulted from the uncanny circumstance that he chanced to run an article in *Freiheit* the day before the assassination entitled "Murder Against Murder," written over fifty years before by the old German Revolutionary, Karl Heinzen. That Most was not acquainted with Czolgosz, and that there was no possible connection between the appearance of the article and the act of terror, carried no weight whatever with the judge or jury. Actually Most withdrew the issue from circulation the moment he heard about the assassination but a single copy of *Freiheit* somehow was obtained by a policeman and it was on this bare thread of evidence that the conviction against Most was obtained, despite the fact that he was defended by the able socialist, Morris Hillquit.[29] Once again sentenced to the dreaded Blackwell's Island, Johann Most had good reason to question whether it was he or the state which unmercifully harrassed him that was the real criminal.

Most's place among the theorists of anarchism is exceedingly difficult to pinpoint, as the historian, E. V. Zenker pointed out long ago.[30] At the outset it must be said that Most was in no way original in his conceptualization of the anarchist idea. But at the same time it must be acknowledged that for all the confusion that seems to have accompanied his practical activity as a revolutionary journalist and speaker, the attitudes he embraced were generally within the scope of the anarchist movement as it developed in America. As a very young man Most had translated parts of Marx's *Kapital* while languishing in prison during one of his numerous internments and had succeeded in getting his excerpt published before the entire work was first issued. Marx, true to form, had nothing but bad things to say about Most's project and accused him of having a poor knowledge of socialist economics. In actuality, any confusion that might have been evident in Johann Most's economic analysis was most likely due to the fact that he was rapidly gyrating away from the theories of scientific socialism developed by Marx and Engels. It was about this time that he became familiar with the writings of Proudhon and Bakunin and from then on he steadily veered toward the idea of economic and political decentralization that is the hallmark of anarchist thought. Most certainly it was under Prodhon's influence that Johann Most wrote that in a free society, "All man's wants are met by associations or groups. These are no longer centralized, and are only cooperative with one another as is necessary for the end sought. Art and science, like production, are advanced through the adjustment of competent minds."[31] In a little-known essay titled "The God Pestilence," Most embraced the sort of libertarian psychology advanced by Proudhon, Bakunin, or any other exponent of the free thought point of view that stands out so distinctly in anarchist writings, holding with them that it is the idea of an all-powerful god that leads men to submit themselves to political and social tyranny and not simply the economic forces that surround them.[32] This shift in perspective was basic to Most's intellectual development and is of the utmost importance in assessing his ideological position. If Emma Goldman was accurate in her recollections, it was while Most still lived in England that he broke forever with the Marxian state idea with its concept of the dictatorship of the proletariat and chose instead the anarchist idea of no state whatever. If Marx proclaimed that Most was hopelessly confused, this meant nothing more than that they had parted ideological company and that their respective views of the world were irreconcilable.

Those who knew Johann Most while he was alive have left us with two conflicting portraits of what he was really like. On the one hand Max Nomad pictures Most as a sort of second-rate socialist thinker fluttering confusedly from one school of thought to another without a clear picture in his mind as to what things were all about.[33] Nomad also charges Most with holding tenaciously to the principle of "an eye for an eye," allowing this precept to color all that he did or wrote about anarchism.[34] Over against Nomad's uncomplementary view we have the picture drawn by Emma Goldman, whom Most loved and despised alternately, depending upon the mood that gripped him at the moment. Much of Most's stormy personality stemmed, undoubtedly, from his thwarted adventures in romance; twice married and twice divorced, Most still yearned for that tenderness and sympathy which only the love of a woman can bring to a man. Contrary to popular notion, Most, according to Emma Goldman, was not a misanthrope at all but a highly sensitive individual whose love for beauty and aesthetic form was the mainspring of his prodigious energy. It was perfectly true that Most passionately hated the ugliness and immorality of capitalist civilization with its callous disregard for the hopes and suffering of the poor. "But his hatred of social wrongs, of ugliness and meanness, was the natural offspring of his love of beauty, of color, or all the vital things."[35] It was from Most that Emma herself had learned to appreciate music, art, and literature with a new intensity, as it was from him that she learned to think deeply in the world of social problems.

Widely read in history and philosophy, Johann Most could hold his own where scholarship was concerned. But here, as in his political activities, his caustic tongue and his cutting wit earned him the enmity of those he challenged, as in the case of his essays which criticized the historical findings of Theodor Mommsen, the widely recognized expert on ancient Rome. Had Most's appearance and personality been less twisted and warped by the personal suffering he experienced, his reputation as a libertarian would certainly have been much higher, for it was always by the public image he projected that he was judged and never by what he actually did or wrote. We cannot, therefore, discount Most's contributions to anarchism until the day that some historian takes the pains to do a definitive study of his thought.[36] Honored in 1898 and again in 1901 by friendly visits to his home by Peter Kropotkin who was on these occasions touring the United States, John Most, as he now preferred to refer to himself, spent his last years eking out a bare existence on the proceeds of *Freiheit,* a lonely but compelling spokesman of anarchism to the end. It was appropriate that death came to John Most on March 17, 1906

NOTES

SECTION V - CHAPTER 1

1. E. C. Walker, "Liberal Thought Among the Jews in New York," *Lucifer the Light Bearer* (September 29, E. M. 297), 305.

2. *Liberty* (March 7, 1896), 3.

3. "Joseph Bovshover," in the Ishill Collection, Houghton Library, Harvard University.

4. Boris Yelensky, *In the Struggle for Equality* (Chicago, 1958). See also: Joseph Cohen, *The Jewish Anarchist Movement in the United States* (Philadelphia, 1945.)

5. Boris Yelensky, "Twenty-five Years of 'Free Society' Activity in Chicago," *The World Scene from the Libertarian Point of View* (Chicago, 1951), p. 13.

6. Samuel Polinow, "Anarchism and the National Spirit," *Man!*, III (April, 1935), 35.

7. G. P. Maximoff, "The State of the World," in *The World Scene from the Libertarian Point of View*, p. 5.

8. Rudolph Rocker, "Introduction," *The Political Philosophy of Bakunin*, ed. by G. P. Maximoff (New York, 1953), p. 25.

9. Samuel Polinow, William Shulman, *Man!*, IV (November-December, 1935), 23.

10. (New York, 1957), p. 68.

11. "The Moral Decay of Our Society," *The World Scene from the Libertarian Point of View*, p. 25.

12. Adolph Eduard Zucker, *Robert Reitzel; A Ph. D. Dissertation Submitted to the University of Pennsylvania* (Philadelphia, 1917), p. 15.

13. "Robert Reitzel," *Man!*, I (July, 1933), 5.

14. Zucker, p. 36.

15. *Ibid.*, p. 45.

16. " 'The Poor Devil'; A Memory of Robert Reitzel," (Detroit, 1909). Reprinted by Joseph Labadee from John Hubert Greusel, *The Detroit News-Tribune* (September 16, 1900).

17. Otto Herman, "Anarchists: Carl Nold," *Man!*, III (January, 1935), 160.

18. *Living My Life*, (New York, 1931), p. 64.

19. Frederick W. Mitchell, "John Most and Freiheit," *Lucifer the Light-Bearer* (December 12, 1900), 385.

20. The European phase of Most's life has been described in a series of six articles by Max Nomad titled: "Johann Most: Terrorist of the Word," *The Modern Monthly,* Vols, IX-X (June, 1936 to April, 1937). Even more valuable is the section on Most in Andrew R. Carlson, *Anarchism in Germany,* Vol. I (Metuchen, N. J., 1972), pp. 173-247.

21. *Ibid.,* p. 235.

22. Johann Most, *The Beast of Property* (New York, 2nd Edition, n.d.), p. 12.

23. George Woodcock, *Anarchism* (Cleveland, 1962), p. 461.

24. "Attentat Reflexionen," *Freiheit* (August 28, 1892), quoted in *The Conspiracy of the Privileged* (New York, 1908), p. 17.

25. Johann Most, *The Social Monster: A Paper on Communism and Anarchism* (New York, 1890), p. 2.

26. "John Most," *Road to Freedom,* IV (March, 1938), 3.

27. Emma Goldman, "Johann Most," *The American Mercury,* VIII (June, 1926), 165.

28. "Authority Blinded," *Liberty,* IV (June, 1886), 4.

29. Morris Hillquit, *Loose Leaves from a Busy Life* (New York, 1934), p. 129.

30. *Anarchism* (London, 1898), p. 191.

31. "Free Society," in *Down with the Anarchists* (n.d. or p.), p. 2.

32. "The God Pestilence," *Man!,* III (January, 1935), 157.

33. "Death Comes to the Anarchist," *Modern Monthly,* X (June, 1938), 9.

34. *Apostles of Revolution* (New York, 1961), p. 257.

35. Goldman, "Johann Most," *op. cit.,* 159.

36. Most's autobiography titled *Eight Years Behind Lock and Bolts* has not yet been published in English. Rudolph Rocker's biographical study of Most was apparently translated into English but all attempts to locate a copy of it have thus far been unsuccessful.

37. Hippolyte Havel, "John Most—The Stormy Petral," *Man!,* II (January, 1934), 5.

CHAPTER 2

Emma Goldman: "High Priestess" of American Anarchism

Undoubtedly the most famous of all American anarchists was Emma Goldman (1869-1940), who for almost thirty years personified the anarchist idea in the minds of Americans and served as the main force for keeping it alive. Immigrating to the United States with her two older sisters in 1886 to escape the tyranny of her father's authoritarian ways, she had an innate thirst for freedom which she never quite managed to quench. Like many another immigrant to these shores, she was possessed by an "exalted idea of American liberties and [a] sincere belief in this country as a haven for the oppressed, with her wonderful equality of opportunity."[1] In her early youth in Russia she had read widely and had acquired considerable familiarity with social and philosophical ideas but felt no need to commit herself to any particular ideological viewpoint. A bright-eyed, vivacious young girl, she wanted nothing more than to love everyone in the world and be loved in turn. Upon witnessing her mother engage in an uncontrollable outburst of hostility against the nihilists based upon a blind devotion to the authoritarian ways of the Tsar, however, Emma suddenly found herself on the side of the executed revolutionaries, despite the fact that she had previously felt revulsion for their terroristic methods. Her mother's brutal suggestion that the Nihilists ought to be exterminated like wild beasts froze her blood and caused her to react strongly. "Something mysterious had awakened compassion for them in me. I wept bitterly over their fate."[2] In the years to come Emma was again and again to find her heart gripped with sympathy for those who dared to fight back against social and political tyranny, even when they resorted to the brutality and terror which were completely alien to her fundamental values. In many respects, the basic outline of her political philosophy was summed up in her proclivity to empathize with anyone whom she felt had been driven to violence by the repression and inhumanity of power-oriented society.

After a brief sojourn in Rochester, New York, and an unhappy marriage broken up by the sexual impotence of her husband whom she had married more out of sympathy than love, she broke completely with conventional society and threw herself into the Yiddish anarchist movement she found in New York City. Here she met Alexander Berkman, her beloved "Sasha," with whom she was destined to work in revolutionary activity for the rest of her life. Equally important to her political education was Johann Most, the recognized leader of anarchist communists in the United States at the time. It was Most, the editor of the German language paper *Freiheit,* who first gave her the self-confidence she needed to advocate the theory of anarchism before a public meeting. Although she and Berkman were to break with Most in 1891 over the question of tactical methods, joining the rival *Autonomie* group led by Joseph Peukert, Otto Rinke, and Claus Timmerman, she remained sympathetic to Most as a person to the very end. But it would be erroneous to believe that Emma Goldman adopted the doctrines of anarchism under the influence of any teacher, Berkman and Most not excluded. Like her friend and comrade, Voltairine de Cleyre, Emma, propelled by her great hatred of injustice, was confirmed in her anarchist beliefs by the farcical trial and tragic execution of Albert Parsons and his companions in Chicago. Rendered a mad young woman by the soul-shaking sympathy she felt for the executed martyrs, she devoted the rest of her life to fighting hypocrisy and injustice wherever she found it. As her friend, lover, and editorial assistant, Hippolyte Havel put it, the execution of the Chicago anarchists convinced her that "no mercy could be expected from the ruling class, that between the Tsarism of Russia and the plutocracy of America there was no difference save in name."[3] If there was anything fundamental that distinguished the foreign-born anarchists from the native American group, it was this experience of tyranny learned in an older but similar culture.

Founding *Mother Earth,* the major vehicle for disseminating the ideas of militant anarchist communism in America, in 1906, Emma Goldman very quickly became a major voice of libertarian philosophy. Although *Mother Earth* had at first received the enthusiastic support of many artists and writers, by the end of the first year of its publication Emma found that her greatest support came not from the literati but from the hard and fast anarchists such as Berkman and Havel.

Apparently the intellectuals who had promised to write for *Mother Earth* were frightened off by Emma's tendency to view art not as a remote exercise in beauty and form but as a product of revolutionary progress and development. Were it not for such broad-visioned souls as Leonard Abbott, Alvin Sanborn, and Sadakichi Hartman, who "regarded life and art as the twin flames of revolt," *Mother Earth* might well have folded in the first year of its life.[4] But Emma Goldman's energy and enthusiasm could not be quenched and she continued to publish the journal until its suppression during the war hysteria of 1917 when she was imprisoned, along with Alexander Berkman, for opposing wartime conscription.

Emma Goldman's duties as editor of *Mother Earth* by no means exhausted all of her tremendous dedication to the idea of anarchy, however. Developing a powerful speaking style and an engaging stage presence, she began a series of lecture tours which carried her all over the United States and made her the catalyst for the many independent radical groups that were to be found in almost every large city. Already well-known among anarchists for her complicity in the *Attentat* directed against Frick at Homestead, she captivated radical audiences everywhere with her fiery manner, her penetrating logic, and her refusal to compromise with injustice and ignorance. Branded with the name "Red Emma" by an unsympathetic popular press, most of what she had to say passed over the heads of the American people without affecting them in the least. Yet for all her devotion to the idea of social revolution, many of her lectures, reflecting the broad interests which made her the anarchist she was, dealt with literature and art rather than political subjects. One of her favorite lecture topics, in fact, dealt with the social implications of George Bernard Shaw's plays. Drawn to the subject of birth control by the training she had had in nursing, Emma frequently talked about the need of working-class women to limit their child-bearing function as a first step in emancipating themselves economically and socially.[5] Far from being the narrow-minded, doctrinaire malcontent the general public thought her to be, she was one of the most vital and far-seeing personalities of her age.

Like Alexander Berkman, from whom she undoubtedly derived many of her arguments relating to the phenomena of violence, Emma Goldman subscribed to a theory of class conflict which owed much to the concept of inevitable social upheaval. Yet the record is clear that aside from her moral support of Berkman in his attempt to take the life of Henry C. Frick for his alleged crimes against labor, violence played no part whatever in her social thought. Much of her reputation as a purveyor of violent social theories stems from her arrest in December, 1894, on a charge of inciting a riot. Addressing a large crowd of workmen in Union Square, New York, on the injustice of a society that permits thousands to suffer starvation while the wealthy few indulge themselves in luxuries, Emma Goldman had quoted Cardinal Manning's famous statement, "Necessity knows no law, and a starving man has a natural right to his neighbor's bread," embellishing it with her own conviction that those who ask in vain for the means of sustaining their own lives should "then take bread" when it is not given. Although her argument was purely rhetorical and did not result in any overt action upon the part of those she addressed, she was convicted of inciting a riot and sentenced to six months in prison. From that point on she was kept under almost constant police surveillance, arrested nearly forty different times, and often locked up for long periods of time without any legitimate reason. And yet, according to Theodore Schroeder, the attorney for the Free Speech League, Emma Goldman never uttered any exhortation to violence other than the innocuous argument she made in her Union Square speech.[6] As one of her contemporaries put it, Emma Goldman "does not advocate violence any more than Ralph Waldo Emerson advocated violence."[7] But how, then, are we to explain the fact that the police apparatus of her day reacted hysterically to her presence, directing almost constant pressure to her as if she were a highly dangerous arch-criminal? Perhaps the most plausible explanation of this enigma was made by another woman, Margaret Goldsmith, who argued that Emma Goldman's highly developed social conscience and her impeccable standards of personal integrity made her "an articulate conscience for the United States," thereby eliciting a negative response from those who are charged with enforcing the law.[8] If the most feared and notorious of all anarchists was as honorable and trustworthy as her personal conduct seemed to suggest, then the whole question of the police as the guarantor of public order and decency would be open for discussion. And this, in fact, is exactly what anarchism does proclaim.

Equally instrumental in her rise to notoriety was her adamant

defense of Leon Czolgosz, the convicted assassin of President William
McKinley. Although she did not know Czolgosz personally, and was
aware that he had little real understanding of social philosophy,
Emma defended the act of the confused young man even against
criticism directed against him by anarchists themselves. It was ridiculous to believe, she maintained, that Czolgosz had acted from
motives of cruelty or any other criminal instinct. "On the contrary,"
she insisted to the consternation of friend and foe alike, "it is mostly
because of a strong social instinct, because of an abundance of love
and an overflow of sympathy with the pain and sorrow around us, a
love which seeks refuge in the embrace of mankind, a love so strong
that it shrinks before no consequence" that a man like Czolgosz can
strike out at the established power structure.[9] To the argument made
by many radicals that the act was "foolish and impractical," Emma
retorted that no human social action, however negative it may appear
to be, is without its logic. Man is a social animal who never acts
irrationally when he listens to his heart, she maintained.

> What absurdity! As if an act of this kind can be measured by its usefulness,
> expediency, or practibility. We might as well ask ourselves of the usefulness of a
> cyclone, tornado, etc. All these forces are the natural results of natural causes,
> which we have not yet been able to explain, but which are nevertheless a part of
> man and beast, developed or checked, according to the pressure and conditions
> of man's understanding.[10]

Throughout the whole realm of the natural order, Emma insisted,
resistance against force is a natural phenomenon. Like the wild beast
who is cornered by his enemy, man, being a part of nature, fights
back when he is pressed. Individuals like Czolgosz do not choose to
engage in violent conduct but are forced into it by the injustice and
oppression of the organized political order. "Force will continue to
be a natural factor just so long as economic slavery, social superiority,
inequality, exploitation, and war continue to destroy all that is good
and noble in man." On the other hand, violence will no longer play
any role in man's actions at the point at which human understanding
progresses to a level where force and compulsion are no longer acceptable methods of maintaining social order and control. Until that time,
she proclaimed, acts of social violence must be viewed as being as
natural as the acts of force by which those in power attempt to maintain control over those they rule.

Much too honest to deceive herself with a "lie of the soul," Emma

Goldman ultimately came to regret her one youthful flirtation with violence during the Homestead *Attentat.* Upon hearing of the death of four of Berkman's acquaintances who had been killed while working with dynamite in a Lexington Avenue flat, she was horrified by the thought; "Comrades, idealists," she exclaimed, "manufacturing a bomb in a congested tenement house! I was aghast at such irresponsibility." But then her mind was flooded with the memory of that moment many years before when she had helped Berkman experiment with making a bomb for the purpose of destroying Henry Frick.

> With accusing clarity I now relived that nerve-racking week in July, 1892. In the zeal of fanaticism I had believed that the end justifies the means! It took years of experience and suffering to emancipate myself from the mad idea. Acts of violence committed as a protest against unbearable social wrongs—I still believed them inevitable. I understood the spiritual forces culminating in such *Attentats* as Sasha's, Bresci's, Angiolillo's, Czolgosz's, and those of others whose lives I had studied. They had been urged on by their great love of humanity and their acute sensitiveness to injustice. I had always taken my place with them as against every form of organized oppression. But though my sympathies were with the man who protested against social crimes by a resort to extreme measures, I nevertheless felt now that I could never again participate in or approve methods that jeopardized innocent lives.[11]

The passage of time also caused her to have second thoughts concerning the human suffering which so often accompanies class conflict. Discussing social ideas in a Parisian cafe with one of her earlier loves, Max Baginski, and Victor Dave, who had been Johann Most's teacher, Emma now acknowledged the "incredible waste of human life involved in the terrible war of the classes in every country," and she confessed to her companions that she no longer believed that violence is justifiable as a means of redressing the social balance. Later she was to admit to Sasha that if she had her way she would have preferred to follow the example of Tolstoy and Gandhi rather than the revolutionary theories of Bakunin, since "violence in whatever form never has and probably never will bring constructive results."[12] As a social theory, she declaimed, anarchism places human life above material things. "All anarchists agree with Tolstoy in this fundamental truth: if the production of any commodity necessitates the sacrifice of human life, society should do without that commodity, but it cannot do without that life."[13]

The most gentle of souls, Emma Goldman, far from approving of violence, was basically anti-war in outlook. Throughout her long career as social reformer she was consistently opposed to military conflict, whoever waged it. One of her most cherished memories was of Randolph Bourne, that bitter-tongued young man who stood firm in the face of the hysteria which swept the nation during World War I and whose diatribe against war had been reprinted in *Mother Earth*. Bourne, along with Roger Baldwin, had earned Emma's hard-to-win approval for his adamant refusal to accept war as conduct becoming of sane men. One of her most heartrending memories, on the other hand, was Kropotkin's unexplainable decision to give moral support to the Allies during the holocaust. For all her devotion to her teacher, she steadfastly criticized Kropotkin's decision and remained firm in her own resolve never to give aid and comfort to the state in its waging of war. Most certainly there is something to be said for her argument that acts of unorganized social violence are almost infinitesimal in importance when compared against the organized bloodshed and destruction of capital and government.[14] And she was on even firmer ground when she maintained that throughout modern times it has been the propertied classes who have indoctrinated the masses in the methods of brutality and violence, even forcing gentle people to fight and kill when they had no stomach for it.[15] Emma Goldman, like Thoreau, may well have shouted shrill defiance at the state and its methods but she was never guilty of organizing any force for aggression or conquest. And she shared the support of all pacifists in her argument that "the contention that a standing army and navy is the best security of peace is about as logical as the claim that the most peaceful citizen is he who goes about heavily armed." Emma Goldman, consistent with her basic libertarian principles, insisted instead that peace is only possible where people disarm themselves and place their trust in the reality of a basically peaceful human nature.

The philosophy of libertarianism outlined in Emma Goldman's writings is not fundamentally pessimistic but instead reflects a sincere commitment to the proposition that humanity may yet overcome the legacy of authoritarianism and tyranny that have plagued it in the past. "The awakening of America's spiritual youth is the safest guarantee for the great libertarian transformation that is yet to take place in that country," Emma wrote from exile. "Governments come and governments go . . . but the spirit of life, of growth, of innovation and idealism goes on forever. I have already pinned my faith to that spirit which is slowly coming into its own in America."[16] Although Kropotkin may have initially inspired her in the formation of her indefatigable idealism, it was from Henry David Thoreau, "the greatest American anarchist," that she learned to think of government as the most fragile of human artifacts. Government, she argued, following the sage of Walden Pond, is but a recent innovation, a mere ephemeral tradition, which lacks the force and vitality necessary for the conduct of real social life. Those who turn to the state as the means of living in harmony with their fellowmen are bound to come to grief, for all government can offer them is a mock theory of social justice in which morality can be nothing more than a slavish obedience to a sterile body of legal rules. Law, as it takes shape in the hands of the legalists, she held, has no power whatever to impart that feeling for justice which is so necessary for the development of a satisfactory social system. To the contrary, those citizens who are predisposed to think positive thoughts toward their fellowmen are soon conditioned by the inexorable logic of law to distrust their basic social sentiments and to accept injustice and inequality as inevitable. "Indeed, the keynote of government is injustice," she proclaimed. "With the arrogance and self-sufficiency of the king who could do no wrong, governments ordain, judge, condemn, and punish the most insignificant offenses, while maintaining themselves by the greatest of all offenses, the annihilation of individual liberty."[17]

It was for its crimes against the individual, and not for any supposed personal reasons of her own, that Emma Goldman engaged in her energetic campaign of criticism against the state. Pointing to the autoritarianism by which all government must necessarily operate to a greater or lesser degree, she charged the state with being the major cause of the social atrophy we find everywhere in modern life. In her view the legal system that is part and parcel of any governmental structure is essentially a device for forcing men and women to live without that freedom which is necessary to their wholesome growth. And this, she insisted, is the real cause of social disunity and disharmony. "Discipline and restraint—are they not back of all the evils in the world? Slavery, submission, poverty, all misery, all social inequities result from discipline and restraint."[18]

It has not been clearly understood in the past that Emma Goldman, far from being the advocate of a stultifying collectivism, was as staunch a champion of individualism as any of the native-born American anarchists. As a delegate to the Second Anarchist Congress held in Amsterdam in 1907, she, along with Max Baginski, poked holes in the commonly accepted theory that the state is the most advanced theory of human organization possible. Rather than being a "true" form of social organization, she argued, the state is an "arbitrary institution cunningly imposed upon the masses." The theory of organization endorsed by anarchism owes nothing to imposed discipline and restraint but maintains instead that all social life must be firmly based upon freedom and must proceed from voluntary cooperation. Anarchists do not subscribe to the erroneous notion that social organization in and of itself leads to the eclipse of individuality. Placing herself in opposition to some of the European anarchists who proclaimed that the theory of mutual aid propounded by Kropotkin led exclusively to a theory of collective organization and away from the theories of individualism found in Ibsen, Emma refused to choose between them. ". . . anarchism does not involve a choice between Kropotkin and Ibsen; it embraces both," she insisted.[19] While Kropotkin was undoubtedly correct in maintaining that social progress is inevitably carried forward by the forces of revolution, Ibsen was equally correct in insisting that the process must be accompanied by "a revolution of the human soul, the revolt of individuality." To choose the one to the exclusion of the other is to render the philosophy of anarchism impotent to effect any fundamental reform of society.

The full extent of Emma Goldman's commitment to individualism was made evident at a farewell party held at Justus Schwab's saloon on First Street, then the gathering place for radicals in New York City. In a heated discussion with the well-known writer, James Huneker, Emma spoke of the deep impression that Nietzsche's writings had made upon her intellectual development and extolled the "aristocracy of spirit" she found everywhere in his writings. It was this aristocratic quality that made Nietzsche an anarchist, she argued, just as "all true anarchists were aristocrats."[20] Reminiscent of some of the argument made by Proudhon, Emma Goldman expressed deep concern for the mass tendencies she found everywhere in modern society. "If I were to give a summary of the tendency of our times," she wrote, "I would say, Quantity. The multitude, the mass spirit, dominates everywhere, destroying quality. Our entire life—production, politics, and education—rests on quantity, on numbers."[21] In direct proportion to the increase of mass social organization in society, she held, the principles and ideals of justice and truth have lost their hold upon the minds of men and have been replaced by an attitude of ethical relativism in which everything appears profane. Exploiting this situation, the modern politician, true to his philosophy of sophism, has erected a system of slavery and subjugation which would put the regimentation of the ancient Pharaohs to shame.

Rather than being a flaw in her thinking, Emma Goldman's attempt to "find a place in her thought for heroes"[22] was a truly remarkable insight into the nature of modern political development. From the very beginning of the evolution of anarchist thought in America, libertarians of all persuasions have recognized that the central problem in the task of establishing a free society is to somehow reverse the tendency toward the further centralization of political power. Under the aegis of democratic ideology, as both Jefferson and Tocqueville had noted, the popular majority becomes a jealous god which permits no other gods before it. At the risk of being misunderstood, Emma Goldman, in harmony with the main thrust of anarchist thought in America, completely denied the wisdom of majority rule, thereby rejecting the notion of democracy as it is popularly conceived. The difficulty with the idea of majority rule, in her opinion, is that "the majority cannot reason; it has no judgement." Placing its trust in the leadership furnished it by politicians and their political parties, the mass inevitably allows itself to be led like a band of little children. Yet, she held, it is not the politician, "parasite" that he is, who bears culpability for this chaotic state of affairs but the mass itself. Clinging to old, established ways in the manner of the insecure child who clings to his pacifier, the mass has an insatiable desire for security which leads it to a blind fury against the innovator who suggests new ways of doing things, whether it be in art, religion, economics, or politics. The mass "clings to its masters, loves the whip, and is the first to cry 'Crucify' the moment a protesting voice is raised against the sacredness of capitalistic authority or any other decayed institution." In an age when the idea of majority rule still played a very large role in the thinking of most Americans, it is easy to see why Emma's words were often thought to be blasphemous.

Although Emma Goldman was never able to bring herself to respect Benjamin Tucker, especially after his priggish attitude when asked to help secure Alexander Berkman's release from prison, she shared the positive response to Max Stirner's philosophy of individualism that Tucker did. It was from Stirner that she had derived the conviction that "man has as much liberty as he is willing to take."[23] Everywhere we turn today, she argued, we find that "the political superstition" holds a vice-like grip upon the minds and hearts of the people, destroying their will to act and transforming them into willing slaves. It was this idea which led her to give her unqualified support to anarchism as the only realistic salvation for mankind in its fight for freedom. "Anarchism is the only philosophy which brings to man the consciousness of himself; which maintains that God, the State, and society are nonexistent, that their promises are null and void, since they can be fulfilled only through man's subordination." Anarchism, far from being the negative force it is often supposed to be, she argued, is "the teacher of the unity of life." Viewing man as a truly social animal, anarchism denies that there is any basic conflict between the individual and the social instincts. To the extent that man discovers the strength within himself to make himself free, men will again find themselves living a true social existence. Working together, rather than against each other, the structure of a harmonious social life will then take form. Under present circumstances, she argued, men turn to the state in the hope that its power will be used to give them comfort and security. But the state, she insisted, far from being a social institution, is an instrument of tyranny and destruction, a veritable Leviathan which consumes all who venture within its grasp. For the state's only technique is force and compulsion, the very things which prevent the development of wholesome social sentiments among people. It is this reliance upon government as the supposed guarantor of social unity that we must destroy.

Very much in the tradition of Proudhon, Emma Goldman decreed that the first step toward the libertarian goal was for man to free himself from the "phantoms that have held him captive." In their fight to free men from the state idea, however, it was imperative for anarchists to avoid the temptation to indulge in utopian thinking. In this regard she wrote:

> . . . I believe that Anarchism can not consistently impose an iron-clad program or method on the future. The things every new generation has to fight, and which it can least overcome, are the burdens of the past which holds us all in a net. Anarchism . . . leaves posterity free to develop its own particular systems, in

harmony with its needs. Our most vivid imagination can not foresee the potential-
ities of a race set free from external restraints. How, then, can anyone assume to
map out a line of conduct for those to come? We, who pay dearly for every breath
of pure, fresh air, must guard against the tendency to fetter the future. If we
succeed in clearing the soil from the rubbish of the past and present, we will
leave to posterity the greatest and safest heritage of all ages.[24]

It was here that Emma Goldman's heroes were to come into play.
While the vast majority of people willingly submit to the dominion
of the state, the church, and the economic system, the anarchist,
secure in his belief that freedom alone can bring society social unity,
calls upon everyone to rise up against their servitude. "Break your
mental fetters, says Anarchism to man, for not until you think and
judge for yourself will you get rid of the dominion of darkness, the
greatest obstacle to all progress." But words without deeds played
no part in Emma's thinking. Heroism, in her opinion, took the form
of direct action against tyranny and injustice. "Direct action against
the authority in the shop, direct action against the authority of
the law, direct action against the invasive, meddlesome authority
of our moral code, is the logical, consistent method of Anarchism."
Emma Goldman's heroes, then, were revolutionaries, such as Johann
Most and Peter Kropotkin, who steadfastly refused to submit to the
yoke of government and called for the absolute rejection of politics
as a means of securing social unity. But she also found room in her
heart for revolutionaries such as Thoreau, Emerson, and Roger
Baldwin who had developed their social thought within a framework
of individualism. As Joseph Ishill, one of Emma's most cherished
friends observed, "If we begin to hear and read more and more
about Walt Whitman, Thoreau and Emerson, it was due to a large
degree to Emma Goldman's emphasizing the consciousness and
greatness of their contributions towards the American arts and
letters."[25] What mattered to her was not whether one called himself
an individualist or collectivist but whether one was committed to a
philosophy of direct action against the abuse of power as it is found
in all authoritarian institutions. "No real social change," she insisted,
"has ever come about without revolution." And since "revolution
is but thought carried into action," any sincere idealist, whatever
label he may have attached to himself, is a hero to the extent that he
acts upon his commitments.

It is not to be supposed, however, that Emma Goldman, in
extolling the merits of heroism, was guilty of abandoning the masses

to their own slothfulness. No one truly understands the philosophy of anarchism who does not understand that there is a strong strain of Platonic idealism running through the social views of all anarchists. In final analysis, Emma Goldman's hero, like Plato's philosopher king, is a genuine lover of truth and beauty. Aware that the mass of men are held captive in the demi-world of darkness and shadow, the hero must turn to art in an attempt to lead them to the light above. For having renounced authority as a social means, the hero, like the philosopher-king, can only appeal to the minds of men by enticing them to accept new conceptions of beauty. In this respect, she maintained, "life in all its variety and fulness is art, the highest art."[26] And the hero, aware of "the tragedy of the millions condemned to a lack of joy and beauty," must attempt to free mass man through an appeal to his imagination. Let men once see that authority and power are bleak and ugly and their natural craving for beauty will lead them out of the cave. This course of action, according to "Red Emma," is the only possible one open to the libertarian. Unless social reformers become artists, she urged, or kings and rulers become libertarians there is no hope that mankind can ever claim the heritage of freedom that rightfully belongs to it. Much more than most people realize, Emma Goldman's interest in art and beauty was not a superficial sideline but a fundamental part of the libertarian philosophy she had worked out over the years.

Far from being the narrow-minded propogandist she was so often depicted as being, Emma Goldman was much more interested in art than she was in politics. For art, as she viewed the subject, was one of man's most potent techniques for bringing about real social and cultural progress. This was why so many of her friends were drawn from the fields of art and literature. Visited during a lecture in Toledo by the well-known painter, Robert Henri, she recognized him at once as a true anarchist. Later, Henri, along with George Bellows and John Sloan, were key figures in the evening classes of the Ferrer Modern School she helped to establish in New York. It was not Henri's great love for Walt Whitman alone that drew her to him but the spirit of freedom which she found so pronounced in his work. Sitting for her portrait in his studio in Gramercy Park, she had many exciting conversations about art, literature, and libertarian education with Henri and his wife. The Henris clearly understood, as Sebastian Faure did, that true social revolution is best accomplished by freeing the imagination of the individual while he is still young. For in final analysis it is the older generation, with its blind reliance upon authority, which is the real cause of the social tyranny that plagues mankind. Among the other libertarians who merited her hard-to-win respect were Elizabeth and Alexis Ferm, founders of the Playhouse, one of the early freedom schools in America. Although the Ferms thought of themselves as single-taxers, Emma Goldman recognized their libertarian educational views as being basically anarchist in flavor. Maintaining a completely un-structured curriculum in their school, they threw out all rules and regulations and encouraged their students to learn for themselves without the aid of textbooks or other imposed authority. The Ferms, she generously admitted, put into practice the social theories which she merely advocated in her speeches and writing.

In no aspect of her social teachings were her libertarian senti-ments more pronounced than in her attitudes toward women's rights. Tilling the soil which had originally been broken by the Heywoods, Emma Goldman stands out as an ardent champion of woman's right to full and unrestricted freedom. Although we must agree with Floyd Dell that her theories in this regard were at basis a mere re-flection of the ideas she had culled from her reading in Ibsen[27], this does not detract from the fact that she possessed tremendous insight into the problem women faced in winning their freedom.

Just as she insisted that labor could hope for no real progress through the ballot, so Emma warned women that they stood to gain nothing at all by winning the franchise in politics. It is by asserting one's self as a woman and not as a voter, she cautioned, that the American female will raise herself up out of slavery.

To the extent that woman resists the false allure of political power, Emma insisted, she can hope to make herself a real force in the evolution of social progress. But her heroism can only take form if she is first successful in breaking free of the stultifying phantoms which have held her captive throughout the ages. Refusing to allow herself to be used as a sex commodity, woman must assert herself as a social personality. No longer must she bear children at the com-mand of husband, church, or state but only when she freely chooses to do so in response to her own natural desires. Formulating the doctrine of "free love" upon which much of her notoriety came to be based, Emma Goldman counselled women to make freedom the central fact in all their relationships. The popular press of Emma's day completely distorted her argument, branding her as the advocate of wanton promiscuity. A careful reading of her words indicates, however, that there was absolutely nothing promiscuous in her viewpoint. Idealist that she was, Emma conceived of the sexual function as a sacred aspect of life. She considered it outrageous that any mature woman should be asked to subordinate her own natural sexual cravings to the demands of artificial institutions such as marriage or social mores. Like life itself, sex could only flourish within an atmosphere of freedom. "Free love? As if love is anything but free," she ejaculated. "Yes, love is free; it can dwell in no other atmosphere. In freedom it gives itself unreservedly, abundantly, completely. All the laws on the statutes, all the courts in the universe, cannot tear it from the soil, once love has taken root." Where men and women are bound together by the cold fetters of artificially contrived matrimonial bonds, on the other hand, sex can produce nothing but bitter fruit. Only freedom can be depended upon as the regulator of mankind's most precious treasure.

Those who do not clearly understand the logic of anarchism have always found it difficult to understand why American anarchists have made sexual freedom the central focus of their theories. But as Hutchins Hapgood pointed out, American anarchists have been more interested in sex than in politics simply because there has always been less freedom allowed the individual in his sexual expression in this country than there has been in Europe.[28] Typical of the libertarian in America, Emma Goldman found Puritanism the most pernicious aspect of the culture of her adopted land. ". . . Puritanism has made life impossible," she held. Life, as she thought of it, "represents beauty in a thousand variations; it is, indeed, a gigantic panorama of eternal change.[29] But Puritanism, she maintained, confined within the Calvanistic ethos which views life as a "curse, imposed upon man by the wrath of God," drains the sexual function of all of its natural content. Laboring under the heavy burden of sin, "man must do constant penance, must repudiate every natural and healthy impulse, and turn his back on joy and beauty." In the tradition of Walt Whitman, Stephen Pearl Andrews and the Ezra Heywoods, Emma Goldman condemned Puritanism because of the deep gloom it cast over American society and the crippling effect it had upon the lives of the men and women who came under its influence.

On a visit to the East in 1903, Abe Isaac, the editor of *Free Society* which was then published in Chicago, stopped off for a brief sojourn at an "anarchist summer resort" in New Jersey to exchange greetings with some of the Eastern comrades. Here Isaac was inspired by the sight of Emma and her uninhibited friends emerging from an early morning dip in the sparkling lake, their naked bodies reflecting the glowing rays of the rising sun.[30] Although nudism plays no official role in the philosophy of anarchism, Emma considered it central to the problem of human freedom. Modern social theory has at last come to realize, she argued, that "nakedness has a hygienic value as well as a spiritual influence" which hits directly at the morbid emotions Puritanism has imposed upon us. Made conscious of our capacity for evil by the teachings of Christianity, we have lost our innocence and consequently our ability to see beauty in nature. To remove one's clothing and cavort in the raw with one's fellows, therefore, was an act of propaganda by deed aimed at the reclamation of our basic humanity.

> The vision of the essential and human form, the nearest thing to us in all the world with its vigor and its beauty and its grace, is one of the prime tonics of life. But the spirit of purism has so perverted the human mind that it has lost the power to appreciate the beauty of nudity, forcing us to hide the natural form under the idea of chastity. Yet chastity itself is but an artificial imposition upon nature, expressive of false shame of the human form. The modern idea of chastity, especially in reference to woman, its greatest victim, is but the sensuous exaggeration of our natural impulses.[31]

True to the spirit of freedom which motivated her to think in libertarian terms, Emma made no attempt to impose her nudist sentiments upon anyone who did not share her ideals. For nudity, like any other aspect of anarchist theory, can only survive where it is adopted voluntarily as a self-imposed discipline based upon sincere conviction. But like her predecessors in the struggle to free man's mind from the debilitating effects of Puritanism, Emma resented the fact that the powers of government were employed in America directly for the purpose of imposing Puritanical values upon the people. "The almost limitless capacity of Puritanism for evil is due to its entrenchment behind the State and its law," she wrote. "Pretending to safeguard the people against 'immorality,' it has impregnated the machinery of government and added to its usurpation of moral guardianship the legal censorship of our views, feeling, and even our conduct." The devil incarnate in this regard, according to Emma, was Anthony Comstock, the high-priest of governmentally regulated morality in America. Waging a relentless battle against all laws which sought to censure the ideas of Americans, whether on the state or in literature, Emma called for a return to the principle of *laissez-faire* in morals. Let freedom reign, she admonished, and evil thoughts will dissipate as the early morning haze evaporates under the warming rays of the sun.

It is not to be concluded, however, that Emma Goldman's advocacy of free love and the unrestricted right of woman to full expression was a mere reflection of the feminist movement in America. Exercising an uncanny intuition into the psychology of human behavior, Emma laid the foundations for many contemporary theories regarding the feminine character. Rather than being a pale imitation of the male, woman, for her, was the source of compassion and pity in the world, the essential ingredients of any well-balanced social system. Completely feminine herself, she insisted that woman can only obtain the full development of her personality by giving expression to the natural traits she derived from her maternal and companionable instincts. To the extent that woman embodies in her life the feminine qualities which are natural to her she may become "a force hitherto unknown in the world, a force for real love, for peace, for harmony; a force of divine fire, of life giving; a creator of free men and women."[32]

Nowhere is Emma Goldman's dedication to the libertarian idea more pronounced than in the criticism of the Bolshevik revolution she spelled out in her two books, *My Disillusionment in Russia* and *My Further Disillusionment in Russia*, the latter made necessary by the fact that her publisher had failed to include the last twelve chapters of the first manuscript she had delivered to him. Originally titled "My Two Years in Russia," her publisher, by giving it the title he did without her permission, made it appear as though she had suddenly become disenchanted with the turn of events that practical Marxism had taken. But Emma, according to her version of the affair, was not a Johnny-come-lately critic of Soviet Communism. "I had always known the Bolsheviki are Marxists," she proclaimed. "For thirty years I fought the Marxian theory as a cold, mechanistic formula."[33] Consistently sympathetic with the persecuted and the misunderstood, it was the repressive measures of the Allied nations of the West which brought her to the defense of the Bolsheviki.

In spite of their Marxism, and not because of it, she came to defend the Russian revolutionaries simply because they were revolutionaries. Always more interested in justice than she was in shallow ideological consistency, she thus exposed herself to the bitter criticism that was bound to follow should she be forced to change her mind again at a later date.

During the first months of her forced sojourn in the Soviet Union, Emma made a valiant attempt to find the brighter side of communism as it was working out in practice. She was thus able to overlook the poverty and human suffering she found on all sides, telling herself that this was largely the result of the blockade imposed by the Allies and the inevitable inefficiency of people when they suddenly find themselves free after a lifetime in slavery. As time went on, however, she became increasingly disturbed by the cold, inhuman attitude of the bureaucracy which was becoming progressively more powerful. Upon learning that large numbers of the intelligentsia had been executed by the Bolsheviks after the October Revolution on the grounds that the revolution itself could not hope to succeed while its enemies continued to live, Emma's hope that something good could come out of practical Marxism was totally shattered. Her sleep disturbed night after night by the sound of gunfire in the distance, she forced herself to the realization that the Bolsheviks, although officially proclaiming an end to the primitive practice of capital punishment, secretly gunned down all political opposition within the country. Confronting Jack Reed, the American Marxist who had expatriated himself to the Soviet Union, with this knowledge, she was shocked to discover that political execution had become an integral part of the Bolshevik program of social revolution. "Any suggestion of the value of human life, quality of character, the importance of revolutionary integrity as the basis of the new social order, was repudiated as 'bourgeois sentimentality,' which had no place in the revolutionary scheme of things."[34] Recoiling in horror from the brutality of this thought, she was forced to thoroughly reevaluate the meaning of the revolution in her own mind. "Is there any change in the world?" she morbidly asked herself. "Or is it all an eternal recurrence of man's inhumanity to man?" Becoming outspoken in her condemnation of the Communist apparatus, Emma Goldman soon became *persona non grata* in the last remaining spot on earth that had promised to give her haven.

While it is true, as the liberal Charles A. Madison charges in his *Critics and Crusaders*, that Emma Goldman and Alexander Berkman unleashed a scathing attack on the Soviet system after leaving the country, it is incorrect to describe their criticism as "fanatic hatred" more "hysterical" than that directed against the Soviets by "the most extreme reactionaries."[35] Never given to soft words, the team of Berkman and Goldman always spoke their minds with vigor and incaution, letting the ideological chips fall where they might. Their criticism of the Bolsheviks was no more bitter than their criticism of the capitalists had been. To claim, moreover, as Madison did, that "had the anarchists [themselves] seized power, they might have been equally cruel and incompetent under the drastic circumstances" is to completely misunderstand the anarchist argument. Of course the anarchists would have been cruel and vicious masters as a ruling elite. But no anarchist has ever deluded himself into believing that the seizure of political power is a feasible course of social revolution. Consistently opposed to the state idea, whether it was proletarian or democratic in form, anarchists are by conviction unwilling to "seize power" under any circumstances. The liberal's inability to understand this fact is due to his proclivity to think of political power as an inevitable aspect of social life, a *non sequitor* if ever there was one from the anarchist point of view. Society itself does not exist, according to the anarchist, so long as political power is relied upon to assume social order. To seize power, therefore, would be to end the revolution before it had even gotten started.

What finally turned Emma Goldman against the Bolsheviks was not their administrative inefficiency but their zealous adoption of the "Jesuitic formula that the end justifies all means." Adapting the military principle to industry during the Ninth Congress in March of 1920, the Communist Party, to Emma's dismay, sought to bring efficiency to the Russian economy by organizing the workers like soldiers. But this, as she pointed out to Jack Reed and anyone else in Russia who would listen to her, was to resurrect the authoritarian notion that force and compulsion are the mainsprings of social progress. But "The authoritarian method has been a failure all through history," she proclaimed, "and it has again failed in the Russian Revolution." Steadfast to the end in her dedication to the libertarian idea, Emma Goldman chose to place her faith in the Proudhonian notion that "man has indeed uttered the highest wisdom

NOTES

SECTION V - CHAPTER 2

1. Emma Goldman, "Johann Most," *American Mercury,* VIII (June, 1926), 158.

2. *Living My Life* (New York, 1931), p. 28.

3. "Biographic Sketch," In Emma Goldman, *Anarchism and Other Essays* (New York, 1910), p. 17.

4. *Living My Life,* p. 395.

5. For a sympathetic evaluation of Emma Goldman, see Eunice Schuster, "Native American Anarchism," Smith College *Studies In History,* XVII (October 1931—July, 1932), 173.

6. Theodore Schroeder, *Free Speech for Radicals* (New York, 1916), p. 13.

7. Floyd Dell, *Woman as World Builders* (Chicago, 1913), p. 59.

8. Margaret Goldsmith, "Emma Goldman," in *Seven Women Against the World* (London, 1935), p. 153.

9. Emma Goldman, "The Tragedy of Buffalo," *The Revolutionary Almanac* (1914), p. 55.

10. *Ibid.,* p. 56.

11. *Living My Life,* p. 536.

12. Quoted in Richard Drinnon's *Rebel in Paradise* (Chicago, 1961), p. 82.

13. *Anarchism and Other Essays,* p. 113.

14. *Anarchism and Other Essays,* p. 140.

15. For a biting condemnation of the class basis of modern warfare, see Bart Deligt, *The Conquest of Violence* (New York, 1938), p. 71.

16. Emma Goldman, "America by Comparison," *Road to Freedom,* II (July 15, 1926), 3.

17. *Anarchism and Other Essays,* p. 63.

18. *Ibid.,* p. 171.

19. *Living My Life,* p. 402.

20. *Ibid.,* p. 194.

21. *Anarchism and Other Essays,* p. 75.

22. *Rebel in Paradise,* p. 107.

23. *Anarchism and Other Essays,* p. 71.

24. *Ibid.,* p. 50.

25. Joseph Ishill, "Emma Goldman," Unpublished Manuscript,

The Houghton Library, Harvard University.

26. *Living My Life,* p. 464.

27. *Woman As World Builders,* p. 62.

28. *An Anarchist Woman* (New York, 1909), p. 154.

29. *Anarchism and Other Essays,* p. 173.

30. "A Little Journey," *Free Society,* X (September 20, 1903), 1.

31. *Anarchism and Other Essays,* p. 177.

32. *Ibid.,* p. 217.

33. *My Disillusionment in Russia* (Garden City, 1923), p. 10.

34. *Ibid.,* p. 110.

35. *Critics and Crusaders* (New York, 1947), p. 233.

36. "A Lesson from Russia," *The Road to Freedom,* II (November, 1925), 2.

37. *My Further Disillusionment in Russia* (Garden City, 1924), p. 169.

CHAPTER 3

Alexander Berkman: A Frustrated Moralist Crying in the Wilderness of American Capitalism

Less notorious than Johann Most or Emma Goldman but equally misunderstood was Alexander Berkman (1870-1936). Born at Vilna, later part of Lithuania, Berkman spent his early youth in comfortable physical surroundings. Well-off financially, as many Russian Jewish families were, the Berkmans enjoyed the luxury of servants and other amenities of life, including pleasant summer vacations spent in a fashionable suburb of St. Petersburg. But Alexander Berkman did not possess a temperament that would permit him to accept the pleasures of class privilege without question. While still in his early teens he precipitated a grave family crisis when he sternly rebuked his mother for slapping a servant for some domestic error, sending her into shock by impudently reminding her that "the low servant girl is as good as you." In later years Berkman again and again gave demonstration of the fact that his sympathies lay primarily with the oppressed and persecuted social minorities of this world rather than with the strong and powerful. Like Rousseau, his compassion for human suffering was not something that was learned but a natural tendency which was well-developed even in his early youth. Viewing the corpse of a Nihilist who had been executed, the sensitive boy was shocked to the core by the brutality and ruthlessness of man, his mind set aflame by burning questions of the why and how of it all. In later years this proclivity to throw himself into the defense of those who were being brutalized by their fellowmen became the prime motive power for all his actions and was the force that sustained him in life.

It would be inaccurate to say, however, that Berkman was already an anarchist during his boyhood in native Russia. While still in school, it is true, he had become something of an iconoclast and religious skeptic, earning the condemnation of his teachers and principal for an essay he wrote repudiating the idea of God. But atheism and anarchism are no more to be equated than are anarchism and violence. If we may take Berkman at his word, he had never even heard the word anarchist before he arrived in this country an immigrant at the age of seventeen. His decision to embrace the anarchist idea was based upon the revulsion he experienced at witnessing the social and economic violence of a rapidly developing industrial nation. It was in search of alternatives to "the methods of tyranny, oppression, and persecution, practiced not only in penitentiaries, but also in the larger prison called the world," Berkman wrote, "that made me an Anarchist who seeks more humane forms of social life."[1]

Unfortunately, Alexander Berkman's name has been inextricably linked to that moment in July of 1892 when, armed with a pistol and dagger, he gained entrance to Henry C. Frick's private office for the purpose of assassinating him. Legally there has never been any doubt that the act was properly classified as a case of premeditated murder. Fortunately for both Frick and for himself, Berkman inadvertently bungled the job, therby sparing their respective lives. Had he succeeded in his mission, the world would never have gained the first insight into Berkman's motives, for he not only refused to avail himself of legal counsel during his trial but he even refused to defend himself. In Berkman's view of things, the legal proceedings he was caught up in were without right or reason, since he did not acknowledge the state or any of its institutions as legitimate. Rather than give sanctity to law by recognizing it, Berkman planned to endure the thing in silence until that moment when he could speak out over the heads of the stuffy officials in the courtroom to the people and allow the anguish and pent-up emotions of his heart to flow out as water gushes forth when the walls of a dam have fallen. In Berkman's mind, the people could understand him where the officials of the state could not; surely they would listen when he poured forth his heart to them. But the presiding judge, whose mind was as firmly fixed in the existing legal system as Mars and Jupiter are fixed in their orbits, refused to give him his moment in court, rewarding him with a harsh prison sentence for his pains. As a consequence, Alexander Berkman's name has largely remained shrouded in darkness and misunderstanding to this day.

When we focus directly on Berkman's social philosophy rather than the deed which he committed under its influence, we gain a totally different picture of the man from the one generally held by the public. Undoubtedly the strongest element of his personality and character was his devotion to the concept of social revolution. "Since my early youth," Berkman wrote toward the end of his life, "revolution—social revolution—was the great hope and aim of my life. It signified to me the Messiah who was to deliver the world from brutality, injustice, and evil, and paved the way for a regenerated humanity of brotherhood, living in peace, liberty, and beauty."[2] Under different circumstances, Alexander Berkman might have dedicated himself to the Church, and, having taken the vow of celibacy, poured all his phenomenal energy into the office of priesthood. Unable to believe in any conventional notion of God, this course was closed to him and he was forced to seek elsewhere for an outlet for his compassion and social dedication. The libertarian idea played the same role in Berkman's life that the idea of Jesus Christ plays in the Christian's, sustaining him in his hour of need and furnishing him with energy and determination in his chosen vocation of social reformer. So serious was he about his mission that he refused to give free play to his basic instincts for fear that they might lead him astray, maintaining that:

> The revolutionist has no personal right to anything. Everything he has or earns belongs to the cause. Everything, even his affections. Indeed, these especially. He must not become too attached to anything. He should guard against strong love or passion. The People should be his only great love, his supreme passion. Mere human sentiment is unworthy of the real revolutionist: he lives for humanity, and he must ever be ready to respond to its call. The soldier of the Revolution must not be lured from the field of battle by the siren song of love.[3]

It is utterly impossible to pronounce absolute judgement upon Alexander Berkman's actions when he sought to take the life of Henry Frick, as the courts of this country attempted to do at the time. His act, to be sure, signified that he was willing to take human life as a means of attaining his social aims. But it does not follow from this, however, that Berkman believed in violence as a legitimate social force or that he was essentially callous regarding the value of human life. Paradoxically, it was because he held life in such high esteem that he was willing to sacrifice it under certain circumstances. ". . . it is at once the greatest tragedy of martyrdom, and the most terrible indictment of society," Berkman wrote, "that it forces the noblest men and women to shed human blood, though their souls shrink from it."[4] These were not crocodile tears but the expression of genuine contrition for the necessity of doing harm to a fellowman. Underneath the hard shell of revolutionary fervor which Berkman encased himself in was a heart which was kindly and warm and which went out to all creatures who suffered. "Who can be happy at a time when *power* (force) means right, and weakness—wrong? When it is a shame to be poor, because the poor is the weaker and the weaker is always wrong. Who, I ask, can be happy while millions of human beings are poor, wretched and miserable," he wrote from his prison cell.[5] Obviously Alexander Berkman was one of those souls who was guilty not of loving too little but of loving too much.

Berkman, like another great heroic figure, John of Salisbury, justified the *Attentat* as a means of obtaining social justice when all other means had failed. In Berkman's mind the workingmen and women of this world alone should inherit the earth. With the coming of capitalism and industrial society the people had been denied their rightful inheritance by the strong and powerful. The ruling classes were parasites, sucking the life blood from the people. Accordingly, Berkman reasoned, they must be destroyed so that the working people of the world might once again go free. But in advocating the employment of force against the oppressors, he was painstakingly careful to distinguish between murder and tyrannicide. In this regard he wrote:

> The removal of a tyrant is not merely justifiable; it is the highest duty of every true revolutionist. Human life is indeed sacred and inviolate. But the killing of a tyrant, of an enemy of the People, is in no way to be considered as the taking of a life. A revolutionist would rather perish a thousand times than be guilty of what is ordinarily called murder. In truth, murder and *Attentat* are to me opposite terms. To remove a tyrant is an act of liberation, the giving of life to an oppressed people.[6]

As the above quotation makes clear, Berkman was well aware that violence of itself is wrong and that to employ it does as much harm to the individual who commits it as it does to society in general. Undoubtedly the ambivalence toward violence that characterizes his thinking was primarily caused by his acceptance of certain strands of revolutionary thought that derived from his upbringing in Czarist Russia where brutality and suffering were everyday experiences. Like Kropotkin and other Russian émigrees, Berkman subscribed to the view that class conflict is a constant fact of life and that a certain degree of violence is inevitable whenever any significant social change takes place. "In all history," he wrote, "the ruling classes never surrendered an iota of their power except through force or fear. Nor did the masters ever cease encroaching upon the liberties of the people until the people revolted in self-defense."[7] As a member of the Pioneers of Liberty, the first Yiddish Anarchist organization to be formed in the United States, Berkman was convinced that open conflict between the wage slaves and their masters is inevitable in capitalist society. But the violence that was certain to ensue was not something the oppressed worker freely chose to engage in but something forced upon him by the system that he was born into. "Our present system of civilization has, by disinheriting millions, made the belly the center of the universe," Berkman complained. And yet, he maintained, while the material facts of history are of crucial importance in the determination of social events, no human action is without its moral implications.

> Man can better stand starvation than the consciousness of injustice. The consciousness that you are treated unjustly will rouse you to protest and rebellion just as quickly as hunger, perhaps even quicker. Hunger may be the immediate cause of every rebellion or uprising, but beneath it is the slumbering antagonism and hatred of injustice and wrong. The truth is that right and justice play a far more important role in our lives than most people are aware of.[8]

At first sight it might appear that Alexander Berkman was guilty of clumsy thinking when he maintained that although violence is always wrong and to be abjured, it is sometimes necessary to the attainment of libertarian social goals. But as he made clear in his major theoretical work, *Now and After* (1929), violence is not a phenomenon that is exclusive to any one class in society but the common possession of the whole social fabric. Like power or love, it is an interpersonal relationship in which the actions of one party are inevitably the cause of the reactions of the other. When captial employs its power to exploit the laboring classes, it ought not to be surprised when resentment and hostility are directed against it in turn. In fact it may well expect to receive social pressure back in proportion to the pressure it exerts itself. When, as in the nineteenth century, the ruling class presses its advantage as hard as it possibly can, the only possible reaction is one of total revolutionary action upon the part of the exploited. Moreover, he argued, when we are perfectly honest with ourselves we must admit, whether we like it or not, that while all of us condemn violence when it is practiced by others, we resort to it ourselves when it is to our advantage. "In fact," Berkman maintained with more truth than liberals and conservatives care to admit, "all the institutions we support and the entire life of present society is based on violence." What is government itself, he queried, other than organized violence in support of the interests of the predominant social and economic groups which support it? It may well be that some slight shift in the power structure takes place from time to time which allows formerly deprived groups to enjoy a new-found affluence. But this does not alter the fact that all government, law, and authority ultimately rest upon a system of force and violence which is directed against those who fail to recognize the propriety of the *status quo.* Wherever we find law we find sanctions which threaten punishment for those who transgress the rules. Throughout the length and breadth of the western political tradition we find that authority has always depended upon punishment, or the fear of punishment, to maintain itself. "Why, even spiritual authority," according to Berkman, "the authority of the church and God rests on force and violence, because it is the fear of divine wrath and vengeance that wields power over you, compels you to obey, and even to believe against your own reason." Like Proudhon, Berkman placed the idea of God on the same plane as the idea of the state and condemned them both as the major source of social confusion in the world.

To a much greater extent than we realize, Berkman wrote, the social atmosphere which is created where force and authority are used to maintain social order makes violence an integral part of all of our lives. Growing up under formal government, we are all conditioned to accept force and compulsion as a normal aspect of existence rather than as the horrible antisocial thing it really is. "We are so steeped in the spirit of violence that we never ask whether violence is right or wrong. We only ask if it is legal, whether the law permits it."[9] Refusing to engage in any semantic gyrations regarding the supposed distinction between legitimate and illegitimate force, Berkman, like all libertarians, pronounced an anathema upon all forms of compulsion. For as he pointed out, those who distinguish between legitimate and illegitimate force actually argue that the difference between the two ultimately rests upon nothing other than a principle of legal rather than moral right. Thus, when governments take life in a time of war or civil insurrection, it is termed "legitimate force," whereas a destitute citizen who inadvertently kills someone while stealing to feed his starving children is deemed to be guilty of "violence." But, as Berkman rigorously argued, to defend the use of force by government is to admit that it is not violence in itself that disturbs us but the employment of violence by those who are not authorized to so employ it.

Caught up as he was in the vanguard of the proletariat, Berkman, like many another Anarchist Communist, was compelled to explain how he himself could employ violence to bring social justice about if the doctrine of anarchism does in fact reject violence and force as a means to its end. In this regard, he argued, we must be clear on the fact that anarchists hold no monopoly on violence. On all sides of the social spectrum—left, right, and center—force and violence are daily occurences. This being so, it can hardly be maintained that anarchism is the only source of violence or even its main source. If conservatives and reactionaries sometimes commit individual acts of violence, how can it be maintained that anarchism as an idea is responsible for the outbreak of violence within society? Individual anarchists, to be sure, like the McNamara brothers, have rebelled against their exploiters and have committed murder as an expression of their social resentment. But is the murder and violence unloosed by oppressed labor any worse than the murder and violence forced upon society by capital? *"You* are the guilty ones, you who uphold the 'law and order' founded on internecine strife, on tyranny and exploitation," Berkman caustically ejaculated. "As long as you defend and continue this murderous system, just so long will the violence of labor be inevitable."[10]

His brain seared by the burning resentment of the social injustice he witnessed everywhere about him, Alexander Berkman stood in danger at times of succumbing to the shallow appeal of terrorism. And even worse, he sometimes seemed to be on the verge of accepting the totally unanarchistic doctrine that the end justifies the means when it gives promise of delivering correct results.[11] But just as Saint Augustine had to live life intensively and dangerously until he found his vocation, so Alexander Berkman at first dabbled in false theories until he finally discovered the true genius of the libertarian idea. Already in his *Prison Memoirs of an Anarchist* (1912) he had some doubts that acts of terror, even when they are genuine social actions of a sincere individual such as Czolgos, contribute anything of worth to the development of humanity. Did the lightning flash set off by Czolgos "really illuminate the social horizon, or merely confuse minds with the succeeding darkness?" he asked. In Berkman's later years he was even more solidly convinced that violence can play no real part in the activities of an anarchist. There was a time, he asserted, when some individual anarchists viewed acts of "propaganda by deed" as a correct method for calling the world's attention to social injustice. But experience has taught us, he continued, that terrorism solves nothing, and, in fact, can only give rise to a further increase of injustice within society. Without professing himself to be a thoroughgoing pacifist, Berkman nevertheless adopted the essential attitude of nonviolence when he proclaimed that violence and terror, however unavoidable they may be in the unfolding of social life, are not legitimate means for bringing about social revolution. Those who criticize Berkman for taking so long in arriving at this basic truth might well reflect upon the fact that no existing government in the world today has yet discarded its prison system, police, or armed forces. To the contrary, the trend everywhere is toward further refinement in the techniques of police control and the instruments of warfare.

Deported to his native Russia with Emma Goldman in 1919, Berkman found in the Communist Party the corrective to his ailing social vision concerning the real effects of violence and the scales soon dropped from his eyes. The Bolsheviks, unable to adopt the libertarian principle of total freedom and individual social control, attempted the impossible feat of bringing about the social revolution by means of terrorism and repression. "But the principles of terrorism unavoidably redound to the fatal injury of liberty and revolution," Berkman argued. Force and violence are a two-headed sword, injuring those who wield it as much as those who have been cut down by it. Where terror is employed to fight the forces of counterrevolution, terror itself becomes the "efficient school" of both parties to the conflict. Traveling all over Russia in search of historical records for a museum of the Revolution, Alexander Berkman and his comrade, Emma Goldman, became intimately acquainted with the fact that violence committed in the name of working-class values is no less objectionable than violence committed by the nobility. It was with utter dejection that he wrote:

> Gray are the passing days. One by one the embers of hope have died out. Terror and despotism have crushed the life born in October. The slogans of the Revolution are foresworn, its ideals stifled in the blood of the people. The breath of yesterday is dooming millions to death; the shadow of today hangs like a pall over the country. Dictatorship is trampling the masses under foot. The revolution is dead; its spirit cries in the wilderness.
>
> High time the truth about the Bolsheviki were told. . . . I have decided to leave Russia.[12]

It is to Alexander Berkman's credit that his disillusionment with the Bolshevik Revolution did not lead to the weakening of his anarchist convictions but instead confirmed him even more in his beliefs concerning the correctness of libertarian methods. In the final form in which the anarchist idea presented itself to his mind, Berkman, like all convinced anarchists, was perfectly clear on the fact that revolution and anarchism are in no way synonymous. Revolution may be the means of bringing anarchism about but it is not in and of itself anarchism. Although he himself had earlier toyed with the idea that the end justifies the means, Berkman recoiled in horror when, upon meeting Lenin, he realized that the chief theoretician of Marxism in Russia was "a 'practical idealist' bent upon the realization of his Communist dream by whatever means, and subordinating it to every ethical and humanitarian consideration."[13] This "Jesuit of the Revolution" would use any means to force mankind to become free in order to make the unfolding of history keep pace with his interpretation of Marxian logic. For the anarchist who values human freedom above every other consideration, it is foolhardy to adopt this formula, Berkman countered. The fact is that ends and means are always conditioned by one another and can no more be of opposite natures than the head can be severed from the body without doing violence to the whole organism. In this connection he wrote:

> Your aims must determine the means. Means and aims are in reality the same: you cannot separate them. It is the means that shape your ends. The means are the seeds which bud into flower and come to fruition. The fruit will always be of the nature of the seed you planted. You can't grow a rose from a cactus seed. No more can you harvest liberty from compulsion, justice and manhood from dictatorship.[14]

Obviously, Alexander Berkman's communism was cut from a very different piece of cloth than were the doctrines of his communist counterparts in the Soviet Union.

Where Berkman fundamentally disagreed with the Bolsheviks was not so much on economic matters of production and distribution but on the basic question of whether the revolution is to be social or political. Lenin and his party, faced with practical necessities, had opted to set the basic liberties of the individual aside in order to consolidate the gains of the revolution they had just carried off. But all they had really succeeded in doing, according to Berkman, was to replace one ruling minority with another. The kind of revolution anarchism calls for, Berkman argued, does not stop after making a mere poltitical change but aims instead at bringing about a fundamental economic, ethical, and cultural transformation of society. The difficulty with most revolutions is that those who engineer them are not convinced of the efficacy of liberty as a means to their end and hence force, terror, and persecution have invariably prevented them from any positive accomplishments. Taking his cue from Kropotkin whom he had met in Russia and whom he greatly admired for his philosophical prowess, Berkman announced that "the time has come to try new methods, new ways" of bringing about the emancipation of humanity. Where the Bolsheviks had sought to create liberty and freedom through the means of compulsion and force, anarchism took its stand on the proposition that "the cure for evil and disorder is *more* liberty, not suppression."[15] For anarchists subscribe to the basic postulate that it is more important for society that justice should be realized than that efficiency of organization be achieved. In this argument his thinking was very much in tune with the viewpoint of the native American anarchists who were his philosophical forebears.

In final analysis, then, Berkman insisted, any conception of revolution which *does not go beyond* the idea of mere physical struggle against a ruling elite is altogether deficient. "The truth is, in modern times revolution does not mean barricades anymore."[16] Revolution is not simply the unleashing of violence and destruction, which are wholly negative phenomena, but a basically constructive social process which aims toward the realization of universal freedom. Drawing upon the genius of that famous anarchist theoretician, Michael Bakunin, Berkman redefined the social revolution as a constructive device which has for its goal the destruction not of any social class but the true enemies of all mankind, authority and servile obedience to ancient myths. It is false beliefs and false values which we anarchists seek to destroy, Berkman proclaimed. Everywhere men and women sit on their haunches and suffer the bonds of economic and social servitude in abject silence, their minds and hearts numbed by the chilling winds of ancient and unexamined prejudices. Like the dumb beast that obeys its master whatever it is ordered to do, they plod straight ahead in the furrows of timeworn habits and customs without ever questioning the myths which harness them to their present ways. Yet Berkman did not conclude from this, as all who accept the statist view of politics do, that mankind is hopelessly condemned to remain in this sad state of affairs. Some few men do break the habits of centuries, discovering the great powers of beauty and social facility which they harbor in the inner recesses of their basic human nature. And while it is foolhardy to suggest that all men might simultaneously break out of their bonds, it is certainly true, Berkman proclaimed, that all men have the potential for discovering the genius of social life, whether or not they ever actually accomplish that difficult feat. The task of the anarchist is not to lament the magnitude of the struggle ahead but to outline the structure of the libertarian idea so that all who have eyes to see can discover it.

Putting his finger on the vital pulse of the anarchist idea, Berkman correctly proclaimed that it is the institution of government itself which has enslaved mankind and destroyed its capacity to live in freedom. Government is "invasive" of the rights and powers of the individual, that is to say, for it invariably accomplishes its goals by force and compulsion rather than voluntary cooperation. Confined within the framework of law and punishment which serves as its life's blood, government must inevitably be a destructive force within society since it largely elicits compliance with its demands by directing the individual to obey whether or not he understands the need for such obedience. In condemnation of such human bondage Berkman wrote:

> More vicious and deadening is compulsory compliance than the most virulent poison. Throughout the ages it has been the greatest impediment to man's advance, hedging him in with a thousand prohibitions and taboos. weighting his mind down with outlived canons and codes, thwarting his will with imperatives of thought and feeling, with 'thou shalt' and 'thou shalt not' of behavior and action. Life, the art of living, has become a dull formula, flat and inert.[17]

In answer to the argument that it is not the law itself that is deficient as a social technique but merely its administration, Berkman refused to accept any part of this notion. Law in Rome is the same as it is in Moscow or Washington; it assumes that the individual does not respond to internal moral imperatives and hence must be bound to his duty by external sanctions administered by government. If the social condition we wish to achieve is a system of slavery, law is well suited for the task. But if we seek to create a free society, Berkman argued, we must learn to live without compulsion or authority. If we wish to live in peace and harmony with one another, we must replace law with attitudes of respect and brotherhood. If we wish to establish a mutually beneficial society in which all share in the fruits of production, we must discover the joys of cooperative labor. For the social revolution, rather than being a mere change in the organization of political life, means the establishment of new human values and patterns of social relationships. Such a transformation in human conditions is not likely to come overnight but only after we have prepared the soil for its growth. "It is a spirit to be cultivated, to be nurtured and reared, as the most delicate flower is, for indeed it is the flower of a new and beautiful existence."[18]

When Benjamin Tucker learned that a man named Alexander Berkman had attempted to snuff out the life of Henry C. Frick, one of the most notorious of all American exploiters of labor, Tucker acknowledged that although he did not know the assailant and did not approve of his use of violence, he believed that he had much in common with him.[19] And indeed the two did share many similar attitudes, for all the differences which stood between the individualist and communist versions of the anarchist idea. For just as much as Tucker, Alexander Berkman maintained that after all is said and done, "the only thing which is real and actual is the unit, the individual."[20] Berkman, to be sure, accepted the communist conclusion that labor must engage in a collective effort of production. But this, in his opinion, did not at all indicate that the individual is to be denied the fruits of his labor. ". . . the question is not whether one has a right to his product," Berkman held, "but whether there is such a thing as an individual product."[21] Under the terms and conditions of modern industry, with its highly specialized yet interrelated techniques and processes, it is impossible to maintain that any one individual produces anything by himself. ". . . all labor and the products of labor are social. The argument, therefore, about the right of the individual to his product has no practical merit." It was the realization of this social fact, and not any supposed differences as to the legitimacy of violence, which separated the philosophical from the communist anarchist.

Focusing upon the social and economic conditions of early twentieth century America, Alexander Berkman clearly understood that the greatest threat to the freedom of the individual lay in the highly centralized nature of industry and production. The free society anarchism hoped for, he believed, could only be brought about to the extent that the centralizing tendencies which had led to such tight concentrations of industry could be reversed.

> The revolution can accomplish the emancipation of labor only by gradual decentralization, by developing the individual worker into a more conscious and determining factor in the processes of industry, by making him the impulse whence proceeds all industrial and social activity. The deep significance of the social revolution lies in the abolition of the mastery of man over man, putting in its place the management of things. Only thus can be achieved industrial and social freedom.[22]

Addressing himself to the often heard statement that anarchists reject absolutely all forms of organization, Berkman labeled such talk sheer nonsense. To the contrary, he maintained, "the whole of life is organization, conscious or unconscious." Without some kind of organization, the social and economic unity which makes life possible would be lacking, thereby rendering individual men and women helpless to rise above a mere subsistence level of production and consumption. Anarchists most certainly do believe in organization. But the kind of organization they demand is one that is consistent with the libertarian idea of freedom which is basic to all anarchist thought. Anarchist communists oppose capitalism primarily because it attempts to organize industrial life on a basis of compulsion and force, treating the individual worker as a mere object to be manipulated and used, Berkman pointed out. The plan of organization favored by anarchism, on the other hand, would be consistent with the idea of a free society. "The libertarian organization, formed voluntarily and in which each member is free and equal, is a sound body and can work well. Such an organization is a free union of equal parts."[23] It is as different from capitalist society as night is different from day.

In basic agreement with the tenets of anarcho-syndicalist thought, Berkman proclaimed that the major reform to be made in industry was to free the worker from control from above. If democracy is to be anything more than a mere empty phrase, he held, it must be reflected in the industrial life of society. "Organization from the bottom up, beginning with the shop and factory, on the foundation of the joint interests of the workers everywhere, irrespective of trade, race, or country, by means of mutual effort and united will, alone can solve the labor question and serve the true emancipation of man."[24] Labor must not seek to find its strength at the polls, he cautioned, for to do so is to accept the erroneous notion that political activity is an answer to its problem. Neither must labor allow itself to seek its strength in union organization, for unionism is merely another kind of political activity. In this regard Berkman wrote:

> . . . the strength of the worker is not in the union meeting-hall; it is in the shop and factory, in the mill and mine. It is *there* that he must organize; there on the job. There he knows what he wants, what his needs are, and it is there that he must concentrate his efforts and his will. Every shop and factory should have its special committee to attend to the wants and requirements of the men, not leaders, but members of the rank and file, from the bench and furnace, to look after the demands and complaints of their fellow employees. Such a committee, being on the spot and constantly under the direction and supervision of the workers, wields no power: it merely carries out instructions. Its members are recalled at will and others selected in their place, according to the need of the moment and the ability required for the task in hand. It is the workers who decide the matters at issue and carry their decisions out through the shop committees.[25]

As labor builds democracy at the grass roots of industry, it will in time acquire the strength to break free from the bonds that now enslave it to its capitalist masters through the mechanism of the *general strike*. Only thus can the worker hope to acquire the full value of his labor and lift his head like a free man, Berkman argued. In time the wage slavery of capitalism will be replaced by a free economy owned and operated by the workers themselves.

Like Kropotkin, upon whose political theory his own was largely patterned, Berkman's conception of democracy was federative in character. The idea of people's cooperatives figured greatly in this arrangement. "Shop and factory committees, organized locally, by district, region, and State, and federated nationally, will be the bodies best suited to carry on revolutionary production."[26] Farmers, organized in cooperatives of their own, will supply the worker's cooperatives in town and city with food and raw materials in exchange for the finished industrial products they need. Berkman was confident that the motive power of such a free economy would be found in the spirit of mutual aid which Kropotkin insisted was basic in all social configurations. Let the people once escape from the chains of capitalist society and their natural propensity to live in freedom with one another would become reality rather than a mere dream.

Had he lived in some era other than the turbulent years of capitalism's expansion in America, Alexander Berkman might well have embraced some other economic theory than the syndicalist notions he did, for the economic ideas which any individual anarchist chooses to champion are largely determined by the social environment that shapes his particular experiences. In an earlier age he would probably have found much in common with Josiah Warren and other exponents of individualism. In respect to his basic attitudes toward freedom, however, Berkman stood steadfast in the mainstream of the libertarian tradition in America—a tradition which values liberty above every other consideration. Underneath the economic determinism that he shared with Marx was an acceptance of Jeffersonian principles which completely destroys the notion that anarchists like Berkman were out to subvert the American heritage of freedom or to introduce values that were alien to the people.

Although Alexander Berkman was influenced in his social thought by the writings of Peter Kropotkin more than by any other single philosopher, it is nevertheless true that he drew heavily upon the ideas of many of the same great exponents of American democracy that had served as the guiding stars of the native American anarchists. In his *Deportation—Its Meaning and Menace,* for example, Berkman frequently quotes from the writings of Lincoln, Garrison, Wendell Phillips, Paine, Stephen Pearl Andrews, Henry George, and Thoreau to substantiate his argument that the people can only be enslaved where they permit themselves to be. Greatly concerned for the welfare of his adopted country, Berkman interpreted his deportation order as the act of a government which had little real knowledge of the American heritage of liberty. "Oh shades of Jefferson, Thomas Paine, and Patrick Henry," he wrote, what has become of freedom that this great country should resort to "sudden seizure, anonymous denunciation, star chamber proceedings, the third degree, secret deportation and banishment to unknown lands."[27] With genuine concern for freedom he called upon Americans to reverse the tide of despotism which he felt was then engulfing the civil liberties so many have fought so hard to build.

> Do not stand supinely by, while every passing day strengthens reaction. Rouse yourselves and others to resent injustice and every outrage on liberty. Demand an open mind and fair hearing for every idea. Hold sacred the right of expression: protect the freedom of speech and press. Suffer not Thought to be forcibly limited and opinions proscribed. Make conscience free, undisciplined. Allow no curtailment of aspirations and ideals. These are the levers of progress, the fountainhead of joy and beauty.[28]

It is not yet too late, he urged, to save the American dream of unrestricted liberty. Let all who love freedom raise their voices in protest of her rape by the despots who have infiltrated your shores.

Whatever other faults he may have had, Alexander Berkman could in no instance be accused of lacking faith in the people. Again like Kropotkin, Berkman was an incorrigible idealist, professing a belief in the social sincerity of the common man that has seldom been equaled in intensity.[29] With all anarchist communists he began with the axiom that true liberty can only come about when the social revolution opens up economic opportunity for all. "In the profoundest sense," he asserted, "liberty is the daughter of economic equality."[30] Yet Berkman was fully aware that economic well-being is not the end of life nor even a guarantee of happiness. Humanity moves forward not on its stomach but on its ideals regarding truth, beauty, and justice. Far in advance of existing patterns of social thought, Berkman embraced the idea of anarchism because he was aware that a new and better humanity could be built only on entirely new foundations. It is not human nature that is brutal and cruel, he maintained, but the institutions which everywhere pervert man's basic social instincts. He fought against government because he realized that government is the chief source of compulsion and force in the world. "It is economic slavery, the savage struggle for a crumb, that has converted mankind into wolves and sheep. In liberty and communism, none would have the will or power 'to make countless thousands mourn.' Verily, it is the system, rather than individuals, that is the source of pollution and degradation."[31] Once the walls of existing institutions of force and compulsion have crumbled, Berkman pleaded, man's spirit will once again breathe freely and a new culture will come into being. "Free to exercise the limitless possibilities of his mind, to pursue his love of knowledge, to apply his inventive genius, to create and to soar on the wings of imagination, man will reach his full stature and become man indeed."[32]

In final analysis, then, Berkman, like all anarchists, was more a child of the Enlightenment than he was a social engineer who would force upon mankind his plans for a more perfect world. "If I were asked to define civilization in a single phrase," he wrote, "I should say that it is the triumph of man over the powers of darkness, natural and human."[33] Throughout his writings there is a constant reference to the human condition and the obstacles which prevent men from realizing their potential powers for social and spiritual growth. Fully within the tradition of native American anarchism, Berkman saw war as the greatest of all of mankind's failures. "War! do you realize what it means?" he queried. "Do you know of any more terrible word in our language?" In specific reference to the Great War of his time, Berkman lamented the purposeless sacrifice of human lives it entailed and the untold suffering it caused to individuals. Reflecting the very same moral indignation that characterized the social thought of Randolph Bourne, Berkman abhorred the fact that intellectuals in America, following the lead of Wall Street, had turned their backs on the country's heritage of freedom and had allowed the fevers of war to push them into the ways of philistinism.

> Shame upon the mighty powers of the human mind! It was the "radical intellectuals" who, as a class, turned traitors to the best interests of humanity, perverted their calling and traditions, and became the bloodiest canines of Mars. With a power of sophistry that the Greek masters of false logic never matched, they cited history, philosophy, science—aye, they called the very Christ to witness that the killing of man by man is a most worthy and respectable occupation, indeed a very Christian institution, and that the wholesale human slaughter, if properly directed and successfully conducted, is a very necessary evolutionary factor, a great blessing in disguise.
>
> It was this "intellectual" element that by perversion of the human mind turned a peace-demanding people into a war-mad mob. . . . Forced service became in their interpretation "equality of contribution for rich and poor alike." The protest of one's conscience against killing was branded by them as high treason. . . . Every expression of humanity, of social sympathy, and understanding was cried down with a Babel of high phrases, in which "patriotism" and "democracy" competed in volume. Oh, the tragedy of the human mind that absorbs fine words and empty phrases, and is deaf to motives and blind to deeds.[34]

Berkman, for his part, would have none of the ethical relativism under the influence of which his contemporaries were castrating freedom in America. Like Martin Luther, he had no stomach for compromise where injustice and hypocrisy are involved. Compromise, in Berkman's opinion, means that one must sacrifice one's basic principles in order to obtain some desired goal of the moment. Where one makes such concessions to expediency, a vital part of one's "better self" must of necessity be destroyed. "This stifling, this violation of our better self, is the real tragedy of man's life," he held.[35] For it is the crushing of the human conscience, the " 'wee' still voice" within us, by which we must determine the difference between right and wrong.

It has long been believed in anarchist circles that Alexander Berkman put an end to himself by suicide while living in Nice in 1936. This notion, no doubt, has been made to appear plausible by the fact that Berkman almost did take his own life after release from his long interment in prison, and that he was given to long periods of depression as a consequence of the hopelessness he felt in the face of the social malaise he found himself surrounded by. But if Max Nomad, a disillusioned anarchist of old can be believed, Berkman's death was not by his own hand but by that of his young mistress who was outraged by his attention to an old flame, Emma Goldman.[36] It is difficult to accept the idea that Alexander Berkman chose to leave this world through so prosaic an act as self-destruction, for his devotion to an idea and his dedication to humanity would hardly have permitted him to participate in so pointless an action. Misunderstood from cradle to grave, Alexander Berkman most likely died in quest of the love and solidarity he had searched for throughout his life but always had been denied. At any rate, his passing robbed the anarchist movement in America of one of its noblest sons.

NOTES

SECTION V - CHAPTER 3

1. *A Fragment of the Prison Experiences of Emma Goldman and Alexander Berkman* (New York, n.d.), p. 19.

2. *The "Anti-Climax": The Concluding Chapter of My Russian Diary "The Bolshevik Myth"* (Berlin, 1925), p. 9.

3. *Prison Memoirs of an Anarchist* (New York, 1912), p. 73. For a critical view of this work by a follower of Johann Most, see F. Thaumazo, The *Martyrdom of Berkman* (Brooklyn, New York, n.d.).

4. *Ibid.,* p. 416.

5. "A Letter from Prison," *Solidarity* (February 9, 1893), 3.

6. *Prison Memoirs of an Anarchist,* p. 7.

7. "Why Revolution," *The Road to Freedom,* I (July, 1925), 5.

8. *Now and After: The A B C of Communist Anarchism* (New York, 1929), p. 191.

9. *Ibid.,* p. 178.

10. "The McNamaras," *The Revolutionary Almanac* (1914), p. 53.

11. *Ibid.,* p. 92.

12. *The Bolshevik Myth* (New York, 1925), p. 319.

13. *Ibid.,* p. 92.

14. *Now and After,* p. 168.

15. *Ibid.,* p. 293.

16. *Ibid.,* p. 230.

17. *Ibid.,* p. 207.

18. *Ibid.,* p. 232.

19. Benjamin R. Tucker, "Save Labor from its Friends," *Liberty,* VIII (July 30, 1892), 2.

20. "The Failure of Compromise," *Road to Freedom,* V (September, 1928), 1.

21. *Now and After,* p. 212.

22. *Ibid.,* p. 288.

23. *Ibid.,* p. 249.

24. *Ibid.,* p. 260.

25. *Ibid.,* pp. 257-8.

26. *Ibid.,* p. 267.

27. *Despotism—Its Meaning and Menace* (New York, n.d.), p. 17.

28. *Ibid.,* p. 23.

29. For a statement of his attitude toward Kropotkin, see

"Kropotkin as an Anarchist," in *Peter Kropotkin: The Rebel, Thinker and Humanitarian* (Berkley Heights, New Jersey, 1923).

30. *Now and After,* p. 265.

31. *Prison Memoirs of an Anarchist,* p. 223.

32. *Now and After,* p. 209.

33. *Ibid.,* p. 219.

34. *Deportation—Its Meaning and Menace,* p. 7.

35. "The Failure of Compromise," p. 1.

36. *Dreamers, Dynamiters, and Demagogues* (New York, 1964), pp. 207-9.

CHAPTER 4

Hippolyte Havel and Marcus Graham:
Two Who Made Social Revolution

If the place of one's birth settled the matter, Hippolyte Havel could make as legitimate a claim to being a native American anarchist as anyone else, for he was born in Chicago (1869), lived most of his life in the United States, and died in New Jersey in 1950 at the age of eighty. When he was very young, however, Havel was taken by his parents to the Bohemian village of Burowski from which they originally came, there to develop an appearance and mannerisms which had a distinct old-world flavor. Although his father was of middle class origins, Havel's mother was a gypsy, and this accounts, perhaps, for the fact that he very early developed a radical point of view. Going off to school in Vienna, Havel was soon calling himself an anarchist and adopted the vocation of radical journalism which he was to follow to the end of his life. At the age of 23 he was imprisoned for eighteen months by the Viennese police for making an inflamatory May Day speech, after which he was deported back to Burowski. A born activist, he then crept off to Germany where he occupied himself in anarchist propaganda. Unhappily, Havel was arrested in Vienna during a visit home to see his family and would have spent the rest of his life in an insane asylum, where the police ingeniously interred him, had it not been for the intervention of the famous psychiatrist, Krafft-Ebing, who pronounced Havel "saner than any of us" after a lengthy discussion with him about psychiatry.[1] Deported once again, Havel worked his way to Paris, then Zurich, and finally to London, where he kept himself alive by doing menial household labor such as shining shoes and sweeping floors. In 1899 Havel's future suddenly brightened, for at a meeting of the *Autonomie Club,* which was organized by German-speaking anarchists residing in London, he fell madly in love with the featured speaker of the evening, Emma Goldman, who was then touring Europe. Emma, equally in love with Havel, provides us with a description of her lover in the pages of her autobiography, *Living My Life*. Small in stature, with large, dark, gleaming eyes and beautiful white teeth, Hippolyte Havel dressed impeccably and impressed Emma as rather "dandyish" for the revolutionist he was. In spite of this, or perhaps because of it, she felt an almost irresistable attraction to the man. Havel, according to Emma, was virtually a walking encyclopedia of the anarchist movement in Europe, and she was fascinated by the East End scenes he guided her to. For all her devotion to anarchism, however, Emma Goldman was first a woman, and it was not long before she and Havel found lighter things to talk about. "London receded," she wrote years later, "the cry of the East End was far away. Only the call of love sounded in our hearts and we listened and yielded to it."[2] Although the intensity of the physical attraction they felt for each other cooled considerably in years to come, Emma and Havel remained close friends and anarchist comrades for the next half century, often finding themselves yoked together in the fight for social revolution and a new social order. Unhappily, Emma and Havel were not perfectly suited to each other in temperament, although like good anarchists they always succeeded in working out some kind of adjustment when personal differences temporarily separated them. The basic difficulty was that Emma was volatile, optimistic, extroverted, with so great a love for life and freedom that she could not bear to make herself the private property of any single man for any length of time; Hippolyte Havel, on the other hand, was quiet, timid, insecure, so that he sought to escape from people in general by fastening himself securely to Emma whom he dearly loved. Undoubtedly there were deep-seated personality problems in Havel's makeup which caused him to display a restlessness which bordered on the morose at times. Emma had early noticed that Havel could not engage in argumentation without showing irritability and bad temper.[2] His standard reaction to such situations was to sulk off by himself, seeking relief in heavy drinking from the turbulence which troubled his psyche. Even as a young man Hippolyte Havel was addicted to the bottle, and in his later years his drinking was a problem which his friends and comrades in the anarchist movement were forced to share with him. This side of his character is described by *Resistance*, which wrote on his death:

> The complex tragedy of his life is not easily understood, especially by those of

us who knew him only as an old man, his powers diminished and useless; nor was justice done him by Eugene O'Neill, whose character evidently patterned after Havel in "The Iceman Cometh," was a brutal caricature. Probably in good and bad senses, Havel was an aristocrat, a natural bohemian, with a brilliant mind, frequently prostituted to his friends to be able to live and drink another day; a tragedy of personality and a tragedy of society.[3]

As editor of the *Revolutionary Almanac of 1914*, which was apparently intended to be an annual publication but never appeared again, Havel took pains to divorce anarchism from the socialist tradition as it had then developed. Socialists everywhere, Havel complained, have yielded to the idea that justice and freedom can be obtained by means of the ballot. "The workingman who casts his vote into the ballot box," Havel insisted, "only throws his initiative and his own power into the gutter."[4] Rather than trust his fate to the politician and the political parties, the workingman would do well to organize himself at his place of work so that he might be ready when the day of revolution arrives. "Stand shoulder to shoulder in international solidarity," he counseled, "and you will be strong enough to liberate the world from the robber capitalism and from the murderous rule of government." Above all, he urged, it is essential that the workingman avoid the pitfall that Kropotkin stumbled into when he allowed his "French patriotism" to lead him to support the Allies in the First World War.[5] Although he was in fundamental agreement with Kropotkin's theories of anarchism, he could not forgive him for yielding to the war hysteria. With bitter wrath, Havel boldly castigated the greatest name in European anarchism for his failure to remain true to his pacifist ideals.

In January of 1916 Hippolyte Havel undertook the task of editing *Revolt*, which vied with Emma Goldman's *Mother Earth* for the title of most famous of all anarchist publications of the early twentieth century. Even if Havel had not been notorious in his own right, the galaxy of flaming radicals he chose to serve as his editorial board—Leonard D. Abbott, Elizabeth Gurley Flynn, Alexander Berkman, Harry Kelly, and Margaret Sanger—would have assured the journal a zesty reputation. But Havel needed no help in stirring up the public, for he seemed to have an innate capacity for stating things in the most vitriolic manner possible. In his debut as editor of *Revolt*, he promised his readers that so long as he was in command the journal would not indulge itself in toleration. "Our whole social, political, and artistic life is corrupted by the philosophy of tolerance," he ejaculated. Unequivocally rejecting all forms of compromise, Havel sarcastically proclaimed that *"Revolt* will not work hand-in-hand with the dear, good, sympathizer, the meek golden-rule people, who say neither yea nor nay, men who preach harmony between capital and labor, those who never want to hurt the enemy."⁶ Sticking to its resolve with a tenacity that must have appeared as viciousness to the anxious authorities, *Revolt* printed articles on the subjects of violence and revolution which went much further than a nation which prided itself on "making the world safe for democracy" could accept, and the entire printing of the seventh issue was locked up by the United States Government. Moving underground, Havel somehow or other brought out the eighth issue on March 11th, but his editorial efforts were to serve as the funeral oration of the journal, for no further issues appeared. Once again it had been demonstrated that freedom of speech and press are extremely difficult to maintain in a democracy, if indeed, it is even realistic to speak of democracy as real. Most certainly the idea had no meaning in the mind and experience of its victims, as Hippolyte Havel, Emma Goldman, and Alexander Berkman were quick to point out.

In October of 1925 Havel commenced publishing the second of his journals, *Road to Freedom.* Now associated with the Modern School at Stelton, New Jersey, he used his power as editor to expose the evils of existing society. Although Havel frequently referred to himself as an anarchist communist, the pages of his journal were entirely free of the kind of doctrinal rigidity which all too often accompanied the running dispute between individualists and collectivists during these years. Reading through the files of *The Road to Freedom* from the vantage point of today, one is struck by the fact that Hippolyte Havel was much closer to the tradition of individualism supported by the native American anarchists than is usually thought. Sounding very much like Emerson or one of the lesser Transcendentalists, he editorialized that "the idea of Anarchy is inherent in the soul of man. To destroy this idea would mean to destroy every aspiration for a higher life, every hope for freedom; it would mean to destroy life itself. Anarchy was from the beginning, is now, and will be forever."⁷ As much as Havel professed himself to be a communist, he nevertheless believed that the essence of life is found in the individual as he responds to nature. "The one purpose of being," he wrote, "is development; in free expression alone is satisfaction. Expression is

growth; growth in freedom, progress. In man alone is progress. Woe
to them when they hinder instead of reflecting the soul. That is
barbarism, slavery."[8] Havel might have been a bad sociologist, judged
by contemporary norms, but he certainly was close to the individualism of Emerson when he argued that were we only to put liberty in
charge of the helm of society, "the better nature of man will assume
control and in the genial warmth of an emancipated race a closer
social feeling will be engendered."

Unlike the Bolshevik, who places all his hope in a centralized
social order in which technological and administrative efficiency are
considered the key to heaven on earth, Havel placed all his faith in
the freedom of ideas rather than the machinery of social control. "The
tyranny of other people's ideas is the most powerful of all tyrannies,"
he wrote. This "is what prevents us from being the large, free, creative,
powerful, infinite being we might be if we knew ourselves as we are, if
we loved freedom as we should love it."[9] Reflecting Bakunin's influence, Havel proclaimed that "Man will have to recover the power
with which his ignorance has invented gods, statesmen, priests, and
politicians, before he can achieve maturity and independence."[10] But
he might equally as well have derived this idea from the influence of
some one of the native American anarchists, like William B. Greene,
Lysander Spooner, or Benjamin Tucker, for this conception is common to all anarchists, however they may be categorized.

That Havel was spiritually as well as ideologically close to the
native American group is further demonstrated by the generosity with
which he gave space to contributors who persisted in extolling the
merits of the mutualist ideas originally conceived by Josiah Warren.
Bearing the thoroughly American name of Donald Crocker, one of
Havel's frequent contributors emphatically repudiated the Marxian
theory of class struggle on the grounds that history does not bear out
the notion that social revolution is a class phenomenon. Social revolution does not proceed on the vigor of a class of people, he argued, but
is brought about by "groups of determined *individuals,* who invariably
are drawn from diverse classes."[11] The anarchist, unlike the Marxian
Socialist, insists that social revolution can never take place "until
a sufficient number of resolute, intelligent rebels WILL to wage one."
Havel in turn argued that well-informed thinkers do not indulge
themselves in idle dreaming when they proclaim anarchy as the
"highest ideal of human society," for this conclusion is in full harmony

with both the tendencies of history and the findings of science.[12] Doggedly loyal to the traditions hewed out by his native American forebears, Havel, despite the frequency with which he labelled himself a communist, was a firm believer in the powers of the individual as opposed to the crowd. To extol the virtues of individualism, he urged, is not to project any fuzzy notions of a

> superhuman race of beings, but appeals to the fundamental traits of average human nature. It demands no exalted self-sacrifice from individuals, but appeals to motives of intelligent self-interest. When we talk of brotherhood, we do not appeal to a mawkish sentimentality. We merely state a fact in nature, on the recognition of which social harmony and the happiness of the individual alike depend."

These sentiments might well have appeared in Tucker's *Liberty* instead of *The Road to Freedom,* so faithfully did they represent the native American experience. Another of Havel's readers was so taken by the spirit of individualism which *The Road to Freedom* had breathed back into the anarchist movement of the late twenties that he praised the Vanguard Press for reprinting the works of the earlier mutualist anarchists and called for more.[13] The American anarchist movement, it would seem, had at last rediscovered the wealth of its heritage.

Rivaling Hippolyte Havel and John Most for the dubious distinction of being the most persecuted of anarchists in America was Marcus Graham who was born in Canada in 1893 under the name of Samuel Marcus. Very little accurate biographical information is obtainable concerning Graham's private life, for the constant legal harrassment he was subjected to during his first years in the United States forced him to keep a cloak of security wrapped tightly around himself, and to this day (August, 1975) he lives in anonymity somewhere on the west coast, communicating with the world through trusted friends who will not reveal his exact whereabouts. A recent statement of his views is contained in *The Match,* one of the many anarchist publications that have started up again after several decades of inactivity.[14]

A staunch pacifist, Marcus Graham dates his political life from the passage of the compulsory conscription statute during World War I, when he spoke at numerous rallies in Montreal under the pseudonym "Robert Parsons," impishly urging that the wellborn professional and businessmen of Canada form a battalion of chauvinists to lead the conscripted troops into battle in dramatic demonstration of the deep patriotism they boasted so much about.[15] Moving to Toronto, he became an active anarchist as editor of an underground paper, *Der Einziger,* which was published in Yiddish, and later took over the helm of an American underground organ, *The Anarchist Soviet Bulletin* (later called *Free Society*); it was for editing the Bulletin that he was first arrested and imprisoned on Ellis Island. Unable to make a sound legal case against him, the authorities were forced to release Graham several weeks after his arrest. The United States Government had no intention of forgetting about him, however, and he was illegally arrested again and again over the years on the very same dog-eared arrest warrant. After spending a year in England, Graham returned to America via Canada, taking up the editorship of *Free Society* again. Once again arrested, this time at Patterson, New Jersey, he was subjected to the third degree and then imprisoned for six months on Ellis Island. When he was not in prison or in hiding from the immigration authorities, Graham spent every moment he could find working long hours in the library of whatever city he happened to be in, compiling an *Anthology of Revolutionary Poetry,* which he brought out in 1929. Deeply interested in the history of the anarchist idea, he was a frequent visitor to the special collections of anarchist materials at the Universities of Michigan and Wisconsin, and his editorship of *Man!* reflects his scholarly interests, providing us with a wealth of biographical material on various members of the movement.

Marcus Graham's most significant contribution to anarchism was the founding of *Man!,* "A Journal of the Anarchist Ideal and Movement," in 1933. Based in Oakland, California, *Man!,* according to Graham, would bridge the gap between the communist and individualist, taking its stand on the common ground shared by all anarchists, whatever they might call themselves. Philosophically, Graham was himself very taken by the logic of the individualist position, and *Man!* advertised the works of Proudhon, Tucker, and other individualists as essential reading for its subscribers, while it often carried articles by the last of the living Tuckerites, Lawrence Labadie and Steven T. Byington. Reflecting something of the fascination with the philosophical outlook of Max Stirner which Tucker's *Liberty* had displayed in its last years, Graham ran an excerpt from *The Ego and Its Own,* indicating that he too subscribed to the Stirnerite proposition that the basic social problems of society depend upon the individual for their solution. However alienated the individual worker might be under the conditions of advanced capitalistic culture, he was still powerful if only he could escape from the "fixed ideas" which from the very earliest of times man has subjected himself to, reducing him to the level of a cipher or pawn. As Stirner put it: "The laborers have the most enormous power in their heads, and, if they once became thoroughly conscious of it and used it, nothing would withstand them; they would only have to stop labor, regard the product of labor as theirs, and enjoy it."[16] The idea that all authority rests ultimately on the acquiescence of the individual and that his refusal to no longer obey unjust or outmoded authority would immediately transform the social relations of society was a widely held precept among anarchists of all persuasions. Marcus Graham was on the right track, therefore, when he urged Max Stirner upon his readers. For if the state has no substance when divested of the "slavery of labor," as Stirner held, then the state must fall when labor refuses to submit to the slavery imposed upon it by capital. Preoccupied as they were in the Thirties by the problem of capital versus labor, anarchists nevertheless found much in Graham's neo-individualism to interest them.

Like many other American individualists, Graham was resolute in his opposition to Marxism, holding that Marx had made the gravest of blunders when he accepted the idea of conventional political action as a possible means of social transformation. Graham, like many other individuals of his day, might be criticized for failing to see the crucial distinction between Marxism and Bolshevism, for it was Lenin and later interpreters of the Marxian idea who actually held to the idea of the state, not Marx, although Marx, of course, might be criticized in turn for failing to make himself explicit on this point. But there was no flaw in Graham's vision when he addressed himself to the subject of Bolshevism, adopting approximately the same stance toward it that Emma Goldman did in her later days. Anarchists, according to Graham, can subscribe to no theory of revolution other than the idea of social revolution which arises spontaneously from the people themselves. No party or government of any kind must be allowed to come between the people and the revolution as has been the case in the Soviet Union. "Bolshevism stands for the submission of the people to the authority of their 'communist' State of 'intellectual' rulers and is therefore opposed to Freedom," he urged. Anarchism, on the other hand, "opposes any form of State or rulership and only suggests Voluntary Association between individuals, groups, and peoples of all countries, and therefore *strives* for, and *aims* at Freedom."[17] Whether rulers rule in the name of capitalism or in the name of the proletariat, Graham insisted, it nevertheless remains true that "rulership has always bred dishonesty, treachery, and wanton murder."[18] Is it not time for self-respecting Communists to admit that "every criticism and accusation made by the Anarchist movement against the Bolshevik Marxian State has now fully been demonstrated as justifiable?" he asked.

Unlike the Burnette G. Haskells and the Albert Parsons who flirted with the organized labor movement under the dangerous rationalization that the real key to social progress lies in bigger and better forms of social power under the control of labor leadership, Graham looked upon organized labor as "a compromising force at the expense of the true interests of the workers."[19] Likewise, Graham held, it is a mistake to place one's faith in any kind of prepared or organized revolution. "As Anarchists we hold forth the very opposite view, contending that the only social rebellions that prove of any significant value in effecting changes for achieving more liberty are those that come about SPONTANEOUSLY."[20] Undoubtedly his opinion in this regard was basically shaped by the influence which the great American radical, Wendell Phillips, exercised over his thinking. So indebted was Graham to Phillips for spiritual guidance that *Man!* carried the motto under its masthead, "If There Is Anything That Cannot Bear Free Thought—Let It Crack," which was a line taken from one of Phillips' celebrated speeches. Like Phillips, Graham clung tenaciously to the democratic theory that people in a free society will generally choose the correct course of social action if left to their own devices. This was not disproven for Graham by the advent of mass society and the capture of the mass mind by the communication media, for as a convinced revolutionary he was secure in the faith that the people will rise up and throw off the yoke of tyranny when their situation warranted such strong measures. Ultimately man will grow tired of the State's powerful grip over life and happiness, as he will grow tired of wars and politicians, Graham insisted. And when that happens, and not until that happens, will centralization of power and command, "the chief prop of capitalism and Marxian socialism," be replaced.[21]

It might be argued against this view that to sing the praises of spontaneous rebellion against social tyranny or oppression is to actually advocate or condone violence. But if we accept the widely held definition of violence as force directed against another individual with intention of doing him harm, social revolution of the kind advocated by both Phillips and Graham would not be placed in that category. One can certainly argue that the political rulers of the world who arm their troops and police for the purpose of suppressing domestic demonstrations aimed against the *status quo* are engaged in the planning of violence, for they know without a shadow of doubt that the military force they prepare is specifically designed to crush legitimate dissent and protest. But to argue that the worker who spontaneously lashes back at those who exploit him is guilty of violence is to engage in the ridiculous. No man has a right to exploit another man and those who do are the true authors of violence. Who today would hold Wendell Phillips guilty of advocating violence when he argued in his own day that the slaveholder gets just what he deserves when he is injured by the actions of his escaping slave? The factor of organization, as all anarchists know, is a crucial one in the area of human relations, and Marcus Graham argued from a very strong position indeed when he suggested that the unplanned interaction of individual to individual and group to group is the most worthy social conception for the libertarian to assume.

The real function of anarchism, in Graham's opinion, was the task of giving man renewed hope in his own ability to create social life. Born free, yet enslaved in a web of binding institutional restrictions, man must somehow achieve liberation from the hopeless condition he is presently in. And this liberation could only come from man himself acting independently of the organized church and state which are in themselves a part of the problem. Of all the enemies man faces in his struggles to liberate himself, Graham held, the institution of war is undoubtedly one of the most formidable of his foes. Born out of the human instinct of fear and the craving for security which resides in every man's breast, war must be eliminated from society before men can achieve their full potential for social development. Writing in 1938 when the clouds of war had not yet darkened beyond the light gray of an early morning mist, Graham warned that "people throughout the world are *today* encircled in a new bloody war. Tomorrow may find the whole world completely encircled by this war."[22] Should the disaster of war overwhelm the world again, he argued, the people of the world will have no one else to blame but themselves, for it would be impossible for the governments of the world to wage war if the men who are asked to fight refuse to do so. Sabastian Faure, the renowned French individualist anarchist, spoke with truth when he asserted that "all those who are totally pacifists are not [necessarily] anarchists; but all anarchists are totally pacifists," Graham urged.[23] Or as Hippolyte Havel, who substituted for Graham whenever the regular editor of *Man!* was in prison, put it: "anti-militarism is the first step on the road to Anarchism."[24] To liberate himself, man must first demand an immediate and final halt to the war-making machine to which governments everywhere devote the lifeblood of their subjects. So consistent in his thinking was Graham on this issue that early in life he adopted the principle of vegetarianism, refusing to eat meat on the grounds that the slaughter of animals is the first step toward the manipulation of man by man. But the libertarian who practices vegetarianism, he argued, "becomes a living symbol of the ethical man of today who once more reaffirms the inviolable right of all living species to life."[25] In terms of its actual effect upon his own life, this meant that Graham was often forced to go without proper food for long periods of time, for the prison authorities gleefully exploited this principle as an additional means of adding to his discomfort during his frequent sessions in jail. In recent years almost all anarchists have come to recognize the correctness of Graham's thinking on the subject of war, although many of them may not be able to share his objection to eating meat.

In terms of the internal squabbles which raged among various anarchist groups in the Thirties and Forties, Graham saw no basic conflict between the followers of Kropotkin and the followers of Stirner or Proudhon, insisting that all schools of anarchist thought come to approximately the same conclusions with respect to freedom and association. The communists, following Kropotkin, sing the praises of the voluntary commune within which each individual is free to come and go as he pleases, whereas the Stirnerites favor the idea of a "union of egoists" which affords the individual exactly the same degree of personal liberty, Graham explained. The one aspect of Kropotkin's social philosophy that Graham took exception to was his attitude toward the machine. "I think that the future will prove that Kropotkin, from an Anarchist point of view, has, in accepting the machine, made one of the gravest of errors," Graham wrote.[26] While the machine has increased the level of mankind's physical wellbeing to the extent that hunger and disease do not present the kind of problem they formerly did, its net effect has been harmful to the human condition in that life is increasingly being mechanized and standardized to the detriment of individuality and originality. "As an Anarchist," Graham asserted, "I am in favor of the destruction of every power on earth that tends to hinder the liberation of mankind from all forms of oppression and rulership." With impressive foresight he recognized that the machine civilization that was rapidly being created by the technicians and scientists of the modern age was as much a threat to the liberation of man as any of the forms of rulership he had suffered in the past. No amount of good the machine may promise us in the area of physical progress can offset the regimentation and standardization it is bound to bring to social life as technology and automation become increasingly more complex and centralized. In Graham's mind there was a necessary conflict between the design imposed upon humanity by the artificially constructed machine and the design pressed upon humanity by the natural currents and rhythms of nature. In a "true civilization," he wrote, "man will discard the insane and suicidal mechanization of human life. He will learn that nature has placed before him the most glorious possibilities for building an earthly paradise—through the use of mother-earth."[27] Where man turns to nature for the pattern of social life, he discovers the healing qualities of love, reconciliation, and cooperation as possible answers to the conflicts that divide nations and groups, whereas all science and technology have to offer is bigger and more efficient schemes of regimentation and coercion. Life is an art rather than a science, Graham urged, and it is the artist and the poet who draws upon the resources of mother nature who is the best guide to social progress. This is why anarchism "looks to art as one of the chief means of social transformation" and stands wary of the "machine monster that is annihilating bit by bit everything that is human within man."[28] Although he was a lonely voice in his day, the events of recent years have led a lot of people to a position close to the one assumed by Marcus Graham as he fought to keep the focus upon man.

NOTES

SECTION V - CHAPTER 4

1. "Hippolyte Havel," *Resistance* (June, July, 1950), 16.
2. *Living My Life,* (New York, 1931), p. 267.
3. *Resistance,* 16.
4. "Don't Vote," *The Revolutionary Almanac,* (1914), p. 3.
5. "Has the International Broken Down," *The Modern School,* II (May, 1915), 55.
6. *Revolt,* I (January 1, 1916), 3.
7. *The Road to Freedom,* I (November, 1924), 7.
8. *What's Anarchism?,* International Anarchist Relation Committee of America, (n.p., 1932), p. 19.
9. "The Truth Shall Make You Free," *The Road to Freedom,* II (May, 1926), 1.
10. *What's Anarchism?,* p. 9.
11. "The Mistake of Marx," *The Road to Freedom,* IV (November, 1927), 7.
12. "Are We Dreamers?" *The Road to Freedom,* IV (April, 1928), 1.
13. T. H. Bell, "What is Mutualism?" *The Road to Freedom,* IV (September, 1927), 3.
14. (October, 1971), 3.
15. Ralph Cheney and Lucia Trent, in Introduction to *An Anthology of Revolutionary Poetry,* ed. by Marcus Graham (New York, 1929), p. 42.
16. "The Ego and Its Own," *Man!,* I (August—September, 1933), 1.
17. *Anarchism and the World Revolution,* published under the pseudonym "Fred S. Graham" (U.S.A., 1921), p. 32.
18. "Rulership's Harvest: The Bolshevik Massacre," *Man!,* III (January, 1935), 153.
19. "Organized Labor and Social Emancipation," *Man!,* VII (January, 1939), 457.
20. "When the People Act," *Man!,* II (June—July, 1934), 123.
21. "Towards an Anarchist Society," *Man!,* VII (January, 1940), 548.
22. "At the Abyss of a New World War," *Man!,* VI (March, 1938), 385.

23. Sebastian Faure, "Anarchists are Totally Pacifists," *Man!*, IV (January, 1936), 233.

24. "Art and Literature," *Man!*, V (February—March, 1937), 7.

25. "Vegetarianism," *Resistance*, VI (March—April, 1948), 13.

26. "What Ought to be the Anarchist Attitude Toward the Machine," *Man!*, II (March, 1934), 102.

27. "Anarchism, Capitalism and Marxism," *Resistance*, VIII (August—September, 1949), 16.

28. *An Anthology of Revolutionary Poetry*, p. 13.

CHAPTER 5

The Modern School and Its Revision of the Anarchist Idea

Many people will find it hard to believe that in the years following World War I the most active agent of American Anarchism was the Modern School, a most unlikely source of the violence and destruction that the American people erroneously came to associate with the anarchist movement. And no one more fully reflected the libertarian spirit of both anarchism and the Modern School than Harry May Kelly (1871-1953). Born of a working-class family in St. Louis, Kelly learned the printing trade as a youth and early joined the great mass of humanity that made its living by the sweat of its brow, thereby becoming something of an authority on the subject of labor unrest.[1] Affiliating with the Knights of Labor, he very soon became an ardent radical and a much beloved comrade to some of the most famous names in American anarchism, including Alexander Berkman and Emma Goldman.

In 1895 Kelly sought to give expression to his anarchist fervor by establishing *The Rebel,* a monthly published from Boston which was devoted to the exposition of anarchist communism. As a skilled printer, Kelly's contribution to the venture was mainly as a member of the "Rebel Group," a cooperative printing association which performed the technical tasks of putting the journal out, the major share of the editorial chores being left to Charles Mowbrey (after Voltairine de Cleyre, having been offered the editorship, had turned it down in an effort to protect her frail health). *The Rebel,* which scarcely lasted a year, joined *The Firebrand* in its crusade against American capitalism, the voice of *The Alarm* having been stifled with Albert Parsons' death on the gallows a short time before. Reflecting the influence of the International Workingman's Association, *The Rebel* chose as its motto the statement: "Educate, in order to understand our true value as workers in society; Agitate, in order to arouse our apathetic fellow workers; Organize, to overthrow the power of government, capitalism, and superstition. . . ."[2] Emma Goldman, with an inimitable burst of enthusiasm, heralded the birth of *The Rebel* as a sign that a renaissance was taking place in anarchist ranks. Her prognostication was not altogether invalid, although the mass movement to anarchism which logically would have to accompany any real ideological renaissance failed to materialize. Later on, Kelly put out a paper of his own called *The Match,* but this, like *The Rebel,* enjoyed only a very brief existence. Some years later Kelly visited Great Britain and became a frequent contributor thereafter to *Freedom,* the authentic voice of English anarchism, as a consequence of the firm friendship which sprang up between its editor, Peter Kropotkin, and himself. In June of 1919 Kelly became editor of an American journal of anarchist communism, also called *Freedom,* which was published from New York City. With Leonard Abbott sitting on his right hand as associate editor, Kelly sought to make *Freedom* live up to its boast that it would be "a journal of constructive anarchism" when he editorialized that the aim of anarchism was to abolish the state not through the seizure of political power but through the practice of voluntary association and free communism.[3]

As his good friend and companion, Hippolyte Havel, once pointed out, Harry Kelly, for all his lack of formal education, was one of the most astute theoreticians of anarchism during the period around World War I. On the one hand, Kelly possessed a toleration for dissenting ideas and differences of opinion which consistently avoided the squabbling that so many anarchists of his era indulged themselves in and thus he found nothing irreconcilable in the various doctrinal formulations exposed by such diverse groups as the Guild Socialists in England, the Syndicalists in France, the Bolsheviks in Russia, and the I.W.W. in America. All these movements possess a common goal, which is to transform society from a highly centralized monolith of industrial and political power to a decentralized society in which the worker shares in the policy formation process at the place of his work, Kelly maintained. "For the benefit of faint hearts and dogmatic theorists," he continued, "it might be added that they are all offsprings of that much maligned and little understood theory, Anarchism."[4] But while he clearly perceived the necessity of defining anarchism in the very broadest of terms so that freedom would not be sacrificed to consistency, he was equally cognizant of the fact that social revolution, as Proudhon had earlier demonstrated, is not inevitable. That tempting myth, according to Kelly, was completely and forever deflated by the horrible sight of worker fighting worker at Verdun and Argonne. And who can remain optimistic concerning the advent of social revolution in the face of the oppressive sluggishness by which the revolutionary idea has circulated among the ranks of the laboring classes. "In this connection there is one thing that is often overlooked," Kelly wrote, "and that is that social changes are conceived always in the first instance by small groups of people, and are adopted by society before the majority understand them or want them; the majority acquiesce in the changes if the majority advocating them is reasonably large and forceful enough, but by the time they are understood society is ripe for other changes."[5] Replacing the chains of ignorance, by which the masses had in former times been kept in subservience to their masters, with the chains of public education which is equally as stultifying to the mind, social change is thwarted. "Perhaps, after all," Kelly wrote in 1925, "the function of the anarchist is *just this and nothing more:* to diffuse opinions among the masses, thus creating an ever increasing number of individuals less susceptible to the wiles of the politician, the priest, and the capitalist." (Italics mine.)[6] And thus, Harry Kelly put anarchism on a smaller gauge track than the one it had followed before but one which possessed far more potential for the reformation of society than many of his contemporaries realized.

As a charter member of the Ferrer Association, which he had organized in June of 1910 along with other anarchists like Alexander Berkman, Kelly was dedicated to the ideals of the martyred Francisco Ferrer y Guardia who had been shot down before a firing squad in Barcelona in October of the previous year. Denied a fair trial, Ferrer was sentenced to death for the supposed crime of teaching the school children in his charge the tactics of revolutionary warfare. Ferrer was, it is true, a revolutionary who dreamed of the overthrow of the corrupt government which was oppressing his countrymen. But as Voltairine de Cleyre pointed out after his execution, the revolutionary techniques he championed had nothing whatever to do with dynamite or guerilla warfare but were based on the much more deadly weapons of critical scholarship and philosophical enlightenment.[7] The major shortcoming of modern educational methods, according to Francisco Ferrer, is that they train the child to respond automatically to authority, thereby turning him into a robot under the command of his teacher. Under these circumstances, there is no hope that the firm grip of the ruling classes can ever be loosened. From top to bottom the structure of modern educational organization is characterized by violence. How else are we to describe educational institutions which "dominate the children physically, morally, and intellectually, in order to control the development of their faculties in the way desired," Ferrer wrote.[8] For thinking and expressing such dangerous thoughts as these, Francisco Ferrer was brutally silenced by the rulers he had offended.

Reaching across the ocean, American anarchism tenderly lifted the libertarian spirit from Ferrer's riddled corpse and raised it high as its new standard. Times were changing, as all anarchists clearly sensed, and the techniques of libertarian social revolution had to be brought into keeping with the new circumstances. Harry Kelly was one of the first to realize that "Libertarian Education and Socialist Education, however idealistic the latter may seem to some people, are incompatible with one another."[9] The socialist, viewing the world through the prism of an economic interpretation of history, declares this to be the keystone of education and insists that all children start from this fundamental truth. "Aside from its humanitarian side and the desire of socialists to establish equality," Kelly reasoned, this is "as fixed and as rigid a dogma as the one of the Immaculate Conception." Stirred by the spirit of freedom which characterized all of Ferrer's ideas on education, Kelly sought to escape from such dogmatism by adopting a pedigogical paradigm that steered clear of all appeal to authority. Throughout history, he insisted, the struggle for freedom has been a struggle to "live one's own life, to grow along the lines of one's own being."[10] The failure of men to realize any of their potential for free development is one of the most difficult of all historical facts to explain. Why had man failed again and again to set himself free from the dogmatisms he has chained himself to? "May it not be because man has forgotten to call to his aid the one ally who could have turned defeat into victory—the children," Kelly queried!

In June of 1910 the Francisco Ferrer Association was established in an old brownstone building in the heart of the Jewish tenement district adjoining Central Park in New York. Its chief organizer was Joseph J. Cohen assisted by such vivacious anarchists as Bolton Hall, Leonard Abbott, Harry Kelly, Alexander Berkman, and the omnipresent Emma Goldman. Dedicated to the propagation of the educational and social ideas of its guiding spirit, Francisco Ferrer, the association's membership was made up of anarchists, libertarians, freethinkers, socialists, syndicalists, and singletaxers.[11] In addition to a day school for children, the association carried on its work through evening lectures and classes for adults conducted by a number of notable authors and professors. Professor Bayard Boyesen, who had been employed as an instructor in literature at Columbia, resigned his position to devote full time to the movement. Boyesen gave a series of lectures on contemporary literary figures, including Tolstoy, Ibsen, Anatole France, Gorky, and others. Will Durant, author of the monumental work, *The Story of Civilization,* gave a preview of the brilliance of his later work in his lectures on philosophy and sex in the Ferrer evening lectures. Another of the star performers in the lecture series was Gilbert E. Roe, at one time a partner in the law office of Wisconsin's Robert La Follette, who held forth on the structure and dynamics of the political system in America. Among others who graced the Ferrer Association's lectern were André Tridon, lecturing on Maeterlinck and Rodin; John Weichsel, speaking on the history of education; Louis Levine, discussing the philosophy of syndicalism; and the famous Clarence Darrow, who packed the hall for his lecture on Voltaire. Perhaps the most notable of all the Ferrer Association's projects were the art classes conducted by Robert Henri and George Bellows of the Ashcan School. Reflecting the libertarian penchant for freedom, Henri gave his students more encouragement than guidance and was credited with conducting one of the best art schools in the country.[12] Henri, true to his vocation as artist, remained aloof from the political currents that swirled about him. But through all his years of teaching at the Modern School from 1911 to 1918, he basically thought of himself as a philosophical anarchist and derived his inspiration from the writings of Bakunin, Emerson, Whitman and Nietszche, just as Emma Goldman and Alexander Berkman did. In fact, it was Emma Goldman who served as "the catalyst that helped him translate his abstract belief in philosophical anarchism into a deeply felt personal creed."[13]

Like the Fabian Society in England, the Ferrer Association exercised much greater influence upon the direction of radical thought in this country than the strength of its membership warranted. Serving as "a sort of foster-mother to all kinds of libertarian and humanitarian movements," the association could claim the distinction of being one of the main centers of radical ferment and enthusiasm in the United

States in the years just preceding World War I. As Leonard Abbott wrote in 1914, the association gave free expression to the forces of liberty which until then had been bottled up within the dark interior of America's puritanical heritage. Francisco Ferrer's body might lay molding in its grave in Spain but "all that is most enduring in his spirit lives on" in the libertarian movements spawned by his mourners in America.

On October 13th of 1911 the Ferrer Association opened a day school in a three story brownstone house on the lower east side of New York. Dedicated to the libertarian conception of education developed by Ferrer, the Modern School started out with one pupil but could soon boast of over twenty. The first principal of the Modern School was Will Durant, who came to it on the rebound from a Roman Catholic seminary which he found to be inhospitable to his radical inclinations. Most people fail to understand the function of radicalism, Durant argued. The radical aims towards the creation of a social system within which those who possess advanced notions or moral responsibility may find room to adjust themselves to reality. Libertarian educational theory is often accused of sacrificing social order and stability to individual license and whim. But Durant insisted that libertarian educational methods are designed to produce real responsibility in the individual by strengthening his powers of self-control, as opposed to slavish conformity to the authority of gods or the policeman inculcated by traditional methods of authoritarian education. When libertarians insist that there can be no genuine morality without freedom, they rest their case upon the proposition that only a free man who possesses full freedom of choice can be thought of as truly responsible. Durant summed up his social philosophy many years later when he wrote: "Order is a means to liberty, and not an end; liberty is priceless, for it is the vital medium of growth."[14] The child raised to adulthood within a process of libertarian education, Durant held, "will be a law unto himself because he will understand that his freedom is dependent upon the continued freedom of others; he will need no other law than this sense of fitness and mutual right."[15] Widely prepared in the classics and philosophy as well as in Latin and French, Durant left the Modern School after teaching its classes in the Spring of 1911 and the following Fall and Winter to become Director of the Labour Temple School, at the same time teaching philosophy at Columbia (1917), and devoting the rest of his prodigious energy to writing. He was succeeded by Cora Bennett Stephenson, a protegé of Eugene Debs and Emma Goldman, and later by Robert E. Hutchinson, a socialist who, along with his wife Delia, was afterwards to found his own school at Story Ford Station, New York.[16] During all the time that the school was located in New York City, the "dangerous" radicals who made up the Ferrer Association initiated fund-raising project after fund-raising project to gather enough money to move the school away from the dirt and gloom of its urban environment. Defying precedent as always, two of the most energetic fund-raisers were "Red Emma" Goldman and the notorious capitalist slayer, Alexander Berkman, who were soon to be deported to the Soviet Union.

When the Modern School celebrated its twenty-fifth anniversary in May of 1940, all those gathered at Stelton were mindful of the many storms which the school had somehow weathered in its quarter-century of precarious existence. It was perhaps a portent of things to come that the move from New York on Sunday, May 16, 1915 was marred by heavy rains which temporarily dampened the spirits of the twenty-five children ushered to Stelton by Joseph J. Cohen, who from the very start had taken a great deal of the burden of the Modern School upon his own shoulders and who remained loyal to it to the very end. With but 52 cents in his pocket after paying the rail fares, Cohen was forced to walk most of the children out to the run-down farm in New Jersey which the Ferrer Association had purchased on time at the suggestion of Harry Kelly. Although many willing hands pitched in to make the delapidated old farmhouse and outbuildings livable, it was several years before the Modern School took on the appearance of permanence and respectability. A colony composed of libertarian families who had followed their children to Stelton soon sprang up around the farm and additional land was later purchased to accommodate additional latecomers. One of the most enthusiastic supporters of the school at Stelton was Leonard D. Abbott who had been converted to revolutionary socialism while a schoolboy in Liverpool, England, as a consequence of reading Robert Blatchford's *Merrie England*. Later Abbott discovered the writings of Whitman, Tolstoy, Henry George, Kropotkin, Marx, Edward Bellamy, Ruskin, and Edward Carpenter, but was most influenced by the ideas of William Morris. In America Abbott served on the advisory board of John Spargo's *The Comrade*, helped edit *Freedom* (New York) along with Harry Kelly, and was a contributing editor to *The Modern School,* which was an attempt to explain the educational experiment being carried on at Stelton.

The purpose of the libertarian education purveyed by the Modern School was to free the child from the bondage which organized society swaddles him in from the time of his birth. "According to our thinking," Abbott wrote, "Francisco Ferrer died in order to set men free,"[17] and so freedom in every aspect of life becomes the primary objective of those who associate themselves with the school. The Modern School, devoted to ideas and ideals which were wholly incompatible with the existing structure of social thought, presented itself as a challenge to the existing order of things. "Until our ideals triumph," Abbott proclaimed, "the spirit of our movement is bound to be mainly one of revolt against accepted traditions and creeds. We fight not to standardize life but to free it in order that it may find its own manifold expression." Like many other anarchists, Abbott saw Walt Whitman as an archtype of the revolutionary spirit and a guide to the kind of freedom of thought and expression that anarchism desires to achieve. As Whitman created a medium through his poetry which was totally subversive of the old forms, thereby attaining a freedom of mind that surpassed anything known in the past, so education patterned after the libertarian model can free the child's mind from the ancient tyrannies of time immemorial.[18] Refraining from any kind of doctrinal activity, the Modern School, as Abbott conceived of it, was to be the vanguard of a new era of libertarian education designed to make freedom a meaningful phase of American life rather than the hollow phrase it had become.

More than most people realize even now, the philosophical foundations which supported the educational theory professed by the Modern School were highly sound. What made it appear unbelievable at the time was the fact that most political theorists were then still under the spell of John Locke's liberal rhetoric, whereas the libertarians who made up the modern school were all adherents to one degree or another of the anarchist frame of reference. Bolton Hall, one of the most faithful of the Modern School group, clearly reflects the political theory of anarchism when he argued that the slavery under which modern man groans and labors is of his own making. "Individually and as a race," Hall wrote, "men begin as slaves, on one side to father, chief, baron, duke, king, or to customs, law, constitution;

and on the other, to nature, ghosts, fetich and superstitution." We
obtain our freedom by asserting our right to be free, by having the
strength and courage to escape from the tyranny of government,
church, or graven image. Unfortunately, Hall maintained, most men
still need some kind of authority to guide their lives and hence remain
content to submit to the rulership under which they find themselves.
Slavery, like childhood, is something the human being must outgrow.
But all too many men never reach the level of adulthood.

But as Will Durant optimistically proclaimed, so long as there
are radicals in the world, the hope remains alive that humanity may
find a revolutionary model to emulate, thereby escaping the tyranny
which perverts its more noble qualities. Reflecting the evolutionary
theory which Kropotkin had bequeathed to the libertarian movement,
Durant held that mankind's hope for freedom lies in its ability to
discover the laws of human progress as they are found in nature so
that men might learn how to be free once again. "Socialism, feminism,
anarchism, so far as they aim at social justice rather than merely a
shift in the incidence of political power and economic emoluments,"
he wrote, "are attempts to meet the task suggested by Huxley,—the
task of so changing by cooperative control, the conditions of selection
in society that the honest man may survive. . . ."[19] When we search for
the root causes of human slavery, according to Durant, we find that it
is the phenomenon of war which has enthroned the chief, the king,
and in turn, the state. In the beginning, "war dissolved primitive
communism and anarchism, introduced organization and discipline,
and led to the enslavement of prisoners, the subordination of classes,
and the growth of government. Property was the mother, war was the
father of the state."[20] Over the years mankind has become so habituated to its condition of servitude that most men cry out in despair and
anger when it is suggested to them that they might live in freedom
from control from above. Durant established one of anarchism's most
vital teachings when he insisted that the most important consideration
in social reform is not to worry about the reformation of society but to
focus primarily upon the more difficult task of remaking our own
character and morality. All too many social reformers start their
humanitarian schemes by concentrating upon the forging of new laws
to straighten out society, whereas their first concern should be with
their own lives and actions. "Real responsibility implies self-control, as
distinct from that control which comes from fear of god or policeman;

and self-control implies freedom of choice. Hence the obvious truth of the anarchist contention that there can be no real morality without freedom."[21]

It was this principle which led the supporters of the Modern School to make freedom the primary consideration in their curriculum. Where children are encouraged to be free social agents, they can be expected to escape from the numbing subservience to authority which traditional methods of education inculcate. Grown to adulthood, children who have been educated under libertarian methods can hopefully fashion a world which lacks the legalism and tyrannical rule which characterizes standard governing procedures. It is to be expected, of course, Durant conceded, that a certain degree of social disorder will accompany any experiment that attempts to throw people upon their own inner resources. This is what has throughout history impeded the development of democracy. "It is the perennial disease of philosophers and statesman that they can not bear disorder." Hence, wherever democracy has been tried, whether in school, church, or civic group, conservatives have cried out against the confusion and lack of unity which inevitably accompanies popular control of the social order. "In a nation where the few who really rule must get some show of popular consent, a special class arises whose function it is, not to govern, but to secure the approval of the people for whatever policy may have been decided upon by that inevitable oligarchy which hides in the heart of every democratic state."[22] The rulers of modern society (or politicians, as Durant dubbed them) inevitably divide into hostile parties and seek to draw the people behind them in support of their respective goals. Unhappily, "the natural party-spirit of mankind makes such organizations easy; they are a survival of warlike tribal loyalties." As a consequence, man, who has been born for freedom, languishes in slavery, not knowing that the cherished liberty he desires lies in his power to overcome his instinct to run with the herd in the trail of its leader. Aware that the politician will not go away of his own accord, and that man is a long way from conquering the passion of fear which makes him prey to the ruler, Will Durant sensibly discarded the argument made by some nineteenth-century anarchists that the state must be done away with at once. Looking forward to the day when government would no longer be necessary or tolerated, Durant accepted its presence much as people in the middle ages accepted the bubonic plague. "The time must come when men will understand that the highest function of government is not to legislate but to educate, to make not laws but schools."[23] When that point in human evolution has been reached, mankind will have learned what Kropotkin and other anarchists already knew in the nineteenth century, viz., that man is a social animal if only he is turned loose to graze upon the nutrition furnished him in freedom.

One of the pioneer founders of the Modern School at Stelton was Joseph J. Ishill, who arrived in the Spring of 1915 and who almost at once became one of its most valuable members. Ishill (1888-1966) landed in the United States in November of 1909, already a veteran of European anarchist thought. Born in Botshani, Romania, he spent his early years on his father's farm where life was physically hard but spiritually pleasant due to the elder Ishill's libertarian inclinations. Enjoying almost unlimited freedom as a youth, Ishill developed a personality which later made him one of the most tolerant and generous individuals who ever called himself an anarchist. At the age of fourteen, Ishill learned the printing trade in his native Botshani, and it was here that his lifelong interest in literature was first awakened.[24] Perhaps because of the personal anguish he suffered when taunted as a boy about his Jewish blood, Ishill early developed a feeling of sympathy for the persecuted and reviled people of the world. A few years before he immigrated to the United States, Ishill was acting editor of a periodical called *The Wandering Jew,* but unfortunately it only lasted for a few issues. When it failed, he took to wandering himself, finding his way to Bucharest where he was put in touch with anarchism through his acquaintance with Panaite Musoiu, editor of the anarchist journal, *Review of Ideas.* For the first few years after his arrival in the United States, Ishill remained detached from any specific group although he was a frequent visitor at all libertarian functions, including Emma Goldman's lectures and the activities at the Ferrer Center in New York. But when the Modern School moved to Stelton, Ishill moved his family to the colony and built a little house with his own hands which his wife christened *The Little Nirvana.* Latter Ishill built a print shop where the children of the school could discover the joys of the art of printing and where *The Modern School* was composed and printed. It was also at Stelton that he first printed the limited editions for which he is widely known.[25] Starting with Oscar Wilde's *Ballard of Reading Goal,* Ishill put the prose and poetry of anarchism and libertarianism into print, including the poems of his wife, Rose Florence Freeman. All of the volumes produced by him, which are universally known for the excellence of their typography and binding, were issued under the imprimiture of The Free Spirit Press and The Oriole Press. From 1919 to the year of his death, Ishill published his many private editions from Berkley Heights, New Jersey, where he supported himself by commuting to an eight hour a day job in order to have his evenings free for his printing. Perhaps his most celebrated edition was his *Peter Kropotkin—The Rebel, Thinker, and Humanitarian* (1928).

It was characteristic of Joseph Ishill that he found room enough in his heart to make himself friend and supporter of all brands of anarchist thought, so long as they were genuinely libertarian in spirit. On the one hand Ishill found Thoreau's individualism decidedly authentic. Although Thoreau was willing to tolerate government as a "necessary evil," he yet held that in the end government, like every other human institution, is to be judged by the effect it has upon the spirit. Basically convinced that the political process as it is traditionally practiced is "unreal, incredible, and insignificant," Thoreau turned to the individual for the stuff out of which society is made, thereby demonstrating his libertarian convictions.[26] Of all Thoreau's pronouncements, the one which Ishill most cherished was his defense of John Brown in the face of the criticism which was heaped on him for his raid on Harper's Ferry. A thoroughly committed pacifist himself, Ishill had no difficulty in understanding what his good friend Emma Goldman so well knew, *viz.*, that violence in the social order is almost always the result of institutional structures of power and not the free choice of individuals like John Brown or Nat Turner. How then could he sit in judgement of Henry David Thoreau who merely expressed what every consistently honest man must acknowledge? Yet at the same time that he embraced Thoreau's doctrine of individualism, Ishill felt himself to be spiritually tied to Peter Kropotkin, the leading advocate of anarchist communism. In Ishill's mind, there was no barrier between the two branches of anarchist thought. It was characteristic of Joseph Ishill that he clearly understood what so many others misunderstood concerning Kropotkin's endorsement of the Allies during World War I. When Kropotkin condemned Germany for its crimes against humanity, it was not because he was under the influence of English nationalism or any other ideological force. Kropotkin's denunciation of Germany, according to Ishill, was directed against those intellectuals and scientists who excused the war on the grounds that Germany's struggle was a mere phase of the struggle for survival, as formulated by Darwin. Kropotkin's *Mutual Aid,* far from accepting armed conflict as a necessary phase of Darwin's survival of the fittest, maintained that human progress is carried foward on the wings of mutual aid and cooperation among men. "Were Kropotkin alive today," Ishill wrote in 1942, "it is certain that he would have allied himself with the United Nations...."[27] For Kropotkin was completely open to all human endeavor and on the side of life whatever form it might take. As an anarchist he was irrevocably opposed to all coercion and compulsion of human beings, and thus opposed to the state. But where men federate together in an effort to extend the boundaries of mutual aid, Kropotkin was ready to give his blessings, even when these efforts were termed "government." For Ishill, as for Kropotkin, what was important was not the name given to things but the spirit in which they were done. Ishill's ability to reconcile apparent inconsistencies was an indication that anarchism had reached maturity and was to at last escape the ideological quibbling which had plagued it so during the thirties.

Another of the important figures in the life of the Modern School was William Thurston Brown (1861-1938). Whereas many anarchists found the martyrdom of Albert Parsons or Sacco and Vanzetti the spark that fired their imaginations, William T. Brown, like Sidney Morse, reached back to Thomas Wentworth Higginson, who reached back to John Brown, for the inspiration which led him to anarchism. While a student at Yale, where he later studied divinity from 1892 to 1895, Brown was carried away by the Phi Beta Kappa oration delivered by Higginson, who was "the intimate friend and kindred spirit of Lowell, Longfellow, Emerson, Whittier, Bryant, George William Curtis, Wendell Phillips, Bronson Alcott, Henry Thoreau, Oliver Wendell Holmes, Theodore Parker, and all the rest who make up the list of America's greatest poets, orators, philosophers, wits and literary men."[28] What endeared Brown to Higginson was the depth and sincerity of the latter's character. In the company of the abolitionists, Higginson had spoken out in no uncertain terms against slavery, thereby demonstrating the authenticity of his moral credentials. "It was he who bore the body of slavery's first hero and martyr, John Brown, from the scaffold of his transfiguration in Virginia to the no less heroic household that waited for its beloved dust among the

Adirondack mountains." Born to the nobility of New England, Higginson's thirst for truth and justice made him one of America's greatest philosopher-kings, a "patriot of patriots," a man to be looked up to. And thus William Thruston Brown was led to join those who perpetually search after justice and who can never be content until they find it.

Born in upstate New York, Brown became minister of the Congregational Church in Madison, Connecticut in 1893. In 1896 heresy charges were instigated against Brown by some of his parishioners but he defended himself successfully and was fully exonerated. Leaving the parish in 1898, Brown steadily veered further and further to the left in both his theological and social views; for several years he lectured full time on socialism, switching over to the ministry of the Unitarian Society, in which he served churches in New York, Massachusetts and Utah, and later became field secretary for the Unitarians in Denver, Colorado. In 1909, Brown, simultaneously with a great many other individuals of anarchist inclination, experienced an event which sharpened the images in the innermost recesses of his social consciousness as they had never been sharpened before. The execution of Francisco Ferrer in Barcalona was the shot which jolted Brown into thinking of himself as an anarchist. The next year he organized a Modern School in Salt Lake City, later repeating that procedure in Portland, Oregon, and Chicago, Illinois. It was in Chicago that he met Voltairine de Cleyre and fell madly in love with the noble idealism which characterized her life and thought. Deeply moved by her death, Brown spoke of her as one who held a secure place "among the morally and intellectually elect of all the years," a woman who possessed "a great soul."[29] Accepting the principalship of the Ferrer Modern School at Stelton, New Jersey, in 1916, Brown worked for the next three years with the stars of twentieth century anarchism—Harry Kelly, Emma Goldman, Alexander Berkman, Joseph and Rose Ishill and others too numerous to mention. Apparently one of the most articulate of all the Modern School people, he developed an impressive body of educational theory to justify his libertarian attitudes. On his death in 1938 his alma mater correctly remembered him as one whose "life was devoted to a militant opposition to the existing order," but it displayed an unfortunate misunderstanding of his ideas when it labeled Brown one who "openly professed Communism and taught its principles, believing that therein lay the solution to most of the ills of modern society. . . ."[30] Brown most certainly professed his socialist beliefs in the open, and he was as devoted to his ideals as it is humanly possible to be. But he never labored under the simplistic notion that all the ills of the world can be cured by the adoption of any economic or social theory, for he knew from reading Plato that it is only through the education of children that society can be saved from itself.

If William Thurston Brown had been capable of throwing bombs, his prime target would have been the public schools, after which he would have aimed at the church and the state in that order. But like all sincere libertarians, he was under no illusion that dynamite can blast down the massive walls of ignorance which mankind has surrounded itself with. "The anarchist, believing that external changes in society are only the outward expression of the state of consciousness of the individuals composing society," he wrote, "lay a great deal of stress not on dynamite bombs, as so many have mistakingly supposed, for such weapons are forged by the cruelties of capitalism and are used chiefly by the innocent but despairing victims of capitalistic oppression—anarchists lay stress rather on *education and direct moral action.*"[31] Horrified by the oppressive methods of public education, Brown was convinced that all reform starts with the school. Created in monarchical times, he argued, the public school embodies the primary principle of authoritarian rule, which is that the pupil must obediently submit to the every command of his teacher and master. The public school does not ask the individual to think but only to obey. This is in part explained by the fact that the public school system is a mere tradition handed down to us from the past, whereas any true education must be experimental. "Life itself," Brown wrote, "is supremely an experiment, and he who knows nothing of experiment and adventure, *morally, ethically, spiritually,* knows nothing of life."[32] Where the school is entrusted to the state, education becomes burdened down with the stultifying methods of authoritarian command and hierarchy, for every human institution necessarily reflects the essential nature of its superstructure. And thus, Brown wrote: "The State will not give us schools that will produce individuals, that will beget freedom. *No State ever wanted individuals or freedom.* The most the State will attempt to do is to turn out a lot of dummies, all infected with the false and paralyzing superstitions of patriotism and culture, both empty, fraudulent, degrading."[33]

Properly defined, education is the most revolutionary of all human activities and the state is the least capable of all in structuring it.

The Modern School, as Brown conceived of it, was a valid instrument of education because it was a truly revolutionary organization. The "flower of the best intelligence and the loftiest idealism of the radical movement of America," the Modern School sought to make education reflect the libertarian principles developed by anarchists everywhere. In a truly democratic society, Brown wrote, the methods adopted by any school "must afford a sense of freedom impossible elsewhere—not a lawless freedom, if such a thing could be, but a freedom inspired by positive purpose, by the sense of happy tasks, of tasks fitted to the character of children and expressing also the sense of social unity."[34] Coupling the principles of both individualist and communist anarchism into a unified whole, Brown thought of education as a process whereby the individual is transformed into a truly social being in conformity with the human nature of which he is an integral part. Freedom is not, on this view, something one is given through artificial institutions such as government but a wholly natural phenomena we must discover within ourselves and apply in our relations with others. ". . . the only thing worthy of being called 'education,' " he held, "is that which starts every human child with the clear sense that the supreme good for him or her is the full and free expression of all the faculties and functions he or she possesses—and in one thing more: *a social consciousness centering in the thought and aim of universal freedom and well-being, and not in some purpose that grows only out of existing society or government.* "[35] Mankind in the past has revolted against oppressive political rule but it has not yet revolted against a far more insidious enemy of human freedom, a tyrannical system of public education which binds the mass of men in their shadowy cave of half-truth and illusion with no hope of liberation. Public educators, having made themselves the high priests of a power complex that places the state in the place of God, treat the individual as a subject to be shaped and molded as they please. It was against this kind of tyranny that anarchists of the stripe of William Thruston Brown pitted their nerve.

Devoted to the libertarian premise that freedom is an integral phase of human life and not something that is given or protected by government, Brown maintained that only the individual who craves freedom for himself can acquire it. ". . . one becomes free only when he does from inner motives the things which at once express his own individuality and recognize the equal rights of other individuals."[36] Like Plato, Brown viewed life as an art which embodied the full range of universal truth and beauty for those capable of mastering its essential philosophical techniques. Art is in fact merely another name for life itself, he argued. "Life is expression, and that is exactly what art is. So that the measure of one's life must inevitably be the measure in which one becomes, in all one does or is, an artist."[37] It came as no surprise to Brown, therefore, that there was nothing that might legitimately be termed art in the America of his day, for the coercive authority of its public institutions crushed out all opportunity for it to grow. "Art cannot exist under the domination of anything. Freedom, complete freedom, is the first requisite for art, and so for life itself." Just as Plato found solace in the hope of education, so Brown, convinced that the hubris of modern life can never be overcome through social engineering or the manipulation of people, turned to the free school as the last wall behind which the philosopher might take refuge.

With Horace Traubel, Brown found the poetry of Walt Whitman the inspiration for his libertarian attitudes toward life. Rejecting the concept of dualism which sees good and evil as opposites, Whitman, according to Brown, affirmed the monistic notion that all human substance is good. "There is no 'base' or 'low' in this nature of ours, and it is only mistaken and degrading human laws that create such ideas in the minds of people."[38] Thus armed by the greatest of America's poets, Brown's religious attitudes reflected the same libertarian flavor that his educational theory did. "I believe in men," he wrote. "And I hold that to profess a belief in God which does not involve the greatest possible belief in men is a contradiction in terms. I hold that the very deepest foundation stone of anything worthy to be called religion is belief in men."[39] The first concern of the truly religious man, according to Brown, is not with life after death but with life here on earth, the only life man can know.

From Whitman Brown also derived the foundations of his libertarian attitudes toward sex. Why is it, Brown asked, that man alone of all animals is troubled by his capacity for sexual activity? The lower animals display none of the troublesome symptoms which disturb human society in this regard. Primitive man, likewise, was not troubled with sexual promiscuity, sexual excesses, or sexual diseases. It is only in advanced civilization that immorality comes between man and woman, robbing them of the full dimension of their natures. The explanation for this, according to Brown, lies in the fact that freedom has been taken away from men and women in the area of sexual relations. Where people are free to determine their own actions, they are capable of controlling themselves intelligently. Whenever sexual immorality is found there will inevitably also be found a lack of personal freedom. "We have prostitution today in civilization because we haven't freedom, not because we have freedom."[40] Criticizing the woman's suffrage movement for its shortsightedness in focusing primarily upon the vote as the lever to make woman free, Brown insisted that the roots of female slavery went much deeper than woman's inability to vote. Woman "will be a commodity and her sex as well, *exactly as long as the system of private ownership of social wealth and the exploitation of man by man remains,*" he proclaimed. While Whitman might have been uncomfortable with the notion of economic determinism implicit in this argument, he would most certainly have concurred in the notion that freedom is as instrumental to a wholesome sexual morality as it is to a functioning social morality.

But Brown, like Whitman, was only secondarily interested in the economic causes of woman's enslavement to man. Of primary concern to him was the larger question of the psychological and spiritual implications of sexual repression. The sex question, he wrote, "is the fundamental question of life itself. In the sex question is bound up every human right, every human possibility, every human fulfillment."[41] One cannot deal with the problem in any intelligent fashion until one approaches it in a wholly revolutionary way. The America of which Whitman sang, according to Brown, was a thoroughly decadent society which shrank back from any honest discussion of sex and its importance to life. Seeing filth and corruption where Whitman only saw beauty and good, the people of America cry foul when his poetry openly discusses the sexual organs and actions of man. Such a gross perversion of human life, according to Brown, can only happen in "a civilization that is rotten to the core, a civilization that smells to heaven, a civilization that no alleged revivals of religion, though converts were numbered by the millions instead of the hundreds, can ever make decent or clean."[42] The only thing such a society deserves is to be overthrown. If we would be free, Brown prophesied, we must come to see, as Whitman did, that "sex is sacred, is divine, is fundamental, is the holiest thing this world contains, is the fountain of all that means anything, of all value, of all poetry, of all truth, of all beauty, of all love, of all life." If men want to be free to enjoy the human potential for beauty they have inherited, they must cease hiding their eyes when sex is mentioned and openly face the fact that only through it can they achieve a healthy social life. Undoubtedly Brown and Whitman were largely responsible for the scenes of innocence at the Modern School in which boys and girls frolicked on the grounds without the benefit of clothing.

Like all libertarians, Brown was as staunchly opposed to war as he was in favor of free education, free love, and a free humanity. The most damning indictment of war, according to him, was that it violates the fundamental principle of individual moral responsibility. "War isn't individuals killing individuals—it is *machines* destroying *machines.*"[43] Those who speak of war to make the world safe for democracy do nothing more than mouth political platitudes which have absolutely no relevance to the real world. "No war conducted by rulers or governments ever was or ever can be a war for democracy," Brown wrote. "Only the people themselves, conscious of their power and conscious of the meaning of democracy, can carry on a war for democracy."[44] Left to himself, the average man is wholly incapable of waging war against his fellowman for the act of taking life in organized fashion is not something natural to him. It is in his role as citizen that man learns to fight. And consequently, it is the state that is responsible for the phenomenon of warfare. Once man gets rid of the "superstition" that "government owes its origin to popular demand, or that it is worth fighting or dying for," mankind will never again wage war. In this aspect of his teachings, Brown reflected the individualism of Thoreau and other exponents of the philosophy of civil disobedience.

But Brown was not oblivious to the changing conditions of industrial America, and the idea of class consciousness, accordingly, finds a prominent place in his thought. On the one hand he insisted that "Human progress is never made en masse." Yet he at the same time argued that human "interests are no longer individual. They are social. They follow the lines of economic classes."[45] The idea of democracy is unreal in the minds of middle class Americans, according to Brown, for the simple reason that middle class people "are unconscious of the need of any struggle for freedom and against oppression." The industrial worker, on the other hand, values democracy to the extent that he has learned the necessity of fighting

NOTES

SECTION V - CHAPTER 5

1. Hippolyte Havel, *Harry Kelly, An Appreciation.* Ferrer Colony (January 23, 1921), p. 1.

2. *The Rebel,* I (September 20, 1895), 1.

3. *Freedom,* I (New York, June, 1919), 1.

4. "Local and National Guilds," *The Modern School,* V (December, 1918), 370.

5. "Worker's College," *The Modern School,* IV (September, 1917), 67.

6. "The Psychology of Fear," *Road to Freedom,* I (August, 1925), 1.

7. *Selected Works,* (New York, 1914), p. 300.

8. *The Origins of Ideals of the Modern School,* translated by Joseph McCabe (New York, 1913), p. 68.

9. "Salute," *The Modern School,* III (May, 1916), 3.

10. "Old Year Reflections," *The Modern School,* II (January, 1915), 1.

11. Leonard D. Abbott, "The Ferrer School in New York," *Everyman,* X (December, 1914), 7.

12. Perhaps the most famous of the artists who associated themselves with the school was the surrealist, Man Ray. Others who were to be found in its studios at one time or another were: Adolph Wolff, Ben Benn, Manuel Komroff, Helen West Keller, Paul Rohland, and Harry Wickey. *Socialism and American Life,* ed. by Donald Drew Egbert and Stow Persons. (Princeton, 1952), p. 715fn.

13. William Innes Homer with the assistance of Violet Organ. *Robert Henri and His Circle* (Ithaca, New York, 1969), p. 180.

14. *The Mansions of Philosophy* (New York, 1929), p. 424.

15. "The Political and Philosophical Bases of Educational Theory-II," *The Modern School,* III (November-December, 1916), 135.

16. *Experimental Schools: Bulletin of the Bureau of Educational Experiments* #5 (New York, 1917), p. 9.

17. "The Background of Our Movement," *The Modern School,* III (May, 1916), 19. See also, Terry Perlin, "Anarchism In New Jersey"; The Ferrer Colony At Stelton," *New Jersey History,* LXXXIX (1971), 133-148.

18. "Whitman as Revolutionary," *The Modern School,* VI (April-May, 1919), 138.

19. "The Political and Philosophical Bases of Educational Theory," *The Modern School,* III (October, 1916), p. 109.

20. *The Foundations of Civilization* (New York, 1936), p. 53.

21. "The Political and Philosophical Bases of Educational Theory," *The Modern School,* III (November-December, 1916), 134. For a recent study of the Modern School, see Laurence Veysey, *The Communal Experience: Anarchist and Mystical Counter-Cultures In America* (New York, 1973).

22. *The Mansions of Philosophy* (New York, 1929), p. 437.

23. *Ibid.,* p. 426.

24. Rudolph Rocker, "Joseph Ishill," *A Way Out,* 23 (October, 1967), 21.

25. Will Ransome, *Private Presses and Their Books* (New York 1963), p. 119.

26. Joseph Ishill, "Thoreau: 'The Cosmic Yankee,' " unpublished manuscript in the Ishill Papers, Houghton Library, Harvard University, Cambridge Massachusetts (n.d.), p. 12.

27. "Peter Kropotkin," unpublished manuscript in the Ishill Papers, Houghton Library, Harvard University, Cambridge, Massachusetts (1924), p. 2.

28. "The Spring and Possibilities of Character," *Free Society,* X (May 31, 1903), 1.

29. "Education in the Light of Present Day Knowledge and Need," *The Modern School,* III (July, 1916), 33.

30. *Yale University Obituary Record,* Class of 1890, p. 56.

31. *What Socialism Means as a Philosophy and a Movement* (Portland, Oregon, n.d.), p. 11.

32. *The Most Important Educational Experiment in America* (Stelton, New Jersey, n.d.), p. 11.

33. "Education in the Light of Present Day Knowledge and Need," p. 33.

34. *Education or Constructive Democracy* (Stelton, New Jersey, n.d.), p. 18.

35. "Education in the Light of Present Day Knowledge and Need," 10.

36. "The Work of a Libertarian School," *The Modern School,* IV (September, 1917), 74.

37. *Socialism and the Individual* (Portland, Oregon, n.d.), p. 24.

38. *Walt Whitman: Poet of the Human Whole* (Portland, Oregon, n.d.), p. 25.

39. *The Real Religion of Today* (Chicago, 1900), p. 7.

40. *The Evolution of Sexual Morality* (Portland, Oregon, n.d.), p. 15.

41. *Ibid.,* p. 11.

42. "Whitman and Sex," *The Modern School,* VI (April-May, 1919), 145.

43. *The Modern School: What It Is and What It Will Do* (Stelton, New Jersey, n.d.), p. 5.

44. *Education for Constructive Democracy,* p. 9.

45. *The Real Religion of Today,* p. 30.

46. "The Springs and Possibilities of Character," p. 2.

Later Day Manifestations of the Anarchist Idea

CHAPTER 1

The "Great Hearts" of Anarchism:
Sacco, Vanzetti, and Rudolf Rocker

On both the East and West coasts of the United States there were before World War II numerous Italian immigrants who professed themselves anarchists and who carried on a vigorous program of propaganda in their native tongue. To date these Italian-speaking anarchists have remained shrouded in the somber shadow cast over America by the judicial murder of Sacco and Vanzetti on August 22, 1927. So brutally did the State of Massachusetts put these two innocents to death for their alleged ideological beliefs that the heart-break brought on by this most infamous deed is still felt by people throughout America; it is impossible for one who is the least bit sensitive to read their letters from prison without a deep emotional experience, for the story of their lives embraces the entire range of human pathos and deserves a place alongside the story of Christ's agony upon the cross.

The facts of this notorious miscarriage of justice are too well-known to be reiterated here in detail, and so we need deal mainly with the quality of the social thought expounded by Sacco and Vanzetti. It is to be noted at the outset that these two sons of Italy were much more interested in living their anarchism than writing about it and hence we have very little published material to go by when assessing their ideas; most of what they did write was penned as letters to friends as they sat in prison through seven long years awaiting execution. Although Nicola Sacco had been in America twelve years before his arrest in May of 1920, he was not at all fluent in English and had an extremely difficult time in making himself understood in both speech and writing. In the south of Italy, where Nicola was raised, he had received no formal education even though his family owned productive olive groves and vineyards in the Province of Foggia. Always close to nature in his outlook and feelings, Nicola Sacco preferred to trust his heart and his emotions rather than his intellect, and so he made little effort to educate himself formally until the State of Massachusetts shut him up in a cell and forced him to find some formal means of self-expression. He worked as a machine operator in a small shoe factory throughout most of his years in America and was just beginning to become interested in political philosophy when he was accused of taking part in the robbery and murder in South Braintree, Massachusetts. When he had first arrived from Italy in 1908 he held quite orthodox political views but his work experience soon led him to socialism and thereafter to anarchism.

Bartolomeo Vanzetti's experience was very similar to Sacco's, except that he was much more intellectual than Sacco and was very quick to pick up and assimilate new ideas. The son of a prosperous farmer in the small village of Villafalleto in Italy's Piedmont region, Vanzetti as a youngster was a quick and eager student. "My earliest memories are of prizes won in school examinations, including a second prize in the religious catechism," he wrote in his auto-biography.[1] For a time Bartolomeo's proud father thought of training his precocious young son for the law but because of the oversupply of lawyers in Italy it was decided that he should be apprenticed as a pastry baker, in which trade he learned what it is like to have nothing to live by other than one's own labor. At the end of six years of back-breaking labor in the searing heat of bakery kitchens in Turin and other Italian cities, Vanzetti came down with pleurisy and was tenderly carried home to his native village to be nursed back to health by his mother and father. Here he remained until in his twentieth year his mother was taken from him by death. The deep heartbreak and personal agony that Vanzetti experienced as he laid his revered mother in her coffin tells a great deal about his personality and character. "I was burying part of myself," he wrote years later, "and the void left has never been filled."[2] Unable to stand the loneliness he felt at home with his mother no longer with him, Vanzetti took leave of his fellow townsmen in a most moving demonstration of love and personal devotion, never to return again.

Coming to America in 1908, Vanzetti, like many another immigrants, soon gained an insight into the nature of the state that is denied to that individual who never leaves his native land. Filled with hope for the future, the immigrant, pushed about by unyielding officials as though he were a part of a herd of cattle, soon loses the idealism that brought him to the new land. Vanzetti perhaps expressed the experience felt by all immigrants to foreign lands when he wrote:

> Until yesterday I was among folks who understood me. This morning I seemed to have awakened in a land where my language meant little more to the native (so far as meaning is concerned) than the pitiful noises of a dumb animal. Where was I to go? What was I to do? Here was the promised land. The elevated rattled by and did not answer. The automobiles and the trolleys sped by, heedless of me.[3]

The unspeakable loneliness he felt intensified during the next dozen years as he made a precarious living as dishwasher, ditch digger, railroad hand, and ice cutter, with long periods of unemployment between jobs. Vanzetti appeared to have found some measure of security peddling fish to his friends in the Italian colony of Plymouth, Massachusetts, when he was accused of the payroll robbery and slaying in South Braintree and a previous armed robbery in Bridgewater. Never having married, Vanzetti threw all his energy while in prison into a self-imposed regimen of education, reading and writing every minute he could squeeze out of the prison routine in an attempt to expand his mind and to explain his social and political attitudes to the world outside. Like Sacco, his character and conduct were exemplary previous to his arrest and both of them were highly respected by all who knew them in the Italian districts in which they lived.

Perhaps the most striking thing about the entire Sacco and Vanzetti affair is that neither of them had any conscious design whatever upon martyrdom or fame and would have been content, had fate allowed it, to live out their lives quietly without ever leaving the circle of their friends and loved ones. But fate was not to allow them any real choice in the matter and hence they were thrust on the stage and made the chief protagonists of one of the most melodramatic moments in the entire history of American anarchism; only the Haymarket incident compares with it in terms of the effect it had over the feelings of American anarchists. Vanzetti undoubtedly felt something of this drama himself when he said to a reporter who was interviewing him:

> If it had not been for these things, I might have lived out my life talking at street corners to scorning men. I might have died, unmarked, unknown, a failure. This is our career and our triumph. Never in our full life could we hope to do such work for tolerance, for justice, for man's understanding of man as now we do by accident. Our words—our lives—our pains—nothing! The taking of our lives—lives of a good shoemaker and a fish-peddler—all! That last moment belongs to us—that agony is our triumph.[4]

When the moment of truth arrived on death row, both of them knew instinctively how they must behave. As David Wieck, editor of *Resistance,* observed, their greatness essentially consisted of having "the power to act greatly when the occasion demanded it" and of having the courage to die nobly for an ideal even though they would have preferred not to have died at all.[5] Or as Roger N. Baldwin, one of those who came to know them intimately during the seven years they suffered in prison, said, "Sacco and Vanzetti lived their faith in every word and act, and it sustained them to the chair."[6] In many respects, therefore, their conception of anarchism is as "authentic" as any that is available to us and we are thus constrained to study their lives carefully if we would hope to achieve any understanding of American anarchism.

When the trauma they experienced from being forced to sit in a courtroom and witness the grotesque travesty of justice take place before their eyes subsided somewhat, Sacco and Vanzetti turned to political philosophy and sought to alleviate the deep hurt they felt by articulating their inner thoughts and emotions. Falsely accused of murder and robbery by the State of Massachusetts, they had difficulty understanding why the truth they spoke through their lawyers was so deliberately distorted by the prosecution and the presiding judge until they realized that what they were being tried for was not any actual act or deed but an ideological position—that of being "anarchists." And not only were they forced to suffer punishment for their beliefs in violation of both the letter and spirit of the American Constitution, but those who stood ready to crucify them for what they believed had only a murky idea at best as to what they believed in. In the summer of 1926, Leonard D. Abbott visited Sacco and Vanzetti in their cells and came away tremendously impressed by the intelligence, charm, and obvious sincerity which they both exuded under the most trying of circumstances.[7] Although Sacco was reticent when it came to public expression, he was an omnivorous reader and devoured everything he could obtain of Dostoevsky's in an effort to reach a more satisfying explanation of man and his social actions toward others. It is likewise significent that he was reading Max Stirner's *The Ego and His Own* a year before the execution. Vanzetti, for his part, had discovered Proudhon while in prison, thereby expanding the range of his understanding of anarchism beyond the writings of Kropotkin, Malatesta, Elisee Reclus and other communist anarchists he had previously been familiar with. Translating Proudhon's *War and Peace* in the gloom of his cramped prison cell, Vanzetti came to see how paradox and a broad view of history can help one better understand the role which mankind's dual nature plays in human affairs, and the sting of what was happening to his personal life was perhaps lessened thereby.

We are not to be misled by the fact that Sacco and Vanzetti faced their execution with psychological calm and philosophical resignation, into believing that they were sheep-like in their social attitudes. Vanzetti put all such accusations to rest forever when he wrote to his friend, Alice Stone Blackwell, that "There is no spirit of sacrifice in this deed. I simply realize to be in merciless hands, and do my utmost to say to my enemy that he is wrong."[8] Like all anarchists, Sacco and Vanzetti longed for a world in which individual freedom would be at a maximum and force and compulsion at a minimum. In their appeal to Governor Fuller which they wrote only to satisfy the consciences of personal friends who argued that the Governor could not act legally in their behalf until this step was taken, Sacco and Vanzetti spelled out the terms of their objection to legal coercion. "We call ourselves libertarians, which means briefly that human perfectability is to be obtained by the largest amount of freedom and not by coercion," they proclaimed.[9] Recognizing that there is little possibility that the basic form and structure of human institutions can be changed radically at once, they nevertheless placed themselves on the side of those who call for more freedom and less coercion on the grounds that only within freedom can the good which lies deep within the human breast find its way into actuality. "That is why we are opposed to every theory of authoritarian communism or socialism," they added, "for they would rivet more or less firmly the chains of coercion on the human spirit, just as we are opposed to the present system, which is based on coercion."

Caught as they were in a legal quagmire from which they could not escape however strenuously their friends and anarchist companions tried to help them, Sacco and Vanzetti probably saw and understood the real nature of American law more clearly than the most learned of jurists can ever hope to do. It was more than personal suffering that led Vanzetti to write one of his confidants that "laws are the codified will of the dominating classes; the laws are made to legalize the State organization of violence. . . ."[10] In branding law the tool of the powerful, Vanzetti was not engaging in a crass oversimplification of subtle philosophical phenomena based solely on his own unfortunate experience; to the contrary, he understood full well the depth of the impersonal social forces that shape the political world and the psychological imperatives that lie behind them. If law is the tool of the powerful, this is so not so much because the powerful few are vile, unprincipled individuals as because they are not individuals at all. Those who come to exercise power over their fellowmen, in his opinion, do what they do because they fail to recognize the destructive elements that are inevitable in all power relationships. Were they once to understand that life cannot be sustained by force and involuntary regimentation, they would not take power when it presents itself.

Throughout the entire period of their incarceration, Vanzetti adamantly held that no new trial would ever be granted them, for if it were, the full depth of the corruption and injustice of the American legal system would be dragged out into the bright light of day so that all would know what kind of social insanity they were caught up in. When Governor Fuller finally appointed an investigation committee to look into the details of the case for the purpose of ascertaining whether justice had been done, Vanzetti recognized at once that this was to be just another scene in the judicial farce the State of Massachusetts was staging. The appointment of the notable political scientist, A. Laurence Lowell, to the committee might have impressed academicians and the bluebloods of Boston as a sign of Fuller's impartiality but Vanzetti never for a moment was fooled by this stratagem. Had the Governor desired that justice be done the investigation would have been conducted out in the open instead of behind closed doors with rigid rules of procedure that excluded any possibility of a confrontation between the prosecution and the defense. Vanzetti spoke harshly but honestly when he claimed that "they convicted us because we are Italian, against war, and anarchist: to succeed they were compelled to the most vile, criminal conduct: and now, to save their faces and uphold their institution they must kill us—also to quench their fears."[11] Looking back at the case from the viewpoint of detachment that time now affords us, who can say that Vanzetti's analysis was not accurate.

The deeper we proceed into the character of Sacco and Vanzetti's social and political thought the more evident it becomes that the basic outline of their thinking was shaped by the libertarian philosophy of the Enlightenment. Having read Proudhon, Vanzetti professed a certain degree of historical pessimism based upon the "blindness of the more [the many], the rascality of the few, and the dreadful unconsciousness of all" who allow the currents of life to become damned and stopped up through inertia and the moral failure to act upon one's convictions. Labelling himself "a voluntarist and an anarchist, that is, the opposite of a fatalist," Vanzetti put his finger upon the vital pulse beat of libertarian thought when he declared himself on the side of those who refuse to allow themselves to drift along on the currents of historical necessity. Writing to Li Pei Kan, a young anarchist in China, Vanzetti was forced to concede that in his opinion "we are actually certainly dragged, with the rest of mankind, toward tyranny and darkness."[12] Yet the outcome of human history is by no means unalterably fixed, for mankind, divided as it is between the forces of tyranny and the forces of freedom, is theoretically capable of spiraling off in either direction. Ultimately, Vanzetti held, the final outcome of civilization depends upon us, since "history will become what we force it to become." Since every individual contains within his nature both the seed of tyranny and the seed of freedom, no one can predict the final result of human evolution until the very end of time. Meanwhile, he implied, this world remains a battlefield on which the forces of light and the forces of darkness joust with one another in a struggle for life and death.

If American anarchism were asked to name two representatives by which its social worthiness might be judged, it could do no better than to ask that it be represented by Nicola Sacco and Bartolomeo Vanzetti. As devoted as Sacco was to his young wife and two small children, his seven years in prison must have been equivalent to an eternity in the fires of hell, so deeply did he long to be at their side. When on the eve of his execution he wrote Dante, his son, to take his mother after he was gone "for a long walk in the quiet country, gather-wild flowers here and there, resting under the shade of trees, between the harmony of the vivid stream and the gentle tranquility of mother nature," he expressed not only his own deep attachment to nature but a side of the anarchist idea that is rarely appreciated by those who view it from the outside. Even while he suffered the torments of hell at the thought that his wife and children would be denied their husband and father for no other reason than that a few short-sighted political figures willed that he should die, he was generous enough to urge his son always to place himself on the side of the weak and persecuted in the struggle in life.[13] Vanzetti, too, realized "what a tragic laughingstock our case and fate are" and yet still held firm to the Enlightenment's libertarian view of nature as the font of all human good. "Nature has gave us unphantomed treasures for the security and elevation of life," he wrote in his inimitable prose; "it breath in our heart an unquenchable long of freedom, and it gifts us of such faculties which, if free an cultivated, would make a wonder of us."[14] Perhaps it was from Emerson's *Essays* and Thoreau's *On Nature*, two of his favorite books until they were lost to him as a consequence of a change in prison cells, that he had derived this dimension of his mind. But from wherever he had received the germ of the thought, Vanzetti placed himself on a plane with the greatest of libertarian thinkers when he wrote that "the dearest manifestation of Nature to me is mankind with his miseries and proudness, his glories and his shames, his smallness and his grandeur."[15] Unable to change the course of history except through the small influence he might exert through his own martyrdom, Vanzetti went to his death with grace and generosity, going so far as to ask that his enemies be forgiven for their trespasses against him. In this, he, along with Sacco, was successful in setting an example for mankind of the great range of humility and nobility that the occasional human being is capable of. Knowing full well that their "execution was in fact an assertion of power against all who believe that our political and economic institutions are the agents of life, which we have molded for our purposes, not obscure, tyrannous deities, whom we must blindly obey,"[16] Sacco and Vanzetti still chose to remain true to the enlightened idea that the only reliable guides to a wholesome social life are the inner feelings of solidarity and justice one intuits from the depths of his being.

Many people have been troubled by the fact that when arrested Vanzetti had a pistol in his pocket along with several shotgun shells, conjecturing from this that there may after all be something to the often repeated assertion that under the skin anarchists are prone to violence and destruction. But when this fact is viewed against the circumstances that accompanied the incident, the charge is seen to be completely without foundation. As a dealer in fish, Vanzetti was compelled to carry several hundred dollars in cash on his person and thus it was not at all strange that he was carrying a pistol. As to the shotgun shells, according to his explanation, these were to be sold and the money used to support the program of education which he and his anarchist companions were engaged in. It is also to be noted that there was a great deal of concern for their personal safety among the Italian immigrants with whom Vanzetti moved, for one of their friends had just been killed by a fall under suspicious circumstances in the jail in which he was being held incommunicado, giving rise to the fear among them that arrest by the police was tantamount to death. When it is recognized that the period with which we are concerned was the period of the Palmer raids in which radicals of all persuasions were mercilessly, and often illegally, hunted down and persecuted for the most tenuous of reasons, it is not at all surprising that Italian immigrants like Sacco and Vanzetti expected very little in the way of justice from the authorities. And very little did they get. When picked up by the police, Sacco and Vanzetti believed that they were only being accused of the political crime of opposition to the state and thus they talked freely, telling a number of fabrications in the hope of escaping the deportation that so many of their radical friends and acquaintances had been subjected to. Had they been immediately informed by the police of their constitutional rights under American law, it would not have been so easy for the prosecution to obtain a conviction against them on the flimsy evidence the state contorted.

Nor was Vanzetti acting inconsistently with his anarchist ideals when he armed himself against attack from his enemies, for anarchism does not claim absolute pacifism as one of its principles but only a refusal to engage in organized systems of force and violence for the perpetuation of order. During World War I Vanzetti, along with Sacco, left the United States for Mexico in order to avoid military service, for they both held firm to the conviction that organized warfare in any of its forms is wrong; although they could not persuade the American people as a whole to refrain from such insanity, they could as individuals keep themselves relatively free of the taint of war's monstrous evils. Likewise, Sacco and Vanzetti made their way through American society acting spontaneously and with good faith toward their fellow citizens; in their personal relations they characteristically displayed trust and warmth to those with whom they had dealings and never sought to force their will upon another via the law or government. When thrust into the grasp of an unyielding and hostile legal system, on the other hand, Vanzetti recognized at once that it was unrealistic to expect any help from any quarter other than one's own strength. Had he the force to break the bars which kept him penned up, he would have done so, for the "slave has the right and duty to rise against his master."[17] This subtle distinction between legitimate and illegitimate force and violence is uniformly present in the thinking of all anarchists and is one of the hallmarks of the basic philosophy of anarchism. The struggle against injustice waged by Sacco and Vanzetti serves as one of the most poignant reminders to mankind that the quality of any social system is no better than the theory of order upon which it is built. Like Christ, Sacco and Vanzetti were executed because the simple message of love and order which they tried to articulate was interpreted by the rich and powerful as the most subversive of doctrines. Although they contributed little in the way of formal political theory, their life experience will live forever among those who value freedom above all else.

The tremendous outpouring of sympathy and support which the Sacco and Vanzetti incident gave rise to almost totally obscured the many Italian-speaking anarchist groups that existed in every large urban center in the period preceding World War II and so the history of this phase of American anarchism has been largely lost.

Perhaps the most well-known of the Italian-speaking anarchists was Carlo Tresca who edited several publications including *L'Avenire* and *Il Martello* from New York City. Lending its support to the I.W.W., his office in Harlem was the meeting place for many of the young Wobblies who sought to bring the meaning of poverty and depression into the churches and meeting places of the rich.[18] A frequent victim of police brutality, Tresca was assassinated in 1943 on the street just as he emerged from his office and the details of his murder remain one of the many unsolved incidents of American violence. It remains for some historian proficient in the Italian language to write a history of the Italian-speaking anarchist in America.

Although Rudolf Rocker (1873-1958) is not known nearly as well as Sacco and Vanzetti, he was the most accomplished political philosopher to affiliate himself with American anarchism prior to World War II and he exerted tremendous philosophical influence over the direction of libertarian thought by virtue of his many published writings. Born on the banks of the Rhine River in Mainz, Germany, he was the son of poor Roman Catholic parents. They died while he was young, however, and his religious education had to be completed by the Catholic orphanage to which his care was entrusted. After running away from the orphanage several times, he was apprenticed to a bookbinder and later traveled around Europe as a journeyman of that trade.[19] Educating himself in political philosophy via the path of free thought, he had come by his eighteenth birthday to think of himself as an anarchist and began to frequent radical groups whenever he could. In 1892 the German authorities pressed him so hard as a consequence of his political opinions that he was forced to flee to Paris from where he made his way to England, settling among the "Jewish" anarchists of London's East End.

It is surely one of the great anomalies of cultural history that Rudolf Rocker, a full-blooded German by birth, should have thrown his lot in with the poor Yiddish-speaking refugees who huddled in London's great slums, but this is exactly what he did. Teaching himself to speak and write Yiddish in a remarkably short time, he was soon established among the Yiddish proletariat as one of their own, attending anarchist meetings at the Grafton Hall club and eeking out a precarious living by virtue of an occasional bookbinding job. During his first years in England he met and fell in love with a young Jewess who had fled to London from her native Ukraine, Milly Witcop, and she subsequently became his lifelong companion. In 1898 these young lovers decided to try their luck in America and they embarked upon the long and uncomfortable journey to the land of hope and promise. Upon reaching America's shores, however, they were met by the immigration officials who refused them admittance unless they would submit to an official wedding ceremony complete with a license from the state and a civil officer to perform the act. The young lovers, pledged to the anarchist idea of individual freedom, idealistically refused to accommodate the puritanical bias of the immigration officials and hence were forced to return to England on the very ship that had brought them. Ironically, the argument that was used against them was that Milly Witcop was bound to be exploited by Rocker unless she had a legal hold upon him.[20] As things worked out, however, nothing short of Milly's death in 1955 could part these lovers; in his personal affairs as in his political philosophy, Rudolf Rocker was completely dedicated to the libertarian conviction that the only legitimate authority is one's own natural desires.

Sharing the poverty and social isolation of the Yiddish-speaking emigrees who sought political shelter in England, Rocker for the next twenty years was a chief figure in the development of the anarchist movement. Becoming editor of *Dos Freie Vort* in Liverpool, in 1898, he soon knew everyone in the Jewish socialist labor movement. After publishing four or five issues of *Dos Freie Vort,* he assumed the editorship of the *Arbeiter Freund,* the leading Jewish anarchist publication in England, and was in constant demand as a speaker for the various groups in the country. Rocker was instrumental in organizing the Yiddish-speaking workers of London's sweatshops into trade unions and was the leader of the first strikes by the Jews against the hard-fisted practices of the clothing industry. Working closely with such outstanding anarchist personalities as Peter Kropotkin, Louise Michel, Errico Malatesta, Gustav Landauer, and Max Nettlau, Rocker developed a profound grasp of libertarian philosophy, producing some of the most outstanding writings to come out of the movement. In addition to the *Arbeiter Freind,* he edited *Germinal,* a Yiddish monthly devoted to art and literature.

In 1914, Rocker, along with the other Germans residing in England, was arrested and interred as an "enemy alien." The fact that he was totally opposed to war, including the one then being waged by his former countrymen, did not alter the mindset of the British authorities and he was forced to endure four long years of imprisonment until he was forceably returned to Germany in 1918. After the war the change in political affairs within defeated Germany permitted him to live safely in Berlin where he completed the greater portion of his major work, *Nationalism and Culture*. With Hitler's rise to power, however, the political situation again shifted and he and Milly were fortunate to get out of the country with the manuscript in their possession. Making their way to the United States, the Rockers found a haven in the Mohegan Colony, an anarchist commune at Crompond, New York, and in the home of Milly's sister in Pennsylvania. In America Rocker found many of the Yiddish-speaking comrades he had worked with in London and before long he was contributing articles to the *Freie Arbeiter Stimme* and speaking before anarchist groups from New York to Los Angeles.

The influence of the Enlightenment is as pronounced in Rocker's political thought as it is in that of the native American anarchists. Displaying an encyclopedic knowledge of philosophy and history, Rocker, much like Voltaire or Paine, decried the fact that organized religion has lulled humanity into moral and philosophical somnambulism. The difficulty with all religious systems, according to Rocker, is that those who exist within them inevitably wind up the creature of the very system they initially created. Allowing his imagination to indulge itself in such fanciful notions as a God with absolute power, man throughout history has progressively found himself enslaved to the idols he has raised. "Always it is the illusion to which the real essence of man is offered as a sacrifice; the creator becomes the slave of his own creature without ever becoming conscious of the tragedy of this."[21] Man's submission to an absolute deity has important social and political consequences, according to Rocker. From the moment that he allows himself to become the subject of a mysterious power over which he had no control, man loses all direction over his own social and moral will. And this condition carries over into the realm of the political and is not confined merely to the world of religion.

In fact, Rocker argued, the model of might and domination that man patterns his religious relationship after is the very model that determines his actions and thought in his political relationship; having submitted himself totally to an all-powerful deity, man finds nothing wrong in submitting himself totally to the political ruler he finds himself under. "Thus we arrive at the foundations of every system of rulership and recognize that all politics is in the last instance religion, and as such tries to hold the spirit of man in the chains of dependence."

More than at any other time in history, according to Rocker, in modern times "religious feeling has assumed political forms."[22] Everywhere today, he complained, nationalism sucks the vital moral energy out of the citizen's heart and people parade about behind their national banners like wooden marionettes, never questioning the brutality and injustice of their government's policies. Pointing to Rousseau as the culprit responsible for much of the false illusion which has come to dull the senses of modern man, Rocker faulted him for creating yet another sacred idol before which men stand powerless. Like a huckster who skillfully entices the unsuspecting to buy his wares, Rousseau holds out the prospect of a "political providence" for those who submit themselves completely to the all-powerful state in the interest of collective security and salvation. In the name of the general will, men are asked to give themselves completely to the nation, thereby assuring themselves power and glory far greater than they ever could achieve as isolated individuals. But in raising the nation to the status of an omnipotent god, Rousseau divested man of all the social strength that is his by nature, Rocker charged.

By Rousseau's definition, the citizen's freedom is subsumed in his duties to the common good as symbolized by the state. But, declared Rocker:

> He who declares the common will to be the absolute sovereign and yields to it unlimited power over all members of the community, sees in freedom nothing more than the duty to obey the law and to submit to the common will. For him the thought of dictatorship has lost its terror. He has long ago in his own mind sacrificed man to a phantom that has no understanding whatever of individual freedom.[23]

If man is ever to be truly free, Rocker urged, it is essential that he free himself from the "curse of power" under the crushing weight of which the human spirit presently lies prostrate. The blind faith which many people place in power is ultimately "a cruel deception," for power in itself has no capability whatever of a creative kind. Rather than serving the needs and aspirations of all the people, power always serves the special interests of the minority that is successful in acquiring a grip upon it. In final analysis, "power always reverts to individuals or groups of individuals" and never to "the people."

When we scrutinize political power carefully, getting behind the aura which ordinarily blinds us to its real nature, we discover that the essential character of power is such that it can never lead to anything positive. In essence, power is basically totalitarian in the sense that it makes absolute demands upon those who are subject to its control. "Power is active consciousness of authority," according to Rocker. "Like God, it cannot endure any other God beside it."[24] Striving always for rigid uniformity, power imposes total control and regulation over everything it touches so that those who come under its influence must always give up their own individual personalities to its demands. "In its stupid desire to order and control all social events according to a definite principle, it is always eager to reduce all human activity to a single pattern." Power, in short, is an unhealthy phenomenon which is to the body politic what cancer is to the human organism.

Advancing the novel thesis that nationalism stands basically opposed to culture, Rocker argued that the nation is not a natural growth arising from the social actions of a people but a wholly artificial one which is in effect imposed upon them by a political minority. "The nation is not the cause, but the result, of the state," as Rocker put it. "It is the state which creates the nation, not the nation the state."[25] No individual, on this view, naturally holds a place within the nation as he holds a place within his family or tribe, for there is no basic social tie which binds him to the political body. "Belonging to a nation is never determined, as is belonging to a people, by profound natural causes; it is always subject to political considerations and based on those reasons of state behind which the interests of privileged minorities always hide." One is trained to think of himself as a member of his nation just as one is trained to think of himself as a member of a church. "National states are political church organizations; the so-called national consciousness is not born in man, but trained into him. It is a religious concept; one is a German, a Frenchman, an Italian, just as one is a Catholic, a Protestant, or a Jew." Those who actively advance the cause of the nation know exactly what they are doing when they cultivate the belief among the people that the citizen has a duty to the state that is similar to his duty to God, Rocker charged.

Denying that there is any fundamental discrepancy between anarchism and socialism, Rocker summed up the entire range of anarchist thought when he pointed out that "the exploitation of man by man and the dominion of man over man are inseparable, and each is the condition of the other."[26] Political rulership arises at the point at which a minority of men, seeking to protect their economic advantage, set out to use force and coercion for their own purposes, he argued. So long as there exists a minority class that possesses property and a majority class that does not, the state will continue to be necessary to protect the wealthy in their economic and social privileges. The Marxist contention that the state will wither away at the point that it is no longer necessary, Rocker wryly quipped, "sounds, in the light of historical experience, almost like a bad joke." The very nature of political power is exhausted in its mission of perpetuating and protecting the privileges of the possessing class; the majority armed with state power would be just as inhospitable and dangerous as the minority presently is in that position. "Only by a fundamental reorganization of labor on the basis of fellowship, serving no other purpose than the satisfaction of the needs of all instead of increasing the profits of individuals as today, can the present economic crisis be overcome and the way cleared for a higher culture."[27] Calling his proposal "anarcho-syndicalism," Rocker placed himself squarely in the tradition of Peter Kropotkin whose call for voluntary federation among the laboring classes of the earth has been the main thrust of libertarian thinking during the twentieth century.

Unlike some other forms of socialism, anarcho-syndicalism, according to Rocker, seeks not to capture the power of the state for its social purposes but to eliminate state power entirely.[28] In this aim, anarcho-syndicalism has its roots in the First International which in 1864 decreed that its chief concern was to break out of the pattern established by the bourgeoise by refraining from perpetuating the structure of political parties as they had then been formed. The members of the First International clearly understood, according to Rocker, that only by making a clear break with political power could a fundamental reshaping of social life be achieved. Thus while the parliamentary labour parties in some European countries attempt to work within the framework of established political power, anarcho-syndicalists place themselves completely outside the establishment, recognizing that freedom is never a gift from those who hold places of power. For, according to Rocker, "Political rights do not originate in parliaments, they are, rather, forced upon parliaments from without."[29] When the people, acting upon deep-seated feelings of injustice, resist further exploitation at the hands of those who control power, their grievances will be listened to and acted upon. Basically no pacifist, Rocker argued that "One compels respect from others when he knows how to defend his dignity as a human being." If the working people in modern industrial society are ever to obtain freedom, their social liberation must be the result of their own determined efforts to throw the boot of the oppressor off their necks. "Not even the most liberal regime confers rights and freedoms upon a nation on its own initiative; it does so only when the resistance of the people can no longer be ignored."[30]

In calling upon the laboring people to organize themselves in resistance to formal power and government, Rocker did not indulge himself in irresponsible or unsocial rhetoric, nor did he call for the violent overthrow of existing political structure in one great cataclysmic event. Recognizing that those who possess power never give it up voluntarily, Rocker, drawing upon the wisdom of Proudhon, nevertheless urged that the coming socialism he called for must be libertarian in character if it is to serve as the catalyst for a new and better culture. It is impossible for human beings conditioned by the brutality and widespread injustice of modern capitalism to suddenly transform themselves into social beings capable of living in communism. Accordingly, Rocker argued, men must tune themselves to the demands of the new social order by gradually withdrawing from existing conditions through a program of voluntary economic and political decentralization. Following Proudhon's concept of independent communes federally associated on the basis of free agreement, anarcho-syndicalists propose that the present system of economic capitalism gradually be replaced by a federation of communities bound together only by mutual agreement and free contract. In effect, then, the fundamental objective of anarchists must be "pre-eminently a work of education to prepare the people intellectually and psychologically for the tasks of their social liberation."[31] And it is to be expected that the reorientation of people to libertarian values cannot realistically be expected to be completed in less than several decades.

It is not to be assumed, however, that the concept of social education proposed by Rocker and other anarcho-syndicalists was a subtle disguise for quiescence. To the contrary, social education for Rocker was synonymous with social action. Holding that "the people owe all the politcal rights and privileges which we enjoy today . . . not to the good will of their governments but to their own strength," Rocker urged upon the workers a vigorous program of direct action in shop and factory. Not only should the laboring people employ the general strike in their wage struggle against capital but they should be ready to use the boycott, industrial sabotage, and "in peculiarly critical cases, such for example, as that of Spain today, armed resistance of the people for the protection of life and liberty."[32] In every epoch of history, Rocker argued, there is a special mode of social and political thought and action that is appropriate to the times. In the modern period, political revolution as a means to social progress and liberation is no longer efficacious. The problem that is most peculiar to modern life, he urged, is that of industrial centralization and monopoly under capitalism, and it is through the solution of this central crisis that the liberation of humanity must take place. "Only in the realm of economy are the workers able to display their full social strength," Rocker proclaimed, "for it is their activity as producers which holds together the whole social structure, and guarantees the existence of society at all."[33]

Forming themselves into trade unions, the exploited thereby penetrate the structure of the existing economic and political order and at the same time create the model for the new socialistic order of the future. In this connection it is highly important to recognize, according to Rocke, that:

> Every new social structure makes organs for itself in the body of the old organism. Without this preliminary any social evolution is unthinkable. Even

revolutions can only develop and mature the germs which already exist and have
made their way into the consciousness of men; they cannot themselves create
these germs or generate new worlds out of nothing.[34]

The kind of trade union supported by anarcho-syndicalism, however, was significantly different from the kind actually developed
in America, and this difference consisted of anarchism's foundations
in enlightened free thought. Had Tom Paine lived on into the
twentieth century, he might well have written, as Rudolf Rocker
did, that the unity of action sought by labor in its war with capital
must be "sprung from inner conviction which finds expression in
the vital solidarity of all. It must be the voluntary spirit, working
from within outward, which does not exhaust itself in mindless
imitation of prescribed patterns permitting no personal initiative."[35]
Outspokenly critical of the centralization which characterizes
the politcal labor parties that have developed in America, anarcho-
syndicalism boasts that the principle of federalism it supports is
characterized by "free combination from below upward, putting
the right of self-determination on every member above everything
else and recognizing only the organic agreement of all on the basis
of like interests and common convictions."[36] For in final analysis,
according to Rocker, "Only freedom can inspire men to great
things and bring about intellectual and social transformation."
For "Freedom is the very essence of life, the impelling force in
all intellectual and social development, the creator of every new
outlook for the future of mankind."[37] Socialism, accordingly,
can measure its forward progress only by the degree of freedom
it brings to mankind and not by the material progress that the
worker enjoys. Rocker adroitly demonstrated the natural com-
patability of socialism with anarchism when he wrote:

> Whoever believes that freedom of the personality can find a substitute in
> equality of possessions has not even grasped the essence of socialism. For freedom
> there is no substitute; there can be no substitute. Equality of economic situation
> for each and all is always a necessary precondition for the freedom of man, but
> never a substitute for it. Whoever transgresses against freedom transgresses
> against the spirit of socialism.[38]

In view of the thoughts expressed above, it is not difficult to
see how Rudolf Rocker, a comparatively late comer on the American
scene and a foreigner by birth, was able to serve as a vital link
between the older tradition of anarchism developed by Josiah Warren

and the newer outlook developed by those who were caught up in the sweat and tears imposed upon humanity by modern technology. In his *Pioneers of American Freedom* which was published in 1949, Rocker correctly pointed out that it was Warren who first developed the theory of value that serves as the foundation for modern socialism and not Marx.[39]

Rocker also cautioned his contemporaries that the greatest evil mankind faces lies in the complacency with which the new scientific and industrial developments are accepted and submitted to by the masses of humanity. "The growth of technology at the expense of human personality, and especially the fatalistic submission with which the great majority surrender to this condition," he warned, "is the reason why the desire for freedom is less alive among men today and has with many of them given place completely to a desire for economic security."[40] Had Rocker lived on into the sixties he would in all likelihood have joined those anarchists who focused their attention upon technology as the central threat to mankind's freedom, just as he had criticized Kropotkin several decades previously for failing to recognize the dangerous implications of the machine to human culture.

It is impossible to overexaggerate the influence that Rocker exerted over American anarchism in the period just preceding World War II. When he came to America in 1933, Rocker was immediately in great demand as a speaker before Yiddish anarchist circles that remembered him for his sparkling performance in England prior to World War I, and before long he was addressing American audiences in English as well as Yiddish and his native German. A magnificent speaker in whatever language he employed, Rocker won over his listeners more by the power of rational persuasion than by flamboyancy or personal charisma, although he was certainly an individual who possessed great charm and human warmth. So profound was his impact upon American libertarians that in December 1939 he shared the honors with Bertrand Russell at a reception in Los Angeles intended to acknowledge their outstanding scholarship and personal courage.[41] It was also in Los Angeles that the Rocker Publications Committee was formed to provide for the translation and distribution of Rocker's numerous books.[42] Not only was *Nationalism and Culture* published in German and English but there was a Spanish and Chinese edition, indicating the cosmopolitan nature of libertarian philosophy.[43] Unhappily Rocker's last years were disturbed by the controversy that raged over his support of the allied offensive against Hitler's Germany, Rocker arguing that World War II is one war that is justifiable in terms of the ultimate preservation of libertarian values. Given the fact that Rocker had opposed his teacher, Peter Kropotkin, for the same sort of rationalization during World War I, his position elicited a particularly bitter reaction from some American anarchists.[44] And still on the occasion of his eightieth birthday dinner held in London in 1953, messages of gratitude for his great intellectual vigor were read from such outstanding personages as Thomas Mann, Albert Einstein, Herbert Read, and Bertrand Russell. After all the pluses and minuses had been balanced off against each other, Rudolf Rocker still stands out as one of the great figures in American anarchism and anyone inclined toward the philosophy of libertarianism would be well advised to make himself familiar with his writings.

NOTES

SECTION VI - CHAPTER 1

1. Bartolomeo Vanzetti, *The Story of a Proletarian Life,* trans. by Eugene Lyons (Boston, 1924), p. 9.

2. *Ibid.,* p. 11.

3. *Ibid.,* p. 13.

4. *The Letters of Sacco and Vanzetti,* ed. by Marion Denman Frankfurter and Gardner Jackson (New York, 1960), p. v.

5. "Catholic Anarchist; A Review of Ammon Hennacy's *Autobiography of a Catholic Anarchist,"* *Resistance,* XII (June, 1954), 12.

6. "Sacco and Vanzetti," *Man!,* VII (August, 1939), 515.

7. "Sacco and Vanzetti as I Knew Them," *The Road to Freedom,* IV (October, 1927), 3.

8. *The Letters of Sacco and Vanzetti,* p. 118.

9. "An Appeal to Governor Fuller," *Road to Freedom,* III (June, 1927), 1.

10. *The Letters of Sacco and Vanzetti,* p. 264.

11. *Ibid.,* p. 269.

12. *Ibid.,* p. 309.

13. *Ibid.,* p. 72.

14. "Vanzetti; An Unpublished Letter," *Resistance,* VII (July-August, 1948), 3.

15. *The Letters of Sacco and Vanzetti,* p. 121.

16. Lewis Mumford, "Massachusett's Day of Shame," *Man!,* II (August, 1934), 130.

17. *The Letters of Sacco and Vanzetti,* p. 121.

18. Carlo Tresca, "The Unemployed and the IWW," *Retort,* II (June, 1944), 23.

19. Emma Goldman, "Rudolph Rocker: On the Occasion of his 50th Birthday," (Berlin, March, 1923), in the Ishill Collection, The Houghton Library, Harvard University.

20. Rudolf Rocker, *The London Years,* trans. by Joseph Leftwich (London, 1956), p. 104. For a glimpse into the depth of the love Rocker felt for his companion, see Rudolf Rocker, *Milly Witcop Rocker* (Berkley Heights, N.J., 1956).

21. *Nationalism and Culture,* trans. by Ray E. Chase (Los Angeles, 1937), p. 45. This book received excellent reviews. See

Crane Brinton, "Contemporary Nationalism," *The Saturday Review,* XVI (September 4, 1937), 17; and Solomon F. Bloom, "The Dilemma of Anarchism," *The New Republic,* XC (September 22, 1937), 192.

22. *Ibid.,* p. 252.

23. *Ibid.,* p. 170.

24. *Ibid.,* p. 63.

25. *Ibid.,* p. 200.

26. *Anarcho-Syndicalism* (London, 1938), p. 23.

27. *Nationalism and Culture,* p. 526.

28. "Kropotkin as a Scientist,"*The Road to Freedom* (February, 1926), 1.

29. *Anarcho-Syndicalism,* p. 111.

30. "Social Rights and Freedoms: Their Vital Worth to Us," in *The World Scene from the Libertarian Point of View,* p. 12.

31. "Anarchism and Anarcho-Syndicalism," in Paul Eltzbacher, *Anarchism,* p. 244.

32. *Anarcho-Syndicalism,* p. 116.

33. *Ibid.,* p. 88.

34. *Ibid.,* p. 89.

35. *Nationalism and Culture,* p. 535.

36. *Anarcho-Syndicalism,* p. 90.

37. *Ibid.,* p. 33.

38. *Nationalism and Culture,* p. 237.

39. Trans. by Arthur E. Briggs (Los Angeles, 1949), p. 57.

40. *Nationalism and Culture,* p. 254.

41. Cassius V. Cook, "What Rocker's Books Mean to Me," *A Testimonial to Rudolf Rocker* (Los Angeles, 1939), p. 30. For a less complimentary view, see W. J. Fishman, "Rudolf Rocker: Anarchist Missionary," *History Today,* XVI (January, 1966), 45-52.

42. In addition to *Nationalism and Culture* and *Anarcho-Syndicalism,* Rocker's published works include: *The Six, Behind Barbed Wires and Bars, The Life and Times of Johann Most,* and his *Autobiography* of which only one part has been translated under the title *The London Years.*

43. "Rudolf Rocker Dead at 85," *The New York Times* (September 11, 1958).

44. David Weick, "To Our Readers," *Resistance,* VII (November-December, 1948), 16.

CHAPTER 2

Christian Anarchists:
Catholic Workers and Other Religious "Extremists"

Although A. J. Muste (1885-1967) at one time described himself as more of a social democrat than an anarchist,[1] no history
of American anarchism would be complete without some analysis
of his thought, for in spite of his own ideological disclaimer, Muste's
social philosophy embraces the very core of what is lasting in
anarchist thinking even while it remains formally removed from
it. And incongruous as it may seem, the tradition of anarchist
thought he most completely belongs within is the movement of
radical Catholicism.

Born in the Netherlands where he was tutored in the catechism
of the Dutch Reformed Church by a devout mother and father,
Abraham Johannes Muste, as he was christened, became so tinged
with the spirit of Christian love that his entire career as an activist
reflected that outlook, even during the period wherein he had
renounced the idea of Christianity and adhered to the Marxist
teachings of Trotsky instead. When A. J. was six, his father gave
up his position as coachman to a noble Dutch provincial family
to shepherd his brood to America where they settled amidst relatives
in Grand Rapids, Michigan. Upon completing an A. B. degree
at Hope College, A. J. entered the Theological Seminary maintained
by the Dutch Reformed Church in New Brunswick, New Jersey,
where he imbibed even more Calvinist piety. He paused long enough
in his arduous Christian labors to get married after graduating
from the seminary in 1909, and then at the age of 24 found himself pastor of Fort Washington Collegiate Church in Upper Manhatten. Always of a studious turn of mind, A. J. read widely and
took additional course work at N.Y.U., Columbia University, and
Union Theological Seminary, receiving a Bachelor of Divinity degree
magna cum laude from Union in 1913. His rumination on the

pacifist writings of Tolstoy, Gandhi and the Quaker, Rufus Jones, however, tended to lead him away from the strict Calvinist position he had been educated to, and in 1914 he formally broke with Calvinism, resigning his pastorate on Washington Heights and moving to Newtonville, just outside of Boston, where he resumed his Christian vocation by taking over a more liberal Congregational Church.

The social and intellectual climate in Boston at first agreed marvelously with Muste's liberal theological disposition and he gratefully found himself basking in the warmth of the libertarian heritage that had carried over from nineteenth century New England. But as America's entry into World War I became imminent, the pacifistic sentiments he had by this time developed increasingly grated upon the nerves of his patriotic parishioners, and it soon became evident that here was little room within the organized Church for one as unorthodox and controversial as he. Leaving the Congregational Church late in 1917 after having been daubed "traitor," he affiliated himself with the newly created American Civil Liberties Union in the work of helping conscientious objectors protect themselves from the self-righteous harrassment directed against them by the government, and then moved on to Providence where he became a minister in the Society of Friends. A. J. found the non-theology of quakerism perfectly suited to his needs and he soon felt an internal glow as warm as the friendly face on the box of Quaker Oats his loving wife, Anna, kept in her kitchen cabinet.

During the later part of 1918 and the first few months of the next year Muste and his family shared a large run-down house on the fringe of Back Bay Boston with a number of other families who together constituted "The Comradeship," a loose grouping of Friends and members of the Fellowship of Reconciliation who found comfort in the communal living arrangement they had devised. Arising mornings at five o'clock, A. J. and his friend, Harold Rotzel, bundled themselves in their overcoats against the chill of the New England winter to read and reflect upon the Sermon on the Mount and other passages from the New Testament. Muste also read John Dewey, G. D. H. Cole, Marx, Lenin, Trotsky and just about any other author who came to his attention and had something to say on the topic of social justice. In January of 1919 rumblings of discontent from the nearby city of Lowell, where the workers in the textile mills were engaged in a violent clash with management, began to catch the attention of The Comradeship, and A. J. and several other clergymen reconnoitered the situation to see if there was anything in it that concerned them as Christians. Before long A. J. was caught up in the fray, and despite the tactics of nonviolence he introduced into the strike, he experienced his first roughing up at the hands of the establishment. During the next seventeen years A. J. expressed his social conscience by working actively as a union organizer, serving as general secretary of the Amalgamated Textile Workers of America and educational director of the Brookwood Labor College where he collaborated with such leading social thinkers as John Strachey, Harry Overstreet, Harry Elmer Barnes, Reinhold Niebuhr, Norman Thomas, and Roger Baldwin. Associated with Louie Bundenz as co-editor of *Labor Age*, A. J. was instrumental in the organization of the Conference for Progressive Labor in 1929, out of which arose the movement for the formation of an American Labor party on the lines of the British Labour Party. Philosophically, A. J. during this period of his life thought of himself as a Trotskyite and the highlight of his career was his meeting with the man himself in 1936. Ironically it was but a few months after his meeting with Leon Trotsky that A. J. experienced another conversion, this time back to the idea of Christianity to which he remained dedicated to the end of his long, active life.

It is surely the height of irony that A. J. Muste's return to Christianity should take place in the Church of St. Sulpice in Paris. Never one for pomp or sham, A. J. clothed his tall, lanky frame in a threadbare suit that usually looked like he had slept in it and he was totally unconcerned with religious ritual and ceremony. Yet sitting amidst the clutter of religious statuary in St. Sulpice, A. J.'s heart was flooded with light and his mind's eye saw clearly the path that he must from henceforth follow. In the case of his friend and socialist companion, Louie Budenz, conversion meant that he must abruptly turn his back upon the Communists with whom he had formerly associated and enter the Roman Catholic Church in total oblation. For A. J., conversion meant simply that he should continue being a socialist with the simple difference that from now on he would look for justification for his activism not in the complicated political doctrine of Marxism but in the simple message of Christ's suffering upon the cross. During the trotskyite phase of his life A. J. had shared the Leftist vision of a world in which social classes and national wars would be eliminated once and for all. Here in a sense, he wrote, "was the true church. Here was the fellowship drawn together and drawn forward by the Judeo-Christian prophetic vision of 'a new earth in which righteousness dwelleth.' "[2] Obviously "the church" for A. J. Muste was more spirit than it was organization, doctrine, and physical structure. Whether he served mankind from within a radical political party or an organized religious association made little difference to him so long as the motives from which he acted were in keeping with the spirit of love and devotion that Christ demonstrated upon the cross.

The fact that A. J. during the Twenties had been active in supporting the Progressive Party campaign of Robert M. LaFollette and that he generally voted the Socialist ticket would tend to suggest that he was miles away from the anarchist's total rejection of political power as a means of effecting social order on this earth. But when one reads deeper into his politcial theory it becomes abundantly evident that A. J. Muste was an implacable foe of all manipulation of man over man, whether the impetus for that manipulation arose on the Left or the Right. Nowhere is this more pronounced than in his realization that the Trotsky that he had so greatly admired for the nobility of his social ideals during his flirtation with Marxism was just as capable of ruthless opportunism as Stalin.[3] It was this stark realization that caused him to write:

> Inextricably mingled with an in the end corrupting, thwarting, largely defeating all that is fine, idealistic, courageous, self-sacrificing in the proletarian movement is the philosophy of power, the will to power, the desire to humiliate and dominate over or destroy the opponent, the acceptance of methods of violence and deceit, the theory that "the end justifies the means." There is a succumbing to the spirit which so largely dominates the existing social and political order and an acceptance of the methods of capitalism at its worst.[4]

While still a practicing trotskyite, A. J. had himself denied the "theory of 'spontaneity' of the masses." "It is our position," he wrote, "that the leadership of the revolutionary Marxian party is indispensable for the success of the proletarian revolution."[5] Three years after his religious experience in St. Sulpice, however, A. J. had come full circle on the question of the necessity of the party. "Lenin," he now held, "was really concerned about two things: the nature and structure of a revolutionary party and how the party might acquire state power."[6] Just as much as Emma Goldman or Alexander Berkman, A. J. found this aspect of Bolshevism thoroughly revolting and from this point to the end of his life he consistently remained opposed to all proposals that suggested that institutionalized political power might be used to serve human good.

One cannot read A. J.'s political essays without receiving the distinct impression that here was one of the most faithful sons the Enlightenment ever produced in America, for not only did he share the Enlightenment's unbounded faith in the individual as the key figure in the struggle for freedom but he was as adamantly opposed to circumscribing the spontaneous revolutionary forces that individualism inevitably gives rise to as were Tom Paine and Elihu Palmer during an earlier age. "We live in a time when the individual is in danger of becoming a cipher," Muste wrote several years after the end of World War II. "He is overwhelmed by the vast and intricate technological machinery around which his working life is organized, by the high-powered propaganda to which he is incessantly subjected, and by the state-machine on which he is increasingly dependent and by which he is increasingly regimented in peace and war."[7] Reacting against the "neo-orthodoxy" of such Christians as Emil Brunner, Reinhold Niebuhr, and Karl Barth, A. J. strongly condemned the pessimistic view that man lacks the strength to fashion a world free from warfare and other forms of mass violence and that he must therefore seek protection from the state, proportedly the only source of law and order on earth. Far from being a force of law and order, A. J. complained, the "war-making power state" of our day is intimately connected with the totalitarianism that presses down upon us like a thick blanket of fog and which has caused us to lose sight of our utlimate goal of human freedom. Long before most liberal thinkers had any inkling whatever that something had gone wrong with democracy, A. J. pronounced the warfare state the major source of the totalitarian systems that have dominated both the socialist and the non-socialist countries since World War II. Those who would work toward peace through the political party should bear in mind that "control over the national government . . . almost always comes to mean control over the machinery of a war-making power state,"

A. J. warned.[8]

Although it was Tolstoy that first turned A. J. in the direction of radical libertarianism, it was his reading in the nonviolent theories of Gandhi that ultimately led him to adopt a basically anarchistic outlook toward power and violence. Implicit in Gandhi's conception of Satyagraha is the outline of a fully developed theory of anarchism that relies upon the free cooperation of individuals against the power-tainted state.[9] It was most certainly under Gandhian influence that A. J. wrote: "Non-conformity, Holy Disobedience, becomes a virtue, indeed a necessary and indispensable measure of spiritual self-preservation in a day when the impulse to conform, to acquiesce, to go along, is used as an instrument to subject men to totalitarian rule and involve them in permanent war."[10] Steeped as he was in the Christian value of love, A. J. yet held that it is impossible to realize the basic religious ideals of Christianity unless the individual shares the same intense moral fervor and dedication that characterized Christ's activism. Liberation, for A. J., was both religious and political at one and the same time, for in his opinion the line between these two human activities is so fine that they really can't be distinguished from one another. "In a world built on violence, one must be a revolutionary before one can be a pacifist," he wrote; "in such a world a non-revolutionary pacifist is a contradiction in terms, a monstrosity."[11] To the objection that Christ was apolitical and that his emphasis of love and understanding denied his followers the right to actively resist their oppressors, A. J. countered by pointing out that there is no contradiction whatever between rebellion against tyranny and the demands of Christian morality, for he argued:

> What Jesus objected to was not the great religious act of human beings moving out of Egypt into Canaan, out of bondage and insecurity into freedom, security and peace. What grieved him was that men were forever moving out of bondage—*into bondage!* They escaped from the violence of another to fasten the chains of violence on themselves. This terrible evil circle must be broken.[12]

In the final analysis A. J.'s philosophy of nonviolence was not an escape from the reality of life but a soberly conceived libertarian technique whereby the individual might directly confront violence and ruthless force and yet avoid the corruption he would have suffered had he taken up arms in emulation of his adversary.[13] Like David facing Goliath, the individual armed only with dedication to nonviolent means appears weak and insignificant as he stands before the powerful super-states of the nuclear age. But for all the advantage the state may appear to possess, A. J. held, it has no power great enough to defeat dedicated individuals who band together to put themselves in determined opposition to its immoral opportunism. Although it was Gandhi and not Thoreau or Bakunin from whom he got the inspiration, A. J. Muste was very much an anarchist when he pointed out that "unjust laws and practices survive because men obey and conform to them." The antidote to the violent fevers of modern totalitarianism, he argued, is to be found in the practice of unserving dedication to the example of Jesus upon the cross." . . . whenever a true Crucifixion takes place, unconquerable power is released into the stream of history," he proclaimed.[14] It may well be that most men lack the courage and conviction to rise to the heights demanded of them by A. J. Muste. But as the dangers of the nuclear era become progressively more frightening, it becomes increasingly clear that the kind of far-reaching social solutions he reached for are the only ones adequate to the crises we face.

One of the surprising turns the anarchist idea has experienced in America has been its adoption in recent years by a number of practicing Roman Catholics, the most famous of whom is Dorothy Day. Born in Bath Beach, Brooklyn in 1897, Dorothy Day very early broke with the middle class values of her father who was a newspaperman, to begin shopping around for a political ideology that would be more satisfying to the compelling inner thirst she felt for spiritual fulfillment. Consuming the writings of Dostoevski and Tolstoy, Kropotkin, Vera Figner, and just about all the social novelists, Dorothy swung further and further to the Left, joining the Socialist Party while a student at the University of Illinois. But there was an indefinable restlessness within her that did not permit her real peace of mind and she continued her search for social fulfillment by reading everything she could get her hands on. Finding the intricacies of Marxist theory a bit too obscure, not to mention dull, she shifted toward the I.W.W. point of view more because it presented an immediate relevancy to the problems of American life then because it definitively answered the pressing social questions that kept her brain throbbing during her youth.[15] Going to work as a reporter, first on the *Call* and later on *The*

Masses, she came to meet and know many of the great and near great of American radicalism, including Hippolyte Havel, Eugene O'Neill, Floyd Dell and Terry Karlin. Although she never officially carried a Communist Party card, many of her friends were either Communists or anarchists and she considered herself generally to be in community with them all, whatever labels they might attach to themselves. In many respects she felt herself to be more a Tolstoyan than anything else, however, for Tolstoy's deep spiritual convictions appealed to her own profound religious yearnings. But as the years followed one another she began to realize that since her attraction to radicalism was essentially a search for community and personal religious fulfillment, she at some point would be compelled to enter the Roman Catholic Church.

On first sight it would appear that Dorothy Day's conversion to Catholicism places her outside the purview of American anarchism with its roots deep in enlightened free thought and radical libertarianism. And indeed it did have this immediate effect in terms of her personal life, for at the time of her conversion she was living happily on the desolate beaches of Staten Island with a free thinking anarchist who abundantly returned the deep love she felt for him until her impending entrance into the Church raised an insurmountable barrier between them. The great paradox of all this, as Dorothy described it in her autobiography, was that the birth of their child which should have tied them more closely together was the occasion for their drifting apart. "No human creature could receive or contain so vast a flood of love and joy as I felt after the birth of my child," Dorothy wrote. "With this came the need to worship, to adore."[16] The choice before her, as Dorothy saw it, was monumental in its consequences; she could continue loving the father of her child and enjoy earthly happiness, or give her love to God in anticipation of a more lasting and profound relationship. Thus it was that she fled into the arms of the Church while her lover and mate, unable to fit her religious conversion into the loosely structured design of the cosmos that he was contained by, took to flight. Whether she was right or wrong in making this decision, she realized, would only appear clear with time; for the moment, all she could do was to pray for strength and keep the faith she had so recently adopted.

After becoming a Catholic, Dorothy was no longer so greatly plagued by the religious longing that had formerly nibbled at her soul but now she suffered from a new torment—the realization that the vast majority of the communicants with whom she shared the mass and other sacraments were hollow creatures without sense or feelings when it came to the crushing social evils that dominate life in America. Temperamentally an activist, Dorothy never enjoyed standing on the sidelines while others did her fighting for her; it was this side of her character that had led to her first jail term during the Suffragette era after the First World War. As a practicing Catholic, therefore, she felt bitter resentment at the thought that the religion she had embraced produced little or no effective social consciousness in the face of the poverty and suffering that appeared on every side following the crash of the stock market and the start of the Great Depression during the early Thirties. On returning to New York after covering the Hunger March on Washington for *The Commonweal,* she found Peter Maurin waiting for her. The event was earthshaking in terms of her own social and religious development, for Peter, a "French peasant," had a message to give her as he happily spoke his mind concerning the things a good Catholic should know and do about poverty and hunger. It was out of this meeting that The Catholic Worker movement originated.

At basis the Catholic Worker Movement was an outgrowth of the personalist religious philosophy Dorothy Day perfected as a practicing Catholic. Fundamental to it was the attitude toward poverty she acquired from Peter Maurin. "I condemn poverty and I advocate it; poverty is simple and complex at once; it is a social pheonomenon and a personal matter," she wrote. "Poverty is an elusive thing, and a paradoxical one."[17] Translated into terms of the actual conduct it gave rise to within her own personal existence, the voluntary acceptance of poverty was living demonstration that Dorothy Day and all those who associated themselves with the Catholic Worker Movement had consecrated their lives to serving God; it was a return to the simple life advocated by Jesus. In its physical aspect, of course, *The Catholic Worker* was a messenger dedicated to spreading the propaganda of radical catholicism to all who would voluntarily accept it. Using the contributions that it has prompted from its readers, the Catholic Worker Movement since its establishment in 1933 has maintained houses of hospitality where the poor could find both physical shelter and spiritual comfort. But while the essential spirit of the movement is Catholic, the ideas it is based on are derived from the anarchism of Peter Kropotkin, Eric Gill, and Peter Maurin himself. It was Maurin who advised Dorothy to take up and read Kropotkin's *Fields, Factories, and Workshops, Mutual Aid,* and *The Conquest of Bread,* and it was Maurin's *Easy Essays* that convinced her that the state has nothing to teach us about the serious business of charity and that this is the one thing above all others that must be left to the people themselves.

Far from being the opiate of the people, religion, in Dorothy Day's hands, was a tool by which she has sought to create a more libertarian world after the idea of anarchism. Religious tradition and ritual, to be sure, play a far greater role in her life than they do in the lives of most other anarchists, and hence it is difficult to fit her into the overall pattern of anarchist thought. Yet when we lay aside the stereotypes we all unconsciously employ to force order upon the disparate and contradictory world we live in, we see that the very attitude of simple faith that characterizes the Catholic Worker Movement is anarchistic in essence. As Dorothy Day views the problem of living in the modern age, the essential task is to somehow penetrate the facade of false security and unthinking complacency that most people hide behind. Bombarded constantly with superficialities from the mass media and the advertising industry, the individual stands in constant danger of becoming made over into the slick image his seducers would like to force upon him; his smoking, his drinking, his lovemaking, and above all his war making, are all more the will of the hucksters who surround him than they are freely willed acts on his part. How, then, are we to make contact with so plastic a being in a day when technology and mass institutions dominate all? The Catholic Worker's answer to this imbroglio is to revert to the simple faith of Jesus in all of one's relationships. Men in the mass may well have been homogonized by the social and political processes of modern life but beneath the superficiality of their collective consciousness they still retain their basic humanity and can freely respond to basic religious truths when they are confronted by them.[18] This is why the doors of the hospices operated by the Catholic Worker Movement are kept open to all without question. The drunk or the petty "criminal" may well be troublesome to deal with but they, too, are capable of responding to simple acts of human kindness or concern and can thereby be made whole again. The "high and the mighty" are more difficult to reach but even they are potentially responsive to personal acts of faith and charity.

However much simplicity and straightforwardness may have been emphasized by Dorothy Day and Peter Maurin, the anarchism contained in the pages of *The Catholic Worker* over the years has been anything but simpleminded. Reviewing such books as Ignace Lepp's *The Christian Failure* (1962), the *Catholic Worker* addressed itself to the problem of how freedom might be attained in a world in which the prevailing mass psychology allows individuals to hide behind such vapid myths as the irrational fear of communism that has gripped both Europe and America since the overthrow of the old Czarist system. Nuclear warfare, the reviewer pointed out, has been made possible by a "psychology of evasion and helplessness, glorified and encouraged by persons in authority who are able to take advantage of it. . . ." Far from being an acceptable Catholic posture, the mass hysteria that prevails everywhere in the face of Communism is "a subservient opportunism which, in reality, has nothing Christian about it, but on the contrary, gives ample scope for the irresponsibility of the mass mind and in the end threatens to destroy both Christian and democratic liberty."[19] Advising his readers to struggle mightily against the myths that blind them to true reality, the reviewer reflected the essential outline of enlightened free thought, however much he argued the wisdom of retaining the basic structure and community of the Roman Catholic Church. Obviously for him as for Tom Paine, the "Church" was essentially a spiritual principle or truth rather than a concrete structure or institution and the means to salvation lay in rational individual judgment and moral courage instead of dumb collective acquiescence or conformity. This broad, sensitive outlook characterizes the whole of the Catholic Worker Movement and permits us to think of it as an outgrowth of libertarianism.

An appealing definition of Catholic anarchism was contributed by Karl Meyer from Chicago where he was active in the labor movement of that city. Categorizing the major principles of Catholic anarchism as "obedience and order," Meyer called upon Christians everywhere to free themselves from the hierarchical structure of their church which they fearfully curled themselves up in as though it were a huge, protective womb that could protect them from all outside dangers. "Anarchist obedience is," according to Meyer, "obedience to reason instead of hierarchy, obedience to love instead of power, obedience freely given instead of coerced, obedience to all men instead of special classes of men."[20] Jesus himself was an anarchist, Meyer proclaimed, because he ignored the power structures of this world and dedicated himself to charity and mercy without any thought of his own vulnerability or powerlessness, and true social order will come on the day that people are allowed to conduct their own lives without interference from rulers or imposed authority. Coercion, in fact, according to Meyer, is "the sign and seed of disorder." An anarchist is one who refuses under any and all circumstances to cooperate with the legal and political systems of this world that attempt to obtain good ends by employing the very same kind of destructive means they have taken upon themselves to judge.

Catholic anarchism, following the tradition of nonviolence practiced by Jesus and his followers, does not call upon the Christian to submit meekly to the evil notions of corrupt and tyrannical governments, however, but to the contrary, calls upon him to resist tyranny with all his moral might. As one contributor of the *Catholic Worker* argued, in order for "Christians to recover the Gospel and the cross today it is necessary that they develop, and learn to live by, a theology of resistance."[21] Such a posture inevitably pits the individual against the government in those instances when it uses its power in immoral and antisocial ways. Tension between the individual and his government is not a wholly new thing to Christianity, for Jesus himself "was killed by the State." It is perfectly true, of course, that governments have come a long way since the crucifixion and rarely in the democracies, at least, are the same crude methods of murder and torture employed that were employed in Jesus' day. But governments still maim and murder as brutally as they always did, only now they operate on a much broader scale and their propaganda ministries make the evil they do look either harmless or so necessary to the common good that no individual can question it. Yet we must question evil and resist it wherever we meet it, especially in an age such as our own when governments undertake wars of extermination against helpless underdeveloped nations without apparent good cause.

Perhaps the charge that has most often been directed at the Catholic Worker Movement, especially by other Catholics, is that its members are a bit too zealous, too ready to offer themselves as martyrs, too impressed with their own importance. But one searches Dorothy Day's writings in vain for any symptom of bloated ego. "People probably do not realize with what fear and trembling I speak or write about the Catholic Worker, our ideas and our point of view," she once wrote.[22] The task of the radical Catholic is not an easy one, she pointed out, for once we have assumed an extreme position, "it is almost as if God says to us, 'do you really mean what you say?,' and then gives us a chance to prove it." In her own life Dorothy Day has demonstrated her devotion to Christian action in a thousand ways. One such instance was her participation in the act of civil disobedience against the mock civil defense exercises staged in New York City during 1957. Arrested along with many others for her part in the action, Dorothy served her time without concern for her own health or comfort, and then wrote that being in jail "gave me a chance to tell the other prisoners about Tolstoy, and how he said that the first move toward reform was to do one's own work."[23] Although our action may not bring the American military machine to its knees, she admitted, at least we are not guilty of the "prevailing sin of our age" which is a feeling of hopelessness and despair at the mere thought of any kind of moral or social endeavor.

Reflecting a simple, unassuming trust in love that seems almost conservative in its adherence to basic religious teachings, Dorothy Day called for a program of direct action that drew directly from the individual's inner resources. "If we do the right thing, unquestioningly; if we pray that God will water the seed that we plant; then we can have faith that He will give the increase," she urged.[24] Yet she is well aware that it is not easy to be certain that one's motives are always pure, even with regard to so basic a virtue as voluntary poverty. Do we really want to live with the poor without money or property, or do we merely seek the luxury of sitting idle in the sun totally without responsibility while we watch the children at play or catch up on the reading that we were unable to do while we were working at our conventional jobs?[25] Like Proudhon before her, Dorothy Day is unafraid of the paradoxical and contradictory, recognizing that life itself is a series of irreconcilable opposites that can only be fully understood at the end of history. We are to be judged not by the ideals we profess to believe in but by the acts that we do in this life, she urged, although we must wait patiently until some time in the future before the ultimate effect of our actions becomes clear. One does not have to wait to recognize, however, that Dorothy Day's steadfast refusal to acknowledge the powerful warmaking states of our day as legitimate agencies of social control makes her libertarian in every sense of the term. Who but a libertarian would renounce all power and trust one's fate to the social forces we share in mutual aid with each other?

If anarchism were given to crowning its great with sainthood, surely Ammon Hennacy (1893-1970) would be among the first to receive that special rank, for his devotion to the cause of freedom was almost superhuman in character. Intensely religious in all that he said and did in life, Ammon Hennacy was yet so unorthodox and unstructured in his personal beliefs that no church was flexible enough to contain him for very long. Born on a farm in Negly, Ohio, Ammon's unorthodoxy was partly determined by the latitudinarianism he was exposed to as a youngster. The name of John Brown was uttered with reverence in the Hennacy household and he was ten years old, he confessed in his autobiography, before he "knew the difference between God, Moses, and John Brown."[26] Stemming from old Quaker stock, Ammon at the age of twelve had himself baptized in the local Baptist Church after experiencing conversion during a moving six week long revival meeting and in his youthful spiritual enthusiasm he fancied himself cut out for the vocation of a missionary. After witnessing the famous Billy Sunday twirl the minds of his gullible followers around like the gold watch on the end of his chain, however, Ammon, a few years after his baptism arose in church and announced to the wide-eyed, open-mouthed congregation that he no longer considered himself a Christian as he had become an athiest and did not believe in the Bible. After attending Hiram College in his freshman year, Ammon enrolled at the University of Wisconsin where he became a Socialist and received some public attention when he was the only individual courageous enough to undertake the task of introducing the notorious Emma Goldman when she came to the campus to speak. Little did he know at the time that he would later join in the crusade against bigotry and organized power that she waged. At the time, however, he was an active participant in the ROTC program at the University and still had much to learn before he could properly refer to himself as an anarchist.

A crucial turning point took place in Ammon Hennacy's political and spiritual development when during World War I he was imprisoned for two years in Atlanta Federal Penitentiary for refusing to register for the draft. Prison for most men is a veritable purgatory in which they live and relive the sins of their youth over and over again. But for Ammon it was more like a religious retreat, for the depressing atmosphere created by the damp stone walls and iron bars that shut him in, released irrepressible spiritual forces within him and from that point on he commenced his "one man revolution" against the deceit and injustice of the organized world without. Brutally confined in solitary for seven months by an inhumane warden for leading a demonstration against the rotten fish served to the prison's inmates, Ammon seriously considered suicide by cutting his wrists with a knife fashioned from a tin spoon and it was only his Irish stubbornness that kept him from going through with this act of self-destruction. The main thing that prevented Ammon from losing his grip on sanity was the brief glimpse he was able to steal every now and then of Alexander Berkman's bald head as he worked in the tailor shop across the way from the solitary confinement cage. Ammon had read Berkman's *Prison Memoirs of an Anarchist* the year before he was sent to Atlanta where Berkman was already imprisoned and he was captivated by the sincerity and nobility Berkman dedicated to his cause. In Ammon Hennacy's opinion there was no greater believer in truth and justice than Alexander Berkman and he determined to make his own life reflect the courage and moral strength demonstrated by his hero.

As difficult as it will be for some to believe, it was this very Alexander Berkman known far and wide as a wild and ferocious slayer of capitalists that first convinced Ammon Hennacy that real revolution is only possible where one has first laid aside his own sword and turned instead to love and understanding. Pacing miserably back and forth one day in the dark confinement of solitary, the true meaning of the Sermon on the Mount suddenly illuminated Hennacy's brain as though it were a flare shot above a battlefield on a dark, moonless night, and in the days that followed he was to read that portion of the Bible over and over again. Just as Alexander Berkman loved even those who tortured him with the loss of his precious personal freedom, so Ammon Hennacy now saw that he must love those who tortured him, even including the narrow-minded warden who showed more mercy toward the rats and mice that plagued the prison than he did toward the human beings who languished in it. It was this experience that led Ammon back to Christianity. Girded now in the impregnable armor of Christian charity and spiritual dedication, he went forth to do battle with the forces of unenlightened authority and repression wherever they might be found.

When Ammon Hennacy decided to do something, he did it with complete abandon until he had exhausted the great store of energy housed within his lean but powerful physical frame, and so it was with his Christian anarchism. Immediately upon his release from prison he pooled his resources with those of an old love, Selma, and together they took to homesteading in Wisconsin on ten acres on which he erected a log cabin. Raising vegetables and chickens along with two daughters that were born to them in 1927 and 1929, Ammon and Selma experienced great happiness together as they sought their independence by waging the green revolution advocated by Tolstoy and other Christian anarchists. After six years of homesteading, however, they were unable to meet their mortgage payments and Ammon was forced to take a job as a social worker in Milwaukee to keep his family alive. It was in Milwaukee that he first met Dorothy Day and fell in love with the radical Christian teachings by which she conducted her own life. In the meanwhile, Selma had found a spiritual faith of her own and the strict regulations of her sect tended to separate Ammon and herself from the commonlaw arrangement that had formed them into a family. As each went his own way, Ammon revamped his life in such a way that he could devote his entire energy to the pursuit of the spiritual goals he had set for himself.

Abstaining from eating meat and refusing to pay taxes to the state so long as it continued to deny the Sermon on the Mount, Ammon accepted only those jobs in which he was paid by the day so that the government could not withhold any part of his wages in support of its prisons, courts, and armies. Practicing the simple, straightforward spiritualism of Tolstoy and Gandhi, he trusted his fate to God, never taking thought of his own interests and never returning hatred when it was directed at him by those who could not understand his philosophy of life. More often than not, those who came into contact with Ammon Hennacy thought him to be some kind of deranged zealot, for he adamantly refused to recognize as legitimate those laws and authorities that the average man accepts as the basic firmament of the social universe. Even Dorothy Day, the most understanding and kindred of souls, had difficulty in accepting the extreme stand he took toward religious authority.

There never was a time, Ammon once confessed to Dorothy, when he was not in love with some woman.[27] When Ammon fell in love with Dorothy, it was the beauty of her spiritual personality rather than her physical attributes that led him to idealize her, and thus he was led to join the Catholic Church within which he remained for fifteen years until he found it too confining with respect to his boundless energy. But if he "had no mind for philosophy or theology," he had dedication and courage far beyond that which most men within the Church or Catholic Worker Movement were able to muster and hence it was Ammon who was among the most steadfast in refusing to own property or violate his basic spiritual principles in any way. Although Ammon only remained with the Catholic Worker Movement from 1953 to 1963, he was with it "long enough to make an impression on that great pagan city of New York," before he went off to start his own mission, The Joe Hill House, in Salt Lake City.

To the charge that he never was a genuine Catholic, Ammon Hennacy wittily replied: "Whether I left the Church or the Church left me depends upon how you look at the question."[28] In one respect, Ammon could not really be said to have accepted the Church's teaching entirely, for his stand toward its organization was far too unyielding to permit that claim. The sacraments, for example, meant nothing whatever to him, and although he was intellectually convinced of the correctness of the Church's stand toward authority in moral and spiritual matters, he never could quite bring himself to give up his independence in deciding for himself what was right and what was not. This often led him to take positions that placed him completely beyond the pale of organized Catholicism. It is to be noted, however, that his criticism of the Catholic Church was not aimed so much at its teachings as it was at the loose way in which its teachings were applied in the everyday lives of those who belonged to it. When he did disagree with one or another of the Church's principles, his disagreement was invariably based upon his own fervent dedication to Christian ideals as he interpreted them. "It is not my fault," he once complained, "that the Church makes itself look foolish by insisting on the wickedness of birth control because it is mechanical when she takes all the rest of the mechanical civilization that goes with it: Atom Bomb and all."[29] Christened "John the Baptist" when he converted to Catholicism, Ammon Hennacy stood ready to trust his fate entirely to God, and unlike most people, he had no hidden mental reservations to keep him from going through with the bargain as he had made it. "God, or Good, as I prefer to spell it," he wrote, "is the only *real* force that exists." Unfortunately, he urged, most people believe more in power than they believe in God, for they actually "put their trust in government, insurance, politicans, medicine, war, and anything but God."[30] Whatever theological indiscretions Ammon Hennacy may have been guilty of, he was too good a Christian to allow himself to take anything but a thoroughgoing libertarian stance in his relationships with his fellowmen.

In many respects, Ammon Hennacy's autobiography, *The Book of Ammon*, is one of the finest sources of anarchist philosophy and theory available. Written in the simple, trusting style that characterized all that he said or did, its pages contain a wealth of information regarding the ways of libertarianism. Anthropologists could journey to such faraway places as the South Seas or the Phillipines in search of primitive man living in pristine harmony with nature but Ammon had no need to travel so far, for he found in the Hopi Indians of Arizona all the data he needed to construct his social theory. Where contemporary Americans turn to science and technology for the means to make themselves happy, the Hopi tune themselves to nature and thus find the key to living harmoniously together. "The major sin they recognize is to try to get even with the neighbor who may have wronged them. Their wholesome culture rests upon each individual's complete acceptance of responsibility for the consequences of his motivations as well as his actions, and their keen awareness of the spiritual significance of life."[31] In effect, according to Ammon, these are the views of Christian anarchism, and the Hopi who have been living this lifestyle in America for over a thousand years are among the oldest libertarians in the country.

With respect to the internecine struggles over doctrine that has so often plagued American anarchists, Ammon Hennacy spoke to the issues in the same straightforward manner that he lived his own life. Anarcho-syndicalists in looking toward organized labor for the strength to change society after a better image were, in his opinion, ill-advised as to technique. "For anarchists to rely upon the organized might of the workers to establish their power, whether by force or by strength of organization, is an illusion," he wrote.[32] Citing Kropotkin and Edward Carpenter as the sources of his bias, Ammon argued that society will be saved not by the machine or science but by the individual who is inspired to break from existing conditions to create the form of a better social world. "Worthwhile social change will only come *voluntarily from within each individual*, and not through groups." he insisted.[33] This, as he interpreted things, was the meaning of Christ's admonition that the Kingdom of God lies within the breast of each one of us. What we must do if we would build a better world, he urged, is to trust to the internal forces we find within our own natures, refusing any longer to rely upon the organized machinery of the state for our security and happiness. And above all we must have the courage to persist in the pursuit of our ideals in the face of brutal and even violent opposition so that those who follow us will recognize the importance of doing the same thing in their own lives.

If devotion to duty is any measure of one's philosophical perspicacity Ammon Hennacy surely stands out as one of the greatest of all American anarchists. Jailed thirty-two times in eight different states for various acts of civil disobedience, he stood as a constant reminder to the authorities that their power as symbolized by the police and military could have little real deterrent force on one who refused to be cowed. With A. J. Muste, Ammon Hennacy went over the fence at Omaha in 1959 to demonstrate to the airforce that all the sophisticated instruments of modern high-level bombing in which the crews never see their human targets cannot hide the immorality of air warfare from those who have the eyes to see it. And it was Ammon Hennacy who stood just behind Rocco Parelli, the innocent bootblack who was herded by the police into a van to be charged with breaking New York State's civil defense laws in June of 1955. The only thing that Rocco Parelli was guilty of was not knowing that it was a criminal offense to fail to take shelter when New York City conducted one of its mock air raids in preparation for nuclear attacks that might come later should the architects of American policy decide to risk World War III. Ammon Hennacy felt that the real crime was for the authorities to lead innocent men, women and children to believe that nuclear warfare is a thinkable alternative to peace, and hence he sent out a call to other brave souls to come join him in mocking Caesar for his irrationality. Supported by Dorothy Day, A. J. Muste, Baynard Rustin, Jackson MacLow, Judith Beck, and twenty-three other individuals of various political outlooks, Ammon Hennacy allowed himself to be jailed as a demonstration of his love of God and humanity. For the next seven years Ammon and company returned to the sidewalks to demonstrate outside of civil defense headquarters until in 1962 the whole affair was recognized as a farce and the authorities were too embarrassed by the ludicrous actions they were caught up in to continue the compulsory air raid drills any longer. That victory may well appear insignificant to some observers but for Ammon Hennacy it was a demonstration of the power of reason over irrationality and ignorance. As for all anarchists, reason is the only power worthy of human concern and the force before which the political kingdoms of this world must eventually fall. Ammon Hennacy was too good an anarchist to talk about the coming kingdom of Utopia; for him the time for reason is while one has the vigor and strength to live one's ideals. And few men have embodied reason in their lives more faithfully than Ammon Hennacy.

NOTES

SECTION VI - CHAPTER 2

1. Nat Hentoff, *Peace Agitator; The Story of A. J. Muste* (New York, 1963), p. 236. See also: Jo Ann Robinson, "A. J. Muste and Ways to Peace," *American Studies,* XIII (Spring, 1972), pp. 95-108.

2. "Sketches for an Autobiography," *The Essays of A. J. Muste,* ed. by Nat Hentoff (Indianapolis, 1967), p. 135.

3. *Ibid.*, p. 169.

4. "Return to Pacifism," *Ibid.*, p. 199.

5. "Trade Unions and the Revolution," *Ibid.*, p. 186.

6. "The True International," *Ibid.*, p. 210.

7. "Pacifism and Perfectionism," *Ibid.*, p. 317.

8. "Pacifism in the Atomic Age," *Not by Might* (New York, 1947), p. 214.

9. Joan V. Bondurant, *Conquest of Violence* (Berkeley, 1965), p. 173.

10. "Of Holy Disobedience," *The Essays of A. J. Muste,* p. 372.

11. "Pacifism and Class War," *Ibid.*, p. 182.

12. "What the Bible Teaches about Freedom," *Ibid.*, p. 284.

13. Colman McCarthy, "Peace, Activism, and A. J. Muste," *The Washington Post* (May 2, 1971), p. 23.

14. "What the Bible Teaches about Freedom," *The Essays of A. J. Muste,* p. 294.

15. *The Long Loneliness, An Autobiography* (Garden City, 1959), p. 60. For a recent study of the movement, see William D. Miller, *A Harsh and Dreadful Love: Dorothy Day and the Catholic Worker Movement* (New York, 1972).

16. *Ibid.*, p. 135.

17. *Loaves and Fishes* (New York, 1963), p. 67. For an analysis of Maurin's social views, see Arthur Sheehan, *Peter Maurin: Gay Believer* (New York, 1959).

18. *The Long Loneliness,* p. 199.

19. "Book Reviews: The Christian Failure," *The Catholic Worker,* XXIX (January, 1963), p. 2.

20. "Catholic Anarchism," *The Catholic Worker,* XXX (OCtober, 1963), p. 3.

21. James Douglass, "Theology of Resistance: Gospel's Revo-

lution Against Violence," *The Catholic Worker,* XXXV (December, 1969), p. 1.

22. "Fear in Our Time," *The Catholic Worker,* XXXIV (April, 1968), 5.

23. "After Prison—Part II," *Liberation,* II (October, 1957), p. 17.

24. "Thoughts after Prison," *Liberation,* II (September, 1957), p. 7.

25. *Loaves and Fishes,* p. 80.

26. *The Book of Ammon* (Salt Lake City, 1970), p. 1.

27. "Ammon Hennacy—'Non-Church' Christian," *The Catholic Worker,* XXXVI (February, 1970), p. 8.

28. *The Book of Ammon,* p. 474.

29. *Ibid.,* p. 273.

30. *Ibid.,* p. 276.

31. *Ibid.,* p. 240.

32. "The Doukhobors," *Retort,* I (December, 1942), p. 38.

33. "The Machine in a Free Society," *Man,* III (January, 1935), p. 154.

CHAPTER 3

The "Green Revolutionaries" and Their Call to Make Hay, Not Laws

One of the most pronounced points at which anarchists and Marxists disagree with regard to socialism, as has already been suggested, has to do with the relative merits of the agrarian life as opposed to an unqualified acceptance of the urbanization that has accompanied advanced capitalist technology and industrialization. Since at least the time of Thomas Jefferson, land in America has been recognized as essential to the development of a free society, and anarchists have been prominent in focusing upon it as the primary means whereby the enslaving powers of government might be brought under control. Pierre-Joseph Proudhon, one of the "most brilliant thinkers of the nineteenth century," stands out as one who realized the immense social damage that takes place when the individual is removed from his natural connection to the soil and the mutualist social groups that spring from it,[1] although others, like Josiah Warren and William B. Greene, expressed the same view even before Proudhon did. Ridiculed by Marx for his failure to recognize the "idiocy" of the agrarian life, the anarchist, like Proudhon, has not received a fair hearing to date. But now that the failures of urbanization are becoming evident for all to see, it is essential that we reconsider what the anarchist has had to say about land and the agrarian way of life.

Outstanding among those who have championed agrarianism was Joshua K. Ingalls (1816-1898). Hailing from Swansea, Massachusetts, Ingalls had been won over to the anarchist idea by the writings of Proudhon and as a consequence later came to know both Josiah Warren and Stephen Pearl Andrews.[2] Associating briefly with several voluntary communities, Ingalls quickly became convinced that social progress lay along the lines of individual rather than collective economic effort and hence he began a search

for a political theory that would lead to the liberation of the individual as opposed to the group. Writing in Ezra H. Heywood's *Word,*
to which he was a regular contributor, Ingalls expressed the view
that only free and unrestricted access to the land could solve the
labor problem, for it is the land that forms the keystone of the
bridge we must build to span the gap that separates rich from poor
in this country.[3] Unless we solve the land problem, he urged, all
tinkering with monetary and social reform must come to nothing.
Moving to New York, Ingalls established *The Landmark,* a journal
devoted to the problem of land reform. Deprived of any formal
education beyond the basics he picked up in a country school,
Ingalls had not even read Adam Smith when he first began to
cogitate concerning the question of social justice as it relates to
land.[4] Becoming acquainted with Victoria Woodhull, he joined
the New York Section of the International Workingmen's Association organized by her and was a frequent participant in the lively
discussions that were held in her parlors; it was there, no doubt, that
Ingalls and Tucker first became known to each other. At any rate,
Ingalls was very early a contributor to Tucker's *Radical Review,*
and in later years his economic and social theories were often the
subject of reviews and articles in *Liberty.*

　　The solution that Ingalls offered to the labor problem was as
ingenious as it was simple—*abolish all laws that give individuals
possession or control over land that they cannot cultivate by their
own labor.* "Did our land laws confine ownership to that which a
man could occupy and cultivate," Ingalls wrote, "rent could not
be obtained."[5] The virtue of this arrangement, according to him,
was that every man in America would thus have access to the
essential means of making his livelihood so long as there remained
unoccupied land that he could put to use for his own sustenance,
and hence the props would be knocked out from under the prevailing
economic system in which those who have capital live off of the labor
of those who do not. One might conceivably have to borrow money
at first to purchase livestock and tools, Ingalls reasoned, but the
enormous indebtedness that newly established farmers must undertake in order to purchase land would be eliminated from the
American economic scene, thereby drawing the fangs of capitalism.

　　In order to carry out this basic land reform, however, Ingalls
urged, "We greatly need to disabuse ourselves of all that nonsense

about absolute *property*. There is no such thing. We have no such property even in our bones and tissues."[6] The only property we have a right to is that which is produced principally from our own labor, making use, of course, of the natural resources furnished us by nature to the extent that our private energy and ingenuity permits. Addressing the sixth annual convention of the American Labor Reform League held in New York in the spring of 1876, Ingalls argued that since labor is the creator of all weath, it should also be the legal justification for the temporary ownership of land.[7] Were all laws protecting those who presently control the land repealed, Ingalls held, the thorny economic problems that plague society would be solved at once, for there would no longer be a shortage of capital to keep the hands of the American working people idle. Thus able to feed and house themselves, the American people would be freed from the debilitating effects of the poverty now pressed upon them by the incessant malfunctioning of capitalistic economic institutions, and large scale social unrest and discontent would soon become a thing of the past.

Another vociferous champion of land reform as the chief means to freedom was Charles T. Fowler (1851-1889) who, like Ingalls, was an associate of Ezra Heywood as well as a disciple of Josiah Warren. Fowler, who lived most of his life in Westport, Missouri, had as a young man been a steady participant in the parlor meetings held by Warren in Boston where he first became acquainted with Benjamin Tucker and Sidney H. Morse.[8] A Unitarian minister at the time, Fowler tended steadily to become more radical in his theology and he soon gave up the ministry altogether to devote himself to radical social and political causes. After moving west to Kansas City, Fowler established *The Sun,* a journal that drew much of its inspiration from the writings of Proudhon and which concerned itself with the problem of equitable land distribution. "He who has a foothold in the soil and the organization of business emanating therefrom," Fowler declared, "is perfectly independent."[9] Like John Beverley Robinson, Fowler was a Member of the American Free Soil Society which had been organized in June of 1883 and thus he subscribed to the Jeffersonian view that only as the citizen lives close to nature and the soil can he maintain a wholesome social existence. Writing to Joseph Labadie, Fowler asserted that the reason he chose to call himself an anarchist was that the philosophy of anarchism was the only social theory that based itself completely upon the laws of nature as they pertain to social life.[10] The full extent of Fowler's commitment to anarchism is revealed in his bold assertion that "we declare the United States Government's laws to be license, and unworthy of the name of laws; its authority usurpation, which it is our bounden duty to disobey."[11] With Thoreau and Jefferson, Fowler envisioned human freedom as something one must be prepared to protect with courage and determination, even it if meant putting oneself in opposition to one's own government. For after all is said and done, Fowler held, it is the land that serves as the basis for all the other freedoms we cherish and hence it is land reform that must be our first concern.

Heir to the libertarian social philosopohy promulgated by Ingalls and Fowler was William Charles Owen (1854-1929). Although he spent 32 years in America, mostly on the west coast, Owen was an Englishman by birth, his father representing the British Empire as head of a large military hospital in India. The senior Owen never saw his son, however, for he died of an uncontrollable fever before William was born. Brought back to England while he was still a baby, William C. Owen received an excellent education, studying law at Wellington College and picking up proficiency in a number of languages, including Greek. But Owen could not bring himself to practice law very long, for his quick and sensitive mind soon convinced him that the legal profession was no place for a completely honest man, and no amount of persuasion on the part of influential friends of his aristocratic family could make him revise his decision.[12]

In 1884 Owen came to San Francisco, supporting himself by representing a firm engaged in compiling credit ratings for business firms.[13] By coincidence, it was Burnette G. Haskell, that erratic dilettante of California radicalism, who first introduced Owen to socialist theory. Owen at the time was active in the Federated Trades Council and was just beginning to think of himself as a socialist when Haskell enticed him to join up with his International Workingmen's Association. But Owen quickly became disenchanted with Haskell when it became apparent that the latter harbored ill will toward Chinese immigrant labor and he sought elsewhere for more serious sources of inspiration for his ideological development. An omnivorous reader, he had soon run through the principal theorists of radical politics, including Kropotkin, Bakunin, Jean Grave, and others, and before long was referring to himself as an anarchist. Discovering Benjamin R. Tucker's writings, Owen found himself "steadily drifting away from Communism" as well as state socialism until he further classified himself as an individualist anarchist.[14]

A lover of the great outdoors, Owen spent a great deal of time tramping the hills and trails of Southern California, then a veritable wilderness. On two occasions he spent months roughing it in a lonely cabin in the frozen barrens of the Klondyke; finding no gold, he nevertheless enjoyed the solitude of the Alaska winter, for it helped put him spiritually in tune with nature. Supporting himself as a journalist with an occasional stint at teaching, Owen came to reflect in his writings a genuine reverence for the land not unlike that of Thomas Jefferson or John Muir. Reverence for the land, of course, was not peculiar to Owen or Jefferson, for that matter; around the middle of the nineteenth century the land question was uppermost in everyone's mind and no radical group was without its theory as to how it should be solved. Elizur Wright, for example, the President of the National Liberal League, called for a convention of "liberals" to be held in Cincinnati in the fall of 1879 for the purpose of setting forth a program with regard to the distribution of the land.[15] 1879 was also the year Henry George's *Progress and Poverty* first made its appearance, and George very rapidly mobilized a large force of American radicals behind his single tax theory by which the advantage that falls to those who control the land was supposedly to be eliminated. Owen, however, was highly critical of George's social theory and turned instead to the more radical solutions offered by the philosophers of American anarchism. A faithful subscriber to *Liberty*, Owen's views on land reform were in all probability derived more from the writings of Ingalls and Fowler than they were from those of Henry George.

Something of a gypsy at heart, Owen rarely stayed more than a few years in any one place, wandering to wherever his taste and finances would permit. The year 1890 found him in New York where he was instrumental in founding the Socialist League and where he first made the acquaintance of two famous anarchists, Malatesta and Merlino.[16] Three years later he was in London, speaking on problems of anarchist theory at the Autonomie Club and writing frequent pieces for *Freedom*. So charmed was Owen with *Freedom's* editor, Peter Kropotkin, that he continued to correspond with him until Kropotkin's death. By 1911 Owen had worked his way to Mexico where he discovered wisdom as well as charm in the social attitudes of the Mexican peasants whom he found to be "tremendously individualistic in certain ways—above all in their fear of any of their co-workers trying to boss them—and absolutely communistic in others."[17] The judicious balancing of the ideas of individualism and collectivism Owen admired in the Mexican peasantry became an outstanding characteristic in his own social philosophy.

Appointed editor of the English section of *Regeneration*, the mouthpiece of the Mexican Liberal Party published from Los Angeles, Owen heralded the Revolution to the South as a genuine event in the history of human liberation. "Nowhere else have tens of thousands risen in arms not merely against the existing government, but against the very idea of government," he wrote in Emma Goldman's *Mother Earth*.[18] Establishing a journal of his own called *Land and Liberty* on May 1st of 1914, Owen called upon the American people to support the struggling revolutionaries beyond the Rio Grande, for they were the vanguard of the universal social revolution yet to come. "Do not let Debs mislead you with twaddle about the necessity of long-continued education" in revolutionary theory, Owen warned his readers. "All effective organization springs spontaneously from discontent and never from the careful calculations of a central ring."[19] The Mexican people, oppressed beyond endurance by the insatiable appetites for wealth of both the indigenous landholders and the foreign capitalists who were pouring into the country from the North, were motivated not by ideology but by genuine outrage against blatant economic and political despotism, he charged. In standing firm against this destruction of their natural liberties, according to Owen, the oppressed Mexicans were true anarchists, for "Anarchism seeks to call into existence free individualities who will neither invade nor tolerate invasion."[20] Joining forces with Ricardo and Enrique Magon, Owen gave his full support to the Mexican people in their struggle against Porfirio Diaz, the dictatorial leader of the Mexican Establishment. When the U.S. Government imprisoned the Magon brothers, Owen took over their duties as chief editor of *Regeneration* until he, too, had to flee when it was learned that a warrant for his arrest had been issued. Going underground, he made his way to New York and by 1916 he was safe at last in England.

Living out his last years in London where he was barely able to keep himself alive on the proceeds of his writing for *The Middleton Guardian,* Owen found solace in the fact that the publisher of the *Guardian* had never altered a single word of his copy but had let him express himself freely on the land question. Never fond of urban life, he endured the hardships of metropolitan London for the sake of his political vocation which he fulfilled by speaking frequently in Hyde Park and Trafalgar Square and with his many contributions to *Freedom, The Commonweal,* and other radical periodicals. In his old age, Owen, who had through life displayed a deep affection in his actions for animals and young children as well as the human race in general, found his generosity of spirit reciprocated by all those who knew him, and he became something of a sage and elder prophet in the anarchist circles he frequented. Neither time nor adversity could dim the glint in Owen's critical eye and it was with a firm voice that he spoke out against the Labour Party, warning his contemporaries that the collective egalitarianism that the members of that party put so much of their faith in was merely another step along the way to the state socialism that anarchists dread so much. Some years before this, Owen had warned his compatriots against the social theories of Herbert Spencer, pointing out that the author of *Social Statics,* however much he might praise the virtues of individualism, was really no libertarian at all. "Anarchists are fond of pointing to Mr. Spencer as one of their most distinguished teachers," Owen caustically observed, "but Mr. Spencer is no Anarchist."[21] In the first place, Spencer does not advocate the complete abolishment of the institution of government but approves of it as a force for the protection of property and contracts as well as the punishment of crime. Those anarchists who look on Spencer with favor conveniently overlook the fact that he subscribed to a thoroughgoing system of land nationalization as a precondition for the individual liberties that were supposedly to follow.[22] But once the individual is divested of his foothold on the land, Owen retorted, it is futile to speak of individual freedom, for the foundations for liberty will have already been eroded.

Unable to find work of any kind after awhile, Owen's personal plight strengthened him in his convictions that to be without land on which to sustain oneself is to be at the mercy of powerful money interests who care nothing for the general welfare or humanitarian concerns. The monopolization of the land by the politically powerful, however, was only the first step in the enslavement of humanity; as masses of people huddle together in their urban slums, Owen prophesied, they become progressively more susceptible to regimentation and manipulation with the consequence that they soon lose all desire to steer their own lives. Revealing his thoughts to his friend, Jo Labadie, another staunch libertarian and lover of nature, there was more than a little anguish in his heart when he wrote:

> In a way I am an incurable optimist, being convinced that man, having risen thus far, is bound to go on rising, and that someday he is bound to become really master of his now enormous resources. On the other hand, this London, this monstrous modern Babylon, which always weighed on my spirit, now sits on me more heavily than ever. It is not merely that it is so huge, and that one's own individual efforts seem to make *no* impression. What I feel all the time is that this mass is so situated that it cannot help being helpless; that its wholly unnatural life distorts all its thought; that, alike by its mental make-up and the constant pressure of its circumstances, it is bound to be ruled.[23]

William C. Owen was no Johnny-Come-Lately when it came to recognizing the dangers of collectivism, for it was as a comparatively young man that he had first warned against giving oneself too completely to the social group. "Freedom for the individual—free access to the means of sustaining and developing life—this is the basic principle," Owen wrote in the *Firebrand* in 1895. Man "must be free to use these means in solitude, or in co-operation with others, just as may seem to him desirable."[24]

Although he had a sincere respect for the thoughts of such notable anarchists as Bakunin, Reclus, and Kropotkin, Owen was wary of following too slavishly their peculiar suggestions for social reform, since to look upon their writings as authoritative would be to violate the very character of the philosophy they espoused. "They are, as must be every true teacher, mere stimulators to self-thought, to self-action, to self-development," he cautioned.[25] It was Peter Kropotkin who had revolutionized Owen, making him see "the necessity of universal revolution" as well as the totally repressive character of the money power as it is supported by the state. Yet Owen was reverently critical of Kropotkin nevertheless, pointing out the weakness of his tendency to credit the masses with positive qualities they do not actually possess. Without taking any of the credit Kropotkin deserved away from him, Owen rejected the emphasis upon the collectivity as central to the advance of libertarian society and turned instead to Stirner and Tucker, the advocates of responsible individualism. From my point of view, Owen wrote, "Kropotkin expects too much from the masses. I believe, on the other hand, that the individual rebel is the greater force. I think events have shown . . . that the unfettered individualism taught by the Nietzsches and Stirners is the true revolutionary philosophy, and that when we tie ourselves to collectivism we tie ourselves to stagnation and consequent reaction.[26]

Although William C. Owen consistently identified himself as an individualist anarchist and had severe reservations concerning the validity of anarchist communism as the ultimate in political theory, he was not by any means without criticism of the philosophical anarchism of Benjamin R. Tucker. "What excellent things Tucker wrote," Owen observed to his friend, Jo Labadie, "and yet somehow today I have more and more feeling that Tucker has always been removed from life, and that his work smacks too much of the fine abstractions philosophers have written from time immemorial."[27] More given to pragmatism than he was to untested philosophical speculation, Owen insisted that the quality of any given anarchist principle is to be judged by the results it brings to the lives of those involved. Mock as we may the "poor and insufficient" philosophical views of the I.W.W., Owen chortled, the willingness of those "roughnecks" to stand firm for what they believe is more valuable to the progress of libertarian ideas than all the books in the universities. In final analysis, Owen held, social progress takes place at the moment that the forces for change become so overwhelming that they can no longer be resisted. Until that moment arrives, human beings, generally too lazy to think or act constructively, will succumb to inertia and thwart all efforts to put things right. In this regard Owen wrote:

> Personally I bank much on necessity, and believe that in our standing armies and navies, our gathering hosts of tramps and habitually-out-of-works, our crowded jails and lunatic asylums, society is staggering under a load it will find it necessary to discard. These seem to me the really potent forces; the great facts that talk more eloquently than words; and I think that the instinct of life will accomplish ultimately what is beyond the power of any human philosophy.[28]

It was indeed a sad day for anarchism when William C. Owen passed away, and his death was mourned by countless comrades on both sides of the Atlantic. Victor B. Neuburg caught the best of Owen's character when he eulogized:

> It is rare to find so generous and lovable a personality combined with so revolutionary and uncompromising a mind. He was the most affectionate of revolutionaries, the kindest of Anarchists. He loved life to the brim, and smoked, sang, drank and yarned like the proud, seasoned Bohemian that he was. Loathing Puritanism in all its disguises, he was a herald of the day when every man will lead a full, free, untrammelled life.[29]

Not all radicals approved so enthusiastically of Owen's free spirit however, as witnessed by the fact that in 1892 he was unceremoniously ejected from the Socialist League of New York which he had helped to organize.[30] The occasion for the League's drastic action against Owen was the breakup of his unoffical second marriage. Leaving the States on a prolonged visit to his native England, Owen, for reasons of his own, left behind his pregnant young common-law wife, later advising her by letter how she might take care of herself and her child. Since Owen had never officially entered into marriage, there was no legal obligation that could be imposed upon him, and all his socialist friends could do was moralize against him for his alleged social irresponsibility. As callous or immoral as his action might have seemed to the members of the Socialist League, however, Owen was acting consistently with reference to his basic social philosophy. When Owen first arrived in San Francisco, his first wife, whom he had married in England, fell in love with one of his socialist compatriots, H. G. Wilshire, and Owen graciously consented to a divorce so that the lovers might consummate their love in freedom. After the divorce, Owen gave demonstration of the deep conviction by which he held his libertarian views by continuing to live in the same house he had previously shared with his former wife, only now it was made a bit more crowded by Wilshire's presence. While this incident may not endear Owen to those who hold marriage a sacred institution, it does indicate the depth of his dedication to the ideals of libertarianism. Unwilling to impose bondage of any kind on any other human being, Owen demanded a similar freedom for himself, and this, of course, made him appear an unprincipled libertine in the eyes of his more conventional-minded contemporaries. But since Owen never proclaimed any value other than freedom to be sacred, he could hardly be charged with moral turpitude, and we are unfair if we judge him by any standard other than his own.

By the end of the first World War, land reform as a practical means to social freedom was largely a dead issue, for the millions of toiling men and women who worked America's farms and fields were too firmly tied to the idea of private property by this time to view land reform as anything more than the most grandiose of radical nostrums, and the names of prophets like Joshua Ingalls, Charles T. Fowler, and William C. Owen very rapidly became embalmed in total obscurity. Besides, the rapid material progress America was experiencing as technology and capitalism teamed up together irresistibly drew people in ever increasing numbers toward the offices and factories of the big cities. During the first two decades of the twentieth century, freedom, for most Americans, meant to get off the land and into the city where opportunity and wealth were theoretically within reach. In the eyes of the typical American, life in the country was a backward, stultifying existence that held no promise for the young or energetic. To live or work on a farm was generally considered the reverse of being free, and land, as Henry George had already aptly demonstrated, was only really valuable as cities became built upon it.

Not all Americans, however, were fooled into believing that the breathtaking material progress and urbanization of early twentieth century America would automatically lead its people to the promised land of personal wealth and contentment. As the hazards of city life became more acute and poverty became more widespread with each passing economic dislocation, some Americans began to have serious doubts that the urbanization of society held all the answers. What did it profit a man to own his own home or business if a sudden reversal of economic forces led to his losing all the equity he had built up over years of back-breaking toil? And how could one speak of being free and happy when life in urban America consisted of a hectic struggle to get from home to factory and back again week after week with monotonous regularity, only to find that decades of faithful devotion to duty did not entitle a worker to any real social security? Gradually many people came to see that the rapid progress America was making in material standards was largely illusory, for soon after finding a working solution for one social problem two were discovered where only one had been before. The bus and subway provided a way to move large numbers of people from one place within the city to another, for example, but it was becoming increasingly evident that every technological advance of this kind had a subsequent impact upon the total environment that was generally negative. Air pollution, street congestion, crime and delinquency all had become pressing problems that threatened to destroy the quality of life in urban America. One could sit and wait for the officials of government to solve these problems through technology, suffering their discomforts in the meantime, or do something on one's own. It was in the face of this crisis that the green revolution took form.

Closely related to American anarchists, green revolutionaries were homesteaders who advocated a return to the soil much as Jefferson before them urged that the true strength of society is to be found in the independent freeholder who makes his living off the land without any great reliance upon government. It is impossible to describe with any accuracy all those who subscribed to this essentially libertarian philosophy, for most of them went about the business of homesteading without any theoretical fuss or fanfare and hence the story of their lives has been lost to history. The best we can do under the circumstances is to select a few outstanding green revolutionaries as typical of the kind of individual who went in for homesteading and relate their basic philosophical assumptions to the ideas expressed by some of the great names in American anarchism.

One of the chief strategists of homesteading as a means to individual security and freedom was Ralph Borsodi, who has written extensively on the philosophical foundations of the movement. Borsodi's commitment to homesteading began when the depression of 1921 left him in precarious financial straights. Looking around for a means of livelihood that would not make them so completely dependent upon the vagaries of the national economy, Borsodi and his wife decided to return to the soil and thus they bought seven acres of farm land close to Suffern, New York, on which they raised fruit and vegetables and kept a cow and chickens.[31] Before long they were manufacturing their own clothes out of homespun fabric they turned out on their loom and were feeding themselves and their children exclusively on fruits and vegetables they canned in their own kitchen. The Borsodis prospered so greatly on their homestead that when the Great Depression hit the country during the early Thirties, Ralph Borsodi organized the Dayton Homestead Colonization Movement near Dayton, Ohio, which operated from 1932 to 1934. Offering individuals the opportunity to set themselves up on cheap land provided by a loan from the national government, the experiment ran into difficulty when Washington insisted upon supervising the management of the project, and Borsodi, who was adamant in his Jeffersonian distrust of formal government, withdrew to return to his own homestead in Suffern.[32] Borsodi was convinced as a consequence of this experience that the first thing that must be done if people are to return to the soil in any large number is to educate the public in the underlying philosophy of homesteading without any assistance from government and hence he decided to dedicate himself to the work of propaganda. In 1936 Borsodi organized The School of Living, a research center dedicated to spreading the idea of homesteading and helping people get started in homestead communities.

Closely allied with Borsodi in The School of Living was Mildred Jensen who had been raised on a Nebraska farm but had been completely urbanized by the time she had received her M.A. degree in Education from Columbia University. After a stint at social work in Chicago during the depression years, she chanced upon Ralph Borsodi's *This Ugly Civilization* (1928), one of his early books in which he laid out the underlying philosophical principles of homesteading.[33] After marrying John Loomis, a transplanted Missouri farmer who had participated in the Dayton Homestead Colonization Movement and later bought his own place near Brookville, Ohio, called Lane's End Homestead, Mildred Loomis, on the suggestion of Borsodi, began to edit *The Interpreter*, a semimonthly newletter intended to keep the many individuals who attended the annual School of Living conferences in touch with one another's homesteading activities. In 1950 most of the activities of the School of Living were brought together under Mildred Loomis' direction at Lane's End and for the next eighteen years she provided the main impetus for the movement, editing two publications, a monthly paper, *The Green Revolution*, and a quarterly journal appropriately named *A Way Out*. During all this time, she and John Loomis provided for themselves by raising their own food and other necessities at Lane's End, giving living demonstration of the fact that it is possible to be self-sufficient even in so highly industrial a society as twentieth century America. It is impossible to determine just how many people found their way back to the land and independence as a consequence of the propaganda work carried on by the School of Living but undoubtedly its influence upon American life has been immense. The names and faces in the "hippie communes" spawned by the contemporary youth culture may be new but the underlying social principles were first developed by the School of Living. Others, of course, such as Scott and Helen Nearing simultaneously discovered and practiced the life-giving dynamics of homesteading elsewhere but this merely bears out anarchism's contention that spontaneity is the essential principle in any functioning libertarian society. Life proceeds not on the command of high officials of the state, libertarians assert, but on the independent exertions of will of the myriad ordinary men and women who together make up society. Real revolution, therefore, takes place as people rediscover their own powers of creativity as they escape from the cities by returning to the land, green revolutionaries hold.

If there is any doubt that the green revolution as it was interpreted by Ralph Borsodi was intimately connected with the philosophy of the Enlightenment, it is surely dispelled by his two volume *Education and Living* (1948), in which he argued that the only possible way modern man can enjoy freedom is to make education instead of government the central institution of society. Sounding very much like an anarchist whether or not he thought of himself as one, Borsodi insisted that "The time has come to end the usurpation of leadership in society—by priests, by soldiers, by plutocrats, by politicians—from which mankind has suffered and continues to suffer so much."[34] If man is ever to be free, he must devise a social system in which control over human activities is in the hands of the people themselves rather than officials of government and their legions of bureaucratic underlings.

Borsodi conceived of education as "a process of cultivation" that develops the whole man after the patterns of right living the "normal" individual inevitably discovers when his emotions and intellect function as they were meant to by nature. "If men are rightly educated," he held, "their perceptions and experiences do not deceive them; their reason and intelligence is not misused by them; their emotions and impulses are not uncontrolled; their wills do not permit them to act abnormally." This was not to argue that all a man need do is trust to social convention or folkways or blindly to follow his raw instincts, for Borsodi held that "right-education" must always proceed upon a correct organizational structure. Like all anarchists, Borsodi did not call for *no* organization but for a *rational* one that was adequate to the task of assuring freedom to those whose lives would be shaped by it. And for him, as for Thomas Jefferson, the only rational social organization was a society of homesteaders living their lives close to nature as they tilled the soil without help or hindrance from impersonal, repressive government. This was what Borsodi had in mind when he wrote that human relations are territorial as well as social, and that true community begins with the spatial configurations we impose upon ourselves as we go about the business of living. Just as it is land that provides the individual with the means of individual survival, so is it the land that provides the group with the means of group survival. So primary a connection does man have to land that those who place themselves outside of a direct relationship with it pay for their mistake by suffering insecurity. "Modern man, who has substituted almost total dependence upon money for dependence upon the direct harvesting of the fruits of the earth, is not only insecure; he fails to obtain what is the just due of his labor or enterprise in almost exact proportion to the degree to which he permits his relationship to land to become indirect," Borsodi warned.[35]

Calling upon his contemporaries to realistically assess the quality of modern life, Borsodi admonished them that progress, correctly defined, is not coterminous with change and innovation. Americans seem to think that because their cities are growing bigger and more materially complex, they automatically enjoy the benefits of progress, Borsodi complained. But progress does not necessarily accompany scientific and industrial advance, he warned, and change in itself is not always for the better. Rather than fixate without question upon "the dictum *that man should devote him-self to going forward,*" we might better ask ourselves whether industrialization actually enhances life or retards it.[36] If the latter be the case, wisdom would dictate that the most rational definition of progress is that social plan that eschews technology and industrialism and turns instead to the land and agriculture for the means of sustaining life.

Here Borsodi introduced a further distinction, the distinction between organic and inorganic production. Organic production, as Borsodi defined it, consists of techniques of agriculture and animal husbandry that employ the genetic and biological patterns found in nature as the means by which raw materials are transformed into finished products for human consumption. "It is a process in which dealing with life is central; in which the machinery and power used, and even the physical and mental labor, are contributory and accessory."[37] The great advantage of an organic system of production over that of an inorganic system is that the former can never be highly standardized and controlled from a central location as can the latter, Borsodi held. Organic production, drawing upon the living genetic and biological differences found in nature, does not lend itself to mass production and regimentation under the direction of central control, whereas inorganic production systems which utilize uniform mechanical and chemical processes are readily fitted into a standardized and regimented mold.

Clearly articulating what Thomas Jefferson only vaguely implied, Borsodi gave modern scientific justification for the cherished American dream of agrarian democracy in which all men, rather than the politically powerful few, share in the fruits of human industry and labor. If freedom is our central goal, he reasoned, no better plan of organization can be found than the kind of agrarian society envisioned by Jefferson in which every man is shaped by the rhythms of nature as he experiences them in everyday encounter with the land and its products. Unlike the ruler who must force his arbitrary will upon his subjects if political control is to be preserved, nature directs those it serves not through blind obedience to rule but only through voluntary acquiescence in the self-evident procedures it functions by. Rational necessity, not authoritarian prescription, is the force that molds the members of an agrarian culture into a functioning libertarian society, and hence a return to the land and nature, as Thoreau predicted, is the most practical step toward freedom that modern man can take.

Giving the lie to the often repeated charge that anarchists have no working solutions to the problems of modern life, Borsodi urged all who cherish freedom to set themselves up as independent centers of libertarian influence by returning to the land and organic farming. Carefully documenting his position with references drawn from professional journals, Borsodi argued that since only five to forty acres of land are enough to support a family, over two hundred million people could support themselves in only one third of the available farming lands found in America,[38] thereby offering a highly workable scheme to break the hold that the wealthy power elite formed by Alexander Hamilton exercises over the American people. The individual finding self-sufficiency on the land directs a more telling blow at the vital control center of modern authoritarianism than all the bricks and bombs hurled at the functionaries of the state by revolutionary terrorists, for his self-sufficiency furnishes him with immunity to government's all-pervasive powers. Quietly but steadily the homesteader commits the most revolutionary of deeds when he opts to leave conventional society behind, since he places himself outside the reach of the minions of power who cannot conceive of life under any other frame of reference than an authoritarian one. The great virtue of homesteading as a revolutionary technique is that those who engage themselves in it make themselves politically invisible at the same time that they constitute themselves a counterforce to the centralizing tendencies of our advanced bureaucratic structures;[39] theirs is a form of guerrilla warfare that no government, however powerful it might be, can suppress.

Not all green revolutionaries adhered so strictly to the tradition of individualism urged by the School of Living, however. When Joseph J. Cohen and confreres drawn from the anarcho-syndicalist groups of New York and other Eastern cities headed for Michigan's Saginaw Valley to establish the Sunrise Co-operative Farm during the early Thirties, the impetus that sent them on their merry way was faith in the conception of the collective ownership and management of the land. Cohen at the time was editor of the *Freie Arbiter Stimme* and the nucleus of people out of whom the farm was formed originally gathered together in response to an ad Cohen ran in that paper. Since all of them were generally advocates of collective action by labor againt management, and since Cohen had previously experienced communal living as one of the founders of the Ferrer Colony at Stelton, New Jersey, it was a foregone conclusion that the experiment should operate according to a communist form of organization.[40]

From 1933 to 1938 the enthusiasts who made up the group struggled mightily to make their dream of unselfish communal living come true, only to discover in the end that there were too many obstacles to overcome. "The plain fact is that we had created conditions in which we could hardly have expected anything better," Cohen regretfully wrote in retrospect. "What we failed to realize was that when a number of people—strangers to each other—are thrown together in such a way that their interests are intertwined, there is bound to be trouble and misunderstanding."[41] Tools and equipment were constantly being lost or abused and the community kitchen proved to be inefficient in both labor and cost; on top of all this the incessant bickering and power struggles of some of the more socially immature members, and the disastrous decision to apply for a loan from the Federal Government in Washington, threw the venture so totally out of equilibrium that it eventually toppled over and died. After things had deteriorated so badly that the farm in Michigan had to be sold, a remnant of enthusiasts gave it one last try in Virginia, but in February of 1940 it was all over and only the obituary of the movement remained to be written, which Cohen undertook in his *In Quest of Heaven*. What had fundamentally caused the downfall of the experiment, according to Cohen, was the inability of any of the participants to feel wanted and respected within the collectivist frame of reference the community had initially chosen to adopt. Under normal social circumstances the average individual receives recognition in the inner circle of his family if not in the greater outside world and hence he finds the energy to keep going. But "At the tiny apex of our social pyramid," Cohen reflected, "there was no room to accommodate all the aspirants to distinction, and in this situation the ordinary man began to lose all sense of his own worth, so that his morale sank rapidly to a low level." All the love they held for the land and the human race could not make up for this organizational weakness and so another phase of the green revolution ended in abortion.

One of the most unexpected sources of enthusiasm for the green revolution came from the Catholic Worker Movement which nestled for most of its early years in the shadows of the foul-smelling, dilapidated tenements of Mott Street in New York's Chinatown district. Dedicated as it was to harboring the human derelicts who drifted on the streets of America's largest metropolis, the Catholic Worker Movement has always projected an urban image and is generally associated with the teeming masses spawned by the great industries of the city. Moreover, Dorothy Day, as suggested in the previous chapter, personally loved life on the Lower East Side of the city and found herself most comfortable living in close proximity to those poverty-stricken individuals the Catholic Worker serves. Largely responsible for the Catholic Worker Movement's adoption of the principles of the green revolution was Peter Maurin, whose upbringing in a peasant village of France led him to look toward the land for a solution to the pressing problems of modern urban civilization. Rarely did Peter allow any discussion to end without mentioning the virtues of farming as a life style. Living on the land is a veritable education in itself, Peter held, and hence those who work it might consider themselves students of an "agronomic university" in which nature and the seasons are the professors and the land the textbooks. There is no real security or comfort in the city, Peter argued, for the bosses who run the mills and offices know nothing other than the rules and regulations of capitalism. Only on the land can a sincere Christian hope to live his faith. "The future of the Church is on the land, not in the city," he wrote.[42] "It is in fact impossible for any culture to be sound and healthy without a proper respect and regard for the soil. . . ."[43] It was in response to Peter's urging that the Catholic Worker Movement established a series of farming communes to which refugees from the urban ghettos and slums could occasionally escape.

The first of the Catholic Worker farms with an eight-room house on Staten Island that overlooked Raritan Bay, was established in 1935. Actually, as Dorothy Day points out, the project was more accurately called a garden commune than a farm, for all the land it incorporated was a single acre.[44] Longer in enthusiasm than they were in skill, the Catholic Workers who sought to release nature's energies for the benefit of the soup lines back in the city found that it took more than willpower to make land produce. Fortunately they had the irrepressible Peter Maurin to spur them on and to teach them the basics of agriculture he had learned on the land as a boy. As in the city, the Catholic Worker movement on Staten Island was plagued by the old division between the "workers and scholars," as Peter jocularly referred to them, the workers losing themselves in labor, and the scholars losing themselves in endless theoretical chatter about how the work might best be done. Peter's cure for this was to take all out to the bean patch for a practical demonstration in how to use a hoe. But Peter was a born teacher and his talk always somehow got back to the fundamental religious issues that were the sinews of his soul, which in turn got him started on a discussion of the ideas of Don Luigi Sturzo, Pierre-Joseph Proudhon, or Peter Kropotkin. With Peter Maurin around, the land was indeed an agronomic university. When the university outgrew its campus on Staten Island at the end of the first year, the operation was moved to a 28 acre place near Easton, Pennsylvania, which was named Maryfarm, and from that point on the Catholic Worker Movement was never without its country retreat to repair the bodies of its urban poor. Steeped in the communal teachings of the Catholic Church, the work arrangements at Maryfarm, Peter Maurin Farm, etc., were communistic, each individual taking what he needed and giving all that he possibly could in love for his fellowman. Things did not always run with perfect efficiency, of course, any more than they did at the Sunrise Co-operative Farm, but the example of piety and devotion set for the others by Dorothy and Peter somehow managed in the long run to carry things off successfully. Not the least part of the Catholic Worker Movement's success were the many farm communes of a like nature started by groups in other parts of the country. Like the true teachers they were, Dorothy and Peter inspired green revolution on all sides and through them countless individuals made their way to freedom via the land. Catholic Workers might not have set any great records for making hay but the kind of love they made has had lasting and profound consequences.

Although Peter Maurin and Dorothy Day were essentially personalists and hence little concerned with articulating the philosophic underpinnings of their faith in the land, *The Catholic Worker* has served as a clearinghouse for green revolutionaries desiring to reach out to others. Hardly an issue of the *Worker* passes that does not contain communications from three or four voluntary communities in various parts of the country that have been established after the example set by other Catholic Worker groups. But the roots of homesteading as a way of life that offers escape from the insanity of contemporary civilization often can be traced to early anarchists and land reformers. The Vale, an intentional community at Yellow Springs, Ohio, implemented the basic teachings of Ingalls, Fowler, Owen, and Henry George in their system of allocating the use of their lands in leaseholds rather than individual ownership and control. As each family of the community is assigned an acre or more of land which it may work for its own living, rent is based not on the improvements made to the property but its intrinsic worth, and the monies thus derived are devoted to the support of libertarian projects selected in common by the members of the community.[45] Like the ghosts that supposedly haunt empty houses, the idea of land reform is far from dead in America, however little known its early prophets may be and however few may practice it.

Perhaps the most perceptive insight into the problem of land and nature was expressed by Thomas Merton who before his death was one of the monks who worked the Trappist fields of Gethsemine, Kentucky. In Merton's opinion, the most destructive of all American myths is the "frontier mythology" which perpetuates the notion of the pioneer as a virile hero whose task it is to civilize and tame the wilderness so that the chosen people who follow may enjoy its bounty in security. There is a pronounced ambivalence in the American's attitude toward land and nature; on the one hand, he professes a deep love for it, while at the very same time he demands its destruction so that civilization may spread unimpeded. This "manichean hostility towards created nature" is most evident in the Puritan's attitude toward the wilderness he faced. Viewing the untamed forests that surrounded them with the same bleak sentiment with which they viewed their internal desire for love or sex, the followers of Calvin in America conceived of the wilderness as an enemy to be slain and hence they cleared the land with vengeance and self-righteousness. For the Calvinist, "The wilderness itself was the domain of moral wickedness," according to Merton. And hence victory over it "was an ascetic triumph over the forces of impulse and of lawless appetite. How could one be content to leave any part of nature just as it was, since nature was 'fallen' and 'corrupt'?"[46]

As Calvinism and capitalism merged so that they became scarcely distinguishable from one another, the mystique that nature was only good when it had been totally tamed and subdued by man became an integral part of the American way of life. And thus it was that generations of American boys were raised on the precept that "you prove your worth by overcoming and dominating the natural world. You justify your existence and you attain bliss (temporal, eternal or both) by transforming nature into wealth." If American capitalism has ravished the land for its own profits, according to Merton, it has done so on this quasi-religious justification based on a poor reading of the Judeo-Christian tradition. Fortunately, Henry David Thoreau and other Transcendentalists "reversed the Puritan prejudice against nature and began to teach that in the forests and mountains God was nearer than in the cities," Merton held. Green revolutionaries who urged a return to the lands and woods may give the most benign of appearances but they walk hand in hand with some of the most profound radical thinkers America has produced, for theirs' is an ideology that has deep roots in the soil.

NOTES

SECTION VI - CHAPTER 3

1. Robert Nisbet, *The Social Philosophers: Community and Conflict in Western Thought* (New York, 1973), p. 367.

2. James Martin, *Men Against the State* (New York, 1957), p. 147.

3. "Labor, Land, and Finance Reforms," *The Word,* V (December, 1876), 1.

4. Joshua K. Ingalls, *Reminiscences of an Octogenarian* (New York, 1897), p. 22.

5. "Positive Limitation of Property," *The Word,* IX (March, 1881), 1.

6. "Letter to Irish World," *Liberty,* II (November 25, 1882), 3.

7. "Land Reform: The Only Logical Solution to the Labor Question," *The Word,* V (August, 1876), 1.

8. Benjamin R. Tucker, "A Reminiscence," *Liberty,* VI (January 25, 1890), 4.

9. *The Sun,* I (May, 1887), 25. Among Fowler's published works were: *Co-operation, Its Laws and Principles; Co-operative Homes; Land Tenure;* and *The Reorganization of Business.*

10. Letter from Charles T. Fowler to Joseph Labadee (Westport, Missouri, 1889), in the Labadee Collection, University of Michigan.

11. "Declaration of Independence of the Working People of the United States," *The Word,* IV (June, 1875), 1.

12. T. H. Keell, "Death of William C. Owen," *Freedom Bulletin* II (September, 1929), 4.

13. Frank Roney, *An Autobiography,* ed. by Ira B. Cross (Berkeley, 1911), p. 445.

14. William C. Owen, "Is Communism Compatible with Liberty," *The Firebrand,* I (August 18, 1895), 1.

15. *Man: A Weekly Journal of Progress and Reform* (August 31, 1879), 1.

16. Keell, *op. cit.,* 4.

17. Letter from William C. Owen to Joseph Labadie (July 23, 1913), in Labadie Collection, University of Michigan.

18. "A Letter from William C. Owen," *Mother Earth,* VI (February, 1912), 381.

19. "Mexican Manifesto," *Land and Liberty,* I (July, 1914), 5.

20. "Against Invaders Only War," *Land and Liberty,* I (October, 1914), 2.

21. William C. Owen, *The Economics of Herbert Spencer* (New York, 1891), p. 145.

22. *Ibid.,* p. 7.

23. Letter from William C. Owen to Joseph Labadie (July 29, 1924), in the Labadie Collection, the University of Michigan.

24. "A Symposium of Anarchist-Communism," *The Firebrand,* I (July 14, 1895), 1.

25. William C. Owen, "Elisee and Elie Reclus: In Memoriam," *The Oracle Press: A Bibliography,* ed. by Joseph Ishill (Berkeley Heights, New Jersey, 1953), p. 87.

26. "Kropotkin," *The Syndicalist,* III (January 1, 1913), 3.

27. Letter from William C. Owen to Joseph Labadie (December 5, 1913), in the Labadie Collection, the University of Michigan.

28. "Tolstoy and the Spirit of Revolt," *Regeneration* (August 17, 1912), 4.

29. "William Charles Owen," *The Freedom Bulletin,* II (September, 1929), 2.

30. "Too Bad for Socialists; W. C. Owen Expelled by Them for Deserting his Young Wife," *The New York Times* (December 2, 1892), 3.

31. *Homestead Notes,* I (September, 1933), 3.

32. David Knoke, "Decentralizing the Great Society," *A Way Out,* XXII (May-June, 1966), 5.

33. See also Borsodi's *Flight from the City* (Suffern, New York, 1947).

34. *Education and Living,* Part I and II (Melbourne, Florida, 1948), p. 15.

35. *Ibid.,* Part III and IV, p. 562.

36. *Ibid.,* Part I and II, p. 195.

37. *Ibid.,* 208.

38. *Ibid.,* Part III and IV, p. 567.

39. For an indication of the depth of the School of Living's commitment to the anarchist idea, see *The Green Revolution,* X (February, 1972), in which the entire issue is devoted to a discussion of anarchist theory.

40. In quest of complete accuracy it should be noted that the

Ferrer Colony at Stelton consisted of one hundred families, each of which possessed its own garden plot on which it sustained itself. Only the Modern School project was operated collectively. Cohen was critical of the principle of individualism after which the land was worked at Stelton and hence he influenced the Sunrise Farm experiment to adopt the collectivist approach to farming.

41. *In Quest of Heaven,* p. 195.

42. "Outdoor Universities," *The Green Revolution; Easy Essays on Catholic Radicalism* (Fresno, California, 1961), p. 129.

43. "Regard for the Soil," *Ibid.,* p. 100.

44. *Loaves and Fishes,* p. 43.

45. "Land Experiment," *The Catholic Worker,* XXXIV (June, 1968), 6.

46. "The Wild Places," *The Catholic Worker,* XXXIV (June, 1968), 4.

CHAPTER 4

Liberation Redefined

The numbing heartbreak that was experienced in anarchist circles in America as a consequence of the execution of Sacco and Vanzetti caused many observers to erroneously conclude that by the thirties, anarchism was dead and buried along with its fallen heroes, but this was far from being true. Starting in 1942, the idea of anarchy received a reinterpretation in the pages of *Retort: A Quarterly of Social Philosophy and the Arts,* which was edited and printed by Holly R. Cantine, Jr., on the press he maintained in the back of his hillside home in upstate New York. The editorial policy proposed by Cantine in the first issue of *Retort* called for a new and critical look at the revolutionary movement in America in the hope of working out a different orientation than it had had in the past.

At the outset, *Retort* found it necessary to deviate from the tradition of communist anarchism in a number of essential ways. For one thing, the "old anarchists" were somewhat too facile in their espousal of such concepts as equality, mutual aid, and social solidarity. The transition from old forms of social organization to a new and free society is a much more difficult problem than many anarchists of the past were aware, Cantine warned his readers. The anarchist of fifty years ago, according to *Retort,* directed his attention directly at the worker, calling for a general revolt against the absurdity of social life as it then existed. But experience demonstrates that the working classes, considered as a collective entity, have no appreciable awareness of the degree to which society is defective, nor are they in any way conscious of their social responsibility to their fellowmen. "Until we come to realize that human well-being is not going to spring full formed from an economic reorganization of society," Cantine editorialized, all efforts to build a new and better world are bound to be futile.[1]

Acknowledging that most anarchists under the age of fifty were more than likely determined in their social outlooks by the combined influence of Marx and Kropotkin, *Retort* nevertheless pointed out that there was much to be gained by looking back to the philosophical patterns of thought established by the older individualist school of Josiah Warren and his followers. Although the typical individualist might have been less revolutionary in spirit than the anarchist communist of later day America, there was a great deal of substance in individualism's underlying social philosophy. "Anarchism as a doctrine must be based on belief in the individual potentiality of the average man; its whole case against the necessity of the state ultimately rests on the assumption that ordinary people can regulate their lives more effectively than any outside agency," Cantine reasoned.[2] And since the individualist school of anarchist thought carries the distrust of government control beyond the point held in communist and syndicalist circles, going so far as to deny that the "individual owes allegiance to anything except himself," the individualists have much to offer modern society in the quest for freedom.

The turn back toward the individualist viewpoint precipitated by *Retort* was greatly determined by the fears its editor, Holly Cantine, harbored in his breast concerning the dangers of technology as it increasingly impinged upon every effort of the individual to protect his cherished personal freedom.[3] To be sure, this was not the first time that anarchism had expressed a concern for the evils inherent in technology. "Man has chased many phantoms and is chasing one now in the belief that machinery will free mankind simply because it increases production," Harry Kelly of the Modern School wrote in 1917.[4] But the thought was not original even with Kelly, nor his teacher, Peter Kropotkin, for that matter, for Pierre-Joseph Proudhon had long before pointed out that the machine is essentially a potential enemy of human freedom. With respect to this, Proudhon wrote:

> For it is with the machine as it is with a piece of artillery: the captain excepted, those whom it occupies are servants and slaves. . . . Accuse me, if you choose, of ill-will towards the most precious invention of our century, nothing shall prevent me from saying that the principal result of railways, after the subjection of petty industry, will be the creation of a population of degraded laborers—signalmen, sweepers, loaders, lumpers, draymen, watchmen, porters, weighers, greasers, cleaners, stokers, firemen, etc.[5]

In focusing once again upon the dangers of technology to human freedom, Retort was continuing in a tradition rather than clearing new ground, however novel the idea may have seemed to its readers in the forties.

In yet another respect Retort was in tune with the philosophical foundations of individualist anarchism and this was with regard to the insistence upon free, voluntary choice as the principal means of effecting the social revolution. The social revolution hoped for by anarchists can best be brought about, Retort urged, by establishing a series of voluntary cooperative communities which will parallel the existing economy and yet lead to a new social consciousness fashioned after the pattern of the libertarian paradigm. "Since both violent revolution and parliamentary activity seem to lead away from the realization of fundamental liberty, a realistic radical movement should concern itself with building up a nucleus of the new society 'within the shell of the old'." The erection of a communitarian society will not immediately transform the whole of society, Retort conceded. But what it will do is to approximate as nearly as possible in daily life the underlying ideals of the social revolution. The radical accomplishes two things through his communitarian efforts. On the one hand, he is engaged in a learning experience from which new insight into the nature of social life and organization may be derived. On the other hand, he is actually engaged in living a revolutionary principle, thereby demonstrating to other men the practicality of the anarchist idea. When an individual enters a communitarian venture, Retort conjectured, he has in effect made a clean break with the values so assiduously supported and cherished by the status quo. And he has given visual demonstration of the fact that there are other values in this world other than the existing ones that the individual might set his social course by. "By living according to these values, he hopes to encourage the workers to follow his example, and by breaking away from existing institutions cause them to collapse."[7]

Although Retort was full of the sound and fury of the revolutionary outlook, the fact that its chief editor was primarily interested in the arts made it inevitable that its orientation would be aesthetic in character. This tendency became especially pronounced after the poet, Dachine Rainer, became associate editor in 1946, joining Jackson MacLow and Paul Goodman who were among the most notable of its contributors. With the Winter issue of 1947, *Retort's* subtitle became "An Anarchist Quarterly of Social Philosophy and the Arts," indicating that the mood of its editors was becoming progressively more radical, although no less interested in art and beauty. Many people are still not aware that anarchism, which possesses many facets, has always had tremendous appeal to the individual of a poetic or artistic temperament.[8] *Retort* proposed to exploit the natural connection that exists between art and anarchism, thereby hoping to find an alternative to the idea of liberal democracy which was in a moribund condition. Within the scope of the "revolutionary movement," its purpose was to work out an orientation that would be as much concerned with the matter of individual liberty as it was with economic security.[9]

A truly anarchistic society, according to *Retort,* will be one in which the arts will not be neglected but rather will be given the prominence they lack everywhere today. Largely eschewing the attitude of direct revolutionary engagement, *Retort* maintained that no satisfactory society can be constructed which does not provide some means whereby the masses may engage in creative self-expression. A true revolution will not be content with merely tampering with the superficial aspects of the economic system while it at the same time leaves the techniques of leadership and social control unaltered. If we are to design a genuine change in social life, the change must affect the basic structure of society. And this can only be done through the arts. If we can bring men to a new social perspective by affecting their appreciation of beauty and form, we can effect a radical change in the social order without any resort to force or compulsion. "It is the duty of revolutionists who sincerely want to make a better world, to work for a more widespread appreciation and practice of the arts, crafts, and sciences; as a means of giving the people ego security without having to depend on leaders to provide it vicariously."[10] And not only must the people be helped to appreciate the "joys of creation" but there must also be a free and unrestricted development of all modes and schools of art, all attempts to reduce it to dogma being rejected, for "only a truly free artistic expression can insure a free people." Here *Retort* gave expression to an aspect of anarchist theory that has always had great appeal to those who understand the power that beauty holds over the lives and destinies of men. Working through the aesthetic faculties, human nature can be changed without violence or force. This, as the late Herbert Read put it, is the "politics of the unpolitical."[11] It is the only kind of politics, according to *Retort,* that an anarchist can legitimately engage in.

Continuing in the pattern of free thought that had germinated in the fertile philosophical matrix of the American Enlightenment, almost all the contributors to *Retort* reflected the healthy conception of nature that Tom Paine and other enlightened thinkers held. When William H. Auden's *Age of Anxiety* was published, Dachine Rainer took him to task for the dismal view of the natural world that he presented to the reading public. Charging Auden with the crime of "anthropomorphizing," nature, Rainer complained that his view of natural phenomena "is an inverted form of pantheism, where instead of finding god in every leaf and flower, man's evil is injected into natural phenomena, so that they appear evil, too."[12] Like most intellectuals, she fussed, Auden has subjectivized the world after the mood of alienation that grips his own consciousness and has thereby reduced it to ashes and bitter fruit. In much the same vein, Paul Goodman warned that those "who separate themselves from nature have to live every minute of their lives without the power, joy, and freedom of nature."[13] Although fully conscious of the danger implicit in any attempt to ape the lifestyle of primitive peoples as many back-to-nature advocates foolishly do,[14] Holly Cantine reflected the essential design of enlightened philosophy when he held that it is the social instinct itself that must serve as the solid foundation of human morality, for apart from the solidarity of the natural group, there is no other basis for good.[15] Until we again learn to see in nature the form and imprint of the beautiful, society cannot hope for relief from the terrible evils that presently beset it. But this means, *Retort* insisted, that all men must become artists, for unless all are included in the act of creation, an elite must impose itself upon the mass to give guidance and direction to social development. Unhappily, Holly Cantine became so involved in practicing the creative arts he advocated that the last issue of *Retort* appeared in 1951 following the lapse of an entire year in which its readers had no words from the editors. Devoting his entire energy to creative writing, Holly Cantine had done his stint at picket duty and now left the defense of anarchism's ramparts to others.

One of the most important, if not *the most important,* voices of American anarchism to speak out during the dark years of World War II was Dwight Macdonald's *Politics* which was issued from 1944 to 1949, starting out as a monthly and winding up as a quarterly. Basically, *Politics* was a "one-man magazine," since it was edited and supported almost completely from Macdonald's own resources, both intellectual and financial. But upon closer examination it becomes clear that *Politics,* however much it may have depended upon Macdonald's personal vitality, had support from a wide spectrum of people on the American left. To start with, there was Macdonald's wife, Nancy, who not only licked postage stamps and served as business manager but also contributed to the support of *Politics* the proceeds of a trust fund that had been set up in her name. Apart from a contribution of one thousand dollars from Margaret De Silver, the widow of Carlo Tresca, the entire financial burden of putting out the journal came from the Macdonalds' own pockets.[16] Beyond the financial aspect, there was a tremendous outpouring of spiritual and literary support from such radical notables as C. Wright Mills, Paul Goodman, Daniel Bell, Milton Mayer, David T. Bazelon, Bruno Bettelheim, Nicola Chiaromonte, George Woodcock, and Niccolo Tucci. Although *Politics* never reached more than five thousand paying readers at any time, it had a tremendous impact upon the American social and political scene, especially among servicemen and youth on college campuses. Having cut his literary teeth as a writer for *Fortune* and editor of *The Partisan Review,* Macdonald had little difficulty in bringing out one of the most attractive radical journals ever published in America.

It was not simply its sparkling format or scintillating list of contributors that made *Politics* a force to be reckoned with during this very crucial period of social and intellectual development; far more important in explaining *Politic's* climb to eminence in American radical circles was its editor's profound grasp of the intricacies of libertarian philosophy and his penetrating analysis of economic and political developments as they began to shape up in the late forties. Completely uninhibited when it came to ripping fig leaves off popular idols, Macdonald took Admiral "Bull" Halsey to task for his moral and intellectual flatulence, as when the Admiral boasted to some Washington journalists that he hated "Japs" so much that if he "met a pregnant Japanese woman, I'd kick her in the belly." An admiral in the United States Navy is free to make such irrational, psychotic statements without facing any of the consequences, Macdonald observed, but if an ordinary citizen did this we would hustle him off to a padded cell.[17] When death finally forced F.D.R. to let loose his tight grip on the reigns of the American political hobbyhorse he had ridden for so long, Macdonald pointed out that the deluge of tears that his death precipitated among Americans, could only have been elicited by the death of one who had become "the Father of His Country" in the full meaning of the Freudean concept of Father. However much we may sympathize with the loved ones of another human being who has slipped from the ranks of the living, the American people may gain socially and politically from their loss, for "rebellion against paternal authority is the road to maturity for society as for the individual. . . ."[18] Feeling increasingly comfortable in the loose, flowing robes of anarchist thought, Macdonald zoomed to prominence as one of the supermen of the badly shattered forces of the American left during the twilight of World War II.

Like most intellectuals who had come of age during the depression era, Macdonald had initially viewed the world in terms of the probing insights bequeathed to the twentieth century by Marx, and hence he understood that the basic problems with which we have to deal are essentially derived from economic relationships. But Macdonald recognized that his view of the world was somewhat distorted by the dense foliage he had to peer through in order to see out from the forest of Marxian ideological propositions he had come to surround himself with during the thirties, and he was not content to discuss political problems in a superficial way. Thus it was that he sought for a new perspective by which he might arrive at a more substantial social position. One of the most popular features of *Politics* was a series of articles titled "New Roads in Politics," the purpose of which was "to criticize the dominant ideology on the left today—which is roughly Marxian— in the light of recent experience, and to suggest and speculate on new approaches to the central problem; how to advance towards a society which shall be humanly satisfying."[19] If American anarchists are indebted to Macdonald, it is for the tremendously effective critique of Marxian philosophy that was incorporated into the pages of *Politics* during the brief six years of its publication. Although many American anarchists had previously sought to establish a rational assessment of Marx's social thought as it relates to the goals and values of libertarian philosophy, no one has been as successful in this as Macdonald.

Although Macdonald continued to think of himself as a socialist and held firm to a great many of the social propositions that Marx had developed, he sharply veered from the attitude that most Marxists then took regarding the individual as he relates to history and social change. One of the most objectionable aspects of Marxism today, Macdonald proclaimed, "is that it is not a philosophy of rebellion and action but rather one of conformity and quietism."[20] To the extent that Marxism views the social world in terms of inexorable patterns of economic and historical progress, the individuals who make up this world are mere cyphers and pawns in a process that is larger than themselves and hence they become hapless victims of an external force. In an effort to reverse the deterministic direction in which Marxism had channeled radical thought, Macdonald announced his own determination to address *Politics* to the crucial problems of demonstrating that the individual is not a powerless being but one who has real potential as a force for social change.

In a series of articles titled "The Root is Man," Macdonald probed into the deep wound that Marxism had inflicted upon the libertarian movement in an attempt to locate the source of the infection. It is not Marx's values that are diseased, Macdonald concluded, but the philosophical over-view that Marx took regarding social reality. When it comes to the question of intent, Marx continues to stand up as one who wished well for mankind and hoped to liberate people from the dreadful consequences of capitalism and advanced industrial society. Where Marx went wrong, Macdonald concluded, is on the question of what is real and what is not. Committed as he was to the Hegelian notion of consciousness, Marx held that the material forces of this world are more substantial and compelling upon the individual than his state of individual consciousness. Underlying all of Marx's social and political conclusions was "the assumption that the only 'real' political action is on a mass scale. . . . This means that, politically, one thinks of people in terms of classes or parties instead of in terms of individual human beings; and also that one's own motivation for action springs from identification with a class or a historical process rather than from one's personal sense of right and true."[21] The inevitable outcome of such a theory of reality, according to Macdonald, is a tendency "to think of peoples as responsible and individuals as irresponsible."[22] Had it not been for this frame of mind, it would have been impossible for the political and military elite that calls the shots in America to have foisted the atomic bomb upon the human race, for no individual as such would have stood for this kind of barbarism without raising a determined opposition. Where the Marxian theory of class consciousness colors all, the individual is reduced to a mere part of a whole, and his ability to act effectively is seriously curtailed. Where all are responsible together, none is responsible in fact, and the injustices and inequities go on piling up in this world like the dirty dishes in a bachelor's sink.

If mankind is to be rescued from the alienation that presently afflicts it, Macdonald conjectured, it is essential that the individual recapture the sense of purpose and power that earlier generations enjoyed, for it is only as individuals that mankind can escape from the mass. "This in turn depends on people entering into direct personal relationships with each other, which in turn means that the political and economic units of society (workshops, exchange of goods, political institutions) are small enough to allow the participant to understand them and to make their individual influence felt."[23] Where socialism is practiced under the terms of a hierarchical party structure as in Stalinist Russia, Macdonald held, the individual suffers from alienation just as much as he does under capitalism; the only thing that is different is the rhetoric by which those in power justify the coercive policies they rule by.

Nowhere is Macdonald's identification with the idea of anarchism more pronounced than in his frequent references to the writings of Randolph Bourne. It was from Bourne's "Unfinished Fragment on the State" that Macdonald found support for the view that the state is not a nebulous fantasy of the radical mind but a concrete socio-political force that shapes and compels all those who fall under its control. The first step towards a science of politics, therefore, is to clearly recognize the nature of the beast with which we have to contend. And here we must not make the mistake of assuming that the state is a neutral force that can be used either for good or evil as the Liberal says it is, Macdonald cautioned.

The difficulty with the "Good-or-for-Evil platitude," as the Marxists have yet to learn, Macdonald argued, is that there is such a thin line between the good and bad aspects of force and power that no mortal being possesses the moral and intellectual balance to walk such a precarious wire without losing his footing. As with the atomic bomb, capitalism, or the state itself, what starts out as a force for human good inevitably becomes twisted into a force for bad when the myriad impulses of life become impeded by some obstacle or other.

Nicola Chiaromonte, one of the many bright stars discovered by Macdonald, helped develop this line of reasoning in *Politics* when he observed that the weakest point in Marx's socialist theory was the vague terms in which he defined the state. Instead of focusing clearly upon the essential properties of the state and its powers, Marx leaves us with a "general implication" that the state may be used by socialism until it is no longer needed and can be allowed to wither away. Since socialism will face many dangers as it struggles to find its footing, according to the Marxist view, it will be necessary to retain the state as an emergency force until the proletariat is strong enough to make it on its own. But here Chiaromonte warned that "the theory of State power as an emergency power has always been the theory of despots. Despots have always maintained that, the more stupendous the aims to be achieved, the more ruthless the use of State power has to be—and also the more ruthless the use of power, the more limited it will be to a definite time, and to the specific necessities of a certain emergency."[24] Thus the ultimate outcome of all attempts to use the power of the state for libertarian purposes must inevitably end in failure so far as the goal of attaining an increased degree of human freedom is concerned; and Chiaromonte, like Macdonald, concluded that the only feasible stance to take toward the state is one of general suspicion and distrust. It was just this kind of hard-nosed reasoning that made *Politics* one of the most vital sources of anarchist inspiration in the years immediately following the war.

During the forties and early fifties the anarchist idea was given additional reinterpretation by *Resistance*, originally published under the title *Why*. David Thoreau Wieck, who was mainly responsible for carrying on the publication of the journal in the last years before it ceased publication in 1954, was staunchly opposed to the tendency of some anarchists to engage in polemics regarding the virtues of either the individualist or collectivist point of view. To place the individual against society is to reduce the level of anarchist philosophy to an absurdly low level, Wieck held.[25] If we are to gain any real insight into the logic of anarchist thought in the United States, he argued, we must see that a reconciliation has taken place between the individualist and collectivist viewpoints. To some extent we may speak of this as being a rediscovery of the idea of individualism and the recognition that the viewpoint of rigid collectivism is no longer viable. What has given renewed prestige to the idea of individualism among anarchists is the realization that a high regard for the value of the free individual is essential in the modern era of impersonalism and alienation. The individualist, in refusing to acknowledge even the authority of the group, makes a real contribution to the anarchist's quest for a science of freedom. Anarchist communism following Kropotkin assumed that the individual would benefit by his participation in the life of the commune, gaining as much as beneficiary of the mutual aid which exists within the social group as he lost by the abandonment of his unqualified individuality. But in the United States the collective idea was largely appropriated by the syndicalists who orgainzed the I.W.W. and dominated the anarchist movement in America during the entire period between World Wars I and II.

Although there may be a strong case to be made for syndicalist theories, most anarchists are unwilling to accept the conclusion that anarchism and syndicalism are synonymous. Writing in *Resistance*, George Woodcock, a leading historian of anarchism, called for a reconsideration of the entire foundation of anarchist thought as it had developed between the two world wars.[26] The syndicalists, emulating Marxism to the extent that they came to conceive of industrial capitalism as the personification of all social evil, organized themselves along the lines of a huge and powerful labor organization. But in doing so, according to Woodcock, syndicalism transformed itself into the very likeness of the evil it fought. When syndicalism adopted the spirit and tactics of the capitalistic trusts, it exposed anarchism to the debilitating forces of regimentation, authoritarianism, and centralism. Those who become obsessed with the grandiose idea of "One Big Union" are in danger of becoming entangled in the psychosis of power they indulge themselves in, Woodcock warned. Over against the centralized and homogeneous organization of the industrial union, Woodcock called for a return to the commune in which the individual worker and consumer is not so easily swallowed up in the vast size of the undertaking he is involved in.

It is instructive to note that at the very moment that professional sociologists and political scientists were frantically searching for more refined methods of "scientific" outlook, the anarchists who wrote for *Resistance* were calling for increased reliance upon the natural instincts and a more revolutionary approach to social problems. Sociologists proclaim that "if we knew more sociology we could change society for the better," but Paul Goodman wryly quipped that the truth is that "if we dared to change society for the better, we should learn more sociology."[27] David Thoreau Wieck spelled out the more precise meaning of the anarchist formula for social progress when he argued that "to give a new tone to our society, a new quality to our life, we must change the central principle of our society—we must learn how to live socially, and work together, without the profit and power motives; without a monopoly property-system; without centralized political authority; without war."[28] Acknowledging that there is no easy solution to social problems, *Resistance* yet maintained that the only hope for success in the task of building a new humanity lies along the route of libertarian philosophy. "We contend that men need to be free of restriction in order to grow to the limit of their powers—and when these powers are released from inhibition, entirely new solutions to our economic, political and social problems will be possible," Wieck editorialized. Decrying the cynicism of those who see only doom in store for the human race, *Resistance* took the stance that anarchism is not so much a political theory as it is a feeling of confidence regarding the social potential of people. The true anarchist is one who has "Joy!, sincere delight in men and women when they are beautiful—sorrow, not bitterness and contempt, when they are not."[29]

Writing in the fifties when a mood of conservative quiescence gripped young and old alike from one end of the country to the other, the anarchist idea as it was presented by *Retort* and *Resistance* largely fell upon deaf ears and the public generally dismissed anarchism as a tale told by idiots and fools. But in retrospect it is clear that anarchists of this period were the harbingers of the cultural revolution that was to start in the sixties. Sounding very much like the young firebrands who later organized Students for a Democratic Society, David Thoreau Wieck virtually called for "participatory democracy" when he suggested to the youth of the country that the real evil we face in America is "power, and the remedy for the evil of power is, not the half-step of Democracy, but the whole step of Freedom."[30] Freedom, as Wieck defined the term, drew heavily upon the concept of individualism which he derived from the writings of native American anarchists of the past. "The individual is powerful when he is free, and more powerful when he is not alone"; Wieck urged, "but he is weak when he is in a mass." In warning anarchists away from mass action as a possible solution to social problems, Wieck merely restated a truth that anarchists of all persuasions had always known—that "freedom means individual responsibility" without which social life is impossible. Anarchism is not opposed to organization in itself, Wieck pointed out, but only to that organization that depends upon the authoritarian principles of command and compulsion for its success. An anarchist society, building upon the social responsibility and initiative of primary groups acting voluntarily, will gradually develop the libertarian social foundations essential for a truly free society. Any shortcut to utopia that bypasses the individual can only end in failure.

Anticipating the charge that anarchism's emphasis of individualism is really a form of elitism, *Resistance* countered by insisting that real revolution can never be the work of an elite leadership but must always build upon the enlightened principle of individual social awakening. That is to say, Wieck argued, "the social revolution for any of us can be the work only of all of us."[31] Only a society that has enjoyed a widespread experience of individual enlightenment can claim any headway toward social and political liberation. In an effort to acquaint the readers of *Resistance* with concrete suggestions as to how this social revolution could proceed, Jackson MacLow, a "young, Chicago-born poet and critic" proposed that American radicals look toward the spontaneity so highly regarded by anarchists such as Godwin and Bakunin for the dynamics of social rejuvenation. Although precise rules for direct action can never be finalized beforehand, MacLow held, there are a number of specific things that libertarians can do to help bring about social revolution. Not only must we relentlessly attack the idols that our fathers have imposed upon our social and political consciousness but we must "affirm the natural world and our common nature (which is a social nature)" by acting directly and spontaneously on the environment that we find ourselves in.[32] The most "atrocious" of all that stand in the way of our social liberation, according to MacLow, is the system of public schools with which America has subverted the natural spontaneity and creativity of the young.[33] So long as we continue to regiment the minds and hearts of the young with the false patriotism of mass education disguised as democracy, the vitality necessary for a real social revolution will be denied us. Although *Resistance* was unable to find the resources to continue publication beyond 1954, its brief existence helped establish the fact that the anarchist idea did in fact have relevance in post World War II America.

Early in 1956, following the circulation of a questionnaire designed by the War Resisters League to ascertain the feelings among radicals and pacifists regarding the feasibility of supporting yet another journal, *Liberation*, an "independent monthly," began publication. The fact that *Liberation* was sponsored by the War Resisters League made it inevitable that its major emphasis should be anarchistic, for the League, although only established at the end of World War I, was spiritual heir of such anarchistic souls as Adin Ballou, Henry C. Wright and William Lloyd Garrison of the New England Peace Society of an earlier era.

If there was any question that *Liberation* was greatly inspired by the anarchist idea, it was dispelled by the lead article of the very first issue, "What I Believe," by Vinoba Bhave.[34] Thinking within the social perspective of the impoverished peasantry of India, Vinoba Bhave called for the bypassing of governmental control and the creation of a new society at the village level where the masses of people have effective existence. Over the years many contributors to *Liberation* were to reaffirm Vinoba Bhave's devotion to the idea of communitarianism and agrarian decentralization. Several members of *Liberation's* editorial board, moreover, were at one time or another involved in intentional communities, making it evident that the journal was solidly grounded in the basic attitudes of American anarchism, although it did not openly advertise itself as an anarchist publication.

Actually, *Liberation* in the early years of its existence was somewhat evenly divided between those who were attracted to Marxian ideas and those who thought along the lines of anarchism. But the ideological orientation of its editors and contributors was secondary to their primary interest in the liberation of mankind. The purpose of *Liberation,* according to its editorial board, is to inspire people to think and act constructively regarding the forces within contemporary society that tend to regiment, corrupt, and dehumanize the individual and deprive him of his freedom. *Liberation* condemned the political act that is not rooted in ethical considerations. It is impossible for a true social revolutionary movement which sincerely seeks for justice to achieve its ends within the structure of political reality as it exists at the contemporary moment, its editors lamented, for conventional society extracts all ethical substance from politics, making it into an exercise in human trivia and futility. Rather than concentrating on the individual's right to vote for meaningless alternatives, *Liberation's* editorial board maintained, emphasis should be placed instead on the "transformation of human society by human decision and action. . ." And here it is evident that the central problem of post World War II society concerns the necessity of finding ways to check and control *both* parties to the international struggle for power who seem determined to win at all costs, even if it means destroying the rest of the world in the process. Facing the question completely without prior commitment to any ideological position, *Liberation* quickly established itself as a truly "independent monthly."

Reflecting the urgency of the times in which it was born, *Liberation* was impatient with the old techniques and methods of radicalism. As Dave Dellinger pointed out, a real social revolution "begins with one's self,"[36] for the problems which face us cannot be solved if we sit idle in wait for ready-made solutions to fall down from the skies. As the original followers of Jesus did, according to Dellinger, we must "start living as brothers now, regardless of the power of Big Business, the oppression of governments, the aggressiveness of our enemies." To join a political party is to avoid social revolution. On the other hand, the act of changing society is inseparable from the act of changing oneself. And one cannot act at all unless it is within the context of existing social relations.

Dellinger's emphasis upon the necessity of individual direct social action was widely shared among the other contributors to *Liberation*. The late A. J. Muste, dean of American pacifists, as an example, had long urged that only a total involvement of the individual in the cause of peace can halt the march toward war that appears to arise anew with each generation. This individualist bias was built into the enrollment form of the War Resisters League which asks each prospective member to voluntarily assent to the declaration that "war is a crime against humanity" and pledges him "not to support any kind of war, international or civil, and to strive for the removal of all the causes of war." Applying the principles of individual direct social action to other areas of life such as civil rights in the South, *Liberation* was quickly recognized as one of the most significant and influential voices of American radicalism, a status that it enjoys to this day. And while *Liberation* did not formally recognize itself as an anarchist journal, the tone of its approach to social and political questions left little doubt where its real sympathies lay.

This is not to suggest that there were not occasional disputes concerning the fine points of anarchism as it relates to other political theories within the editorial group that was responsible for *Liberation's* publication. Dave Dellinger, succeeding A. J. Muste as chief editor, precipitated one such controversy when he insisted against considerable opposition from other board members that *Liberation* should maintain a sympathetic attitude toward Castro and the Cuban Revolutionary movement which had just come into public focus. Dellinger argued in the best tradition of radicalism that libertarians must remain completely tolerant and open to all peoples so that truth and justice would not be sacrificed once again to power and expediency. At times Dellinger found himself in the position of insisting that the violence resorted to by libertarian movements in developing nations such as Cuba and Vietnam is somehow different from the violence waged by the American military-industrial complex.[37] In the initial stages of the controversy, Roy Finch, one of the original editors who considered himself an anarchist, was critical of Dellinger's position on the ground that in his opinion it violated one of anarchism's most fundamental principles. Finch argued that the libertarian can never support a political leader who entrenches himself within a power structure and begins to assemble bureaucratic as well as popular support for his policies, as Castro was then doing. Anarchism, according to Finch, has always been opposed to power politics, whether it was waged by rightists or leftists. The fact that the Cuban revolution has raised the standard of living for the vast majority of Cuban people does not make it any more acceptable in the eyes of the anarchists than the Bolshevik revolution was, he argued. The seizure of political power is definitely not the social revolution advocated by anarchism, Finch proclaimed, nor is the anarchist capable of rationalizing away the violence which the Castro regime has directed at its political enemies; Castro has established a regime which, although less brutal and corrupt than the Batista regime, is a dictatorship nonetheless. Finch's resignation from the editorial board over this issue in 1961 is indicative of the depth to which this disagreement went.[38] In retrospect it is clear that the controversy between Finch and Dellinger was more one of emphasis and personal understanding than of fundamental philosophical disagreement. Finch was perfectly correct when he argued that no anarchist may take up the sword to put down his adversaries in the struggle for power, while Dellinger was equally correct when he insisted that those who are enslaved by the powerful are perfectly in the right when they leap at their captors for the purpose of gaining their freedom. As Pierre-Joseph Proudhon, a master of paradox and contradiction, had pointed out long before, power and violence are as inevitable in human society as they are despised, which explains why two men of equally good faith can engage in heated dispute over their relative value; it is only time that can bring into focus the true significance of human passions. *Liberation*, like anarchism itself, sought for a politics of social justice and right, not a politics of power, and hence it could tolerate the expression of completely diverse points of view and still remain clear as to its libertarian mission.

As the fifties gave way to the sixties, a plethora of journals carrying the message of anarchism appeared to demonstrate the fact that the seed planted earlier by thousands of American anarchists had not lain fallow. *View and Comments* (later titled *Towards Anarchism*) published by the Libertarian League was in fact largely the handiwork of Esther and Sam Dolgoff, the latter of whom writes under the pseudonym Sam Weiner. Schooled in the theories of anarchism through their association with the Libertarian Book Club and the editorial board of the *Freie Arbeiter Stimme*, Sam and Esther are typical of the thousands of thinking Americans whose sentiments and affiliations are anarchistic and who have kept the idea of anarchism alive through the precarious era of world wars, depression, and centralized governmental power. Although the Libertarian League embraced very few people in terms of actual numbers, it has had a tremendous impact on American radical thought to the extent that it is the heir to the tradition of anarcho-syndicalism honed out by Emma Goldman and later Rudolf Rocker. For people like Sam and Esther, anarchism is not so much a theory to be talked about but an idea to be practiced in one's life. If the idea of anarchism has survived against impossible odds, it is because of the courage and determination of people like these.

During the late sixties the anarchist idea was given one of the most intelligent interpretations it has ever had by the pen of Murray Bookchin, who sometimes wrote under the pseudonym, Lewis Herber. A member of the anarchos group in New York City, Bookchin was one of the founders of *Anarchos*, an occasional journal of contemporary anarchist theory. Referring to himself as an "anarchist communist," Bookchin tacitly acknowledged the wisdom implicit in the individualist view when he wrote: "The problem of what social forms will replace existing ones is basically a problem of the relations free men will establish between themselves. Every personal relationship has a social dimension; every social relationship has a deeply personal aspect to it."[39] When we focus clearly on this fact, Bookchin urged, we see that the long awaited liberation of mankind will come about not at the barricades or in the halls of organized power but as a consequence of the kind of personal social relationships people build for themselves. Bookchin firmly established himself among libertarians as one to take notice of when he made the important observation that "If we define 'power' as the power of man over man, power can only be destroyed by the very process in which man acquires power over his own life and in which he not only 'discovers' himself but, more meaningfully, formulates his selfhood in all its social dimensions."[40] American anarchists, to be sure, had been voicing this crucial insight over the years with regularity, but never before had the general public tuned to a frequency that permitted them to fully appreciate its meaning or its importance to the process of social change. Presenting the anarchist idea in terms of the contemporary problem of ecological survival, Bookchin made anarchism relevant to people who had previously appeared deaf, dumb, and blind, and he at once became one to be listened to by youth.

It is not too much to say that Bookchin's essay, "Listen Marxist!," is a definitive statement of the anarchist position with regard to Marxism. To the extent that Marxism relies upon an organized party structure, Bookchin held, it aligns itself with the bourgeoise model of hierarchy and centralized power and lays the foundations for the ultimate corruption of the proletariat. "Karl Marx and Fredrich Engels were centralists—not only politically, but socially and economically. They never denied this fact and their writings are studded with gleaming encomiums to political, organizational, and economic centralization."[41] When the Bolsheviks later adopted the party as the central focus of their revolutionary effort, the Russian Revolution was doomed to failure, for they had made the grievous error of holding tenaciously to the state in practice, just as Marx and Engels before them had held tenaciously to it in theory. The difficulty with Marxism in terms of its ability to liberate mankind from poverty and oppression, according to Bookchin, is that it reaches back into the past for the means of bringing about the future. Just as the monarchs of old celebrated power as the touchstone of life, so the Marxist is incapable of thinking outside the framework of organized power and social control for his design of utopia. In this, the Marxists of the present are no better nor worse than the authoritarians of the past, and we are constrained to look for social and philosophical substance somewhere other than in the theory and practice of Marxism.

Unlike the establishment people who see only gloom and doom in the social unrest that currently disturbs contemporary society, Bookchin sees the turmoil we are experiencing as a sign that the spirit of the Enlightenment is once again at work and that we may look forward to a better day when many of the problems we face today will be solved. From one perspective, the widespread disrespect toward institutional codes and goals we see all around us is an indication that the bourgeoise culture of the last several centuries is tottering and will soon collapse. Viewed from the opposite perspective, however, this unrest and cultural breakdown, according to Bookchin, are the first crude movements of life as the society of tomorrow struggles to draw in breath and establish itself as a living organism. It is true that people have taken to the streets, circumventing the established political institutions that ordinarily are supposed to assure social and economic transition from one historical moment to another. But the mass demonstrations and "riots" we witness are indications that the human beings of which they are composed are searching for their respective individual personalities and are no longer willing to be exploited and used by an elite of property and power. Social unrest and philosophical confusion are the birthpains that usher in a new era of human development and we should rejoice that we are experiencing them rather than lament the discomfort they cause us.

The most distinctive aspect of Bookchin's interpretation of the anarchist idea is the deft analogy he constructs between anarchism and ecology. Building upon the philosophical foundations laid by nineteenth century anarchist theoreticians such as Kropotkin, Malatesta, and the Reclus brothers, Bookchin points out that the evolutionary process we find in physical nature has its counterpart in social development, and that we ignore this truth at our own peril. For both the ecologist and the anarchist, the most striking characteristic of nature is the spontaneity that lies at the bottom of every natural growth pattern. Natural living processes atrophy and die to the extent that they are artificially restricted and caged within imposed regimens of force and restraint, Bookchin argues, whereas they flourish and progress whenever left to their own internal resources. Bookchin aptly sums up the major thrust of the evolutionary theory initially formulated by Kropotkin when he writes:

> The ecologist, insofar as he is more than a technician, tends to reject the notion of 'power over nature.' He speaks, instead, of 'steering' his way through an ecological situation, of managing rather than *recreating* an ecosystem. The anarchist, in turn, speaks in terms of social spontaneity, of releasing the potentialities of society and humanity, of giving free and unfettered rein to the creativity of people. Both, in their own way, regard authority as inhibitory, as a weight limiting the creative potential of a natural and social situation. Their object is not to *rule* a domain, but to *release* it.

As the above makes clear, anarchism draws its inspiration not from the modern world of science but from the idea of nature as it has always been interpreted during previous periods of enlightened thought. Nature, on this view, is not a defective system that needs to be discarded but a highly ordered living process that merely needs to be relieved of its artificial restraints to become the magnificent thing it is. Just as ecology seeks to right the balance of physical nature by allowing it to revert back to its natural patterns of growth, so anarchism seeks to right the balance of human society by allowing people to express their inner social inclinations. There is a vital truth contained in ecology, according to Bookchin, and this is that "if we wish to advance the unity and stability of the natural world, if we wish to harmonize it, we must conserve and promote variety."[43] If Bookchin's theory appears strikingly similar to the theory of laissez-faire formulated by the enlightened thinkers of the eighteenth century, we should not be surprised, for the philosophical foundations of all anarchists stem from the same source.

NOTES

SECTION VI - CHAPTER 4

1. "Towards a Revolutionary Morality," *Retort,* I (Spring, 1943), 48.

2. "The Individualists," *Resistance,* XII (December, 1954), 9.

3. "Technology and Socialism," *Retort,* II (November, 1943), 8.

4. "Specialization and the Modern School," *The Modern School,* IV (October, 1917), 108.

5. *System of Economical Contradictions,* trans. by Benjamin R. Tucker (Boston, 1888), p. 203.

6. "The Mechanics of Class Development," *Retort,* I (June, 1942), 13.

7. "Editorials," *Retort,* II (Winter, 1945), 8.

8. For a perceptive treatment of the aesthetic interests of outstanding anarchists such as Josiah Warren, Pierre-Joseph Proudhon, and Peter Kropotkin, see Donald Drew Egbert, *Social Radicalism and the Arts; A Cultural History from the French Revolution to 1968* (New York, 1970).

9. "Editorial Statement," *Retort,* I (Winter, 1942), 7.

10. "Egoism and Revolution," *Retort,* I (Winter, 1942), 29.

11. For an appreciation of Read's contribution to anarchist thought, see William O. Reichert, "The 'Unpolitical Philosophy' of Sir Herbert Read," *Arts in Society* (Summer, 1968), pp. 129-141.

12. "Auden: A Note of Anxiety," *Retort,* IV (Winter, 1949), 38.

13. "On Treason against Natural Societies," *Retort,* III (Fall, 1945), 40.

14. "The Environment of Freedom," *Retort,* III (Spring, 1946), 13.

15. "Towards a Revolutionary Morality," 46.

16. "Publisher's Preface," *Politics, in Radical Periodicals in the United States, 1890-1960* (New York, 1968), II. The best of Macdonald's essays have recently been reprinted in *Politics Past,* formerly published under the title, *Memoirs of a Revolutionist* (New York, 1970).

17. "Atrocities of the Mind," *Politics,* II (August, 1945), 22.

18. "Comment," *Politics,* II (May, 1945), 134.

19. "New Roads in Politics," *Politics,* II (December, 1945), 369.

20. "Here and Now: The Uncommon People," *Politics,* VI

(Winter, 1949), 60.

21. "The Root is Man—Part II," *Politics,* III (July, 1946), 207. Since published in book form under the same title.

22. "The Bomb," *Politics,* II (September, 1945), 260.

23. "The Root is Man—Part II," *Politics,* III (July, 1946), 209.

24. "On the Kind of Socialism Called 'Scientific,' " *Politics,* III (February, 1946), 42.

25. "In Reply," *Resistance,* XII (August-October, 1954), 13.

26. "The Commune; A Factor in a Free Society," *Resistance,* VI (June, 1947). 3.

27. "Statistical Methods in Sociology," *Resistance,* VIII (August-September, 1949), 5.

28. "Essentials of Anarchism," *Resistance,* XI (August, 1953), 5.

29. "Anarchism without Dogma," *Resistance,* VI (December, 1947), 6.

30. "From Politics to Social Revolution," *Resistance,* XII (April, 1954), 3.

31. "The Crime of Revolution," *Resistance,* VIII (December, 1949), 2.

32. "Affirm the Real Thing," *Resistance,* VI (July, 1947), 7.

33. "Affirm the Real Thing—Part II," *Resistance,* VI (August, 1947), 10.

34. *Liberation,* I (March, 1956), 7-10.

35. "Tract for the Times," *Liberation,* I (March, 1956), 3.

36. "The Here and Now Revolution," *Liberation,* I (June, 1956), 17.

37. "The March on Washington and its Critics," *Liberation,* X (May, 1965), 31.

38. "Cuba and Revolution," *Liberation,* VI (May, 1961), 3.

39. "The Forms of Freedom," *Anarchos,* II (Spring, 1968), 23. This essay, along with most of Bookchin's other important writings, has been published under the title, *Post-Scarcity Anarchism* (Berkeley, 1971).

40. *Ibid.,* 40.

41. "Listen Marxist!," *Anarchos* (May, 1969), 23.

42. "Ecology and Revolutionary Thought," *Post-Scarcity Anarchism,* pp. 77-8.

43. *Ibid.,* p. 76.

CHAPTER 5

Randolph Bourne and Paul Goodman:
"Corrupters" of American Youth

Although Randolph Bourne (1886-1918) and Paul Goodman (1911-1972) belonged to entirely different generations, they developed such strikingly similar conceptions of the anarchist idea that they deserve to be treated in the same chapter. Essentially artists by temperament, both of them were moved by strong feelings of beauty to employ their imaginations in the search for a new and better kind of social world. Both of them were also highly vocal critics of the state and its tendency to make war at the expense of the youth. Apostates from the liberalism they had picked up by rote in their early years, both of them declared themselves libertarians instead and extolled the merits of the kind of democracy we might have had under different circumstances. Finally, both of them demonstrated outstanding concern for the destiny of the human race and unusual devotion to the demands of civic responsibility despite the trenchant social and political criticism they raised as writers and intellectuals. If anarchism in America can make any claim to having produced genius along the way, Randolph Bourne and Paul Goodman will surely be recognized as two of its most outstanding representatives in that regard.

A gnome-like figure with his short, stunted body, hunched back, unusually large head, and heavy facial features, Bourne was a highly sensitive, creative individual who learned early in life that his physical disability caused by a fall during infancy was more than compensated for by the keen mind and free spirit housed in his twisted frame. After attending public school in Bloomfield, New Jersey, he worked for a manufacturer of automatic pianos for a time but after some years grew restless as a result of the inactivity his intellect was forced to endure in these circumstances. In 1909 when he was 23, Bourne entered Columbia University where he was stimulated by the brilliant lectures of Charles A. Beard, graduating in 1912 with a Phi Beta Kappa key and the William Mitchell Fellowship which permitted him to do graduate work in political science and sociology. Upon the completion of his studies in 1913 he published the first of his many collections of essays, *Youth and Life,* and then set sail for Europe where he rounded off his education by a year of deep contemplation. His first job after returning home was as a contributor to the *New Republic* in whose pages he valiantly tried to keep alive the liberal faith he had acquired at the feet of John Dewey. But as Professor Louis Filler points out, the "promise of American life" which its editor, Herbert Croly, proferred was actually much different from the hopes and dreams which Randolph Bourne wished for his country, and it was not long before Bourne's frequent visits to Croly's office were chilled by the widening ideological gulf that separated them.[1] Bit by bit Bourne veered away from the liberalism his teachers had taught him. The bone upon which Bourne gagged, causing him to regurgitate all the political theory that had been stuffed into him over the years, was the tempting falsehood that society could be reformed by a series of piecemeal measures which glossed over the surface but did not disturb the underpinnings. As John Dos Passos put it, Bourne "picked rosy glasses out of the turgid jamber of John Dewey's teaching through which he saw clear and sharp the skinny capital of reformed democracy; but he was too good a mathematician, he had to work the equations out."[2] Finding that Dewey and the other learned guardians of liberal democracy were not only deficient in arithmetic but were also practically illiterate when it came to ethical propositions, Randolph Bourne went off to think on his own, thereby giving us some of the finest political theory ever to have been produced by an American anarchist.

In the early stages of his intellectual development, Bourne was influenced by the writings of Henry George to adopt the general attitude of socialism toward economic problems.[3] The degree to which Bourne adhered to the teachings of socialism is demonstrated by the fact that he stood out almost alone among his well-educated contemporaries in recognizing the IWW as a worthy step in the direction of industrial democracy. While abroad, Bourne took a close look at the realities of English economic and political institutions and was appalled by the dismal conditions which the upper orders permitted the working classes to suffer. After he witnessed a general strike in Rome in which the normally happy Italian worker marched in sullen protest against the reactionary policies of his government, his admiration for the doctrine of syndicalism was greatly strengthened and it would not be incorrect to say that he had become something of a socialist himself, at least in spirit.[4] But Bourne was only interested in economic theory to the extent that it led to the liberation of mankind, and hence he focused on the larger issue of social change and the sociological circumstances that accompanied it, leaving doctrinal matters concerning economic questions to others.

Although Bourne was vitrolic in his criticism of American democratic institutions, his real purpose was not to destroy the idea of democracy but to find ways to bring it to realization in this country. In his famous essay, "The War and the Intellectuals," Bourne issued the warning that the function of the democrat is "to divide, confuse, disturb, keep the intellectual waters constantly in motion" as intellectuals and politicians persist in the folly of pushing the bankrupt ideas of moribund liberalism off on the gullible American public.[5] From his point of view the only thing that could save America was the adoption of a thoroughgoing policy of participatory democracy which would take power back from the politicians. Far from being an elitist, Bourne stood ready to turn the control of life over to the people, for "Democracy means a belief that the people are worthy; it means trust in the good faith and the dignity of the average man." Essentially a Jeffersonian democrat, Bourne faithfully reflected the teachings of libertarianism when he proclaimed that no progress whatever could be expected in the direction of democracy until society puts its complete faith in the individual citizen and ceases its dependence upon formal political institutions for the order that is essential to life. Who but a confirmed libertarian could write that:

> The great crime of the past has been that mankind has never been willing to trust itself, or men each other. We have tied ourselves up with laws and traditions, and devised a thousand ways to prevent men from being thrown on their own responsibility and cultivating their own powers. Our society has been constituted on the principle that men must be saved from themselves. We have surrounded ourselves with so many moral hedges, have imposed upon ourselves so many checks and balances, that life has been smothered.[6]

It is to be noted, however, that when Bourne expressed the need to place trust in man, it was not the older generation that he put his faith in but youth.

The theme that ties together the threads of Bourne's political theory is the argument that youth is the one and only force capable of saving humanity from itself.[7] This was more than a social theory, for Bourne, although he had withdrawn a great distance from the Christian teachings he had been tutored in during his childhood, was essentially a religious man in the same sense that Kropotkin or Proudhon could be called religious men. "Really to believe in human nature while striving to know the thousand forces that warp it from its ideal development—to call for and expect much from men and women, and not to be disappointed and embittered if they fall short—to try to do good with people rather than to them—this is my religion on its human side," Bourne wrote.[8] In common with the youth of the present generation, Bourne sought for a spiritual content in the universe that would fill the void he felt at the thought of the injustice and inhumanity which men through the ages had heaped upon one another. Unlike today's average young person, perhaps, Bourne was willing to speak positively about the idea of God, and thus he made reference to a cosmic force that exists in the universe, exerting an influence over our lives to the extent that we are conscious that it exists.[9] But far from accepting the Sunday school morality that so many of his contemporaries contented themselves with, Randolph Bourne was staunchly opposed to the practice of indoctrinating the young in the rights and wrongs of morality. "From home and Sunday-school, children of a slightly timid disposition get moral wounds, the scars of which never heal," Bourne warned. "They enter a bondage from which they can never free themselves; their moral judgment in youth is warped and blighted in a thousand ways, and they pass through life" without ever really learning what right and wrong really mean.[10] "When moral instruction is given," Bourne argued, "a criminal advantage is taken of the child's suggestibility, and all possibility of an individual moral life, growing naturally and spontaneously as the young soul meets the real emergencies and problems that life will present to it, are lost." No less than Proudhon or Bakunin, Bourne shared the conviction that structured moral codes are the greatest enemy of a real moral development and so he stood ready to ban them at once.

It was not the cleric who caught the full brunt of his criticism,

however, but the teacher and philosopher. Making reference to those
intellectuals of his day who stood off from the smoldering issues
of social and political discontent so that their robes would not become contaminated by the acrid fumes which billowed up from
them, Bourne expressed bitter scorn for all who are too timid to
enter the social fray on the side of those whom they deem to be in the
right. "Our distrust of their whole spiritual fabric becomes fundamental. We can no longer take most of them seriously," Bourne
angrily wrote. "We classify people by new categories. We look for
personality, for sincerity, for social sympathy, for democratic feelings, for social productiveness, and we interpret success in terms of
these attainments."[11] Educated men, Bourne complained, destroy
all hope that youth can take them seriously when they defend utterly
antiquated laws and ideals based upon outmoded myths and irrelevant sentiments. "Most of our leaders and molders of public
opinion speak simply as puppets pulled by the strings of the conservative bigotry of their class or group."[12] Their highest ambition is
to obtain the approval of their peers and superiors without regard to
truth or right. If young people have nothing but contempt for their
elders, Bourne lamented, the defect is plainly in the character of
the elders rather than in the character of the young.

    In calling for a social revolution upon the part of the youth,
Bourne actually advocated the establishment of a new and different
kind of religion based upon a fresh view of the essential values of
human experience.[13] American culture was moribund and could only
be revived by a massive transfusion of vital moral energy from the
uncontaminated souls of its young people. But life, even for youth,
is no path of roses, for there are corrupting pressures and influences
to be dodged if the young person is to avoid being destroyed by the
same evils that overcome his elders. Calling upon the young to
exercise their untapped powers of imagination, Bourne pronounced
the established social and political system a snare and urged young
people to avoid becoming implicated in it as though it were the most
deadly of evils. "Man does not live by politics alone," he prophesied
with deep libertarian conviction. Dedicated to the goal of creating
a kingdom of true humanity upon earth, Bourne urged youth to aim
high. If America were to be saved from the corruptions that then
beset it, a new and better culture must be generated along the lines
of libertarian social teachings. Bourne's dogged opposition to World

War I is to a great extent explained by the fact that he saw the war as a block in the way of the cultural renaissance he envisioned.[14]

Ironically, it was during the Second World War that Professor Louis Filler, one of the few historians who have fully appreciated Bourne's ability as a political thinker, made the observation that Bourne's most glaring error was to reject the concept of the state completely.[15] When we look backward some decades later, and with the Vietnamese debacle fresh in mind, Bourne's rejection of the state might appear more plausible to Professor Filler, as it does to so many of the youth of today. For Bourne, like Thorstein Veblen, clearly understood the Rasputin-like hold which the state exercises over the lives and destinies of a people. "To understand the American State of the Twentieth Century we have to realize," Bourne wrote, "that it is a direct descendant of the early English monarchy." In the mind of the average American, monarchy and democracy are poles apart, but on closer examination the perceptive political theorist will note that the concept of the state about which both forms of government cluster is essentially the same.

> The State in its inception is pure and undiluted monarchy; it is armed power, culminating in a single head, bent on one primary object, the reducing to subjection, to unconditional unqualified loyalty all the people of a certain territory. This is the primary striving of the State, and it is a striving that the State never loses, through all of its myriad transformations.[16]

Once established, the realities of politics necessitate that the base of power be broadened so that more and more people come to enjoy the privileges which the control of government always brings to the powerful, Bourne urged. But it is the sheerest of deceptions to hold that the democratic state, unlike anarchy, has the unqualified and enthusiastic devotion of all the people. Working upon the "herd instinct" which all men possess to some degree, the ruling class of any nation maintains itself in power by turning the majority of the people against that small radical minority that would question the legitimacy of the entire enterprise.

Most men must experience the horror and insanity of war at first hand before they can understand the futility of it all. But Bourne, with the penetrating perception of genius, saw clearly without ever hearing a shot fired that war, which is the "health of the state," is the matrix out of which all social illness grows. "The State is intimately connected with war," Bourne wrote, "for it is the organization of the collective community when it acts in a political manner, and to act in a political manner toward a rival group has meant, throughout all history—war."[17] Although Bourne's anarchism has on occasion been questioned,[18] no one has more clearly grasped the essential meaning of that idea than he did when he argued that in order to crusade against war it is first necessary to crusade against the state. In this regard Bourne was spiritual heir to the founders of the American peace movement—stalwart souls such as Adin Ballou, Henry C. Wright, and Henry David Thoreau—who early in the nation's history discovered that war is to the state what oxygen is to fire. "The State is the organization of the herd to act offensively or defensively against another herd similarly organized," Bourne candidly observed. Representative of all the latent hostility, coercion, and autocratic feelings which rumble through the bowels of any social group, the state serves as an outlet for these destructive, antisocial forces, permitting men in wartime to express all the animal instincts which are ordinarily denied them. Acting under the rationale of self-defense, the citizens of the state achieve a social unity and sense of purpose which parallels that of the wolf who runs and fights with the pack for its food. Left to themselves, Bourne maintained, people may fight among themselves over matters of individual difference and personal antagonism, but it is preposterous to suggest that they might under any circumstances organize themselves for the waging of formal warfare in which the main purpose is to utterly destroy one another. But people in modern industrial society are never left to themselves; they are politically organized under the direction of a ruling elite that is expert in the business of manipulating mass opinion and action. And war is the symbol by which all the strings that motivate the citizen are tied. Let the politician merely whisper the word "war," Bourne lamented, and the people rise like an obedient genie to carry out the every wish of its master.

Carefully distinguishing between the concepts of country and nation, Bourne did political theory a great service when he argued that the two are essentially different things. "Our idea of Country concerns itself with the non-political aspects of a people, its ways of living, its personal traits, its literature and art, its characteristic attitudes toward life," he wrote. One's country, besides being the geographical place in which one happens to have been born, is a social group within which one develops his cultural potential. One shares a common lot with kinsmen and friends and thereby acquires a deeply rooted set of values and commitments that give meaning and direction to life. "Country is a concept of peace, of tolerance, of living and letting live."[19] It may ultimately prove burdensome to the individual who has outgrown the cultural qualities it embodies but it can never really imprison him, for it exerts no compelling pressure over his life that he cannot escape by an act of individual will. The state or nation, on the other hand, "is essentially a concept of power" and cannot consequently be escaped as easily as country. Country, to the extent that one freely feels himself a part of it, impels one through love and common feelings of loyalty; one is devoted to it because it is the basic polity to which he belongs and within which he feels his social existence. But "the State is the country acting as a political unit, it is the group acting as a repository of force, determiner of law, arbiter of justice." Totally unwilling to confine its operations to those which can be effected through the instrumentality of love and feelings of kinship, as country does, the state employs force and compulsion, punishment and sanction, to compel the individual to give it his loyalty. If he will not freely do so, it imprisons him or otherwise punishes him for his refusal to obey its demands. In final analysis, the state holds absolute power over the life of the individual which in its ultimate form consists of nothing more than brute force and blind allegiance.

The history of America as a country is quite different from that of America as a state, Bourne observed. As a country, it is a drama of "the struggle of economic classes." But as a state, America has made its way in the world along the pathways of war and political power, competing with all comers for a place of superiority and glory. Unlike the parent whose love dictates that he send his children from him when they come of age, the state, knowing nothing of love, wages war to prevent itself from being divided as a consequence of the economic and religious conflicts that take place internally between one group and another. On the matter of civil obedience, "the State is a jealous God and will brook no rivals." All must bow down before it and stand ready to devote their lives to its objectives when national survival dictates. Far from being the servant of the people, the state is more aptly described as their master, for its needs and goals inevitably take precedence over those of the private individuals who together make up the people.

Were it not for war, Bourne argued, the state could not elicit the total obedience from the individual that it does. Statesmen, however, are skilled in the technique of presenting war as a serious threat to the continued survival of the social group, thereby winning the support of men and women who would otherwise view war as the most reprehensible of actions. Enthusiasm for war seems to arise spontaneously from the people, Bourne urged, but on close examination it becomes clear that it is really only the "state obsessed portion of the public" that genuinely desires armed conflict. "Militarism expresses the desires and satisfies the major impulse only of this class. The other classes, left to themselves, have too many necessities and interests and ambitions, to concern themselves with so expensive and destructive a game."[20]

Bourne's political philosophy precociously anticipates the theory of power politics developed after World War II. As Bourne viewed the international scene, the state exists as a special form of political phenomena that reflects a definite body of laws that explain its nature. States vie with each other, he held, not because the people who make them up are brutal and violent but because it is the state's fundamental character to wage war with other states when power conditions demand it. "Indeed," Bourne exclaimed, "it is not too much to say that the normal relations of States is war."[21] Whereas the prevailing view among political scientists is that diplomacy is a normal phase of international relations that takes place within conditions of peace, Bourne thought of it as "disguised war, in which States seek to gain by barter and intrigue, by the cleverness of wits, the objectives which they would have to gain more clumsily by means of war." Man's chief enemy, on this view, is the state, and hence the duty of every right thinking man is to withdraw his allegiance from it. The somewhat intemperate language Bourne employed in condemning the state as the primary source of violence tends to obscure the real depth of his social criticism, and hence he has not been as widely read in America as he deserves to be. Those who take the trouble to read Bourne carefully, however, recognize him as a true libertarian and one of the most perceptive social critics America has ever produced, even if the demands he made upon his fellow Americans may have been more than their patriotism could bear. When contemporary sociologists point out that "there is a close and lasting affinity between war and the state,"[22] their research findings clearly reflect the earlier sociological efforts of Randolph Bourne as he labored to liberate his countrymen from the tyranny he felt they were enslaved by.

Undoubtedly the most important theorist among American anarchists in the second half of the twentieth century was Bourne's counterpart, Paul Goodman, whose writings brilliantly elaborate the socio-political themes initially roughed out by his ideological forebear. Goodman's essays and books stand as an excellent compendium of libertarian thought and are essential reading for anyone interested in focusing upon the sociological and psychological foundations of the anarchist tradition.

Born in Greenwich Village the youngest of three children, Goodman was free to roam the sidewalks of New York and "the wild rocks of the Hudson" after the family was abandoned by the father shortly after Paul's birth. After attending the public schools in the city, Goodman graduated from The City College of New York in 1931 and then attended graduate school in a spasmodic fashion, journeying to Harvard and other intellectual centers to hear an occasional lecture as the spirit moved him but without officially registering for classes. During the last half of the 'thirties' Goodman was invited by Professor Richard McKeon, one of the teachers who early recognized his brilliance, to lecture in English literature at the University of Chicago while working on a Ph. D. degree on the side. But shortly before the final defense of his dissertation in 1940 he was let go from the faculty for "nonconformist sexual behavior," never again to establish any kind of long-term affiliation with a major American university.[23] Goodman was bisexual from the age of twelve, and this encounter with hard-bound prejudice and un-yielding moral self-righteousness might well have crushed a less philosophical individual, for the event must have caused him consider-able personal anguish. But again like Randolph Bourne, what might have been considered a "physical affliction" to another man was to Paul Goodman a phenomenon of nature that must be carefully examined and explained to be understood, and hence we are the richer for a long series of writings which address themselves to the nature and function of sexuality as it relates to the liberation of mankind.

It is impossible to describe the libertarian sentiments of Paul

Goodman, the anarchist, apart from the intimate sexual life of Paul Goodman, the man, for the basic game plan he deliberately followed in his writing was a totally frank and open discussion of every thought that entered his head, whether it had to do with politics or his own private erotic desires. To a greater or lesser degree every essay he wrote was autobiographical, and he held back nothing in his fanatical effort to achieve a basic honesty in all that he said. Far from being the reflection of an egomaniacal desire to draw attention to himself by shocking the sensitivity of his reader, this practice was in line with his belief that the primary function of philosophy is to facilitate human understanding by bringing thought out into the open. As he put it, "The best use of philosophy has been to get rid of silence and superstition; that is, to simplify the situation just by its being said."[24] Too long has humanity permitted itself to remain in abject slavery to unexamined prejudice so that the best part of its nature has been stunted as a consequence. When we recognize that the conventional language we use in everyday discourse is really one of the "strongest of glues" binding people together within established institutions, and that the "nature of things is amenable to being manipulated by words," Goodman argued, we can readily understand why it is essential to speak with total honesty when discussing the basic facts of human nature.[25] And thus it was in his book, *Five Years,* which was essentially a detailed chronicle of his intimate thoughts during the difficult period between 1945 and 1950 when he hungered in vain for any crumb of recognition, that he described how he felt when huddled in the back of a truck engaged in homosexual activity with some drifter he chanced to pick up; while in the very next paragraph he discussed the state of social disintegration in America. To speak openly of one's homosexual thoughts is to remind people that homosexuality, like life itself, is dirty, Goodman intoned. But "In a society as middle class, orderly, and technological as ours, it is essential to break down squeamishness, which is an important factor in what is called racism, as well as in cruelty to children and the sterile putting away of the sick and aged."[26] One cannot help but admire Goodman's honesty in this regard; like Socrates, he loved the polis too much to debase it with anything less than complete and serious-minded candor, however much risk he faced in having his sociological theories misunderstood. No student of modern social psychology can afford to ignore Goodman's writings, for they introduce a view of life that cuts through the ignorance and superstition of past ages with the sharpness of a surgeon's scalpel.

Stimulated by the writings of Wilhelm Reich, Goodman perfected himself in post-Freudian psychological theory and by 1955 had become a practicing psychotherapist affiliated with the New York Institute for Gestalt Therapy[27] on which subject he collaborated in writing a basic text.[28] The fundamental postulate of his psychological theory was that there is a direct linkage between the degree of erotic release enjoyed by the individual and the general level of social liberation experienced by society, and it was in pursuit of knowledge relating to the correct balance between these two vital forces that Goodman explored the forbidden realm of sexuality. In defiance of both the popular belief that the bisexual individual has been stunted in his sexual development and the existential conclusion that there is nothing spiritually meaningful to cling to in the universe, Goodman proclaimed both his animal nature and his spiritual values to be "unquestionably worthwhile and justified."[29] In his view a healthy society is one in which sexual inhibition has been reduced to the point that the real social characteristics of human nature are permitted to rise to the surface instead of remaining submerged in the dark recesses of unexplored life. And it was as an anarchist that he was able to clearly understand this sociological subtlety. "Anarchism is grounded in a rather definite social-psychological hypothesis: that forceful, graceful, and intelligent behavior occurs only when there is an uncoerced and direct response to the physical and social environment," Goodman wrote.[30] So long as the sexual natures of both young and old alike are kept in "anxious submissiveness to authority" there is no hope that the human race will free itself from symbol and rite long enough to make the difficult transition to an unstructured free society in which full expression of human nature would be permitted. In final analysis, Goodman warned, *"it is only free positive action that makes history,* revealing the depths of our common powers."[31] There is no choice open to us if we would live in freedom, therefore, other than the libertarian demand that we eliminate all authority at once and learn to conduct ourselves according to the social resources we find within human nature, even in so perilous an area as the deep-seated sexual drives that course beneath the surface of our conscious lives.

Publishing the first of his three novels in 1942, Goodman produced a long string of essays and books which have finally established him as one of the most original thinkers of this century, although it is only in recent years that he gained wide acceptance outside of libertarian circles. Contributing frequently to *Commentary, Liberation, The Partisan Review, The New York Review of Books,* and the anarchist journals, *Resistance* and *Politics,* Goodman hacked away for years on the theme that there is something terribly wrong with a society that does not permit its young to grow up sensibly so that the full range of its social powers become developed, only to have his argument fall upon tightly closed ears. It was not until the publication of his widely acclaimed *Growing Up Absurd* in the 'Sixties' that he was recognized as having something of importance to say to American youth. The trouble seems to have been in part that Goodman's theories for awhile were out of joint with the times. As Lionel Abel put it, "In the period when people were bent on being sensible, Goodman's wild theories could hardly interest. Now that there was wildness everywhere, it was suddenly noticed that he was sensible. . . ."[32] But even more important in explaining his failure to gain wide attention was the inability of people to accept the simple truths that were contained in his message. Goodman's work, it has been argued, "was to make life satisfying for human beings, largely by demonstrating that their social world is man-made and, therefore, man changeable" and that "the resources for change are in man himself."[33] For a libertarian thinker like Paul Goodman, this was axiomatic; but for a world that considers the foundations of the social firmament to be centered in the institutions of formal government, this was worse than incredible—it was heresy.

Paradoxically, the school of anarchist thought within which Paul Goodman is most precisely located is the Jeffersonian wing which prides itself on its practical thought and its foundations in the everyday activities of people as they go about the business of living together close to nature. Unfortunately, Goodman argues, we Americans "have lost the horse sense for which we were once noted" and have lapsed into a kind of "mindlessness induced by empty institutions" from which we seem unable to extricate ourselves.[34] Sounding very much like Randolph Bourne, Goodman insists that the "fault is not with democracy, but that we have failed to have enough of it."[35] If the political arts have died out in America, he opined, this is because we have not followed in the tradition of the town meeting and the neighborhood communes so much in evidence in the early development of the country, but have turned increasingly to the politician and the bureaucrat for formal leadership. Taking issue with those who totally condemn politics because it has come to be equated with coercion directed against people by those who control the state apparatus, Goodman called for a much broader definition of the concept. Throughout the length and breadth of the western political experience, he argued, "politics along with art and theory has been the noble activity of free men" and not the exclusive tool of those who would impose themselves upon their fellowmen through coercion.[36] "Let us try to define politics as a free act, belonging to free societies," he urged.

It is essential in this regard, according to Goodman, to clearly sort out in our minds the subtle sociological distinctions that surround the problem of coercion as a political phenomenon. On the one hand the anarchist stands firm behind the proposition that blind force and official violence directed against the individual citizen is always to be condemned, for these are primarily negative forces making for even more anomie and alienation and the further breakdown of community. But all coercion is not *prima facia* bad, according to Goodman, for coercion is in itself one of the natural forces that is essential to the functioning of society. Carefully distinguishing between "natural" and "unnatural" politics, Goodman argued that those ideas and principles which "naturally coerce social forces into action" are legitimate forms of libertarian action, whereas those that "invariably inhibit or destroy natural forces" making for human solidarity are authoritarian and therefore illegitimate.[37]

In the same vein, Goodman continued, we must clearly understand that violence, too, is an integral aspect of nature and hence not without its proper uses. With Tolstoy and Ghandi, Goodman held firm on the principle that organized warfare is totally inadmissable as a form of human behavior and hence he always stood ready to join forces with the pacifist camp in its anti-war activities. Yet in equally complete accord with Emma Goldman and Alexander Berkman, he insisted that violence, to the extent that it is found in nature, is a perfectly legitimate phase of human conduct so long as it arises as a consequence of the expression of genuine human emotions. "Natural violence," as Goodman defined it, "is the destruction of habits or second natures in the interest of regaining the primary experiences of birth, infantile anxiety, grief and mourning for death, simple sexuality, etc.."[38] When Goodman referred to himself as a "neolithic Conservative," it was a reflection of his basic agreement with Burke and other conservatives who argued that man's first freedom consists of the right to protect his fundamental ties with nature. Since organized government is only a secondary form of human association, it has no right to coerce the individual into violating his social responsibility to primary social attachments such as peer group, family, and community. As Goodman put it, "Resistance—patience—firmness—duty: these are not negative nor even passive virtues; they are not the restraint of force; they are actions of the more elemental forces of primary nature; of time and clinging to one's place." When the individual engaged spontaneously in violent acts initiated as a consequence of the natural desire to preserve his integrity and his hunger for social integration, we ought to recognize his conduct as a legitimate phase of human growth rather than an abnormal kind of behavior, Goodman urged.

Admittedly it is difficult to draw a precise line between legitimate and illegitimate coercion, Goodman acknowledges, but it is of the utmost importance that we do so. Coercion is legitimate as a social act only when it is "the correlative of natural voluntary dependency," as when a child relies for guidance upon a parent or teacher whose actions are dictated by shared love and social concern. So long as the teacher or parent confine the coercion they exert over their charges to the essential functions of the social role they fill, they are in no sense acting outside the limits of legitimate coercion. Making adequate judgements in this realm is difficult, to be sure, but to fail to try is to shirk our responsibility as social beings, Goodman charges. It is helpful in this regard, according to Goodman, to understand that the "defining property of free political action is potential unanimity, drawing on common nature and undercutting the conflict of interest."[39] That political act is legitimate that has as its goal those objectives and purposes about which there is unanimous agreement. Where unanimity is present, there is no coercion when people decide to act collectively to achieve an agreed upon goal. But where unanimity is lacking, the plan of action adopted by a libertarian society must be structured in an altogether different way.

Flying in the face of contemporary liberal-democratic theory which grounds itself on the principle of majority rule advanced by theorists such as Locke and Hobbes, Goodman totally abandoned the idea of democratic consensus and individual rights and projected in their place the libertarian notion of freedom. Where liberal democrats would restrict the freedom of the individual to those areas of action that can be guaranteed to him by a protective government, Goodman called for a definition of freedom that would have as its perimeters only the libertarian conception of "initiating activity." The only viable justification for individual freedom that will stand careful scrutiny, according to Goodman, is that an *unrestricted* right to initiate meaningful social activity is essential to the development of a rational social order. In the early stages of liberal thought, "Freedom meant freedom to enterprise, to bear witness, to initiate and govern," and it is this spirit we must recapture if we are to save America from the social atrophy that presently grips it.[40] Put into different terms, what we must do, according to Goodman, is to invent new programs whereby we might reverse the anti-democratic forces that have led us away from the goal of freedom our forefathers set for us when they broke finally with tyrannical government imposed upon them from without.

Like all anarchists, Goodman, although he was in basic agreement with the social psychology of Marxism, declared himself totally at odds with the political program offered by Marx and Engels when they called for political revolution against the existing order. And he chided contemporary activists for their proclivity to romanticize revolution. Although he was one of the heroes of the New Left and had spoken on invitation to several hundred university convocations during the period of unrest on American college campuses caused by the Vietnam War, Goodman outspokenly criticized the young for their ignorance of American political history. Employing the pungent terms of Marxian revolutionary thought while they at the very same time demonstrate a living devotion to anarchist social postulates in their actions, the youth of America "cannot remember the correct name for what they in fact do."[41] Whether they know the philosophical origins of their actions or not, Goodman scolded, the young in America who protest against the brutal power machinations of the military-industrial machine "are anarchists because they are in a historical situation in which Anarchism is their only possible response." Not only is social life in America carried on in a wholly immoral way, according to Goodman, but those in authority display a "functional incompetence" that is unforgivable at this late date in history. Pointing to the thoroughly decadent condition of contemporary culture in America, Goodman called upon youth to repudiate the cultural bankruptcy of their elders. It is to be noted, however, that his emphasis is always upon rational self-persuasion and free education rather than the manipulation of people and mass movement psychology. In fact, Goodman was outspokenly critical of those young militants on the Left who would radicalize people against the Establishment by deliberately maneuvering them into crowd situations wherein they come to have their heads broken by the batons of the police. "It is Anarchist for people to act on principle and learn, the hard way, that the powers that be are brutal and unjust," he wrote, "but it is authoritarian for people to be expended for the cause of somebody else's strategy."[42] Like Benjamin Tucker and other earlier libertarians, he insisted that non-invasion is the essential principle of all anarchist thought and that no action can have good results that does not conform to that spirit.

With penetrating analysis that has scarcely been equalled by contemporary social theorists, Goodman went right to the heart of anarchist thought when he pointed out that the word "revolution" in anarchist theory "means the process by which the grip of authority is loosed, so that the functions of life can go on freely, without direction or hindrance."[43] Unlike both the liberal and Marxist who view revolution as the opportunity for a new regime to seize power and restructure the institutions of government after its own peculiar ideological values and interests, the anarchist thinks of coup d'etat as a counterrevolutionary act and condemns it because he recognizes that power has not been eliminated at all but has merely been centralized in new hands. The purpose of revolution, as the anarchist views it, is to eliminate power altogether and not to transfer it from one group to another. Not until a social revolution of the proper kind takes place can we begin to lay the foundations of the libertarian society the world so desperately needs.

In the tradition of Proudhon, Goodman maintained that the

only truly meaningful kind of freedom available to the contemporary individual is to be found in "the expression of the natural animal and social groups to which he in fact belongs."[44] Recognizing that any social scheme that pits the individual against the collectivity is misleading because it distorts the balance that is everywhere found in nature, Goodman cautioned against disturbing the essential patterns of life. The individual is a social animal in the sense that he functions best in concert with those to whom he is naturally tied by virtue of his basic human emotions and instincts, Goodman urged, and any interference in this process is a treasonable act against free society. In anticipation of the criticism that inevitably comes from those political scientists who hold that the individual in final analysis is nothing more than the sum total of the interests which motivate him to act, Goodman held that "The free man does not seek to influence groups but to act in the natural groups essential to him—for most human action is the action of groups."[45] In his own life, Goodman was tied to those he loved—his second wife by common law with whom he lived for over twenty-five years and his son and two daughters—by strong feelings of kinship while he at the same time thought of himself as primarily responsible in his social actions to the larger community of man. When his son, Matthew, was killed while mountain climbing during a vacation from college, Goodman expressed deep parental love and suffering in an article he wrote for *Liberation,* indicating the extent to which he was himself motivated by natural emotions.[46] Like all anarchists, Paul Goodman recognized no institutional arrangements as legitimate other than those that stemmed from his own natural social proclivities. Driven by deep-seated homosexual urges to seek for ever more intimate love and companionship with other men, Goodman at the same time demonstrated the extent to which man is a social animal by nature when he continued voluntarily to recognize the family commitments he had made as worthy of his fidelity. The ultimate social justification for homosexuality as for any other kind of free human behavior, according to Goodman, is that "it is damaging for societies to check any spontaneous vitality."[47] And this cardinal principle of free society is inviolable and must be scrupulously honored if our professions in favor of liberty are to be taken seriously.

That Paul Goodman was not a mere libertine selfishly demanding license for himself that he would hypocritically deny to others is

seen in a piece he wrote during the Second World War with reference
to the correct stance for youth to take when faced with conscription.
However much he was himself opposed to organized warfare as a
consequence of his libertarian convictions, Goodman was unwilling
to advise a young man to accept any penalty the state might impose
upon him in order to avoid military service. That youth should firmly
resist the war and the draft was not a question open to debate; no
other decision was ethically acceptable, and Goodman would have
been sorely disappointed had his own son come up with any other
alternative. But Goodman was greatly concerned about the young
man who was intent upon "enlisting in jail" as if he "approved more
highly of penal institutions than of the army."[48] His thinking here
obviously structured by the egoism of Max Stirner and the eroticism
of Wilhelm Reich, Goodman warned the young to resist the urge to
moralistically expose themselves to severe punishment for the sake
of principle. It was not that one should not act on principle but
that the young have not yet had enough experience with life to be
certain as to what principles they should honor. "Right principles
are the statements of deep impulses, intuitions, insights into our
underlying natures," and we all have a duty to live freely so that
we may mature and develop the moral forces implicit in our being.
The young man who willingly exposes himself to heavy penalties is
violating his primary duty as a young person "to seek for animal
and social satisfactions" that are essential to his development. "You
do not have the right to postpone these satisfactions" that are a
natural phase of growing up, Goodman proclaimed. "To the extent
that the State or anything else tries to make you postpone them,"
Goodman urged in true libertarian fashion, "you must fight for
them by force, cunning, recalcitrance, camouflage, playing dead,
flight, etc., like any other healthy creatures we may observe in
nature." If Goodman filled a special niche in the hall of fame of the
Resistance that sprang up in America during the Vietnam War, it
was for the kind of clear libertarian thought he displayed here.

Of all of Goodman's many contributions to social thought,
none is more valuable than his insistent warning against the modern
trend toward ever more centralization of both economic and political
society. Most certainly Goodman aptly summed up the whole force
of the anarchist tradition in America and brought it into sharp
contemporary focus when he wrote that "What is peculiar about our

times is that, because of the complexity of social, technical, and urban organization, perhaps *no* central authority can be legitimate; it is bound to render the citizens powerless and to be dehumanizing."[49] Faced with this kind of compelling circumstance, the only sane course of action open to us, according to Goodman, "is to stop thinking in terms of power altogether," and hence it was that he rejected the revolutionary solutions offered by Lenin along with the pseudo-democratic proposals of the Trumans and Eisenhowers and turned toward the brilliant truths of Jeffersonian philosophy.

Echoing Randolph Bourne's condemnation of nationalism as a crude form of erstaz patriotism, Goodman, like his predecessor, called for the creation of a true patriotic community in America in which the individual would be free to develop his natural social inclinations rather than the superficial attachments to national interests the politician urges upon him. When reading the writings of our democratic forebears of the eighteenth century, Goodman observed, the fact that stands out above all others is that great patriots such as Jefferson, Madison, and Adams "speak as citizens who embody the polity and are creating it as an existential act of their natures."[50] Their real personalities were not yet swallowed up in the political party system that scheming politicians subsequently devised to rob the citizen of his civic patrimony. The central fact about Jeffersonian democracy that has been lost to the modern age, according to Goodman, was that self-education within the Enlightenment conception of free thought was the essential condition for the preservation of political liberty. Democracy is synonymous with the existence of an informed citizenry dedicated to its own instruction in the rights and wrongs of civic affairs in which all have an obligation to participate. Unfortunately, according to Goodman:

> With the Jacksonian revolution, as Tocqueville was quick to see, the democratic idea was already abandoned, for the power now resided in the majority of the people *as they were*, with their passions and prejudices uneducated by the responsible give-and-take in a face-to-face meeting that had to make practical decisions and use tax money. Instead the people would merely vote on issues and party programs. This was an invitation for demagogues and party leaders to get power, and for lobbying interests, that could deliver votes and cash, to influence the policians for their own power.[51]

After one hundred and fifty years of shameful neglect, it is not at all strange that the idea of democracy shows little sign of life in America.

In calling upon the young to turn their backs upon Lenin's

conception of a revolutionary party as the vanguard of popular rule, Goodman, with the subtlety that was characteristic of his thought, argued that "The young do have an authentic demand for young people's power, the right to take part in initiating and deciding the functions of society that concern them, as well as governing their own lives which are nobody else's business."[52] Breaking themselves down into natural social groupings, people must take back from elected officials and appointed bureaucrats the control of community problems such as schooling and urban development that have been taken from them. The energy for the momentous social reform called for by Goodman could come from only one source, in his opinion, and that was the shared concerns and natural sentiments of patriotic individuals steeped in local political matters. As Goodman put it, "it is impossible for the young to grow up *without* a community or local patriotism, for the locality is their only real environment."[53] And hence the primary social reform that all others rest upon is the decentralization of political power within the context of the urban technology the modern age has wrought. Goodman would not abandon science and technology altogether, or even government, for that matter, but merely make them responsive to the critical judgement of people operating on the social level of commune and factory, shop and home, in the tradition of anarcho-syndicalism. In every instance, however, the only legitimate form of power would be the individual citizen acting upon genuine social concerns of his own without interference from organized law or the state. Since this was the original design of the American republic, Goodman urges, it can hardly be called radical or impractical. And as for the exact terms of how we are to bring this "utopian proposal" about, Goodman in all seriousness suggested that the young make love, not power politics, thereby approaching the problem of social change at the only level at which real change might conceivably take place. It is for gems of wisdom such as these that the anarchist Paul Goodman is likely to be recognized by generations to come as one of their most patriotic and constructive philosophers, as well as one of their most perspicacious critics.[54]

NOTES

SECTION VI - CHAPTER 5

1. *Randolph Bourne* (Washington, D. C., 1943), p. 61.

2. *U.S.A. Nineteen Nineteen* (Boston, 1930), p. 117.

3. "A Philosophy of Handicap," *Youth and Life* (Boston, 1913), p. 352.

4. Filler, *op. cit.,* p. 51. It has been argued that Bourne was shoved in the direction of Marxism by his war experiences. For an example of this point of view, see Sidney Kaplan, "Social Engineers as Saviors: Effects of World War I on Some American Liberals," *Journal of the History of Ideas,* XVII (June, 1956). 369.

5. "The War and the Intellectuals," *Untimely Papers* (New York, 1919), p. 46.

6. "The Virtues and Seasons of Life," *Youth and Life,* pp. 86-87.

7. Van Wyck Brooks, *Emerson and Others* (New York, 1927), p. 125.

8. "A Philosophy of Handicap," *Youth and Life,* p. 355.

9. "Some Thoughts on Religion," *Youth and Life,* p. 198.

10. "The Virtues and Seasons of Life," *Youth and Life,* p. 51.

11. "For Radicals," *Youth and Life,* p. 295.

12. "The Dodging of Pressures," *Youth and Life,* p. 278.

13. On this question, see: A. F. Beringause, "The Double Martyrdom of Randolph Bourne," *The Journal of the History of Ideas,* XVIII (October, 1957).

14. Max Lerner, "Randolph Bourne and Two Generations," *Ideas for the Ice Age* (New York, 1941), p. 128.

15. *Randolph Bourne,* p. vii.

16. "Unfinished Fragment on the State," *Untimely Papers,* p. 191.

17. *Ibid.,* p. 148.

18. H. W. Morton, "Randolph Bourne vs. the State," *Anarchy* 31 (September, 1963).

19. "Unfinished Fragment on the State," p. 228.

20. *Ibid.,* p. 169.

21. *Ibid.,* p. 180.

22. Robert Nisbet, *The Social Philosophers: Community and Conflict in Western Thought* (New York, 1973), p. 12.

23. Michael T. Kaufman, "A Universal Humanist," *The New York Times* (August 4, 1972), 34.

24. *Five Years* (New York, 1966), p. 16.

25. *Speaking and Language: Defense of Poetry* (New York, 1971), p. 26.

26. "Memoirs of An Ancient Anarchist," *Anarchy* II (March, 1971), 31.

27. George Steiner, "On Paul Goodman," *Commentary* (July, 1963), 162.

28. Frederick S. Perls and Paul Goodman, *Gestalt Therapy: Excitement and Growth in the Human Personality* (New York, 1965).

29. *Utopian Essays and Practical Proposals* (New York, 1962), p. 116.

30. "The Empty Society," *Commentary* (November, 1966), 60.

31. *Drawing the Line* (New York, 1962), p. 26.

32. "Seven Heroes of the New Left," *The New York Times Magazine* (May 5, 1968), 128.

33. George Levine, "Paul Goodman, Outsider Looking In," *The New York Times Book Review* (February 18, 1973), 5.

34. Like a Conquered Province: *The Moral Ambiguity of America* (New York, 1966), p. 20.

35. *Growing Up Absurd* (New York, 1960), p. 107.

36. *Art and Social Nature* (New York, 1946), p. 44.

37. *Ibid.,* p. 46.

38. *Drawing the Line,* p. 26.

39. *Ibid.,* p. 40.

40. "Reply on Pornography and Censorship," *Commentary,* Vol. XXXII (August, 1961), 160.

41. "The Black Flag of Anarchy," *The New York Times Magazine* (July 14, 1968), 10.

42. *Ibid.,* 15.

43. *The New Reformation: Notes of a Neolithic Conservative* (New York, 1970), p. 159.

44. *Drawing the Line,* p. 22.

45. *Ibid.,* p. 11.

46. "A Young Pacifist" *Liberation* (September, 1967), 75-79.

47. "Memoirs of An Ancient Anarchist," p. 31.

48. "To Young Resisters," *Resistance* (March, 1949), 8.

49. *The New Reformation,* p. 163.

50. *Drawing the Line,* p. 50.

51. *Ibid.,* pp. 69-70.

52. *The New Reformation,* p. 91.

53. *Like A Conquered Province,* p. 83.

54. For an illuminating discussion of his personal position with reference to anarchism written shortly before his death, see "Politics Within Limits," *The New York Review of Books* (August 10, 1972), 31-34.

EPILOGUE

Although those in America who have chosen to call themselves anarchists have been extremely diverse and argumentive in their viewpoints, it is not impossible to find clearly defined patterns of thought that all anarchists share to a greater or lesser degree, depending upon their individual experiences and positions in space and time. To start with, American anarchists have been as one in holding to the view that human freedom is unattainable except within a society in which individual men and women are permitted to control themselves and to interact with their fellows through unstructured social intercourse. Adhering to the original and basic meaning of *laissez-faire* as it was formulated by Adam Smith, William Godwin, Thomas Paine, Elihu Palmer, and other enlightened thinkers, anarchists have projected a social theory that places the responsibility for law and order wholly upon the free individual as he stands in nature, and not upon formal government. It is this tradition, the libertarian tradition, that is the real genius of American political life and not the individual rights school of thought stemming from the social contract theories of Hobbes and Locke. It is indeed strange that political scientists and historians have almost completely ignored the libertarian tradition, despite the great number of everyday Americans who have sung its praises.

In characterizing the anarchist idea in America primarily as a reflection of the conception of rational necessity developed by the Enlightenment, we have in effect defined anarchism as being synonymous with the philosophical outlook of radical libertarianism which holds that human freedom derives from an unstructured and spontaneous response to the universal patterns of right order every man may discover for himself in the interstices of his own social being. Freedom, on this view, is dependent upon only one right—the right to determine one's own actions without supervision or restriction from any imposed rule by others acting in an official capacity as agents of organized power. This does not mean that anarchism

581

totally rejects authority, if by authority we mean those eternal social and moral verities which have throughout all ages of history appealed to the rational judgements of sensitive men. Anarchists believe that the only adequate definition of freedom is one that stems from a spontaneous and trusting response to the natural order that surrounds us. To be free, in the anarchist view, is to be capable of living life according to the rational imperatives of nature that are prior to human intelligence and organization. Far from believing that there is no order in the universe, anarchists hold that there is a necessary universal order that obligates all reasonable creatures to acknowledge certain natural dictates as real.[1] Those who fail to understand this basic postulate of anarchist thought can arrive at only the most superficial of interpretations as to its essential meaning and its significance to American social life.

Fundamental to American anarchist thought is the philosophical rejection of the most artificial and destructive of all imposed institutions, the modern nation state. When anarchists call for the elimination of the state, they do so not because they are destructive on principle but because they subscribe to the thoroughly sound philosophical argument that the modern state is fundamentally negative and antisocial in its implications. The origins of this aspect of American anarchist thought is again centered in the Enlightenment and the social developments that arose out of it. The historian, Carlton J. H. Hayes, points out that "the era of the Enlightenment, which witnessed . . . the growth of skepticism about Christianity, witnessed also a substitute exaltation—a sanctification, as it were, of the secular state, especially of the national state."[2] In this crucial bifurcation of American political life lie the origins of the contemporary struggle between libertarianism, with its faith in social man, and authoritarianism, with its faith in the repressive state. Conscious of the fact that the modern nation state is primarily a "sectarian religion" which in its very nature must be jealous of any other ethical loyalty, anarchists cry out against the state and call for its end as the main force of control over man in society. Their action is motivated by social and cultural concerns and not political appetite. The advocates of modern authoritarianism, on the other hand, exalt the state and tend to accept it as a sacred force without which human life would be impossible. Unalterably determined in the view that man does not have the inner social resources to control himself, the authoritarian stands ready to turn the entire control of life over to the state with its vast apparatus of coercion and force. These two major socio-political persuasions—the authoritarian and the libertarian—are the real antipodes between which all political thought ranges itself in America, whatever existing textbooks may tell us to the contrary.

When we focus upon rational necessity stemming from nature as the essence of the social program advanced by anarchists, we can more readily understand why anarchist thought in America has been embraced by Catholics and freethinkers, individualists and mutualists, Tolstoyans and egoists without fear of contradiction. Catholics like Dorothy Day or Daniel and Phillip Berrigan who find the state an oppressive force in their quest for religious fulfillment have much in common with freethinkers like William B. Greene or Henry C. Wright who thought of the state as a mortal enemy in their quest for individual perfection. All of these individuals in their own way want only the freedom to respond to the forces they find in nature rather than the laws imposed upon them by the profane state, which is what leads us to claim them for anarchism. This is why all American anarchists have ultimately been committed to the outlook of individualist rather than collectivist thought, for only the free, autonomous individual can cope with the state which is constructed out of the irrational fears and frustrations of collective man.

One of the most pronounced themes to be found in American anarchist thought is a deep suspicion of mass man as he has evolved out of our industrial-technological culture. Some observers who have noticed this critical attitude toward mass man in anarchist writings have concluded that anarchism subscribes to the principles of political elitism and that the anarchist is therefore anti-democratic,[3] but this formulation of the problem entirely misses the point of the anarchist argument. When the anarchist condemns mass man, he does so not because he feels that the "common man" is basically lacking in social or moral qualities but because the average man has not chosen to exercise the social and moral potential he naturally possesses. Everywhere in the modern world today, the anarchist holds, the individual faces social and moral oblivion to the extent that life becomes increasingly dominated by the monolithic nation state. We are caught up in a collective madness that complacently sanctions the absorption of the individual with his private passions and feelings into the huge, amorphous apparatus the state supports with its power. Anarchists argue that modern technological society, touted to be the source of comfort and material well-being for the individual, has proven to be an oppressive monster that sucks the vitality from his character as the leech sucks blood from the body. At the center of this apparatus stands the state, a mythical structure built out of the fears and ignorance of men that has been building since the first cunning medicine men of some tribe lost to history exercised control over his fellowmen through black magic and other forms of deception. In ever widening circles that control has been reaching out over the centuries until today the vast majority of men have been totally caught up in its pulsations of power. Only the individual standing squarely on his own power as a social being remains free to warn us against the enemy we face. And since everyone has the same potential to break free of the myths that bind us, there is nothing whatever to the accusation that the anarchist is elitist in his social views.

In this regard anarchists are in total agreement with Karl Jaspers who warns that the state "is the guarantor of the extant form of mass order."[4] Whether we like it or not, it has been evident from at least the time of Tocqueville that the state apparatus in America has been taken over by the masses who use it for their egalitarian purposes. Were this egalitarianism motivated by the appetitive desire to level wealth so that each and every individual in America shared equally with all others, the anarchist would not necessarily regurgitate the conception. But far from aiming toward any kind of universal equality, mass society in America is actually based upon a blatant form of political elitism in which the few who control power claim privileges far beyond the reach of the average man. Whatever the rhetoric of popular democracy may assert, anarchists argue, the fact is that it is the politically powerful few who manipulate the masses for their own self-serving ends. Democratic politicians, of course, make a great show of denying this, solemnly swearing before their gods in heaven that their desire to rule their fellowmen is based upon the most altruistic of motives. It is to be noted, however, that the basic skill of the politician is not the ability to speak honestly and openly to the crucial social issues of the day whatever the political consequences to himself may be but to "secure the approval of the people for whatever policy may have been decided upon by that inevitable oligarchy which hides in the heart of every democratic state."[5] Dividing men into political parties, politicians ride forth to do battle with one another under the colors of competing ideological truths. When the dust has settled and the collective passions of the masses involved have subsided, however, sober judgement leads inevitably to the conclusion that the social professions of politicians are merely another tactical maneuver designed to deceive the public. Totally lacking in faith in the social qualities of the average man, the politician brazenly asserts his own right to rule by default. This is as true of the intelligent, literate politician such as Edmund Burke as it is of the crude ward boss of the large city who wastes no time in dreaming up idealistic deceptions to hide his base motives from view. Nowhere in modern society does anyone take the idea of democracy seriously, for the average man is looked upon as a gullible automaton who is easily led into the most transparent of deceptions. If men can be deceived into giving their sons to the state to be sacrificed on the field of battle in one shoddy national adventure after another, what politician can doubt that "the people" will meekly submit their own miserable necks to the yoke when exhorted to do so.

The dynamics of mass society, to be sure, are subtle and hence not quickly visible to the naked eye. Under the aegis of compulsory universal education and the patriotic duty to defend one's fatherland, people are hypnotized, as Tolstoy points out, to believe in the most monstrous superstitions. The process "begins in their earliest years in the compulsory schools, created for this purpose, in which the children have instilled into them the ideas of life of their ancestors."[6] Once the individual has been conditioned to substitute the authoritarian precepts forced upon him within the formal educational process for the spontaneous internal reactions he naturally feels in the face of social stimuli, he is susceptible to any authoritarian pronouncements, however farfetched they might have otherwise appeared to him. This is why all modern national states have been so eager to guarantee universal popular education and to gather the little children to sit at the feet of their political functionaries. "For it is through education that the human beings are produced who in due course have to sustain the State," Karl Jaspers argues. This is why "Basic opinions are inculcated with the fixity of religious dogmas, knowledge and accomplishments being drilled into the learner as ways of feeling and valuing."[7] The one thing above all others that the state seeks to prevent in its citizens is a free, unstructured contact with the forces of nature, for it is by this that true rebels are made.

Even more than anarchists elsewhere, American anarchists from the very beginning have stood squarely with Sebastian Faure, the French libertarian, who put his finger on the vital pulse of anarchist thought when he wrote: "All those who are totally pacifists are not [necessarily] anarchists; but all anarchists are totally pacifists."[8] The anarchist's refusal to accept war as a legitimate mode of human action is not so much based on moral grounds as it is on an anthropological conviction that the basis of all slavery and oppression is centered in the state and its proclivity to make war. "It is war that makes the chief, the king and the state, just as it is these that make war," Will Durant has written. If "Property was the mother, war was the father of the state."[9] To eliminate the state, anarchists hold, it is first necessary to eliminate organized warfare, for were it not for the argument that the state is necessary to the physical survival of people in the face of their enemies, they would never have submitted themselves to the brutal regimentation and coercion exercised over their lives by government. In this respect it is important to recognize that "war is an historical, not a biological phenomenon: It is not a consequence of human nature as such but of certain social, economic and political conditions which at a certain time have come into being, and which are bound later to disappear."[10] The average man may consider the anarchist unrealistic for urging a world without organized coercion or armed conflict but the historian and anthropologist well know that the anarchist is on solid ground when he refuses to recognize any aspect of human conduct as absolutely determined and therefore permanent. Human nature is what the human imagination will permit it to be; the anarchist's claim to a "science of society" is grounded in this proposition, and it is on this that his philosophical prowess must be judged and not the vague and abstract fears about human nature that fill the head of the statists who condemn him.

In their adamant refusal to consider organized warfare a legitimate form of human activity, anarchists argue, they give demonstration of true social responsibility. As many perceptive social commentators have observed, what the world needs more than anything else today is the resolute individual who refuses to bend his knee to power and force when these are employed for anti-humanitarian purposes. To stand firm against the powers that be, to disobey authority and command when there are genuine social reasons for doing so, is not to destroy civilization but to further it. Modern warfare, supported as it is by the blind devotion of super-patriotism and the consciousless demands of capitalistic industrial enterprise in which the masses play a passive but crucial role, is not only a conspiracy against life by the few but it is also a form of collective madness. Everywhere in modern society—the communist countries as well as the democracies—men and women meekly submit themselves to mass political organization and regimentation. Conditioned from earliest childhood to "respect authority" without question, it never dawns upon the masses when war comes that the activity they are caught up in is insanely unreal in terms of their own basic social natures. The most rational act a man may commit in this situation, according to the anarchist, is to assert his true social being against the artificial political morality of the state by refusing to abandon his individual judgement and responsibility.

Rather than constituting a negative act, civil disobedience, in the mind of the anarchist, is an essential step in the direction of social revolution and therefore a highly commendable thing. The English sociologist, Alex Comfort, sums up anarchist thinking in this regard when he wrote, "Western civilization is not moribund as a result of the failure of its social organization; it is far more probably moribund through the failure of the individual to assert his resistance to organization of an irresponsible kind."[11] Erich Fromm supports this position when he observes that "If the capacity for disobedience constituted the beginning of human history, obedience might cause the end of human history."[12] When the anarchist calls for revolution, the furthest thing from his mind is a seizure of political power and another attempt to usher in the millennium by reorganizing men within a new administrative structure. There is only one kind of viable revolution, according to the anarchist, and that is the permanent social revolution urged by Proudhon in which the individual stands in perpetual rebellion against the demands of power. Man may never finally eliminate the instinct for power from his basic nature but the libertarian must always guard against submission to the artificial political morality of the state by refusing to submit to the herd instinct upon which all modern warfare rests. Such a course may not bring us to utopia, the anarchist argues, but it will protect our sanity and our freedom to act creatively, which, after all is said and done, is the only freedom man really needs or wants.

Although anarchism in the past has not generally been taken seriously by political theorists, it is currently undergoing reassessment in the light of new insights which time has brought. As we become increasingly familiar with the writings of such libertarians as Lysander Spooner, Emma Goldman, and Joseph Labadee, it becomes clear that the revolutionary sentiments expressed by American anarchists have not been completely outside the conception of freedom developed during the early years of the republic, as once was thought, but squarely within it. Consider, for example, the anarchist's total rejection of the political party as a proper vehicle for carrying forward the people's right to be free and his insistence that freedom is the alpha and omega of any liberated society. As Hanna Arendt points out, nothing is more fundamental to the conception of the American republic which developed out of the rebellion against English misrule over the colonies than the understanding that "political freedom . . . means the right 'to be a participator in government,' or it means nothing." For most political scientists, of course, the party system connotes the substance of democracy and hence they embrace the political party as the chief means of bringing freedom to the masses. But there is considerable substance to Professor Arendt's conviction that the political party, rather than being a vehicle for the attainment of self-government by the people, is actually the device by which their enslavement is invariably brought about. For, as she points out, "it is indeed in the very nature of the party system to replace the formula 'government by the people' by this formula: 'government of the people *by an elite sprung from the people.*' "[14] For years the anarchist stood almost alone in warning that true freedom is not to be found by turning over power to the professional politician but by an active and dedicated involvement of the private individual in public affairs at the level at which he can best participate. Those who have looked at the American past with a clear eye, however, have always recognized that the real meaning of the American

Revolution was an adamant refusal to trust public order and virtue to professional politicians, for those who make their living from politics must perforce exert their wills over the people and use them as the motive power of their own private fortunes and careers. To refer to the conventional political process as anything other than an elitist form of rule is to stretch words beyond acceptable credulity.

In final analysis, then, anarchism is not so much a social or political doctrine or a definite collection of principles as it is an essential way of viewing mankind and the world. In America, the lenses through which the anarchist perceives things were ground primarily after the prescription written by the philosophers of the Eighteenth Century Enlightenment. Unimpressed by the extravagant claims liberals made for empiricism, the philosophers of the Enlightenment developed a methodology which was based on a principle diametrically opposed to the sensationalism of Locke and others who viewed truth as the direct consequence of the senses. Truth and reality for the anarchist is not the concrete world of hard empirical facts our senses convey to our brains but the world we would know should we succeed in clearing from our minds the misconceptions and myths mankind has imposed upon itself almost from the beginnings of human history. The basic epistemological foundation upon which the anarchist view of reality rests is the "symbolic system" described by Ernst Cassirer in which man's view of the world is seen to be filtered through a translucent net constructed out of "the tangled web of human experiences."[15] Structured in his conceptualization of reality by the language, myth, and religion bequeathed to him by his ancestors, man has the difficult task of clearing his mind of the symbolic "truths" that shape his vision and prevent him from realizing his essential social nature. This is why all American anarchists have been freethinkers, for they have intuitively recognized that the first essential step toward rational thought must start with the clearing away of the accumulated myth patterns imposed upon humanity by the past.

As the preceding pages have sought to demonstrate, the perimeters of anarchist thought in America have been extremely broad and fluid, just as the Enlightenment upon which it is based was flexible and loose with regard to its basic philosophical postulates. While this has been a liability to the extent that the shape of anarchist thought has appeared unusually nebulous and indefinite to those who have viewed it from a distance, it has also been a strength to the extent that it has allowed its adherents to keep pace with the changing circumstances and developments of American society. Following Proudhon and William B. Greene who were among the first to urge the view that consistency for its own sake is "the hobgoblin of little minds," anarchists in America have demonstrated a remarkable intellectual vitality that has found them riding the crest of every forward-looking social current of American life, including the counterculture of the contemporary youth movement. Far from being dead as a force in American political life as some historians have imagined, anarchism as a theory of human liberation is just now coming into its own.

NOTES

EPILOGUE

1. Herbert Read, "The Necessity of Anarchism, Part II," *The Modern Monthly*, X (February, 1938), 11.

2. *Nationalism, A Religion* (New York, 1960), p. 45.

3. See for example, Benjamin R. Barber, *Superman and Commen Men: Freedom Anarchy, and the Revolution* (New York, 1971); and, Isaak Kramnick, "On Anarchism and the Real World: William Godwin and Radical England," *The American Political Science Review*, LXVI (March, 1972), 114-128.

4. *Man in the Modern Age*, trans. by Edan and Cedar Paul (Garden City, 1957), p. 115.

5. Will Durant, *The Mansions of Philosophy* (New York, 1929), p. 437.

6. "The Dream Shattered Over Sixty Years Ago," in *Citizens of One World*, Vol. IV (New York, 1960), p. 76.

7. *Man in the Modern Age*, p. 116.

8. "Anarchists are Totally Pacifists," *Man!*, IV (January, 1936), 233.

9. *The Foundations of Civilization* (New York, 1936), pp. 51-3.

10. Bart DeLigt, *The Conquest of Violence: An Essay on War and Revolution* (London, 1937), p. 24.

11. *Art and Social Responsibility* (London, 1946), p. 26.

12. *Beyond the Chains of Illusion: My Encounter with Marx and Freud* (New York, 1962), p. 181.

13. *On Revolution* (New York, 1965), p. 221.

14. *Ibid.*, p. 281.

15. *An Essay on Man* (New Haven, 1944), p. 25.

SELECTED BIBLIOGRAPHY

"Anarchists: Joseph A. Labadie," *Match* 4 (January, 1973), 6.

"Anarchists: Robert Reitzel," *Match* 4 (December, 1972), 10.

Andrews, Stephen Pearl, *Love, Marriage and Divorce and the Sovereignty of the Individual.* New York: Source Book Press, 1972.

_____, *The Science of Society*, intro. by Charles Shively. Weston, Mass.: M & S Press, 1970.

Ashbaugh, Carolyn, *Lucy Parsons: American Revolutionary.* Chicago: Charles H. Kerr Publishing Co., 1976.

Autobiography of the Haymarket Martyrs, ed. by Philip S. Foner. New York: American Institute of Marxist Studies, 1969.

Avrich, Paul, "Anarchists: Daniel Duerin," *Match* 5 (January, 1974), 8.

Baker, James Thomas, *Thomas Merton: Social Critic.* Lexington: University of Kentucky Press, 1971.

Barclay, Harold, "Josiah Warren: The Incomplete Anarchist," *Anarchy* 85 (March, 1968), 90-96.

Buhle, Paul, *Marxism In The United States, 1900-1940.* Unpublished Ph. D. Dissertation, The University of Wisconsin, 1975.

Coles, Robert and Erikson, Jon, *A Spectacle Unto The World: The Catholic Worker Movement.* New York: The Viking Press, 1973.

Cort, John C., "Dorothy Day at 75," *Commonweal* 97 (February 23, 1973), 475-476.

Day, Dorothy, *Meditations,* selected and arranged by Stanley Vishnewski. New York: Newman Press, 1970.

_____, *On Pilgrimage: The Sixties.* New York: Curtis, 1972.

Dejacque, Joseph, "A bas les Chefs," ed. by Valentin Pelosse, Classics of Subversion Series. Paris: Editions Champs Libre, 1971. Reprinted in *Anarchy* 12 (1972), 17-19.

Dickens, Bob, "Thoreau On Slavery, Economy and Alienation," *Anarchy* 8 (1971), 18-24.

Egbert, Donald Drew, *Social Radicalism and the Arts: A Cultural History from the French Revolution to 1968.* New York: Knopf, 1970.

_____, *Socialism and Art in the Light of European Utopianism,*

Marxism, and Anarchism. Princeton: Princeton University Press, 1967.

"Emma Goldman," *Ramparts* 10 (February, 1972), 10-12.

Fishman, W. J. "Rudolph Rocker: Anarchist Missionary," *History Today* 16 (January, 1966), 45-52.

Gallego, Jack, "Wilhelm Reich's Work Theory," *Anarchy* 1 (1971) 25-28.

Gianakos, Perry E., "Ernest Howard Crosby: A Forgotten Tolstoyan Anti-Militarist and Anti-Imperialist," *American Studies* 13 (Spring, 1972), 11-29.

Gibson, Morgan, *Kenneth Rexroth.* New York: Twayne Publishers, 1972.

Goldberg, H., *The Anarchists View The Russian Revolution, 1918-1922.* Unpublished Ph. D. Dissertation, The University of Wisconsin, 1973.

Goodman, Paul, "Memoirs of an Ancient Anarchist," *Anarchy* 2 (March, 1971), 29-32.

_____, "Politics Within Limits," *New York Review of Books* (August 10, 1972), 31-34.

Graham, Marcus, "A Revisionist's Attack Anarchism and Its Movement," *Anarchy* 10 (1971), 9-11.

Guerin, Daniel, *Anarchism: From Theory to Practice,* trans. by Mary Klopper. New York: Monthly Review Press, 1970.

Hacker, Andrew, "Anarchism," in *International Encyclopedia of the Social Sciences* I, ed. by David L. Sills. New York: Macmillan Co. and the Free Press, 1968.

Halbrook, Steve, "Northamerican Anarchism," *Anarchy* 8 (1971), 4-7.

Hall, B., "The Economic Theory of Stephen Pearl Andrews: Neglected Utopian Writer," *South African Journal of Eonomics* (March, 1975), 43-55.

Hall, Constance Margaret, *The Sociology of Pierre-Joseph Proudhon.* New York: Philosophical Library, 1971.

Hess, Karl, *Dear America.* New York: William Morrow and Co., 1975.

Hospers, John, *Libertarianism: A Political Philosophy For Tomorrow.* Los Angeles: Nash Publishers, 1971.

Issel, William H., "Ralph Borsodi and the Agrarian Response to Modern America," *Agricultural History* 41 (April, 1967),

155-166.

Johnston, Johanna, *Mrs. Satan.* New York: Popular Library, 1967.

Karpick, J., "Anarchism: The Russian Movement in America," *Match* 5 (October, 1974), 5-6.

———, "Anarchists: The Russian Movement in America, II," *Match* 5 (November, 1974), 6-7.

Kindilien, Carlin T., "A Neglected Colby Poet: Harry Lyman Koopman, *Colby Library Quarterly* (February, 1954), 201-210.

Lavine, Doug, "40 Years of Mercy," *National Catholic Reporter* 9 (June 8, 1973), 1-19.

Lehning, Arthur, "Anarchism," in *Dictionary of the History of Ideas* I, ed. by Philip P. Wiener. New York: Charles Scribner's Sons, 1968, 70-76.

Leon, David Henry, *The American as Anarchist: A Socio-Historical Interpretation.* Unpublished Ph. D. Dissertation, The University of Iowa, 1972.

Lynd, Staughton, *Intellectual Origins of American Radicalism.* New York: Pantheon Books, 1968.

Lynn, Kenneth S., "Reconsiderations: Living My Life," *New Republic* 168 (November 27, 1971), 26-28.

Miller, William D., *A Harsh and Dreadful Love: Dorothy Day and the Catholic Worker Movement.* New York: Liveright, 1973.

Newell, Peter E., "Who Killed Carlo Tresca," *Anarchy* 13 (1972), 8-12.

Newfield, Jack, *A Prophetic Minority.* New York: New American Library, 1966.

Nisbet, Robert, *The Social Philosophers: Community and Conflict in Western Thought.* New York: Crowell, 1973.

Nowhere at Home; Letters from Exile of E. Goldman and A. Berkman, ed. by Richard and Anna Drinnon. New York: Schocken Books, 1975.

Parker, S. E., "Anarchists: Max Stirner," *The Match* 4 (October, 1973), 8-9.

Parsons, Lucy, *Famous Speeches of the Eight Chicago Anarchists.* New York: Arno Press, 1969.

Perlin, Terry, "Anarchism and the Scholars," *Match* 5 (November 1974), 8.

———, "Anarchism in New Jersey: The Ferrer Colony at Stelton,"

New Jersey History 89 (1971), 133-148.

Perry, Lewis, "Adin Ballou's Hopedale Community and the Theology of Antislavery," *Church History* 34 (September, 1975), 372-390.

_____, *Radical Abolitionism: Anarchy and the Government of God in Antislavery Thought.* Ithaca: Cornell University Press, 1973.

_____, "Versions of Anarchism in the Antislavery Movement," *American Quarterly* 20 (Winter, 1968), 768-782.

_____, " 'We Have Had Conversations in the World': The Abolitionists and Spontaneity," *Canadian Review of American Studies* 6 (Spring, 1975), 3-26.

Reichert, William O., "Anarchism, Freedom, and Power," *Ethics* 79 (January, 1969), 139-149.

_____, "Art, Nature, and Revolution," *Arts In Society* 9 (Fall-Winter, 1972), 399-409.

_____, "The Melancholy Political Thought of Morrison I. Swift," *New England Quarterly* 49 (December, 1976).

_____, "Towards A New Understanding of Anarchism," *Western Political Quarterly* 20 (December, 1967), 856-865.

Robinson, JoAnn, "A. J. Muste and Ways To Peace," *American Studies* 13 (Spring, 1972), 95-108.

Rothard, Murray N., *Egalitarianism As A Revolt Against Nature and Other Essays.* Washington, D.C.: Libertarian Review Press, 1974.

_____, *For A New Liberty.* New York: Macmillan, 1973.

Sheehan, Arthur, *Peter Maurin: Gay Believer.* Garden City: Hanover House, 1959.

Shively, Charles, "An Option for Freedom in Texas, 1840-1844," *Journal of Negro History* 50 (April, 1965), 77-96.

Shulman, Alix Kates, *Red Emma Speaks.* New York: Random House, 1972.

Souchy, Agustin, "Anarchists: Rudolf Rocker," *Match* 4 (December, 1973), 8-9.

Spooner, Lysander, *The Unconstitutionality of Slavery.* New York: B. Franklin, 1965.

_____, *An Essay On the Trial By Jury.* New York: DaCapo Press, 1971.

_____, *Poverty: Its Legal Causes and Legal Cure.* New York:

DaCapo Press, 1971.

———, *Collected Works of Lysander Spooner,* with biography and introduction by Charles Shively. Weston, Mass.: M & S Press, 1971.

Stern, Madeleine B., *The Pantarch.* Austin: University of Texas Press, 1968.

Stevenson, Billie Jeanne Hackley, *The Ideology of American Anarchism.* Unpublished Ph. D. Dissertation, The University of Iowa, 1971.

The Essays of A. J. Muste, ed. by Nat Hentoff. Indianapolis: Bobbs-Merrill, 1967.

Tuccille, Jerome, *Radical Libertarianism: A Right Wing Alternative.* Indianapolis: Bobbs-Merrill, 1970.

Vallance, Margaret, "Rudolf Rocker—A Biolgraphical Sketch," *Journal of Contemporary History* 8 (July, 1973), 75-95.

Veysey, Laurence, *The Communal Experience: Anarchist and Mystical Counter-Cultures in America.* New York: Harper and Row, 1973.

Walter, Nicolas, "Anarchism In Print: Yesterday and Today," in *Anarchism Today,* ed. by David E. Apter and James Joll. London: Macmillan Press, 1971, 127-144.

———, "Figures in Anarchism: A. Bellagarrigue," *Match* (September, 1975), 8.

Ward, Colin, *Anarchy In Action.* New York: Harper and Row, 1973.

Warren, Josiah, *True Civilization An Immediate Necessity and the Last Ground of Hope for Mankind.* New York: B. Franklin, 1967.

West, Eileen, "Anarchists: Albert R. Parsons," *Match* 5 (September, 1974), 6.

Wieck, David, "About Malatesta," *Anarchy* 8 (1971), 25-31.

Woodcock, George, "Anarchism Revisited," *Commentary* 46 (August, 1968), 54-60.

Woodworth, Cheryl, "Anarchists: Emma Goldman," *Match* 5 (June, 1974), 11-12.

Woodworth, Fred, "Anarchists: Boris Yelensky," *Match* 5 (August, 1974), 8-9.

———, "Problems of Anarchism Today," *Match* 5 (August, 1974), 4-7.

Wreszin, Michael, *Albert Jay Nock: The Superfluous Anarchist.* Providence: Brown University Press, 1971.

Yelensky, Boris, "Anarchists: Morris Berezin," *Match* 5 (April, 1974), 6.

_____, "A Visit With Kropotkin," *Match* 5 (August, 1974), 9-10.

INDEX